GOD'S BLENDED FAMILY

Clarity, Biblical Understanding, Spiritual Warfare Strategies and Healing for Biological, Blended/Step, Single-Parent, Adopted and other types of Families so they can Successfully Relate, Stay Intact and Function Victoriously in Everyday Life

Introducing God's Blended Family; plus a Bonus of the Author's Blended Family's Testimony

AUDREY L. DICKEY, PH.D.

Copyright © 2012 by Audrey L. Dickey, Ph.D.

All rights reserved. No part of this book may be reproduced in any form or by any means - electronic, mechanical, photocopy, recording, or otherwise including information in storage and retrieval systems, without the prior written permission of the publisher.

Unless otherwise indicated, all Scripture quotations are taken from The Amplified® Bible. Copyright © 1954, 1962, 1965, 1987 by The Lockman Foundation. Used by permission.

Scripture quotations marked (NKJV) are taken from the New King James Version, Copyright © 1979, 1980, 1982 by Thomas Nelson, Inc. Used by permission.

Scriptures marked (KJV) are taken from the King James Version of the Bible.

Scripture quotations marked (NIV) are taken from the Holy Bible, New International Version, Copyright © 1973, 1978, 1984 by International Bible Society. Used by permission of Zondervan Publishing House. All rights reserved.

Scripture quotations marked (NLT) are taken from the New Living Translation; Holy Bible, People's Parallel Edition, Copyright © 1997 by Tyndale House Publishers, Inc.; Holy Bible, New Living Translation, Copyright © 1996 by Tyndale Charitable Trust; and from NLT Parallel Study Bible, Copyright © 2011 by Tyndale House Publishers. All rights reserved. Used by permission.

Scripture taken from The One New Man Bible, Copyright © 2011 William J. Morford. Used by permission of True Potential Publishing, Inc.

Scripture quotations marked (NAS) are taken from the New American Standard Bible. Copyright © 1960, 1962, 1963, 1968, 1971, 1972, 1973, 1975, 1977 by the Lockman Foundation. Used by permission.

Scripture quotations marked (The Message) are taken from The Message: The Bible in Contemporary English, Copyright ©1993, 1994, 1995, 1996, 2000, 2001, 2002. Used by permission of Nav Press Publishing Group.

Scripture quotations marked (The Book) are taken from The Book. Copyright © 1999 by Tyndale House Publishing. All rights reserved. Used by permission.

ISBN: 1468052942
ISBN 13: 9781468052947

Library of Congress Control Number: 2011962798
CreateSpace, North Charleston, SC

Christian Life/ Marriage and Family/ Spiritual Warfare

DEDICATION

FRIENDS COME AND FRIENDS GO
BUT FAMILY *SHOULD* BE FOREVER!

I dedicate this book to ***JESUS,*** my Lord and Savior of whose family I am, love and serve and Who is my closest and dearest Friend Who I trust with my very life and soul.

To my immediate family because they fulfill an important part of the purpose God intended and destined for my life. To my loving and dear husband, **Robert,** an anointed faithful man of God, husband and father; thank you for your dedication and support of this long endeavor. Also, to our five children that God *chose* to bless us with: ***Camille, Christa, Brandon, Kevin*** and ***Melinda*** who all have a heart of gold, a heart for God and of whom I love very dearly.

I thank God for my loving and dear late parents, ***Mr. and Mrs. Henry W.*** and ***Lillian C. Jones,*** who were an inspiration and true example of Godly and loving parents who gifted their children with the love they shared for each other for fifty-eight years as husband and wife, companions and best friends.

To my siblings for your impartation into my life and all the wonderful memories we share: ***Harold, Deborah, Sharon, Belinda, Michael, Lynn, Jacqueline, Glenna*** and ***Sean.***

I thank my family for their patience and love over the years as we have traveled on this extraordinary journey which enabled us to take hold of our destiny.

TABLE OF CONTENTS

Introduction ix
CHAPTER

1) **What is the Biblical Definition for Marriage?**
   (And How God by His Grace Gave us a Covenant to Seal it) .1

   - What is a Covenant? 6
   - The Blood Covenant, an Eternal Unbreakable Covenant 9
   - The Covenant God Established through Abraham 13
   - Will God Ever Break His Covenant with Mankind? 19
   - How Does the Covenant Affect Marriages Today? 26
   - Cleaving and Becoming One 30
   - The Marriage Protocol from Ancient Times to
     Today's Marriages 37
   - Love is the Essence of Marriage 49
   - Understanding Reasons for Marriage 56
   - Key Tips for a *Successful* Marriage God's Way 58

2) **What is the Biblical Definition for Divorce?**
   (And Things the Bible has to Say about it) 75

   - Frequently asked Questions Regarding Divorce and
     Remarriage 78
   - Regulations that Protect a Divorced Woman's Reputation .. 81
   - The Reasons Divorces are Allowed or Occur 91
   - Remarriage and what the Bible Says about it 104
   - Clarifying Remarriage and whether or *Not* Divorce
     is a Sin 109
   - Is There a Right Time to Remarry? 130
   - Is There a Wrong Time to Remarry? 134
   - Defining Fornication *Beyond* Sexual
     Immorality 139
   - Is Co-Habiting another Form of Fornication? 147

- Clarifying Sin and its Contribution to a
  Divorce 148
- Clarifying Forgiveness 173
- Clarifying Repentance... 185
- General Information Regarding a
  Divorce 194
- No-Fault Divorce Laws and How they are Not of God 198
- Key Measures Given *Before* Marriage to *Prevent* a
  Divorce 202
- Key Measures to *Prevent* a Divorce
  During Marriage 207

3) What is the Biblical Definition for Family? (Also Healthy and Strong Qualities it *Should Possess*) 215

- Who is Sanctioned as a Family and Who is Not? 217
- The Family Home is not Separate from its Nation............. 219
- Qualities and Attributes Found in a Healthy and Strong
  Family 224

4) Various Family Types that Exist in Our Society Today.. 235

- Various Natural Family Types 236
- Co-Habiting and Different Types of Unions....................... 240
- How Television Families Affected Society......................... 243
- The "True Family" as Described by Our Lord 256
- *Family Types that Exist in the Kingdom of God Today
  and Introducing God's Blended Family*................................ 261
- The One New Man... 263
- Defining a Christian and Christianity 266
- Defining the Anointing of God 277

5) Insight as to How God Views a Blended Family, the Challenges it May Encounter and Methods on How to Resolve them 287

- How God Views a Blended Parent 290

- Some Adolescents Reject a Blended Parent 292
- Calling the New Parent Dad or Mom 294
- The Importance of a Child Remaining in their Role 295
- Children Searching for their Identity or Place in the Blended Family 297
- Many Children and Adolescents *Do* Welcome a New Parent 299
- Rebuilding a Strong Home and a Sense of Security in your Family 300
- The Difference between Discipline and Punishment 303
- Visitation Rights and Children Living between Two Homes 308
- Establish New Family Customs and Traditions 312
- Additional Methods on How to Resolve Certain Challenges in Order to make Life in your Home a more Enjoyable One 316
- Was Jesus a Member of a Blended Family? 324

6) Is your Family Functioning According to God's Order and their God-Given Roles? 327

- Roles Assist Us on How to Function in Everyday Life 336
- Biblical Instructions for the Role of a Husband 340
- As the Priest and Protector of His Home 341
- Biblical Instructions for the Role of a Wife 354
- The Importance of a Help Meet and Spiritual Partner 356
- Her Key Functions Are Not Her Only Functions 360
- Biblical Instructions for the Role of a Child 367
- Does a Parent have the Right to Speak to their Adult Children about what they are Accomplishing in their Lives? 374
- Extended Family and Divine Friendships 376
- When Role Models are Outside of Your Home 380
- Continue to Show Adolescents Affection 381
- Suggestions to Help Children make Adjustments 387
- Delegated Authority is Part of God's Order 390
- Information Regarding Family Order and Roles 395

7) **Walk in Victory and Authority through Effective Spiritual Warfare Against Demonic Attacks Assigned to Your Marriage and Family (see Sections One, Two and Three below); It's Not Over Till God Says It's Over! 401**

- **SECTION ONE:** Who is the Adversary and What are His Devices?..411
- We Must Know Who Our Enemy Is 413
- Order and Information about the Satanic Kingdom of Darkness 421
- Be Aware of Devices, Tactics and Weapons that are Sent to Destroy Your Family 423
- Tactics and Attacks Designed to Wear People Out.............429

- **SECTION TWO:** Take the Victory by Force using God's Spiritual Warfare Weapons..433
- We Must Decide *We Want* the Victory Then Take it by Force 435
- Discover "26" Spiritual Warfare Weapons, Tools and Strategies that the Master Strategist has given us *To Use* 441
- Details Regarding Our Spiritual Warfare Weapons, Tools and Strategies..444
- Clarity about Spirits and the Spiritual Kingdom 523
- Kingdom Economics (Godly Principles) Resist the Enemy and Allows Financial Progress..532
- The World's Economic System and Why Some Suffer Lack 533
- God's Prosperity is a Part of His Kingdom and it Differs from the World's Economic System 550
- Covenant People that God Made Rich..............................553
- When Income is Applied to Biblical Truths and Principles Your Seed will Resist the Adversary and Allow Supernatural Increase or Financial Progress 558
- How to Come out of Debt by Using Spiritual and Natural Instruments..561
- All Societies are in the Process of Experiencing a Transfer of Wealth 567

- **SECTION THREE:** Discover Who has the Real Power to Change Hearts, Lives and Circumstances as well as the Power to Restore, Revive and Reconstruct........................573
- Who Is The Holy Spirit? 578
- Attributes of God The Holy Spirit..584
- Illustration of Progress in One's Life with The Holy Spirit 586
- Angel Movement Chart...587
- The Five Divisions of Angels 590
- A Description of Angels and what their Purpose is............593
- A Review of Building and Embracing a Personal Relationship with God 597
- A Quick Review of What *Should* be in Place to Keep God First 599
- A Brief History and the Wonderful Works of the King of kings 603
- Prophecies the Messiah Fulfilled..610
- What was Finished and Accomplished at the Cross?..........613
- What is Salvation? (A Prayer for Salvation) 617

Appendix.. 625
Bonus: Our Blended Family's Testimony

- How God Blended and Bonded Our Two Families Together through Obstacles and Love with a Pre-Schooler, Three Teens, One Young Adult and Gave Us a New Beginning....625
- Introduction to Our Testimony..627
- Our Blended Family's Testimony 631
- A Scripture Passage that Qualifies an Anointed Family of God 710
- **A Prayer for Salvation and the Infilling of the Holy Spirit**..…..713

Endnotes...715
About the Author..719
Contact Information 720

INTRODUCTION

Many years have passed since I received my first prophetic word from a prophet God placed across my path with a word in his mouth to "write a book." Since then there have been several prophets, male and female that did not know one another cross my path with the same word, "write the book." There was an appointed time to begin the manuscript and the word finally came in 1998 through, Melinda, a prophetess in my own home that I was to start the book that summer.

I did, *September 19, 1998* was the day I put pen to the paper and on and off for the next twelve years as I was directed by the Holy Spirit I wrote what was in my heart. I gained more experience in order to complete the book, did additional research, studied and received numerous additional confirmations that this book was to be written. *Finally on September 19, 2010 exactly twelve years later to the day I was in the midst of adding the last section that would end this difficult yet exciting journey.* Only God could have timed this, I had no idea it would be so many years not to mention an additional year or so for revisions and publishing to complete the process. But as I look back it was required to gain the insight, revelation and training necessary to carry the type of anointing God was placing on this writing for marriages and families during the End Times when God will accomplish a great work with those who belong to Him.

As explained in Chapter seven under Kingdom Economics (Godly Principles) regarding financial matters, God is in the process of His people experiencing a transfer of *wealth into the Kingdom of God* by businesses starting, being acquired, promotions, gifts, inheritances, supernatural favor, profound physical healings and so forth. This transfer will also include homes being restored: Restoration for existing marriages and families, at the same time new beginnings for the divorced as well as first time marriages coming forth.

In the beginning when God gave me the name of this book, *God's Blended Family,* I assumed it was about my own Blended Family's experience but as I began writing more and conducting research and because of the way the Holy Spirit was leading me I soon realized this really was not only about my Blended Family's experience but about other Blended Families and their challenges as well.

In addition, **a Divine Perspective of '*God's Blended Family*'** was also given by the inspiration of the Holy Spirit and is discussed in Chapter four. **For instance, this family is larger than what we would perceive or consider as within the limits of a usual or customary family. It would encompass people from all over the world and it crosses all barriers as people are included in this family regardless of race, creed, ethnic group, color, culture, status or former religion, making it the most powerful family on the face of the earth.**

This is a type of family that God calls "HIS OWN" as people are ingrafted by adoption into the family through Christ which is 'God's Blended Family,' one that will function as **The One New Man** *in the Kingdom of God.*

Now, more insight from the usual or customary family's perspective of the Blended Family which normally comes about as the result of a prior marriage that has been dissolved. Although as explained in this resource there are other ways a Blended Family could come into existence.

Most *Blended Families start with strikes against them,* deadly emotions such as anger, unforgiveness, hurt, grief and other negative emotions which means they usually bring a lot of baggage from their past that is not only generated from the married couple but also from the children; because this type of family involves everyone from the beginning of the marriage. So what are the chances of a Blended Family functioning and surviving in today's society?

The Blended Family's chances of survival today are the same as any other family type, they are all at risk. As explained inside of this resource people have an adversary that is very interested in their destruction. The *adversary* has increased his pace in attempting to destroy what God loves because his time is short and he wishes to do as much damage as possible. He is attempting to destroy societies of people with *attacks against the institution of marriage in order to weaken the foundation of the family which in turn will weaken the foundation of society. But there is only one thing wrong with this plan and that is in order for it to be successful one would have to overtake God Himself. As we know there is no weapon or anyone powerful enough to destroy Almighty God and when they try, they try in vain.*

God is the foundation of marriage, the man within the marriage is the foundation of the family and the family is the foundation of society, therefore, for all those in God, it shall stand! As mentioned in chapter one God gave man a covenant with Him that will serve as a protection for him while he is on the earth. The subtitle on this resource's cover is in the shape of a rainbow which was given to me by God in a vision. This rainbow in the clouds is a reminder and a sign of the covenant that God made between He and mankind that still stands today as we look into the heavens and see His rainbow in the sky, (Gen. 9:11-16).

We need to pray for those who are so deceived and being used by the adversary that try to bring destruction to marriages and families. They have been ensnared, knowingly or unknowingly and are in a huge trap and will reap exactly what they have sown. Furthermore, the Lord is causing His people, His family to rise up and be a "light" to those who are in darkness and show them the way.

Many people are not taking the institution of marriage seriously and many more are making a mockery of it directly or indirectly, declaring that family ties really do not matter. Those in the kingdom of darkness do not understand that God Himself put the family in place and it will take more than a fallen archangel to permanently remove it.

I've added history regarding the marriage protocol from ancient times to today's marriages and by addressing this issue hopefully it will spark new interest and thinking in this area. Also, information defining a covenant and how it affects our marriages today plus key tips that include strategies for a successful marriage God's way.

In addition, I have also been given insight into the scriptures regarding divorce and why some people refuse to remarry based on religious rules that have nothing to do with God. Further, why some have remarried and live in guilt every day of their lives. The Holy Spirit has revealed so much to set the captives free from all guilt and condemnation so they can take their rightful place in the Kingdom of God, so they can live by faith and with confidence then go and take back what was stolen by the adversary and enjoy their lives.

At the time my Blended Family began there was very little material to research regarding godly or secular *Blended Families*, therefore, much of what I have written came from the Word of God, life experiences and how The Holy Spirit taught us to overcome challenges. Having been married before and now in a Blended Family for nearly twenty years at the time of this writing, I know first hand what it will take to make it successful. *All of the natural things that people do to take care of their marriage and family is wonderful but in this hour it is going to take more than family traditions, a family dinner, a cute nightie, a date night and going to the kids sports or musical events or even helping them with homework.*

I came from a home where my parents were married for fifty-eight (58), nearly sixty years until my father went to be with the Lord, therefore, I have something to compare to. I have seen how a couple who genuinely loved one another and could stay married for years and raise a family compared to how families are bombarded today from every side and give up. From past experiences I have learned how Satan operates with his ugly ways and devices and have defeated him in many storms with the help of The Holy Spirit. God also directed me through various resources such as: tests, anointed selective books, conferences, prayer meetings, audio electronics, and mentors. In addition, over the years, to counseling singles, married couples with terrible marriages and family issues more insight was revealed.

The advantage that God's Blended Family has is great, and what they have can benefit any family whether it is a Biological, Traditional Nuclear, Single-Parent, Family by Adoption, Child-Free or Foster-Parent Family, the type does not matter, what matters is, if they choose God they will acquire an anointing and strategies that can only be taught by the Master Strategist on how to use effective spiritual warfare against the destruction that has targeted their home. **They will ultimately win the battles and the war and save their family which is a gift and blessing from God in heaven.**

My desire is to share these strategies that were given to my husband and me, as we were both determined that Satan would not rob us in this area of our lives again. We have also included our Blended Family's detailed testimony of how God blended and bonded our two families together through obstacles and love with a pre-schooler, three teens and one young adult and gave us a new beginning. In addition, at the beginning of my testimony I reveal some of the strategies and miracles God performed for me while I was separated and functioning as a single-parent between six and seven years before remarrying nearly twenty years ago at the time of this writing.

Over the years the Holy Spirit had to lead and instruct my husband and me because neither one of us knew anything about Blended/Step Families both having come from intact Biological (two-parent) Families. We did not have a clue about Blended Families and what to expect, what to avoid, what were the pitfalls or danger zones. We had absolutely no knowledge of what was to be. The Holy Spirit literally took us by the hand and walked us through some of the most difficult years of our lives and some of the *greatest!* We basically kept our joy knowing that God was at the head of our family and He was giving us the strength and wisdom necessary for it to be successful. We knew that we would emerge the better for it and come out victorious.

There is an anointing on this book that God will use to destroy yokes of evil that are on assignment against marriages and families. We faced many obstacles and challenges over the years especially within the last seven months of preparation to bring this project to completion and release the manuscript to the publishers. My husband, Robert and I had to make sure everything was covered by the blood of Jesus because as soon as I would begin writing and/or inputting into the computer information that would bring me closer to completion as I listed key strategies or spiritual warfare weapons to use against the kingdom of darkness a part of my computer equipment would fail.

My CPU fan stopped working and once repaired, then the printer stopped, up again then the monitor went out and we are not talking old equipment. We replaced the computer with a brand new one then a Trojan virus broke into my system while I was working on this very material. I tried to back everything up but my drive was full and fortunately my husband came in from a dental meeting and quickly backed everything up on his drive minutes before it shut down for good with all of my files including this manuscript. God supernaturally held it until everything was backed-up. (I always keep a hard copy of everything I do but it would not have been enough time to manually input all of the material and complete all of it by the completion date that had been set). Until we finally submitted everything to the publishers there were attacks against my computer. Meaning, demonic forces would try to block and hinder to cause discouragement and depression so I would give up. But when you understand what is taking place if you would press in that much more and resist the enemy you will have the victory (see Chapter 7, Section One regarding the kingdom of darkness and how it operates with devices that work against you and your home).

I have said all of this to say, the reason the adversary and his evil followers could not stop this from coming to fruition is because it does not belong to me it belongs to God, this is His work and His Holy Spirit directed it every step of the way and through every obstacle. This work is for the new season in which God is beginning to show Himself strong and a strange anointing is going to hit the earth like never before to do signs and wonders wherein these last of the last days of the church age in which we live we will do greater works than He.

The most significant motive for writing this book is to set people free from their past mistakes and condemnation, to live a full and enjoyable life, full of confidence, faith and feeling good about themselves. My hope is that marriages and families can be strong and free from demonic oppression so that people can be about the Father's business for their lives with a peace of mind and the fruit and the gifts of the Spirit, with full authority and power to accomplish much for the Kingdom of God.

This resource will bring clarity, understanding, revelation, healing, restoration, deliverance and salvation to marriages and families as well as impart to singles guidance and preparation for their future families.

Christian Marriages and Blended Families no longer have to fall because of the same old tactics and devices of the enemy. They and other types of families can stop the enemy when they operate as Anointed Families. They can do this by successfully using the spiritual warfare weapons and strategies The Holy Spirit taught us over the years. The Holy Spirit has instructed me through this book to share with millions of people who are serious about their marriages and families staying intact. This also holds true for those who are starting fresh with a new beginning after divorce or even those first time marriages that want to start by doing things God's way.

It is time for the Body of Christ to come into position to be without spot or wrinkle and be a light to a lost and dying world. *Jesus is real and He is ready to fulfill His promises to people as He said He would.*

We are not to be concerned about the past and how we missed God. When a righteous man falls God will raise him up again because God is always there. He said He would never leave us nor forsake us. When Abraham fell he got up; when Job fell he got up; when David fell he got up; when Paul fell he got up and every one of them knew how to encourage himself and to continue with the Lord. Many others have completed their course, finished the race and received their rewards. You and I are no different, if we fall we need to get up and if we fall again, get up again, and continue to get up until we have the victory and then not let it go!

This book will also educate you with foundational information that will give you hope and understanding so when you make a decision to take a stand you can stand and not be moved! However, only families who have a desire to know God and choose to walk in His authority and power will be able to receive and benefit the most from this teaching. It promises the life God intended for all of us to live. *In order to receive the full benefit from this writing it will have to be done by committed Christian Believers who are serious about their current marriage or remarriage and their families who desire good success and the victory that has already been won!*

I would like to share a few of the prophecies I received from others over the years regarding God's intentions and purpose as to why He used this vessel to go through and come out victorious so that others would know how to walk in their full authority and power in regards to their marriage and family:

> **November 30, 1995**: The book that I have commissioned will come forth very soon, saith God. I have healed and delivered my children from distress and pain for all those who trust in Me shall live and be free. A just life can be given to all those who willingly seek Me, saith God.
>
> **March 4, 1996:** Begin to write my words and see the mysteries and marvelous things that will unfold. I will reveal much to thee for many will be set free in Me. I am here, I have come to dwell amongst My people, know when I am present for I never leave thee. Abide in Me in this place and see My Word as living water to

quench the thirst of life itself. Read, read and write My words, saith God.

May 17, 1996: Part of this book, your testimony, it will be a part of this book. A book of faith showing people how to trust in the Lord. Help a lot of people get started, build godly character. Given each measure at a time, give pieces here and there for different chapters of the book.

June 7, 2000: Write, write, write…until you finish for I have ordained healing and clarity to come about, completeness and wholeness.

August 10, 2000: Book published by your writing deep things that happened, prophetic writing in this book.

September 28, 2006: Anointing, bless people with writing…

March 4, 2007: As you write the books, as you write the books…I will speak to you, I will speak to you, I will speak to you. As your hand hits the paper, as your pen touches the paper, as the ink flows, I will flow out of you…I will give you the words, open your mouth, open your mouth and utter my voice, and utter my voice.

April 23, 2011: …and the Lord says, all that is in that book is My wisdom…I see a book with a halo on top of the book resting about twelve inches above it. It is sitting on high because it is going to heal people, and bring things together, what was once broken will be mended. I see restoration, a restoration book that is going to stand; it is a restoration book…God says, it is My book I'm going to release it, I'm going to release it…

My prayer is that this resource will enable families to be set free, reconciled where needed, healed of their past, and allow them to live a whole, prosperous and enjoyable life, with God's grace, forgiveness, and favor. Also that they will come to know The Holy Spirit as their Helper and source of everything and a lifeline to a Savior who is a Friend and a loving God who is a Father that truly cares about them and their family in Jesus' name. Amen.

CHAPTER I

WHAT IS THE BIBLICAL DEFINITION FOR MARRIAGE?

(AND HOW GOD BY HIS GRACE GAVE US A COVENANT TO SEAL IT)

Before we can explore the Biblical definition of God's Family we must first start with the definition of what a **"Biblical Marriage"** is according to the Word of God because **the *first family* was the direct result of a *marriage taking place*. *Marriage takes precedence over child parent ties as illustrated by what God chose to create first as the foundation of a family.*** He could have created an entire "family" rather than only a man and a woman but He chose to start with a marriage and build from there. His ways and thoughts are always higher than ours, He has a better plan and ultimately whatever He does is done for the good of humanity (Genesis 1:26-28; Genesis 2:21-25; Isaiah 55:8-9; Jeremiah 29:11).

Understanding the origin of marriage will give more of an appreciation and an awareness of how important marriage is and that it is to be taken very seriously. Divine revelation knowledge is powerful and this information will build a strong foundation so when it is time for your marriage or family to take a stand against opposition it will be able to stand the test and win the battle. *That means your marriage and family will not only survive they will thrive.*

Marriage on earth is a type and shadow, a pattern if you will, of the *Spiritual marriage between God and His bride Israel.* Marriage, as everything else, starts in the spiritual realm *first* and is then manifested into the earthly realm.

God chose Abraham and rose up the nation of Israel and **He not only rose up a nation but God said He would be** *married* **to this nation and to this people.**

Isaiah 54:5-6 says,

> For your Maker is your Husband – the Lord of hosts is His name – and the Holy One of Israel is your Redeemer; the God of the whole earth He is called. For the Lord has called you like a woman forsaken, grieved in spirit, and heartsore even a wife [wooed and won] in youth…

Isaiah 62:5 says,

> For as a young man marries a virgin [O Jerusalem], so shall your sons marry you; and as the bridegroom rejoices over the bride, so shall your God rejoice over you.

The rendering of several words and phrases in the Hebrew and Greek referring to marriage are as follows: to be "master;" to "take," that is, a wife; to "magnify" or "lift up" a woman; to "contract;" to "dwell together;" to "perform the duty of brother;" and to "become," that is, the wife of one. In all the Hebrew Scriptures there is no single word for the estate of marriage or to express the abstract idea of *wedlock* [1] (paraphrased).

God is the Creator, and "To create" is always an act of God, whether it is a spiritual creation or a natural creation. *"God has both the sovereign power and the purposive intelligence to bring forth creation in an orderly, designed fashion, so that it is pleasing to Him…* the Word of God was the effective tool or instrument of God for creating, blessing or chastising…**God created through His Word. In creating, God brought things into existence out of nothingness.** He did not take previously existing matter and transform it into new kinds of material objects. He began with nothing and ended with the whole of existence brought into being out of His powerful Word."[3] (Genesis 1:3 through 2:25).

Whoever creates a thing is the *owner* and knows what the *true* purpose of what it was created for:

> Revelation 4:11 says,
>> Worthy are You, our Lord and God, to receive the glory and the honor and dominion, **for You created *all things*;** by Your will they were [brought into being] and were created.
>
> Genesis 1:1 says,
>> In the Beginning God (prepared, formed, fashioned and) **created the heavens and the earth.**
>
> Psalm 19:1 NLT says,
>> The heavens tell of the glory of God. The skies display His marvelous craftsmanship.
>
> Genesis 1:26-28 says,
>> God said, Let Us [Father, Son and Holy Spirit] make mankind in Our image, after Our likeness, and let them have complete authority over the fish of the sea, the birds of the air, the [tame] beasts, and over all of the earth, and over everything that creeps upon the earth. **So God created man in His own image, in the image and likeness of God** *He created him; male and female He created them. And God blessed them and said to them,*

Be fruitful, multiply, and fill the earth, and subdue it [using all its vast resources in the service of God and man; and have dominion over the fish of the sea, the birds of the air; and over every living creature that moves upon the earth.(Author's addition – **The Lord's creation was a male and female married couple** whom He created, blessed and spoke to from the beginning even though at the time He spoke the "male" man was the only one present before Him in a physical body. The "female" man was very present but as a *hidden support* who was brought forth and formed in Gen. 2:21-22. Discussed further in Chapter 6 under The Importance of a Help Meet and Spiritual Partner).

Now that we have established that God is the Creator according to His Holy Scriptures He gave instructions so that what He created could fulfill their full purpose and function well on the earth.

After God brought the Israelites, whom He married, out of Egypt to be a people unto Himself (Exodus 6:7), *He offered a covenant and said I will give you My promises if you will give Me your heart, soul, mind, strength and serve Me with your entire being and Israel agreed.*

Exodus 19:4-5 says,

You have seen what I did to the Egyptians, and how I bore you on eagles' wings and brought you to Myself. Now therefore, if you will obey My voice in truth and keep My covenant, then you shall be My own peculiar possession and treasure from among and above all peoples; for *all* the earth is Mine.

Deuteronomy 6:5 says,

> And you shall love the Lord your God with all your [mind and] heart and with your entire being and with all your might. (Also see Deuteronomy 11:13).

The Lord we love has not changed; **the New Covenant (that of Grace) existed from the beginning.**

Now I will expound on information regarding a covenant because it is key that we understand that **God uses a covenant to seal the very foundation of marriage, family and our entire existence with our Maker. Without a covenant, marriage is just another arrangement that offers no substance, depth or true value.** God gave the marriage covenant to be the anchor which maintains a stable marriage because the covenant is based on their relationship with the Messiah.

The command God gave to the Israelites in the book of Deuteronomy 6:5 and in Deuteronomy 11:13 is the same command He gives in the New Covenant which allows God to extend His grace.

In Matthew 22:37-39 it says:

> …You shall love the Lord your God with all your heart and with all your soul and with all your mind (intellect). This is the great (most important, principal) and first commandment. And a second is like it: You shall love your neighbor as [you do] yourself. (Also see Luke 10:27).

It was never meant to be *a relationship* of rules, regulations and laws that drain the very life out of people. The laws or written codes must be balanced with the Spirit of God otherwise you will have legalism. To fully understand how to love God simply *receive* the Greater Love first, I John 4:7-12.

God always intended for His grace to bring forth the type of relationship He so desired with mankind and under grace there will always be a balance of the letter of the Word and His Spirit whether we are referring to the "Old Testament" (The Tanakh in

Hebrew) or the "New Testament" (B'rit Hadashah in Hebrew) also respectively called the Old Covenant and New Covenant.

God has given a New Covenant, one of grace and all those that receive will richly benefit from it. For "He has made us competent as ministers of a new covenant – not of **the letter but of the Spirit; for the letter kills, but the Spirit gives life and liberty"** (2 Corinthians 3:6, 17 NIV).

Basically the marriage relationship between God and Israel as well as marriage between a man and a woman rest on a *Covenant,* therefore, let's explore the meaning of a covenant in the following parts:

(1) **What is a Covenant?**
(2) **The Blood Covenant, an Eternal Unbreakable Covenant;**
(3) **The Covenant God Established through Abraham;**
(4) **Will God Ever Break His Covenant with Mankind?**
(5) **How Does the Covenant Affect Marriages Today?**

WHAT IS A COVENANT?

A covenant is an agreement or a decision to keep a promise that is made "...either between tribes or nations; or between individuals in which each party bound himself to fulfill certain conditions and was promised certain advantages."[1]

"Why a Covenant is more than a promise. Covenant is a word we use today, but fail to grasp its full meaning. Many think of it as a promise, but a covenant is far more. It is a total commitment, an absolute requirement, to do or not do something, even at the cost of one's life. Commitment, in terms of life or death, is difficult for us to comprehend, but a covenant is exactly that. When cutting, making a covenant, each party says, "Everything I have is yours!" That is exactly what we are to do with God."[7]

How does a covenant relate between God and man? "In making covenants God was solemnly *invoked as a witness,* whence the expression 'a covenant of the Lord' and an oath was sworn. Therefore, it is improperly used of a covenant between God and man. As man is not in the position of an independent covenanting party, such a covenant is not strictly a mutual compact but a *promise on the part of God* to arrange His providences for the welfare of those who should render Him obedience" [1] (paraphrased). To further this explanation, it is stated that "in the 'covenant,' *man's response contributes to covenant fulfillment; yet man's action is not causative* (what brings about the result nor is he the principle or movement to support it). God's grace always goes before and produces man's response."[2] In other words, even though it is stated **"the covenant between God and Abraham" or "God and David" or God and anyone, it is to be remembered that the outcome is always the result of God's strong hand and man's part is to Love the Lord and follow through with his instructions from God in obedience to Him.**

Furthermore, there are three different types of covenants in the Bible: a covenant is either conditional or unconditional or used to strengthen or support the two previous types of covenants mentioned. A *Conditional Covenant* requires both parties to agree to fulfill a set of conditions in order for the covenant to exist. If either party does not deliver their part then the covenant is broken and invalid. An *Unconditional Covenant* is only when one party is required to keep the promise and nothing is required of the other party. "The Unconditional is given by God and is an Eternal Promise not requiring certain behaviors from its beneficiaries. These are identifiable by the use of the verbs *give* and *establish*. When God **gives** or **establishes** a covenant, it is unconditional. An exception to this is Lev. 26:1-13, which is conditional. When He **cuts** a covenant, it is conditional." [7]

"The 'Old Testament' and the 'New Testament' as the names for the two sections of the Bible indicate that **God's 'covenant' is central to the entire Bible.** The Bible relates God's 'covenant' purpose, that a man be joined to Him in loving service and know eternal fellowship with Him through the redemption that is in Jesus Christ." [2]

"The Hebrew word meaning a 'covenant' or agreement (from a verb signifying 'to cut or divide,' in allusion to a sacrificial custom in connection with 'covenant-making' or where blood flows." [2] "The English word 'covenant' signifies a mutual undertaking between two parties or more, each binding himself to fulfill obligations, it does not in itself contain the idea of joint obligation; it mostly signifies an obligation undertaken by a single person." [2] *A covenant can be referred to by different names or terms such as league, treaty, an agreement, a promise, vow, pledge and sometimes it is translated as testament.*

"Men (mankind) 'enter into' (Deut. 29:12) or 'join' (Jeremiah 50:5) God's covenant..." **God's *covenant* is a relationship of love and loyalty between the Lord and His chosen people,** [2] (paraphrased). The people are to cooperate with and observe carefully the statutes and ordinances of the covenant (Deuteronomy 4:5-8, paraphrased). However, as stated earlier, *above all else, God said that the greatest command which is a part of His covenant is that His people love Him with their all, their entire being*[2] Deuteronomy 6:5 (paraphrased).

There are twenty-two various covenants in scripture but I will only elaborate on the following three: The **"Shoe Covenant"** found in the book of Ruth 4:7 NIV which says, "Now in earlier times in Israel, for the redemption and transfer of property to become final, one party took off his sandal and gave it to the other. This was the method of legalizing transactions in Israel." In the book of Ruth it also shows that a covenant regarding a marriage to a widow of an Israelite involved intricate covenant regulations. It says that, "Boaz showed loyalty to God's covenant, respect and love for Ruth and concern for the near kinsman as he worked through the legal process to gain his wife. Such commitment is necessary in marriage" (Ruth 3:1–4:12). [3]

The **"Salt Covenant"** is a covenant which involved people in a loyal act. The salt covenant was a symbol of permanence and preservation. "All of life relates to the commitment we make to God. Certain regulations were part of the covenant along with other provisions. Putting valuable salt on offerings signified costly sacrifice and commitment to God's covenant as well as freedom from impurity" (Leviticus 2:13).[3] In addition, "covenanting parties were accustomed to partake of salt, thus making a covenant of salt, one that was inviolably sure

(Numbers 18:19; 2 Chron. 13:5). The meaning appears to have been that the salt, with its power to strengthen food and keep it from decay, symbolized the unbending truthfulness of that self-surrender to the Lord embodied in the sacrifice, by which all impurity and hypocrisy were repelled." [1]

THE "BLOOD COVENANT" AN ETERNAL UNBREAKABLE COVENANT:

Mankind was redeemed by the price of blood. *The New Covenant in Christ differs from the old covenant because it is eternal* – **the Lamb of God, the Lord Jesus shed His blood to seal this covenant forever making it the strongest covenant in the earth today.** Because of His sacrifice this covenant also blesses us with every spiritual blessing in the heavenly realm, (Ephesians 1:3).

Hebrews 13:20-21 says,

> Now may the God of peace [Who is the Author and the Giver of peace], Who brought again from among the dead our Lord Jesus, that great Shepherd of the sheep, by **the blood [that sealed, ratified] the everlasting agreement (covenant, testament),** strengthen (complete, perfect) and make you what you ought to be and equip you with everything good that you may carry out His will; [while He Himself] works in you and accomplishes that which is pleasing in His sight, through Jesus Christ (the Messiah); to Whom be the glory forever and ever (to the ages of the ages) Amen (so be it).

2 Chronicles 13:5 says,

> Ought you not to know that the Lord, the God of Israel, gave the kingship over Israel to

David forever, even to him and to his sons by a covenant of salt?

Why is the blood of Jesus so important? Because it was foretold in the Holy Scriptures that a virgin would give birth to the Son of God (Isaiah 7:14; Luke 1:34-35 and Matthew 1:18) and he would be sent not to condemn the world but rather that the world through Him might be saved (find salvation and be made safe and sound through Him, John 3:16-17). **And because He was the Son of God His blood was *WITHOUT* the Adamic stain of sin.**

The Heavenly Father prepared Him a body that would have blood that was <u>not</u> corrupted by the curse that was released on mankind after the first Adam disobeyed God (Heb. 10:5-10; Genesis 3). So when this blood was sacrificed through the obedience of Jesus the Heavenly Father received it and reconciled mankind back to Himself (Romans 5:19).

Hebrews 10:5-10 explains the reason that *God <u>prepared a body for Jesus:</u>*

> Hence, when He [Christ] entered into the world, He said, Sacrifices and offerings You have not desired, but instead You have *made ready a body for Me [to offer]*;

> In burnt offerings and sin offerings You have taken no delight. Then I said, Behold, here I am, coming to do Your will, O God –[to fulfill] what is written of Me in the volume of the Book...Thus He does away with and annuls the first (former) order [as a means of expiating sin] so that He might inaugurate and establish the second (latter) order.

> And in accordance with this will [of God], we have been made holy (consecrated and sanctified) through the offering made *once* for all of the body of Jesus Christ (the Anointed One).

In the book, *The Power of the Blood*, the author further explains how God the Father prepared a body for His Son that had perfect blood: [4]

> His blood was perfect and the Holy Spirit was the Divine Agent who caused Jesus' conception in Mary's womb. This, therefore, was **not a normal conception, but a supernatural act of God in planting the life of his already existent Son right in the womb of Mary,** *with no* **normal conception of a male spermatozoon with the female ovum of Mary.** As the blood type of the Son of God was a separate and precious type, it is inconceivable that Mary could have supplied any of her Adamic blood for the spotless Lamb of God. **All the Child's Blood came from His Father in heaven by a supernatural creative act of God. Jesus' Blood was without the Adamic stain of sin.**
>
> The idea by a few that Mary supplied the ovum and that the Holy Spirit supplied the spiritual spermatozoon would mean that Jesus would have been conceived with mixed blood, part of Adam and part of God, which is repugnant to God's plan of salvation for a fallen human race.
>
> The fact of the matter is that God says in the Bible that He prepared a body for His Son. It was that body that was created in Mary's womb.

Jesus' conception was not normal but supernatural. The following is that of a normal conception: [4]

> The female ovum itself has no blood, neither has the male spermatozoon; but it is when these come together in the fallopian tube that conception takes place, and a new life begins.

The blood cells in this new creation are from both father and mother and the blood type is determined at the moment of conception and is thereafter protected by the placenta from any flow of the mother's blood into the fetus.

The reason His blood had to be perfect and not mixed with the first Adam (Paraphrased): [4]

> Of course the obvious is that Jesus' blood could not be tainted with the cursed blood if He was to accomplish His mission and He did. Therefore, when God created man, He formed a body from the dust of the ground (Gen. 3:19) –from the substances and chemicals of this planet. Then *He breathed into this body the breath of life.* In other words, He breathed into this chemical composition some of His own spiritual life, and that life was held in the chemical substance we call blood.
>
> So, you see, **blood is not life, but it carries life.** This becomes quite clear by observing what happens at death. Immediately after expiration, the person is still warm, and will remain so for a brief time. Yet that person is dead because the mysterious *life* has departed from the blood. The life of man is carried in his blood stream. **Life itself is spiritual, but it must have a physical carrier, and this carrier is the blood.** Our blood has the capacity to carry the life of God, the contact between the Divine and the human rests in the blood stream.
>
> Jesus was the only begotten of the Father (John 1:14) and His body was formed and fashioned wonderfully in the womb of Mary His mother; but **the Life that was in Jesus**

Christ came alone from the Father by the Holy Spirit. No wonder He said I am the LIFE (John 14:6).

When disobedience corrupted the life in our blood it was no longer that pure breath of life from God and it was causing us to die but because of God's mercy, *desire for a family*, fellowship and His love for all of us He sent His only begotten Son and the result of it is that we can overcome evil by the blood of the Lamb, Revelation 12:11.

To *further explain the meaning of a covenant* one must understand there were ceremonies involved to seal them. However, they had to be repeated regularly and for man's sins repeated yearly until the blood covenant put a stop to it forever which we will explain after a quick definition of what a ceremony would entail.

"Covenants were not only concluded with an oath (Gen. 26:28; 31:53; Josh. 9:15), but, after an ancient custom, confirmed by slaughtering and cutting a victim into two halves between which the parties passed, to intimate that if either of them broke the covenant it would fare with him as with the slain and divided beast. Moreover, the covenanting parties often partook of a common meal (Gen. 26:30; 31:54) or at least of some grains of salt." [1]

"According to the Mosaic ritual, the blood of the victim was divided into halves; one-half was sprinkled upon the altar and the other upon the people (Ex. 24:6-8). The meaning of this seems to be that, in the sprinkling of the blood upon the altar, the people were introduced into gracious fellowship with God, and atonement made for their sin. Through the sprinkling of the blood upon the people Israel was formally consecrated to the position of God's covenant people." [1]

THE COVENANT GOD ESTABLISHED THROUGH ABRAHAM:

In Genesis 6:18-20 God established and ratified a covenant with Noah before the flood occurred that lasted for forty days and forty nights. The next covenant God established with mankind was with a *Hebrew named Abram* in Genesis 15:5, 9-21. However, before the covenant was established Abram was called by God and the Lord told him in Genesis 12:1-3:

> Now [in Haran] the Lord said to Abram, Go for yourself [for your own advantage] away from your country, from your relatives and your father's house, to the land that I will show you. [Hebrews 11:8-10].
>
> And I will make of you a *great nation*, and I will bless you [with *abundant increase* of favors] and make your *name famous* and distinguished, and *you will be a blessing* [dispensing good to others].
>
> **And** *I will bless those who bless you* **who confer prosperity or happiness upon you]** **and** *curse him who curses or uses insolent language toward you*; in you will families and kindred of the earth be blessed [and by you they will bless themselves]. [Gal. 3:8].

God also told him to "look now toward the heavens and count the stars– if you are able to number them. Then He said to him, So shall your descendants be" in other words, he would have so many descendants that he could not count them (Gen. 15:5 and Hebrews 11:12).

Fourteen years later God renewed the covenant with Abram and changed his name from Abram which means *exalted father* to Abraham which means *father of many* and established circumcision as a part of the covenant, Genesis 17:4-21.

God made a promise to Abraham that is still in effect to this day. This covenant is unconditional because God will never fail to do His required part of keeping His promise, therefore, the Abrahamic covenant will never be broken. The main features of the Abrahamic covenant were basically for a nation and a land: (1) The promise of the descendants; (2) the promise of the land;

and (3) the promise of blessing and redemption. And *one of the key principles of the Abrahamic covenant is that when a person or a nation obeys God concerning the moral truths found in the Holy Bible that person or nation would be blessed; to be blessed means to increase.*

When God gave Abraham a covenant, it was a covenant of grace and faith for Abraham also increased greatly as God made him extremely rich in livestock, in silver and in gold (Genesis 13:2). God also gave land to his posterity (succeeding generations) Genesis 12:7 and in Genesis 17:7 which says:

> And I will establish My covenant between Me and you and your descendants after you throughout their generations for an everlasting, solemn pledge, to be a God to you and to your posterity after you.

This passage shows that God not only made a covenant with Abraham but also with Abraham's descendants through his marriage to Sarai whose name was also changed as quoted below.

Genesis 17:15-21:

> And God said to Abraham, As for Sarai your wife, you shall not call her name Sarai, but Sarah [Princess] her name shall be. **And *I will bless her and give you a son also by her.*** Yes, I will bless her, and she shall be a mother of nations; kings of peoples shall come from her.
>
> Then Abraham fell on his face and laughed and said in his heart, Shall a child be born to a man who is a hundred years old? And shall Sarah, who is ninety years old, bear a son? And [he] said to God, Oh, that Ishmael might live before You!
>
> But God said, Sarah your wife shall bear you a son indeed, and you shall *call his name Isaac* [laughter]; and I will **establish My covenant**

> **or solemn pledge** *with him for an everlasting covenant and with his posterity after him.* And as for Ishmael, I have heard and heeded you: behold, I will bless him and will make him fruitful and will multiply him exceedingly; He will be the father of twelve princes, and I will make him a great nation. [Fulfilled in Gen. 25:12-18].
>
> *But My covenant, My promise and pledge, I will establish with Isaac, whom Sarah will bear to you at this season next year.*

Taking this a step further, the Lord made it clear that the covenant would be throughout generations for an everlasting, solemn pledge which brings us in remembrance that *this covenant will not be broken because it is sealed with the blood of Jesus (Yeshua) Who is the Heir of the covenant made between God and Abraham.*

Galatians 3:16 states:

> Now the promises (covenants, agreements) were decreed and made to Abraham and his Seed (his Offspring, his Heir). He [God] does not say, And to seeds (descendants, heirs), as if referring to many persons, but And to your Seed (your Descendant, your Heir), obviously referring to one individual, Who is [none other than] Christ (the Messiah).

Galatians 3:16 above states that the Heir is Jesus and all connected to Him are part of the succeeding generations, I listed this scripture to prove later that **when you are a descendant of Abraham you are entitled to receive the** *Blessings of Abraham because of the covenant that was made between God and Abraham.* This blessing will be greatly appreciated when you are standing on and believing from the Word of God to receive your inheritance which will include your marriage and family having the peace and prosperity God chose for you to have as heirs of the covenant of Abraham.

God is mindful of us and will bless us, the Word says, "May the Lord give you increase more and more you and your children" (Psalms 115:12-16). **Material blessings were a part of the covenant of increase for Abraham and his descendants to enjoy while they were here on this earth. The *Blessing of Abraham* also includes the blessings that were received for obedience found in Deuteronomy 28:1-14.** All of these material blessings were enjoyed by Abraham and his children because *they never became their god.* God was first in Abraham's life not the material riches; therefore, God did not mind him and his family enjoying the blessings on this earth that brought comfort into their lives.

The same holds true for all succeeding generations in Christ. In the book of Galatians it makes reference to this in chapter 3:26-29:

> For in Christ Jesus you are all sons of God through faith. For as many [of you] as were baptized into Christ [into a spiritual union and communion with Christ, the Anointed One, the Messiah] have put on (clothed yourselves with) Christ. There is [now no distinction] neither Jew nor Greek, there is neither slave nor free, there is not male and female; for you are all one in Christ Jesus. **And if you belong to Christ [are in Him Who is Abraham's Seed], then you are Abraham's offspring and [spiritual] heirs according to promise.**

The Lord reminds us not to be a stranger to our covenant and promises because we receive our hope from the covenant God made with Abraham. The covenant reminds us that we are not alone without hope or without God in this world but are close because of the blood of Jesus (Ephesians 2:12-14).

History about one's self whether it is spiritual or in the natural is always helpful in receiving one's destiny and preventing it from being stolen. When you can walk or live with confidence knowing your rights, in this case rights of an inheritance because of who you are in Christ, it makes one aware that there is more to life than they could have ever imagined and it gives life more meaning and understanding. To think that God in the Heavens made a *covenant with your forefather* (if you are a descendant of Abraham) *that still stands today* and that covenant is eternal and carries with it physical and tangible blessings to make your life enjoyable on earth as the process of His restoring families takes place.

Lastly, God gave a **sign with each covenant.** A sign is *evidence of God's promises (*He has done something in the realm of the physical to let us know He is present and involved) *(*2 Cor. 1:20); examples of signs are given below and follow throughout the chapter. For example, one of the signs of accepting and ratifying the covenant God made with Abraham was the circumcision of all males (Genesis 17:11-13) and this is still in effect to this day, however, circumcision is no longer used to show or prove a covenant exists today for all those in Christ according to Colossians 2:11 which says:

> In Him also you were circumcised with a circumcision not made with hands, but in a [spiritual] circumcision [performed by] Christ by stripping off the body of the flesh (the whole corrupt, carnal nature with its passions and lusts).

Another example, God established a covenant with Noah, with his descendants and with every living creature that was with him: the birds, the livestock and all the wild animals, all those that came out of the ark with him. And He said "never again will all life be cut off by the waters of a flood; never again will there be a flood to destroy the earth" (Genesis 9:9-11 NIV). **And God said that He set a *rainbow in the clouds* and that it will be a *sign* of the everlasting covenant between Him and mankind** and all living creatures of every kind on the earth (Gen. 9:11-16) and *to my knowledge rainbows still exist to this day which means the covenant still stands today.*

In addition to God giving signs to His people to show evidence of His promises, He will also give signs to show them the correct way to go as they make their way through the wilderness period of life on their journey to their promise land, destiny or the fulfillment of a dream that is in their heart.

God does not consider these signs wicked but He gives direction because of His love and mercy. What *displeases* Him are people who *demand* a sign to prove He is who He claims to be (Matthew 12:38-39). They need to exercise faith by taking Him at His Word and in doing so they will please a living and loving God who will out of His mercy and grace give them a sign or signs to help increase their faith and to make their journey a more pleasant one.

WILL GOD *EVER* BREAK HIS COVENANT WITH MANKIND?

In His Word it says "For the Lord your God is a merciful God; He will not fail you or destroy you or forget the covenant of your fathers, which He swore to them" (Deuteronomy 4:31). Under the Old Covenant God was *with us* and under the New Covenant God is *in us*.

In Leviticus 26:42-45 the Lord said:

> Then will I [earnestly] remember My covenant with Jacob, My covenant with Isaac, and My covenant with Abraham and [earnestly] remember the land... v 45 says, But I will for their sake [earnestly] remember the covenant with their forefathers whom I brought forth out of the land of Egypt in the sight of the nations, that I might be their God. I am the Lord.

God takes His covenants very seriously. "To make a promise to God and not carry through represents lack of gratitude or trust in God. We must not make promises to God lightly. He does not take His words or ours lightly. He expects us to do what we promise, no turning back" (Ecclesiastes 5:4-6 NIV). [3] In His Word He tells us "when you vow a vow or make a pledge to God, do not put off or delay in fulfilling or paying it;" because His Word says, "He has no pleasure in fools (those who witlessly mock Him)... for it is better that you should not vow than that you should vow and not pay." Ecclesiastes 5:4-5 (paraphrased from the NIV and AMP).

Therefore, a man *can* break his covenant with God as will be demonstrated in this chapter. However, let's look at what God said He would do with His covenant between Himself and His people that would cause it to last forever.

Jeremiah 31:31-34 states:

> Behold, the days are coming, says the Lord, when I will make a new covenant with the house of Israel and with the house of Judah. Not according to the covenant which I made with their fathers in the day when I took them by the hand to bring them out of the land of Egypt, My covenant which they broke, although I was their Husband, says the Lord. **But this is the covenant which I will make with the house of Israel: After those days, says the Lord, I will put My law within them, and on their hearts will I write it; and I will be their God, and they will be My people.** And they will no more teach each man his neighbor and each man his brother, saying, Know the Lord, for they will all know Me [recognize, understand, and be acquainted with Me], from the least of them to the greatest, says the Lord. For I will forgive their iniquity, and I will [seriously] remember their sin no more.

Because of the New Covenant which God said He would make with the house of Israel and with the house of Judah when anything man does to jeopardize or break the covenant between God and mankind can quickly be restored by asking for forgiveness and with true repentance.

Furthermore, in the book of Jeremiah 33:20-26 the Lord explains that you cannot break His covenant with the day or His covenant with the night and just as that will be forever so shall it be a sign that the covenant He made with David and the covenant He made with the Levitical priests and His ministers cannot be broken either and will be forever.

Not only was the New Covenant spoken of in the Old Testament but the *New Testament* as well as we find the same words that were written in the book of Jeremiah 31:31-34 were also listed in the book of Hebrews 8:8-12 as a reminder and to reinforce the covenant. In the book of Hebrews 8:8 it says to whom the covenant is directed to "…I will make and ratify a new covenant or agreement with the house of Israel and with the house of Judah." **In the book of Hebrews 10:16-18 the Lord makes the agreement plain:** "This is the agreement (testament, covenant) that I will set up and conclude with them after those days, says the Lord: I will imprint My laws upon their hearts, and I will inscribe them on their minds (on their inmost thoughts and understanding), …and their sins and their lawbreaking I will remember no more. Now where there is absolute remission (forgiveness and cancellation of the penalty) of these [sins and lawbreaking], there is no longer any offering made to atone for sin."

Why is there no longer any yearly offering made to atone for sin? Because there is now "full freedom and confidence to enter into the [Holy of] Holies [by the power and virtue] in the blood of Jesus" (Hebrews 10:19; 9:11-28). The door was opened when the veil was torn from top to bottom by God Himself after the price was paid to redeem man and reconcile him back to God and re-establish fellowship that day on Calvary. Because of the sacrifice, the covenant was restored and made new and we are welcome to be a part of it because of His grace to receive all by faith (to simply trust and take Him at His Word) Ephesians 2:5 and John 3:14-17.

The following scripture found in the book of Isaiah 9:6-7 also confirms that God set a new covenant in place that *will not* be broken by Him:

> For to us a Child is born, to us a Son is given; and the government shall be upon His shoulder, and His name shall be called Wonderful Counselor, Mighty God, Everlasting Father [of Eternity], Prince of Peace. Of the increase of His government and of peace there shall be no end, upon the *throne of David* and over his kingdom, to establish it and to uphold it with justice and with righteousness from the [latter] time forth, even *forevermore*. The zeal of the Lord of hosts will perform this. (Daniel 2:44; Hebrews 1:8 and I Corinthians 15:25-28).

"That hope looked for a future king who would bring about the reign of God and the redemption of His people. This passage describes the hoped – for messianic ruler to reign on the *throne of David*. His kingdom would be established on the basis of justice and righteousness. It would be a lasting kingdom, taking the Lord Almighty Himself to accomplish it. The *New Testament (Covenant)* recognized Jesus as the fulfillment of this hope, the Inaugurator of God's ideal reign, who will return to consummate it." [3]

Further, *"the Covenant with David was in reality but another and more specific form of the covenant with Abraham*; its main object was to mark with greater exactness the line through which 'The Blessing' promised in the Abrahamic covenant was to find it's accomplishment. The royal *Seed* was from then on to be in the house of David (2 Samuel 7:12; 22:51), and especially in connection with the *One* who was to be preeminently the Child of promise in that house, all good, *first* to Israel and then to all nations, should be realized" (Psalms 2; 22; Isaiah 9:6-7).[1] Also in the book of Matthew 1:1-16 in the genealogy of Jesus with emphasis on verse sixteen, this passage too clearly gives the connection where it proves *Jesus came through the line of King David who was from the line of Abraham.* Abraham's covenant was for a nation and a land whereas David's covenant was for a throne and a city, Jerusalem; all constructed to enable the Child of promise to come forth and rule forever.

The Lord always as mentioned earlier gives **a** *sign to confirm or show evidence that He has made a covenant.* The following scripture shows that God gave a *sign* that demonstrates that He established a New Covenant with King David that would last forever.

Psalms 89:34-37 says,

> My covenant will I not break or profane, nor alter the thing that is gone out of My lips. Once [for all] have I sworn by My holiness, which cannot be violated; I will not lie to David: His Offspring shall endure forever, and his throne [shall continue] as the sun before Me. [Isa. 9:7; Gal. 3:16]. It shall be established forever as the moon, the faithful witness in the heavens. [Rev. 1:5, 3:14].

The *New Covenant was also sealed* and that is why it was received by the Father in Heaven as the final sacrifice to redeem mankind. From the book of Hebrews 9:11-28, I have listed verses 11, 12 and 15 to make this point:

> But [that appointed time came] when Christ (the Messiah) appeared as a High Priest of the better things that have come and are to come. [Then] through the greater and more perfect tabernacle not made with [human] hands, that is not a part of this material creation. v12 - **He went once for all into the [Holy of] Holies [of Heaven], not by virtue of the blood of goats and calves [by which to make reconciliation between**

God and man], but His own blood, having found and secured a complete redemption (an everlasting release for us). v15 – [Christ, the Messiah] is therefore the Negotiator and Mediator of an [entirely] new agreement (testament, covenant), so that those who are called and offered it may receive the fulfillment of the promised everlasting inheritance –since a death has taken place which rescues and delivers and redeems them from the transgressions committed under the [old] first agreement.

God is not a God that He should lie and He is faithful to His Word. If He said it He will do it. This is why we place our trust in Him and in His Word. 2 Timothy 2:13 in the Message Bible says this in regards to His faithfulness:

> If we give up on Him, He does not give up – for there's no way He can be false to Himself.

Furthermore, *God is so faithful from the beginning to the end*, He demonstrates His faithfulness as He called us to salvation, as He calls us to be sanctified He knows we cannot achieve these things in our own power and wisdom, so He graces us with His grace (ability and empowerment) and gives us His wisdom to show His faithfulness and in order to fulfill His promises to us. Therefore, we have no need to fear the judgment which the world (people who are without salvation in Christ Jesus) will face at the appointed time.

I Thessalonians 5:24 says,

> Faithful is He Who is calling you [to Himself] and utterly trustworthy, and He will also do it [fulfill His call by hallowing and keeping you].

In concluding this portion on will God break His covenant with mankind, the fact was established that He will not. However, *it was mentioned earlier that man on the other hand* <u>*could*</u>

break his covenant with the living God. King Solomon was able to break the covenant God had with him. But, because of God's <u>faithfulness</u> to His Word, God had *already protected* the covenant by making a new covenant with Solomon's father King David. To illustrate the fact that King Solomon had nullified his covenant with God is explained in the following passage:

From I Chronicles 28:9 KJV/AMP Parallel version states in their footnote:

God's promises to men and women invariably are dependent upon the other party to the covenant meeting His conditions, whether He says so at the time or not. In I Chronicles 28:7 we find Him promising to establish Solomon's Kingdom forever. Yet *in I Kings 11:9-11 we find that God became angry with Solomon for all his degenerate and abominable conduct and his treachery of heart toward Him; and without mercy, except for David's sake, God declared that the kingdom would be torn from him.*

Was God breaking His covenant with Solomon? No, Solomon had broken and nullified that covenant long before; it no longer existed. There was now no promise for God to keep.

Some Christians are prone to think that God will keep His part of a bargain whether they do or not, but the wisest man who ever lived died knowing that God is not mocked. "[He inevitably deludes himself who attempts to delude God.] For whatever a man sows, that only is what he will reap" (Galatians 6:7). "If you seek Him [inquiring for and of Him and requiring Him as your first and vital necessity], you will find Him; but if you forsake Him, He will cast you off forever! (Author's addition – "But whoever denies and disowns Me before men, I also will deny and disown him before My Father Who is in heaven," Matthew 10:33).

Unfortunately in all of Solomon's wisdom he failed to comprehend that "Something greater and more exalted and more majestic than the temple is here!" And Someone more and greater than Solomon is here, (Matthew 12:6, 42).

People of God must realize that when the "God" of the third heaven created us by His power and grace in His own image, He gave everyone a free will. He will not violate that, He will not make us love Him, obey Him or do anything else. However, He will lead us into all righteousness through Christ Jesus by His Holy Spirit Who was sent to help keep us on track but if we choose to ignore His Holy Spirit and His plan for our lives (which is greater than any we could ever possibly come up with ourselves) then He has no choice because of our free will except to allow us to proceed in whatever we decide to do which can and will be influenced by the adversary.

These are some of the reasons God takes His covenants very seriously, His Word is His bond, they are living words, containers of power that are not to be taken lightly. He will remain faithful to His Word even when we are not.

HOW DOES THE COVENANT AFFECT MARRIAGES TODAY?

We have shown that the new covenant God made was through the line of David and it will last forever. This is important because the essential core for **the entire marriage covenant between a man and a woman is modeled after the marriage of God and Israel, therefore, if that covenant still stands so does the covenant God validates for today's marriages.**

Remember two things, (first) that the new covenant made through the line of David not only does it include the covenant made with our forefather's Abraham, Isaac and Jacob but the *land of Israel* is also mentioned in the new covenant in several passages as a reminder that God does not forget His promises; (secondly) Jesus showed all of us throughout time the importance of the wedding and marriage covenant when He did *His very first miracle* at a wedding feast (John 2:1-11).

Marriage is a divine institution formed by a "blood covenant" which is validated *only* **by God, simply because He created it.** It is between one man and one woman and their God. Why? Because at the time God was restoring the earth, the Lord God formed mankind (male and female) from the dust of the ground and breathed into his nostrils the Spirit of life (Genesis 2:7; Gen.1:27). He created mankind in His own image or likeness and said He gave **them** complete authority over all the earth (Genesis 1:26). Shortly after God formed man He brought forth his wife who was hidden inside of him because God said it was not good (sufficient, satisfactory) that the man should be alone... (Genesis 2:18).

Therefore, "the Lord God caused a deep sleep to fall upon Adam; and while he slept, He took one of his ribs or a part of his side and closed up the [places with] flesh" (Genesis 2:21). "And the rib or part of his side which the Lord God had taken from the man He *built up* and *made* into a *woman,* and He *brought her to the man*" (Genesis 2:22). **Notice that when the Lord opened and closed Adam's side the blood that was shed formed a blood covenant for this new institution called marriage.**

Many believe that on the wedding night if the woman is a virgin during intercourse she may experience some bleeding (which is normal because the hymen which is a fold of mucous membrane partly closing the vagina is broken) and this has become to some a part of forming a blood covenant for *that* marriage. But what about the couples where the young ladies have already experienced bleeding from the hymen being broken before marriage because of participating in strenuous sports events or other activities or they lost their virginity before marriage due to pre-marital sex or because of abuse? Or the women who have entered into a subsequent marriage? Are these marriages not protected by a blood covenant once the vows have been exchanged? Of course they are! As shown above the marriage covenant between God, a man and a woman which is also a blood covenant was formed for *all future marriages in the Lord* when He opened Adam up and Adam bled as the Lord took out a rib and formed it into a woman and the first marriage took place on the face of the earth.

Furthermore, the marriage is consummated by the wedding vows and not necessarily by the act of intercourse (John 3:29) which will be explained later in this chapter under 'The Marriage Protocol from Ancient Times to Today's Marriages.' **Note: A woman changing her name to her husband's name was also a part of the marriage covenant.** When God formed Adam's wife they were both called Adam and it was Adam who renamed his wife "Eve" (Gen. 3:20); he also called his wife "woman" (Gen. 2:23). When God made a covenant with people He often changed their names so they would be called by that which He declared for their destiny, for example, Abram to Abraham who became the father of many nations and Jacob to Israel who became the father of twelve sons who would become the twelve tribes of Israel and Eve which means life spring because she was the mother of all the living. Once a couple marries then the wife acquires her husband's name that is significant in declaring the household of which she has become.

When God said He *brought* her to the man, thereby, causing the first marriage between one man and one woman the Lord of Glory validated the first marriage and ordained the first Blood Covenant that was made on earth between God and mankind. In a biblical wedding ceremony the woman is escorted usually by her father down the aisle and is presented or *brought* to her husband. Here again is another model that was adapted by man from God's protocol of God and Israel, God said "He *brought* Israel to Himself" (Exodus 19:4).

Furthermore, **God called her a "helper meet,"** in the KJV she is called a "help meet." *A help meet is a married woman who is* *a confidante, encourager, an inward strength, her husband's helper, a comforter, an aid suitable for him;* someone who is sent by God to help him fulfill his purpose and vision while on this earth. The "helper" does not mean inferior but describes a "function" and not "worth." It can and does include more than birthing children and managing a home according to the Word of God (Proverbs 31:10-31; Ps 68:11; Esther 4:14; and so on). These are *very important* functions but they are not the only functions that God purposed as a woman's part in being her husband's helper, but she may also be a woman who has an assignment or mandate from God to fulfill. (See Chapter 6 for more details regarding a biblical woman and/or wife).

As we know the Holy Spirit, the Third Person of the Godhead is also called a "Helper" and Jesus refers to Himself as a "Helper." As a helper the woman is in Good company and is equipped and anointed by God to help her husband. A willingness to help others in a loving manner is the very thing God loves and desires of all His children.

In John 14:16, Jesus is speaking about Himself and the Holy Spirit,

> I will ask the Father, and He will give you *another* Comforter (Counselor, *Helper*, Intercessor, Advocate, Strengthener and Standby), that He may remain with you forever...

A woman as a help meet is found in Genesis 2:18,

> Now the Lord God said, It is not good (sufficient, satisfactory) that the man should be alone; I will make him a helper meet (suitable, adapted, complementary) for him.

A woman is given wisdom and strength to be a man's spiritual partner in the task of obedience to God. She is the "female" man, the counterpart of the "male" man. When God created "Adam" He created mankind (the male and female), the very name Adam means "man, mankind or natural man." When the Lord God tailor made a woman for this man and presented her to him at that moment *God established a covenant between the two of them and Himself.* And because it was intended for a *lifetime* it is still so for today and what made it work then is powerful enough to cause it to work today. (See Chapter 6 under The Importance of a Help Meet and Spiritual Partner for additional information regarding the wife as a man's spiritual partner and how both were created at the same time).

When a man and woman exchange their wedding vows (oath) which are repeated before an officiant and witnesses, who are generally family and friends, *they seal and establish a sacred lifetime covenant with one another and with God.*

God takes the wedding covenant seriously even when we do not. Wedding vows are a promise to love, honor, respect, cherish and a lot more and the Lord expects us to fulfill our vows or to say the very least make a great attempt at fulfilling them. Whatever the Lord asks of someone He has equipped them to do it. The key is to know Him and to know His will in a certain matter. Once that is accomplished following His instructions to cause something to work will be a lot easier. But understand this, in a marriage covenant you are dealing with two people which both possess a "free will" and one cannot "make" the other do anything against their free will without causing damage to the relationship. So with that in mind, how would these two separate individuals who have been supernaturally joined by the Spirit of God and are now *one* in God's eyes become *one* in the natural? God will help them make it happen as along as He is the head in *their* marriage covenant with Him.

CLEAVING AND BECOMING ONE:

One of the first things to learn is to *cleave to the* **marriage covenant** and realize that when we are married we are no longer two, but one flesh (one mind that should be walking or living together in agreement). "What therefore .God has joined together, let not man put asunder (separate)," Matthew 19:6. The word **Cleave** literally means to "stick like glue." Having left your family home with parent(s) or the single life you now bond with your spouse and become one flesh. As you marry you become one in the spirit supernaturally once your vows are spoken and you learn to cleave in the natural with that person you are now *one* with. As we cleave we should set our priorities to place our marriages at the top of the list right after our own personal relationship with our Maker.

When God is first and as we grow closer to Him as individuals it will draw us closer together with a better meaning and understanding for our marriage and each other. This pattern or method will always keep God at the center of the relationship and cause one to cleave in a cheerful way. A person will gain greater insight and strategy from a holy God Who loves you and wants to see your marriage succeed because He loves what He created and always desires the best.

If your spouse is not willing to really seek God in order to keep the marriage sound by staying out of danger zones and to do their part to help cleave to the marriage covenant, then allow them to see you doing your part by walking in love, forgiveness, understanding and communicating with good body language, facial expressions and using a calm voice tone. Let them see your consideration of them when they know they don't deserve it as well as allowing them to see you seek God for yourself. And also that you are willing to wait on God for instructions without making any rash decisions about your marriage something God takes very seriously (this can be accomplished by a man or a woman) I Peter 3:1, paraphrased. Of course I am not speaking about people enduring physical abuse they may need other options.

During the cleaving process we should set priorities to keep God first; keep Godly principles and set quality time to spend with your spouse, to touch basis with them during the day and at other times to keep them in your heart not thinking on the negative but cleaving to the positive that may have brought you together in the first place.

According to Pastor Ed Young, **"When a man and woman leave and cleave, they become one."** "What is important to your spouse is important to you; what troubles your spouse, insults your spouse or hurts your spouse you will feel the weight of these things too. He goes on to say, we strengthen each other, we encourage each other and we hold each other. In other words, we cleave, in both good times and in bad. We are covenant partners." He added, *"When you leave parents, people, problems and places of your past and cleave to the sacred covenant of marriage, the principles of God, and your mate you will have unity, you are one flesh. If you are to have this oneness in your marriage then he says you must do everything you can to cleave to your mate physically, emotionally, and spiritually."*[5]

One must be ready to emotionally leave home realizing that leaving father and mother to cleave to their spouse does not mean that you no longer have anything to do with your parents; you should always love, honor, enjoy and respect them. **Leaving your father and mother simply means that now your spouse is the exalted person in your life.** Married people are the two closest people in the world because *they have become one* in the spirit in the eyes of God and with that are added benefits. For example, if they pray together in agreement, and their prayer is in God's will, then *their prayer is the most powerful prayer in the universe*. This is one reason Satan fights marriage because prayers that are in agreement come against his kingdom of darkness (discussed in Chapter 7, Section One).

The New Ungers Bible Dictionary has this to say about a *Christian marriage and oneness*:

…The original appointment of monogamy is confirmed.

The presence of Jesus at the wedding in Cana happily

illustrates the feeling and teaching of Christianity respecting marriage. Christ taught the divine origin and sacredness of this institution. It is more than filial duty. It is unifying. *The husband and wife become one through the purity and intensity of mutual love; common interests are necessitated by common affection...* Furthermore, marriage is not binding upon every member of the race, and that devotion or discretion may make it expedient to renounce or defer it...

They are no longer two, but one in the flesh in the eyes of God (Matthew 19:6). When they are in agreement and keep the Lord as the head of their marriage through their relationship with Him, it will strengthen and preserve their marriage. The Bible says in Ecclesiastes 4:12, "And though a man might prevail against him who is alone, two will withstand him. A threefold cord is not quickly broken."

Joyce Meyer said the following about *"Becoming One:"*

If both people in a marriage relationship are born again, then the spiritual union is in place. The most difficult part of the "becoming one" process is usually the uniting of two souls –the joining of two minds, wills, and sets of emotions. Most marital problems in the arena of the soul result from strife over lack of communication, sexual misunderstanding, money, goals, and the disciplining of children. All of these things need to be worked out in the soulish realm of the marriage union, and in order to become one in that area, a husband and a wife need to give their issues to God and say, "Father, change my mind or my will if I'm wrong." God is the One Who will bring them into agreement with His will and purpose. *If each marriage partner is willing to be brought into agreement with the other, they no longer try to force each other to be someone they are not, but realize they need each other to be exactly* *who God created them to be. They no longer pick on each other's weaknesses. Instead, they partake of their strengths, they enjoy one another, and they enjoy the process of becoming one.*

As we remember that marriage is a divine institution designed to form a permanent union between a man and a woman we must look to God for it to function properly in order to receive all of the promises of the covenant which includes a healthy, long and loving marriage.

In addition, in the marriage covenant we have vowed to God to do certain things, but as we all know just like any other commandment, teaching or cut and dry rules and regulations that are legalistic will not prevent people from falling short because the "hard fast rule" will become destructive when it is without the Spirit of God which gives life and brings balance (2 Corinthians 3:6).

For example, when Moses brought the Israelites out of Egypt it was by *God's Grace* **(Spirit, power and enablement).** At that time they were all *miraculously healed* after they ate the roasted lamb whose blood was shed and placed over the door and the two side posts of their homes on the night they were delivered out of Egypt (Exodus 12:22). He also caused them to have *great favor* and before they departed they were also made *wealthy* with jewels, silver, gold and clothing from the Egyptians (Exodus 12:35-36). *He did many miracles for them by His Spirit and they were blessed, empowered, favored and kept by His Grace, not the laws and regulations.* The Lord in Heaven did it all and all they really had to do to continue to benefit under His grace was to follow the leading of His Holy Spirit Who at that time was present with them in a cloud during the day and a pillar of fire at night to lead them and Who had also anointed their leaders to hear Him for instructions and directions.

Even though some were still complaining and in fear (as people are today) their wilderness experience was the beginning of trusting Almighty God who created them and who loved them but who had also been silent for four hundred years while they were in captivity. Thus as a people they had to learn of Him and His ways once again.

To further illustrate *God's grace, before the law was introduced,* we see that **grace is needed to effectively fight and be victorious in spiritual warfare**; there has to be an understanding of the contrast between the Law and the Spirit of Grace and how one should use the written letter of the Word in conjunction with the power of the Spirit of God. For example, when the Israelites were brought out of Egypt there were no deaths; when they complained to Moses at the Red Sea it parted; there were no deaths or backlash when they complained about food, **God just gave them what they needed,** water came from a rock, food from heaven and clothes and shoes that grew as they grew. They experienced miracle after miracle. Why? Because they **were under and** *protected by His grace.* When the Ten Commandments were introduced they were meant to instruct as a father would instruct his child for his well-being, Exodus 20. It was also given with the intention that people would learn that in and of themselves it was impossible to keep the law with its code of written regulations and that they would need to receive and live by His grace once again.

In Romans 7:6 NIV it says, "But now, by dying to what once bound us, we have been released from the law so that we serve in the new way of the Spirit, and not in the old way of the written code." So when the old covenant drew to a point God brought forth a *New Covenant* to *complete or fulfill the old by using a Holy Scripture that He first gave* them when He brought them out of bondage and it was simply, "...love your God with all your heart, soul, strength and mind as you love your neighbor as you do yourself" (Deut. 6:5; Luke 10:27 paraphrased) and in doing so you will do all that God ask of you. *God's Spirit and His Word must flow in your life together* in order for you to live the life God intended and purposed for you to have. If we are doing all that He ask of us which is to love Him, love ourselves in a healthy way and love each other then we will honor our father and mother and we won't commit murder, adultery, steal, lie and covet someone else's things but live a life of liberty and fulfillment in Christ.

People will need the grace of God, coupled with a relationship with Him to acquire supernatural help *to **keep them in a supernatural covenant, a covenant that has the power to cause two people to become one**.*

When couples incorporate the Spirit of God and look to Him daily to help them with their covenant that they have made before a living God, He is just and faithful to help them sustain and enjoy it and each other. Of course, it would make things easier if people would *first* pray about the man or woman God has for them. Some may think and feel this is foolish because after all we are grown and quite capable of finding a mate for ourselves, and so on. Well, statistics coupled with my experience and along with speaking to many others over the years is that, that is not always the case. Many people hide things and information as they lie about their true motives and themselves.

God will give His children the ability to *discern* by the Spirit of God the true motives of someone else because only He can see the true heart of an individual and reveal it. Only He knows the ins and outs of a person as He has stated in His Word, He has even counted the number of hairs on an individual's head. Only God knows what He purposed for that which He created. When someone does not know the purpose of a thing or person it won't be long before they will abuse it.

Since God made you and marriage, He understands what it will take to keep it. Then why not go to Him first and allow Him to "set it up," bring it to pass and then be a part of it to help keep it on course so that your marriage covenant could be for a lifetime with joy as so many are experiencing in spite of the number of divorces in the world today.

Is that to say every marriage arranged by God is perfect and successful? I would like to answer that with a reminder, if you know that your marriage was orchestrated by the Heavenly Father and confirmed by His Spirit that you are with the right person yet everything seems to be going wrong, especially in the early stages when you are becoming "one" remember this, *His Word* will be *tested and tried*. If you withstand the test and *flow with* the Holy Spirit and not work against Him at the appointed time, deliverance, the help needed whether it is a change of heart, a new attitude, finances, healing or whatever, will come and will be "right-on-time" and it will refresh you and even deepen your love for one another, enlighten you as a couple, and enhance your relationship and bond.

Yes, when the couple remembers that they are in a covenant with Christ Jesus Who is at the head of the relationship that the adversary is trying his best to devour, then they can experience a peace as they seek Him for their help. Then follow His instructions and wait on Him to bring their relationship to what it should be, strengthen it and prepare it to go to a greater level. Also keep in mind that His instructions may require forgiveness, seeing a Christian marriage counselor or to stop some destructive habit that is opening doors for demonic oppression and as you are *willing* to change things you can expect the victory.

THE MARRIAGE PROTOCOL FROM ANCIENT TIMES TO TODAY'S MARRIAGES:

Now that we have defined and clarified what a covenant is to a great degree and we know that Israel continues to have a covenant with God, this section will describe the **protocol of how God married Israel and how and why that protocol has a great influence on marriages today.**

First there was the *covenant* (**contract**) *from the Lord to Israel* (Exodus 24:1-7). This contract was called the Torah (the first five books of the Bible, which in Hebrew means "teaching" as it gives "instructions" and is also known as the "Law." **Second**, Israel *agreed* to the contract (covenant). **Third**, God told Israel to *sanctify herself*, to be set apart for Him. This was done when they bathed and washed their clothes in order to come into God's presence (Exodus 19:10). **Fourth**, God came down upon Mount Sinai [in a cloud] in the sight of all the people (Exo.19:11) and became a *covering* for the people He loves as they went to the Promise Land (Deuteronomy 33:2-3). God was a *covering* to Israel as a man is a covering for his wife. The cloud also represented the huppa or canopy under which the ancient Jewish couple were blessed by the Rabbi during their wedding ceremony.

The Marriage protocol between God and Israel was the model and pattern for the Ancient Jewish Wedding. The Jewish wedding originally had fourteen different stages but only *key points will briefly be discussed as we compare the protocol from ancient Jewish weddings, the marriage between Christ and His Church,*[6] *to today's marriages between one man and one woman.*

The *couple met* usually in the market place while the virgins were shopping. The *man approached her*, they briefly spoke and he took her name and later made arrangements for her to come to his father's house for a *meeting*.

Once the meeting arrangements were prepared she went and took her friends with her who waited outside in anticipation of the outcome of this meeting.

To make a long story short, the two of them sat down at a table with the man's father in the center and a *contract* was read to them by the man. The contract listed the obligations of the husband and the wife and it also named the *price* of the bride. The biblical obligation to one another especially for the husband was extensive. According to the Jewish Bible the husband must provide for his wife and show respect for her. (Judaism was the first religion that obligated the husband to provide financially for his wife in the event of his death).

Once she *agreed* to the contract and they both signed it, *gifts* were also offered to the woman that could include jewelry (Abraham the father of Isaac sent his servant with gifts to find his son's wife, Genesis 24:10). They *sealed* all with a sip of wine (wine represented that it was sealed with a *blood covenant*) given to them by the man's father in a silver cup (silver being the color of *redemption)*. This process legally binds the man and the woman together because "betrothal vows were binding as married even though the couple did not live together until the wedding" [3] Matthew 1:18-19. They both realized at this point they were considered to be in the first stage of their marriage, known as the *"betrothal stage"* in this stage she is called a "wife" (Deut. 22:24). We today would refer to this stage as **the** *engagement* **period**. However, if she *did not drink of the cup* then he collected his things and they parted never to come together again. (Revelation of a mystery that is concealed in the Old Testament and later revealed in the New Testament – if we refuse the invitation to become a part of God's family by rejecting His Son, this would be tantamount to rejecting your invitation to the Marriage Supper of the Lamb with your Bridegroom, Jesus Christ, Rev. 19:9).

If agreement was reached then during the betrothal stage they did not contact each other; they did not speak, date or do any of those things. She was *sanctifying* herself in preparation for their marriage. The Hebrew term for marriage is Kiddushin which comes from a root word meaning "holy" and implies sanctification. Part of this sanctification included wearing a veil across her face in the market place signifying she is no longer available, that she has been *set apart* and belongs to someone else. (Wearing the veil was similar in other cultures to wearing an *engagement ring* signifying you are no longer available and are now set apart and you belong to someone else).

They are now considered *one* for the next twelve months or so. He left to go and *prepare a place for her in his father's house.* If he were asked when will the big day be? He said I don't know only my father knows. **Only the father knew the day** the chamber would be ready (Matthew 24:36) and when the father said it was ready the groom went for his bride at *night* with others and one in the party would go ahead and shout their coming (I Thessalonians 4:16 and I Corinthians 15:52, Matt. 25:6) and she and her girls would be ready to go.

They stayed ready with a little lamp burning each night while waiting for him to come (Matt. 25:1-13 and Matthew 24:44). Then all were taken to the bridal chamber at his father's house. (Revelation – notice the correlation with the groom leaving to prepare a place for his bride and what happened after Jesus was resurrected: He walked the earth for forty days and was seen by over five hundred witnesses and then ascended in front of witnesses into the heavens *to go and prepare a place for His bride in His Father's house* (I Cor. 15:6 and Matthew 28:1-15). What was acted out in the Old Testament is a truth and mystery that was concealed (hidden) and later revealed in the New Testament (I Corinthians 2:7). The Word says, *no one knows the day nor the hour (Matthew 25:13)* but God has given to each man who can discern the times and season, the season of His return. All those who are *prepared* and received the sacrifice that Jesus made (Luke 23:33) will be with Him as the bride will be with the bridegroom. The young girls are to be prepared with the oil which is a symbol of the Holy Spirit and this instruction shows us that it is part of the preparation which is to stay close to the Holy Spirit and be sensitive to His leading especially in these last days!

Now it is time to *complete the process of their marriage*, the *final* and second stage known as the **"Consummation Stage."** It took place in the open under a canopy (called a huppa) which symbolizes the bridal chamber in the presence of God's love that is always protecting the couple. The groom arriving first, then the bride was carried to the bridegroom in a large decorated box like the priest carried the Ark of the Covenant. The groom gives the bride a wedding ring and in the presence of two witnesses they exchange the traditional wedding vows which are followed by a procession and a big festival which lasted for seven days with family, friends and neighbors, all part of the wedding festival. (Revelation – the festival that they enjoyed would be equivalent to our celebrating at the wedding reception. Again, this is a type and shadow of a hidden truth or mystery in the Old Testament that is revealed in the New Testament: the *Consummation or final stage* is one of the steps done during *Passover* which is the first feast given by God to His people and is to be enjoyed and celebrated by Jews and Christians alike, Exodus 12:14-15 and I Corinthians 5:7-8). The word *feast* means that God set an appointed time for His people to meet with Him.

What is revealed in the final stage: During the Passover Seder (the ceremonial evening meal) with which Passover (Pesach) begins in Jewish and Christian homes (observed by both but celebrated differently). In the Jewish home four cups of red wine are included and each with spiritual significance and blessings. The fourth cup is called the "**Cup of** *Consummation*" which is the cup of the *final thing*. When Yeshua (which is Jesus' Hebrew name) an Orthodox Jewish Rabbi observed the *Passover Meal* at the *Last* Supper with His disciples, He did not drink of this cup but set it down and said "I will not drink of the fruit of the vine until the Kingdom of God comes;" in other words, I will not drink of it until we are together again (Luke 22:15-18). The redemption process of redeeming God's people from this world is **hidden** in the stages leading up to a biblical wedding and marriage which is revealed in the book of Revelation as well as other books of the Bible.

I would also like to add that many people believe that in order to consummate a marriage, to bring it to its final stage the couple *must* engage in sexual intercourse based on such scriptures as John 3:29 and Song of Solomon 5:1. When they became husband and wife they were now considered one in the flesh (like thinking), Matthew 19:6. The Hebrew and Greek terms are usually translated "flesh" in regards to the whole human being rather than merely to the sensual or physical aspect of human nature. Becoming one flesh is said to be established through sexual union, but the implications of the term are more than sexual. *This type of union creates a spiritual and psychological interrelationship in which the couple establishes a bond that is more than physical. Therefore, the one flesh union also establishes bonding of two people because they think in agreement, which is fundamental to a lasting marriage and fundamental to taking dominion and ruling the earth.*

So then, the *final stage to consummate a marriage is the exchange of marriage vows because they are" words" and there is power in the spoken word as demonstrated by God Himself. Surely intimacy has its part and can be seen as perfecting the final thing but it is not in itself necessary to finalize the union in matrimony.* Take for instance people who marry by exchanging wedding vows and one is on their death bed; or another couple marry just before their spouse is shipped overseas immediately after the ceremony; or a spouse is incarcerated or a spouse is paralyzed, none of these couples would have had the opportunity to participate in sexual intercourse, therefore, are they not considered married? According to God and the laws of the land they are spiritually and legally married when they have completed their wedding vows.

As they have supernaturally become one in the spirit at the time they repeat their marriage vows, they are also seen as one in the flesh in the eyes of God. From there they begin to think alike and over the years grow closer together until their relationship truly becomes connected by their hearts, minds and other character traits they individually posses that will make them unique as a couple.

The following is a **breakdown of these four stages** (*a covenant, agreement, sanctification and consummation*) which are mentioned above in some detail *that led to a biblical wedding and marriage*. These four stages are given below and were placed in the following order to illustrate that *God's protocol or pattern has never changed*. The protocol which covers these four stages is applied to the marriages between *God and Israel*; a *Jewish man* and a *Jewish woman*; *Christ* and *His Church*; and *a wedding* between *one man* and *one woman* **married today in Christ (The Messiah, the Anointed One).**

- **The Marriage Protocol regarding God and Israel:**

    First, God *chose* Israel, arranged a *meeting* with Moses and gave a contract (a *covenant*) and a *gift* of "My Promises" from His Word to Israel;

    Second, Israel *agreed* to the contract (covenant);

    Third, God told Israel to *sanctify herself* and she bathed and washed her garments;

    Fourth, God came down upon Mount Sinai in a cloud and became Israel's *covering* which was the *final stage* of the wedding. (Under the huppa or canopy which is a covering where the vows were exchanged).

- **The Protocol of an ancient Jewish wedding and marriage between <u>a Jewish man and a Jewish woman</u>:**

    First, he *chose* her and arranged a *meeting* and gave her a *contract* which included the *price* he would give for a wife;

    Second, she *agreed* to the contract and also received *gifts* he prepared for her;

    Third, she *sanctified herself* later when she would bathe surrounded by her virgins;

    Fourth, he came to pick her up and no one knew the day or hour because he had to wait till his father said the place that was being prepared was ready. So she stayed *prepared* in an anticipation of his coming. They were *married (final thing)* and *seven blessings were recited to seal* the marriage followed by seven days of *celebration* with family, friends and others.

Under the New Testament there was another spiritual marriage that took place when Christ took the Church as His Bride. Under the Old Testament <u>Israel is the Bride of Father God</u> and under the New Testament <u>The Church is the Bride of Christ</u>. Both covenants illustrate a spiritual marriage between God and His people.

2 Corinthians 11:2, the Apostle Paul teaches,

> For I am zealous for you with a godly eagerness and a divine jealousy, for I have betrothed you to one Husband, to present you as a chaste virgin to Christ.

Romans 7:4 says,

Likewise, my brethren, you have undergone death as to the Law through the [crucified] body of Christ, so that now you may belong to Another, to Him Who was raised from the dead in order that we may bear fruit for God.

- **Please notice that the same Protocol is now used for the spiritual wedding and marriage between Christ and His Church:**

First, Christ *chose* us (we are the church) John 15:16-20;

He gave us a *covenant* (**contract**) called the New Testament;

and He paid a *price* (the cross) for His new bride (1 Co. 7:23);

He also gave us spiritual *gifts* of the Holy Spirit – the manifestations of Revelation, Utterance and Power

(I Corinthians 12:7-11);

Second, we *agreed* to the covenant (contract) when we accepted Jesus Christ as our Lord and Savior (Romans 10:9-10);

Third, Part of our *sanctification* is to be baptized in water (the ancient Jewish woman bathed in water as part of sanctifying herself as did the Israelites bathed and washed their garments to sanctify themselves). In addition, when we receive the Baptism or the Infilling of the Holy Spirit as well, this will assist us as Believers in living a sanctified lifestyle as we obey the teachings in the Word of God and live by the fruit of the Spirit. He expects us to be consecrated, set apart, having holy behavior, and devout with godly qualities (2 Peter 3:11);

Fourth, Jesus is coming back for His bride (*consummation, final thing*) to receive what He paid the price for and redeem her out of this world. Therefore, He has asked His bride to be *prepared* for His coming, to be without spot or blemish and at peace [in serene confidence, free from fears and agitating passions and moral conflicts] (2 Peter 3:14). Jesus is the **covering** for His bride. This spiritual marriage was **sealed** by the blood that was shed by Jesus (Hebrews 13:20). [He has also appropriated and acknowledged us as His by] putting His **seal** upon us and giving us His [Holy] Spirit in our hearts... 2 Cor.1:22; Eph. 4:30. The wedding *celebration* will be at the Marriage Supper of the Lamb which will take place in Heaven and will last until we come back to reign with Him (Revelation 19:7-9 KJV).

I would also add that the tradition of wearing a "**white wedding gown**" **or dress is biblical.** "White garments represent being in a state of spiritual preparedness, from Ecc. 9:8, Let your garments be always white..." [7] In the book of Revelation 19:8 it explains that when Jesus returns for His bride she should be arrayed (dressed in especially, splendidly, rich clothing) in fine linen, clean and white:

Revelation 19:8 says,

> **She has been permitted to dress in fine (radiant) linen, dazzling and white – for the fine linen is (signifies, represents) the righteousness** (the upright, just, and godly living, deeds, and conduct, and right standing with God) of the saints (God's holy people).

During the traditional Jewish Wedding the bride and groom wear white symbolizing that their sins are forgiven and that they will begin married life with a clean slate.

God's holy people are not people who do everything right for it is not in *their* righteousness but because of <u>Who is in them</u> that makes them holy and righteous.

Many cultures use different models from the beginning of a relationship to the day of the wedding. But in our society and many around the world the same biblical pattern is still used today.

- **When it comes to an important event like a wedding and <u>marriage between one man and one woman</u> the Protocol is still honored today***:*

First, the man generally is the one that *chooses* the woman for his wife (Proverbs 18:22). There is a courtship and within the course of this he may propose marriage (the ***betrothal*** stage); they may discuss how to handle the obligations/responsibilities for their home and what will be expected of one another. They may also discuss such things as where they will live; careers/work; how many children are expected in this union; what faith will they follow; and so forth. This portion would be the oral *contract* of the proposal. He will offer a ring to represent their engagement and this would be his ***gift;***

Second, she *agrees* to the proposal (the plan he presented for consideration) the **covenant** (**contract**);

Third, she starts to *prepare* herself spiritually, physically, emotionally and makes preparation for the wedding ceremony. Her new attire is set aside (*set apart*) from other garments for this special occasion and she will wear her *engagement ring* (replaces the ancient veil) to further demonstrate that she is set apart and not available. She may even remove herself from old activities, people, places and distractions as preparation for the new thing that is about to happen in her life (these are all forms of *sanctification*);

Fourth, during a biblical wedding ceremony the groom is positioned near the minister of the Gospel of Jesus Christ, or the Rabbi or the Priest and so forth, while the bride is escorted in on the right side of her father, a place of honor, as he will present her to her husband. (Just as God built up Adam's rib and made it into a woman and brought her to her husband, Gen. 2:22). They will exchange marital vows (*consummate* their marriage) before God (who will validate it) and witnesses; then they will *seal* it with a kiss. The reception (festival, *celebration*) follows next as part of ending the final stage as well as serving as the beginning of a beautiful marriage. The Holy Spirit is the "Promised *Gift*" and is a *covering* for the marriage as part of the covenant (Acts 1:4). The guests will bring **gifts** which is also biblical; gifts confirm that a covenant has been made (Genesis 21:30 and Genesis 31:52).

The latter two marriages, one being spiritual and the other in the natural followed the same pattern as the Old Testament marriages *because the foundation of the New Testament is the Old Testament*. And the fact that God said He is the same yesterday, today and forever still stands (Heb. 13:8). **What was sacred to God then is sacred to God now!**

You see the Old Testament conceals within it events that were to come and these events are revealed in the New Testament as to why certain things were performed or done a certain way in the Old Testament ("But rather what we are setting forth is a wisdom of God once *hidden* [from the human understanding] and *now revealed* to us by God..." I Corinthians 2:7).

Jewish ancient customs based on the Word of God were in existence thousands of years before Christianity came into being. The Word of God laid a strong foundation as well as prophetic words that went forth of which most have already come to pass. Many of the negative events occurring in our society today, were spoken forth thousands of years ago, and are recorded in the Holy Scriptures. These negative events are affecting our marriages, families, cities, and countries primarily because the basic fundamentals of God's Word for living are being distorted, changed, altered, and ignored (2 Timothy 3 and Matthew 24:1-44).

Under the Old Testament, issues of life were dealt with mostly by using man's senses, mind and responding to an occasional prophetic word from a prophet or a word or an inspired instruction from a priest or king who were empowered with an anointing to lead others if they obeyed God. Under the New Testament we were given a better covenant as far as how to live and deal with life's issues day in and day out where people are growing weary and are tempted to give up on their marriages and other concerns in their lives.

Under the new covenant Believers are anointed or *empowered from the inside* by the Spirit of God which brings an inner strength, fresh revelation and insight with the ability to live or walk by faith in trusting the leading of the Holy Spirit. We are also given the ability to daily receive: wisdom, revelation, insight, help, direction and so forth as received from the Holy Spirit Who is our Teacher, Counselor, Comforter, Helper, Strengthener and Deliverer amongst other things. The Holy Spirit is the One who heals us, preserves us, directs our path, delivers us and the same One who is the **Gift of the *Promise*** that Father God gave to mankind when He married Israel (Acts 1:4-5). And He dwells in us today if we receive the Father's Son. He will turn things around as we seek Him, listen for instructions and act on His Word. He is faithful and He will preserve our marriages, families, homes, careers, employment, businesses or whatever we have been empowered with favor to possess. He has the ability to save whatever we need, if we receive our Father's Gift, the Holy Spirit, Who is The Third Person of the God Head, the Trinity (See Chapter 7, Section Three).

LOVE IS THE ESSENCE OF MARRIAGE:

God is the very essence of Marriage for God "is" Love (I John 4:16). He created people to have someone to love and return that love to Him, so He made someone in His likeness who could relate to Him and who would relate to each other with godly love and character. And the greatest expression of His love should flow from His creation of marriage and the family throughout the world.

The following passages explain biblically how a husband is to love and respect his wife and how a wife is to respect and love her husband.

I Peter 3:7 says,

> In the same way you married men should live considerately with [your wives], with an intelligent recognition [of the marriage relation], honoring the woman as [physically] the weaker, but [realizing that you] are joint heirs of the grace (God's unmerited favor) of life, in order that your prayers may not be hindered and cut off. [Otherwise you cannot pray effectively.]

Ephesians 5:33 says,

> However, let each man of you [without exception] love his wife as [being in a sense] his very own self; and let the wife see that she respects and reverences her husband [that

she notices him, regards him, honors him, prefers him, venerates, and esteems him; and that she defers to him, praises him, and loves and admires him exceedingly]. See also I Peter 3:2.

Ephesians 5:21-28 says,

> Submitting yourselves *one to another* in the fear of God (v 21 KJV).

> Be *subject to one another* out of reverence for Christ (the Messiah, the Anointed One) (v 21).

> **Wives,** be subject (be submissive and adapt yourselves) to your own husbands as [a service] to the Lord. For the husband is head of the wife as Christ is the Head of the church, Himself the Savior of [His] body. As the church is subject to Christ, so let wives also be subject in everything to their husbands (v 22-24).

> **Husbands** love your wives, as Christ loved the church and gave Himself up for her. So that He might sanctify her, having cleansed her by the washing of water with the Word. That He might present the church to Himself in glorious splendor, without spot or wrinkle or any such things [that she might be holy and faultless]. Even so husbands should love their wives as [being in a sense] their own bodies. He who loves his own wife loves himself (v 25-28).

Love is a major key in having success in all relationships especially a marital relationship. *When we choose to yield or submit ourselves one to another it means we are simply choosing to honor and respect the other person.* When you walk or live a life of love, you are walking with God, **to walk**

with God is to *stay in step* **with His Holy Spirit.** According to I Peter 1:22 the Holy Spirit is the One Who purifies our hearts so that the pure sincere love of God can flow through us and out to others. "As we allow the love of God to work or flow through us it will enable us to ever be filled with the Holy Spirit. We are to walk as children of Light and be filled with the Spirit because the fruit of the Light or the Spirit [consists] in every form of kindly goodness, uprightness of heart, and trueness of life" (Ephesians 5:8-9, paraphrased).

Some of the things we are *not to do* **if we are to be subject to one another** are for husbands not to expect their wives to be subservient (so self-abasing as to lack a proper degree of personal dignity or to be useful as a means or instrument) but rather receive her as a partner to share in mutual biblical submission; wives *are not to* try to influence, manipulate or reject their husbands to gain control or ground to force an issue in their favor. All of these childish tactics are not a part of biblical submission and they will only lead to heartache and possibly separation when one or both partners have had *enough*. *When you decide in your heart to do things man's way and not God's way you have made a decision for your marriage to fail to be all that it could be.*

Paul tried to guard the institution of marriage which God loves dearly and in doing so, Paul gave advice to those who were joined to unbelievers not to disturb their relationship. However, for the good of a marriage both parties should be in agreement to stay married realizing marriage is not merely a civil contract when the scriptures make it very clear that it is the most sacred relationship in life (I Corinthians 7:13-14).

As you choose love over bitterness, strife or some other demonic spirit you will have the victory every time because love is the most powerful weapon, tool, device or spirit any person could ever possess. When love is expressed through kindness, thoughtfulness, forgiveness, respect, humility, self-control, honor, gentleness, goodness, peace, patience, faithfulness, caring actions and deeds you are then walking in His love and thereby abiding in Him which will result in a loving and good marriage.

Without love nothing will be long term in your life because God is Love and apart from Him you can do nothing (John 15:5). God said in His Word that without faith we cannot please Him, well love activates faith. You cannot even use your faith to its greatest potential if you are not expressing and receiving the love of God.

God tells us how to love Him with His first and principal commandment and that is that you *must* "love the Lord your God with all your heart and with all your soul and with all your strength and with all your mind; and your neighbor as yourself" (Luke 10:27). This is part of our marital covenant with the Lord and as we do our part, He will certainly do His. He is the only one that can change hearts and all of His commandments can be fulfilled when we keep the Commandant of Love:

I John 3:23-24 The Message states:

> Again, this is God's command: to believe in his personally named Son, Jesus Christ. He told us to love each other, in line with the original command. As we keep His commands, we live deeply and surely in Him, and He lives in us. And this is how we experience His deep and abiding presence in us: by the Spirit He gave us.

God is all about love, He is a Holy God, and He is a Loving God, He is Love (I John 4:16). He set the pace and pattern for marriage and has given us powerful tools to maintain it and the same holds true for any type of relationship we are in, if we simply choose to model after Him and stay in the love of God (I John 4:10-11).

The Law of Love is found in Luke 6:27-31 and it basically tells us how to express love to those who have come against us. For example verse 27 tells us to make it a practice to love our enemies by doing *good* to those who hate us. One of the first things we are to do is to pray for them. When this is done you open a door for God to heal your heart because of your obedience to a spiritual principle and command. And in Luke 6:31 (NAS) the Golden Rule says, "And just as you want people to treat you, treat them in the same way." When we choose to obey God we free ourselves up from bondage to whatever or whomever.

We can avoid many negative things from coming into our lives if we would just humble ourselves and follow His spiritual instructions that may not make sense to the natural mind, but if done, it will cause things to turn around for our good. One example of an instruction or command that makes absolutely no sense to the natural mind (I Corinthians 2:14) is to forgive those who have wronged you so that the Lord can then forgive you of the things you have done that were wrong, *your failings and shortcomings* (Mark 11:25-26).

But if you would follow through and obey, even though it does not make any sense to you, you will find because of that step of faith that it works, because it will allow you to enter into the supernatural and receive a supernatural healing from a Supernatural God. Healing in any area of your life where it is needed is connected to your being able to forgive others which in turn will close doors that the enemy has access to. But most importantly when we choose to release anger, unforgiveness and bitterness we prevent our blessings from being blocked. Let God be God, He said vengeance is His, He will repay (Romans 12:19); so cast your care, stay in a loving frame of mind and move on (I Peter 5:7 and Psalm 55:22, this issue is discussed further in Chapter 2 under Clarifying Forgiveness).

In continuing our discussion on love, The Song of Solomon illustrates the love between God and Israel, His bride. Just as the book of I Corinthians, Chapter 13 illustrates the love we should have for each other. When we can love the way God says to love, then we will love our Maker and Creator the way He says to love Him (I John 3:23, 24; John 14:15). The Lord says, when you do anything for the least of these in Christ you have done it unto Him (Matthew 25:40).

Guard love; take care of it, because it is the most valuable tool or weapon you will ever have. There is no weapon that is formed against it that will be able to stand. I once heard someone say, "It is the Father's business to judge; it is the Holy Spirit's business to convict; and it is our business to Love!"

Great characteristics of **true or mature love** are found in the Love Chapter, I Corinthians 13:4-8:
In "The Book:"

> Love is very patient and kind, never jealous or envious, never boastful or proud, never haughty or selfish or rude. Love does not demand its own way. It is not irritable or touchy. It does not hold grudges and will hardly even notice when others do it wrong. It is never glad about injustice, but rejoices *whenever* truth wins out. If you love someone you will be loyal to him no matter what the cost. You will always believe in him, always expect the best of him, and always stand your ground in defending him.

In the Amplified Bible vv. 7 and 8 are powerfully stated as well:

> Love bears up under anything and everything that comes, is ever ready to believe the best of every person, its hopes are fadeless under all circumstances, and it endures everything [without weakening]. Love never fails...

The Love Chapter describes God's idea of mature love. Take notice, it has included in it: Patience, Kindness, being Joyful with Truth, Trusting, Loyal, Full of Hope and Enduring or Totally Committed. Unconditional Love will allow you to accept your husband or wife or children and others as they are while allowing God to work on any changes that need to be done. **If your goal or motive is to really show someone else love then**

you should remember that if it is not *unconditional love* then it really is not love at all. Also remember that if it is a "heart" issue only God can change a human heart to line up with what is righteous. In doing so He will not violate the person's free will nor will He answer any prayers that will violate that person's free will.

But you are anxious to see changes in the person while you are trying very hard to "overlook" all of these faults *you* have determined that they have and need to change. So what is your part in helping that come about since you cannot nag, force and you have decided to show unconditional love? **You are to stand in the gap with your prayers and if you receive instructions to confront in a loving way, assist, or to continue to be silent and led by your heart as the Spirit of God fills it with the right things to say and/or do.**

In the meantime pray only prayers that are in the will of God about the other person. **Never pray prayers that are soulish prayers. These are prayers that try to dictate to God what you want to see happen in another person's life that may be against their will or wrong for them.** They are controlling prayers which are not of God. God does not answer these types of prayers because they do not line up with the will of God or His Word. *Instead of trying to control someone else through your prayers pray that they will hear God for themselves and listen as He leads them.* And do not allow anyone in your presence to pray controlling prayers over your life either. In other words do not allow someone to use prayer to try and manipulate you into doing what they think you should do. Always go with the peace in your heart and if there is no peace and you know it is not the will of God for your life then make the choice to do God's will.

An unknown author wrote this about love, "Everyone says love hurts, but that is not true. Loneliness hurts. Rejection hurts. Losing someone hurts. Envy hurts. Everyone gets these things confused with love, but in reality love is the only thing in this world that covers up all pain and makes someone feel wonderful again. Love is the only thing in this world that does not hurt…God is Love!"

The Bible states that, "God is Love" and God loves us so much that He chooses to make His home in us, in our hearts. *So as you Go with Love, Love will Go with you!*

UNDERSTANDING REASONS FOR MARRIAGE:

- According to the principles we have read, marriage is not merely a civil contract; **the Scriptures make it the most sacred relationship of life and the most powerful union on earth in the sight of God.** "Moses presents it as the deepest, corporeal and spiritual unity of man and woman in monogamy" (Genesis 2:24; Matthew 19:5). [1]
- Two of the things that God gave for our good were (1) the Sabbath to preserve His church (the assembly of persons who worship Him and receive Him as their Lord and Savior) and (2) **marriage to preserve mankind.**
- One of God's basic purposes for marriage is companionship; it is not good for anyone to be too lonely and if marriage is for you and there is good communication within your relationship this would offer **great companionship**.
- Without the martial tie the family circle, family institution, and parental love and care would have been altogether unknown.
- When your marriage is a priority and is secure on solid ground your **children will feel more loved, more secure**, be stronger and have more confidence in themselves.
- Another benefit of marriage is that it **causes men to be more productive** because they have wives to encourage and remind them of certain social obligations; she may influence him to start a business; encourage him to handle responsibilities around the house, or to buy a house if they

did not own one; bring to him things they need to do with their children and with the extended family and so forth. As a result the man is more productive in areas he probably would not think much about if he were single.
- **Marriage helps regulate sexuality in any society.** Every society needs sexual guide posts or a way to monitor sex so that society won't fail and die out like the Roman and Greek societies did. When any society erases their sexual morals, sexual values and allows all types of sexual behavior it is just a matter of time before judgment on that society will occur, causing it to collapse. Each man having his own wife helps to keep the society holy (sanctified) and on the up and up doing more good than evil (I Corinthians 7:2).
- **Marriage protects women by enforcing monogamy.** Society's most serious problem is the unattached male. Women need to be protected from *some* men who are aggressive, self-centered male chauvinist. The danger is of women becoming commodities to be used and traded into slavery for sex and other services (which does exist illegally today in many countries). Marriage makes sure that there are men and women connected as much as possible to care for and protect one another.
- Another benefit of marriage is that because it has to do with the procreation of children **it provides fathers and mothers** as well as protection for children. Most people are more determined to stay together in order to raise their children.
- When a man and woman marry and procreate children then nurture and train them up in the way they *should* go, parents can rest in the fact that when their children are older they will not depart from it (Proverbs 22:6). The result is

with the Word of God as the foundation you will raise decent and well adjusted human beings. Marriage has the potential to produce the next generation of producers, workers, good citizens and good parents with godly character. With this in mind, marriage plays a significant and important social role in any society. And a society has the God-given right to protect children and to have children brought up in nurturing families and homes.

- **A society where marriage is *honored* is a society that has a lower rate of domestic violence.** However, in our world today there is so much pressure on marriage and families which come from outside of their homes through other natural and spiritual influences and the affects of that pressure is shown by the rate of domestic violence and divorces that are reported each day. **One of the major reasons for the increase is that** *people are trying to live in a godly institution without God.*

KEY TIPS FOR A *SUCCESSFUL* MARRIAGE GOD'S WAY:

- A successful marriage requires being **sensitive to the leading of the Holy Spirit** (being sensitive to what is in your heart for the good of the relationship) to receive God's instructions for guidance and His timing to carry it out in order to receive breakthroughs and deliverance. **To walk (live) with God is to stay in step with His Holy Spirit;** in other words continue to flow with Him as He continues to lead you. One reason this is important is because **people change over time and some grow together whereas others grow a part.** Even though they are both growing one may grow faster than the other; or they may grow in two entirely different directions.

For example, one could experience growth because they were influenced by the Word of God and the other more so about worldly matters and opinions of men. If they are to remain in agreement they will both need to receive growth from the same source.
- **Maintain Godly principles** found in His Word regarding marriage and all other areas that are relevant to everyday life and this will help to *keep God first* in your relationship and enhance your lifestyle.
- **When God is first He becomes the center of your marriage, home and your joy. As a result the household will *know* where their source is for love, strength, relief, hope, wisdom, healing, faith, self-esteem, security, justice and so forth.** They will know not to put hope for these things in *man* whether it is their spouse, parent, sibling or someone else but to trust only the One who can truly give them these things by His Grace through them exercising their faith – knowing that He will do it for them.
- **Wisdom and Revelation Knowledge** are keys that will empower you in the proper handling of whatever arises. Using the "instruction manual" is going to the source which can only benefit and enhance the proper and full use of what is being used, operated or studied. Our instruction manual is the Holy Bible and from it we can:

Get Wisdom and *Understanding*, Proverbs 4:7-13 says,

> The beginning of Wisdom is: get Wisdom (skillful and *godly Wisdom*)! **[For skillful and godly Wisdom is the principal thing.] And with all you have gotten, get *understanding*** (discernment, comprehension, and interpretation). Prize Wisdom highly and exalt her, and she will exalt and promote you; **she will bring you to honor when you embrace her.** She shall give to your head a wreath of gracefulness; a crown of beauty and glory will she deliver to you. Hear, O My son, and receive My sayings,

and the years of your life shall be many. I have taught you in the way of skillful and godly Wisdom [which is comprehensive insight into the ways and purposes of God]; I have led you in paths of uprightness. When you walk, your steps shall not be hampered [your path will be clear and open]; and when you run, you shall not stumble. *Take firm hold of instruction, do not let go; guard her, for she is your life.*

Proverbs 2:2-8 NLT says,

"My child, listen to Me and treasure My instructions. **Tune your ears to wisdom, and concentrate on understanding.** Cry out for insight and understanding. Search for them as you would for lost money or hidden treasure. Then you will understand what it means to fear the Lord, and you will gain knowledge of God. For the Lord grants wisdom! From His mouth come knowledge and understanding. **He grants a treasure of good sense to the godly. He is their shield, protecting those who walk with integrity.** He guards the paths of justice and protects those who are faithful to Him."

- As we **express our love** towards our spouse, the choice of our **words are extremely important** in order **to accomplish this** because words are a very powerful and effective tool. As we are able to express our feelings, love and appreciation for our spouse through our words they can become a blessing to them. Words can be used to honor a person because all people have God-given worth and assets and something nice *can* be said about anyone.

- Words are not some empty sound that just floats out of our mouths, **words are *"spirit"*** *they are alive and can give life or if we use them improperly with our tongues they can bring death* (Proverbs 18:21). God said He is a *Spirit* (John 4:24) we are made in His likeness and are a spirit being that has a soul and lives in a body (I Thess. 5:23). He created "man" and man means "spirit being." When God communicates with us He speaks directly to our spirit man through the Holy Spirit. He does not speak to our bodies or our soul (mind, will and emotions) He speaks to our spirit and our spirit conveys it to our mind which controls our body through our brain. Therefore, when we speak to our spouse our spirit (which is the part of us that is the real person) is speaking to their spirit and the choice of our words will bring life or death, build them up or tear them down literally because the words are alive and have power. So speak uplifting words and bless your husband or wife (Hebrews 4:12).
- The Bible says, **God's words will not return to Him void** (Isaiah 55:11), therefore, if we speak His words "over" *or* "to" our spouse those *words will produce a harvest* by accomplishing what they were sent to do and things will come to pass, they will manifest as a result of the words we have spoken whether they are God-given words or negative words. Why? Words bring us into our destiny. Someone once said, "watch your <u>thoughts</u> because they become <u>words</u>; choose your <u>words</u> because they become <u>action</u>; understand your <u>actions</u> because they become <u>habits</u>; study your <u>habits</u> because they become your <u>character</u>; develop your <u>character</u> because it becomes your <u>destiny</u>." Your gifts and talents can open a door of opportunity but your character is what will

sustain you once you are there. It all starts with speaking out our thoughts. The first action taken is *releasing* the *words* because thoughts do not produce so we have the option of casting down the wrong thoughts and only speaking the correct ones, therefore, it is your choice as to whether they are words that will bring life or words that will bring death, it is up to you.

- **If the words that are spoken are constantly negative** then once released from our mouths into the atmosphere they will *not* be used by the Holy Spirit but instead an evil force will pick those words up and will bring those words to pass. Therefore, speak godly, uplifting positive words to prevent receiving a negative harvest.
- Some of the most successful and joyous couples say, *I love you to each other*. It sets the atmosphere to continuously build on a solid foundation and since their words have power they are *releasing or sending* their love to that person every time they speak those words into the atmosphere because those are *godly words*. **At the same time you are *instructing* the Holy Spirit to fill you with a love towards your spouse when you say the words, I love you.** Why does this happen? Because the words you spoke were in line with God's will, therefore, it is set to come to pass. You are also *strengthening the commitment* you have for one another when you speak godly words. No one can have a true and lasting love for their spouse without making a strong commitment.
- *Attentive listening* **encourages and blesses the speaker**. Even if some women go on and on and on about the same subject, if a husband can just listen and acknowledge she is speaking by making a *remark* every now and then, for example by saying "really" or "wow" or "yes dear" any sound

to let her know he is still paying attention to her as she attempts to express or vent something that she needs to release. He does not always need to "fix" something but just have a listening ear. She will eventually move on to another topic having fulfilled this desire to express what was in her heart. **BUT, if *she* continues with the same subject far beyond reason she may require more than just a listening ear.** Therefore, he may gently suggest a third party like a good friend or mother, or father, or Christian counselor, etc. listen for a while to get their opinion. Sometimes the person speaking repeatedly about an issue either needs an answer, a need met, healing in a certain area or to forgive, therefore, they may need to seek another reliable ear before they wear their spouse out.

- *Communication is a skill* which develops with practice and encouragement from one another. Prayer is extremely important to keep the interpretation of what is actually being said or intended, to not become distorted or misinterpreted to the hearer. When you ask the Holy Spirit to help you understand or give you clarity in understanding your spouse and plead the blood of Jesus over your ears in prayer from time to time, you will find that it will be easier to get the true meaning of what they are actually saying and hopefully before someone arrives at the wrong conclusions or becomes offended.
- Remember there is **an *assignment against marriage*** from Satan who hates it and will do all that he can to cause confusion and misunderstandings by sending negative thoughts to one or both partners in order to keep strife in the home. Therefore, think before you speak, you do not have to say everything that comes to your mind

especially if it is negative. Ask God to guard your mouth, "Set a guard, O Lord, before my mouth; keep watch at the door of my lips" (Psalms 141:3) or "Take control of what I say, O Lord, and keep my lips sealed" (Psalms 141:3 NLT). If you feel you must say something then ask the Holy Spirit to help you word it so it will be received well. The Holy Spirit will help you develop and exercise control over your language (Proverbs 21:23; Proverbs 18:21; Proverbs 15:1; Proverbs 16:24; James 1:19; and Proverbs 19:14).

Colossians 4:6 says:

Let your speech at all times be gracious (pleasant and winsome), seasoned [as it were] with salt, [so that you may never be at a loss] to know how you ought to answer anyone [who puts a question to you].

Ephesians 4:29-32:

Let no foul or polluting language, nor evil word nor unwholesome or worthless talk [ever] come out of your mouth, but only such [speech] as is good and beneficial to the spiritual progress of others, as is fitting to the need and the occasion, that it may be a blessing and give grace (God's favor) to those who hear it....And do not grieve the Holy Spirit of God...Let all bitterness and indignation and wrath (passion, rage, bad temper) and resentment (anger, animosity) and quarreling (brawling, clamor, contention) and slander (evil speaking, abusive or blasphemous language) be banished from you, with all malice (spite, ill will, or baseness of any kind). And become useful and helpful and kind to one another, tenderhearted (compassionate, understanding, loving-hearted), forgiving one another [readily and freely], as God in Christ forgave her.

- A *lack of communication* is one of the main reasons people separate or divorce. In most cases it can be resolved with proper skill in communicating which involves *listening* and *speaking* in the right tones and so forth. In communicating the couple should welcome and be able to discuss any topic especially those about their marriage, children, work, friends, extended family, finances, their business, etc. and be considerate of the point the other person is making. Try to discuss one topic at a time.
- A *key point* is to **agree to talk** at a time when they are in a relaxed atmosphere if at all possible. They *can also agree to disagree* peacefully and be willing to discuss any disagreements further until they come to some sort of resolution. They should be aware of their voice, facial expressions and keeping in mind to show their spouse respect whether they agree or not. I would like to add if the atmosphere does change and barriers go up such as offense, pride, anger, guilt making it difficult to express personal feelings or emotions then it would be better to terminate the conversation and not allow it to turn into an argument or even an attack on the other person by speaking words that may be regretted later. If the both of you can – pray and thank God you got this far and ask Him to help you reach an understanding and then in agreement set up a continuation for the discussion at a specified date, time and place. Maybe somewhere casual or relaxing where you can finish and hopefully develop a strategy that will resolve the issue.
- It is always better to at least try to communicate and **work it out even if a *professional third party***

or someone you really trust has to be brought to the table because every marriage is worth saving, restoring and renewing if at all possible. Seeking outside help from a qualified counselor or someone knowledgeable that you can trust, realize that a mediator can bring a different perspective, be more objective since they are not emotionally involved and can hear and see more clearly how to reach a successful resolution to your problem. (Proverbs 15:22).

- *Selfishness* **is at the heart of almost every marital problem** so practice giving and helping to take the attention off of yourself for a while and try thinking about others first. Ask God how you can be a blessing to someone else especially your spouse, children and extended family.
- **Strive to keep** *strife* **out** *of your marriage and entire household. It is a killer. It will rob you of your peace, joy, your faith, miracles and any power you have as a couple especially if you are praying together.* **Strife is bickering, arguing, heated disagreements, and an angry undercurrent and the enemy will use these tools to do damage to your relationship.** It is dangerous and destructive and it will spread rapidly unless it is confronted and stopped. Since all couples argue from time to time I suggest being very watchful and monitor the strife (the *constant* bickering and arguing) and instead pray, use wisdom, constructive advice from outside help, books, tools and other methods for making your point in order to control or stop the strife from becoming more frequent. (2 Timothy 2:23-24, Isaiah 32:18; Proverbs 16:32; Proverbs 17:14; and James 1:19-20).
- Married people should spend as much *leisure time together* as possible. Date nights or date breakfasts or date lunches, once or twice a week,

are always nice and they remind a couple that they are a romantic couple *before* they are parents, business partners or before any other demand that is placed on their relationship. On these dates or just at home spending leisure time together or going for walks, exercising together or having a snack together <u>remember</u> to keep the conversation "light" during these leisure times so you won't discourage one another from spending these healthy, joyful times together for fear of constant reminders of great or heavy responsibilities. There should be other times set aside to pray together as well as set times to discuss finances, management of your home, family and so forth.

- **Couples with strong marriages also recognize that they are *still individuals* and need to permit each other to express themselves while they are developing common bonds and shared interest together.** Doing things of interest for themselves, having lunch with friends or extended family, sports events, shopping or taking a class and so forth will help to strengthen the union and keep balance in the relationship which is very important.
- **Proper management of finances** is very important to maintain a strong marriage. For information regarding finances see Chapter 7, Section Two.
- *Physical intimacy* won't be all that it could be without first the proper usage of words and how we communicate with each other during the day. *Words and deeds give a relationship meaning,* what we say and do does matter because sex apart from any meaningful relationship will eventually get "old" because if the relationship's foundation is only built on sex, people will eventually move on. *Sexual intercourse is a holy*

gift from God to be used within matrimony and when coupled with meaningful loving words and deeds this will only add worth and pleasure to the intimacy between a husband and his wife.
- Like everything else, especially things concerning marriage, couples should pray and ask God to give them **wisdom and show them how to bring balance and pure pleasure into the** *sexual part of their marriage.* In being considerate and loving to one another finding a healthy balance to engage in *sex that pleases both partners* where one does not feel as if they are being taken for granted or taken advantage of or being used just to satisfy the sexual needs of their spouse when they have needs or desires in other areas of their marriage that are being totally neglected or rejected.
- Bringing a balance will further help to prevent over taxing each other, making unreasonable demands or being inconsiderate by violating their spouse's rest. Also adding further stress by asking their spouse to bring into their marriage bed certain sexual acts one of them may have been exposed to because of experiencing multiple partners before marriage that their spouse does not choose to participate in.
- In addition, if both of you have a **heavy work schedule** (even if Mom or Dad is a homemaker that is still considered a heavy work schedule) then there are solutions to resolve these issues listed above so people do not burn out and want to give up on the entire marriage because one or two areas need to be "fixed" or given more consideration.
- In helping to resolve the above issues keeping a *balance in your sexual life* **by planning the best time to come together sexually** whether it should be at night, early morning or whenever and

having an appointed day(s) in a given week and *being in agreement* and only making exceptions if both are in agreement will relieve a tremendous amount of stress from over worked individuals. Stress is basically a part of most cultures now because of the pace of the society they live in. One must take charge of their life and finances and happiness because successful things just "don't happen" *they are planned.*

- This may seem silly to a number of people or couples who think this will interfere with the romantic side of their relationship, but actually it will enhance it. With **appointed or joint committed times** for sexual union people can plan ahead to be rested and prepare to make their time together special, joyful, wonderful, creative and a blessing for one another.
- Overall **a well balanced healthy sexual relationship** with your spouse could actually pro-long your life span as well as strengthen your marriage. In most cases your spouse should not need to "wander or stray" outside of the home for fulfillment. Small things like holding hands, kissing, hugging, touching one another will help draw you closer to your mate and encourage intimacy. Some of the fruit of the Spirit such as love, gentleness, kindness, faithfulness, meekness and joy along with understanding and self-sacrificing in a good way can lead to sexual fulfillment.
- **The purpose of sex is more than for procreation and pleasure it is also to keep us holy. That is why it was created only for those who are married.** Sex engages our bodies and it touches our souls. *A transfer of spirits takes place when people are not married and soul ties are formed.* Sexual intimacy is a physical act that is part of a marriage

relationship and if it is detached from the relationship, the relationship could become spiritually bankrupt. Sex is a physical act but it is also spiritual and it should be guarded and protected by the married couple by not opening a door for any demonic activity to have place in their marriage.
- When people do not understand the purpose of something they can easily misuse it and then find out later after everything has fallen a part what the true purpose was. When you are about to use a new DVD player you read the manual first so you can get the full benefit of the product and to not use it inappropriately and cause some type of breakage. Right? How much more important do you think your sexual life is to God. Follow the manual from the Creator He knows the purpose of all things including sex and its importance for the marriage bed.
- **Coming together is also a form of spiritual warfare** because it will protect most marriages when or if you or your spouse is overpowered with temptation according to I Corinthians 7:5. The reason I say "most" is because I know of cases where the couples were having relations several times a week and their spouse still committed adultery primarily because there were other major issues in the marriage or with that particular person. **However, succumbing to temptation would not be the norm when people are truly committed to God, love one another and are reading the instruction manual (the Bible).**
- Another area of concern is the **over taxing of one spouse when the other has a strong sexual drive**. Unfortunately most couples have been *taught*, even through religion, that their spouse's body is given upon request regardless of the emotional state or if one is exhausted or busy. The teaching

or what has been implied is that it is *wrong* to deny, "say no" to your spouse's request for sex <u>anytime they ask</u> because it has been implied that it is a *command* from God for them to respond regardless of circumstances or feelings because their body is not their own and since their bodies belong "one to another" they cannot refuse (I Corinthians 7:4). This scripture has been misused and misquoted for the marriage bed for decades.

I Corinthians 7: 2-6 says,

2-But because of the temptation to impurity and to avoid immorality, let each [man] have his own wife and let each [woman] have her own husband.

3-The husband should give to his wife her conjugal rights (goodwill, kindness, and what is due her as his wife), and likewise the wise to her husband.

4-*For the wife does not have [exclusive] authority and control over her own body*, but the husband [has his rights]; likewise also *the husband does not have [exclusive] authority and control over his body*, but the wife [has her rights].

5-Do not refuse and deprive and defraud each other [of your due marital rights], except perhaps by mutual consent for a time, so that you may devote yourselves unhindered to prayer. But afterwards resume marital relations, lest Satan tempt you [to sin] through your lack of restraint of sexual desire.

6-But I am saying this more as a matter of *permission* **and** *concession,* **not as a command or regulation.**

- As seen in the above passage, verse number six (6) clearly shows that in verses number four (4) and five (5) **that this is** *not a command from God nor is it a regulation* **but that a** *request* **for sex is** *granted by permission and concession* (conceding means to grant a right or privilege; or to yield) and thereby *the woman or the man has the right and choice of saying "yes" or "no."* **However, in verse five (5) there is a warning that if you deprive your spouse of affection** *for a time without mutual consent* **(consent here in the Greek means agreement) that Satan will use the temptations of the culture to become overpowering** and you will run the risk of your spouse being tempted because of a lack of sexual restraint and falling (committing adultery) which will greatly impact your marriage. *Therefore, you should continually not deprive one another.*
- Because these scriptures have been misunderstood or misquoted out of context or not quoted in its entirety it has caused guilt, shame and people to be taken advantage of. People especially women have been made to feel guilty as if they were committing a *sin* because on occasions they told their husband's "no" for whatever reason they gave. Some people have been made to feel ashamed because they have done certain sexual acts that violated their own conscience or upbringing simply because they were told that their body is not their own once they were married. Still others are taken advantage of to the point of abuse. How? Some not knowingly were possibly trying to satisfy a *spirit of perversion* that is in or on their spouse

which means that no matter what they did sexually or how many times they yielded, they could not satisfy their mate's desires because that person was being driven by a demonic spirit.
- The **Strongman Spirit of Perversion** is another concern. It has demons attached to it such as sexual perversion; sexual violence/torture; adultery, pornography; fornication; immorality; incest; seduction, lying and a host of others. **One way that different spirits transfer to people is when they participate in pre-marital sex and form ungodly soul ties with various partners.** Unless these people get deliverance these demonic spirits stay with them and are present during their marriage. And the spirit of perversion could be on assignment to work against the tired spouse through their sex driven spouse by *wearing them out* (lack of rest because of daily schedules coupled with lustful demands) so that Satan can get a foothold in their life. He loves to attack or push himself on people when they are tired, this is one of his tactics.
- Now everyone that enjoys sex does not have a demon. **Sex is a gift from God for the marriage bed.** What I am talking about are people who seem to be "unreasonable with their demand for sexual intercourse from their spouse on a constant basis when they know the person is not in favor of this arrangement and may have voiced it and the partner who has the strong sexual drive refuses to compromise or listen. You would have to discern if this were the case, pray and ask God to show you and then confirm it to you and if you find that this is the case or maybe it is just sexual abuse, professional help from a *Christian sex therapist or deliverance ministry* may be the solution. You can also see Chapter 7.
- **There is an old saying – "The grass is greener on the other side" but if you water your own grass**

it will be green too. In other words, if you take care of your relationship with God's help, doing things decently and in order your marriage will flourish beyond your expectations.

CHAPTER 2

WHAT IS THE BIBLICAL DEFINITION FOR DIVORCE?
(AND THINGS THE BIBLE HAS TO SAY ABOUT IT)

Basically the word **"Divorce"** has been misused and has a great deal of negative connotations associated with it that needs to be addressed, clarified and the reason for its existence explained. Also, in this chapter is knowledge on how to begin recovery as a result of having gone through a divorce and to begin to have a full and well adjusted joyful future as one proceeds with their life.

God has *permitted* divorce yet He said, "I hate divorce." To stay within the *context* in which He said this in Malachi 2:16, it is explained in verse 11 NLT which says, "In Judah, in Israel, and in Jerusalem there is treachery, for the men of Judah have defiled the Lord's beloved sanctuary by marrying women who worship idols." They were **unequally yoked** with these women because they worshipped foreign gods and this was causing the men to be pagan in their concepts. This disturbed the Lord as it is written in the book of Malachi 2:14-16 NLT which says, "You cry out, 'Why has the Lord abandoned us?' I'll tell you why! Because the Lord witnessed the vows you and your wife made to each other on your wedding day when you were young. But you have been disloyal to her, though she remained your faithful companion, the wife of your marriage vows. Didn't the Lord make you one with your wife? In body and spirit you are His. And what does He want? Godly children from your union. So guard yourself; remain loyal to the wife of your youth. For I hate divorce! Says the Lord, the God of Israel." An additional answer is found in Deuteronomy 7:6 as it says, "For you are a holy and set-apart people to the Lord your God; the Lord your God has chosen you to be a special people to Himself out of *all the peoples* on the face of the earth."

He also stated in Malachi 2:16 that He hated *marital separation* **and those who had** *violence towards their wives.* These acts were leading His people in the wrong direction causing them to be in sin (which separated them from God) and **which resulted in a divorce** because these acts were against the will of God.

Read Malachi 2:10-16 in the Amplified version in its entirety as it **explains why God said "I hate divorce"** in verse 16:

> Have we not all one Father? Has not one God created us?
>
> Why then do we deal faithlessly and treacherously each against his brother, profaning the covenant of [God with] our fathers? ...Judah has been faithless... and has **married the daughter of a foreign god....** The Lord will cast out of the tents of Jacob to the last man those who do this [evil thing]...And this you do with double guilt; you cover the altar of the Lord with **tears [shed by your unoffending wives, divorced by you that you might take heathen wives]**...Yet you ask, *Why does He reject it? Because the Lord was witness [to the covenant made at your marriage]* between you and the wife of your youth, against whom you have dealt treacherously and to whom

you were faithless. Yet she is your companion and the wife of your covenant [made by your marriage vows]. And did not God make [you and your wife] one [flesh]? ...For the Lord, the God of Israel, says: **I hate divorce and marital separation and him who covers his garment [his wife] with violence.** Therefore keep a watch upon your spirit [that it may be controlled by My Spirit], that you deal not treacherously and faithlessly [with your marriage mate].

Furthermore, <u>He hates it because</u> it causes so much pain and hurt to the adults and children of these unions of which many are seriously damaged or disturbed for years as a result of the spiritual and emotional ties being severed causing them to feel torn apart, rejected, used, hurt, empty and lost. It can literally bring your life to a complete halt. But we also know that many can be seriously damaged mentally and/or physically or even killed if they stay in some of these marriages. *Each marriage or case is different and has to be dealt with where that particular marriage is,* even though God hated divorce then and He hates it now because He created marriage to be permanent, *He understands (He has Wisdom) that some marriages will warrant a divorce, which will be shown and explained later in this chapter.*

Many people never fully recover, having to deal with a number of emotions and in many cases demonic oppression that causes great pain. Some have chosen to live in anger, fear, depression, guilt, shame, bitterness, loneliness, unforgiveness, rejection, grief, regret, self-pity, confusion and so forth especially those that do not turn to God for healing and restoration. *The good news* is that all those who do turn to God *and follow His plan,* which will include the Holy Spirit empowering and leading them into all truth (John 16:13), they may obtain the guidance, as well as spiritual, emotional and physical help that is needed and available from Him and through others divinely sent by Him. In addition, He will divinely connect them to a number of resources for healing and total restoration.

We've defined what the Holy Scriptures had to say about marriage, an institution created by God and intended to *last*. We have also discussed why He hates divorce. Therefore, *if a divorce is the first line of defense or resolution then it has been improperly used*. Nevertheless, if a marriage must be dissolved, we will explore certain aspects of the process and how it relates to scripture.

FREQUENTLY ASKED QUESTIONS REGARDING DIVORCE AND REMARRIAGE:

The most frequently asked questions by people who are contemplating divorce are listed below. They will be discussed throughout the pages in this chapter. These questions primarily come from people that have a relationship with God, those who are aware of the traditional options or biblical scriptures on how God feels about the subject and they do not want to offend Him. However, many people in the world (those without Christ in their lives) seem to not be bothered as much about how it looks and pretty much accept whatever happens and do whatever they want when it comes to marriage, divorce and remarriage unless of course they have strong morals. Morals originated from godly principles and laws and these moral values are to be kept to this day. Moral laws do not change only the way they are dealt within a given society changes.

- **Does the Bible make it clear whether or not people are permitted or have the right to divorce or remarry?**
- **Why was divorce instituted in the first place?**
- **Is divorce a sin?**
- **If I remarry will I be living in sin?**
- **Will God still bless me after a divorce or if I remarry?**
- **If I divorced for the wrong reasons will this be held against me for the rest of my life?**
- **Is there a right time or a wrong time to remarry?**
- **If we divorced for the wrong reasons and are still both single and wish to try again can we remarry and still be in God's will?**

WHAT IS THE BIBLICAL DEFINITION FOR DIVORCE?

- If I divorce will I have to lose my position in the ministry and step down for a while or permanently?
- Should I remain single for the rest of my life in order to be pleasing to God?

We will begin by giving the origin of divorce and by defining its biblical meaning. But in addition to knowing the origin and definition of divorce it is most important to know how the term "Law" is defined by God because it is used both in the Old and New Testaments in relating to marriage. The term "Law" today is seen as a lot of rules, regulations or ordinances that govern under an authoritative administration and are binding with no room for teaching or for them to be broken. Is this what God intended when God gave His Word to Moses (what the Jewish people refer to as the Torah) to His people *for teaching and/or biblical revelation?* We will attempt to answer this question in this chapter as well.

Polygamy (one man having possession of many wives *all* at the same time) **was the reason Divorce was instituted.** God did not want men to live a lifestyle of Polygamy because God's plan was **Monogamy** (one male husband with one female wife at one time). With the advent of the Messianic period the Jewish followers (Believers) were already aware of God's moral laws but the Gentile followers were not and had to be taught by the Apostles.

Because of corruption, polygamy and having concubines became common place amongst the Gentile societies who believed in **polytheism** (the worship of many gods and none being the One True God). Because of their belief they did not live within the boundaries or safety of a covenant with God. Therefore, the Gentiles did not receive righteous instructions or protection nor did they have godly character or behavior. Because it became common that it was considered not wrong in ancient times. Even after the divine law was given the Gentiles were not governed by it and continued in their polygamous ways and therefore they did not depart from the law because they never gave their consent to the law.

Polygamy was tolerated but never given God's approval. God tolerated Abraham with his wife's maidservant, Hagar, as his subordinate wife (Genesis 16:3) and Jacob with Leah the wife he was tricked into marrying and then he married his true love, Rachel, and was married to the both of them at the same time (Gen. 29:15-30). In addition to that he took both of their handmaids because of the rivalry between the two sisters.

People inferred from such stories like these found in the book of Genesis and throughout the Bible that it was alright to have more than one wife. But the Bible says, in the beginning when God gave a man a wife, *it was one wife.* God also said that the man would leave his father and mother and be joined to his wife and they shall become one flesh. He further said in Proverbs 18:22, He who finds a [true] *wife* finds a good thing and obtains favor from the Lord.

Polygamy produced jealousies and quarrels (strife). Also, along with the purchase of wives and the small liberties allowed daughters in the choice of husbands probably resulted in unhappy unions. Therefore, God allowed divorce because the men would have resulted to more of this behavior. In some cultures **polyandry** was practiced where there would be one wife and many husbands *all* at the same time. These arrangements are not from our heavenly Father and cause great distress and confusion for everyone involved especially the children. Even though they are brought up in the culture and accept it they still notice the jealousy, favorites given to other wives or husbands and children. The emotions that arise from this behavior only play right into the plan of Satan whose goal is to destroy marriage and families.

In many cases during ancient times and still in some cultures today, when the laws were written wives were categorized together with slaves, cattle and other possessions. An owner could give up his property but the property could not leave its owner, therefore, a wife had no rights in this area. **Wives were not allowed to divorce their husbands** for fornication until the New Testament or New Covenant (Mark 10:12).

REGULATIONS THAT PROTECT A DIVORCED WOMAN'S REPUTATION:

Divorce Defined According to The New Ungers Bible Dictionary in the "*Old* Testament" or as it is referred to in Hebrew "The Tanakh:"

The word divorce means "cutting," "separating," under the **Jewish Law** a legal separation between man and wife by means of a formal process of some sort. As the ordinances respecting marriage have in view the hallowing (holiness) of the relationship, so also was the Mosaic regulation in respect of divorce. A man finding in his wife something shameful or offensive, dismissed her from his house with a certificate of divorce. Causes of divorce seem to have been accepted by Moses by hereditary usage and allowed because of the people's hardness of heart. The question of divorce entirely at the will of the husband; the *wife*, not possessing equal privileges with the husband, had no right of divorce.

Ground of divorce – there have been many interpretations of the expression "anything indecent" given as the ground of divorce. Based on Deuteronomy 23:14, things that profane the camp of Israel, and denotes something shameful or offensive. Adultery, to which some of the rabbis would restrict the expression, is not to be thought of, because such was to be punished with death. It is necessary, therefore, to understand by the phrase in question *something besides adultery*, although something perhaps tending in that direction, something that would cause jealousy or distrust in the mind of the husband and destroy the prospect of true conjugal affection and harmony between him and his wife. *A good deal was left to the discretion, and it might be the foolish caprice*

of the husband. **Our Lord admitted its imperfection and threw upon the defective moral condition of the people the blame of a legislation so unsatisfactory in itself and so evidently liable to abuse.**

The Law provided Regulations "to guard against a thoughtless and hasty divorce," therefore, "the law provided **if a man dismissed his wife, and she became the wife of another man**, *he must not again take her as his wife*, not even if the second husband had divorced her, or even if he had died." *Why?* For the **FIRST husband** to *remarry* his former wife who is now a **"*Divorced Woman*"** "is to be regarded as a **pollution**, or on the same level with *fornication,* and **the law condemns the reunion of such a divorced one with her FIRST husband** as an 'an abomination before Jehovah,' because thereby fornication is carried still further, and marriage is degraded to the mere satisfaction of sexual passion."

Because of the regulation which was **a law instituted by men *to safe guard against thoughtless and hasty divorces on the part of the husband*** and to make sure that her *first husband* gave serious consideration for his decision to divorce her because he would never be able to remarry her once he dismissed her and she married another man even if that man dismissed her or died. If she, as a divorced woman did remarry her first husband she was labeled an adulteress because this was regarded as a pollution, or on the same level with fornication, therefore, THIS remarriage by a divorced woman was the marriage that would make her an adulteress and cause her husband to commit adultery with her in the Old Testament. In the New Testament regarding Mark 10:12 and Luke 16:18 it states how a woman becomes an adulteress. The findings to explain these scriptures are found further in this chapter under Examining and Exposing Scriptures that have caused Mass Confusion in Christendom.

Deuteronomy 24:2 KJV explains that when she was dismissed by her first husband and she remarried she was not labeled an "adulteress:"

> **And when she is departed out of his house,
> she may go and be another man's wife.**

She was not labeled an "adulteress" when she was dismissed (divorced) and she remarried, no, that label was given to *her if she remarried her first husband after* **she had remarried and was divorced by someone else or became a widow.** This was done to make her first husband think twice before he divorced her and took another woman because of the lust in his eyes or for whatever reason that he gave her a bill of divorce. Also, *if she had never remarried after she was divorced from her first husband* then if he wanted to remarry her and she agreed that would have been acceptable and perfectly *legal.*

One additional point about **protecting the woman's name and reputation**, in Deuteronomy 22:13-21 this passage explains that if a man slanders his virgin wife's name and he was found guilty he had to pay her father a fine and stay married to her without the possibility of ever acquiring a divorce.

In any event **adultery defiles the marriage bed.** Adultery occurs when either of the married couple becomes sexually involved with a person outside of their marriage (Hebrews 13:4).

The One New Man Bible explains the passage regarding the woman caught in adultery and how it takes two not one to be caught in the act (John 8:1-11). "If you catch someone in adultery, you have to catch two because one person cannot commit adultery. Yet only the woman was brought to be punished. That was the practice of the societies of the ancient world, except for Judaism. In all the other societies, except for a few that were matriarchal, the wife was a chattel, a possession of the husband, so if she was caught in adultery it was a crime against her husband and he could punish her any way he wished. She was just like any other possession, to be treated like furniture or a slave. Adultery to those societies was not sin, just a crime against the husband. **Only in Judaism was adultery a sin against God."**

"Because it was a sin against God both participants were to be stoned – it was not a lesser sin for one than for the other. Lev. 20:10 and Deut. 22:22 say *If a man is found lying with a woman married to a husband, then they will both of them die, both the man who lay with the woman, and the woman; so you will put away evil from Israel.* Although the verses, John 7:53-8:11, were added long after the New Testament Scriptures were written, we need to keep the basic message of the addition, that we are to love the sinner, but hate the sin. It is more important for each of us to focus on his own shortcomings rather than on the shortcomings of others," (The One New Man Bible).

Divorce Defined According to The New Ungers Bible Dictionary in the "*New* Testament" or as it is referred to in Hebrew "B'rit Hadashah:"

Under the **Christian Law** the teachings of Jesus on the subject of divorce are **(1)** the liberty given to a man by the Mosaic Law to put away his wife (Deuteronomy 24:1-4) was because of the hardness of the Jewish heart. **(2) He who divorces his wife,** *except* **for fornication, and marries another commits adultery (Matthew 19:9) and leads her to commit the same crime (Matthew 5:32). (3)** He who marries a divorced woman commits adultery, and the woman who puts away her husband and marries another man (Mark 10:12) incurs the same kind of guilt. (Note: the wife might also be the divorcing party because during the time of this writing this was a custom among the Greeks and Romans).

Ground of divorce – In Matthew 19:9 the one exception in favor of divorce is given, namely, **fornication,** *perhaps* some form of sexual immorality, although **the meaning of the term is uncertain. It was evidently not adultery, which is described by a different word.**

In reference to number two (2) above, *Jesus "warned husbands not to ruin a wife's reputation by divorcing her. He charged husbands with adultery when they divorced an innocent wife and remarried."* [3] Matthew 19:3-9.

Later in this chapter we will **define and explore what** *fornication entails* **because it certainly is** *not limited* **to** "sexual" **immorality.** Thereby opening the door to additional allowances for a *biblical divorce* and at the same time setting many people free from the condemnation they have carried for years because of a lack of knowledge on their part, on the part of leadership or just the truth being withheld because of religious spirits that believe others have to suffer for past mistakes for the rest of their lives or better yet for past sins that have already been removed by the Blood of a Wonderful Savior who does not condemn them or even remember their sins Himself. Ephesians 1:7 KJV says, "In whom we have redemption through His blood, the forgiveness of sins, according to the riches of His grace."

Many in today's society see the above definitions as outdated and they choose not to follow the new covenant's reasoning, commands and explanations regarding grounds for a divorce which as we can now see has resulted *in a record breaking number of people divorcing one another because of any and everything.* This has left families, Christian and Non-Christian alike, broken and some literally destroyed for decades if not permanently.

Ladies and gentlemen, God is a just God, He knows better than we, and yes He allows divorce but as we will find, His grounds for divorce as explained in length will help many of you to understand why certain laws are necessary and for many of you to know that **remarriage** *is* **an option** *after* **divorce.**

Whatever situation you may find yourself in whether it is happily married, struggling in your marriage, separated or even divorced, always remember *it is not over till God says it is over!* I have found that God always has a ram in the bush, a plan "B" if you will. *Never give up hope but press on and seek God for the plan that He has for your life that will bring hope and not despair, freedom and not bondage, relationship and not religion.*

Notice in the passage that God said He made a New Covenant with the house of Israel, this transpired and is found in the book of Luke 22:20 where it is recorded that Jesus took the (communion) cup during the Passover Seder (meal) which He observed being a Jewish Rabbi with His Jewish disciples (Christians are familiar with this meal as "The Last Supper"). Jesus said, "This cup is the New Testament or *Covenant* [ratified] in My blood which is shed (poured out) for you." **God is recognizing that the New Covenant He made for the house of Israel** *extends* **to His** *Adopted Family* which are all those who receive Him as their Lord and Savior; they have been <u>ingrafted</u> into the family of God according to Ephesians 1:5, "For He foreordained us (destined us, planned in love for us) to be *adopted* (revealed) as His own children through Jesus Christ, in accordance with the purpose of His will [because it pleased Him and was His kind intent]." Also according to 2 Corinthians 5:17-19 states **we were** *ingrafted* **in:**

> Therefore if any person is [ingrafted] in Christ (the Messiah) is a new creation (a new creature altogether); the old [previous moral and spiritual condition] has passed away. Behold, the fresh and new has come...

Even though divorce involves missing the will of God, He does not want people to carry guilt and shame as a result of a divorce nor does He desire for people to remain alone the rest of their life, nor for a single parent to raise their children alone. In addition, because of their thinking **the condemnation will be used by the adversary to**

weaken their authority. How? Because of a lack of confidence and thinking that God is displeased with them they are unable to walk (live) or move in their full authority.

So let's start with some foundational information according to the Word of God that will be helpful in releasing years of pain from the aftermath of a divorce so that healing can come forth to all parties involved adults and children alike.

What is a "Bill of Divorce" – A Certificate "book" of Divorce. It requires the intervention of a Levite to secure the formal correctness of the instrument. This would bring the matter under the cognizance of legal authority and tend to check the rash exercise of the right of a husband.

Deuteronomy 24:1 says,

> When a man takes a wife and marries her, if then she finds no favor in his eyes because he has found some indecency in her, and he writes her **a *bill of divorce*,** puts it in her hand and sends her out of his house.

Matthew 5:31 says,

> It has also been said, whoever divorces his wife must give her **a *certificate of divorce.***

"The process of divorce was between families rather than being a legal matter at this time. If the woman was guilty of misconduct, her father would have to forfeit her dowry. If she was divorced without blame, he could demand the return of some of it." [3] 24:1-4.

The bill of divorce is a document or tool that is used to dissolve and finalize a legal contract or an agreement regarding a marriage. And because the divorce is recognized by God the covenant between them will no longer exist. And since it is recognized by the laws of the land and God, therefore, it means that the formerly married couple has dismissed (divorced) each other and they are not to continue to have sexual relations with one another and if they do they are committing sexual immorality which is a form of fornication. (See the section in this chapter on Remarriage for more details).

There are numerous **terms used in the Bible to indicate divorce** and they are according to Vine's Complete Expository Dictionary as follows:

> "to let loose from," "let go free," "is put away," "a standing off," "to cause to withdraw," "a writing or bill of divorcement," and "to dismiss"

The term or word **"Law"** is used in both the Old and New Testaments in relating to marriage, therefore, it is necessary to express how it is used when relating to marriage and God's people. God first gave the Law, Torah, to Moses.

According to Jewish writings sent through **Rabbi Yisrael Ben Avraham** the following is a partial definition of **Torah** and a summary of how the term *Law* was *intended to be used in relating to people:*

The *Torah* the body of history, which includes the commandments, are the first five books of the Bible. *The Torah is the most important collection of writings within the Hebrew faith in the Bible as it remains today to the Jewish community.* It is known as the Five Books of Moshe (Moses), or the Law of Moshe; it is also known as Humshei Torah "[the] five fifths/parts [of the] Torah" or simply the Humash (Chumash) and known as Sefer Torah. **The commandments of the Lord are often mistakenly seen as "*law*" in Christian western thinking.** This term though technical has caused much confusion within Greek thinkers. **Torah is not law as seen in the Pauline letters.** It is critical that we keep in context the historical life of Paul. Remember he considers himself a Hebrew of Hebrews according to Philippians 3:4-6 and in Acts we see Rav Shaul (Paul) speak regarding his identity as he spoke in the language of Hebrew though this is written in the Greek text. The word law for Paul was not as it is for Christians, if it were then why does he still observe it in the books of Acts?

Torah again is not law. The word Torah comes from the Hebrew root word "yarah," a verb that means, "to flow or throw something." This can be a flowing of an arrow from an archer's bow, or the flowing of a finger to point out a direction. The Hebraic definition of Torah is *"a set of instructions," from a father to his children*. If the teaching is not adhered then there is discipline to foster obedience and train his children. *Torah is to teach and bring the children to maturity.*

Laws are rules, regulations or ordinances that govern under some authoritative administration and are binding on a community. Violations of the rules require punishment. With this type of law, there is no room for teaching, either the law was broken with the penalty of punishment or it was not broken.

God, as our heavenly Father, gives his children His Torah in the same manner as parents give their Torah to their children, not in the manner as a government does to its citizens.

The founding document of Jewish law is split into two parts: the Written Law and the Oral Law. The two serve as a sort of "constitution" for the legal system, except that this constitution may never be amended or changed.

The "Written Law" is found in the Torah, also known as the *Pentateuch*. The "Oral Law" is to clarify, compliment and supplement the laws written in the Torah. *The Oral Law provides guidance on the nature and applications of the Written Law and a reference to the Written Law without a reference to the Oral Law will almost never accurately describe the complete valid and current Jewish legal position on a given subject.*

Please Note: *The Lord gave four different types of Laws in the scriptures from the beginning. Some we no longer practice, some never change.* The Holy Spirit is available to help bring balance, clarity and the discipline we need to stay in right standing with God: (1) **Ceremonial Law,** which is no longer practiced. It involved sacrificing animals for their sins; today a child of God would ask God to forgive them for their sin which is something that is not to be taken lightly; (2) **Judicial Law,** which determines the type of punishment for certain behavior. For example, under the Old Testament people were stoned to death for committing adultery and under the New Testament people are divorced for committing adultery. The act is still considered wrong just dealt with in a different way; (3) **Moral Law,** God told the people the things that were wrong and those do not change unless He changes them. For example, He said murder was wrong, stealing was wrong, adultery was wrong, lying was wrong and so on, <u>these Moral Laws never changed</u> but the penalty on how they are dealt with may; and (4) **Social Law,** how we seal a contract (covenant). For example, before men would take off a sandal and give it to someone to seal the purchase of property. Now we sign a contract and have it notarized by a notary in order to seal it.

This is very important in order to get the full understanding of what God intended for His people. He gave the Torah, the law as a guide of instructions to help men live holy and decent lives based on truth and godly principles. He also gave balance between the written word and the oral word. **The law regarding marriage** and people in general was **never intended as hard nosed rules**

and regulations but instructions to help us move forward and live in a loving manner with authority over our enemies as we obeyed God and spent time with Him.

When you examine this it relates to us today because we to have been given a Written Word which is balanced with the leading of the Holy Spirit. They work together to bring accuracy, justice and clarity. The Written Word alone will kill just as religion will kill, but the Written Word working with the Spirit will bring life, guidance, peace and success.

God's Word will truly preserve, it is written and the Holy Spirit will put all into action to see that it is done.

Exodus 24:12 says this about the Law:

> And the Lord said to Moses, Come up to Me into the mountain and be there, and I will give you tables of stone, with the law and the commandments which I have written that you may *teach* them. (2 Corinthians 3:2, 3)

Romans 3:20 says,

> For no person will be justified (made righteous, acquitted, and judged acceptable) in His sight by observing the works prescribed by the Law. For [the real function of] the Law is to make men recognize and be conscious of sin [not mere perception, but an acquaintance with sin which works toward repentance, faith, and holy character].

THE REASONS DIVORCES ARE ALLOWED OR OCCUR:

The first reason is for the HARDNESS of HEARTS and how it relates to a divorce. Because of the hardness of the husband's heart (women were not allowed to divorce their husbands under the Old Testament) God allowed a divorce to take place.

The stubbornness and perversity or unreasonably contrary attitude that he had was the reason that God granted a bill of divorce.

Matthew 19:8 states:

> He said to them, **Because of the hardness (stubbornness and perversity) of your hearts** Moses permitted you to dismiss and repudiate and divorce your wives; but from the beginning it has not been so [ordained]. Also see Deut. 24:1.

Mark 10:5 states:

> But Jesus said to them, **Because of your hardness of heart** [your condition of insensibility to the call of God] he wrote you this precept in your Law.

A hardened heart by one or both spouses refuses to yield to the Spirit of God or to righteousness, is insensitive, unfaithful and unwilling to change or compromise and is dead to the things of the Living God. **Your heart or will is being ruled primarily by your soul (mind, will and emotions) and not by your spirit.** The Spirit gives life, it brings about true love and compassion that would cause your heart to line up with the will of God instead of your own will and mind which can be heavily influenced by Satan's temptations.

Some people would say, well I go to church; I read the Word of God all the time and now look at my life? My question would be do you have religion or do you have a personal relationship that would include the leading of the Holy Spirit? **Many people are not sensitive to His Spirit and they miss opportunities to avoid traps set by the enemy.** Jesus said He sent the Holy Spirit to comfort us, to teach us, to direct us, to help us and for a host of many other reasons. But if we choose to ignore the full counsel of His Word then we miss a lot of valuable insight and revelation. The letter of the Word alone kills but the Spirit makes alive, so if you use them both it will bring balance and more protection for your marital relationship (2 Cor. 3:6 and John 16:7, 13).

God gave us all a choice to choose in each situation or circumstance that arises in our lives. We can either choose life or choose death. We make the choice when we make our decision. *If your decision is for life* you will have a peace and strength as well as other help from the Holy Spirit to resolve the matter and get back on track or move forward. But *if your decision is death* there will probably be very little peace coupled with guilt, shame, regret, pride, unforgiveness and things we allow to torment us and/or to justify our decision. Furthermore, the Holy Spirit will not help because He has been rejected by your decision which He will not violate or override; and because the atmosphere you have created around yourself is not one that He moves or operates in.

If your decision is in favor of your flesh (your plans and ideas apart from God) then evil forces move into your situation to cause even more havoc, chaos, confusion, pain, suffering, loss and so on. A hardened heart is rooted in stubbornness (witchcraft) rebellion, lack of knowledge and fear so in the long run a person will only be lead into further bondage until they wake up and do something to turn their situation around. That something should start with repenting and trusting God. He can speak to a heart that is willing and obedient and turn things completely around for all those who love Him and are called according to His design and purpose (Romans 8:28).

A hardened heart starts with a bruised heart and instead of forgiveness or talking it out it is left to grow cold and hard. This is why the Bible says do not go to bed angry but to resolve whatever the problem is (Eph. 4:26). If you do not resolve it then you open a door for the adversary to feed negative thoughts and make matters worse.

If a heart is bruised and cold it is the *husband's responsibility* as the head of the house to work on the forgiveness to clear the atmosphere and let peace remain. He is called the "head" therefore he is responsible for the leadership in the home. He must lead in the right things to do according to the Word of God (Ephesians 5:23).

He should be the first to seek forgiveness, the first to confess his problems and/or the first to seek to bring reconciliation. This will help solve the bruised heart and prevent it from going to the next stage. God called men to love their wives *as Christ loves the church* and gave His all for it, which included giving His life. However, if a woman is the first to work on forgiveness that is alright too, especially if she knows in her heart that is what the Lord is prompting her to do or she knows that is the right thing to do. *The point is forgiveness needs to come about;* **<u>but if no one steps forth</u> then God has ordained the man as the head to step out and lead his wife and children in the righteousness of God.**

The hard heartedness is usually the result of failure to humble oneself, forgive others, ask for forgiveness and repent while seeking God for strength, guidance, instructions and deliverance from any issue that is dominating a person's life and causing tremendous damage to their marriage and family. Once again, if there is no change of heart and they exercise their *free will* and make the wrong choice, then God by His grace, has permitted a man or a woman to be set free by divorce. *Keep in mind that the spouse who is following instructions from the Lord to obey God's will for their life and has attempted to do all that God would have them to do in their marriage will be given a peace about the matter and strength to move on totally free from any bondage.*

Only God knows the heart and He knows that the person with the hardened heart has <u>chosen</u> not to change, therefore, **by *His Spirit*** God will direct His child out of their present marriage *if that is their heart's desire* and/or what is best for their protection and overall being. In some cases there is an assignment on someone's life from God who has to do a work for Him that would be hindered from coming forth if they were to stay in this relationship. Therefore, The Holy Spirit will guide them out of the relationship at the appointed time and onto the correct path to fulfill their destiny.

Another reason for divorce is for PHYSICAL and/or MENTAL ABUSE due to a lack of obedience in yielding to biblical principles for marriage the result could lead to great distress, abandonment, heavy addictions and so forth.

If a person is **living in an extremely controlling environment,** one that has *physical, mental, emotional or sexual abuse there needs to be godly confrontation and the matter addressed and boundaries drawn.* If confrontation is not wise, or if confrontation in a Godly way has not helped and the abuse continues it is not against God and it is not a sin to leave the situation by separating and seeking professional help while you are seeking God for instructions, directions and healing whether it is emotional, physical or both.

Anyone living in fear for their life is not obligated to submit or be subject in that situation to anyone or for any reason. God asks a couple to submit (honor and respect) *one another* out of reverence for Christ (Ephesians 5:21), and that the husband is to love his wife as Christ loves the church. *God laid His life down for the Church He did not tear it down, reject or beat it. He loved it with an unconditional love.* There is liberty in Christ not lording over someone watching and dictating their every move (2 Corinthians 3:17). The Bible further says that, "Even so husbands should love their wives as [being in a sense] their own bodies. He who loves his own wife loves himself. For no man ever hated his own flesh, but nourishes and carefully protects and cherishes it, as Christ does the church" (Ephesians 5:28-29).

By the same token *if* a wife is constantly nagging and making demands on her husband and not handling things the way the bible would say to do so then she is creating a situation that can lead to a divorce. She is to be subject to her husband and far more precious than jewels in his sight, in other words she is to respect and reverence her husband (love him, notice him, regard him, prefer him, honor him, comfort and encourage him, Ephesians 5:33 and Proverbs 31:10-12). Is that to say that she can never have an opinion or make a decision on her own? Of course not, it is good advice and suggestions that offer wisdom that will keep the adversary out of your marriage and it should be welcomed by both parties, (Eph. 5:21).

Being UNEQUALLY YOKED is another major reason couples divorce. Many family issues are not resolved because of a lack of agreement regarding beliefs, morals and the handling of funds God's way.

The Word of God says in 2 Corinthians 6:14 that people should not be unequally yoked:

> Do not be unequally yoked with unbelievers [do not make mismated alliances with them or come under a different yoke with them, **inconsistent with your faith**]. For what partnership have right living and right standing with God with iniquity and lawlessness? Or how can light have fellowship with darkness?

Malachi 2:11 also says that people should not be unequally yoked:

> Judah has been faithless and dealt treacherously, and an abomination has been committed in Israel and in Jerusalem;

> For Judah has profaned the holy sanctuary of the Lord which He loves, and has married the daughter of a foreign god... (Also see Jeremiah 2:3).

"A Christian should marry a Christian. Since Christ through the Holy Spirit dwells within the Believer, Christians are not to marry unbelievers and participate in their false worship. Marriage should strengthen Christian faith" [3] (2 Co. 6:14-18).

When both parties within the marriage have a personal relationship with Jesus then each can go to God in their separate prayer closets (ones place of prayer) and receive instructions and guidance for their marriage. **Once they have prayed separately and then come together to pray if they both have a**

personal relationship with God they should be able to come in agreement using the Word of God as their Mediator. This is one major reason why it is extremely important not to be unequally yoked with someone, in this case married to an unbeliever, because then if only one of the partners has a personal relationship with Jesus then God the Holy Spirit has access to that one and not the other because He will not force Himself on the unbelieving spouse who does not know Him or is sensitive to His Spirit.

Furthermore, when they are <u>not</u> both in a place in their relationship with God where they can hear from God it is probably because they do not have a prayer life, nor share in the things which are biblical that would save their marriage. People who have a personal relationship with the Lord and are led by His Holy Spirit will have the greater advantage.

Note: Many people stay together for various reasons: obligations, children, finances and other responsibilities, fear of loneliness, poverty, or for whatever reason knowing that these things do not necessarily dictate that they are happy together, content or satisfied with their marriage. However, when you stay because what you are doing is unto God first and secondly because you are committed to one another not out of duty but out of genuine love then peace, joy and true satisfaction will be in your marriage.

With the day in and day out routines and living life in general it will require more to sustain the love you have for another person. Feelings alone can change and fade or be diminished in your eyes; tests and emotions get involved but when God is first He has the ability to keep it fresh and new; to keep everything in its right perspective so that the love you have for one another will remain alive and well.

God commanded divorce in the cases of men from Israel who were marrying foreign wives who worshipped foreign gods and this was causing the men to be pagan in their concepts and to turn away from God.

Ezra 10:2-5 says,

...We have **broken faith and dealt treacherously against our God and have married foreign women** of the peoples of the land... Therefore let us make a **covenant with our God to put away all the foreign wives and their children**...Arise, for it is your duty, and we are with you. Be strong and brave and do it. Then Ezra arose and made the chiefs of the priests, the Levites, and all Israel swear that they would do as had been said. So they took the oath.

Again, people have a free will and if they choose not to do it His way, they haven't realized that His way is the only way and their plans will more than likely fall to the ground. Why such a strong statement? Because a person cannot *change* the heart of another person, only God can do that and when we yield and give Him first place, His plan cannot fail because He is a God of miracles. This could be just what your marriage needs, a fresh word and a miracle from God.

Christians with unequally yoked partners are marriages not *instituted by God* but as they come together anyway some are successful. Was God's blessing on it from the onset? Or did God know something we did not know when we judged by outer appearances only because we were not able see a person's true heart, true intentions or true motive? Only God knew for sure that one day they would come into the Kingdom of God, (John 7:24). Keep in mind though this is a chance that you take when you marry outside of your faith. Ask God to give you discernment to see their true motive because some people will lie about their faith just to marry you.

An unequally yoked couple is referred to as Inter-marriage when Christians *are married to "followers of other religions and is universally condemned in the Word because of the temptation of idolatry within the family relationship"* [3] Paraphrased Deuteronomy 7:3-4. **Intermarriage is not based on:** *the division of mankind, on hereditary traits, color of skin, race, people of a nation of the same type or culture but* **based only upon differences in <u>belief</u>.** The same holds true for the New Testament as seen in my quote of 2 Corinthians 6:14 where it is indicated you are not to be with someone who is inconsistent with your faith.

Intermarriages usually come about from the wrong motives such as self gain, the appearance of the other person was extremely pleasing to their eye (could be based only on lust so be careful); they needed financial support or another parent in the home or for some other selfish desire. However, one reason some are successful is because many of these couples "find God" or receive salvation while in these marriages. Father God knew that they would receive Him and *many of them are indeed married to the right person* even though they were attracted to the person for the wrong reasons or even married for the wrong reasons. God has a way of turning things around for our good and/or *revealing* certain things we need to know when we are mature enough to receive it.

I would like to add that some individuals of certain races or cultures placed **interracial or biracial marriages** *in this category and condemned these marriages because the people were of a different race having a different color of skin or their cultures were different.* If these people are both Believers sharing the same faith and worship the same God who is of the Holy Scriptures then they are indeed "equally yoked." **It is perfectly fine and legal for them to marry.** Not all couples are in the same place in the spiritual realm or their walk with God (how strong their personal relationship is with God, how obedient they are to go to certain levels with Him or in living true to the Word of God) but this does not mean that they cannot grow and mature. As long as the person is open to renew their mind in the scriptures by studying the Word of God there should not be any major problem in this area.

The truth of the matter is that interracial or biracial marriages are pleasing to God who created all mankind in His image and this is validated throughout the Holy Scriptures whether you call it the Bible, Torah or the Tanakh it is God's Word and it will never change. Briefly, I will give examples of several couples who God used mightily and who were all in interracial marriages. God does not do anything by accident or chance He knew from the beginning that they would be with people of a different race and culture yet He used these relationships to help others and at the same time make history by one or both spouses being recorded in the Bible and elsewhere. And these marriages were as follows: **(1)** After Sarah passed Abraham remarried. Abraham and Keturah and she bore him six sons (Gen.25:1-2); **(2)** Moses and Zipporah, his Ethiopian, Cushite wife (Numbers 12:1; Ex. 2:21); **(3)** King David and Bathsheba the daughter of Eliam and the former wife of Uriah the Hittite (2 Sam. 11:26, 27, 3). King David and Bathsheba had a son (2 Sam. 12:24), who grew up to be King Solomon who built the Temple for God. Now King Solomon fathered a son, Menelek with the Queen of Sheba also known as the Queen of Ethiopia who was very wealthy (I Kings 10:1-2, 10) and who was a direct descendant of Ham and Shem, this was another interracial couple and it did not stop God from using Solomon mightily during his reign; **(4)** Queen Esther (Hadassah is her Jewish name) and the Persian King Ahasueru (Esther 2:15-17; Est.1:2); **(5)** Joseph and Asenath daughter of Potiphera, priest of On (Gen. 41:45); and **(6)**Ruth, a Moabite and Boaz, a Jew, their son Obed was the father of Jesse who was the father of King David [the ancestor of Jesus Christ] (Ruth 4:13,17).

He created the variations in color and formed different cultures that were pleasing to Him. People have distorted what God began by setting rules, regulations and laws that God was never in or never spoke. Some people have allowed Satan to dictate to them and place others in bondage. There is liberty in Christ and He is pleased when all people love one another and show due respect to each other's cultures as long as that culture's traditions line up with His will for mankind.

A child once asked "what color was Jesus?" The mother answered, He is the Light of the World which is "Pure Light" and all the colors of the rainbow are in this light. So all people regardless of their color who were made in His image are apart of Him, the Living God!

In addition to that, once any two people unite in marriage they must be confident that there is hope for their marriage to survive. **God does not fight against marriage He accepts it; He instituted it and works with you to achieve success in it.** The believing spouse can hope for the unbeliever and a divorce does not need to occur unless the unbelieving partner desires it (I Corinthians 7:15). The believing spouse also is a type of covering for the unbeliever and the children of this union as seen in:

I Corinthians 7:14 NIV where it says,

> For the unbelieving husband has been sanctified through his wife, and the unbelieving wife has been sanctified through her believing husband. Otherwise your children would be unclean, but as it is, they are holy.

ABANDONMENT is another reason Divorce is allowed:

The Bible is clear, it says in I Corinthians 7:15,

> But if the unbelieving partner [actually] leaves, let him do so; in such [cases the remaining] brother or sister is not morally bound. But God has called us to peace. In the King James version it says, But if the unbelieving depart, let him depart. A brother or a sister is not under bondage in such cases: but God hath called us to peace.

If a spouse has chosen to leave you and it is clear they do not plan to return because of the hardness of their heart and they have moved on with their life, then you have been given permission to continue with your life and keep peace in your heart and your surroundings. In order for you to go on with your life this would include a divorce which will enable you to have a fresh start.

The divorce may not be because of any sin on your part; for instance, if *the part you contributed which lead up to the divorce* was that you chose to be a Believer, to be Born-again, and they did not choose to become Born-again (John 3:3, 7; a new, from above) that means that their spirit was not alive with the presence of God and you could not truly fellowship as *one* because you were unequally yoked. Then your divorce will not be because of any sin that you did because you chose righteousness and they chose whatever sin that lured them out of "that door." Of course, this is just one example, but on the other hand, if you know that you had a part in pushing them out then you can still have a fresh start and handle the guilt and all that comes with it the same way as you would handle any other mistake, negative situation or sin and be set free (See this Chapter under Clarifying Sin).

God said He called us to peace. Peace also means to be whole, nothing broken and nothing missing. Allow God to rebuild your life, **seek Him first and <u>wait on Him.</u>** As you are seeking God for new direction, fellowship with people who have like faith, through divine connections and remain uplifted, hopeful and in expectation of a better tomorrow. Remember, He will be faithful to complete the restoration process that He starts in you because He is faithful (Phi.1:6; 2 Timothy 2:13).

ADDICTION is another reason Divorce is allowed:

Refusing to seek God and/or professional help for addictions to alcohol, drugs, sex, pornography, gambling, wrong food choices that could cause health issues and obesity which may place financial stress on the family because of medical bills and so on; things that are clearly destroying their lives, their marriage, their family and their health falls under the category of a hardened heart which is ground for a divorce. O.K. you may ask whatever happened to "for better or for worst?" – nothing happened to it. One spouse has decided to breach the covenant (contract) with their addiction so the **"worst" is not beyond their control**, *it is by their choice.*

If they would make a decision to change and get the proper help needed their spouse could continue with a peace to remain in this marriage without being a co-dependent or an enabler. Some spouses will continue no matter what because they love their spouse and the parent of their children but *that is their choice* if they want to invest untold years of praying and believing. We know that God can certainly do it and change the hardened heart if the addicted spouse is willing and obedient. To stay is strictly up to them and what God has placed in their hearts to do for their spouse who is caught in some type of an addiction. Be prayerful, and seek God in this matter and be willing to be led by the Holy Spirit and get confirmation and make sure you have the peace of God before making any major decisions.

I can share this information from first hand experience and I share it only to show that if we trust God He knows what is best for us, do not shut Him out but receive Him into your life and welcome His Holy Spirit and your life will never be the same.

I was married to someone that God did not send into my life and others looking in from the outside thought we had a pretty good marriage, I would say above average. We were both saved but neither one of us attended church regularly. At this point we had been married for years with two children and buying a home before I discovered he had a strong substance abuse addiction. Once I rededicated my life to the Lord because of "trouble" as so many do, I made the decision to stand for my marriage and to pray consistently about it and wait on God while still being a faithful wife. Even though he had already **abandoned** the family to move in with a female drug supplier, was committing **adultery,** freely using *chemical substances* in her house and using his income to support his habit, I was still determined to wait and hope for the best for the sake of our marriage and the children being raised by their natural father.

And the Lord sent His prophets (male and female and more than one and none of which knew one another) to tell me that

God had a "husband" for me (in the midst of my standing and believing for, at that time, my husband to be delivered). Of course, I rejected every one who told me to let it go and move on or to receive the "new" thing God was about to do in my life. *I could not see or discern that the person I had taken a stand for had no mindset to stop doing what he was doing and change, therefore, I would have wasted even more years and missed the blessing that God was bringing into my life.* God does not play when it comes to matters like this that concern His children because He is serious about their well-being. He was warning me that I was going to miss what He really had for my life because this was not it. This was an assignment from hell to cause me to miss what God really had purposed for my life. To make a long story short I decided to go with God and I do not regret that decision at all. Sure, it was a great sacrifice and extremely painful but God gave me the strength, He comforted me, He became the Father of my children, He supernaturally provided for me and showed me the way. At the appointed time the word that His prophets' spoke declaring "God had a husband for me" did come to pass. I am grateful to this day that I trusted and *waited on God. (In the Appendix our "Blended Family's Testimony" is more fully explained regarding how God did the miraculous in so many ways to guide, protect and change our course to bring us out of a bad situation and into His divine plan for our lives).*

REMARRIAGE AND WHAT THE BIBLE SAYS ABOUT IT:

Before we explore what the Bible has to say about remarriage, first, we will look at a few of the **negative connotations that follow the words, "divorce and remarriage"** in regard to what some religious organizations and people in general think about those who divorce and remarry. Secondly, with the help of the Holy Spirit, **clarity on this subject** whether it is a religious person in an organization, people in the Kingdom of God or people in the world seeking truth about this subject, they will find answers that will help them make a sound decision and bring comfort to their souls as well as see divorcees in a different way. Thirdly, Questions and Answers not addressed in the body of this chapter.

Those in the world may still feel condemnation and great pain and all the other feelings and emotions that come with divorce but not to the extent where it will be a torment like it would for a Christian who is about to take this step for the first, second or whatever time it is for them. Keeping in mind that we are not making light of the number of times a person has gone through the painful process of a divorce and remarriage. But realizing that they need answers that will break and stop the cycle such as weapons on how to fight in the spirit because they are in the midst of an agenda that is designed to destroy their life (Ephesians 6:12 and see Chapter 7 under Spiritual Weapons).

Some of the Negative Connotations that come with the words Divorce and Remarriage:

"*Religious* denominations (different sects of the church), seminaries, Christian universities and so forth in Christendom as well as Christian individuals strongly disagree over issues regarding divorce and remarriage. Many of them **persecute people who are divorced by limiting their involvement in ministry; leadership roles; they are asked to step down from certain offices and positions either for a season or permanently;** some universities won't even admit them; sometimes they are barred from teaching the Word of God on any level and even looked at by other members of a congregation as a backslider. In some families they are treated like an outcast and purposely left out of certain functions as if they had a disease," [8] (paraphrased).

Let's begin by *clarifying some attitudes that are not biblically justified*. A denomination, seminary, Christian university, Christian business or whatever its entity or whatever a person's position is within Christendom, **THEY ARE NOT GOD,** nor is what they say the **FINAL AUTHORITY** when it does not line up with the Word of God. They are people who are *called to represent* and *serve God* and His people with a heart of God that will demonstrate His love, compassion, mercy, forgiveness and leadership.

People have been hurt unjustifiably by **"religious"** spirits that operate through <u>some</u> people in <u>some</u> of the religious organizations (I am referring to those who are strictly legalistic, unyielding in following the letter of the Word without any balance or justification from the Holy Spirit). Remember, **Not *All* Christian denominations, universities, business people and so forth feel this way toward divorcees**.

If you are experiencing persecution it is strongly suggested that you ask for a meeting with the Pastor or President or someone in authority. *Ask them to verify their position or their policy with the Word of God along with guidance and direction from the Holy Spirit.* Then ask for an opportunity to give them the facts and if they are not willing to listen or are unreasonable once having heard your side of the story and they have no scriptural basis for their attitude or decision then you should ask God what it is that He would have you to do about the present situation. To stay and be a light or go and He will direct you to another place where there is liberty in Christ or whatever you need? **For those who do act ungodly by imposing unjust rules and regulations towards people who are divorced and remarried only demonstrates that they do not understand the Word of God regarding this matter.** Most of the time they are simply judging without facts and driving people further away from the house of God, our schools, Christian institutions, businesses and most of all out of the Kingdom of God even as others give up their precious gift of salvation from God because of their hurt. There are many churches and Christian organizations that have a personal relationship with God that are more understanding, knowledgeable and open to extend His grace to the divorcee. *God is faithful and I would not give up on God because of poor representation.* For every poor leader there is a great one somewhere. Seek God and He will direct your footsteps.

Still there are those that are very religious with rules and regulations without balance from the Spirit of God. Some of these churches and organizations <u>still</u> set their standard for leadership today based on Lev. 21:7 which states, *If they were a Priest in God's Temple they were not allowed to marry a divorced person because they were required to marry a virgin* because the Priest was set apart unto God (Lev. 21:13-14). **However, the New Testament says that a leader must be a husband to one wife and in Greek it says, "A one woman man, devoted to the woman he marries,"** I Tim. 3:2, 12 *and no other stipulation is made.* **Many religious churches and organizations call divorce a sin when the Bible does not support this.** We must all remember we are called to love people, God is the Judge. Therefore, it is **a dangerous thing for anyone to sit in judgment over someone else's marriage or divorce.** The true sin in the eyes of God are those sitting in judgment about a matter they don't have a right to judge. God has said, "Vengeance is Mine, I will repay..." (Romans 12:19). If someone or something is out of order the Holy Spirit knows how to convict them for their own good and send five fold ministers with a heart for God into their situation and across their path to bring correction if it is needed. We are called to love our neighbor as we love ourselves and to treat others with respect and dignity.

As stated earlier in this chapter, divorce was instituted in the Jewish Law in the Old Testament and is modified by the Messiah in the New Testament. *Later man-made doctrines added many restrictions to prevent people from marrying again* primarily because of a lack of understanding and misinterpretation in this area leaving others to believe that they would be in violation of the scriptures and out of the will of God if they were to remarry.

These are real scriptures that have been taken out of context and presented "alone" as a final word from the Lord (2 Timothy 3:16). They are cut and dry, black and white, they indicate that she or he can divorce their spouse but when they do and remarry they are not only going to be living in sin but the person they marry will be living in sin with them. No wonder institutions and people shun divorcees and look down on others for being in second or third marriages as if these people had committed the unpardonable sin which they have not (Matthew 12:31-32).

As a result this has caused thousands upon thousands to live alone as singles or with a roommate and if they are a single parent they are left alone to raise their children. Furthermore, because of their decision not to remarry (much of it based in fear) many people are living with the guilt and torment of a divorce and some with the disgrace of living in sin because they are living with someone without the benefit of marriage which brings more havoc and chaos into their homes and unfortunately in front of their children.

This lifestyle also gives their children the message that it is alright to live together without marriage or it is alright to have different people sleeping in your bed from time to time of which you may never see again. This message is reinforced with the help of the media, internet and whatever the latest technology is. Our young people and all ages for that matter are exposed to these *messages on a daily basis giving the impression that everyone is doing it so it must be alright.*

Many *religious* "churches" are thought by many to be a place people could receive refugee, understanding and guidance for such a painful and major turning point in their lives but instead were judged, condemned, and many were told just to forgive (with or without instructions on how to do so) stay and make the best of it while you pray because divorce will be worse, costly and will cause you to be in sin and on and on. **I firmly believe that all attempts should be made to reconcile first and that divorce should be** *the very last resort. However, if the situation is impossible and many are, people need to know that God has permitted divorce, God will still love them, He will forgive them, bless them and help them make the necessary changes while healing their hearts and changing their circumstances. He will give them a fresh start in their new beginning.*

Joshua 1:8-9 says,

> ...Have not I commanded you? Be strong, vigorous, and very courageous. Be not afraid, neither be dismayed, for the Lord your God is with you wherever you go.

Isaiah 41:10 says,

> Fear not [there is nothing to fear], for I am with you; do not look around you in terror and be dismayed, for I am your God. I will strengthen and harden you to difficulties, yes I will help you; yes, I will hold you up and retain you with My [victorious] right hand of rightness and justice.

CLARIFYING REMARRIAGE AND WHETHER OR *NOT* DIVORCE IS A SIN:

Remarriage *is* an option *after* divorce because there is *life after divorce*. God Himself gave us the example when He married Israel (Isaiah 54:5-6) and later divorced her as recorded in Jeremiah 3:8 and remarried her, Jeremiah 31:31-33 and Hebrews 8:8-10.

Jeremiah 3:8:

> And I saw, even though [Judah knew] that for this very cause of committing adultery (idolatry) I [the Lord] had put faithless Israel away and given her **a bill of divorce**... (see Isaiah 54:7-10).

This shows us that **divorce in and of itself is *not* a sin because God cannot and does not sin.** God told Moses to tell the men they could give their wives a Bill of Divorcement and God would never tell His people to do anything that would bring them *into sin* and out of His will for their lives (Deut. 24:1 and Matthew 5:31). "Furthermore, divorce never appears on any list of sin in the Bible." [8]

Divorce is recognized by God and the laws of the land, therefore, the marriage covenant no longer existed for the divorced couple. Which means that the **formerly married couple have dismissed (divorced) each other** and they are not to continue to have sexual relations with one another and if they do they will be committing sexual immorality which is a form of fornication.

Divorce is neither righteous nor unrighteous but is a document or tool that is used to dissolve and finalize a legal contract or an agreement regarding a marriage. Marriage causes a covenant between two people to exist and it brings about a legal right for a couple to live together as man and wife. *Marriage is a righteous institution, yet if the marriage bed is defiled by one or both partners does that change the status or definition of what marriage is or does (Hebrews 13:4)?* Of course not, however, <u>the status of that particular marriage in question has changed from a place of honor to dishonor</u>. Nevertheless, if they are Born-again and ask for forgiveness and truly repent for defiling the marriage bed (someone committed adultery) then it returns to its place of honor because they are forgiven (Eph. 1:7). God no longer sees the defiled bed because of what Jesus did at the cross.

Another example to make this point is that some people may say that money is evil; well we know that is not true, *for the love of money is what is evil* because it makes money a god and places it before the Most High God. *Money in and of its self is neither good nor evil* but whosoever hands it is in determines if it will be used for good or for evil.

Sin not repented of in one or both partners will more than likely result in a divorce. **Divorce is not an institution, as stated it is a document that dissolves a marriage, it is not sinful but someone's sin caused it and they need to deal with their sin.** *Once they have dealt with it* the way the Bible says to deal with sin, *it is forgiven* and under the Blood of Jesus. This *leaves no room for them to be judged by a past sin when they are a Child of God.*

If someone went through a divorce and it was not sin on his or her part that caused the divorce because that person remained righteous (in right standing with God throughout the entire process and because a person is in Christ he or she is the righteousness of God) **then he or she is being judged and persecuted by people and not by God.** *The people who are judging, are actually the ones in sin* according to Matthew 7:1-2 which says, "Do not judge and criticize and condemn others, so that you may not be judged and criticized and condemned yourselves. For just as you judge and criticize and condemn others, you will be judged and criticized and condemned, and in accordance with the measure you [use to] deal out to others, it will be dealt out again to you."

In the matter of **God and Israel's divorce that was <u>not</u> the end of the story**, God said He would make and ratify a *new* **covenant** with the house of Israel and the house of Judah…and He will be their God and they shall be His people (Hebrews 8:8-10). **God in essence <u>remarried</u>** (gave them a new covenant, a new agreement) and extended His covenant with the house of Israel through *Abraham's descendants* making the *second time* even better with a better covenant that is still in existence today.

Jeremiah 31:31-33 says,

> Behold, the days are coming, says the Lord, when I will make **a *new covenant*** with the house of Israel and with the house of Judah (Luke 22:20; I Corinthians 11:25). Not according to the covenant which I made with their fathers in the day when I took them by the hand to bring them out of the land of Egypt, My covenant which they broke, although I was their Husband, says the Lord. But this is the covenant which I will make with the house of Israel: After those days, says the Lord, I will put My law within them, and on their hearts will I write it; and *I will be their God*, and they will be My people.

Remarriage can last **like any other marriage,** it all depends upon the couple and how they approach daily life issues together and the *decisions* instituted during their marriage and of course the *miracles* that God will send for any marriage because of His love for people and faithfulness to His Word. No marriage whether it is your first, second, third, etc. will work successfully without

God and the use of basic biblical principles. (See Chapter 6, God's Order of Authority and the family's given roles for insight on how to function within the marriage and family).

As Paul said in I Corinthians 7:28 **"But if you do marry, you do not sin [in doing so]…" Paul was addressing remarriage.** He would not have needed to make this statement if this were a first time marriage. God led Paul to address this issue because **God understands there is an enemy of marriage** and that enemy is a demonic spiritual force and it will take another Spirit, a Spirit that is Greater to intervene and strengthen the couple as they resist the attacks against their new marriage. This is why a threefold cord relationship (God, the husband and the wife) is so important for the well-being of any marriage.

When God told Israel "I will be your God," He was making a declaration that He would be all things to them and whatever they needed He could supply it; in other words, He declared that *He would work miracles (do the supernatural) in their lives.* Well, if you are a Christian then you share the same covenant because you are a descendant of Abraham also and when God declared He would work miracles for them that was also extended to you because you were ingrafted into the family of God.

Of course **there are other reasons for not wanting to remarry but I am dealing primarily with the one that** *states* **it is a sin to remarry**, meaning if you have gone through a divorce and it was not for the "right reason," a reason that is biblically allowed.

From the beginning God intended for marriage to be a permanent union. But because of polygamy God told His servant Moses to permit divorce. Even though God hated divorce He still *permitted it for their safety*, since they were determined to have other women even though this was not His perfect will He permitted them to divorce their wives so that they could be free to remarry and their former wives could be free to remarry as well (see Deut. 24:1 below) and *neither of them would be living in sin because they would be with one spouse and not committing adultery before God for He is a Holy God.*

WHAT IS THE BIBLICAL DEFINITION FOR DIVORCE?

The following scriptures are often quoted to explain divorce and remarriage or why remarriage should not take place; and very often some of the wording in the scriptures are misinterpreted or taken out of context which causes misunderstandings and confusion as well as judging divorced people and remarried couples:

Deuteronomy 24:1-4 KJV says,

> When a man hath taken a wife, and married her, and it come to pass that she find no favour in his eyes, because he hath **found some uncleanness in her**: then let him *write her a bill of divorcement*, and give it in her hand, and send her out of his house. **(v.2)** And when she is departed out of his house, she <u>may</u> go and be another man's wife. **(v.3)** And if the latter husband hate her, and write her a bill of divorcement, and giveth it in her hand, and sendeth her out of his house; or if the latter husband die, which took her to be his wife; **(v.4) Her former husband, which sent her away, may not take her again to be his wife**, after that she is defiled; for that is **abomination before the Lord**: and thou shalt not cause the land to sin, which the Lord thy God giveth thee for an inheritance.

Deuteronomy 24:1 AMP says,

> When a man takes a wife and marries her, if then she finds no favor in his eyes because he has **found some indecency in her**, and he writes her a bill of divorce, put it in her hand, and sends her out of his house.

Matthew 19:9 KJV says,

And I say unto you, Whosoever shall put away his wife, **except** *it* be for **fornication**, and shall **marry another**, committeth adultery: and whoso **marrieth her** which is put away doth **commit adultery.**

Matthew 5:32 KJV says,

But I say unto you, That whosoever shall put away his wife, saving for the cause of **fornication**, causeth her to commit adultery: and whosoever shall marry her that is divorced **committeth adultery.**

Matthew 5:32 AMP says,

But I tell you, whoever dismisses and repudiates and divorces his wife, except on the grounds of **unfaithfulness (sexual immorality), causes her to commit adultery**, and whoever marries a woman who has been divorced commits adultery. [Deut. 24:1-4.]

Note: Deut. 24:1-4 in the Amplified Bible (seen above) was listed as a reference for scripture in Mt. 5:32 and in it the author translated from Deut. 24:1"found some indecency in her" to Mt. 5:32 her having "unfaithfulness (sexual immorality), which causes her to commit adultery." **Why was it translated with such a strong difference from indecency to adultery?** See explanation further on.

Mark 10:11 AMP says,

And He said to them, Whoever dismisses (repudiates and divorces) his wife and marries another **commits adultery** against her;

Mark 10:12 AMP says,

> And if a woman dismisses (repudiates and divorces) her husband and marries another, she **commits adultery.**

Luke 16:18 AMP says,

> Whoever divorces (dismisses and repudiates) his wife and marries another commits adultery, and he who marries a woman who is divorced from her husband commits adultery.

Matthew 5:27-28 AMP says,

> You have heard that it was said, You shall not commit adultery. But I say to you that everyone who so much as **looks at a woman with evil desire for her has already committed adultery with her in his heart.**

I Corinthians 7:39 AMP says,

> A wife is **bound to her husband by law as long as he lives. If the husband dies, she is free to be married** to whom she will, only [provided that he too is] in the Lord. (Explained further on in this section); Also see Ro. 7:2.

Romans 7:3 AMP says,

> Accordingly, she will be held an **adulteress if she unites herself to another man while her husband lives.** But if her husband dies, the marriage law no longer is binding on her [she is free from that law]; and if she unites herself to another man, she is not an adulteress.

Examining and Exposing the Above Scriptures that have for Centuries caused Mass Confusion in Christendom as well as in the World:
I would like to first point out that according to Deuteronomy 24:1 *KJV* it says regarding the wife that there was **"found some uncleanness in her"** in Deut. 24:1 the *Amplified version* says that there was **"found some indecency in her"** followed by the New Testament in Matthew 19:9 KJV and Matthew 5:32 KJV using the word for her dismissal or divorce **"fornication"** to Matthew 5:32 Amplified version using the words **"unfaithfulness (sexual immorality) which caused her to commit adultery."**

In addition, the scripture Matthew 5:32 Amplified version makes reference to Deuteronomy 24:1-4. The author translated **"found some indecency in her"** to mean a wife was unfaithful and indulged in sexual immorality. But since the author is using Deuteronomy 24:1-4 as her reference point it is safe to say that she probably interpreted it this way because the KJV calls it **"fornication"** and *the belief is that all fornication is sexual immorality.*

The Old Testament usage of the words **"uncleanness and some indecency"** are *more accurate to use* because they do not indicate that the wife was given a divorce because of sexual immorality for the mere fact **that in that time or era she would have been stoned to death not punished with merely a bill of divorcement.** Therefore, her husband was given the right to dismiss her and give her a bill of divorce for *some indecency, something other than sexual fornication or adultery.*

And since both parties can give a bill of divorce beginning in the New Testament (Mark 10:11-12) the wife has the right to put away her husband but according to these scriptures **they are both charged with committing adultery** if they dismiss their spouse.

My Question is: If both the man and the woman were given permission to remarry in Deuteronomy 24:1 after their divorce, how is it that neither can remarry according to Mark 10:11-12 without committing adultery? And in Mark 10:11-12 it does not specify the reason for the divorce yet it makes it clear that if either remarries they have both committed adultery, How and Why?

To begin to answer this question lets look at Matthew 19:9 KJV which says, "**whosoever shall put away his wife, except it be for fornication, and shall marry another, committeth adultery and whoso marrieth her which is put away doth commit adultery.**" Realize that Mark 10:11-12 is basically stating the same message that is in Matthew 19:9. These scriptures as explained earlier were given by Jesus as a warning about divorcing innocent people. *Jesus "warned husbands not to ruin a wife's reputation by divorcing her. He charged husbands with adultery when they divorced an innocent wife and remarried."* [3]

According to Matthew 19:9 and Mark 10:11-12 once someone innocent is divorced the innocent person is also charged with committing adultery as well if they remarry, therefore, is the Lord saying that the innocent person cannot ever remarry? Of course not. What the Bible says as stated earlier in this chapter under 'The Reasons Divorces are Allowed or Occur' is that God grants divorce because of a hardness of hearts, abandonment and so forth. When a spouse divorces an innocent person this would fall under a hardness of heart and therefore the innocent person is free to repent for their part in the divorce and go on with their life and remarry if they so choose to do so. *They need to realize that their former spouse made a choice and it affected their life but because of the Grace of God they have every right to have peace and joy in their life, to have all their needs met, to enjoy being in the presence of God and to fulfill their purpose in this life; in other words they have a right to go on with their life and live it to the fullest!*

Regarding Luke 16:18 says, "Whoever divorces (dismisses and repudiates) his wife and marries another commits adultery, and he who marries a woman who is divorced from her husband commits adultery." This scripture has a combination of a two part answer. The answer to the first part of this is the same one given for Matthew 19:9 where Jesus gives the warning for divorcing an innocent woman. The second part of this scripture was answered in the beginning of this chapter regarding Deut.

24:2. I have listed it below to answer part two of the Luke 16:18 scripture because it bears repeating to give clarity as to what is being said.

Because of the regulation which was **a law instituted by men** *to safe guard against thoughtless and hasty divorces on the part of the husband* and to make sure that her *first husband* gave serious consideration for his decision to divorce her because he would never be able to remarry her once he dismissed her *and she married another man* even if that man dismissed her or died. If she, as a divorced woman did remarry her first husband she was labeled an adulteress because this was regarded as a pollution, or on the same level with fornication, therefore, THIS remarriage by a divorced woman was the marriage that would make her an adulteress and cause her husband to commit adultery with her in the Old Testament. In the New Testament **we** have explained above scriptures Mark 10:12 and Luke 16:18 that talk about how a woman commits adultery.

Deuteronomy 24:2 KJV explains that when she was dismissed by her first husband and if she remarried she was not labeled an "adulteress:"

> And when she is departed out of his house,
> **she may go and be another man's wife**.

She was not labeled an **"adulteress"** when she was dismissed (divorced) and she remarried, **no, that label was given to** *her if she remarried her first husband* after she had remarried **and was divorced by someone else or became a widow**. As I said earlier in this chapter, this was done to make her first husband think twice before he divorced her and took another woman because of the lust in his eyes or for whatever reason that he gave her a bill of divorce. Also**, if she had never remarried** after she was divorced from her first husband then if he wanted to remarry her and she agreed that would have been acceptable and perfectly *legal*.

Looking at **Matthew 5:27-28** in the Amplified Bible, Jesus has declared that if a *man "so much as looks at a woman* with evil desire for her, he has already *committed adultery* with her in his heart" (Even though "actual adultery is a physical act; but sin begins as a thought, desire, or plan in one's heart or mind" ³ Matthew 5:27-30). The Bible also says in Proverbs 6:32 "But whoever commits adultery with a woman lacks heart and understanding (moral principle and prudence); he who does it is destroying his own life."

Before we continue to the last scripture, let's look at **another illustrated scripture that has also caused a great deal of confusion and heartache because it has been taken out of context.**

I Corinthians 7:39 says,

> A wife is bound to her husband by law as long as he lives. If the husband dies, she is free to be married to whom she will, only [provided that he too is] in the Lord.

First of all this verse is <u>not</u> speaking about a *"divorced woman"* but a married woman. Paul says in v. 40, "But in my opinion **[a widow]** is happier (more blessed and to be envied) if she does not remarry…" Where it is stated "<u>a wife is</u> <u>bound to her husband by law as long as he lives</u>" this is referring to a **"married woman,"** she and her husband are bound together by a marriage covenant (contract) for the rest of their lives because from the beginning marriage was intended to be permanent; and *as long as he lives* he will be married to her unless he divorces her or he dies or she divorces him.

And where it says, *"only in the Lord"* is telling her not to be unequally yoked if she remarries. One additional point regarding this is found in Deuteronomy 24:1-4 where God told Moses to permit the husband to give his wife a bill of divorcement, <u>she was "free" to go and marry another man while the husband who divorced her was "still alive."</u> How do we know this? In v. 4 it says that the first husband was not allowed to ever marry her again even if she were free to remarry so the implication is that he is still alive and forbidden or prohibited from remarrying his first wife if she is <u>again</u> a divorcee (if she remarried after their divorce).

Further notice what is said in this same chapter but in a different verse:

I Corinthians 7:27-28 says,

> *Are you <u>bound</u> to a wife?* Do not seek to be free. Are you free from a wife? Do not seek a wife. But **if you do marry, you do not sin [in doing so]**...Yet those who marry will have physical and earthly troubles, and I would like to spare you that.

Verse 27 says, <u>"Are you bound to a wife?"</u> (This verse is referring to a **married man**) ... "Do not seek to be free" (divorced). "Are you free from a wife?" (Are you divorced?) "Do not seek a wife" (Advising him not to *remarry*). <u>"But if you do marry, you do not sin [in doing so]"</u>... (**If you <u>remarry</u> you are not in sin**). *Paul would not have had to tell a single person who has never been married that if they marry they are not in sin. He was speaking to a divorced man and letting him know that if he remarried he was not in sin.* (In the beginning of this Chapter there is a list of terms that indicate divorce and "let go free" is one of them).

Why is Paul making it a point for everyone to stay as they are in Chapter seven? Because in I Corinthians 7:31 *Paul believed that the present world order was passing away* and a person was better off to stay in whatever state they were in (vv. 24, 26 and 29). He thought it best if a man was single and a woman was single and a woman was a virgin, and someone was a slave and so forth that everyone should remain the way they were to worship and be devoted to God in this changing and distressful time (vv.32, 34, 26, and 21). But Paul admits that <u>he had no command of the Lord</u> but this was <u>his opinion</u> <u>and advice</u> (v. 25) and if the people wanted to marry and divorce that was up to them.

As far as **a man committing adultery** we have mentioned it above, see Matthew 5:27-28 and Mark 10:11. But for more examples let's look at the marriage violations primarily regarding the male in Deuteronomy 22:13-29. In vv.13-21 this passage of scriptures explains about a man slandering his virgin wife by giving her a bad name in order to dismiss her so he could be free to remarry and the men who were found to be guilty were punished by paying a fine to his wife's father and he could not ever divorce her. In addition, vv. 22-27, explains that it was wrong for men to sleep with another man's wife even if she was only betrothed at the time. *In this case he was found to have committed a sexual sin and was stoned to death.* If the woman was not innocent because she did not scream for help then she was stoned to death with him. And vv.28-29 explains that it was wrong for a man to rape a virgin who was not engaged to be married or in the betrothal stage and he was punished at that time by paying a fine to the girl's father and he had to marry her because he had violated her and he could never divorce her as long as he lived.

In today's society these are still considered offenses/ crimes and are still considered wrong because they violate moral laws that were set in place by God which have not changed. The only difference is how these men and women are punished for these crimes – for rape it is prison and for adultery it may be divorce or forgiveness instead of being stoned to death.

Bottom Line as mentioned earlier – **Adultery occurs when** either the husband or the wife becomes sexually involved with a person outside of their marriage. Adultery is what causes the marriage bed to become defiled:

> **Hebrews 13:4 says,**
>
> **Let marriage be held in honor (esteemed worthy, precious, of great price, and especially dear) in all things. And thus let the marriage bed be undefiled (kept undishonored); for God will judge and punish the unchaste [all guilty of sexual vice] and adulterous.**

How to avoid fornication is another challenge for people especially in today's society where people are taught almost everywhere that fornication is alright and it is a natural part of life. But what does the Word of God have to say about it? The Word clearly tells one how *to avoid it* as it is recorded in I Corinthians 7:2 KJV where it says, "Nevertheless, to avoid fornication, let every man have his own wife, and let every woman have her own husband."

Furthermore, **we need to define what the Biblical definition of "fornication"** is in order to make sure that the woman or man who is divorced and remarried knows that they are not committing adultery in their next marriage because their former marriage did not end because of sexual immorality.

God said **"Except it be for fornication"**… well fornication includes more than sexual immorality which would bring us to a place that would involve more than sexual sin. To cover this information and definition in great detail *please see my next section on "Defining Fornication Beyond Sexual Immorality."* Hopefully, you will see and receive the revelation that was shown to me which brought clarity to this entire matter and share with others who suffer with torment and are living in fear that they are in violation of God's will by living in sin and thus living under condemnation which is not of God. We cannot be a strong army for the Lord if we are going to continue to attack each other, be unforgiving towards each other and cause people to live in bondage when Christ Jesus has already set us free.

My overall point is this, God did not intend for people to remain single after a divorce except by choice because He gave them the liberty through Christ to remarry. Judging strictly by the letter of the Word especially with this subject is unwise being that it is not really clear. Because it is not clear it leaves room for the Holy Spirit to bring clarity, balance and the restoration necessary for each individual divorce and remarriage.

> **Our Lord admitted its imperfection** and threw upon the defective moral condition of the people the blame of a legislation so unsatisfactory in itself and so evidently liable to abuse. [1] (See the definition of Divorce in the New Ungers Bible Dictionary in the Old Testament at the beginning of this Chapter).

In addition to the above revelation, God has given us His grace and He has given us a new covenant which allows us to **function by the leading of the Holy Spirit in conjunction with His Word, therefore, we are not to live solely by the written Word which will only lead to destruction.**

Our last illustrated scripture explains that "...**we serve not under [obedience to] the old code of written regulations, but (under obedience to the Promptings] of the Spirit in newness [of life].**"

Romans 7:1-6 says,

> **1.** Do you not know, brethren –for I am speaking to men who are acquainted with the Law – that legal claims have power over a person only for as long as he is alive?
>
> **2.** For [instance] a married woman is bound by law to her husband as long as he lives; but if her husband dies, she is loosed and discharged from the law concerning her husband.
>
> **3.** Accordingly, she will be held an adulteress if she **unites** herself to another man while her husband lives. But if her husband dies, the marriage law no longer is binding on her [she is free from that law]; and if she **unites** herself to another man, she is not an adulteress. *
>
> **4. Likewise, my brethren, you have undergone death as to the Law through the [crucified] body of Christ, so that now you may belong to Another, to Him Who was raised from the dead in order that we may bear fruit for God.**

5. When we were living in the flesh (mere physical lives), the sinful passions that were awakened and aroused up by [what] the Law [makes sin] were constantly operating in our natural powers (in our bodily organs, in the sensitive appetites and wills of the flesh), so that we bore fruit for death.

6. But now we are *discharged from the Law* **and have terminated all intercourse with it, having died to what once restrained and held us captive.** *So now we serve not under [obedience to] the old code of written regulations, but (under obedience to the Promptings] of the Spirit in newness [of life].*

Romans 7:6 Message Bible interprets it like this,

But now that we're no longer shackled to that domineering mate of sin, and out from under all those oppressive regulations and fine print, we're free to live a new life in the freedom of God.

Romans 7:4-6 NIV expresses it this way: [3]

Human life may be dominated by either legalism or *God's Spirit.* *Legalism leads us to test the law and follow the impulses of our flesh.* The flesh represents our basic human nature dominated by worldly desires rather than spiritual goals. When we follow the flesh, we deserve and receive death. *Christ frees us from the domination of sinful nature and lets us follow the guidance of God's Spirit* away from death to eternal life. Obeying God is not a dreaded, impossible duty but a natural result of the Spirit in us... **Christians are**

WHAT IS THE BIBLICAL DEFINITION FOR DIVORCE?

set free from (attempting to be justified by) the law, just so we will be free to serve Christ by serving other people... The Spirit is not a passive observer of the lives of Christians, He is actively at work in all believers to transform us into the kind of person God wants us to be. **This means new service in a new freedom with a fuller understanding**, (John 15:15).

* In addressing **number 3 listed above in Romans 7:1-6, v.3** starts with "Accordingly, she will be held an adulteress if she unites herself to another man while her husband lives..." Explanation, if a married woman *is not divorced* and she unites herself with another man while her husband is still alive then she is an adulteress. The usage of the word "unites" used in the beginning of v. 3 demonstrates this fact. This **unites** according to the New Webster's Dictionary of the English Language means "to bring together in *common cause*; to cause to become attached; to become one **or** *as if one*." The **first unites** is speaking about a married woman attaching herself to someone other than her husband. The **second unites** in this passage is defined by the same dictionary as "*to bring together by a legal or moral bond*; to bring together so as to make one." This "unites" is making reference about a former wife who has a legal right to be united (remarried) with another man because her *former husband* is dead or if he is alive they are divorced.

Furthermore, Paul did not mention divorce her in v.3 because he was making a point about old relationships being removed by "death" to illustrate his point in v. 4 of the same passage which speaks about the body of Christ being dead to the old and receiving the new so they could belong to "Another," to Christ Jesus.

When we apply the Written Word and the Holy Spirit to our marriages there is always hope; when we do not have both in our marriages there may not always be a divorce but there certainly will not be true peace, harmony and agreement.

An **excellent illustration of a story that shows the Grace of God** as well as the usage of **the Word of God and the Holy Spirit working together** to bring clarity, balance and understanding *to a situation that in the natural "looked like sin"* but because of the intervention of the *Spirit of God along with the help of an angel truth* was revealed and all were found to be innocent and what was done was found to be *justified and righteous*.

Matthew 1:18-23 tells a story of God's grace in action:

> Now the birth of Jesus Christ took place under these circumstances: When His mother Mary had been promised in marriage to Joseph, *before they came together, she was found to be pregnant [through the power] of the Holy Spirit.* And her [promised] husband Joseph, *being a just and upright man* and not willing to expose her publicly and to shame and disgrace her, *decided to repudiate and dismiss (divorce) her quietly and secretly.* But as he was thinking this over, behold, *an angel of the Lord appeared to him in a dream, saying,* Joseph, descendant of David, do not be afraid to take Mary [as] your wife, for that which is conceived in her is of (from, out of) the Holy Spirit. *She will bear a Son, and you shall call His name Jesus* [the Greek form of the Hebrew Joshua, which means Savior], for *He will save His people from their sins* [that is, prevent them from failing and missing the true end and scope of life, which is God]. All this took place that it might be fulfilled which the Lord had spoken through the prophet, Behold, the virgin shall become pregnant and give birth to a Son...

This story also reveals how Joseph and Mary who were in the *first stage of a Jewish marriage* (the Betrothal Stage which was as binding as marriage even though the couple did not live together), and **how Joseph had** *planned to divorce Mary* **because of the** appearance **that she committed sexual sin (John 7:24)**. **God called Joseph a righteous man** when he wanted to divorce Mary rather than have her publicly exposed and experience capital punishment by stoning her to death. Because Jesus taught that the acceptable grounds for divorce was sexual immorality (Matthew 5:31-32), Joseph, had permission for a divorce and this is why Joseph was called righteous. But after his visitation from an angel he changed his mind about divorce and in vv. 24-25 it says "Then Joseph, being aroused from his sleep, did as the angel of the Lord had commanded him: **he took [her to his side as] his wife**. But he had no union with her as her husband until she had borne her firstborn Son: and he called His name Jesus."

We all need the written Word *and* **the Spirit of God to help us make the right decisions in order to live holy righteous lives**. People try to feel spiritual by obeying religious laws. But they hardly ever feel good about themselves because there will always be one more law to follow. This is why God does not define our righteousness by our works, but by our *faith* in Jesus knowing He took our sin and gave us His Righteousness. **For the law of the Spirit of life [which is] in Christ Jesus [the law of our new being] has freed me from the law of sin and of death, (Romans 8:2).**

Romans 7:7-8 clarifies whether the Law is sin or not?

> What then do we conclude? *Is the Law identical with sin? Certainly not!* Nevertheless, if it had not been for the law, I should not have recognized sin or have known its meaning. [For instance] I would not have known about covetousness [would have had no consciousness of sin or sense of guilt] if the Law had not [repeatedly] said, You shall not covet and have an evil desire [for one thing and another].

The following Scriptures further tell us biblically that one should balance the written Word of God with the Spirit of God to receive revelation that is full of life and not of death.

> 2 Corinthians 3:6 KJV says,
>
> Who also hath made us able ministers of the New Testament; Not of the letter, but of the Spirit: For the letter killeth, but the Spirit giveth life.
>
> Galatians 2:19 says,
>
> For I through the Law [under the operation of the curse of the Law] have [in Christ's death for me] myself died to the Law and all the Law's demands upon me, so that I may [henceforth] live to and for God.
>
> Galatians 2:20 KJV says,
>
> *I am crucified with Christ: nevertheless I live; yet not I, but Christ liveth in me; and the life which I now live in the flesh I live by the faith of the Son of God, who loved me, and gave Himself for me.*
>
> Acts 13:39 says,
>
> And that through Him everyone who believes [who acknowledges Jesus as his Savior and devotes himself to Him] is absolved (cleared and freed) from every charge from which he could not be justified and freed by the Law of Moses and given right standing with God.

Answers to Frequently Asked Questions not Addressed thus far:

- **Question**: If we divorced for the wrong reasons and are still both single and wish to try again can we remarry and still be in God's perfect will?
- **Answer**: Yes. I have heard many testimonies where people divorced and the Lord spoke to one or both of them and told them to remarry. There is nothing biblically wrong with this. If God has told some people to return to their former spouse, if it were a sin He would be in violation of His own Word. The Lord realizes that they were deceived and evidently He intended for them to be together. He is faithful to His Word. Follow the leading of the Holy Spirit along with scripture. (See also the book of Hosea in the Bible).
- **Question:** Is there a right time or a wrong time to remarry?
- **Answer:** Yes. See the following explanation:

The divorced or widowed person's desire to remarry or not to remarry may be for various reasons. *My response, however, is directed to those who desire to remarry.* Some just love marriage and they do not desire to live any other way. They love the companionship, having that special someone in their lives, being in a long term relationship and they enjoy the benefits of marriage. God placed that desire in their hearts because it is good and just that people marry. Yet still many remarry for other various reasons such as having a partner to share in parenting and household responsibilities, finances, fulfilling dreams, to avoid fornicating, for fear of being exposed to diseases from having multiple partners or they are tired of just living together with someone and want to bring real meaning to their relationship, (See Chapter 1, under 'Understanding Reasons for Marriage' for additional reasons).

No matter what the reason or motive is for remarriage the number one consideration is to be mindful with the mind of Christ about who you marry, why you are marrying them and that you marry the person because you are willing to commit to the relationship and loving them with an unconditional love.

Once the above is settled this brings us to the answer of the question: **Is there a right time or a wrong time to remarry?** Yes is the answer for both parts of this question. Below you will find listed a few items to consider in regards to this question.

IS THERE A RIGHT TIME TO REMARRY? Yes and preparation is a key word and your preparation should include the following:

- If you feel that your former marriage was either dissolved for the wrong reason(s) or you still have love or strong feelings for your former spouse and both of you are still <u>single</u> even though divorced, it is **never too late to attempt reconciliation**. Maybe something will come of it or maybe not but at least you know in your heart that you have done all that you could do. And now sufficient closure can be reached (if it was not done before the divorce); you have a peace of mind about it whereas you will not carry any regrets but can move forward with your life with a clear conscious.

- Pray and make sure that you are with the right person (ask God to confirm it for you). Make sure there is a peace in your heart about the marriage if there is any wavering or doubting it should be dealt with first. **Make sure you are equally yoked both choosing to worship the same God.** *It is not wise to marry when you know you are <u>not</u> both of the same biblical belief or faith..* Sharing the same beliefs and the way they will function in your lives is key. Such as, if one believes in the gifts of the spirit and healing and miracles and the other does not and could care less you will have a problem. If one believes you can enjoy a personal relationship with God and the other is just religious, again there will be a problem. *The problem may not manifest right away but these truths and beliefs are strong and come out in times of testing.* If you are at odds about them then you will not be able to come in agreement and fight life's problems together because you will be too busy fighting with each other about who is right and the way it should be resolved. *It is biblical to be equally yoked* with the person you marry otherwise it is unwise and lays the foundation for failure. See if one is willing to change so you will not be unequally yoked (2 Corinthians 6:14). Keep in mind this is a big step and some people are just a little cautious about the unknown and from the examples they have seen from other marriages. No two marriages are the same, what you do will determine your outcome not what someone else experienced.

- As much as possible humble yourself and **release the past**. This means to understand that many times we need God to help us do this. By doing so, in releasing the past, you can drop off excessive emotional baggage that some of you have been carrying since your divorce. One example: Make sure you have forgiven your former spouse because if you have not you run the risk of bringing a lot of baggage that may include unforgiveness, bitterness and resentment into your new marriage. This could cause problems with your present spouse. You could unknowingly be wearing them down from your complaining about your past or you could constantly be telling the same stories over and over (which could be wearing in itself). As you complain you will begin to project a side of yourself that your present spouse may not have seen. Eventually old emotions will surface and it could change the atmosphere in your home and cause damage in your present relationship. The best way to avoid this is to choose to forgive and let God do the rest in you to bring you to a place of total forgiveness and healing.

- Enroll in *pre-marital classes* and study the institution of marriage; read Christian books on the subject to get God's perspective; study out the words in the marriage vows to get a clear understanding of what vows you are making before God and repeating to one another. Most of all read the scriptures for yourself that pertain to marriage in the Bible and ask God to give you revelation and a deep understanding of the commitment you are about to make. These classes should bring to the forefront issues that should be dealt with before and after marriage. If your church does not have such classes look around for who has a good track record or contact the ministry of Family Life, www.familylife.com they hold conferences for thousands of couples called a *"Weekend to Remember" that travel to various cities each year.* ***They are anointed to minister to engaged couples and young marriages* as well as successfully minister to all stages of marriage**. They have a long and excellent track record.

- If you are believing God for a *future husband or wife* the best way to do it is to not be anxious for anything but put all of your energy and trust in God for that person to come into your life at the appointed time. In the meantime, concentrate on the Kingdom of God and your assignment from the Lord as well as your current responsibilities and helping others reach their goals. As you are mindful to complete what He is asking of you (which is probably preparing you for your mate as well) God will receive the seed you have planted and it shall harvest with a spouse straight from the throne. In other words if you take care of His business He will take care of yours (Philippians 4:6 and Matthew 6:27).
- Sometimes remarriage may seem easier for a person whose **spouse is deceased** once they are past mourning. They do not always carry the stigma or guilt of a divorce. However, if a partner has committed suicide many times the living spouse may not want to give the cause of death because narrow minded people may insinuate or hint that they possibly had something to do with it and that their marriage was a failure. Remarriage may be a little harder for them if they are being tormented or believing the lies. Again, this is all a matter of choice we can choose to believe the truth or choose to

believe the lie and allow it to affect our future. Christian Counseling is always an option to come to that healthy place and remarry if that is your desire. (*The American Association of Christian Counselors* is the largest of its kind in the USA and their record shows that they have qualified people and they care, www.aacc.net).

- **Knowing in your heart that the wait is over and it is time to remarry.** You will have a complete peace about it. I mention this because I have read where **some counselors or ministers have advised people to continue to wait for their former spouse to come back even if the former spouse has remarried.** Their reasoning is that God did not recognize their former spouse's new marriage because the past divorce from you was done for the wrong reasons. Therefore, your former spouse is not really married to their new spouse and you are not free to remarry anyone else either. This kind of advice is based out of ignorance of God's Word because: **(1)** They do not know if your former spouse has asked for forgiveness and repented for their part in the divorce from you. Because if they have and they are Born-again they are forgiven (I John 1:9). **(2)** When your former spouse remarried *after* **your divorce was final, God and the laws of the land recognized their new marriage** and in order for them to come back to you they would have to go through another divorce. In addition, the only way they would not have to go through a divorce would be if they remarried *before* your divorce was actually final. Then they would be free to leave without any attachments. However, many states have a form that will back date their new marriage with a date showing they remarried *after* the final date was issued for their former marriage thus making their new marriage legal. Therefore, if you continue to pursue this matter you are committing a sin because you are trying to take a married person from their spouse which is adultery. **(3) If you received this logical and legalistic instruction, to** wait for them to leave their new spouse and come back to you and if they never do you just remain alone, then you need to point out to *whoever* told you to do this, that in Deuteronomy 24:3-4 it states that when a man divorces his wife he cannot remarry her once she has been remarried and divorced again, because if they do marry it will cause the both of them to commit adultery. (This answer is for the legalistic people. Keep in mind this was under the old code of law and when Jesus modified and changed it we must balance the Word of God in the Bible with the leading of the Holy Spirit to get the whole truth of a matter that would apply to what each individual couple should and can do to remain in the will of God concerning this issue. Remember also, that women were not allowed to divorce their husbands until the New Covenant therefore in this case the man being dismissed or divorced and remarrying would have the same affect if you were to go strictly with the scriptures stated above, (Also see this Chapter under Examining and Exposing Scriptures).

IS THERE A WRONG TIME TO REMARRY? YES.

- Out of **fear of growing older and not being married**. This decision is rooted in fear and will produce the harvest of something you do not want. Panic and anxiety may be involved and cause you to make all types of wrong decisions.
- **Rushing to the altar because your biological clock for having a child is running out is a deception and a trick.** Again this is fear based and it could cause you to marry just any man for the sake of having a child today and a miserable life tomorrow. God knows your heart and if you allow Him to prepare you He will send the right person at the appointed time and give you the desires of your heart. Note: there are examples in the Bible and in today's news of women having healthy babies in midlife

if it comes to that. God can do anything, yield to His ways and watch Him move on your behalf. Also, I understand many women are choosing to have babies out of wedlock and raise them alone, this is done all the time, although it is not God's perfect will and may require more sacrifices than you thought you wanted to make. Keep in mind that God is not obligated to help with something He did not start.

- If you **have not made an attempt to resolve your bad habits or vices** especially those that aided in the break up of your last marriage you may need to consider waiting before you cause more heartache for yourself and someone else. Seek God and Christian counseling to begin the healing and deliverance process first. Otherwise it will rise up again in your new marriage and start the cycle again.
- As mentioned earlier if you know in your heart that **you did not do everything you could to reconcile** your former marriage and both of you are still single and still in love then take that step **to at least try and if all fails then move forward with a clear conscience and a peace of mind.**
- If you have **a strong desire to remain single** and have no great interest in remarriage, then don't. Do not allow anyone to pressure you into a marriage for any reason. Only remarry because you desire to. Apostle Paul exalted the single person, saying they would have more time for worship and were able to devote more time to God and His Kingdom than a married person with shared responsibilities (I Cor. 7:32-35 also see Mt. 19:12). When we take our minds off of ourselves and circumstances and seek God for His purpose and reach out unselfishly to others that can be so fulfilling and rewarding in itself. And later if your mind changes and you decide to remarry you would have taken care of God's house and His business and surely He will take care of yours.

Divorce in many ways is like a death. Someone you are connected to and seen as "one" in the spirit in the eyes of God; someone you have grown to love and shared your life with is suddenly gone. It can be as painful, hard to bear and grievous as if a sudden death has occurred. If the process was a long drawn out separation with a trial period and so forth, that could have the same heartache, depression and hurt as a loved one dying a slow death. And on top of this if there is a third party such as "another woman" or "another man" emotions get involved such as rejection, fear, jealousy and anger which could start to build inside of you.

- There is such a thing as an *unhealthy mourning process* where instead of moving through the grief to a place of wellness and restoration the person grieving gets "stuck" in one of the stages which could prevent or hinder their healing and future.
- In our culture people are taught not to grieve but instead display how strong and self-sufficient they are, that they are in control of their emotions at all times. Not understanding that it is alright to show emotions when a person needs to. God gave us emotions and we do not have to be ashamed to use them at the appropriate time. When people keep emotions bottled-up inside of them when they *need* to be released it can cause health issues later in life. Statistics show that more men die earlier because they have been taught not to show emotions, cry or show any sign of what society calls a weakness. God gave men tears like he gave them to everyone else and when there is a need to cry it takes a "real" man someone who is secure to express his emotions in front of others and do what needs to be done to relieve himself of grief, great pain or distress at any given moment. How much a person expresses their emotions is up to them, but everyone has a God-given right to do so. Jesus "borne our griefs (sicknesses, weaknesses, and distresses) and carried our sorrows and pains…" this indicates we are all capable of feeling these emotions but it also means we can give

them back to Jesus because He has already taken them to the cross and given us a peace and comfort that we can experience immediately when needed (Isaiah 53:4).

- If people do not grieve their loss <u>when they need to</u> in their own way and instead keep pretending that they are not hurting when they are and need to **release that grief of a failed marriage or the loss of their children to their spouse or the loss of their home or married friends because they are now single and don't quite fit in** then it will come out in other ways such as anger, fear, depression, bitterness, overeating, etc. *Our example is, Jesus, He cried and grieved with Martha and Mary when their brother died even though He knew He was going to raise Lazarus, their brother, from the dead (John 11:17-44).* He was sensitive to where others were and He felt their pain and had compassion and wept with them. He did not condemn them for crying, He cried with them because of their pain and He cried because they doubted Him and was angry with Him because He did not come *sooner* and help in their distress. He wanted them to know that they could trust Him and He gave them a miracle and brought their brother back to life. Another example is with the death of Moses, once he passed God gave the Israelites thirty days to grieve his death. Therefore, we can control the process of grieving. Death opens the door for grief and if we allow it to get out of balance or grieve for extended periods of time we will certainly open the door for additional problems that will have to be dealt with. **God wants us to trust Him** and know that **He can resurrect what seems to be dead** and bring it back to life, maybe not with the old but in a new way it shall live again: your marriage, family and circumstances with a life that has security, love and meaning. He may not be early and He promises not to be late but He will be right on time!

These simple instructions show people how to stay healthy, move forward and not get "stuck." The following are basic stages of grief which most people whether it is an adult or a child experience when they have suffered a loss, especially a major loss in their lives. Many times it is worse for a child because they have not fully learned the difference between what reality is and is not. Recognize that it is normal to have certain types of emotions after a trauma but keep moving through them and come to that place where you have accepted the loss and are ready to move forward and rebuild. **These are the stages of grief one usually experiences before true healing can occur: shock, denial, anger, bargaining (trying to intervene by bargaining with God), depression and acceptance.**

With the loss of a marriage many get stuck in anger, unforgiveness and bitterness and it hinders especially a Christian because it affects their walk (life) with God and limits what He can do in their lives to bring complete restoration.

Please realize that even when your heart is breaking you can still trust and rest in His unfailing love and watch Him turn a dying or dead situation that the enemy meant for evil to work for your good, as He said He would do (Genesis 50:20).

Psalms 143:8 says:

> Cause me to hear Your loving-kindness in the morning, for on You do I lean and in You do I trust. Cause me to know the way wherein I should walk, for I lift up my inner self to You.

I will cast this care upon you and I will not be anxious, fearful or worried about anything because you said when I cast my care on You, You will establish me (I Peter 5:7 and Philippians 4:6). You will give me a great peace, a peace that transcends all understanding shall be mine (John 14:27 and Philippians 4:7). **"Practice what you have learned and received and heard and seen in me, and model your way of living on it, and the God of peace will be with you" (Philippians 4:9).**

DEFINING FORNICATION *BEYOND* SEXUAL IMMORALITY:

In Matthew 19:9, it mentioned that **fornication** or unchaste was the other reason given that a man could put away his wife.

Matthew 19:9 KJV:

> And I say unto you, Whoever shall put away his wife, except it be **for fornication**, and shall marry committteth adultery: and whoso marrieth her which is put away doth commit adultery.

Matthew 19:9 says:

> I say to you: whoever dismisses (repudiates, divorces) his wife, except **for unchastity**, and marries commits adultery, and he who marries a divorced woman commits adultery.

People make decisions based on the information they have before them and if the information is wrong, incomplete, taken out of context or not clear they cannot make a fair assessment or decision. In order for people to be set free to remarry, to be treated with respect after a divorce or freed from a life of guilt and disgrace because of a divorce they need truth and clarification. Many of the younger people have been so conditioned by the media and so forth that they probably don't see nor feel the full impact of what some of the more mature in age or professionals or people in ministry have to deal with as a result of the stigma of divorce. The Bible says, wisdom is the principle thing; therefore, get wisdom: *and with all thy getting get understanding* to have the right mind set (Proverbs 4:7). The Word also says the *truth* will set you free as you receive it and act on it.

The Bible teaches us to flee (run away from or shun) fornication. Like Joseph ran from Potiphar's wife (Genesis 39:11-21) when she approached him to commit sexual fornication or in her case commit adultery because she was a married woman and still living with her husband who was very much alive (I Cor. 7:39). I Corinthians 6:18 KJV says to "Flee fornication..."

I Corinthians 6:18-20 NKJV teaches us the following about sexual fornication:

> **Flee sexual immorality. Every sin that a man does is outside the body, but he who commits sexual immorality sins against his own body.** Or do you not know that your body is the temple of the Holy Spirit *Who* is in you, whom you have from God, and you are not your own? For you were bought at a price (Jesus' blood paid the price); therefore glorify God in your body and in your spirit, which are God's.

The Bible tells us that *sexual immorality is wrong* because it will lead to so many problems in our lives. The Lord warns us for our good because He loves us. Unlike what many believe that He is just trying to stop our so-called "fun" which many already know that there is nothing funny about the consequences of sexual fornication or immorality.

I Thessalonians 4:1-8 NIV, tells us how to live in this area to please God,

> Finally, brothers, we instructed you **how to live in order to please God**, as in fact you are living. Now we ask you and urge you in the Lord Jesus to do this more and more. For you know what instructions we gave you by the authority of the Lord. **It is God's will** that you should be sanctified: **that you should avoid sexual immorality; that each of you should learn to control his own body** in a way that is holy and honorable, not in passionate lust like the heathen, who do not know God; *and in this matter no one should wrong his brother or take advantage of him.* The Lord will punish me for all such sins,

as we have already told you and warned you. **For God did not call us to be impure, but to live a holy life.** Therefore, he who rejects this instruction does not reject man but God, who gives you his Holy Spirit.

However, in this writing I will present my understanding as it was revealed to me by the Holy Spirit and discuss the fact, that **in regards to <u>fornication</u> being a <u>ground</u> <u>for divorce</u> by defining it and how <u>it *extends beyond*</u> illicit sexual intercourse (sexual immorality).**

Fornicating is more than indulging in an unlawful sexual relationship. If you are a Christian and in this type of situation of *illicit sexual intercourse this is one form of fornication* and you have placed yourself in a position that is operating outside of the will, blessing and sanction of Almighty God because you are having sexual intercourse with someone outside of marriage. It is out of order and knowingly or not you have opened a door for Satan to now have access into your life. You have caused the hand of God and His angels to stop protecting you because you are outside of the realm of safety and operating outside the scope of God's divine order. You have cut off your "blessing" line straight from the throne room because it is sin and it will lead to destruction, spiritual death and in some cases physical death. Also sin allows demons to attack, torment and speak into your life because you have opened this door.

God will not protect the areas of your life where there is sin because you have a free will to choose to have or not have sin in your life. However, **God still loves you and will give you a way of escape through forgiveness and repentance**. He may even simply, because He is sovereign, show His mercy and send His grace when this situation back-fires on you but again that is the *chance* that you take. His power works in conjunction with His Word and even though He may not judge you His Word will (John 5:22 and John 12:47-48). Why? Because He is a God that cannot lie and His Word will not return to Him void. The scriptures say we reap what we sow.

Note: singles who are involved in illicit sexual intercourse with other single people, the same results apply. However, if you are single and a Christian and believe that you have the person in your life that was sent by God, realize that you and the person have a great start and your relationship is a blessing from God, therefore, take precautions not to have intercourse with the person. Pray for strength and use wisdom in where you go on a date, stay around other people, etc. because if you open that door even though they may be the right person, more than likely the relationship will change for the worst because you have invited the adversary into something that is holy and was a gift from a Holy God to you.

Many people feel that since they have divorced and remarried but *sexual* fornication or adultery was **not** the reason for their prior divorce and they are a child of God and are now weighed down with condemnation because they feel they have sinned against God or *they may feel that since things in their lives are not going well that God must be angry with them and punishing them because they remarried, this simply is not true.*

People who are Born-again and *living under this kind of condemnation cannot successfully hear from God* even if He tried to tell them or show them that **His love for them is unconditional**. If there is something wrong that was done on their part, He would alert them to repent and receive forgiveness because of what Jesus did nearly two thousand years ago has already paid the price for and set them free. They must *also realize that what they are dealing with in life does not have to be related to the fact that they remarried* but that they are human and in this life there will be challenges and trials. We learn to deal with it by taking authority over it when we are a child of God or we learn to cope with it when we are not because of a lack of authority to do so. (See Chapter 7, Spiritual Weapon number 17).

Yet others need to be aware that many times your greatest trials or attacks come when you are doing something "right." People are not just attacked (persecuted) when they are doing something that they know or think is wrong.

There are many who are afraid to remarry because they divorced and fornication *was not the reason.* As mentioned earlier many of them have chosen to remain single or to be single parents and struggle through life raising their children basically alone with occasional help from family or friends. Possibly going from one relationship to another in hopes of finding genuine love but hopeless because they do not feel they are worthy or in a position where they can remarry or possibly that they can remarry and still serve God and attend their church.

As I stated earlier, fornication <u>*extends beyond sexual sin*</u>, therefore, if this is your concern as you read on and receive revelation be aware that your divorce is probably legitimate in the eyes of God.

When God Himself <u>*divorced*</u> Israel, He listed His reason as *adultery* but it was not limited to the reference of sex but of <u>spiritual adultery</u> that Israel committed <u>Idolatry</u> in the face of God.

Jeremiah 5:7 says:

> Why should I and how can I pass over this and forgive you for it? Your children have forsaken Me and sworn by those that are no gods. When I had fed them to the full and bound them to Me by oath, **they committed [spiritual] adultery**, assembling themselves in troops, at the houses of **[idol]** harlots.

It further says in Jeremiah 3:8,

> And I saw, even though [Judah knew] that for this very cause of committing **adultery (idolatry)** I [the Lord] had put faithless Israel away and given her a **bill of divorce...**

God divorced Israel because of adultery. In this case the type of adultery was idolatry which was not sexual but their worship to lesser gods *put something else* **before God.** Israel's priorities had changed and God was no longer first in their lives at this point. But as shown earlier God did make a New Covenant with Israel, **(remarried her)**, and said I will be their God and they will be My people, Jeremiah 31:31-33.

Just as many of your former marriages had changed and the priorities were out of order. **The worship of other things (which include inanimate objects), not placing or keeping God first in His institution of marriage and** *putting other things* **(idolatry) before your spouse and/or family brought the marriage out of balance and out of order so that the strain of it coupled with** *a hardened heart (not wanting to make the necessary changes to put things back in order) was the sin that led to the divorce.*

According to the New Webster's Dictionary of the English Language, International Edition, [5] "fornication is voluntary sexual intercourse between an unmarried man and unmarried woman." Intercourse between any two people that are not married is considered fornication, **although adultery can also fall under the heading of fornication**. If a married person is having sexual intercourse with an unmarried person it is still **adultery/fornication** because fornication includes illicit sexual intercourse and illicit means "not lawful."

Furthermore, in addition to fornication including adultery; according to the Vine's Complete Expository Dictionary, *fornication also includes idolatry*.

According to The New Ungers Bible Dictionary Idolatry was defined as follows:

> "Idolatry is the paying of divine honor to any created thing; the ascription of divine power to natural agencies. Idolatry may be classified as follows: (1) the worship of *inanimate objects*, such as stones, trees, rivers, etc.; (2) of animals; (3) of the higher powers of nature, such as the sun, moon, stars, and the forces of nature, as air, fire, etc.); (4) hero worship or of deceased ancestors; (5) idealism, or the

worship of abstractions or mental qualities, such as justice. Another classification is suggestive: (1) worship of Jehovah under image or symbol; (2) the worship of other gods under image or symbol; (3) the worship of the image or symbol itself. Each of these forms of idolatry had its peculiar immoral tendency." [1]

The worshipping of an idol or idols: an idol is the worship of a person or object with intense admiration or love. In short, if someone is paying attention to something that is causing other things in their life to be placed on hold or neglected because of their intense obsession with this *person or object* then they are involved in idolatry.

In the case of a marriage if an idol has caused a spouse (whether male or female) to harden their heart so as to continue with the idol (this kind of adultery is also a form of fornication) this idolatry could cause enough damage that could lead to a separation and possibly a divorce if no relief is found.

Acts 15:20 says,

> But we should send word to them in writing to abstain from and avoid anything that has been polluted by being offered to idols, and all sexual impurity, and [eating meat of animals] that have been strangled, and [tasting of] blood.

The idol could be someone lusting after anything (sex, food, things, people); it could be the use of illegal drugs (substance abuse) or excessive alcohol by a spouse who lives in denial and has no heart to change (hardened heart); it could the misuse of finances or putting money before all else, working extended hours to make money instead of trusting God and setting proper boundaries so there is time for your marriage and children; *whatever has brought about a drastic change for the worse, it needs to be corrected because it has become an idol.*

I Corinthians 10:32 supports the fact that sin includes other things beside sexual immorality. God said one needs to change their lifestyle if it is allowing sin to destroy their life which would include their marriage.

I Corinthians 10:32 says,

> Do not let yourselves be [hindrances by giving] an offense to the Jews or to the Greeks or to the church of God [do not lead others into sin by *your mode of life*].

All healing and change of heart can only be successful with the Holy Spirit. Pray for your spouse and your situation. God will give you an answer and a peace along with His answer. If that answer is to forgive, reconcile and trust God then do so; if that answer is to divorce and you have confirmation and a peace about your decision then God will instruct you and make provision for it. Remember never do something like this on your own (unless you are in a life threatening situation) wait for God's leading by the Holy Spirit and peace with your decision before taking any action.

God is the One who said to Moses write the bill of divorce because of the hardness of the heart. It was not a commandment because you can always choose to forgive but Moses permitted divorce *because God permitted it*. If someone refuses to stop fornicating (which we know includes idolatry) because of their hardened heart God will release you from this marriage and you do not have to live with guilt, shame or fear, He is with you.

The Word says in Romans 8:1,

> Therefore, [there is] now no condemnation (no adjudging guilty of wrong) for those who are in Christ Jesus, who live [and] walk not after the dictates of the flesh, but after the dictates of the Spirit. [John 3:18].

Remember earlier it was stated, we are not under the law but under grace and even though we receive and act on God's Word it *has* to be balanced with His Spirit or the letter (the written Word) alone will cause legalism and destruction.

IS CO-HABITING ANOTHER FORM OF FORNICATION?

When a couple decides to live together they feel they can still have all the benefits that come with marriage *without* being married. Listen, God is not obligated to protect nor help anything He did not start or ordain. Living together in His eyes is sin (harmful and destructive) it will leave Him out of your relationship because it is not of Him, He is holy. One of the reasons God asks couples not to live together without the benefit of marriage is because things will come up and things will happen, that is a part of life and unfortunately you have tied His hands, preventing His best from coming forth to your aid because you have shut Him out and opened a door and invited the adversary in. What He asks of one is what He asks of all He is no respecter of persons, and those who choose to do things His way will reap the benefit and rewards that will come with that decision. So to answer the question is co-habiting another form of fornication the answer is yes it is.

Some may argue that they have a nice home, money in the bank, and so forth as if that is proof that God is blessing the couple that lives together without marriage. The world (ungodly people) know how to make money and purchase things, that does not prove anything. The question is do you have peace, is there true trust in your relationship? Can you honestly say you can go to Father God and ask in the name of His Son Jesus and in the power of the Holy Spirit to come and give you all the promises of His Word with a clear conscious and expect them? Think about it.

You may think, well I know married couples who are struggling and not doing as well as the couple who are living together. Yes that may be true *but at least they have the option to call on His name and expect Him to come into their situation.* Because many Christians do not know how to walk in their authority and demand certain things to change in their lives or lifestyle does not mean they cannot get the revelation and do so. It is always up to an individual as to how far they choose to go with God and seek Him not just for things but seek Him to know Him and fellowship with Him, which will release everything else because that is what He promised (Heb. 4:16; James 4:8).

The Bible says as we seek first the Kingdom of God and His righteousness (His way of doing and being right) *then all these things will be added to us* (Matthew 6:33). These things include a great marriage and home; work, a career or business; finances; good relationships in our lives; a peace of mind; eternal life; the Holy Spirit with us to guide and lead us; the angels to protect us and so forth. You know God can and does protect us even when we do not know Him but as He reveals Himself to us and we reject Him then we limit what He can and will do in our lives.

The Following Three Remaining Sections in this Chapter will offer Clarification of Sin, Forgiveness and Repentance which will Aid in the Process of Recovering from a Divorce.

CLARIFYING SIN AND ITS CONTRIBUTION TO A DIVORCE:

Many denominations consider divorce in and of itself a sin yet the Bible does not support this. Different denominations have different doctrines of men that they interpret as truth usually based on one scripture that *may* have been taken out of context and then labeled "sin." Yet sin in regards to leading up to a divorce, as seen earlier, could be for various reasons but keep in mind that the bottom line is, in the eyes of God **"sin is sin"** and none is really greater than another although some would argue that sexual sin is worse because the Holy Spirit dwells in our bodies if we have invited Jesus into our hearts.

In this section we will (1) Define condemnation and its ramifications (2) As well as define and clarify sin and its purpose according to the Bible; (3) Explore how Father God feels about

sin which affects how we respond to it; and (4) If your sin contributed to your divorce what you can do about it.

Some of us really do not know **what sin is** especially if we think the only sin in the world is associated with breaking the moral commandments (adultery, murder, lying, stealing, and so forth), drinking heavily, fighting, offensive language, and sexual immorality. If we do not understand what sin or its purpose is according to God's Word, then more than likely we will not ask God to forgive us because we are not aware that we need forgiveness nor are we aware of the importance of forgiveness. **Many of us fail to realize we have sinned against God because we are not aware of what God said sin is and that *all* sin is against God.**

Furthermore, much of the sin that most people dwell in is sin that comes from within.

Mark 7:20-23 says,

> And He said, **What comes out of a man is what makes a man unclean and renders [him] unhallowed**. For from within, [that is] out of the hearts of men, come base and wicked thoughts, sexual immorality, stealing, murder, adultery, coveting (a greedy desire to have more wealth), dangerous and destructive wickedness, deceit; unrestrained (indecent) conduct; an evil eye (envy), slander (evil speaking, malicious misrepresentation, abusiveness), pride (the sin of an uplifted heart against God and man), foolishness (folly, lack of sense, recklessness, thoughtlessness). All these evil [purposes and desires] come from within, and they make the man unclean and render him unhallowed. (Also see Romans 7:18-25).

We were all born in sin because of corrupt blood and trespassing is what we do. *God sees the heart so whether it is a sin that is outwardly shown or a sin that dwells in our hearts God knows and*

He chose to forgive us for every sin through eternity because of The Finished Work on the Cross (Eph. 1:7). That is why it is important not to dwell in sin consciousness because our hearts can become hardened and that will make it more difficult to seek God and ask Him to forgive our sins. Therefore, we run the risk of being cut-off from our Heavenly Father Who in reality is our only hope of deliverance and restoration.

Isaiah 59: 1-2 says,

> Behold, the Lord's hand is not shortened at all, that it cannot save, nor His ear dull with deafness, that it cannot hear. *But your iniquities have made a separation between you and your God…*

Not realizing it, but because of the sin we are harboring many of us have opened a door for **condemnation** if we are <u>not</u> a Believer and **conviction** from the Holy Spirit if we are a Believer. There is a difference between condemnation and conviction. **Condemnation condemns <u>you</u> as a person while conviction from the Holy Spirit condemns <u>your behavior</u> and not you.** Condemnation leads to bondage whereas when the name of Jesus is confessed the results of conviction will bring freedom and release. Conviction makes the Child of God aware of something that has the potential to harm or that has pulled them out from under that place of protection with the Holy Spirit. Even though during this process they did not lose their salvation, their righteousness in God because they were Born-again, however, they still need to be in His will. When they were made aware through conviction that if they would ask for forgiveness for that particular sin, repent and receive God's forgiveness this would place them back under the hedge of protection and back in His will.

Conviction is also an opportunity to change whatever is coming against the will of God for your life so that you can continue in faith doing what is right. The end result of conviction is fulfillment and destiny. The end result of condemnation is being full of guilt and fear about losing something or something happening which leads to stress and stress can lead to health problems or other issues. By allowing the root cause of these problems which is condemnation to remain in your life you are working along side Satan to condemn you and at this point you are running the risk of also destroying your mental health.

Condemnation also has a *false guilt* that comes with it that is based on the lies that the enemy feeds to you, things that God never said about you yet many have chosen to believe the lie. As you believe the lie and keep making the same mistakes over and over without any relief it deepens the condemnation and the negative feelings just get stronger which of course leads many to take chemical substances or engage in immorality to escape their pain of which these choices only compound their problems. Whereas *true guilt* is guilt based on the sin and the sin has been forgiven and therefore removed the condemnation.

As a matter of fact, since Jesus became the second Adam and "has entered into heaven itself, now to appear in the [very] presence of God on our behalf," (Hebrews 9:24), Satan can no longer come before the throne of God to accuse anyone of anything. He now comes to us on earth and accuses us in our minds, for the battle rages in our thoughts; or he will have others slander or accuse us. He uses deception because he has no real power against us since "God disarmed the principalities and powers that were ranged against us and made a bold display and public example of them, in triumphing over them in Him and in it [the cross]," (Colossians 2:15). (Read more about Satan and his devices in Chapter 7, Section One).

Therefore, Satan tells us lies about our circumstances, sickness, poverty, guilt, poor relationships and so forth that it is punishment from God for our sins and past mistakes and that God must be angry with us. Whereas in reality we have access to the throne of grace to receive God's mercy but instead many Christians are allowing themselves to be mentally tormented by Satan (Hebrews 4:16) because they do not understand the authority that has been given to them. [6]

The final difference between the two **(condemnation and conviction)** *is simply this, the Believer knows that at the cross all their sins* *were put on Jesus' body and His body was condemned so the curse would not have to manifest in their life.* They know that when evil comes they can resist it because of what Jesus did, they don't have to carry the guilt and the shame as the world (the unsaved) does, they are free. The person who lives under condemnation does not know this so they try to carry the weight of their sin that will eventually destroy their life.

Romans 8:1-3 NAS tells us that **we are not to receive condemnation**:

> **There is therefore now no condemnation for those who are in Christ Jesus.** For the law of the Spirit of life in Christ Jesus has set you free from the law of sin and death. For what the Law could not do, weak as it was through the flesh, God *did*: sending His own Son in the likeness of sinful flesh and as an offering for sin, He condemned sin in the flesh.

When Christ condemned sin in the flesh the Amplified Bible says in v. 3 He "subdued, overcame, deprived it of its power over all who accept that sacrifice." *A person's conscience can be totally set free from sin when they understand that He was totally condemned for all the sin of the <u>world throughout eternity</u>.* **Being conscious of your sins is to have a guilty (evil) conscience (Hebrews 10:22). His work of purging our sins is completely finished and perfect, therefore, to dwell in sin consciousness or condemnation is a sin in itself (we are to cast those thoughts down and out according to 2 Cor. 10:5).** Instead thank Jesus for His finished work at the cross and know that you are covered and have been reconciled back to God and your sins forgiven. When Father God sees you all He sees is the blood that cleansed you, He sees you holy and perfect. So that leaves nothing for you to do about your sin except (1) ask for forgiveness and mean it; repent; and (2) receive the gift of no condemnation by the words Jesus spoke *"Neither do I condemn thee; go and sin no more"* (John 8:11 KJV).

He further said in I John 2:1-2:

> My Little Children, I write you these things so that you may not violate God's law and sin. **But if anyone should sin, we have an Advocate (One Who will intercede for us) with the Father – [it is] Jesus Christ [the all] righteous** [upright, just, Who conforms to the Father's will in every purpose, thought, and action]. And He [that same Jesus Himself] is the propitiation (the atoning sacrifice) for our sins, and not for ours alone but also for [the sins of] the whole world.

In addition to this the Word of God makes it very clear in Romans 5:19 where it says:

> For just as by <u>one man's disobedience</u> (failing to hear, heedlessness, and carelessness) the many were constituted sinners, so by <u>one Man's obedience</u> the many will be constituted righteous (made acceptable to God, brought into right standing with Him).

Here the Word is speaking about one man's disobedience, the first Adam, who caused a curse to come upon all of mankind but the second Adam, **Jesus Christ, caused the curse to be removed and all sin forever forgiven.** *"We know that we are human and we will sin and make mistakes again but hopefully through our love for God and what He did for us including giving us the power to stop sinning and realize He is not waiting to punish us for our mistakes and failures but that He is there to encourage and strengthen us to rise up in our authority and say, that is it! Enough is enough! God is calling for His people to be righteous and holy. Therefore, we receive the 'gift of no condemnation' that has given us the power to 'sin no more' because **we no longer desire to sin against the One who loves us so dearly, and we will not receive nor keep a guilty conscience but will*** *instead cast down any and all vain imaginations"* (Col. 3:12; 2 Cor. 5:21 and 2 Cor. 10:5) [6] Paraphrased.

A lack of knowledge and not fully understanding how sin affects our lives does not change the fact that even though **Father God does not judge us (John 5:22-23); His Word will judge us in the last day if we reject His Son and will not receive His Word and His teachings (John 12:47-48).** As we stated dwelling in sin separates you from God and His Word (Isaiah 59:1-2). Please take note, His Word is already activated and principles and laws are already in existence and when we violate a law or principle the Word automatically goes into affect. This is another reason to clear our conscience and to come back into right standing with God and to maintain that position as much as possible.

For example, gravity is a law; if we jump off of a building and with the law being in effect it will automatically respond to our action and we will proceed downwards. God is no respecter of persons and He is a God that cannot lie, therefore, He will not violate His own Word which includes His teachings, laws, principles and precepts. *One exception to this statement is that God will violate His natural laws to accomplish His spiritual purposes of performing the supernatural (miracles) such as when He walked on water (Matthew 14:25-27); multiplied resources supernaturally by the anointing (Matthew 14:15-22; Matthew 15:33-38); when the sun stood still for one day (Joshua 10:12-14) and how He replaced the sun with the radiance of His glory* (Revelation 21:23; Isa 24:23) and so forth. There are consequences for right and wrong choices and the consequences will either be good and work for us or unfavorable and work against us. In a court of law the ignorance of judicial laws are without excuse, well ignorance of the principles, laws, precepts and teachings located in the Word of God are without excuse as well and these are set up by a much higher authority.

In James 4:4 it says, "...Do you not know that being the world's friend is being God's enemy? So whoever chooses to be a friend of the world takes his stand as an enemy of God."

In other words, knowingly doing things that are not right or consistently being with people who are not righteous in Christ meaning they choose to remain strictly worldly with no desire to change whatsoever, causes you to place a principle of the Lord's on hold for personal reasons. Because some people are searching for fulfillment and are trying to fill that void with friends, fashion, fornication, false faith, drugs and so forth they end up ignoring the wisdom of God by rejecting the One who will fill their emptiness and set themselves up for what is an inevitably negative consequence.

Hosea 4:6-7 says,

> **My people are destroyed for lack of knowledge**; because you [the priestly nation] have rejected knowledge, I will also reject you that you shall be no priest to Me; seeing you have forgotten the law of your God, I will also forget your children. The more they increased and multiplied, the more they sinned against Me; I will change their glory into shame.

"There is a way which seems right to a man and appears straight before him, but at the end of it is the way of death. **Fools make a mock of sin and sin mocks the fools** [who are its victims; a sin offering made by them only mocks them, bringing them disappointment and disfavor]…" (Proverbs 14:12, 9); "…for the wages of sin is death…" Romans 6:23 KJV). However, when we consider the price that was paid for us to have a new covenant that would show us mercy and not operate under the old code to punish sins which were cut and dry, black and white, but at the same time, realizing that *even under grace sin is still sin but God's mercy and grace will be with you because it is part of His Finished Work.* This will cause the consequences that were meant for evil to turn in your favor and turn for your good. A man of God once said, *"Sin will take you farther than you want to go, keep you longer than you want to stay and cost you more than you want to pay."*

According to the New Ungers Bible Dictionary SIN is:

A falling away from or missing the right path. The underlying idea of sin is that of law and of a lawgiver. The lawgiver is God. Hence *sin is everything in the disposition and purpose and conduct of God's moral creatures that is contrary to the expressed will of God.* **The sinfulness of sin lies in the fact that it is against God,** even when the wrong we do is to others or ourselves. The being and law of God are perfectly harmonious, for "God is Love." The sum of all the commandments likewise is love; sin in its nature is egotism and selfishness. Self is put in the place of God (Ro. 15:3; I Co 13:5; and 2 Tim. 3:2, 4). Selfishness is at the bottom of all disobedience, and it becomes hostility to God when it collides with His law.

According to the Vine's Complete Expository Dictionary SIN is (paraphrased):

A missing of the mark. It is the most comprehensive term for moral obliquity (departure from sound moral principle or behavior). **Christ who had no sin was made to be sin** in order to deal with it as a sin and guilt offering. **Sin leads to death so He died and dealt with it and redeemed man from it.** (Ro 6:23 and 2 Cor. 5:21). We can sin against our own bodies by fornication and against others, but **ultimately all sin is against God.**

Sin comes about because of evil deeds; therefore, what is the origin of evil? "EVIL" defined according to the Disciples Study Bible NIV, Genesis 1:1-3 is as follows: [3]

God created a good world. God did not create any part of the world to be intrinsically evil but left evil as a possibility, since He wanted humans to be free to love and serve Him. Such freedom required the possibility of sin and its evil consequences. As Creator, God is responsible for the world in which evil occurs. He allows evil; but being good, He does not act in an evil way. *Evil is whatever or whoever disrupts the goodness of God's world.* The direct cause of evil and suffering may be human beings, or Satan, or demons. These are all created beings who can cause evil and suffering. *Evil and suffering were not part of the original creation but are a perversion of that created order.* Evil is not an eternal power or person equal to God.

Proverbs 6:16-19 lists Seven Sins God Hates:

These six things the Lord hates, indeed, seven are an abomination to Him:

- A proud look [the spirit that makes one overestimate himself and underestimate others];
- A lying tongue (person who constantly lies);
- Hands that shed innocent blood (murder);
- A heart that manufactures wicked thoughts and plans;
- Feet that are swift in running to evil;
- A false witness who breathes out lies [even under oath]; (false religions);
- He who sows discord (causes disagreement and a lack of harmony) among the saints.

The following are a **few devices or sins (tools and weapons of the adversary)** that are sent across our path that we are to resist and not receive. (A more extensive list is given in Chapter 7, Section One).

Unforgiveness, Bitterness, Fear, Doubt, Misery, Complaining, Strife, Gossip, Cheating, Not Praying, Rejection, Jealousy, Immorality, Not Walking in Love, Grumbling, Murmuring, Pride, Laziness or Procrastination, Offense, Depression, Not being Thankful, Selfishness, Rebellion, Witchcraft, Sin while Angry and Self-Pity.

As we expect the mercy of God, God tells us to not judge but extend mercy to others as well, one reason being all have sinned and the other being, "…judgment is without mercy to the one who has shown no mercy. Mercy triumphs over judgment." (James 2:8-13).

Another point the Bible makes about sin is: **whatever is not of faith is sin** and who is to pass judgment on whether you are in faith or not? *Only God has the privilege of passing judgment on issues based solely on what is in a person's heart* because only He can truly see and know their motives. Only He truly knows someone's weaknesses and strengths; and still there is another aspect of this as seen in Romans 14.

Romans 14:1-23 addresses the weak and strong, faith and sin and how our actions affect others. It is an example of what a person believes produces *faith* and the lack of faith (doubt) can produce *sin* and our response to it. It also demonstrates that "fellowship should be a fundamental concern to all Christians. We should live in the sensitive awareness of the weaknesses of others so we do not lead another into sin. Christians need to know that behavior can have destructive consequences on fellow Believers. Further, we should accept other Christians without passing judgment upon centralities of their faith. We can still love one another even while disagreeing so as not to give Satan a foothold through division"[3] Romans 14:1-13. Those who used their faith did so for the Kingdom of God (righteousness, peace and joy in the Holy Spirit). However, the *end result is whatever does not originate and proceed from faith is sin (Romans 14:23)*.

[After all] **the Kingdom of God** is not a matter of [getting the] food and drink [one likes], but instead it **is righteousness** (that state which makes a person acceptable to God) and [heart] **peace and joy in the Holy Spirit**. He who serves Christ in this way is acceptable and pleasing to God and is approved by men. So let us then definitely aim for and eagerly pursue what makes for harmony and for mutual upbuilding (edification and development) of one another...Your personal convictions [on such matters] exercise [them] as in God's presence, keeping them to yourself [striving only to know the truth and obey His will]. Blessed (happy, to be envied) is he who has no reason to judge himself for what he approves [who does not convict himself by what he chooses to do]. *But the man who has doubts (misgivings, an uneasy conscience) about things and then does them (perhaps because of you), stands condemned [before God], because he is not true to his convictions and he does not act from faith. <u>For whatever does not originate and proceed from faith is sin</u>* [whatever is done without a conviction of its approval by God is sinful]. vv.17-19; 22-23 paraphrased.

In reference to vv. 19-23, "Apostle Paul claimed his freedom in Christ (I Cor. 1:19 and I Cor. 10:25-33), he still highlighted the need to be sensitive to others' consciences. Our conscience may not be violated by a particular action, but such an action may be perceived as immoral by other individuals living out of another level of ethical maturity. For them moral confusion may set in. Does one live life, but continually bends to the dictates of others' consciences? **Yes,** when the motivation is to nurture others in the understanding of the Kingdom of God and to bring honor to God. **No,** when the bending limits or alters our own sense of maturity in God. A fragile balance results, and constant vigilance to such a tension is necessary. We must avoid an attitude of condemnation and a feeling of guilt. We must seek to mature and help others mature. Above all, we must seek to avoid quarrels and division (strife) in God's church." ³ Romans 14:19-23.

In Romans 4:5 it says Abraham's …"faith is credited to him as righteousness (the standing acceptable to God)." And in v.13 it says, "**For the promise or his posterity, that he should inherit the world, did not come through [observing the commands of] the Law but through the righteousness of faith.**" Righteousness comes from faith not our works and you will have to *use your faith to declare you are the righteousness of God in Christ* after you have sinned or missed the mark when condemnation tries to enter in; or your mind is attacked by Satan or if you are recovering from some type of failure that occurred in your life. In some cases you will have to declare to yourself, who you are in Christ to gain the strength that will be necessary to continue with Him (Also see 2 Corinthians 5:21). King David encouraged himself, sometimes that is all you have, is yourself to encourage you and the best way to do this is with the Word of God and what Christ has said about you.

"**God is a just God. He neither does evil, causes evil, nor tempts anyone to do evil. Righteousness is such a part of God that He will not tempt any person to do wrong.** His desire is to bring every person to do what is right. We must accept responsibility for our sin. God did not make us do it." ³ James 1:13-14. One of the things the Lord desires is to make all of us become like Jesus, "Those whom He foreknew…He also destined from the beginning [foreordaining them] to be molded into the image of His Son," Romans 8:29. *Because of our free will, He will never force anyone to love, obey or serve Him.*

"God is not the author of sin. A person must accept responsibility for personal sinful acts. Someone cannot evade responsibility for sinful acts by saying, 'God made me that way. I cannot help myself.' Similarly, no one can blame a sin problem on Satan. Satan tempts us to do evil, but we make the choice to sin and must accept responsibility of our evil choices. Physical, emotional, and psychological desires lead to sinful acts. There is no invisible force that <u>makes</u> persons sin *against their wills.* Sin is a consciously-chosen path, not an outwardly determined reflex." [3] James 1:13-15.

James 1:13-15 further explains that God does not tempt us but rather we are drawn away into sin by what is in our own hearts because sin is an individual choice:

> Let no one say when he is tempted, I am tempted from God; for God is incapable of being tempted by [what is] evil and He Himself tempts no one. **But every person is tempted when he is drawn away, enticed and baited by his own evil desire** (lust, passions). Then the evil desire, when it has conceived, gives birth to sin, and sin, when it is fully matured, brings forth death.

Furthermore, **Satan can blind the spiritual eyes of a person who makes a decision to live in sin** so that they cannot see truth and therefore know right from wrong. Satan will do everything in his power to cause a person to remain in this state, hopefully in his thinking, until they pass from this earth and join him in his kingdom of darkness for eternity.

2 Corinthians 4:4 speaks about spiritual blindness,

> **For the god of this world has blinded the unbelievers' minds [that they should not discern the truth],** preventing them from seeing the illuminating light of the Gospel of the glory of Christ (the Messiah), Who is the Image and Likeness of God. (Also see John 12:40 and Isaiah 42:18-20).

The Bible says in Romans 6:16, "Do you not know that if you continually surrender yourselves to anyone to do his will, you are the slaves of him whom you obey, whether that be to sin, which leads to death, or to obedience which leads to righteousness (right doing and right standing with God)." **Even though** we once were slaves to sin we can become obedient with all of our heart to follow righteousness and be set totally free as Believers. The Bible says, "Let not sin rule as king in your mortal bodies, to make you yield to its cravings and be subject to its lusts and evil passions...but rather offer and yield yourselves to God as though you have been raised from the dead to life..." (Romans 6:12-13).

Obedience keeps us from defiling our conscience. When we choose to obey we are choosing to live in God's glory. In Isaiah 11:2 it says the Spirit of the Lord will help us to discern by giving us "the Spirit of wisdom and understanding, the Spirit of counsel and might (His power to overcome), the Spirit of knowledge and of the reverential and obedient fear of the Lord" which will enable us to stay on track and in God's will and not be easily deceived nor will we dwell in confusion which is not of God.

When we make the choice to yield to the ways of God then it says, "For I will be merciful and gracious toward their sins and *I will remember their deeds of unrighteousness no more"* in another passage it is written, *"And their sins and their lawbreaking I will remember no more."* And in another it says, *"For I will forgive their iniquity, and I will [seriously] remember their sin no more"* (Hebrews 8:12; 10:17; Jeremiah. 31:33-34). His ways are not our ways; God will give instant forgiveness, show mercy, restore and remove from His mind any and all sin you have committed. *In return* **He asks of us to** *make a conscious decision* **not to sin against Him**. And if we sin know that He has already paid the price and given us a way of escape and has never stopped loving us no matter what state we were in. Although keep in mind, He expects us to grow and mature in our relationship with Him as we learn the things of the Spirit as we are taught by our Comforter and by studying His Word to increase in the knowledge of Who He is. Then our sin nature will decrease and weaken because of the renewing of our minds according to Romans 12:2.

When you feel uneasy *in your heart* (your spirit) about doing something and then decide to ignore it and do it anyway and what you did turns out to be sinful, notice your spirit man was warning you that something was wrong and you were about to make the wrong decision. We could learn from this experience and be sensitive the next time we feel uneasy and choose not to yield and wait until we sense a peace about what it is we are about to do and if we do not get that "peace" then let it go. Whether it is for ourselves or for the benefit of being an example at that moment for someone else, whenever we decide not to trust and rest in God we are more than likely going to do things that would later cause condemnation.

The Bible says, *"No temptation has overtaken you except such as is common to man; but God is faithful, who will not allow you to be tempted beyond what you are able, but with the temptation will also make the way of escape, that you may be able to bear it."* (I Cor. 10:13 NKJV) and in the NIV it ends by saying, *"...But when you are tempted, He will also provide a way out so that you can stand up under it."* God never allows more than what we can bear and He reveals what is not of Him *because He loves us.* Know that *when you are in Christ you are dead to sin, sin is not dead, you are dead to it.* Temptation will always be an issue because evil is in this world. We are to express our love for God (John 14:15) which will help us to make the choice of not participating in sin.

We are to exercise our authority and not allow nor receive condemnation because the more guilt a person has the more a person will sin; On the other hand the more of God's grace a person receives the less sin they will have in their life. This is confirmed in Romans 6:12-14 KJV which says, "Therefore, do not let sin reign in your mortal body, that you should obey it in its lusts. And do not present your members as instruments of unrighteousness to sin...**for** *sin shall not have dominion over you, for you are not under law but under grace."*

Each person is traveling on a path in this life with a specific purpose whether they realize it or not or whether they know what their purpose is or not. Nothing is done in vain and no one is a mistake. Everyone from Ministers of the Word of God; Presidents or Prime Ministers; Parents or Teachers; Scientist or Corporate CEO's to the smallest most insignificant positions (in man's eyes because all honest work is considered worthy in God's eyes, Luke 10:7 and I Timothy 5:18) on this earth, we have all made mistakes, all have sinned, and fallen short of the glory of God (the manifestation of His excellence in your life) and *no one* is perfect or has done everything totally right.

Romans 3:23 KJV and v. 24 Amplified says,

> **For all have sinned**, and come short of the glory of God. [All] are justified and made upright and in right standing with God, freely and gratuitously by His grace (His unmerited favor and mercy), through the redemption which is [provided] in Christ Jesus.

Notice it says **all have sinned and missed the mark**. We came into this world as *sinners* because the blood of mankind became corrupt throughout the ages when the first "Adam" fell from God's glory because of sin (Genesis Chapter 3).

This is why Jesus had to shed His blood which was of *no human man*. Because of this act all those in Christ are justified, just as if we have never sinned. His blood was used to redeem and to reconcile us back into that place of glory with our Heavenly Father and seal the covenant that we still enjoy to this day. (See the Chapter 1 under What is a Covenant).

Jesus became the "Second Adam" who did not sin so that His blood could reverse the curse that came upon mankind caused by the first Adam (Genesis 3:14-19). **This one sacrifice of the eternal blood from the Son of God has forever removed our sins and cleansed us of all unrighteousness.**

2 Corinthians 5:21 says,

> **For our sake He made Christ [virtually] to be sin Who knew no sin**, so that in and through

Him we might become [endued with, viewed as being in, and examples of] the righteousness of God [what we ought to be, approved and acceptable and in right relationship with Him, by His goodness].

In the Old Testament a sin offering was brought to the High Priest, *he examined the sin offering* (lamb, bull or whatever) *he did not examine the person* who brought the offering and if it was acceptable it was offered to the Most High God to cover their sins for a time, usually one year. Well the same holds true for us who are protected under the Blood of Jesus. **Our High Priest, Jesus, took His blood to the Most High God and presented it as a sin offering** and it was received so our sins were forgiven and washed away *forever.*

So how do we activate this in our present everyday life? By confessing our sins to God, He looks at the sin and then He looks for the sacrifice to take care of the sin. *He does not examine us* but instead *He examines our sin offering* which is the *King of kings and the Lord of lords* and when **He sees the blood that is perfect** without corruption and He remembers the sacrifice of this sin offering and on that merit alone He has forgiven us of all our sins. There is nothing more that needs to be done by us because it has already been paid in full.

Ephesians 1:7 says,

> In Him we have redemption (deliverance and salvation) through His blood, the remission (forgiveness) of our offenses (shortcomings and trespasses), in accordance with the riches and the generosity of His gracious favor.

Psalms 103:3-6 adds,

> Who forgives [every one of] all your iniquities, Who heals [each one of] all your diseases, Who redeems your life from the pit and corruption, Who beautifies, dignifies,

and crowns you with loving-kindness and tender mercy; Who satisfies your mouth [your necessity and desire at your personal age and situation] with good so that your youth, renewed, is like the eagle's [strong, overcoming, soaring]! The Lord executes righteousness and justice [not for me only, but] for all who are oppressed.

The shedding of His blood paved the way and gave redemption, **now God's grace will sustain you** because as you receive His grace it will destroy the sin in your life. **You cannot stop sin with mere will power but as you realize that your sin cannot stop God's grace on your life you can finally understand how deep and wide His love is for you** and how much He desires that you live a righteous life in Christ because that will protect you. God desires this for you because He knows that sin will only destroy your life, your relationships, your body and your overall wellbeing. Receive His grace and let it conquer the sin nature for you. "…where sin increased and abounded, grace (God's unmerited favor) has surpassed it and increased the more and superabounded, so that, [just] as sin has reigned in death, [so] grace (His unearned and underserved favor) might reign also through righteousness (right standing with God) which issues in eternal life through Jesus Christ (the Messiah, the Anointed One) our Lord," (Romans 5:20-21).

Read Romans 6:14-23 and see vv.14-16 as follows:

> For sin shall not [any longer] exert dominion over you, since now you are not under Law [as slaves], but under grace [as subjects of God's favor and mercy]. What then [are we to conclude]? Shall we sin because we live not under law but under God's favor and mercy? Certainly not! Do you not know that if you continually surrender yourselves to anyone to do his will, you are the slaves of him

whom you obey, whether that be to sin, which leads to death (v.23) or to obedience which leads to righteousness (right doing and right standing with God)?

And because of what He did for all those who receive Him, He said "your sins and lawless deeds I will by no means remember." God placed it in the sea of forgetfulness. He no longer remembers so why do we still carry the guilt, worry and all that came with it when He Himself has forgotten?

As long as people are conscious of or consistently thinking about their sins they are unable to receive forgiveness from the Lord or any healing that is needed, whether it is in their body, family, relationships, finances or wherever it is needed because of the condemnation. Because of this many do not feel worthy of blessings, however, *some Christians believe that God has forgiven some of their past sins but maybe not the sins of their entire life* or the sins they feel are so terrible they are beyond His forgiveness. Because they are in unbelief, that it is all done for them, many of them choose to suffer continuously in areas where the Lord has already taken care of it when He paid the sin debt.

Some people are in so much bondage from condemnation that they do not realize when Jesus paid the price for our eternal life that in our salvation is everything we need **including payment for our sin debt**. They may think or say, I know He redeemed my life and gave me eternal life and took the sting out of death for me; I know He took my sickness and all infirmity when He took the strips on His back and gave me health; I know He took poverty upon Himself so I could be rich; I even realize when they placed the crown of thorns upon His head He gave me a peace of mind and wisdom as He took away torment and confusion intended for me. They also know He took their weaknesses and gave them His strength; yet in all that He did to take all these curses off of our lives it is still difficult for some to understand and believe that **He took away** *all of our sins for eternity?* But it is true, He took all of my sins and He gave us His Righteousness, He took our punishment and gave me forgiveness and He called Himself the Son of man so we could be called the sons of God (Matthew 5:9). And when it was all said and done, He said, "It Is Finished!"

Therefore, when you choose to remain sin-conscious, *constantly searching your own heart or finding fault with yourself* **for past mistakes and sins, know that this is a tradition or a way of men and not of God.** God's way is to have <u>Him</u> search your heart as King David asked the Lord to search his heart to try him and know his thoughts to find out if there was any wicked way in him so the Lord could lead him in the way of everlasting (Psalms 139:23-24 and Psalm 26:2). Why is this so important? Because if we remain sin-conscious we are saying what He did for us fell short, it was not enough and we need to compensate by remembering our own sin and punishing ourselves even though He has chosen to forget it once we have asked for forgiveness.

On the other hand there are occasions where we are asked to examine our own hearts. For instance, Paul asked us to examine and evaluate ourselves in I Corinthians 11:28 before we partake of communion (Chapter 7 under Spiritual Warfare weapon number 16). And in 2 Corinthians 13:5 it says, "Examine and test and evaluate your own selves to see whether you are holding to your faith and showing the proper fruits of it..." **When we take the time to examine ourselves we are <u>not</u> doing this to bring up past sins that would cause guilt and condemnation but it is to examine where we currently are** and to ask for forgiveness of current sin or where we have made a mistake and wish to sincerely ask the Lord for forgiveness. **It is also to ask as a reminder or a safety for us, as we ask: am I forgiving, patient, and generous; do I yield to the leading of the Holy Spirit; am I spending quality time with God and my family and so on.** This will aid in keeping us free from being sin-conscious and giving Satan a place to rob us of our faith or in some other area. We can remain confident that we are in Christ and are anointed to go forth and do all that He is asking of us. One last good point, as you examine yourself and are merciful with yourself remember to show mercy to others and not judge or criticize them but make an effort to show love and forgiveness. *In regards to judging people, I keep a check on myself when I see something negative that I could comment on by saying or reciting the phrase, "except for the grace of God, there go I."*

Furthermore, we are saying even though "a voice came from Heaven," and said "You are My Beloved Son, in whom I am well pleased" (Mark 1:11 KJV); and even though Jesus was obedient to death so we could all have life and have it to the abundance, **some of us actually think that we can add to what He did** by keeping our suffering sick bodies, remaining in marriages that are life threatening, dealing with wayward children alone and keeping our depressed minds and backslidden ways. **All of this because we cannot comprehend that Someone could love us so much and make it so easy that all we have to do is believe, receive and say thank You** for all that You did for me. No, that would be too simple and not religious enough for most and it does not make any sense for others. The bottom line is this, it is not humility but false pride, fear and self-righteousness for those who choose to suffer for the enemy instead of walking in wholeness and life with Christ. I did not say a life without any struggles or pain or suffering but it will not be the same type of suffering that the adversary places in your path by any means.

Isaiah 53:5 completes it:

> But He was wounded for our transgressions, He was **bruised for our guilt and iniquities**; the chastisement [needful to obtain] peace and well-being for us was upon Him, and with the stripes [that wounded] Him we are healed and made whole.

For all of those <u>who can receive</u> and do understand that His Word is true that the penalty of sin is no longer on us, you will be set free as soon as you take hold of the revelation that your sins are forever forgiven because of what Christ did. So thank and praise Him because of His grace, for who the Son has set free is free indeed. It is a gift, just receive it.

There are some who will **chose <u>not</u> to receive the free gift of salvation that was paid for with a price** as it says in I Corinthians 6:20, "You were bought with a price [purchased with a preciousness and paid for, made His own]. So then honor God and bring glory to Him in your body]." And for those who chose not to receive the free gift and are committing sexual immorality they will find that *they will have to take care of their sin themselves (which they cannot do)* simply because they rejected the One who took care of it for them. You might say they as well as all others who sin for various reasons **and who have refused the free gift are now on their own**.

Romans 1:21-32 explains what happens when you are left to take care of your own sin:

> **Because when they knew and recognized Him as God, they did not honor and glorify Him as God or give Him thanks. But instead they became futile and godless in their thinking** [with vain imaginings, foolish reasoning, and stupid speculations] and their senseless minds were darkened. *Claiming to be wise, they became fools [professing to be smart, they made simpletons of themselves].* And by them the glory and majesty and excellence of the immortal God were exchanged for and represented by images, resembling mortal man and birds and beasts and reptiles. **Therefore God gave them up in the lusts of their [own] hearts to sexual impurity, to the dishonoring of their bodies among themselves** [abandoning them to the degrading power of sin], **Because they exchanged the truth of God for a lie** and worshiped and served the creature rather than the Creator, Who is blessed forever! Amen.

For this reason God gave them over and abandoned them to vile affections and degrading passions. For their women exchanged their natural function for an unnatural and abnormal one, And the men also turned from natural relations with women and were set ablaze (burning out, consumed) with lust for one another – men committing shameful acts with men and suffering in their own bodies and personalities the inevitable consequences and penalty of their wrong-doing and going astray, which was [their] fitting retribution. **And so, since they did not see fit to acknowledge God or approve of Him or consider Him worth the knowing, God gave them over to a base and condemned mind to do things not proper or decent but loathsome,** until they were filled (permeated and saturated) with every kind of unrighteousness, iniquity, grasping and covetous greed, and malice...*hateful to and hating God...boasting...*They were without understanding, conscienceless, and faithless, heartless and loveless [and merciless...they not only do them themselves but approve and applaud others who practice them.

IF YOUR SIN CONTRIBUTED TO THE DIVORCE, WHAT THEN?

So what can or should you do if your divorce has already taken place and you have discovered that *part* of the reason for the divorce was because you had a hardened-heart or something else that may have been done by you that contributed to the separation and divorce? Or if you divorced before you became a Christian and now feel guilty, what can you do about it? **First** of all, realize that it takes two people to cause a marriage to be successful and it takes two people to cause it to be unsuccessful because it is *never* one hundred percent one person's fault.

Each person had *a part* in the outcome, for example, even if your part was not sinful because you took a stand to do things God's way and the other party chose not to stand but to leave. **Secondly**, understand that condemnation, guilt and torment are not from the Heavenly Father and if you are a new creature in Christ Jesus**,** *all old things have passed away:* "Therefore, if any person is [ingrafted] in Christ (The Messiah) he is a new creation (a new creature altogether); the old [previous moral and spiritual condition] has passed away. Behold, the fresh and new has come!" (2 Corinthians 5:17).

Your negative actions or sins were a part of your past so you would handle that behavior from your past like you would any other bad behavior or sin once you came into the knowledge of Christ. He has given all who follow Him a way out and shown us how to get back on track if we have missed the mark as well as redeemed our time.

During or after a divorce **if you feel in your heart that your sin contributed to the divorce** you would deal with it the same way you would deal with any other sin in your life as follows:

- Ask God to forgive you for your sin (s);
- Repent of your ways (sins) with true remorse;
- *Receive* His forgiveness;
- Forgive yourself;
- Forgive others (Matthew 6:14-15);
- Forgive God if you believe He is partially to blame;
- If it is *possible,* ask the other party to forgive you or you make some type of restitution. (Restitution is not necessarily reconciliation but whatever you can do to bring some comfort to the overall situation helps);
- Another suggestion would be to write them a letter with the intent to bring closure;
- But if restitution is not possible, then place the entire matter in God's hands by releasing that care to Him, placing this behind you forever and moving forward with your life (I Peter 5:7).

Forgiveness is an important step and forgiving yourself is important for this process. Why? Because if you choose not to forgive yourself and cannot see yourself the way God sees you and love yourself in a healthy balanced way, you won't be able to sincerely forgive others, see them as God sees them nor love them with the love of the Lord. This is simply because you cannot give someone else what you do not "first" have.

CLARIFYING FORGIVENESS:

Before we approach Father God with true sorrow and humility when asking for forgiveness of our sins we must first as mentioned earlier confess or admit our sins before our Heavenly Father because we are troubled by them and we need to clear our hearts of the sin and break its power of sin-consciousness.

Forgiveness is the next step that leads to reconciliation with God which will result in healing and full recovery. Let's remember that our sins were forever forgiven because of the finished work at the cross. We are always to know that we are forgiven and that we come before God and ask for forgiveness to clear our hearts and conscience to speak boldly and fellowship freely with our God and so that the adversary will not gain ground in our lives because we are harboring unforgiveness.

Let's not cause what He did for us to be in vain as we confess our sins and ask for forgiveness and know it is accomplished. We rest in that knowledge because we are conscious of His love and sacrifice.

If He had not shed one drop of His precious blood we never would have been forgiven and therefore never would have qualified to come before God the Father. **"In Him we have redemption (deliverance and salvation) through His blood, the remission (forgiveness) of our offenses** (shortcomings and trespasses), in accordance with the riches and the generosity of His gracious favor" (Eph.1:17).

The Bible says we can confess our sins one to another (confessing to people we trust and have our best interest at heart) this is designed to remove the weight of carrying the sin and exposing it. Exposing the sin and then praying about it will begin the process of freeing a person up and give them relief and/or healing. Satan likes to make others think they are the only ones who sin or have a particular "problem" and when you carry this burden or secret you will never really be free or receive deliverance. Once we are Born-again if we sin being sin-conscious will cause different levels of condemnation therefore it is best to not think on past sins once you have asked for forgiveness, receive it and go on. *I John 1:9 was designed for the unbeliever because the Believer does not lose their righteousness if they sin, they are still righteous in Christ but need to ask for forgiveness, repent, receive forgiveness and continue in Christ.*

I John 1:9 says,

> **If we [freely] admit that we have sinned** and **confess our sins**, *He is faithful and just* (true to His own nature and promises) *and will forgive our sins* [dismiss our lawlessness] and [continuously] cleanse us from all **unrighteousness** [everything not in conformity to His will in purpose, thought, and action].

I John 5:17 says,

> All wrongdoing is sin, and there is sin which does not [involve] death [that may be **repented of and forgiven**].

As we ask for forgiveness of our sins we break sin's power. Once we *repent* then we need to *receive His forgiveness* knowing in our hearts we are truly forgiven. *God loves us with an unconditional love* and in that love is complete forgiveness. I once heard someone say "I get to *live* forgiven." This means that once you are a Believer and you put your **faith in His blood that keeps you cleansed from all your sins** as you continue to walk in the ways of righteousness the devil cannot win because he has already been defeated by the Blood of the Lamb.

I John 1:7 says,

> But if we [really are living and walking in the Light, as He [Himself] is in the Light, we have [true, unbroken] fellowship with one another, and the blood of Jesus Christ His Son cleanses (removes) us from all sin and guilt [keeps us cleansed from sin in all forms and manifestations].

Once that is cleared up we need to **forgive others**. When we forgive we are making a *conscious decision to choose to pardon* someone or something for an offense that was directed towards us or someone we love. **We must understand that our feelings really do not have much to do with it because it is about a decision of our will to be obedient to God.** We are led by the Spirit of God not by our feelings. If we decide to forgive, a spirit of forgiveness helps us and we receive healing in our hearts. The Holy Spirit will also tell us when it is necessary for us to confront. The key is to be led on how to handle a situation the way He would have us to do it. Otherwise you could wear yourself out fighting every battle or being offended about everything without knowing how to let it go and just choose to forgive and cast your care.

As stated above in I John 1:9 He is a faithful God who is faithful to us regardless of how we act because that is His nature (2 Tim. 2:13) and He asks us to be faithful as well because we were created in His likeness and should desire to have godly character (Psalm 31:23 and Proverbs 28:20).

Therefore, regardless of the offense against us and how we feel we should be willing to make a decision to forgive others knowing forgiveness is not for people who deserve it but it is the right thing to do because we have an opportunity to extend God's grace to someone else just like God extended undeserved grace and favor to us. Once the decision is made to forgive it will open a door for God to heal our hearts toward them which will free us up from bitterness and other negative emotions that would be the result of unforgiveness.

Mark 11:25-26 says,

> And whenever you stand praying, if you have anything against anyone, *forgive them and let it drop* (leave it, let it go), *in order that your Father Who is in heaven may also forgive you* your [own] failings and shortcomings and let them drop. **But if you do not forgive, neither will your Father in heaven forgive your failings and shortcomings.**

Yes, it is equally important *to choose to forgive others* and this would include the spouse that you feel betrayed you. In addition to forgiving them pray for your former spouse. You may ask why would I want to forgive and pray for someone who ruined my life? **To *choose* to forgive and *pray* for your former spouse or anyone for that matter is another major key in the process of forgiveness** which is to pray for a blessing for your "enemies" because God says to "Bless those who persecute you [who are cruel in their attitude toward you]; bless and do not curse them" (Romans 12:14). In this context the word "bless" means "to speak well of." **It is extending mercy to people who do not deserve it.** One reason God would have you pray for them or whoever is because *this blessing is for them to be blessed spiritually in order to bring truth and revelation so they will be willing to repent and be set free from their sins as well.*

The greater thing is knowing that Jesus Christ would have us to show compassion for one another because He does not desire for anyone to be lost for eternity. The two greatest commands are to love God and to love your neighbor as you love yourself. Love yourself enough to receive Jesus, for He is *Love*, He is God; and love your neighbor enough to forgive and be like Jesus. It also means you are learning to forgive those who came against you and release the matter into God's hands.

We have to exercise our faith to forgive and trust God to heal and turn situations around. **Faith pleases God and forgiveness releases His power.** As you by faith forgive based on His Word the power of the Holy Spirit will be released to heal, correct and avenge. *Furthermore, the foundation for the fruit of the Spirit is Love (Gal. 5:22-23) and part of the fruit of love is forgiveness. When you reject forgiving others you are rejecting love. God said, He is love, therefore, you are really rejecting Him and His ways* and placing a wedge between God and yourself which could jeopardize your healing and redemption if reconciliation has not been achieved before passing into eternity (Mark 11:25-26; I John 4:16).

Mark 6:14-15 NLT says,

> If you forgive those who sin against you, your heavenly Father will forgive you. But if you refuse to forgive others, your Father will not forgive your sins.

Born-again people have a right to eternal life it is a promise from God. Our sin was taken care of by the Finished Work at the Cross but in order to receive it we must confess Jesus as our Lord and Savior. Furthermore, to continue to receive the Lords forgiveness we must forgive others and if we refuse then we shut the door to our sins being forgiven as well.

Matthew 18:21-22 tells us how often we are to forgive someone:

Then Peter came to Him and said, Lord, how many times may my brother sin against me and I forgive him, and let it go? [As many as] up to seven times?

Jesus answered him, I tell you, not up to seven times, but seventy times seven! (Genesis 4:24).

There are rewards for choosing God's way of letting it go instead of nursing and rehearsing in your mind the offense (what they said or did to you) by tormenting yourself or even worse plotting ways of revenge. One of those rewards is that you have a greater peace of mind and the anointing of God can increase on your life because you put your flesh (what you wanted to do) under subjection to the will of God.

Romans 12:19-21 breaks it down for you and clearly shows you that God does not want you to avenge yourself:

> **Beloved, never avenge yourselves, but leave the way open for [God's] wrath; for it is written, Vengeance is Mine**, I will repay (requite), says the Lord. But if your enemy is hungry, feed him; if he is thirsty, give him drink; for by so doing you will heap burning coals upon his head. **Do not let yourself be overcome by evil, but overcome (master) evil with good.**

So why should we be at odds with God when He said to drop it and let it go? God doesn't ask us to do anything without first equipping us to do it. By remembering what they did to you over and over again, you are running the risk of blocking your blessings and help from the Lord when you could instead just follow the example of God by letting it go, knowing that He is faithful to repay any injustice at the appointed time. How and when is His business not ours. Why? Because He told us to love our enemies and do good to them and He will take care of the matter, just trust Him. I am not saying this so you can think, oh boy, God will get them now! No, I am saying this because if you continue to hold onto the pain and hurt it has the potential of driving you out of your mind. Some people never bounce back if they get "stuck" in the past.

It is also extremely important that *we forgive ourselves*. We could pray a simple prayer like this: I choose to forgive myself of ___ (you can be specific) that I did, that was an offense and sin against You, Heavenly Father and that grieved the Holy Spirit (I Thessalonians 5:19). I repent of my ways. I thank You and I receive Your forgiveness for ___. Now, I refuse to remember something that God has chosen to forget. He said, "For I will forgive their iniquity, and I will remember their sin no more" Jeremiah 31:34; Hebrews 10:17. Forgiving yourself is the opposite of what the adversary wants you to do. For one thing it will bring you into a safety zone; it will be one of the things that will keep you under the protection of God and give Him space to work on your behalf.

In the area of forgiveness some people become bitter towards God and need to *forgive God as well*. They tend to blame Him because they feel He is in control and the One with all the power to stop bad things from happening or make things happen for their good. Well He is the One that is all powerful, all knowing and everywhere, but He is also the same One who gave us a free will to choose who we would serve. Many people refuse to believe they have an enemy named Satan and because of their unbelief or denial they end up serving him directly or indirectly because he will use them without their consent. They have given Satan place in their lives because of their ignorance of the Word of God (Hosea 4:6-7). And as a result of this God the Father is blamed for any and everything that happens under the sun.

Please understand that God the Father, His Son Jesus and the Holy Spirit loves you, are there for you and are willing to assist you in this life. We do not need to hold a grudge or have unforgiveness against the very One that is here to help us and set us free from all our distresses. **Choose to forgive God** if you think He is the problem so you can set things in their proper order and receive His mercy, grace, strength and help.

Satan does not want you to forgive, *especially forgive yourself.* He knows that unforgiveness automatically pulls you out from under the umbrella of protection from God. He fights this with all he has because he cannot successfully do the damage he wants as long as you are striving to do things God's way. He wants you full of anger, hatred, afraid, miserable, resentful and living in self-imposed bondage because under these conditions you are no threat to him whatsoever, you are too consumed with yourself to be concerned about others or your surroundings. And the resentment will cause you to repeatedly think on the event that brought the offense which will cause a stronghold in your mind and lead to other issues. It is easier to do what the Word of God says and cast down these vain imaginations from your mind (2 Corinthians 10:5).

If you choose not to forgive yourself these are some of the reasons why and some of the consequences you will encounter: [4]

"**(1)** It may have something to do with being self-righteous (we are all born with this because of the fall of the first Adam Gen. 3:9-13; Ps 51:5), because of self-righteousness we are spiritually blinded to the truth about ourselves and the way of the Lord (2 Cor. 4:4), deceived into believing we are wise enough, good enough, know enough and can handle anything (I Cor. 3:18-19). We think we do not need a Savior or the help of the Holy Spirit. We trust in our own good works and self-righteousness for approval instead of Christ's blood and His Righteousness.

(2) Some are afraid to forgive themselves because they feel responsible (or partially responsible) for their past. A part of them knows that God has forgiven them yet they may feel He needs them to pay or punish themselves for their past sins or wrong doing to justify their part in their current situation.

(3) Self-righteousness and self-pity work hand in hand. They both lead you away from forgiving yourself one hundred percent. Self-pity makes you feel sorry for yourself because you may feel that God allowed a situation to happen that does not make any sense to you. Self-pity is also selfish and has anger towards God. So you blame God while feeling sorry for yourself. It will also cause you to demand that God help you, speak or do something on your behalf.

(4) Not forgiving yourself can stop or paralyze you by causing you to live in despair over your past and in so many other ways and areas of your life at home, at work or doing things for yourself. It is a sin against God not to forgive yourself just as if you would refuse to forgive another person.

When we choose not to forgive in general it will cause us to stay in guilt, shame, doubt, anger, bitterness, resentment, depression, and so on. It will also hinder our personal relationship with God if we are Christians. When we hold a grudge and unforgiveness long enough in our hearts it can translate into a disease and affect our health physically, emotionally, mentally and spiritually by grieving the Holy Spirit within us."

Ephesians 4:30-32 NIV explains,

> And do not grieve the Holy Spirit of God, with whom you were sealed for the day of redemption. Get rid of all bitterness, rage and anger, brawling and slander, along with every form of malice. **Be kind and compassionate to one another, forgiving each other, just as Christ God forgave you.**

God did not create us to hate others or ourselves. But He did tell us to hate what is evil and love what is good (Amos 5:15). That is why we were given the emotion of anger, it is for righteous indignation to express anger when there is wrong doing but not to express it to the point that we sin while angry. God said to love one another (our neighbor) as we are to love ourselves (Luke 10:27 and Matthew 22:39). We are to speak well of each other, encourage one another, pray for and do good to and for one another.

Forgiveness will enable us to be able to do that; it will help us fulfill our destiny and our purpose in life. It can make us like and treat ourselves better and thus enable us to do the same towards others. Forgiveness will bring us to that place of inner peace and set us free from bitterness and other negative emotions and evil forces that come with unforgiveness. **It all starts with *making a decision* to forgive, expect and then accepting the Holy Spirit to bring Truth and healing into our hearts thereafter.**

What happens *if we decide that we have not sinned* in relation to our divorce and we do not need to ask for forgiveness nor offer forgiveness to our spouse or anyone else because we feel that we were the ones who were wronged in the process of the divorce? If you know that there was *absolutely no sin* on your part in regards to your divorce and you are not harboring any ill wishes, feelings, bitterness or unforgiveness and you *have a complete peace* about the whole matter then "fine." However, if you claimed you have not sinned in regards to your divorce but you do have unforgiveness towards your former spouse, children, blended-family children, in-laws or anyone connected and you **refuse to forgive** *then it has become sin on your part.* **Unforgiveness is sin in the eyes of God**. You may say, well after all **"I"** was the one who was lied about and lied to, betrayed, whose name was slandered, and so forth and you just cannot forgive them for what they did to you. You have just licensed the enemy to torment you, keep you in bondage and stop you from moving forward with your life in peace. By refusing to forgive you have made a decision not to do things God's way as the sinners (unbelievers) have and you have opened a wide door for the adversary to operate in your life.

I John 1:10 states:

> If we say (claim) we have not sinned, we contradict His Word and make Him out to be false and a liar, and His Word is not in us [the divine message of the Gospel is not in our hearts].

Galatians 6:7-9 is addressed to all Sinners and Believers as it says,

> Do not be deceived and deluded and misled; God will not allow Himself to be sneered at (scorned, disdained, or mocked by mere pretensions or professions, or by His precepts being set aside.) [He inevitably deludes himself who attempts to delude God.] For whatever a man sows, that and that only is what he will reap.

Matthew 6:14-15 is for every Believer:

> For if you forgive people their trespasses [their reckless and willful sins, leaving them, letting them go, and giving up resentment], your heavenly Father will also forgive you. But if you do not forgive others their trespasses [their reckless and willful sins, leaving

them, letting them go, and giving up resentment], neither will your Father forgive you your trespasses.

It all starts with forgiveness, help Him forgive you of your trespasses by simply receiving His forgiveness, forgiving yourself and forgiving others. And then watch the peace, love and doors open on your behalf because you desire and wish to do things His way not because someone is threatening you to do so or trying to frighten you into doing so but simply because you have come into the knowledge of what it means to have a Wonderful, Loving and Living God who really cares about you and wants to be a part of your life. Remember in His forgiveness is all of your healing in every area of your life, relationships, your health, your finances and so forth.

When we fully understand that His entire plan was built around us and how He lifted us up and seated us with Him in heavenly places in order to give us His name so we could conquer, have authority and be victorious. After all *who* was going to make God love us? Who was going to make Him deliver us, empower and gift us? Who was going to cause Him to treat us with justice? There is none equal to Him that could make Him do anything; He Who is all powerful and all knowing. He did it because He loves us and for no other reason.

He took the punishment so we could have forgiveness. He came into this world as one of us and *willfully went through and suffered with us then suffered for us.* Are we going to tell Jesus that it was all in vain, for nothing? He has demonstrated and He has declared His love for us and made a way through His grace for us to receive His love, His kindness, His fruit and character as well as His gifts (Ps. 130:3, 4). We can receive all of His promises through His Grace as we use our faith.

When we know that we know in our hearts that He is our Father, He is our Mother, He is our Brother, He is our Friend, He is our very source of life and when we know how badly He wants us to succeed we should want to please Him, we should want to be His Friend, we should want what He wants for our lives.

If we do make a decision to at least try and trust the Holy Spirit to heal our hearts, remove past hurts, restore us and give us a fresh start, not only will He do this for us but He will keep us and as long as we strive to continue in Him we need never fall, according to 2 Peter 1:3-10 NIV:

His divine power has given us everything we need for life and godliness through our knowledge of him who called us by His own glory and goodness. Through these He has given us His very great and precious promises, so that through them you may participate in the divine nature and escape the corruption in the world caused by evil desires.

For this very reason, make every effort to add to your faith goodness; and to goodness, knowledge; and to knowledge, self-control; and to self-control, perseverance; and to perseverance, godliness; and to godliness, brotherly kindness; and to brotherly kindness, love. For if you possess these qualities in increasing measure, *they will keep you* from being ineffective and unproductive in your knowledge of our Lord Jesus Christ. But if anyone does not have them, he is nearsighted and blind, and has forgotten that he **has been cleansed from his past sins**.

Therefore…, if you do these things, you will *never fall,* and you will receive a rich welcome into the eternal Kingdom of our Lord and Savior Jesus Christ.

A Summary of the Steps for the Process of Forgiveness:

- Ask God to search your heart for any wicked way that may be in you (Ps. 139:23-24);

- Ask God with true remorse and sorrow to forgive you of your sins;
- Repent of your ways (sins);
- Receive God's forgiveness for your sins;
- Forgive yourself;
- Forgive others;
- Forgive God if you believe He is to blame;
- Make an attempt at restitution to bring comfort and/or closure;
- Strive to keep your heart and motives pure before God so your past will not be a hindrance for your future;
- Cast down vain imaginations (reasoning and negative thoughts) 2 Corinthians 10:5;
- Cast your care (give it to God and leave it there) if it comes up again cast it down and do not entertain negative thoughts. You have already done your part there is nothing left to do, God will do the rest in this area (I Peter 5:7).

CLARIFYING REPENTANCE:

The major and final step in the process that will bring you back into right standing with God is Repentance. Because of repentance we do not have to live with condemnation, guilt, anger, shame or torment of past regrets. The Blood of the Lamb washes away our sin and we are set free to be peaceful and live a life of *joy and abundance even after a divorce.*
The New Unger's Bible Dictionary defines Repentance:

> **A "change" of mind. A fundamental and thorough change in the hearts of men from sin and toward God.** Although faith alone is the condition for salvation, repentance is bound up with faith and inseparable from it, since without some measure of faith no one can truly repent, and repentance never attains to its deepest character till the sinner realizes through saving faith how great is the

grace of God against whom he has sinned. On the other hand, there can be no saving faith without true repentance.

Repentance contains as essential elements (1) **a genuine sorrow toward God on account of sin** (2) an inward repugnance to sin necessarily followed by the actual forsaking of it; and (3) humble self-surrender to the will and service of God.

It becomes more complete and powerful in those who have experienced the saving grace of God and thus realize more fully the enormity of sin and the depths of the divine compassion that has been operative in their salvation. **Repentance is the gift of God.** But as with faith so with repentance – it is left with men to make for themselves the great decision.

Once we have recognized we have sinned against God we are to come to Him with a sorrowful heart.
2 Corinthians 7:10 says,

> For **godly grief** and the pain God is permitted to direct, **produce a repentance** that leads and contributes to salvation and deliverance from evil, and it never brings regret; but **worldly grief** (the hopeless sorrow that is characteristic of the pagan world) is deadly [breeding and ending in death].

Once we ask for forgiveness **we are now ready to repent of our ways**.
2 Peter 3:9 NIV tells us to come to Him for God wants everyone to repent:

> The Lord is not slow in keeping His promise, as some understand slowness. He is patient

with you, *not wanting anyone to perish, but everyone to come to repentance.*

First of all, you must understand that in the last days scoffers will come, scoffing and following their own evil desires. They will say, "Where is this 'coming' He promised? Ever since our fathers died, everything goes on as it has since the beginning of creation." "But they deliberately forget that long ago by God's Word the heavens existed and the earth was formed out of water and by (in) water. By these waters also the world of that time was deluged and destroyed" (2 Peter 3:3-6 NIV). At that time "every living thing that moved on the earth perished... everything on dry land that had the breath of life in its nostrils died. And everything living on the face of the earth was wiped out. Only Noah was left, and those with him in the ark." (Genesis 7:21-23).

People are so quick to call the Word of God a history book or a fantasy book yet nearly every prophecy from the Old Testament has already been fulfilled and some are in the making as I write. **The Lord's love and mercy are the only motives He has for asking people to repent and come away from a lifestyle that will leave them out and leave them behind**. He said He was coming again and He is; He always keeps His Word and He does not desire that anyone should perish but that we all have life. If we choose not to repent of our sins, which will be contrary to the loving Father's will and can only lead to judgment, it will be with great regret to all those who choose this path.

Acts 5:29-31 says,

> ...**We must obey God rather than men**. The God of our forefathers raised up Jesus... God exalted Him to His right hand to be Prince and Leader and Savior and Deliverer and Preserver, in order to grant *repentance* to Israel and bestow forgiveness and release from sins.

The Disciple's Study Bible NIV Psalm 38:1-22: [3]

Repentance for sin is the escape route from divine punishment. *David was sick and sought healing. He was not in grief for his circumstances but for his sin.* The vivid description of physical suffering and oppression from without demonstration that **sin intensifies the pain of outer circumstances. David had removed himself from God's protective presence.** Only he could pray for restoration to the Lord's presence. *Sin produced anger in Cain (Gen. 4:5) and terror in Saul (I Sam. 28:5-6) but repentance in David.*

The word repent: "re" means to turn around, go back; "Pent" means the highest. **When we repent to God we are returning to the highest place of relationship mankind had with Him.** In other words, we are now ready to come back to our place of glory and be seated together in heavenly places in Christ Jesus.

Ephesians 2:6 says,

And He raised us up together with Him and made us sit down together [giving us joint seating with Him] in the heavenly sphere [by virtue of our being] in Christ Jesus (the Messiah, the Anointed One).

When we *turn from the direction we were going* after having realized our sins and repenting we come back into right standing with God, into a place of fellowship and worship with the Most High God. Our praises and prayers are heard, it is a place where broken hearts are mended, and a place where healing and peace can finally be found. It is a place of authority of knowing who we are in Christ and the power we have over our enemy, the accuser.

When we come to Him as we are, He wants us to remember that He took our sins to the cross and *He gave us His Righteousness*. Therefore, our righteousness is in Christ Jesus and not in ourselves or our merits or anything we have done. His Righteousness is what we can put our faith in, and once we believe and do this, then we will progressively display more and more right behavior because of the love He showed towards us and because of revelation knowledge **we finally understand what He gave us**. So when your past sins come up in your mind or through others and you are a child of God, as mentioned earlier, remember the price was already paid and your sins were *removed permanently* and you are now filled with His Righteousness and seated in high places (Hebrews 10:14). So as they come up to you rebuke it from your mind with your mouth and worship God because He is your Forgiver. If you like, you can even remind the adversary of his future, that his time is short (Revelation 12:12) and because he deceives and seduces people to go astray he will be hurled into the Lake of Fire tormented day and night forever and ever (Revelation 20:10).

So if you have made a mistake or sinned, repent and get back into your position of authority where God placed you when He died and took the keys to death, hell and the grave and then rose to give them to you and set you free (Genesis 1:26; Luke 10:19).

Remember through repentance you come back into that place where you fell from, however, *that something* that was put into motion in the spiritual realm by your words or deeds before you realized you needed to repent and turn around and go in the direction God would have had you to go, it will still have a consequence and produce a harvest because it was put into motion with a seed (your words or your actions or both) which will produce a harvest (Gen. 8:22). Keep in mind too, that because of forgiveness and repentance it can stop a lot of bad harvest even though we have put things into motion because what the devil meant for evil God is still able to turn it around for our good (Gen. 50:20).

Also in many cases we can dig up wrong words that have been spoken and put them under the blood of Jesus before they harvest but in other cases the words or our actions have already developed in the spiritual realm, therefore, the harvest will manifest whether a good seed or a bad seed was planted.

For an example: Repentance after becoming pregnant out of wedlock is all well and good but the harvest will still manifest and produce in nine months and be loved by you and others because no one is an accident. Another example is, if you divorced your spouse because of your pride or lust for other things or someone and then you repent later that is good and yes you are forgiven and restored to that place with God seated with Him in heavenly places (Eph. 2:6) but the consequence is your former spouse has since remarried and you have lost your marriage plus your family to a certain degree.

Even though Esau repented for selling His birth right, he never got it back, for his birth right went to his brother Jacob who was blessed in a tremendous way because of it.

Hebrews 12:16-17 says:

> That no one may become guilty of sexual vice, or become a profane (godless and sacrilegious) person as Esau did, who sold his own birthright for a single meal, [Gen. 25:29-34]. **For you understand that later on, when he wanted [to regain title to] his inheritance of the blessing, he was rejected (disqualified and set aside), for he could find no opportunity to repair by repentance [what he had done**, no chance to recall the choice he had made], **although he sought for it carefully with [bitter] tears,** [Gen. 27:30-40].

The moral of the above examples is that, yes you always have the option to repent and turn around and go in a way that God would have you to live, but will it be too late for some things that He intended for you to have in your life? God will not force us to listen to Him but give us every opportunity and even bring us to the end of ourselves so we can see that we need a Savior in our lives as well as guidance from the Holy Spirit and protection from His angels and so forth but if we do not receive Him then He will not force the issue and leave us to ourselves.

I have been told by various people that they will not go to church or ask Jesus into their lives because **they do not want to be a hypocrite** like those they see in church. **Well,** *I interpret that as,* **they plan to make themselves righteous, become holy (be sanctified and set apart) and prevent themselves from ever going to hell <u>before</u> they can come to the Lord's house to worship and partake of "His Goodness."** They feel once all of this is done *by them* then it will be alright, and they won't be a hypocrite. **Evidently they failed to understand that they can never do these things for themselves that is why we needed a Savior** to come into this world in the first place. You see, it is because of His Goodness and Kindness that He offers repentance but the blind and deceived never see that attribute of a loving heart because they can only see the negative and use it as an excuse to pro-long, stay-in and continue with their plan and their lifestyle that comes against His will for their lives. Some also use self-justification to justify their sin(s) so they do not have a need to repent. The longer people go without repenting the deeper it is rooted and it will be difficult later because the person's heart can become hardened as well. They do not understand that "in His love God is kind and patient and does not judge and punish people for sins. As mentioned earlier, His Word will judge. His kindness is not softness towards sin but love for sinners seeking to provide time to change." [3]

Romans 2:4 says,

> Or are you [so blind as to] trifle with and presume upon and despise and underestimate the wealth of His kindness and forbearance and long-suffering patience? Are you unmindful or actually ignorant [of the fact] that God's kindness is intended to lead you to repent (to change your mind and inner man to accept God's will)?

Well I'm sorry to say it but they have already missed the mark. They have already been blinded and deceived into believing that they could save themselves from their own sins and that their goodness and their self-righteousness was all that was needed to please a Holy God and allow them entrance into the Kingdom of God with all its promises and eternal life. John 14:6 states that "**Jesus said to him, I am the Way and the Truth and the Life; <u>no one</u> comes to the Father except by (through) Me.**"

Furthermore, they are expressing that Jesus' sacrifice (which was no ordinary sacrifice) was done in vain because as far as they are concerned human beings have the power, the wisdom and know how to acquire from and please the true and Living God of Heaven. And they have a brain and know how to purchase and have many things without the benefit of God being in their lives.

After all, according to a number of them there are other ways to heaven besides Jesus (even after He clearly stated that He is the Way, the only way). And so they feel why cut your "fun" short "attempting" to live a *holy life* when our experience has shown us that the best of Christians make mistakes, sin and *still* call themselves Believers and **we just *refuse* to be a hypocrite like them**. Maybe in their eyes we are a bunch of looney tunes without a clue and that we are just a lot of weak hypocrites trying to justify our existence on this earth.

Well it goes without saying that this frame of mind or way of thinking will cause a person to more than likely never come to know God through salvation and have a personal relationship with Him nor receive *His forgiveness.* Because of the unbeliever's pride and arrogance which they hide behind, we know that pride comes before the fall (Proverbs 18:12). **Who then is the true hypocrite**, *those who are in church seeking to know God and His Righteousness knowing that their mistakes and sins are forgiven or rather those who refuse to even seek forgiveness where it can be found and deceives themselves that they can 'save' themselves.* They will never come to the point where they have it all together to handle what God conquered in order to totally deliver themselves from various vices, sin, total destruction and eternal death. They simply have not realized that they do not have the power or ability (the grace) to do so.

And as for the people you see as missing the mark and still in the "church" or "family of God" many of them have come to the realization that they cannot do anything without a Savior and Lord (John 15:5) and **they know they may continue to make mistakes and sin but they are covered and protected in the midst of it all.**

When they miss it they already know that they can sincerely ask for forgiveness and be forgiven then repent and come back into that high place with Him. They already know that when He died for them He not only took their sin but He took death, sickness, poverty, torment, grief and shame and gave them eternal life, health, wealth, a peace of mind, purpose, protection and victory in every area of their lives. **They already know that just one Word from Him has the ability to change their lives forever.** Sounds crazy? Well, we serve a tremendous and awesome God who does extraordinary things that are called *supernatural miracles* and He will do one anywhere or anytime to protect and/or restore what belongs to Him. Having a repentant heart is one sure way to release a miracle from God (See Chapter 7, Section Three under A Brief History… of the King of kings).

Truth is the only thing that sets people free. When we have wisdom, knowledge, understanding and revelation of a thing, we can discern what is right from what is wrong and have the option to base our decisions on the truth. But those who cannot discern what is right from wrong, their eyes will not be opened spiritually until they come to the knowledge of the "Truth" nor will they have an opportunity to repent if they never first, *just come as they are* (John 16:13; John 17:17) .

Matthew 3:8-9 says, "Bring forth fruit that is consistent with repentance [let your lives prove your change of heart]; and do not presume to say to yourselves, We have Abraham for our forefather; for I tell you, God is able to raise up descendants for Abraham from these stones!" In other words this is not a time to be proud and think you have all of the answers or have it all together, but it is a time to simply humble yourself, <u>repent</u>

and come into right standing and be seated in glory with Him (Ephesians 2:6).

See Mark 1:15 NLT and NKJV because time is shorter than you think!

> At last the time has come! He announced. The Kingdom of God is near! Turn from your sins and believe this Good News!
>
> The time is fulfilled, and the Kingdom of God is at hand. Repent, and believe in the Gospel.

GENERAL INFORMATION REGARDING A DIVORCE:

Most people really need time to heal after a divorce. Remember God knows all things so if he or she chooses to go directly to Him and not another source, He is able to direct them through His Word and by His Spirit with whatever is concerning them and prepare and keep them "daily" until they fully recover.

However, speaking to a pastor, a rabbi, a Christian counselor, a good friend or relative who can be trusted, should allow the healing to come forth in a more natural time frame and hopefully with more balance and understanding. Getting things out into the open with the right people is a great form of healing instead of burying them and carrying around regrets and fears. For many men this may take longer because as a rule they prefer not to be in touch with their emotions. Therefore, they won't be as open to discuss this painful and private part of their lives. There are resources out there where either party can study on their own for clarity and understanding that will enable them to move forward in a decent time frame.

Divorce is the same as suffering any loss and sometimes it could feel worse than a death in the family (at least you know where they are). Grief and pain are natural after a separation and/or divorce as long as you are able to process through the grieving stages and allow yourself and your children to heal. The amount of time will vary for each person and household, however, it should not go for an extended time such as two years and beyond without professional assistance. This will be even more harmful because you run the risk of opening doors for oppression from demonic spirits such as prolong depression, suicidal thoughts, indulging in comfort foods which can cause obesity, diseases and poor health, withdrawing and many other conditions and/or issues that are destructive. Recognize that Jesus through the power of His Blood and with the help of the Holy Spirit nothing is too hard to overcome.

At the time of this writing it was estimated that it takes a woman seven point three (7.3) years to usually recover financially and about the same amount of time to recover spiritually. This of course depends on the woman and her relationship with the Lord. God can do a quick work as we cooperate with the Holy Spirit.

SIMPLIFYING THE DIVORCE PROCESS ONLY HELPED TO INCREASE THE NUMBER OF DIVORCES:

Forms are used to simplify and speed up the process of divorce but they cannot stop the emotional attachment of trauma, grief, rejection, hurt, confusion or any other type of personal feelings or emotions attached to a divorce. The simplicity of these forms helps to encourage divorce because it makes the process on paper much easier in comparison to prior years. *Marriage is handled in the secular world as if it were just another partnership being dissolved, when in fact the Scriptures make it the most sacred relationship of life and because of the spiritual tie there is nothing simple about it.*

As one can see below it is a cut and dry process usually handled by an attorney, paralegal or because it has been made so simple you can handle your own divorce in pro per (represent yourself in court) if you choose to do so. Many couples do not know the history of marriage, what a covenant means in

relationship to marriage or any of the sacred or spiritual attachments that come with marriage. They receive the short definition as described in The New Webster's Dictionary about divorce and believe that it is just a formality that will give them their freedom from their current marital status and circumstances.

The New Webster's Dictionary definition regarding Divorce:[5]

> A legal dissolution of marriage to end a marriage between two people legally by divorce.
>
> To repudiate (refuse to have anything to do with) one's wife or husband by divorce.

An example of what a Dissolution form may ask a married couple considering the *grounds* for a divorce in our society is as follows:

Dissolution of the marriage based on:

Irreconcilable differences; or Incurable insanity

Nullity of void marriage based on:

Incestuous marriage; or Bigamous marriage

Nullity of voidable marriage based on:

(1) Respondent's age at time of marriage

(2) Prior existing marriage

(3) Unsound mind

(4) Fraud

(5) Force

(6) Physical incapacity

Custody arrangements of the children are dependant upon the paper work that is filed. There are different types of custody arrangements that are used which are no longer an option when filing "Irreconcilable Differences," a No-Fault Divorce as you will discover as you read on. Depending upon the papers filed these are the custody choices: "*Sole Custody; Joint Custody; Joint Legal Custody, Joint Physical Custody and Split Custody.* **Sole Custody** -the child lives with one parent, who has sole responsibility for physically raising the child and making all decisions regarding his or her upbringing. **Joint Custody** –Legal and physical: **Joint Legal Custody** –the children live primarily with one parent, but both share jointly in decisions about their children's education, religious training, and general upbringing. **Joint physical custody** –the children live with both parents, dividing time more-or-less equally between the two households. **Split Custody** –the children are divided between the two parents; the mother usually takes the girls and the father, the boys. This form of custody often has harmful effects on sibling bonds and should be entered into cautiously. For many people going into court for custody is too risky, too expensive, too time consuming" and too painful [7] paraphrased.

In a number of cases a mediator in the system would interview the family and give their advice as to the placement of the children. And still in other cases one of the family members would kidnap the child most of the time for a few days but it could extend to months or years.

Many years ago it was neither a quick nor easy process to acquire a divorce. One had to hire an attorney and have specific reasons usually based on biblical grounds and proven with documentation and sometimes photos from investigators before a divorce was granted. If it were not granted the parties "had to stay married" but of course they could choose to live a part and I'm sure they could appeal the court's decision. However, this was costly and exhausting for the family but at the same time it caused people to look at their actions, re-evaluate their situation and forgiveness could become an option but in any event they had *time* to seek proper help because a judgment in the case was not issued in s*ix months or less* (except for special arrangements such as going to Reno for a quick divorce or something on that order).

This encouraged many couples to hang in there and wait it out as they continued to work things out if at all possible. Many could attest that it was for the best in the long run as I am sure just as many could say it was wrong and prevented them from going forward with their lives. Because they were not free to remarry some lived in adulterous arrangements for years or just remained alone. Each case would be different because when dealing with marriage and divorce issues we are dealing with human beings and nothing is cut and dry about decisions regarding one's emotions, future and happiness. God designed marriage with permanence in mind. At the same time in all of His infinite wisdom He knew that because people were different, with different motives and heart issues that a provision would be necessary that would give some the choice to dissolve their marital union.

In earlier times the majority of people did not have a mindset for "instant" gratification but "longevity" was the more popular thing and most marriages lasted much longer than they do today and everyone in those marriages **were not** miserable and "just putting up with each other." I witnessed first hand with my parent's marriage the love and devotion they had for each other for fifty-eight years until the passing of my father. They had ten children together, myself being the first born, which kept them young and active and in constant communication with each other on a daily basis. The overall experience of growing up in a large family as I remember translated into "fun." Sure there were some difficult times too, especially with my Dad being the only provider in the house; my Mother was a stay-at-home Mom, but the love within the family and the family traditions out weighed them all!

NO-FAULT DIVORCE LAWS AND HOW THEY ARE NOT OF GOD:

In regards to the illustration of forms shown above, "Irreconcilable Differences" is given as one of the options for divorce which meant a No-Fault Divorce making it extremely easy to file and be successful at divorcing your spouse and not assuming biblical responsibility for one's actions that brought the marriage to this point or the responsibility of division of care for children or distribution of property and so forth.

According to *"The Marriage and Family Experience" by Strong and DeVault,* they have listed the definition and arrangements that are considered and followed when one cites *Irreconcilable Differences* as cause for their divorce. [7] (Paraphrased):

> Since 1970, beginning with California's Family Law Act, other states have adopted no-fault (while still providing for "legal grounds" divorce when applicable). This changed four basic aspects of divorce.
>
> **No-fault divorce is the legal dissolution of a marriage in which guilt or fault by one or both spouses does not have to be established…**
>
> Change number **(1)** It has eliminated the idea of fault-based grounds. **Under no-fault divorce, no one is accused of desertion, cruelty, adultery, impotence, crime, insanity, or a host of other melodramatic acts or omissions. Neither party is found guilty of anything**; rather, the **marriage is declared unworkable** and is dissolved. Husband and wife must agree that they have irreconcilable differences (which they need not describe) and that they believe it is impossible for their marriage to survive the differences.
>
> Change number **(2)** No-fault divorce **eliminates the legal adversary process**. Divorces settled out of court in many cases.
>
> Change number **(3)** The bases for no-fault settlements are equity, equality, and need

rather than fault or gender. **It is no longer assumed that women need to be supported by men.** Community property is to be divided equally, reflecting the belief that marriage is a partnership with each partner's contributing equally, if differently. The criteria for **child custody are based on a sex-neutral standard of the "best interests of the child" rather than on a preference for the mother.**

Change number **(4)** No-fault divorce laws are intended to promote gender equality by redefining the responsibilities of husbands and wives. **The husband is no longer considered head of the household but is an equal partner with his wife. The husband is no longer solely responsible for support, nor is the wife solely responsible for the care of the children.** The limitations placed on alimony assume that a woman will work.

As you can see these changes are in direct opposition to what God has stated regarding a man being the head of the household (Ephesians 5:23); people having certain grounds for divorce such as adultery; and other biblical mandates are ignored by man's policies instead of as in the past using God's Word as the standard. **But the most serious violation of the Word of God is the way women and fatherless children are treated within this system. The system pretty much relieves the former husband of nearly all of his responsibilities as a father unless he has been given custody of the children.** Unless he is an individual that will step up and do what is right towards his children otherwise the law will not automatically enforce his responsibilities. In lieu of this, most women find it difficult to recover from or enforce the former spouse to meet his responsibilities. In addition, most will find that her financial resources are not sufficient for attorney fees which would enable her to receive immediate relief for her household.

God warns those (including those in a system that produces policies and acts such as the Family Law Act) against committing evil acts in taking advantage of the helpless. God is not only opposing what is wrong, but He is also vigorously upholding what is right, the gracious protection of those who cannot protect themselves.

It says in Exodus 22:22-24,

You shall not afflict any widow or fatherless child. If you afflict them in any way and they cry at all to Me, I will surely hear their cry…

God said He is "a father of the fatherless and a judge and protector of the widows…" (Psalm 68:5). A single Mother also falls in the category of a widow because she is no longer with her husband. **Man did not create marriage, it does not belong to him, he cannot change the rules or laws of its existence or how it is dissolved. This new system systematically impoverishes divorced women and the children**. Following a divorce with the changes set forth in conjunction with *Irreconcilable Differences,* women are primarily responsible for both child rearing and the finances to support the family.

This puts the woman at a greater risk for poverty or a dramatic downward turn in her economic condition which may take her years to recover. This arrangement that has *made it so easy to get a divorce* puts most single-parent families in long periods of financial hardship. The no-fault divorce's gender-neutral rules incorporated to make men and women *"equal"* (another thing God never said) places older women who may have been out of the work force for years to rear a family most of the time with outdated experience, out of touch with updated skills that are needed to secure work that would offer decent and workable wages.

The mother with young school age children is at a great economic disadvantage. Not to mention many women are choosing to home school and work from home for the protection of their children and the ability to increase their finances are also in jeopardy. As government grows it tries to remove home schooling because it removes funds from the public school system and children from being raised with the State's agenda which includes all kinds of views and doctrines that are far removed from biblical principles. Home schooling or private schools puts the control of what a child will learn back into the hands of the parent where it belongs. Furthermore, it will help the single Mother cut cost and the stress of looking for quality child care.

In regard to thinking of and/or considering a divorce, at low points in any given relationship because of stress or pressure on the marital couple, separation and divorce could cross anyone's mind but it does not have to become a reality if the couple have first made up their minds *that a divorce was not an option* and truly look at all the other options and seek the proper help, they may be surprised and relieved years later when they are still together and everything made a one hundred and eighty degree turn in their favor.

People in the past were more selective about their mates and even welcomed in many cases the advice from their parents and other people they respected such as family members, people in their place of worship or community. People married at an earlier age than they do now which prevented a lot of different partners, risk of contracting a disease or being hurt repeatedly until marriage no longer seemed or was desired to be an option for them. People also came into their marital relationship with far less baggage because they avoided so much negativity by getting married in their early to mid-twenties.

KEY MEASURES GIVEN *BEFORE* MARRIAGE TO *PREVENT* A DIVORCE:

If your future spouse has a real problem with more than two of the items listed it may be a "**red flag**" for you to stop and pay attention to what is really being said or not said.

- **For additional information, in this Chapter under *Remarriage* see the question, Is There a Right Time to Remarry?**
- *Introduce perspective marriage partners* to parents, family, close friends and most of all pray about the relationship and make sure you have a complete peace in your heart before going any further.
- *Both agree that God will be a part of your life*, discuss how you plan to celebrate and worship Him in your home and community. Discuss how you plan to bring your future children up in the Word of God so nothing will be a surprise or assumed once you come to that place in your life.
- A marriage is between three (3) persons the husband, the wife and the Person of the Holy Spirit who will watch over the relationship and help them sustain it in a loving and beautiful way.
- *Be transparent* with each other in discussions about things that are important to you: marriage, children, where to live, in-laws, career, sharing responsibility in the home, discussing money issues and spending plans, whether or not single friends will remain in your life and you will continue to go out with them leaving your spouse at home? All these things and much more serve as a point of reference to build your marriage on.
- Many times people *think they can change the other person* by convincing them or influencing them or showing them what a great catch they are or that the two of them have something special and it could be better if only they would… **Red Flag, time out,** Please realize that you cannot change another person's heart and God will not allow you to override their free will that would be in violation of His Word and not even He will violate His Word in order to *make* anyone

do anything against their free will. What will possibly happen after years of wasted time is that you finally realize that you cannot change anyone; you cannot get "someone saved." These things are reserved for God through what His Son did and the power of the Holy Spirit to draw them and then change them as they follow His leading. For example, if you are living your life for God and they have a carnal mind of flesh [which is sense and reason without the Holy Spirit] and you are expecting them to act, believe and think like you it is not going to happen. "So then they that are in the flesh cannot please God. But ye are not in the flesh, but in the Spirit…the Spirit is life because of righteousness" (Romans 8:5-10 KJV). Therefore, you are unequally yoked and unless they *desire* to change you need to move on.

- *Guard and protect what you see, hear and speak as to anything* that will go into your heart and mind and then grow. If it is junk that you are feeding on, that junk will grow inside of you and you will have a type of character that will be unbecoming to your spouse especially if you do this after you are married. For instance, if you suddenly take an interest in pornography on the internet, which may seem harmless in the beginning but the visual, will soon turn into a desire to touch. This could change you and lead you astray into adultery, sexual abuse with other people whether younger or older, bisexuality or homosexuality and perverted sex. **Guard what you are watching and hearing or you will allow influence and access to your soul (mind, will and emotions) from demonic spirits you really do not want to have to deal with.**
- When dating *avoid premarital sex* even if you are engaged to marry the person. It is great

wisdom that you also avoid living with the person as if you are married. If you have something that is beautiful and especially someone that you feel God sent into your life then why open a door for demonic oppression to have access in your relationship. **A premarital relationship that carries over into a marital relationship can affect your marriage later with "trust" issues that will have to be worked through when this could have been avoided during the courtship.** Couples should develop together in this area after marriage making it something special between the two of them without a lot of excess baggage from their past. And without giving space for Satan to play with their minds about them having premarital sex and what is to stop them from being with someone else once they marry (if they get married).Virginity is still the best way to be and the Bible supports this for more reasons than just being pure. But even if divorced or having had a number of earlier partners, with a period of being abstinent it is giving honor to God to wait until marriage and it is like being a virgin in His eyes once again.

- Freddie M. Flewelen wrote about abstinence before marriage: *"Experience shows that sexual intercourse, instead of deepening and enriching friendship, is more likely to destroy the relationship. They are not 'giving themselves to each other,' but are cheating themselves of the 'essence' of sexual love.* They are getting only a fragment and the real love is never achieved. There is no emotional security in such an arrangement. Emotional security which goes with marriage is one of its most important features, and that this cannot be found outside of marriage. The concealment, secrecy, deceit, sneaking, condoms and birth control pills deprive the relationship of the joy that it might have had under more favorable conditions. But suppose there is a deep and permanent feeling, what is going to happen to it? Disillusionment and cynicism are likely to follow, and then the personality deteriorates. In short, one of the handicaps of premarital coitus is that 'there is no future in it.' **Some psychologists** would say that the human body is compelled to indulge in the sexual act between man and woman. Be not deceived, sex is a mental attitude. There is little, if any, organic motivation of sexual cohabitation between male and female. This frustrating sickness is the source of hundreds of forms of diverted sexual involvement with animals, machines, homosexuality, lesbianism and even murder are applied to sex in the name of *natural love*. **Behavioral scientists would say**, that a person who refrains from sexual intercourse for the present, as a means of preparing for something better in the future, is deprived of a physical sex outlet, but not frustrated and has strengthened self-esteem. This self-esteem has been damaged and may resort to various adventures in order to reassure themselves that they are normal and sexually appealing. **THE FACT IS** that the **Word of God** and **Christian psychologists' views are contrary to humanistic philosophy**. We stand firm that self-control until marriage not only is no insufferable hardship, but avoids many difficulties at the time and makes life more worthwhile when you comply with God's Word. One must be naive indeed to believe that other things being equal, the abandonment of virginity improves one's chances of successful marriage. Often people have feelings of guilt which interferes with subsequent marriage. More than likely they think 'I've gone so far now that I can't turn back.' So each adventure increases the chance of you contracting a disease or an unexpected pregnancy...One moment you thought it was real love and the next moment you saw it for what it really was. It is then that these two realize that this stolen pleasure has brought them no lasting enjoyment but guilt, shame and sinfulness of sin. Ephesians 5:3 says, this should not be found among the saints (God's consecrated people). If it is in your life or has been, know this that everyday is new in Christ and He is merciful and just, if your desire is to change then seek His forgiveness and repent, renew your mind in the Word and be restored in Jesus' name."

KEY MEASURES TO *PREVENT* A DIVORCE *DURING* MARRIAGE:

- For additional information, **see Chapter One under Key Tips for a** *Successful* **Marriage God's way.**
- **These basics truths should be a part of your marriage at all times**: Each spouse develops a personal relationship with God, pray together, exercise integrity, listen, have patience with each other, forgive, repent, and speak well of and enjoy each other's company, be committed to one another, set marital goals together and have a vision for your future together as a loving couple.
- Dr. Tim Clinton and Dr. John Trent of the American Association of Christian Counselors (AACC) had this to say about making a marital relationship healthy and secure: That it requires a commitment and an investment of time and effort to put meaningful work into one's

marriage relationship before there is a serious problem. Realize it is an ongoing process, a dedicated way of living in marriage that nurtures the relationship, making it progressively stronger and more intimate. Even if a marriage is already troubled, the principles of prevention can still bring the marriage back to a place of wellness [9] (paraphrased).

- **Wives with emotionally detached husbands,** a few quick pointers and if followed through will probably make a huge difference and improve communication. If the wife desires to: engage in emotional conversations -things that involve life and causes one to get involved with their own feelings; buy books or CD's, etc. to share for growth as a couple or for the family; seek opportunities for quality time if the both of you do not have any date time or have made your time together for conversation a priority, then she needs to make her desires known to her husband. If it seems that you are the one making all the effort to converse and **your husband's response is** resistance, excuses, avoidance, his mind is somewhere else and he is totally distracted with things such as work, sports, sleep, freedom and flexibility in order to hide in his "man cave" a place where he can hide out either emotionally or physically or both and not be bothered, nagged, pushed into a corner, pinned in, forced to read the materials you purchased or listen to audios, and not get involved with the kids or extended relatives as much as he should then always remember to pray about it first and simply ask for wisdom and guidance. Pointers: **Do not participate in the routine, the pattern of going back and forth when he decides to emotionally shut down.** You as the wife should not need to nag, force, plot, manipulate, have a fit, or talk on the phone with twenty other people about. **See it from a different perspective.** He belongs or should belong to God, see him as God sees him. This man is the head of your family, the father of your children, someone you are to honor and respect. Once that is in perspective and you make a conscious decision to do things God's way, then "let him have it!" (I'm just kidding). Instead of falling into the same routine of nagging and so forth, *realize he is wired differently from you* and he cannot take a lot of the emotions, the high pitch voice or yelling, or negative body language such as bad facial expressions or throwing dishes and so on because **it all adds up in his mind to disrespect.** First of all **you are his help meet and should be praying for him daily in your daily prayers, wives are called to do this (Proverbs 31:15).** Now you are **ready to confront** the issues, approach him when he is rested and in an atmosphere where it is calm (be creative, send the kids outside or give them something to do so your conversation won't be interrupted, go for a walk together, prepare a nice lunch, do something that relaxes the both of you so you can talk). **Speak in a calm and clear voice tone, make your point, say what you really mean and don't always expect him to read your mind, or read between the lines but be clear with your request.** You can even come with paper and pencil to leave a note with him so he won't have to remember it all and you keep a copy so you will remember what you requested of him. Next both of you agree on a time in which the list should be carried out or responded to. Try not to speak to him as if he is a child; don't make him feel incompetent by telling him step by step how to solve things. **Try not to interrupt him if he is talking, with your quick ready made answer, it** will only cause him to withdraw even more. Just try to listen and allow him the freedom to open up and answer in his timing. **Do not rush him while he is speaking; be patient!** Also do not bother to judge, criticize, condemn or do any name calling if you expect an answer. **Once you are done leave it alone, he will need time for his brain to take it all in and process it.** If he does not get back to you with an answer or follow through within the **time frame you both discussed** that you would like something done, one or two reminders will be o.k. *if* you are consistent with a calm voice, being clear and to the point. **After that leave it in God's hands and the Lord will deal with his heart**. You continue to do your part and have the right attitude towards him. If this is a serious situation, you can also encourage **Christian counseling** to help the two of you get back on track with a fresh start. Also there are ministries that have **prayer lines** that you can leave a request with if you do not wish to leave your request with your home church. **Avoid calling people** just to gossip about your husband, this is totally disrespectful to him and to your marriage. If you are calling someone you can trust to vent because you need to do this, make sure that, that person has your best interest at heart and enough integrity that they will keep your business to themselves. **To sum it all up, be a Godly Proverbs 31 woman it will make all the difference in your marriage. See Proverbs 31:10-31 and the selective scriptures below:**

v. 11 The heart of *her husband trusts in her confidently and relies on and believes in her securely, so that he has no lack of* [honest] *gain or need of* [dishonest] *spoil.*

v. 12 *She comforts, encourages, and does him only good* as long as there is life within her.

v. 15 She rises while it is yet night and gets [spiritual] food for her household and assigns her maids their tasks. *(She rises early to pray).*

v. 26 *She opens her mouth in skillful and godly Wisdom,* and on her tongue is the law of kindness [giving counsel and instruction]. *(Mothers are teachers in the home).*

v. 28 Her children rise up and call her blessed; and *her husband boasts of and praises her.*

v. 30 Charm and grace are deceptive, and beauty is vain [because it is not lasting], but *a woman who reverently and worshipfully fears the Lord, she shall be praised!* (This is the beginning of Wisdom and is put forth as the true foundation for a life which is valued by God and her husband as 'far above rubies or pearls,' author's addition).

- If things become unbearable and one or both want out even though this is **not a very good option, separation or legal separation may be necessary for some married couples.** Separation is when spouses are living apart, yet still legally married to one another. A legal separation helps to protect your credit and assets when separated; it may offer a temporary safety net by declaring what is yours apart from your spouse or if they make a purchase you may not be totally liable (consult an attorney or paralegal for details). Ways this could help the couple in distress **(1)** For some it could serve as a means to get the attention of the spouse who is disregarding the marital vows and used as a wake up call. A time to reflect, think before making rash decisions about the future of their marriage and hopefully come to sound godly terms in a friendly manner. **(2)** An agreement about the purpose of the separation is made and with a mutual time frame set to discuss what is going to be done so they can make plans to either continue in the marriage or dissolve it. Precautions should be taken before one or both of them become emotionally and/or sexually involved with other people which then only brings other issues to the table or someone drifts or is lured off and nothing of significance is accomplished from the separation. **(3)** Separations can be dangerous to the marriage and guidelines need to be followed if the purpose is to reconcile. Remember that reconciliation requires that both parties make an effort to reconcile; it cannot happen unless both are in agreement and committed to the relationship. If they both have a relationship with God that will work greatly to strengthen their position and get them back on track, locate where they got off and build from there.

- **As some would say be aware and understand that Divorce is a permanent solution to what may be a temporary problem.** One day you **may feel like** you are no longer in love with your spouse because things happen in life and people grow weary, grow a part or negative feelings set in. But **you should never base anything especially this important just on your feelings because feelings change, feelings can fool you and feelings can be manipulated by the adversary. If you change your perspective and mind and behavior your feelings will follow the lead.** Base what you do on the truth of God's Word, doing what He says to save a situation before just doing what would finalize something that really could have been saved. Even if the facts dictate divorce God's truth can change this fact with forgiveness and considering the consequences of wrong decisions. This may help some arrive at another solution if in deed it is a problem that can truly be worked out in order to make a decision that would give you the victory in the area(s) needed and by you continually working on the problem until it is no longer a threat to your marriage and family. One thing to **keep in mind that is very important is that children even though they can adjust, why put them through the ordeal if the two of you can work it out** with the help of God's Word, a counselor, making adjustments and changes that are for the better. Otherwise when children are involved, the problem is now compounded with them possibly not doing as well in school; being sick more often for attention; in fear of losing their parents or the one parent they are with and being left totally alone; being isolated or withdrawn; or never having any faith in any relationships anymore. **These are problems that may or may not arise, it will depend on how rooted the family is in the Word of God and how much communication and love is shown in the family and so forth. Children should know that even though Mom and Dad's marriage may be in trouble, each one of them can still say,** *I can call on my heavenly Father to make sure that I stay on a path that will keep me sound, safe and prosperous for my life while I pray for my parents and siblings.* If the family members have a personal relationship with Jesus even though the parents may divorce, Jesus has sent the Comforter to heal, guide and restore but most of all, He will be there for them and be the Friend that they will need in this hour.

CHAPTER 3

WHAT IS THE BIBLICAL DEFINITION FOR FAMILY?
(ALSO HEALTHY AND STRONG QUALITIES IT *SHOULD* POSSESS)

"In the beginning [before all time] was the Word (Christ), and the Word was with God, and the Word was God Himself. He was present originally with God. *All things were made and came into existence through Him*; and without Him was not even one thing made that has come into being" (John 1:1-3).

In Genesis 2:7 it tells us that **God created the first family** by forming mankind from the dust of the ground and breathing into his nostrils the breath or Spirit of life. And thereafter this new creation which consisted of a "male and female" became a living being (Genesis 1:26; Colossians 3:10). *God then performed surgery, removing a part (the rib) from the male body which was already equipped with the female at the time He created the male but she needed to be formed which took place when God "built-up and made" the female for Adam from the part of his body that was removed.* This female partner was to be with him for the rest of his life and **this was the beginning of the family** as we know it on earth. They were a Child-Free Family until the birth of their son.

The Bible verifies this in Genesis 2:21-23,

> And the Lord God caused a deep sleep to fall upon Adam; and while he slept, He took one of his ribs or a part of his side and closed up the place [place with] flesh. And the rib or part of his side which the Lord God had taken from the man He **built up and made into a woman, and He brought her to the man.** Then Adam said, This [creature] is now bone of my bones and flesh of my flesh; she shall be called **wo-man**, because she was taken out of a **man.**

He who created them from the beginning made them male and female to be joined in marriage. And God said, "For this reason a man shall leave his father and mother and shall be united firmly (joined inseparably) to his wife, and the two shall become one flesh?" (Matthew 19:4-5). **This is the strongest union in the world because it is in covenant with Almighty God. The family/mishpochah (Hebrew) is the strongest institution built by God.** Without the marital tie the family circle, family institution and parental love and care would have been altogether unknown.

Proverbs 24:3-4 says,

> Through skillful and godly Wisdom is a house (a life, a home, a family) built, and by understanding it is established [on a sound and good foundation], And by knowledge shall its chambers [of every area] be filled with all precious and pleasant riches.

This scripture clearly outlines that the intent God had for the family was for them to walk and **live with godly wisdom** for their lives and families. He said **the family is established on a sound and good foundation which is the Word of God.** Knowledge (divine revelation) will cause their home to increase and be filled with precious and pleasant riches. Rich in love, rich in God's presence, rich in good relationships, rich in the anointing, rich in health, rich in wealth, rich in good strategies for business, rich in success, *and rich in every area of its chambers (home) which shall be filled with precious and pleasant riches.*

"**Joy is a distinctive quality of biblical faith in the Old and New Testaments.** Joy was intended to be shared whether in worship or in family togetherness. Because of the relationship with Christ the Christian family amplifies joy which is a fruit and characteristic of the Holy Spirit who was given to guide the family. Therefore, *uniting the family in Christian faith results in joy for the family* (Acts 16:34). Happy experiences can be shared in joy. *Joy is a gift from God.* Joyful experiences shared by the family create memories that continue through life. Families need to guard against letting the difficulties of daily tasks rob them of time to plan enjoyable experiences together," [3] (John 15:13-15).

WHO IS SANCTIONED AS A FAMILY AND WHO IS NOT?

The family relationship *that was instituted by God* is the very foundation of all human societies as well as it occupies a prominent place throughout scripture. The germ or source and representative of every fellowship known to mankind came through a family.

"When the atmosphere of the home and the parent's attitude is good plus the marriage is secure, **then that family is a core or base** *where a person's character is formed, integrity is born, values we live by are made clear, goals are set and attitudes are formed that last a life time"* as so well stated by Dr. Billy Graham *(paraphrased).*

A body of people living together such as roommates, friends, fraternities, sororities, college dormitories, sport teams, convents, military personnel, firemen, gangs and similar groups may refer to themselves *"as a family"* and they may even have some of the same functions, traditions, develop soul ties and become best of friends really caring and loving one another but **they are not what God has sanctioned as a "family."** *A family does not exist merely to fill a void of loneliness, share expenses, experiences, work or even house rules.* If this is not enough proof know that even people in the world (non-Believers) know the difference. For instance, if someone became ill and a family member had to provide family history, or insurance documents, or allowed in the intensive care unit of a hospital what is the probability of a close friend having this information or even allowed in? Even if they had the information what is the possibility of them having the authority to make decisions about a non-family member's wellbeing? It is almost nil because one of the first questions that is asked is are you a member of the family, are you related?

What God sanctions or approves of as a family in addition to what He refers to as the True Family is designed to train up and produce people with godly character to function a certain way in the Kingdom of God within their given society. They are to bring into place a unit of individuals with like thinking and shared godly morals. In addition, each family member is anointed by God to cause positive change that will affect generations to come.

I might add that even though they may have disagreements among themselves basically no one else from outside of that family unit will have the same privilege.

Core values help discover each person's sense of self and to develop his identity. It is the family that is considered to be the essential **building block of any nation**; one reason being is that the family is focused on creating benefits for the next generation. **Therefore, a community is then formed from strong families thus growing into a city which then produces a society of people.**

Genesis 14:14 NIV [3] is an example of a **Biblical household during ancient times**:

> The household in biblical times included the primary family, servants and other family members and persons entrusted with various

responsibilities for maintaining the household. Thus, in the household of Abram, children of servants were educated as soldiers from their youth. *Education is a basic task of the household.* The wisdom literature of the Old Testament is particularly focused in the nurture and education of children in the household.

The family being the foundation and one of the components or institutions that help form and shape society is currently being attacked on all sides along with other institutions that help shape our society. These other institutions include the church or the Kingdom of God; the educational system; the political system; the economic or financial system; the business industry; and the arts and entertainment industries. They have all been attacked because we live in a fallen society due to the sin that entered in after the fall of mankind and has now been magnified because of the time and season we are currently living in (the End of Days or the Last Days; not the end of the world but the end of an age as we know it, 2 Timothy 3:1-9 and Matthew 24:1-44). Because of this the family, like all of the other components that shape our society are dysfunctional and are heavily affected.

THE FAMILY HOME IS NOT SEPARATE FROM ITS NATION:

The home is a basic unit and cannot be separated from the health of its nation. If the home goes the nation will follow. The church, or on a broader scale, the Kingdom of God is the only institution that is lifting-up the USA with prayer into a great "Awakening" (people returning to God and making Him and His ways first in their lives). As a result of these prayers from *church families* which are made up of *individual families*, these prayers will cause God to move greatly on this country's behalf and in the lives of those who believe. So even though a society has declined the Believer can still experience peace, joy, abundance, good health and on the overall be blessed in the midst of any storm that life brings. Because **the Kingdom of God expands beyond the USA because all Christians around the world are a part of the Kingdom of God** and whatever country or individual that has prayer coverage *God is no respecter of persons* and He will answer with an "Awakening" for that nation and for those individuals as well.

The Kingdom of God, which is also a type of government, is primarily made-up from family units within the Kingdom or Christendom. Like any government their role is to protect one's rights to pursue legitimate goods (in this case spiritual and natural). *The Kingdom of God will do its part for its citizens (the Believers) because it shows the most promise to do so having the Spirit of God at the forefront.* How is that? Because the Kingdom of God is located within each Born-again Believer and its attributes are righteousness, peace and joy in the Holy Spirit (Romans 14:17). Therefore, it will always strive to do what is right and what is right is the will of God. When the will of God is in effect it will change the individual, the family and the society the family dwells in.

The family is the backbone for all societies. God through His Kingdom of people "the Church" not a building or denomination, but individuals who follow Christ and pray will strengthen our nation again, help purify and restore it **by giving way to a new more productive society.** Because education is an essential component of any society a more godly and productive educational system will be produced as well. As a result godly education will produce godly citizens which will produce godly political representatives and in turn produce godly government. Also as godly judges *regain* positions in the higher courts, these actions altogether will affect the well-being of a biblical or Godly family.

Since our Lord and Savior is *about <u>Relationship</u> and not <u>religion</u>*, any family that chooses the biblical guidelines, chooses *God's way*, will have qualities that can produce successful results and cause their families to continue to prosper (be whole in every area) and to have a wonderful home in a time when most families will be totally dysfunctional and falling completely apart.

The biblical family is how God intended a family to function with definite roles and goals. If the leaders (parents) know how to relate to one another it strengthens the family. Having the understanding and knowledge of how to relate in a relationship as a couple; as parents; as a parent to a child and a child to a parent; siblings to one another and to extended family members in a loving and positive way is the result of following biblical principles. (See Chapter 6, for roles and functions discussed in detail).

The biblical family should exercise many different qualities that are based on the Word of God that will literally <u>strengthen</u> them as individuals, as a married couple and as a family. The following information and list are a good start for **strengthening and recovery** and a reminder of what should be included in the biblical family structure:

Always remember to place God first, Mark 12:30 says:

> And you shall love the Lord your God out of and with your whole heart and out of and with all your soul (your life) and out of and with all your mind (with your faculty of thought and your moral understanding) and out of and with all your <u>strength</u>.

As you love God with all your strength you will be strengthened. To love God with all your <u>strength</u> is to use your possessions, wealth as well as your influence and your position in life that you were blessed with to bless others by sharing and helping someone else. In doing so you are honoring and showing love towards God. Your hands are His hands on this earth. (One interpretation of hands is that it represents the work of the ministry which is not limited to the four walls of a church building but is for every Believer).

Next is the *Love* that we should express towards one another. As seen in the Love Chapter's teaching found in I Corinthians 13:4-8 as follows:

Love endures long and is patient and kind; **love never is** envious nor boils over with jealousy, is not boastful or vainglorious, does not display itself haughtily. It is not conceited (arrogant and inflated with pride); it is not rude (unmannerly) and does not act unbecomingly. Love (God's love in us) does not insist on its own rights or its own way, for it is not self-seeking; it is not touchy or fretful or resentful; it takes no account of the evil done to it [it pays no attention to a suffered wrong]. It does not rejoice at injustice and unrighteousness, but **rejoices when right and truth prevail**. Love bears up under anything and everything that comes, is ever **ready to believe the best of every person**, its hopes are fadeless under all circumstances, and it endures everything [without weakening]. Love never fails [never fades out or becomes obsolete or comes to an end]…

The following qualities are components listed by many Christian authors that are necessary to have for a strong marriage:

Commitment; Communication; Acceptance; Adjustment; Respect; Responsibility; Empathy; Encouragement; Forgiveness; Sacrifice, Quality time and a Sense of Humor.

These components are necessary to have a healthy and balanced marriage in your household and when both partners have these qualities first for their marriage and second for their family they will have the beginning stages of a healthy family structure.

I have elaborated on a few of the qualities listed above from *Marriage & Family, A Christian Journal of the American Association of Christian Counselors* and what it briefly says about commitment, communication and respect:

Commitment *– is an unconditional promise, a pledge to a permanent union.* It is not a contract that requires reciprocal action by the partner but a covenant enacted without reservation. ***A prenuptial agreement has no place in a Christian union.***

Communication *–* is shared meaning, occurring both verbally and non-verbally. *Only through open communication can effective decision-making, problem solving and conflict resolution occur.*

Listening attentively facilitates understanding and earns the privilege to speak. Talking is more than the words uttered – the message greatly influenced by the tone and style of expression.

Respect *–* is to hold in high regard or esteem. It does not require agreement with or acceptance of opinion. **It does demand courtesy and politeness at all times** (Ephesians 5:33 and I Peter 3:7).

These are just a few of the instructions found in the Word of God to benefit a household. *The faithful application of biblical principles can bring new life and vitality to any household* **no matter what stage the family is in, whether it be a household in strife, full of rebellious children, an unfaithful spouse and so forth.** When we yield to build a healthy and strong marriage based on God's principles and commands we acquire the wisdom of God to carry it through and allow it to be the example for the family unit that it needs to be.

Building on a Solid Foundation, Luke 6:46-49:

So why do you call Me 'Lord,' when you won't obey Me? I will show you what it's like when someone comes to Me, listens to My teaching and then obeys Me. **It is like a person who builds a house on a strong foundation laid upon the underlying rock.** When the floodwaters rise and break against the house, it stands firm because it is well built. **But anyone who listens and doesn't obey is like a person who builds a house without a foundation. When the floods sweep down against that house it will crumble into a heap of ruins.**

QUALITIES AND ATTRIBUTES FOUND IN A HEALTHY AND STRONG FAMILY:

1. A relationship with God which starts with salvation
2. God's order within your home
3. Respect for one another
4. An understanding of delegated authority
5. Our trust in God makes it easier to trust each other
6. Cohesiveness – having a closeness within the family unit, quality time
7. Adaptability – to be able to make changes and be flexible
8. Communication skills
9. Empathy – think and feel as the other person; new perspective
10. Commitment - integrity, soundness, honesty and keeping your word
11. Creative use of Conflict -searching your heart and motive before confronting
12. Affirmation - affirming one another; respect and trust; asserting positively
13. Role Modeling - having good role models and examples in the home
14. Play and Leisure Time – balance in one's life and individual time is important
15. Discipline and Responsibility – maturity and strength; taking ownership

16. Self Respect - love yourself in a healthy way so you can love others. Take care of your health, appearance and do things for yourself without becoming self-centered and selfish
17. Traditions - foundations, godly beliefs passed from generation to generation
18. A Sense of Family History - roots, know your strengths and challenges
19. A willingness to be humble enough to seek and ask for help in a time of crisis
20. Extended family ties in your life
21. Godly friends outside of the family
22. An understanding of managing finances using godly principles
23. Community Involvement – involved with some aspect of your society
24. Political or Government Commitment – God requires that we pray and vote for godly leaders

The Following *Elaborates* on Some of the Listed Qualities and Attributes Found in a Healthy and Strong Family (NOT IN CONSECUTIVE ORDER WITH THE ABOVE LIST):

1. **Relationship with God** – Are members of your family including children Believers (Born-again Christians, John 3:3, 7)? In other words, from the age of accountability (somewhere around the age of twelve even though some children receive the Lord at an earlier age) have they received Jesus Christ as their Lord and Savior according to Romans 10:9? Are the parents saved and serving God in the area He called them to, which the person is equipped and anointed to serve God, whether it is as a minister, businessman or businesswoman, a homemaker, an entrepreneur, a blue collar worker, an entertainer or whatever your calling (assignment and purpose) might be? God has purposed a specific assignment for each and every person's life.

Strong biblical families encourage the spiritual development of their members preferably bringing their children up in the Word of God. The Bible says to, "train up a child in the way he should go, and when he is old he will not depart from it," (Proverbs 22:6); and "All your children shall be taught by the Lord, and great shall be the peace (wholeness) of your children," (Isaiah 54:13). Part of bringing them up in the Word of God is taking them to a good *Bible Teaching Word Church* that believes in the *Gifts of the Spirit* and receives all the promises of God. Seek God as a couple or family and pray about which house of God should be your church home (Gifts of the Spirit: I Cor.12:7-11; Eph. 4:11-12; Romans 12:6-15 and Romans 11:29).

"**Many families have their own ethical standards**" such as reverence for life, the earth, morals, setting good examples and role models for one another and their children. Godly principles will work for whoever puts them into motion. Ethical standards will give wise guidelines, hope, stability, morals and sound direction to help mold a person for the better. By having peace and understanding about many things in life, these principles can become a part of their lifestyle making it possible to live a blessed life.

However, the **"biblical principles, rules and guidelines *from the Word of God have been set in place by God to use in the home as The Standard.*"** With the benefit of *Salvation* these biblical principles, rules and guidelines from the Holy Scriptures will give each Born-again member of the family the authority, power (grace) and right to exercise the principles in the Word of God and receive the benefits to its fullest extent. Please realize that principles, morals, rules, laws, guidelines, and standards *alone without Salvation* cannot ever offer eternal life nor all that comes with having Salvation to function in the Kingdom of God while here on the earth. Our Lord and Savior has a plan for our lives (Jeremiah 29:11). His plan involves living a life of peace, joy, abundance, fullness, wholeness and victory having all the fruit of the Spirit, the gifts of the Spirit and fulfilling one's heart's desires. **God is interested in our family being whole and we will find that complete wholeness is included in our Salvation.**

Functioning with godly principles but *without Salvation* can be compared to functioning in self-righteousness which is righteousness without power and being full of self and pride. Believing that because you are doing the "right" things you are entitled to all that God has promised you, forgetting that a "price" was paid for the Righteousness that comes with Salvation. In addition to eternal life, Salvation also gives godly authority, power, favor, mercy, protection, provision, deliverance, prosperity, promises fulfilled, health, peace of mind, godly relationships and many more blessings. This cannot be earned by any person; therefore, Salvation was given as a gift to be taken by faith through the grace of God. (If you are ready to give your life to Christ please see Chapter 7, Section Three under A Prayer for Salvation).

Only then after receiving Jesus and studying His Word, learning of Him and His ways will a person not be moved by every doctrine that comes across their path. Furthermore, they will not have to be blown like a wave of the sea driven and tossed by the wind for it says, "a double minded man is unstable in all his ways," (James 1:6-8 KJV), (See Chapter 7, Section Three under A Brief History and the Wonderful Works of the King of kings).

2. Cohesiveness - Cohesion is an emotional bonding that family members have towards one another. It is more than just time together. Members feel close when they are together and not lonely and disconnected. They feel bonded but not "stuck together," but because they chose to "stick together," they have a sense of unity without a loss of individuality; and is a coalition that performs expected functions without interference. Honesty, listening, openness, verbal affection, sensitivity, supportiveness are a part of the closeness felt between family members who have healthy emotional bonds.

Also, spending time together is necessary to develop adequate communication and to build cohesion. **Family traditions require family time. Children and spouses learn they are appreciated, valued, and have self-worth when other members spend time with them.** The modeling and teaching that parents provide for their children requires shared time, as does showing support to family members by attending school events and other occasions of special significance in the lives of family members.

Time taken to play and relax with our loved ones pays off in ways that keeping work caught up or the house clean never can. When we are realistic we see that the paper work never ends and there will always be something to do in the home, but our children and our mates will never again be as they are right now. If we don't take the time now to enjoy our families, we lose an opportunity forever. *Healthy families know this and give play and leisure time high priority.* Note, if you are a family that did not have a lot of time together while the children were growing up, know that God is a God that redeems time, a God of restoration and He will give back to you and your family that which was stolen by the enemy, all you need to do is ask!

3. Adaptability – Healthy families continually change and adapt as they grow through the life cycle. They have the ability to change in response to situational and developmental stress (children becoming adolescents, a wife becoming employed, a family member becoming ill or a sudden death, love ones losing their way or backsliding, husband suddenly unemployed and so on).

There will always be changes in families that will need attention and require members to adapt. Changes which cause the family to focus or adapt can affect individual members of the family who have to participate in the adjusting to what another member is dealing with or going through if it is something that will affect the entire household. Some elements to help adapt to these changes are: (1) reading the Word of God and acting on His Word; (2) having good leadership for guidance and direction to aid with family decision making. Good leadership is having the head of the family who is listening to and obeying God and is open to receive input from other members of the family but most importantly respecting the input (godly wisdom) from their spouse.

Keeping in mind when input is expressed, a healthy family member's request and feelings are without fear and intimidation. A healthy family will allow for individual self-confidence and self-expression as contributions are made towards decisions and directions for the family.

4. Discipline and Responsibility - Is definitely a part of family structure, it helps to set limits and create the framework for desired family behavior. The Word of God says, to "Train up a child in the way he should go [and in keeping with his individual gift or bent], and when he is old he will not depart from it." To train up is to take the responsibility of training, teaching and disciplining your child in the knowledge, understanding and wisdom of God which will empower them to discern and make wise choices in life. As we know, one wrong choice can ruin years of a person's life regardless of their age.

Discipline also demonstrates the love you have for your children by taking the time to care enough to correct their ways or actions in a firm but loving way. It sets boundaries for them and gives them a sense of security. Discipline for children is done on an individual basis because each child requires different action to be taken at various times. Why? Because they are individuals, each situation is to be dealt with according to what is appropriate for that particular child. (See Chapter 5 under the Difference between Discipline and Punishment).

5. Communication Skills – Our tone of voice, body language, eye contact, silence, a touch, a hug or a gift are all forms of communication. In strong families communication usually is direct and often. They have much to share and they enjoy sharing. They trust one another and are good listeners. When family members have truly been heard – not just the words, but their feelings acknowledged, they feel and sense a respect and appreciation because of the attention and empathy of the listener.

In communicating rules for example, strong healthy families discuss rules along with the reasons for them. Rules should never be hidden or changed without acknowledgement from each family member. In our family we called rules "guidelines." We realized that the word "rules" is used a lot in schools, with sports and in different places. The word rules can be a very "negative" word and seen as rigid and will automatically shut some people down when they hear the word, therefore, to receive cooperation from the entire family, guidelines or another similar word would be a better choice.

During conflict, strong healthy families seem to have the ability to keep their communication open and to be able to stay focused on the issues rather than on the person or persons with whom they are speaking. (See the end of Chapters 1 and 2 for additional information regarding communication).

Forgiveness is one of God's major tools to keep communication lines open. Many times as we *choose* to forgive we can look and hear beyond the person or persons we are having conflict with and realize that they may be reaching out for help because they are hurting, or in some kind of bondage and/or fear that is preventing them from being able to communicate effectively or openly.

If we would just *choose to forgive*, take our focus off of the person or what was done and pray, then God would be in a position to intervene in the situation by giving us wisdom, direction, guidance, healing and miracles as needed to aid all parties involved in the conflict. When we ask for help He is faithful to answer, then we must be faithful to receive it. (For additional information on forgiveness, see Chapter 2 under Clarifying Forgiveness).

6. Commitment – When an individual is committed to his or her family, motivation is high to solve problems and to deal with conditions that threaten the family. **When families become busy and fragmented, those with high levels of commitment take the initiative to review the family's priorities and activities and make changes that will relieve the problem and/or condition that threatens the family.** The members deliberately work together to set priorities for the use of family time. Commitment involves the promotion of the growth of other family members. Family members are concerned for one another's happiness and well-being. Commitment involves working on behalf of one's family and wanting the best for each other. It is not about anyone being self-centered but a family member's feeling that he or she is a part of something larger than themselves.

If the members of your family have received their salvation, then they should be committed to the ways of God as it is written in His Word, which is a process and it entails the renewing of the mind (Romans 12:2). If they are committed to God and His ways then they will be committed and faithful in everyday life going about doing good (what is right, decent and in order), keeping their lives in tack by guarding what they watch, hear and say as much as possible and asking the Holy Spirit to help them accomplish this.

When committed they will also be led to pray for the family on a daily basis especially for those who do not know the Lord. They will be accessible to others in the family; they will strive to avoid taking anyone in the family for granted and instead will think of creative or possible ways to bless the family as a whole or individuals within it. And they won't mind examining their actions and attitudes toward other family members and are willing to make any necessary adjustments so that love can be expressed. *And last but not least, they will realize that they will reap what they have invested in their family.*

7. Affirmation, Respect and Trust – For most of us the phrase that we like best is "I love you," it can go a long ways toward soothing a hurt, drying a tear, restoring a crumbling sense of self-worth, and maintaining a feeling of satisfaction and well-being when spoken with sincerity from the heart. *Supporting others in our family, letting them know we're interested in their projects, problems, feelings and opinions and being supportive and affirmed in return is essential to family health.*

We must learn to give respect for a family member's uniqueness and differences, even if we may not necessarily understand or agree with him or her. **Criticism, ridicule, and rejection** undermine self-esteem and severely restrict individual growth. In addition, exhibiting respect for others, **a healthy family member should also insist on being respected in return.**

Children in healthy families are allowed to earn trust as deemed appropriate by their parents. Children who know they are trusted are then able to develop self- confidence and a sense of responsibility for themselves and others.

It is equally important for parents to be realistic in their promises to children and honest about their own mistakes and shortcomings. Parents are to be willing and open to ask one another for forgiveness or to be able to apologize. It is also important for children to see that their parents trust and love each other. It is also important for parents to ask their children for forgiveness when they have made a mistake or misjudged.

A loving relationship between parents breeds security in the children, and in turn fosters the ability to take risks to reach out to others, to search for their own answers, become independent, and develop a good self-image. The more children observe their elders in situations that demonstrate mutual trust, respect, and care, the more they are encouraged to incorporate these successful and satisfying behaviors into their own lives. (See Chapter 6 for additional information concerning family members).

8. Traditions – Especially those rooted in our cultural background help give us a sense of who we are as a family and as a community. Through tradition families find a link to the past and, consequently, a hope for the future.

Most successful families have someone who maintains and transmits the family story. They have traditions that help them keep alive their identity as a family. The traditions may vary greatly, from elaborate holiday celebrations to daily or weekly routines.

Blended families may benefit particularly from the creation of new traditions which can generate a feeling of closeness and provide fuel for weathering the more difficult times. Traditions, special practices, customs and techniques unique to the family whether they are ways of celebrating birthdays or just having dinner together imprint their family identity in the hearts and memories of its members.

9. An Understanding of Delegated Authority - Bottom line, if we place God before our family, then follow the order of God and obey the delegated authority He has placed before us, whether it be a parent, an employer, a state official, a teacher, a church leader or whomever it is in authority over us at the time, *when we render respect towards that person and follow the leading of the Holy Spirit and are obedient to God's Word then we will experience a supernatural strength*, love and divine wisdom that God Himself will pour into us. This will help us to maintain and have a joyful victorious family lifestyle. (See Chapter 6 under Delegated Authority which is Part of God's Order).

10. Biblical Economics - Is another major area required in order for a family to be healthy and strong. How a couple manages their finances is extremely important since most marriages fail as a result of poor management of the family income(s). Marriage is *between a husband, a wife and God*, therefore, all that concerns the couple is also a concern to God. His principles when applied to their finances will assist tremendously in giving the wisdom needed for management. Once a couple realizes that everything belongs to God and He makes them trustees of His possessions, it will be easier to operate within His economic system. They will understand that they are stewards (they are His partners who manage what He has entrusted to them). This knowledge makes it easier to come in agreement with Deuteronomy 8:18 and Malachi 3:6-12 and other instructions that the Lord has designated for their finances in order to increase their family financially. (See Chapter 7, Section Two regarding Kingdom Economics).

CHAPTER 4

VARIOUS FAMILY TYPES THAT EXIST IN *OUR SOCIETY* TODAY

QUESTION: WHICH CATEGORY DESCRIBES YOUR FAMILY AND IS YOUR FAMILY TYPE RECOGNIZED IN THE EYES OF GOD OR IS IT A MAN-JOINED UNIT OF PEOPLE SIMPLY LIVING TOGETHER?

In our society we tend to think that the "True" family is the Nuclear or Biological Family or even the Traditional Nuclear Family. The Nuclear Family is a family that consists of a father, a mother and their biological children. **But the Nuclear Family,** if you will, **is merely an idea or model used as a standard rule of what a family is.** The term Nuclear Family was coined by the anthropologist, Robert Murdock in 1949.

The Traditional Nuclear Family is considered middle class in which a woman's primary roles are wife and mother, and a man's primary roles are husband and bread winner.

Because **people believe that the Traditional Nuclear Family is the "True" Family**, they compared all other types of families against this model. **The Traditional Nuclear Family does not describe the reality of many families.** In fact, the Nuclear Family is only one of many natural family types in most major societies today.

VARIOUS NATURAL FAMILY TYPES:
- **Nuclear or Biological Family** – Father, Mother with biological children;
- **Traditional Nuclear Family** – A middle class biological family;
- **Blended Family** – Remarried couple with biological children; An unmarried parent with children that marries for the first time;
- **Single-Parent Family** – Single-Parent with biological or adopted children;
- **Child-Free Family** – Married couple without children;
- **Family by Adoption** – Parents with adopted children;
- **Foster-Parent Family** – Children living in a Foster Care Home;
- **Immediate Family** – Father, Mother, their children, their children's spouses and their grandchildren;
- **Extended Family** – From the Immediate Family the Extended Family is extended from both the father and the mother and includes other relatives related by blood or marriage: your parents, siblings, grandparents, great grandparents, uncles, aunts, cousins, and in-laws.

Yet *none* of these family types in and of themselves were modeled after what Jesus referred to as the "True Family" which will be discussed further on.

The most widespread family types in our society today are the intact two-parent family homes: Biological, Blended and

Adopted and the Single-Parent Families with biological or adopted children. However, there are more Blended/step Families than any other family group. The current fifty percent rate of divorces occurring whether people are Christians or non-Christians has much to do with the Blended Family growth. A Blended Family not only takes place when a marriage dissolves and there is a remarriage but it could also take place when an unmarried woman gives birth and later marries a man that is *not* the biological father. Or an unmarried man with children marries a woman other than the children's mother. Because of these circumstances less than half of all families are the Traditional Nuclear Family. The Blended Family is no longer the exception but the norm.

When God formed the first family He started it with two parents because it was designed to function in a certain manner. Since the seventies, **Single-Parent Families** have been increasing at four to five times the rate of two-parent families. In addition, many families that are headed by single mothers, single fathers, grandparents or some other family member are not exactly what He intended, however, God will bless, prosper and work mightily in these families as well. While I was separated I functioned as a Single-Parent and I watched God become my husband and provide, protect and love me as He led me by His Holy Spirit and met all of my needs. (See Our Blended Family's Testimony for further details).

Many single people feel as if they do not have any family because in many cases they have lost family members due to death, divorce or a long term separation. But they are still a part of a family if they are someone's adult child, someone's mother or father or sibling, and most of all if they are a Child of God then they are a part of the Family of God. In many cases God will give single people a Spiritual Family because it is not always about the physical blood ties but more about the spiritual ties which in some cases are stronger connections.

Even though this information was shared in the previous chapter the importance of this point needs to be re-emphasized. A body of people living together such as roommates, friends, fraternities, sororities, college dormitories, sport teams, convents, military personnel, firemen, gangs and similar groups may refer to themselves *as a* "family" and may even have some of the same functions, traditions, develop soul ties and become best of friends really caring and loving one another but nevertheless **they are not what God has sanctioned as a "family."** *A family does not exist merely to fill a void of loneliness, share expenses, experiences, work or even house rules.* If this is not enough proof know that even people in the world (non-Believers) know the difference. For instance, if someone became ill and a family member had to provide family history, or insurance documents, or allowed in the intensive care unit of a hospital what is the probability of a close friend having this information or even allowed in? Even if they had the information what is the possibility of them having the authority to make decisions about a non-family member's wellbeing? It is almost nil because one of the first questions that is asked is are you a member of the family, are you related?

What God sanctions or approves of as a family in addition to what He refers to as the True Family is designed to train up and produce people with godly character to function a certain way in the Kingdom of God within their given society. They are to bring into place a unit of individuals with like thinking and shared godly morals. In addition, each family member is anointed by God to cause positive change that will affect generations to come.

Unfortunately there is a great attack both spiritually and in the natural against its very foundation. It has been a subtle attack chipping away at its moral fiber since the fall of mankind but over the last forty years or so it has become very apparent. Basic things like joy, peace, relationships, abundance, homes, resources, and so on have been withheld and made extremely difficult to acquire for the average family. There is always the exception but my experience shows that even if the physical needs are met for the family household the emotional and spiritual needs are usually lacking. What should be wonderful memories of one's childhood as an adult are instead painful, stressful, and sad. So many have been robbed of their childhoods and quite frankly aren't doing much better in their adulthood stage but are still acquiring a string of regrets and wishing that things were different. Things will only change and the negative cycle will only stop when they decide to do something different in order to make that happen! Even if the attacks (financial problems, rebellious kids, foreclosure, illnesses, betrayal, etc.) continue on a large scale towards all families to singling out individual households the attacks do not have to come near them in such a way that they can do any real harm or damage. The Bible says, "A thousand may fall at your side, and ten thousand at your right hand, but it shall not come near you" (Ps. 91:7), just choose to believe it.

Thank God that He always gives His own a way of escape and will never allow more than someone can bear. Since most of you have been robbed in the area of a wholesome family **the Lord has provided for many of you a new family and a fresh start with a "True Family" just waiting for you at your command. I am not speaking about acquiring a brand new physical family (even though for some that will happen) but I am speaking about your current family coming alive and being brand new.** Sounds crazy! Well when you join God's Family you will begin to sense and feel that something has truly changed. Many will receive an immediate breakthrough, miracles, peace and joy with this change. But for most others it may not happen overnight, there may even be challenges in the beginning as you adjust, grow and mature into your new lifestyle but *one thing is for sure* once everything comes full circle you will find that you are no longer living with regrets but with hope in a future you probably never thought would happen to you. As we choose to trust Him at His Word He "is able [to carry out His purpose and] do superabundantly, far over and above all that we [dare] ask or think [infinitely beyond our highest prayers, desires, thoughts, hopes, or dreams] to Him be the glory…" Ephesians 3:20.

C0-HABITING AND DIFFERENT TYPES OF UNIONS:

Now moving forward in regards to the different types of unions, **Families that are formed by consanguineous marriages** (marriages that are between people who are blood related, descended from the same ancestor) especially first and second cousins or brothers and sisters are forbidden by God (Leviticus Chapter 18:6-22). The chances of children coming into the world deformed because of blood ties being so close is a risk factor that doesn't need to be. Certain families especially of royalty practiced these types of marriages often to keep the royal blood and resources within the royal family. And other well-to-do families for similar reasons are taking the risk of their grandchildren being deformed at birth. However, fourth or fifth generation of relatives marrying is less likely to produce such an outcome.

The terms Co-Habiting or Non-Traditional Families are used in some texts to give the impression that people who choose to simply live together have now become a family. **This is not biblical and they are not a family that has been sanctioned or approved by God even though God still loves them because He is a God of love, still He will not go against His Word**. Therefore, they are roommates, friends who share a dwelling and they can certainly do the things that families do but **they are not recognized as a family in the eyes of God nor everywhere by the laws of the land. They are not a Spiritual Family either because a Spiritual Family takes heed (pays attention) to the teachings of the Lord.** There are forms in place in certain States for couples who choose to cohabit or live together to receive special privileges and benefits <u>as if they were</u> a family unit, such as medical and dental coverage. Also, "Common Law" is applied and practiced in certain States to protect an individual's rights, but none of these documents in and of themselves constitute (establish) or fall under the definition of what a "family" is. Be mindful that whatever God declares and does it is always for our good. This is where faith and trust come in, you may not understand

His ways but you trust Him at His Word because of Who He is (Luke 5:5).

Secular teaching in schools and universities teach young people that there has been a change in the nature of the family because there has been a shift from an agricultural society to an industrial one that weakened or gradually and secretly removed many of the family's traditional functions. They say that many of the functions of the family are now handled by schools, hospitals, government agencies, peers and hired help mainly because now the family purchases goods and services rather than producing or providing them itself, (Notice how many different resources they speculated it would take to replace the *family* as if it were possible). *They are also taught that the family is no longer a necessity but rather that it is simply one of many choices they have.*

In addition to the schools and universities the media also encourages adolescents and young adults to forego marriage and instead co-habit which is considered the main alternative for marriage, stating that it is faster, easier and without a strong commitment of any kind. *Their instructions indirectly give them permission to live outside of the Judeo-Christian biblical guidelines which were set in place by God Himself for the protection of people through marriage and families.* They took it upon themselves to teach a way of life that will lead these students astray and leave them empty. God has not changed, He is the same yesterday, today and forever (Hebrew 13:8), and He will continue to love us and lead us by His Holy Spirit if we continue to seek Him for truth and the abundant life He promises to those who will seek and receive Him as their own.

In some cases the influence from the sixties and seventies where people who were fed up with the Traditional Nuclear Family that seemed to not be going anywhere and decided to experiment with open marriages, communal living, trial marriages of living together of which all sounded appealing but later it was discovered over a thirty-five year period that the result of these experimental relationships were empty of value or meaning.

People were misplaced within the unit of the household (they did not understand their role or function) and strong family units overall were not formed. As a major result of this, today many young people are afraid of being a part of a meaningful relationship with real commitment. **They may desire it but they also fear it because they do not know what a committed relationship *really* is,** for a lack of role models and where it is going, in other words what is its true purpose or destination? *With a lack of commitment which these types of relationships were about, people raised in them learned to be afraid of commitment, the marital contract, and even the marriage covenant because they did not believe it could work.* Nor do they believe there is anything to it or the people who raised them would not have fought so hard to make a permanent impression that marriage is not the way to go.

Because God's purposes were ignored and not being focused on training up a child in the Word of God (Proverbs 22:6) which would have *instilled purpose, hope and faith in the future,* **instead a great number of Non-Traditional Families lost the true meaning of their existence and as a result lost their way.**

When these types of unions form, in actuality their reason for their lifestyle being outside of the marital covenant ends up fighting against "marriage" and they are not just fighting against a lifestyle of living in a traditional setting, but *they end up coming against the very core and height of what a relationship should and can be.* Therefore, they never really find out what they are depriving themselves of in relationship to what God had for them. They do not realize that God only gives the best and He does everything with excellence! He created and formed marriage. If we wait on Him and marry the person He sends and operate within the marriage according to His plan then we can experience the joy, peace, love and wholeness that comes with the marriage bond.

This leads me to my next point, why is it that some marriages and families have a better chance at living a fulfilled life than others? A Traditional Biological or Nuclear Family functions differently and is different from a Biblical or Godly

Family. Although they may look and seem very similar the difference is still there and very real. Many of the foundational standards, qualities, values and guidelines that a Traditional Nuclear Family has come from the Bible and this is one reason they seem similar. However, *the Traditional Nuclear Family's values are primarily formed from man's thoughts and from the exposure that families had while watching television programs spanning from the fifties and sixties to the seventies and eighties,* thereby making the "Traditional Nuclear Family" the primary role model used to describe what a family is *supposed* to be and as a result of this, all other types of families are compared to it and fall short.

Later, we will rediscover what type of family according to the Word of God is the kind of family that others *should* compare themselves to – **a family that has the *ability and power* to stay intact, is more real, more loving, and a family that God can place His blessing upon** and has more going for it than any other form of family including what the "Traditional Nuclear Family" could ever have to offer.

HOW TELEVISION FAMILIES AFFECTED SOCIETY:

Going back for a moment let's look at how specific *family* programs on television affected society, I would like to add that many of the television programs had a significant influence in shaping many of our ideas, values and beliefs about how a family would relate to one another: within the household, to how its members functioned in the work place, in the educational system and in society at large. *The media is an extremely strong and powerful tool that can influence for the better or worse.* Know and guard what you see and hear especially on the television, the internet and other media because it will make a difference in your soul and the soul of your child. But most of all it will make a difference in how you perceive information and what you receive into your heart (your spirit).

Prime time television programs such as "Leave It to Beaver," "Father Knows Best," and "The Donna Reed Show" to "The Brady Bunch" and "The Huxtables" greatly helped to shape the idea of what the "Traditional and Blended Families" in the USA were.[4]

By the same token, many have rejected it over the years because it didn't seem "real" it seemed too many, unattainable or there was some kind of an imbalance in the way it was presented for everyday life. **Although these shows were for entertainment we have to question the mindset that was formed because of their influence**. When these sitcoms and others on their order presented a problem it was usually solved through humor within a thirty minute span of time and the families never dealt with any serious issues regarding finances, divorce, in-law problems or serious illnesses just to name a few; these and other important topics that affect many families were never an issue.

The *I Love Lucy* television program**,** which was extremely funny in one aspect but it also, taught many women that the only way to obtain what they wanted in a marital relationship was to manipulate, lie, play games and to deceive their spouse in a round about way which was considered alright because it seemed innocent. As a result some young women may think if a husband calls all the shots, and I cannot ever have my way or that my opinion or suggestions never have any real value then I would rather stay single before I resort to all the tactics of her character.

The truth is, the Lord has given a wife to be a help meet, she has the divine wisdom God has given her to enable and help her husband, therefore, she has to be heard by her husband in order for him to receive the gifts God placed on the inside of her for their marriage, the upkeep of their home, raising their children and accomplishing their dreams and visions. **Therefore, television like so many other media resources make it their place to portray everything but what was *Biblically written* that would truly entertain as well as give depth and truth that would help relationships instead of harm them.**

One reason this happens is because the adversary affects the air waves because people of God don't take dominion over it as it is released on this earth. God gave us dominion but it doesn't do us any good if we do not know how to exercise our authority (Gen. 1:26).

There is one older film that comes to mind that was successful in capturing some of the reality that is involved with a Blended Family probably because it was based on a true story. That movie is called, *Yours, Mine and Ours*, staring Lucille Ball and Henry Fonda. At the time I first watched this film I was a part of a Traditional Nuclear Family, happily married with two young children. Little did I imagine that one day I would be functioning in a Blended Family as I was viewing on the screen. That movie was somewhat of a comfort and a model for me once I came into that position since I really had no where else to draw the experience from or any books to read in depth on the subject and none from a biblical perspective.

This is why it is important to really guard what you watch and listen to. The industry needs to take more responsibility in the hiring of those they entrust to write stories for families. Programs should not be written without any real research or experience and/or receiving from the *One* who has all the answers especially on this subject.

Things that were expected of couples and people were expectations that were based on the opinions of a room full of writers primarily sharing their own views, opinions, backgrounds, experiences, education and lifestyle as opposed to people writing with an understanding of what was written from reliable research about marriage and families. Bottom-line, whatever is not based on Truth – God's Word – will eventually fall.

Therefore, today we have a worse situation, the opinions of most writers giving their views, opinions, background, experiences, education and lifestyle to the public is the same process but its contents is even further from the truth. I would say based on the billboard ads that I see while driving or some commercials during sports events that I watch with my husband from time to time (we now fast forward through the commercials or mute them) that **there is an assignment that is in operation to carry people away from what a marriage, family or a meaningful relationship could ever be.**

I have also noticed from the type of material that is portrayed on the air and in the theatres that much of it is being written by people who are hurting, who come from broken and very hurtful childhoods and do not seem to have a clue as to what a marriage or family is, how it should function or what its true purpose is. It appears evident that many of the secular writers have no connection to truth or reality; therefore, they have no foundation to work from except their own bad experiences and the demonic forces that have influenced their lives.

The argument to justify their position would be that boring unrealistic family lifestyle programs do not "sell" and make money so we give the people exciting programs full of lies, gossip, sex, sin and bloody murders. The public according to this minor group of people in the industry think that the majority of the public love their work or they simply have been deceived or maybe they just do not care what the public thinks. On the contrary most people crave decent and wholesome programs especially to watch with their family. Surveys have been conducted that show that the majority of Americans do believe in God and are hungry for good clean entertainment. **Most people know right from wrong but they have become so accustom to the nonsense that what is wrong seems right and what is right is now seen as out-dated, boring, bias, hateful and wrong**. This is the result of the influence from a portion of the media because not all media people participate in the attempted destruction of society as we know it.

However, there are decent programs and movies out there as well by anointed writers, producers, directors, actors and a host of behind the scenes people. For the sake of our young families we have to search them out on Christian sites and from other advertisements because their work is not boring and out-dated and will help reset healthy family entertainment, (See Chapter 4 under Defining the Anointing).

Now going back to some of the history that formed the ideas of what a family should be and how it should function, we notice that unlike true Biblical values or roles, *the Traditional Nuclear Family accepted values, ways and roles that harmed people in the long run* because of major flaws that were hidden within its institution. **For instance television role models regarding marriage and the family gave somewhat of a distortion of what God originally intended.** In some of the programs during the fifties and sixties there were a number of absentee fathers, devalued mothers and tolerance on both parts from couples to exist for the sake of acquiring this dream life that really did not exist for the masses except on paper.

What do we mean by this, the appearance was wholesome with loving homes that were perfect and stress-free, there were almost never any financial struggles, arguing or major disagreements; their appearance, especially the mothers, was always perfect, as well as the children's manners. The family seems to survive quite well without extended family (which can be a great support system especially when a young family has small children) but they had a neighbor who would pop in from time to time, for the most part, and all schedules worked beautifully each and everyday.

Although during this era, it certainly was not as much "drama" or stress that is in daily life as it is now, but at the same time it was not as "calm" for all families because we have *always had an adversary that came against the family.* His tactics during those days were more subtle because evil stood out and righteousness was the norm, therefore, evil could easily be recognized. The enemy of mankind and families has many devices to destroy them. These devices are not always recognizable simply because unlike years ago where righteousness was the norm, now it stands out and is easily identified, while evil is now the norm and it seems to be everywhere and because of this it is not easily identified because of deception, nowadays you must discern by the Spirit of God (I Cor. 12:10).

During those times **in the fifties and sixties even though there was more of a peace in the overall atmosphere, there was** an undercurrent of plots to destroy taking place. Seeds were being planted that manifested slowly but surely and today we are experiencing the results of subtle movements of compromising and living lives that were based on lies and not on truth. In addition, we are now seeing and experiencing the fruit of a number of events such as prayer being taken out of schools and certain negative legislation and bills being passed over the years that brought corruption into society.

To further my point the Traditional Nuclear Family was not flawless and did set trends that later during the eighties had to be dealt with by society. Another hidden reality was the importance of the male in the home in the programs regarding a Traditional Nuclear Family. The father either worked too much with long hours that kept him out of the home on business trips, or overnight in the city to avoid the long drive to the suburb. And when he was home he was either in his study, or with his neighbor, on occasion with the children, usually only to correct or instruct or having conversations with his wife discussing decisions that needed immediate addressing for the household or children. Usually when he was physically present, emotionally he was somewhere else. No one complained because he was the 'bread winner' who was expected to supply this great life for his family. The problem, however, was that the father's absence created an irreplaceable void in the home. **He was encouraged and allowed to love his family by neglecting them in order to earn a living to achieve a career and financial success.**

This detachment was devastating. Why? **The father's presence is extremely important to validate and affirm his wife and children. He is the source and sustainer, the head, the protector, teacher, leader, primary one that disciplines, he is a nurturer, and he is the very foundation of his family.** When a father speaks his voice usually commands a certain amount of respect and not out of fear but a reverence for his position in the family. This position was given to him by God and we are to respect God's order. **This man's wife was never intended to replace him but to help him in his functions and endeavors** to achieve the desired results and goals set-up by God for him in his primary role as a *family* man.

Needless to say the father in the television program is portrayed as an idiot in most shows if he even exists at all. This is a spiritual attack on the structure and order for the family that was set up by God. And also notice that most of the children in some of these programs know more than their fathers.

Furthermore, the man who for whatever reason could not earn a living (not shown on the television programs till the eighties), the pressure of no income was difficult and embarrassing as seen in programs such as "Good Times." In this particular program the father stayed with his family but was unsuccessful in securing work to properly take care of them. The program was so negative and really exploited the African-American male to the point where the father was eventually written out of the script and the television series wife and children carried on without him which created even a more negative role model for the African-American family.

During the sixties the Welfare system began. Because of a lack of work many men were unable to marry women they loved and to take care of their children because the women were told by the *governmental system* that the fathers could not stay in the same home with their wives or marry their girl friends and she continue receiving state funds. Since neither of them were employed and that check was the only income for their family the men were *trained* to stay away so this "small check" could take care of basic needs. **Many people from all walks of life, backgrounds and races become entangled with this system in their youth because of teen-age pregnancies**. This system encourages women to have children out of wedlock in order to secure a 'paycheck' and to be able to be a stay home mom.

Note: this is a system of bondage one that strips people of their dignity and decision making and the sooner anyone is able to leave it and pursue work which is given by God, the better their life will be. If you are on it change your perspective and see it only as a stepping stone until a door opens for your work to begin. Pray and ask God for your purpose and what it is that He would have you to do; He will surely answer you if you *really* desire to know (Matthew 7:7; Jerem. 29:11). Then ask Him for instructions on how to obtain your purpose or goals and write them down (Hab. 2:2-3). You may be led to enroll in some type of trade, college, apprenticeship program, or start a business, who knows, there are so many options and if you have the wisdom and favor of God *nothing is impossible.*

Likewise in some of the early sitcoms such as the Ozzie and Harriet Show men were at home all the time and never went to work neither did the program ever explain how they acquired an income because the wife was a stay-at-home mom or known today as a homemaker.

Yes, a destructive plot was in the making that was larger than any human man's system. There is an enemy that is fighting to keep the man out of the home and to destroy the lives of his children. Without a father role model many sons never experience the presence of a father in a way that helps him to learn what it means to be a whole man, one who is secure with himself, one who is happy to be a man, one who has healthy and proper thinking about what a man is and about his responsibilities as a husband, provider and father.

Even though it was the early programs that contributed to start the ball rolling on the depreciation of the family structure, the so-called current family programs as mentioned earlier not only attack the father figure as head of his family but they teach young people to disrespect both parents. They are being taught to reject authority in the home and in the society in which they live. This is another tactic of Satan; he too rebelled against his authority when he was the most beautiful angel with the most responsibility of all the archangels. He became jealous of Almighty God and decided he would make himself *like* the Most High God. As it is told he ascended to heaven from the earth where he was living and ruling at the time to exalt himself and was instead met by another archangel, Michael, and was thrown out of heaven with a third of the angels who came with him and who had already been deceived by him (Isaiah 14:12-16), (See Chapter 7, Section One under Who is the Adversary and What are His Devices? And see Chapter 6 under Delegated Authority...).

If our young people continue watching these distorted programs they will set their lives up for much more confusion, frustration, pain and grief because no good thing can come out of anything that fights the very plan of God. That is the same as fighting God Himself and He said, "He who is not with Me is against Me, and he who does not gather with Me scatters abroad" (Matt. 12:30). But the Word also says, "If God is for us, who [can be] against us? (Romans 8:31).

I would like to mention a couple of distortions regarding women in these early programs that were also hidden and we have seen the outburst from women in society as a result. Women were devalued in the Traditional Nuclear Family. Her primary and in most cases *only* role was to support her husband in his career and to raise her children. And there is nothing wrong with that, it is a part of her function if she is a wife and mother. However, when her value and identity were measured *only* with reference to her husband and children never in terms of herself as an individual with self worth, goals, desires or dreams she became and felt increasingly as a person with no identity.

During this era in the media she was a person who was unsupported, isolated and considered unimportant by the world's standard and many times bored with the same routine. *We understand that God desires that a wife's highest priority is her family and her home but is that her only priority?* Except for the fulfillment that she was a good wife and mother, **which is highly commended** especially for the strengthening of the family in any society, this is enough for some women *but is it enough for every woman?*

The Traditional Nuclear Family introduced into our society undue imbalance and suppression of women and why some women felt there was a need to 'rebel' against an unjust world that placed so many limitations on their self-worth and choices in this supposedly perfect situation.

Bottom line, the wives were limited and/or devalued and the husbands were distracted from what was really important. The true examples and uniqueness of both these roles were distorted and neglected. Both the husband and wife in the roles of the Traditional Nuclear Family's priorities were distorted simply because people that wrote the scripts wrote their own cultural values into the structure of the family rather than looking at God's Word (the standard that we should live by) Who originally designed and formed it to succeed [4] Paraphrased.

Because the Traditional Nuclear Family was based on their own experiences and cultural values it did not benefit the family at large in a real society. *We all would have been better off having a sense of fulfillment by seeing a strong foundation and/or support system to build from and the satisfaction of knowing we were accomplishing something that would bear good fruit and would last for generations to come.* This would have been believable and received as well instead of just focusing on that one household that affected that one generation which in and of itself displayed no roots or foundation and possibly very little future.

Sometimes people think you are making too much out of a simple television program and my response would be, just look around at society and then ask yourself what is one of the most profound influences in people's lives? Regardless of what is said or read **the media is the second greatest influence in our lives coming in second only to watching and listening to what our parents say and do.** It is the strongest influence as we all watch day in and day out the primary example before us as we are growing up. Children learn about marriage the same way, is it no wonder with all the pressure on families that children witnessed growing up and once an adult they decide to remain single. Because whether they see the Traditional Nuclear Family obtainable or not, it is seen as a hopeless situation to most. Because some will obtain "the dream" and find that even those that have acquired the "good life" are still empty inside. Others may see it as something that is too far to reach or believe for because of their background and where they are starting from and will not even try to obtain it.

What they do not realize is that *any lifestyle will be hopeless* without the Hope Giver, without faith and strong beliefs in "Someone" that is real and can fill any void in one's life. The confirmation of this is that the programming of that era and even now is extremely void of any reference to God and/or church in their scripts except on occasion using the extremely religious denominations.

The media in all forms and capacities, especially the internet that is currently working to depreciate marriages with pornography, luring teens into sex trafficking and illicit relationships not to mention all the different types of shams and robberies directed at homes and the list goes on. In all fairness the internet can be used for good as well and it does connect people all over the world. *Again, if we would heed (pay attention) to the advice of a Wise Savior who says, guard what you watch, ear, say and where you go, this simple advice would save lives and certainly assist in saving the family structure.*

Both parents are very important, God designed it that way. The father and mother carry different responsibilities and when coupled with the Word of God as the foundation for their principles and actions within their home they will be able to function with confidence and assurance and thereby form and develop well rounded and whole human beings.

Even though there were problems with the Traditional Nuclear Family many of the children grew up and were very successful and basically had normal lives. Every type of family has its problems and out of it there will be those who succeed in life regardless of the flaws and those who won't.

Still the issues with some of the children that grew up in a Traditional Nuclear Family and how they themselves felt the injustice of this imperfect arrangement and how their decisions affect our lives today will be addressed now. **Many from that era tried to find alternatives for themselves.** As mentioned earlier some of those alternatives included open marriages, communal living, trial marriages of living together which only helped to lead us to where we are today with more people living together and higher divorce rates and even though many of these couples did eventually marry after possibly years of living together, still many divorced later.

One reason so many marriages have failed after cohabiting and then marrying is because a spiritual law goes into effect and the entire relationship "changes once married." A connection was established by God that made them *one in the spirit* whereas before marriage there was only a soul tie. The spiritual tie or connection is greater and once married everything becomes "new" the old is gone. However, because we have an enemy that fights against marriage, he will remind the now married couple of their past so they will become suspicious and a lack of trust can develop; if it were not already there, causing their minds to wonder, think and question about their spouses faithfulness. For example, one partner may become suspicious and say or think, after all you "slept with me" how can I trust you not to sleep with someone else or have an affair now that we are married? This is one of the many devices Satan uses to destroy relationships. He is the father of lies and he is the deceiver. Your part is to stay encouraged; you did the right thing by marrying. If both of you turn to God and invite Him into your marriage and resist the lies of the enemy, God will work through the both of you to change any negative situation around (James 4:7).

Of course this is not the only reason for the high volume of divorces, there are many other factors and issues involved that cause divorces as well as those mentioned in Chapter Two. With the prevailing lack of or desire to marry or have a real commitment of any kind with one person for fear of failure and the consequences of a divorce by most, people that wish to be in a meaningful relationship are now faced with a whole new set of issues and problems that are in our culture at large.

Then there are others who choose to simplify the matter by calling it a day and purchasing a pet! For any age from a child to an adult, single or married, pets are important emotional figures and have been so since the prehistoric times. Because the need for intimacy is so strong and powerful some people tend to rely upon their pet to meet their "companion" needs. However, people have pets for different reasons and they can be great company, less maintenance and inexpensive compared to raising children. For instance, a dog's welcoming and greeting behaviors can even make one forget they had a bad day. We know first hand because of our daughter Melinda's pet dog, "Alex" who was fourteen years of age and lived with us thirteen of those fourteen years. He was greatly loved and especially by our daughter who cared for him as if he was her very own child. He was small and faithful and always ready to greet you at the door. So I dedicate this portion to him who was company for all of us during the many years of bringing this altogether. We miss you, Alex, and we know you are in our future, so until then our little friend, you will always be in our heart and memory!

If you have chosen a pet to fill a void your pet may become less important once you are in a meaningful relationship or marry (unless you see the pet as your child, which happens a lot) it is normal for your priorities at this point to shift. *A pet is useful for some and life changing for others. It is one alternative but the greatest alternative for a lonely heart is to really know the "Life Giver" and to allow Him to take you on the journey of your life. What He does will not decrease in your life when something or someone else comes along but instead fulfill it and be a permanent Friend, Comforter, Companion, Counselor, Helper, Strengthener or whatever you need Him to be.* God meets everyone where they are and supplies for them what they need on the way to where they are going and in some cases it will be a trusting little friend, like a pet!

We must realize that anything that goes against the written Word of God will not succeed but when it is used properly it will bring success. All things that are for your good and that bring life into a given situation will come through God (Rev 4:11; Ps.19:1; Ps 24:1-2). Life produces life and death produces death, therefore, we must choose one or the other because no one will have both (Deuteronomy 30:19).

With due respect to all the variations of the different types of families mentioned above that exist in our society today (the Nuclear or Biological; Traditional Nuclear; Blended; Single-Parent; Child-Free; Adoption; Foster or Extended) **regardless of the family type, what is the core result from our observance of a "family" in general? We could say,** *yes the outward appearance is certainly there,* **the husband, the wife, children, pet, house, cars, vacations, business and so on.** However, there are several questions which come to mind. How is each person relating within themselves? Is there inner turmoil, anger, pride, bitterness or unhappiness? How do they relate to one another if they relate at all? For even though the appearance is great there may be adultery in the picture, rebellious children, neglect and little or no communication in the household. Are the members of the family taken for granted, are their basic emotional needs being met? Is there poverty or over indulgence? Is there constant strife in the atmosphere between the family members or is there a balance and peace in their home? *With all things being considered are they relating to one another in a loving manner?* **In many cases yes, in most cases no. To many people having a family is the ultimate foundational achievement of success as far as relationships are concerned. However, all of the above family types may face some or all of the above problems. Then, do we wonder why so many in today's society would rather find an alternative lifestyle, because in the mind of most, there has to be more to having a family than this,** *and there is!*

THE "TRUE FAMILY" AS DESCRIBED BY OUR LORD:

Now looking beyond the different types of families that were mentioned earlier, there is still *another type of family, that is greater than all of these listed.* Furthermore, the True Family can be applied and incorporated into each and every one of the listed family types. *It is a type of family that is overlooked by most societies when defining what a family is. Because the True Family does not fit into the scope of traditional thinking or customs, limitations were set and many people were dismissed, forgotten, left out and persecuted for His name sake in their natural family circle because of ignorance of who God refers to as the 'True Family,' (Matthew 12:46-50 and Mark 3:31-35).*

There are families called the **Family of God** or the **Biblical Family.** The term Family of God can be used to describe the natural Jewish relationship with God and the Body of Christ which includes anyone who has received Jesus (Yeshua) as Lord and Savior. *But also on a much smaller and personal scale it describes a type of family located within an individual home.*

The "True Family" is the Biblical Family or Family of God. It is at the forefront of marriage, family values, traditions and customs, because it is not based *on traditions and morals alone* **but on the fact that at the** *Head* **of this type of family there is a** *High Priest* **that is the same yesterday, today and forevermore and Who understands family.** His name is Jesus and He has the power to perfect these unions when willing hearts are involved. (Read further for the Scriptural Definition of a True Family and see Chapter 7, Section Three under A Brief History…of the King of kings for more information about this High Priest).

In our hearts when we are willing to live by faith we can be successful in our families. Remember, it is not only what you believe that matters, it is how you behave in accordance with what you believe that will make the difference.

God did not design marriage with a basic contract in mind. He drew up a contract between a man and a woman, and He sees a covenant where two separate wills are willing to die to themselves and take on the faith of Christ.

Galatians 2:20 says,

> I have been crucified with Christ [in Him I have shared His crucifixion]; it is no longer I who live, but Christ (the Messiah) lives in me; **and the life I now live in the body I live by faith** in (by adherence to and reliance on

and complete trust in) the Son of God, Who loved me and gave Himself up for me.

Then they are to look to Jesus as their Head and trust that the Holy Spirit will be there to teach them and bring them into all truth about everything that concerns their lives and the lives of their love ones.

When operating with biblical principles your priorities change, your interests change, values change and habits change for the good. Love, trust and fairness are handled differently and there is less taking each other for granted, less isolation, rejection and ignoring of children. **As a matter of fact, one of the greatest things a father can do for his children is to love their mother (his wife).**

When God is in the picture and people in the family have their own personal relationship, reverence and respect for Him and they are humble enough (admitting to themselves that they need a Savior) to receive instructions from His Spirit, then the Holy Spirit will enable (grace) them to do what He has asked them to do and that will make all the difference in the world for their household. Where there is relationship, people are more prone to want to please God rather than spend a lot of time trying to be a people pleaser.

God is first in the Family of God which is the "True" family. He will cause everything to line up and move into position at the appointed time so that whatever is needed for your life, it can be released. In this type of family your focus changes and everything is seen more clearly and the result is less stress, less worry because you will become more trusting (leaning on, relying on and having confidence) as you rest in the Lord (Prov. 3:5-7).

The Family of God or the Biblical Family should: make better choices; forgive easier; cooperate faster; extend grace to one another; attitudes can quickly change for the better; personalities can flourish and have more inner joy; members of the family will exercise the fruit of the Spirit more readily; understand better how they are suppose to function; know how to take authority over their circumstances; know how to set the atmosphere in their home; shake-off demonic assignments that are attached to their family and remove distractions. They will also learn how to be more considerate in their speech with the right tone and attitude towards others; and most of all be more at peace, understanding, trusting and less insecure. We could go on and on about the advantages of being in this type of family.

The only way to become a member in the family of God that offers eternal life with outstanding benefits is to be adopted by God the Father when you receive His only begotten son, Jesus (Yeshua).

>John 3:16-17 KJV says,
>
>>For God so loved the world, that He gave His only begotten
>>
>>Son, that whoever believeth in Him should not perish, but have everlasting life. For God sent not His Son into the world to condemn the world; but that the world through Him might be saved.

In this family you are never alone, you are never forsaken or forgotten and that is why we may boldly say: "The Lord is my Helper…I will not fear… What can man do to me?" (Hebrews 13:6). You will always be loved and protected. Security and provision is available when and if you need it, all you have to do is ask and your Father in Heaven will provide it for you ("Ask, and it will be given to you; seek, and you will find; knock, and it will be opened to you. Everyone who asks receives and he who seeks finds, and to him who knocks it will be opened" (Matthew 7:7-8). In this family there is opportunity to have peace beyond your understanding (John 14:27).

Hope is given to all in the Biblical Family because even though you are a unit of people within the home each person who has a personal relationship with the Lord is anointed and entitled to prosper in health, joy, peace, wealth, strength and confidence knowing who they are in Christ, knowing what their assignment is, being assured that all the promises of God are theirs. Thus each person being secure in the knowledge of Christ for themselves sets a great atmosphere in their home. As a result, they will be perceived as a family, an anointed family, a family which was formed by the Heavenly Father.

When God is at the head of *any type of family* that places that family in the category of being a Family of God, a Biblical Family or a Spiritual Family because they have become set apart for His purpose.

Psalms 128:1-6 is a description of a God-fearing Family:

> **Blessed** (Happy, fortunate, to be envied) is everyone who fears, reveres, and worships the Lord, who walks in His ways and lives according to His commandments. For you shall eat [the fruit] of the labor of your hands; **happy** (blessed, fortunate, enviable) shall you be, and it shall be well with you. **Your wife** shall be like a fruitful vine in the innermost parts of your house; **your children** shall be like olive plants round about your table. Behold, thus shall **the man be blessed who reverently and worshipfully fears the Lord.** May the Lord bless you out of Zion [His sanctuary], and may you see the prosperity of Jerusalem all the days of your life; Yes, may you see your children's children. Peace be upon Israel! (Also see Psalms 1:1, 2)

The difference is the "Anointing" that is now on these families because they became Children of God and have placed Father God, His Word and the Holy Spirit in first place before their own families and have chosen to follow Him. The anointing will destroy bondages and yokes and cause the new and refreshed to come alive. How can the anointing do all of this? Because the anointing comes from the **Anointed One Who is the Messiah and Who** can do what is impossible for men but not impossible for God. What the power of God will do for one family He can and will do for another as long as they acknowledge that He is the Anointed One and invite Him in when He knocks!

However, once they invite Him in some have asked how will their family be different from other families and from the way they were? **For instance, in the natural,** if they were a Biological or Blended Family they still are; if they were a Single-Parent, a Family by Adoption, Child-Free or a Foster Family they remain so. But **spiritually speaking** if any of them become a *Family in Christ* they are now a Family of God or a Godly Family. **This is only an illustration to show that the physical structure of your family has not changed but who they *are* has because of *Who* they serve.** For example, one could say we are a Biological Family of God or a Blended Family of God or a Single-Parent Family of God, just to give an illustration. Actually nothing really needs to be said, for the *change on the inside* will soon speak for itself.

FAMILY TYPES THAT EXIST IN THE *KINGDOM OF GOD* TODAY AND INTRODUCING GOD'S BLENDED FAMILY:

- The Family of God, (a Godly or Biblical Family) includes: Both the Jewish (Gen.12:3; Gen.15:5-14; Exo. 6:7) **and non-Jewish** people who are members of the **Body of Christ** (all those ingrafted or adopted from both groups into God's family through Christ, Eph.1:5; 2 Cor. 5:17; Gal. 3:24); and **The Church Family or an Immediate Family that is Born-Again**, an individual family located within the Body of Christ (Genesis 17:7; Romans 8:17; Gal. 3:16; Psalms 128:1-6; John 3:3; I Cor. 6:20).
- A Spiritual Family: Saved people who are **divinely connected as a family by God,** that may or may not be biologically related; that may or may not

be related by marriage; that may or may not dwell in the same home and "does the things God wills…" (Matthew 12:46-50; Mark 3:31-35).
- **The God-Blended Family:** A family that is formed from one man with or without children and one woman with one or more children or vice versa who are Born-again Christians, have the *Infilling of the Holy Spirit, Anointed with the Authority and Power of God* who are blended together in marriage under the direction of the Holy Spirit (Psalms 128:1-6, **the God-Fearing Family).**
- **God's Blended Family from a Divine Perspective:** This family is larger than what we would perceive or consider as within the limits of a usual or customary family. On a much broader scale, *God's Blended Family encompasses people from all over the world that are blended together* as one big joyous family in His sight, under His protection and authority. *He is our Parent as we belong to His household by choice.* His ultimate Blended Family crosses all barriers as people are united regardless of race, creed, ethnic group, color, culture, status or former religion. Those in God's Family are ingrafted in by adoption by the blood of Jesus/Yeshua who have become one in Him and have formed the *One New Man*, thus becoming a member of *God's Blended Family!* (Eph. 2:14; Ro.11; Eph. 1:5; 2 Cor. 5:17). This *Spiritual Family* could also be referred to as the *Body of Christ,* the same people which make up *the Kingdom of God.*

All people were created by God so He is their Creator but to those who are Saved (have received Salvation) He becomes their "Father" as they are ingrafted into His Family (Ro.10:9-10; I John 2:2, 12; Eph. 1:5).

"He died for everyone so that those who receive his new life will no longer live to please themselves. Instead, they will live to please Christ, who died and was raised for them," (2 Cor. 5:15 NLT).

We exist because God is a Divine Person and He desired to be in a family relationship with all of us! He told Abraham from the beginning how many descendants he would have which would include God's Family through Christ Jesus as well as others, (Psalm 89:34). Genesis 15:5 says, "And He brought him outside [his tent into the starlight] and said, Look now toward the heavens and count the stars – if you are able to number them. Then He said to him, So shall your descendants be."

In Genesis 22:17-18 God told Abraham the following about his Seed and his Descendants:

In blessing I will bless you and in multiplying I will multiply your descendants like the stars of the heavens and like the sand on the seashore. And your Seed (Heir) will possess the gate of His enemies. And in your Seed [Christ] shall all the nations of the earth be blessed and [by Him] bless themselves, because you have heard and obeyed My voice.

THE ONE NEW MAN:

If you consider yourself to be a part of the **Family of God** because of the Finished Work the Messiah did at the Cross it would mean that you have declared that you are a part of the **One New Man.** Furthermore, as this One New Man in the Kingdom of God you would be referred to as a Christian; a Believer; a Messianic Jew; Born-again; a Saint; an Evangelical; a Child of God; Saved; a son or daughter of God; and sister or brother in the Lord to name a few terms used in Christendom. But before Christendom began all of the first Believers were Jewish followers of the Messiah, the Anointed One of Israel.

Ephesians 2:12-20 says,

[Remember] that you were at that time separated (living apart) from Christ [excluded from all part in Him], utterly estranged and outlawed from the rights of Israel as a nation, and strangers with no share in the sacred compacts of the [Messianic] promise [with no knowledge of or right in God's agreements, His covenants]. *And you had no hope (no promise); you were in the world without God. But now in Christ Jesus, you who once were [so] far away, through (by, in) the blood of Christ have been brought near.* For He is [Himself] our peace (our bond of unity and harmony). **He has made us both [Jew and Gentile] one [body], and has broken down (destroyed, abolished) the hostile dividing wall between us,** by abolishing in His [own crucified] flesh the enmity [caused by] the Law with its decrees and ordinances [which He annulled]; that He from the two might create in Himself **ONE NEW MAN** [one new quality of humanity out of the two], so making peace. And **[He designed] to reconcile to God both [Jew and Gentile, united] in a single body by means of His cross, thereby killing the mutual enmity and bringing the feud to an end.** And He came and preached the glad tidings of peace to you who were afar off and [peace] to those who were near. For it is through Him that we both [whether far off or near] now have an introduction (access) by one [Holy] Spirit to the Father [so that we are able to approach Him]. Therefore you are no longer outsiders (exiles, migrants, and aliens, excluded from the rights of citizens), but you now share citizenship with the saints (God's own people, consecrated and set apart for Himself); and you belong to God's [own] household. You are built upon the foundation of the apostles and prophets with Christ Jesus Himself the chief Cornerstone.

"**Christ destroyed the division between Jews and non-Jews, providing all people the opportunity to be saved by grace.** In His death He reconciled sinners to God, destroying our hatred for Him. Thus Jesus/Yeshua opened the way for us to live in God's presence. The Holy Spirit is that presence of God with us. Jesus founded the church and is the uniting power for it" [3] Ephesians 2:14-22.

One of the devices Satan used to cause division between the Church and Jews was **Replacement Theology**, an erroneous teaching which misinformed Christians and resulted in some Christians (or in some cases those who were Christians in name only) mistreating Jewish people. This teaching was especially done during the Dark Ages when the common people had to rely on their leadership for their teaching. At that time the leadership was under orders to teach the lie that God was done with the Jews and that the Church was to replace them. **But the truth of the matter is, the Bible says that Christians are 'adopted' into the family of God, Ephesians 1:5; Romans 8:15; Psalm 27:10 and are 'ingrafted' into the family according to 2 Corinthians 5:17.**

"No New Testament author suggested in any way that the Hebrew Scriptures were obsolete, and neither did Y'shua. Y'shua/Jesus is quoted in Jn. 10:16 as saying, But I also have sheep which are not from this sheepfold: and it is necessary for Me to lead those and they will hear My voice, and they will become one flock, one shepherd. Y'shua was speaking to the Jewish people referring to the heathens as the other flock. In Matt. 5:18 Y'shua said that not one yod or vav would drop from Torah until the sky and the earth would pass away." (The One New Man Bible); (Yod and Vav are the two smallest letters in the Hebrew alphabet).

To further make this point, the following is an illustration of a family which has children and chooses to adopt other children. Does the adopted child(ren) *replace* the natural children? Of course not, the adopted children are a welcome addition into the family. Even if the adopted child(ren) came *first,* once a child is born into the family the natural biological addition does not replace the adopted first child in the home. On the contrary, they have the opportunity of becoming one big happy family! (Ephesians 2:14-20).

Jewish people are forerunners that went through the *storm* so we Christians would know what to do by their examples of faith, success and failures. If they were perfect there would not have been anything to write about. I don't know of any perfect Christians, but I do know that we all need a Savior, Jews, Gentiles and Christians alike. *(If you would like to receive Yeshua/Jesus as your Lord and Savior please see Chapter 7, Section Three under, What is Salvation? A Prayer for Salvation).*

DEFINING A CHRISTIAN AND CHRISTIANITY:

A **Christian** according to The New Webster's Dictionary:

> A person who believes in the doctrines of Jesus and acknowledges His divinity and is also a person having the qualities expected of one who professes Christianity.

A **Christian** according to the Vines Complete Expository Dictionary:

> Christianos, "Christian" a word formed after the Roman style, signifying an adherent of Jesus, was first applied to such by the Gentiles and is found in Acts 11:26; 26:28; I Peter 4:16. Though the word rendered **"were called"*** in Acts11:26 might be used of a name adopted by oneself or given by others, the "Christians"

do not seem to have adopted it for themselves in the times of the apostles. In I Peter 4:16, the apostle is speaking from the point of view of the persecutor; cf. "as a thief," "as a murderer." Nor is it likely that the appellation was given by Jews. As applied by Gentiles there was no doubt an implication of scorn, as in Agrippa's statement in Acts 26:28. Tacitus, writing near the end of the first century, says, "The vulgar call them Christians. The author or origin of this denomination, Christus, had, in the reign of Tiberius, been executed by the procurator, Pontius Pilate" (Annals xv. 44). *From the second century onward the term was accepted by believers as a title of honor.*

* **The word "Call"** according to Vines – *Kaleo*, derived from the root *kal*, whence Eng. "call" and "clamor" is used with a personal object, "to call anyone, invite, summon," e.g., Matt. 20:8; 25:14; it is used particularly of the divine call to partake of the blessings of redemption, e.g.; Rom. 8:30; I Cor. 1:9; I Thess. 2:12; and Heb. 9:15.

A **Christian** according to The New Ungers Bible Dictionary:

A Christian is a believer in and a follower of Jesus Christ the Messiah. This name is more widely employed than any other designation of those who believe unto salvation. However, it occurs in the Scriptures only three times: "And the disciples were first called Christians in Antioch" (Acts 11:26); "and Agrippa replied to Paul, 'In a short time you will persuade me to become a Christian' " (26:28); "If anyone suffers as a Christian, let him not feel ashamed" (I Peter 4:16). **The term Christian is clearly a Gentile designation for believers because the word Christ,**

upon which the term was constructed suggests recognition of the Messiah, which no <u>unbelieving</u> Jew was prepared to do. Becoming a Christian, according to the New Testament, is a definite act with significant results. According to Lewis Sperry Chafer, no fewer than thirty-three (33) simultaneous and instantaneous divine undertakings and transformations, which collectively constitute the salvation of a soul, take place the moment one exercises faith in Christ and is saved. *Among these is that a believer in Christ has the guilt of his sins removed.* Second, he is taken out of Adam, the sphere of condemnation, and placed in Christ, the sphere of righteousness and justification. Third, he is given a new standing by virtue of his being placed "in Christ" by the Spirit's baptizing work (I Cor.12:13; Rom.6:3-4). A Christian then, as Chafer says, "Is not one who does certain things for God but…one for whom God has done certain things; he is not so much one who conforms to a certain manner of life as he is one who has received the gift of eternal life; he is not one who depends upon a hopelessly imperfect state but rather one who has reached a perfect standing before God as being in Christ."

To become a Christian is to partake in a spiritual miracle because all of the above is done supernaturally by exercising one's faith, which every person is born with a measure of in order to receive their salvation which is a free gift from God and is given by grace through faith (Eph 2:8-9). This cannot be done in the natural using any natural senses or means, that is why it is classified as a "miracle" – something that is *super- natural.* Also noted in the above quote, there are thirty-three (33) divine undertakings and transformations that take place at the time of Salvation, this is the same age Jesus was when He died on the cross and rose three days later.

From the beginning of Christianity, Christians have been persecuted not only for following the Anointed One but because they themselves are anointed at the time they receive their salvation. Christ (ian) means Christ (like), we are persecuted because His Spirit dwells in us. The unbeliever's spirit, those with a spirit of religion, those practicing only traditions and customs recognize the Spirit of God in the Christian, the Believer in Christ Jesus. Their spirit is no comparison for the anointing (Christ) which displays the true power of Almighty God. "Because He Who lives in you is greater (mightier) than he who is in the world" (I John 4:4). The world (unbelievers) hated Him and they will hate you. In addition to this, instead of embracing the miracles and good works that followed Jesus they hated Him for it. Even today when miracles and good works are done in the name of Jesus by His sons and daughters (mature Christians/Believers) in the faith who operate in the fruit and gifts of God, they are hated and persecuted for it as well.

Jesus said in John 15:18-20; 24-25:

> **If the world hates you, know that it hated Me before it hated you.** If you belonged to the world, the world would treat you with affection and would love you as its own. But because you are not of the world [no longer one with it], but I have chosen (selected) you out of the world, the world hates (detests) you. Remember that I told you, A servant is not greater than his master [is not superior to him]. **If they persecuted Me, they will also persecute you;** if they kept My Word and obeyed My teachings, they will also keep and obey yours.
>
> If I had not done (accomplished) among them the works which no one else ever did, they would not be guilty of sin. But [**the fact**

is] now they have both seen [these works] and have hated both Me and My Father.** But [this is so] that the word written in their Law might be fulfilled, **They hated Me without a cause.**

Furthermore, this leads to *the suffering that Christians are called to endure because of their stance for Christ. This type of suffering <u>does not entail</u> sickness, poverty and tragedies, those things are sent from the enemy and Christians are to resist those forms of evil* (James 4:7). The kind of suffering Believers encounter from others in the world is called <u>persecution</u> and it may first entail hatred towards their Messiah, Jesus Christ. It would also include hatred towards them because they receive and are committed to Him; they are hated because they are not of this world but of another Kingdom and a part of God's Family; they are hated because they take a stand for Israel; they are hated because people of the world are jealous of what they have in Christ; many of them detest Christians and pursue them aggressively with the intent to destroy them, and so forth (I Peter 4:12-19 and Luke 6:22; I John 3:13).

Because they are hated by those who do not know Father God their names are slandered, they are lied upon, left out of events, isolated and separated from others. Some try to make them feel ashamed of the Gospel and what they believe because they have chosen to embrace Truth. **When Christians maintain their love for others in spite of the persecution they grow closer to God, they receive an inner joy and God's favor on their lives (Luke 6:21). They also become more anointed to the point they walk in His glory and do mightier works (John 17:22-23).** This is what is meant when it is said that a Believer takes up his cross and follows Jesus. As you continue to love the Lord and endure the persecution you are strengthened with faith and a force of patience working on the inside of you that will enable you to stand until your answer or instructions come (2 Thess. 1:4). When you take the position to stand bold, stay strong and focused you are counted as a blessed person, "When a man's ways please the Lord, He makes even his enemies to be at peace with him" (Prov. 16:7) and he is rewarded in heaven (Luke 6:22-23).

He will also honor you as you make a conscious decision to take a stand, and not be moved from your position of righteousness but remain rooted and grounded in love, His Word, faith and patience. As you continue to spread the good news that salvation is available: to bless others; to pray for others; and not allow persecution to distract you and get you off course from your mandate from God, He will give you the strength and wisdom that you will need in order to continue in Him to cross the finish line and receive the prize (to be supremely blessed, I Peter 4:14).

The signs and wonders that followed Jesus then, follow His children now, except greater works will be done in these last days (John 14:12). Some of the works that Jesus did and that His followers still do today are: Raise the dead, heal the sick, open blind eyes and deaf ears, limbs grow out, the lame walk, weight supernaturally falls off, teeth supernaturally restored, supernatural debt cancellations occur, marriages are supernaturally restored, families are restored, and barren women conceive and have children. They also set people free from bondage and torment by casting out evil demonic spirits. These are just a few of the different types of recorded miracles that take place around the world today. Unfortunately they are seen as threats to some unbelievers and religious people (all religion and no personal relationship with God) those who have chosen the ways of men with their traditions, customs and religious spirits. **They prefer to receive the glory of men rather than the glory of God.** The bottom line, Jesus Christ's church will prevail and come forth without spot or wrinkle, as He has said, while we patiently await His return. (Mark 16:17; 1:31, 34; Luke 8:49-55; Rev. 3:10-11; Romans 5:1-5; Matt. 9:1-25).

> **The meaning of *Children of God* according to The Ungers Bible Dictionary:**
>
> > The Believer's relationship to God as a child, accordingly, issues from the new birth (John

1:12-13). But all regenerated people are not only children, (that is, born again) but adult sons as well, children of God

receiving a place as sons (Galatians 4:5) by adoption. The indwelling Spirit (Holy Spirit) gives to the child of God the realization of his sonship or spiritual adulthood (Gal. 4:1-6). Since mankind is fallen, a person becomes a child only by faith in Christ and only members of the *Father's family* are brothers in any vital spiritual sense.

The following is a great illustration of The Father's Family or God's Family as demonstrated by Jesus when He defines who is in His **Spiritual Family** which He also referred to as His **"True family."**

Matthew 12:46-50 (also see Mark 3:31-35):

Jesus was still speaking to the people when behold, His mother and brothers stood outside, seeking to speak to Him.

Someone said to Him, Listen! Your mother and Your brothers are standing outside, seeking to speak to You.

But He replied to the man who told Him, Who is My mother, and who are My brothers? And stretching out His hand toward [not only the twelve disciples but all] His adherents, He said, Here are My mother and My brothers. **For *whoever* does the will of My Father in heaven is My brother and sister and mother!**

God said let Us [Father, Son and Holy Spirit] make mankind in Our image, after Our likeness…(Genesis 1:26) and in John 4:24 it says, ***God is a Spirit*** **(a Spiritual Being)** and we are spiritual beings as well, who possess a soul (mind, will, emotions, intellect, and imagination) and who live in a body. We are part spirit, soul and body as stated in the book of I Thessalonians 5:23 and are of a Spiritual Family based primarily on the fact of what God said in:

John 4:23-24,

> A time will come, however, indeed it is already here, when the true (genuine) worshipers will worship the Father in spirit and in truth (reality); for the Father is seeking just such people as these as His worshipers. **God is a Spirit (a Spiritual Being)** and those who worship Him must worship Him in spirit and in truth (reality).

As a Spiritual Being the Holy Spirit communicates with our spirit once we receive our Salvation and are Born-again and it will increase in different ways once we have the *Infilling of the Holy Spirit* (after we are baptized with the Holy Spirit), Acts 1:5, 8.

Briefly what it means to have the **Infilling of the Holy Spirit** which is also known as the **Baptism in the Holy Spirit (Acts 2:1-4)** as listed above it is one of the key qualities a Family of God has. We know that the "church" is the person who is in Christ not the building, although the building is also referred to as the church. After Salvation the Infilling of the Holy Spirit is the second most important impartation from God to all Believers. "The church received the Spirit at a moment God chose. The church had not become more committed, prayerful, or spiritual in and of itself. *The gift of the Spirit was entirely a matter of grace.* In the Upper Room the Spirit was *given each person*, as the *tongues of fire* separating and resting on each person demonstrated. The Spirit represented *a new commitment of God to the covenant relationship* summarized in Lev. 26:12. Three miraculous signs accompanied the giving of the Spirit: the sound of a wind (Greek pneuma means both wind and Spirit); tongues of fire (tongues point to the worldwide mission of the church to preach the gospel); and speaking 'in other tongues,' which also pointed to the preaching mission." [3] Acts 2:1-4 paraphrased.

Speaking in an unknown tongue is a supernatural spiritual language that is for *all who are Born-again Believers.* It is a language that is of men and angels which reveals the mysteries of God no one understands except God, also it offers great benefits to whosoever receives and uses it (I Cor.13:1; 14:2). (See Chapter 7, Section Two under Details Regarding Our Spiritual Weapons number 4 for additional information regarding your supernatural spiritual language).

Furthermore, as we live and walk by the Spirit looking to the Holy Spirit to help us become more and more like Jesus, it is during this process that we experience a renewing of our minds (Romans12:2) and as we begin to die to the flesh (the old way of thinking) we start to take on the will of Christ and walk in the Spirit of God as stated in the following verse:

Galatians 5:16-26:

> (...walk and live [habitually] in the [Holy] Spirit [responsive to and controlled and guided by the Spirit]; then you will certainly not gratify the cravings and desires of the flesh (of human nature without God)...

This is how other people will know we are a part of the Family of God because we will have the glory of God on us as we demonstrate the fruit of the Spirit (Galatians 5:22-23).

God's family is spiritual and they are alive to Him. "People who are not saved are spiritually dead. This means they are not able to enjoy communion with God or perceive and follow the intuitive promptings of the Holy Spirit. These people are limited to their natural or intellectual knowledge and to their common sense; they cannot enjoy the privilege and power of living by revelation. But, when we have been Born-again and are alive spiritually, God can speak to us and show us things we could not know without divine revelation...If you will be diligent to seek Him and listen to His voice, He will lead you supernaturally. He will teach you how to fulfill His purposes for your life – and they may be far greater than anything you are currently trained to do or could ever imagine." [6]

Christianity as defined by The Ungers Bible Dictionary says:

> The body of doctrine that consists of the teachings and way of life made possible by the death, burial, and resurrection of Christ and the giving of the Holy Spirit. *Christianity although having its roots in Judaism, is not Judaism or a mixture of Judaism. It is a way of life, of salvation, the full expression of the gospel of the grace of God* for this age in which God is visiting the Gentiles and "taking from among [them a people for His name" (Acts 15:14). After this period Christ will return and "rebuild the Tabernacle of David which has fallen" (Acts 15:16).
>
> To many, Christianity is a general term descriptive of all that is not Jewish. To others it is synonymous with Christendom. In such cases, little attention is given to the distinctive features of Christian truth.

Christianity as defined by The New Webster's Dictionary says:

The religion of those who accept Jesus Christ as God incarnate (body, flesh) are guided by the Holy Spirit, and participate in the fellowship of the Christian church.

Christianity came into being 30 A.D. when the Apostles received the power of the Holy Spirit to preach the resurrection and gospel of Christ. *Christianity has molded the shape of Western Civilization and has been carried by missionaries to nearly all the countries of the world.*

Only **God-joined relationships are by divine connection**. In these relationships when people remain with the connection or family that God has ordained the result is that they prosper in all areas including peace, health, and wholeness. God is at the head of it and you are in His will, therefore, as you ask He will answer. But if you choose to separate yourself from the divine connections set by God without asking Him and subsequently connect yourself to someone, for instance in marriage, without seeking God first you could possibly bring a person not sent by God into your life. This decision could possibly not only ruin your own life by robbing you of many precious years and unnecessary hardship but ruin the life of your family, all because you decided to have a man-joined relationship instead of a God-joined relationship.

An example of a **man-joined relationship** would be the story of the prodigal son. He joined himself to a citizen of that country, who sent him into his fields to feed swine. And he filled his belly with the husks that the swine ate; and no man gave unto him (Luke 15:15-16). This young man got into trouble because he joined himself in a relationship which was not God's will for his life. He lost all his money and nearly starved to death before he went back to the family and relationship God had placed him in. If on your own initiative you choose to break loose from someone or some group which God has joined you to, you can become impoverished.

The Bible says in 2 Corinthians 6:14-16,

> Do not be unequally yoked together with unbelievers. For what fellowship has righteousness with lawlessness? And what communion has light with darkness?

Thus a man-joined unit of people has the opportunity in the eyes of God to seek Him for their salvation, ask for forgiveness and repent for bonding with people God may not have intended for them to be with. This simple act of obedience and faith will give God the opportunity to now make changes wherever it is necessary by changing hearts, circumstances, situations and so forth so you may experience a better life and a better family.

DEFINING THE ANOINTING OF GOD:

An Anointed or Spiritual Family functions according to the Word of God as they choose to live a Christian (Christ-like) lifestyle. The word Christian also means the anointed ones. To further understand what it means to be in the Family of God, operating as such we must first understand the meaning of these terms, for the Bible says, "in all your getting, get understanding" (Proverbs 4:7 NKJV) and it says, for a lack of understanding or knowledge, people will be destroyed (Hosea 4:6). Therefore, *it is extremely important to have a clear understanding of who you are so that when you confess to be something, you should at least know what it means and what you stand for in order to take a strong stance for what you believe or do not believe to be true in your heart.*

I John 2:27 speaks about the anointing that dwells in us:

> But as for you, **the anointing** (the sacred appointment, the unction) which you received from Him abides [permanently] in you; [so] then you have no need that anyone should instruct you. But just as **His anointing teaches you concerning everything** and is true and is no falsehood, so you must abide in (live in, never depart from) Him [being rooted in Him, knit to Him], just as [His anointing] has taught you [to do].

The definition for the Anointing as given in the Vine's Complete Expository Dictionary (Paraphrased) says:

Believers (Christians, people who are Christ-like) have "an anointing from the Holy One" indicates that this anointing renders them holy, separating them to God. The Holy Spirit is the all efficient means of enabling believers to possess knowledge of the truth.

Thou shalt take of the oil of the anointing, in Ex. 30:25, etc.; it is spoken of as **"a holy anointing oil."**

Masah "to anoint, smear, consecrate." A common word in both ancient and modern Hebrew, masah is also found in ancient Ugaritic. The basic meaning of the word, however, is simply to "smear" something on an object. Usually oil is involved, but it could be other substances.

The Old Testament most commonly uses masah to indicate "anointing" in the sense of a **special setting apart for an office or function**. Christ as the Anointed of God signifies "The Anointed One" (Luke 4:18 and Isaiah 61:1). Also the anointing of Prophets, Priests and Kings; Elisha was anointed to be a prophet (I Kings 19:16); David refused to harm Saul because Saul was "the Lord's Anointed" (I Sam.24:6). Jesus **"...**formed us into a Kingdom, kings (a royal race) and priests to His God and Father..." Rev. 1:6.

Vessels used in the worship as the sacred shrine (both tabernacle and temple) were consecrated for use by "anointing" them (Ex. 29:36; 30:26; 40:9-10).

The Anointing is within you, He is the Holy Spirit helping you with His power in love that will enable you to do things you could not do on your own. The **Anointing is from God and is only for covenant people.** Dr. Joyce Meyer adds this revelation about the Anointing (paraphrased): "I do not have anything to offer people except the anointing (presence and power)...I must have God's anointing in order to do what He has called me to do...*I have learned that I will not carry God's anointing if I do not walk in love, because God does not anoint the flesh* (our own desires and selfish attitudes or behaviors). God does not anoint carnal behavior. We really must walk in love because that aids and increases the anointing on our lives, and the anointing is what empowers us to do what God has called us to do. God's anointing is His presence and power and it enables us to do with ease what we could never accomplish with any amount of struggle on our own. We all need God's anointing...We need it to be good parents, to have successful marriages, to be good friends, and literally in everything we do." [6]

Christ means, "The Anointed One and His Anointing" and we are the "anointed-ones" because Christ came to live in us when we became Christians.

Acts 10:38 explains Jesus acquired the Anointing through God:

> ...God anointed and consecrated Jesus of Nazareth with the [Holy] Spirit and with strength and ability and power; how He went about doing good and, in particular, curing all who were harassed and oppressed by [the power of] the devil, for God was with Him.

Through His anointing we are given authority and might. Our anointed family is brought to victory because of the anointing acquired through Salvation and acknowledging God (Prov. 3:6). **There are different kinds, different levels and measures of the anointing,** therefore, even though we have authority (John 1:12) we will not walk in certain levels of power until we become a mature Christian or **sons of God.** They speak "...skillful and godly Wisdom which is more precious than rubies...Her ways are highways of pleasantness, and all her paths are peace" (Prov. 3:13-17). The ones who "speak wisdom among those who are mature, yet not the wisdom of this age, nor of the rulers of this age, who are coming to nothing" (I Cor. 2:6 NKJV; Romans 8:14). "And because you [really] are [His] sons, God has sent the [Holy] Spirit of His Son into our hearts, crying, Abba (Father)! Father!" (Galatians 4:6). **As sons of God begin to live your life as an heir of God through Christ.** As an heir of God you inherit all the blessings of God that Jesus inherited that came with the finished work He accomplished at the cross which includes your salvation, healing, wholeness, favor, prosperity, prayers answered and a personal relationship with God. Remember an heir of God through Christ also means you are joint-heirs with Jesus (Romans 8:17).

God confirms and makes us steadfast and establishes us [in joint fellowship] with Christ, He consecrated and anointed us [enduing us with the gifts of the Holy Spirit] (2 Cor. 1:21) paraphrased. These gifts will place us in a position to handle the power that comes with the anointing on higher levels or dimensions placed on our lives as we grow in Him.

The Bible says in Psalms 23:5 "...You anoint my head with oil; my [brimming] cup runs over." *One of the symbols of the Anointing is the Anointing Oil.* "He also made the holy anointing oil [symbol of the Holy Spirit] and the pure, fragrant incense, after the perfumer's art" Ex. 37:29. Throughout the Bible the anointing oil was used for powerful times of ministry (Mark 6:13).

The anointing is God's burden-removing, yoke-destroying power according to Isaiah 10:27 which declares what happens when the anointing (oil) is used. The oil in and of itself has no power in it but when used in accordance with the Word of God it releases your faith and as you pray in **Jesus' name it will release the anointing (power) of God into your situation for whatever reason within the will of God** you are using the anointing oil. It says in Isaiah 10:27 KJV, *"And it shall come to pass in that day, that his burden shall be taken away from off thy shoulder, and his yoke from off thy neck, and the yoke shall be destroyed because of the anointing."* The yoke is the "device" that keeps you clamped to your burden.

The anointing oil is also used when laying hands on the sick. It says once anointed and the prayer of faith goes forth they will be "saved him who is sick, and the Lord will restore him (raise him up); and if he has committed sins, he will be forgiven" (James 5:14-15). Note: if you do not have oil with you and you wish to pray for someone you are "anointed" so go forth and pray and the anointing will still be released. Using anointing oil and laying hands is only one way of praying for the sick.

The holy anointing oil was also used to consecrate people for higher office as they were appointed by God (Psalm 89:20-21). In the Old Testament the holy oil was poured over heads of prophets, priest and kings (I Kings 19:16) as well as vessels and objects inside the tabernacle and temple. In the book of **Isaiah 61:1 Jesus located Himself in the scriptures** as He announced in the synagogue "The Spirit of the Lord God is upon Me, because the Lord has *anointed* and qualified Me to preach the Gospel…" It is written in the New Testament as well, that "The Spirit of the Lord [is] upon Me, because He has anointed Me [the Anointed One, the Messiah] to preach the good news (the Gospel) …" (Luke 4:18). **As He was confirmed to be anointed we are anointed as well because His Holy Spirit dwells in us.**

In the New Testament we see the disciples and apostles using the oil to anoint and pray for the sick. Therefore, the practice of using the anointing oil was extended beyond the use of only anointing prophets, priest and kings; it is for whoever desires to benefit from this type of consecration. In both the O.T. and the N. T. one way the anointing could be transferred was by the laying on of hands (Deut. 34:9 and Mark 16:18). Furthermore, anyone that is Born-again has the right to use blessed holy oil. You do not have to wait for leadership from the church to bless your oil (extra virgin olive oil) or for you to anoint and bless your home, business, bank accounts, work place or pray for a sick family member or any other person. In Mark 16:16 it says "He who believes…" and v. 18 says "…they will lay their hands on the sick, and they will get well." David anointed himself (2 Samuel 12:20).

Anyone and anything anointed is set apart for God's purpose and use. The Holy Spirit Who is The Teacher of all things (John 14:26) is represented in I John 2:27 as it speaks about the "Anointing" Who is God the Holy Spirit. It says, "…<u>you must abide in</u> (live in, never depart from) Him [being rooted in Him, knit to Him], just as [His anointing] has taught you [to do].

Unfortunately there are Believers who do not receive the "Infilling of the Holy Spirit" (Baptism in the Holy Spirit) nor do they desire to be sons of God but settle to be "saved and no more." Reading the Word of God especially when Filled to the brim with His Spirit you will receive deeper revelation of the mysteries in the Word. When you are not renewing your mind and you have stopped seeking, asking, and fellowshipping with God you will start to lose or decrease whatever you received from the Kingdom of God as the world's ways start to increase in you and your life. This may leave you with a form of religion but with no real authority or power.

2 Timothy 3:5 says,

> For [although] they hold a form of piety (true religion), they deny and reject and are strangers to the power of it [their conduct belies the genuineness of their profession]. Avoid [all] such people [turn away from them].

"The Holy Spirit distinctly and expressly declares that in latter times some will turn away from the faith, **giving attention to deluding and seducing spirits and doctrines that demons teach,** through the hypocrisy and pretensions of liars whose consciences are seared…"(I Timothy 4:1-2). **This will hinder and choke off the anointing** you received with salvation from flowing in your life and being of benefit to you. Seduction requires two parties a seducer and someone to seduce. *When you are participating with <u>unholy alliances</u> you have opened a door for the seducer to lead you astray and away from the anointing of God.*

What are some of the unholy alliances we need to guard against in order to protect the anointing on our lives? As listed in Ephesians 4 starting at v. 25, they are: **Lying** (which has become a lifestyle for many Believers); **Anger** (anger is an emotion not a sin, it can become a sin if we sin while angry. If you go to bed angry you give the devil opportunity to come in); **Stealing** (example: taking supplies from work, not really working as you should but still expecting full pay, overpayment from a cashier and you say nothing, and refusing to give tithes and offerings if you are Born-again, Malachi 3:8-9); **Corrupt Communication** that proceeds out of your mouth (not just foul language but doubt in God's Word or ability, negative, murmuring and complaining words or any speech that is counter to the Word of God). (Further explanation regarding unholy alliances can be found in Dr. Creflo A. Dollar's book, *The Anointing to Live).*

Satan fears the anointing on the lives of Believers. He knows he is no match for Christ. When he comes with his devices of unholy alliances (example of those spirits listed above and the following: strife, bitterness, slander, gossip, being offended, self-pity, jealousy, depression, lust and suicidal spirits) they are sent to quench or stop the anointing in your life from flowing and to hinder your spiritual growth. All a Believer has to do is release "God's Word in faith" which is an "Anointed Spirit" in the name of Jesus and it will destroy the yoke or device at the root. Remember godly words are containers of spiritual power for a Born-again Christian.

In the Book of Psalms 20:6 it says, "Now I know that the Lord saves His anointed; He will answer him from His holy heaven with the saving strength of His right hand." In Psalm 105:15 it says, **"Touch not My anointed, and do My prophets no harm."** I have quoted these two scriptures to show that *God knows how to* *protect His own and He will.* One way is for Him to first instruct His children, His sons and daughters on how to live before Him and in such a way that they stay out of harms way. When others are deliberately trying to harm you He will protect you for He will avenge His own (Romans 12:19). He also gives a strong word or a warning to those outside of His family when they choose to harm His chosen (Genesis 12:3; John 15:16).

A note to the Believers: Are you aware that people can operate in the anointing and still sin? But they cannot continue to operate in the glory and sin and not repent. Born-again Christians need the glory of God to stand and remain righteous for this latter season or age that God has transitioned people into (Haggai 2:7-9; Psalm 24:6-7). We know that the anointing is for every Believer and it will keep your mind (I Cor. 2:16) and give you understanding and the revelation of the mysteries of God that are in His Word. But **the glory of God is designed to protect you** because the anointing will still work in a corrupt person as it works in a person of honor because you can be anointed without the glory of God being on your life.

Jesus was anointed and consecrated with the Holy Spirit and with power as He went about doing good (Acts. 10:38). He was trusted with all levels of authority and power. *When we walk in His righteousness as sons of God* (male or female, because this is a spiritual term and there is no gender in the spirit) it will bring the glory on our lives as well and we can be trusted with higher levels of authority and His power because of the glory. This supersedes having an anointing to do a work. That is why some people have authority but no power. In addition, there is **a greater power coming to the earth** that no one has stepped into as of yet that will have such awesome miracles, that many have never seen before and the time is very, very close. Why do I mention this? Because we are in an hour (a time) where these words are about to come to pass: **Jesus says** *if anyone believes in Him, "he will himself be able to do the things that I do; and he will do even greater things than these…"* (John 14:12).

To have the glory and an anointing, someone demonstrated what this would be like by using this illustration: "when the first Adam lived in the garden before the fall of man he had the glory of God on him and he operated by divine revelation and did not really need the anointing to understand God's Word." The anointing has limitations because as mentioned earlier there are different kinds, different levels and measures of the anointing. Therefore, we want to always strive to draw near to God knowing Him by having a personal relationship with Him which will enable His glory to come upon our lives and work with the anointing in us to do even greater works for the Kingdom of God. (For additional information on how to protect the Anointing see Chapter 7, Section Two under Details Regarding Our Spiritual Warfare Weapons… number 8).

CHAPTER 5

INSIGHT AS TO HOW GOD VIEWS A BLENDED FAMILY, THE CHALLENGES IT MAY ENCOUNTER AND METHODS ON HOW TO RESOLVE THEM

God loves families because He loves people! *All people are created equally, made in His image, having the same opportunity to call on His name by faith and see the same results. God sees **all families** the same way, they all have the same opportunity to call on His name by faith and see the same results* – His Glory, because **He loves them all the same – *unconditionally!***

John 3:16 says this about God's love for all people:

> For God so greatly loved and dearly prized the world that He [even] gave up His only begotten (unique) Son, so that whoever believes in (trusts in, clings to, relies on) Him shall not perish (come to destruction, be lost) but have eternal (everlasting) life.

Families may differ in their size, income, social status, whether they are a Biological, Blended, Traditional, Single-Parent, Child-Free, Adopted, Foster or members of an Extended Family, it does not matter how they differ or the type they are, when they apply God's principles because they chose to follow His Word (instructions, precepts and teachings), in other words His Ways of doing things, *any family has the same opportunity* because **His ways** *work* **regardless of the circumstances that they are facing.**

All the **promises of God** that come with our covenant are available to individuals as well as families (groups of related individuals by blood, marriage or the Spirit of God) that follow Him.

2 Corinthians 1:20-22 says,

> For as many as are the *promises of God*, they all find their Yes [answer] in Him [Christ]. For this reason we also utter the Amen (so be it) to God through Him [in His Person and by His agency] to the glory of God.
>
> But it is God Who confirms and makes us steadfast and establishes us [in joint fellowship] with you in Christ, and has consecrated and anointed us [enduing us with the gifts of the Holy Spirit]; [He has also appropriated and acknowledged us as His by] putting His seal upon us and giving us His [Holy] Spirit in our hearts as the security deposit and guarantee [of the fulfillment of His promise].

Our promises include wholeness, nothing broken, nothing missing. This would include peace, healing, provision, abundance, protection, divine wisdom, revelation, prosperity and godly relationships.

Every family or household (which includes your extended family) has the same advantage when in Christ. According to scripture if one person believes and received Christ as their Lord and Savior the Holy Spirit will draw the rest of the family and each member will be given an opportunity to receive their Salvation and become Saved, a Born-again Believer.

Acts 16:31 says,

> And they answered, Believe in the Lord Jesus Christ [give yourself up to Him, take yourself out of your own keeping and entrust yourself into His keeping] and **you will be saved, [and this applies both to] you and your household as well.**

The Blended or Traditional Nuclear Family resemble one another and are similar because they are a two-parent household with biological children, not usually adopted or foster children nor are they a Single-Parent household. However, unlike the Nuclear (biological or natural) Family the Blended Family goes through a honeymoon phase then reality sets in.

When a couple marries that have children they are starting their family with multiple people not just two. After the honeymoon phase is over each family member's true personality surfaces and all family members start to see the 'real' person in each other. Suddenly different and/or more complicated personalities are shown in various family members that must be gently dealt with, confronted boldly or with help from the outside, it all depends on how severe a person (adult, adolescent or child) has been injured in their soul. Put another way, how much they are hurting emotionally from the past or the divorce that took place before your marriage occurred.

With the Biological Family there are always gradual adjustments, but with the Blended Family the roles need to be defined and settled into. This is a process that will need time. In Galatians 5:22-23 God has given us the fruit of His Spirit to help us and patience and self-control are two of those fruit that can be applied to help get through this process.

Children raised-up in the Word of God and that have a personal relationship with Him usually learn that Father God is a Father to the fatherless (Psalm 68:5) which includes those who need a mother, because God is of no gender and He loves all of His children. His sons and daughters should know that they can come to Him first to deal with their heart issues and receive healing where needed. They should have learned how to forgive and treat others because that is a part of God's will for their healing. They understand that even though Dad and Mom's marriage did not continue they can still call on their heavenly Father (Daddy) to make sure that they stay on a path that will keep them sound, safe and prosperous. Also, they can continue to pray for themselves, their natural and blended parents as well as their siblings. However, this is <u>not</u> the norm for most. Many Christian homes in today's society are not training their children and bringing them up in the Word of God and thus the children do not have this revelation knowledge or help to fall back on if needed later.

HOW GOD VIEWS A BLENDED PARENT:

The Blended Parent that assumes the responsibility and the role of a parent should know that God does not see nor does He make a distinction regarding a "parent" whether they reside over a biological, blended, single-parent, adopted or any other family type, to God a parent is a parent. For example, if you are a husband it does not matter whether you are a husband for the first time or the third time you are still a "husband" and you should assume the responsibilities that come with that role along with seeking wisdom and guidance from the Holy Spirit.

If you are functioning as a parent then find out how to be an *excellent* parent by letting the Word of God be your standard. Also read Christian material on parenting and find out what are the responsibilities of a parent. Just because you may be one it does not mean you are a good one. Many times when we parent others it is based on how our parents raised us and that may have been good or it may have been just alright or even badly. You want to strive to be a person of excellence and that would include being an excellent parent, *we did not say a perfect parent but one of excellence, someone who is doing their best in whatever they endeavor.*

If you have not as of yet stepped into the shoes of a "parent" and have chosen to be a "friend" to your spouse's child or teen since functioning as a parent would include discipline and this would be difficult for you since you do not have a relationship with the child (because discipline without relationship only leads to rebellion) then being a friend may be a wise decision for now. Once your relationship with the child develops then you and your spouse should agree when it is time for you to step into the role of a parent which includes a disciplinary role. Giving the child or teen a chance to grow to like, respect and *hopefully* trust you for who you are and what you represent in your home. (The word hopefully was used in this last sentence because many people who are wounded or angry with God will not trust *anyone* and that includes God).

Legally the blended parent has the right to speak their mind in a loving and direct way like any other parent because they are married to the blended child's parent and this is what gives them the authority in the household in the eyes of God and before the law. However, the blended parent must still use wisdom as to timing and be in agreement with their spouse so the natural parent will be able to give them the support they will need to make the transition as easy as possible so their spouse can exercise their parental rights.

If you came into the union without children of your own it may take a while to learn about and adjust to having children but with patience, love, wisdom, guidance and the anointing from the Holy Spirit it certainly can be done. *Nothing is impossible with God, things are only impossible with men.* God will give you a supernatural love for the child or adolescent. Give them your undivided attention by making yourself available to them, making time in your schedule for them. Then listen and begin to learn about them by listening for their likes, dislikes and interests.

Volunteer to help them with school work, school activities, and drive them to the mall and places they enjoy. You and the child or teen can enjoy lunch with the family or just the two of you have some quality time together. Be creative if and when possible or simply offer to be of assistance, not doing the work or project for them, but working *with them* in areas of their interests or obligations.

Do not ignore that the former family has been split in half and the fact that a divorce is a past reality for both of your families. You should be able to understand if you have come into the marriage with children yourself. Because of the split in the two former families there will be feelings of loss, grief, rejection, alienation, anger, helplessness and sometimes shame. **Like any other loss allow people, regardless of their age, time to heal**. When they truly heal they will be able to receive their new life and a new family a lot easier. *In the meantime realize that the new parent is an adult and they should strive to be more mature and understanding to allow room for healing and growth in the children.*

All members of the family should keep in mind that in many instances the parents are probably still healing from the past as well and because of their role they will usually put their wounds and hurts on the backburner for the sake of their children but at some point they need to receive their total healing as well. **Everyone will need patience and understanding and God's assistance for this process to be successful.** Over time with God's unconditional love in the household everyone will heal that <u>wants</u> to be healed.

Children from a divorced home that are still grieving over the lost of a parent (divorce can be as painful as a death in the family) a loyalty to the biological parent that is not in the home may occur if the child is rushed to adjust to his or her new environment or because of the love they have for their parent which should be respected regardless of the problems their parent's marriage suffered.

SOME ADOLESCENTS REJECT A BLENDED PARENT:

Blended parents can be at a disadvantage especially with those who have acquired adolescents with their new marriage. The teen often will dismiss a step or blended parent as having no authority in their life although they still may desire them to assume their adult responsibilities and be a parent in every other sense – provider, homemaker, chauffeur, support system, etc.

The blended parent in many cases is then limited in accommodating them because of the boundaries the teen has set as to how close they will allow them to come into a given situation and how much, if any, they will let them assist with the problems that occur in their lives. It can take time for kids to attach, trust and respect. The time frame will depend of course on the child, adolescent (teen to young adult) and the parents involved.

Usually the new "parent" is unprepared for resistance from their spouse's children and may be surprised and even discouraged by the conflicts they have with these new relationships. For example the child, teen or young adult (the age really doesn't matter), they have become a step or Blended Family child and they are finding ways to adjust and adapt. They may try to dismiss the blended parent by telling them they are not "their" parent or by ignoring them altogether and only addressing the natural parent in regards to their needs, wants and desires.

They may choose to introduce you to their friends or whoever as "this is my father's wife" or the new husband as "this is my mother's husband," making it clear that this is something my parent chose to do and it had nothing to do with me, they do not receive their parent's decision nor do they have to accept or support it. Sometimes this behavior is a protective wall. They may feel like they trusted in their parent's decisions before and look what happened. Thus because the divorce process was so painful the child (regardless of their age) is doing what is natural to protect themselves from further hurt by putting up guards and walls so they won't be subject to that kind of pain again. You may be dealing with a person who has experienced a great deal of trauma and are now faced with hurt, anger, grief, depression, sadness or sorrow and in many cases they have lost faith in their parents, marriage and God.

Children or adolescents do not have enough experience to know that when things go wrong in a "big way," things can still *turn around* and become fine once again. It is not always the end of the world as young people tend to perceive it.

CALLING THE NEW PARENT DAD OR MOM:

Adjustments have to happen, but if they are forced to adjust or if they adjust too quickly it could become a problem. When forced to adjust by: being instructed that we will be together all the time; or trying to make someone address a new parent as Dad or Mom; or if one spouse tries to include the new spouse in every conversation and so forth, this may create resentment or animosity. When people are pressured and they don't have a relationship with each other, there is an irritation or frustration in the air as they are going through the motions of doing what needs to be done and as a result you will more than likely see the opposite of what you desire to see. If the family flows with the Holy Spirit (moves along at a pace that gives you and everyone else a peace not a discomfort) they will adjust and eventually everyone will be able to accept healing and move forward. One cannot set a pace or rate of progress for healing a broken heart or a tormented mind, just know if you follow the leading of the Holy Spirit each family member will heal at the appropriate time for them. The Holy Spirit may lead your family for outside Christian counseling. It may be necessary for the family as a whole or individuals within the family that may need that little extra in the beginning stages of the adjustment. Keep in mind that time, love and communicating are powerful tools for healing a broken heart.

As far as showing the parents respect in the home from the children and vice versa no one should be forced to call a Blended Parent, Dad or Mom. This can be very difficult for some children because they may feel a loyalty to their natural parent is being violated. They may not choose to call the new parent by these "dear" terms which people either associate with love for someone they value or with someone who highly disappointed them and they may feel let them down. **When and if the child or adolescent feels that person is a "parent"**

in their life and they are comfortable with saying it they will address them as Dad or Mom on their own. In the meantime all should agree on what name they should call the new parent in their household whether it is for the husband or the wife. For example, call them by their first name, or if that seems disrespectful because of the age difference and their position in the family, then either replace their name with another term of endearment or along with it or use a nick name, it just depends on whatever everyone is in favor of and comfortable with, especially that particular parent and child.

There is no need for the blended parent to feel resentment or confusion or let it bother them or attack their self-worth. Most of the time it isn't even about you. The child needs to process through different emotions or stages to make the changes easier to deal with for themselves. Again, the parent figure needs to be more mature and understanding in giving time and space where it is needed. You do not have all of the facts, you may not know everything that that child has been through or what they are feeling especially if they came from a home where they were neglected, abandoned or abused and not necessarily by a parent, it could have been an extended family member, close friend or neighbor. Prayer, time, love along with hope can develop into faith and faith can resolve conflicts.

THE IMPORTANCE OF A CHILD REMAINING IN THEIR ROLE:

Another adjustment problem that could occur is if a child or teen willingly moves or is forced into the role of the adult who has departed through separation, divorce or death and as the child or teen steps out of the role of a child into the role of "mom" or "dad" to **replace the one who left later they may become displaced and confused as to what their role or function in the family is. Caution to single parents with children, it is important for** a child or teen to continue in the role of a child or teen and not be robbed of their childhood as much as possible. If they are taking on too many adult responsibilities and losing their childhood they may not complain or even be aware of the seriousness of the matter of taking on and walking in a role that is not theirs. Instead they may be glad that they can be of assistance to the parent who stayed. At the same time, **they run the risk of being misplaced from** *their role as a child* **and becoming confused about their** *function* **in the family.**

If the child or teen had moved into the role of the missing parent, and the blended parent has now filled that role, the child may resent it, may develop unforgiveness and if not dealt with bitterness will also occur. They may also have some fears, insecurities and confusion as to where they fit or belong in the family, if at all. They may be unwilling or unable to return to their role as a child or teen especially if they were a teen and are now an adult, the transition may be to confusing or painful. Some may even see this as some form of rejection by indirectly saying to them that they did not do a good job when they stepped into the role of the parent who had departed.

In a case like this where rejection, low self-esteem and insecurities have now given the enemy room to come in and torment, it is best to give that child or adolescent quality time and appreciate them for who they are as a person and explain to them how you appreciated what they did and the wonderful job they did when they stepped up to the plate and functioned in a role that was designed for a person much older than themselves and required a great deal of experience.

Children especially teens secretly desire for their parents to reunite. Much of this is based on what they feel in their heart from their past. Most teens idolize the way things were when their parents were still together but in most instances they have forgotten or blocked out all the ugliness, isolation and pain that may have also been a part of their natural parent's marriage. In a case like this where the blended parent is present and has started a new life with that child's natural parent this child or teen may see the new parent as an obstacle to that desire or dream being fulfilled. The parent(s) should not take it personally for everyone's good. I would also like to mention that if there was cruelty or violence in the former home some children are glad that is over with and in time welcome a new parent.

CHILDREN SEARCHING FOR THEIR IDENTITY OR PLACE IN THE BLENDED FAMILY:

When they resist your presence or rebel by being rude, defiant, disrespectful or ignoring you, choose to forgive each time and give the matter to God and ask the Holy Spirit to keep you in the right frame of mind and to guard your heart so you won't dislike the child and become bitter. They are doing what is a normal response for them because of where they are spiritually and emotionally and the situation they now find themselves in. Some are really handling things the best that they know how to handle it. Many times when people are going through something it is not their intention or motive to hurt you, or any family member for that matter, they are doing what is necessary to help themselves, guard their heart or try to change a situation they really have no control over but because you are so close in the same house you will feel or be hurt by some of their actions or words. Sometimes they are just searching for their identity or their place in this family structure while they are still concerned about the parent who no longer lives with them. They may also be secretly in fear that this "new thing" may fail and the trauma starts all over again; or that it may succeed which will bring closure to their past life and launch them into a new somewhat scary and unknown future.

Therefore, the Holy Spirit will keep you and give you insight and wisdom as to how to work with the situation. *His way will usually include forgiveness and showing them love. This does not mean you become a door mat. You let them know what you disapprove of but that you also love them and will still be there for them.* There is no weapon formed that can prosper against love. In the meantime you confront when you are led by the Holy Spirit, forgive the rest and continue to leave it in God's hands. When you turn the child loose in given areas especially an adult child they will come back and will probably be closer than ever.

In addition, discuss resolutions with your spouse **before** you have any confrontation with his or her natural child when there has been a great deal of resistance in the past. Because misunderstandings could arise if they think you are mistreating their natural child or showing favoritism toward your own children. **So as to avoid allowing the child to play you one against the other, both parents should pray about the situation and always be transparent in their relationship about the child in question.** Your children regardless of age did not have a lot of control in the matter of your getting married so when they are rebellious these are ways they can express how they feel. Even if they were informed and included they still may choose to give input and communicate indirectly about what happened because their thinking could be, "after all this did affect my life too."

Furthermore, never allow the children to play you against each other, by manipulating you to take sides that will cause division with the two of you. For instance, if a child comes to one of you with a request telling you that your spouse agreed and it is fine with them so you should agree also, tell them after you speak to your spouse then you will make your decision. This way the two of you are letting them know you communicate and you choose to be in agreement and they can save their tricks and their testing of the waters.

Some things need to be mandatory to get things done and other things need to be announced in advance, if possible, so the child or teen is given an opportunity to see if they would like to participate or not in what has been or about to be planned. *Many things can be announced or discussed at family meetings where there is an open forum with freedom to express one's feelings, ideas, family plans, grievances and complaints. The meeting should include a plan of action and a follow-up family meeting to monitor progress in the areas where a reasonable change has been requested by a family member.* (Family meetings are discussed further on under Additional Methods on how to Resolve Challenges…).

The parents should instill godly principles by first, being a godly example themselves and secondly, by taking the time to build relationships within the family and thirdly, by teaching the Word in the home as well as the family attending church and bible study. Also a good youth program wouldn't hurt. However, **if you are not living a godly lifestyle, don't try to teach it, especially in a hostile environment.** In your case just pray and let God move and give you instructions or send you help. *Kids see through phoney people and actions, they can discern very well, it is hard to fool a child when it comes to the true character of a person.* Another thing, never be afraid to ask for help outside of the home from Christians who are experienced with children and have a record of success as well as seeking godly advice from Christian counselors, youth pastors, and so forth.

Also realize that not everyone in the family desires to make the transition or adjustment, some may prefer it the way "it used to be." Some people do not want to listen or obey a new parent or be a part of a Blended Family. The adolescents or adult children that were not raised in the Blended Family but were older will definitely have to settle this in their own hearts especially if they are unprepared to deal with another parent or strongly desired for their biological parents to reunite. *The blended parents have no reason to take these things personally, the child has to want what God has done and/or desire that change in their own heart. Their decision is between them and God and you are out of it. Your part at this point is to continue to show love and be respectful of their decision. God gave each person a free will to choose.*

MANY CHILDREN AND ADOLESCENTS DO WELCOME A NEW PARENT:

On the other hand, there will be those who do welcome a new parent with open arms. This could occur at any age, it depends on the child, their need and their openness to it or expectations of having a parent in the role that has been missing in their home whether it is a father or a mother some will just be excited about being in a two parent family again or for the first time.

The younger the child the better it will work in favor of a blended parent because younger children are primarily more trusting, loving and flexible and they are not old enough to be stuck in their ways. Furthermore, the younger children are more than likely not living with pro-longed disappointments, hurts or past memories of "how it used to be in the good old days."

Sometimes when older children are hurting and want relief from painful thoughts which are fed to their minds usually from the adversary about the good times there will be no remembrance of the bad, the deception that is being fed to them is causing their emotions to come out of balance which is causing them to grieve for the past. Then other thoughts are fed to their mind, if only the new parent was not in the way we could all be so happy again. **The trick or the deception by Satan is to cause people to stay stuck in a past that they can do nothing about at this point and to miss the future that is right before them.** And since Satan cannot stop what God is doing he will try his best to rob you of your joy in receiving what God has done so that when you have it you will not enjoy it. Little by little he will take your strength so he can get to any hope you may have in your heart that can develop into strong faith and trust in God. He will work this on any family member adult or child who is living in the past or prolonged grief. (Other tactics the enemy has is further discussed in Chapter 7, Section One).

REBUILDING A STRONG HOME AND A SENSE OF SECURITY IN YOUR FAMILY:

To rebuild a sense of security in your family as well as a strong home, the more love expressed through mutual respect, appreciation and thoughtfulness, plus pleasant words and deeds, coupled with kindness, consideration and a humble spirit expressed between the husband and wife will set an atmosphere of love and build a strong foundation in your home. The children will begin to feel safe and secure again. Hope can be rebuilt and interest will spark. If the couple prays together on a regular basis and the family is exposed to this it would set an example and explain where their love, strength and help are coming from. The children can also learn where to go for help if they need it. *They need to see your love and respect for each other before you will have their full attention and hope of any real breakthroughs.*

With Blended Families it is best to think and speak of each spouse's natural children as "our" children, not as your child or my child. The responsibility is joint and it should be one's mindset that it will be that way. Team work between the couple is essential to give the children the love, time, attention, training and the self-sacrifice it will take to focus on each child as an individual and the overall family as a whole. It is very important for unity and agreement to be in the house. Luke 11:17 NIV says, **"Any kingdom divided against itself will be ruined, and a house divided against itself will fall."** For example, if a Blended Family has four children, each parent brought two and one spouse responds when asked how many children do you have, and they respond, "I have two children." He or she is indirectly rejecting their spouse's two children for whatever reason. Even though their spouse nor that spouse's children may say anything they perceive that you have not received them in your heart. Therefore, true unity will have a difficult time in this household. Small things add up and will prevent the progress of strong unity in the family. The parent that is directly or indirectly rejecting the other two children has opened a door for the adversary to come in. One thing that is needed, when someone is saying something that is disturbing your heart or you have a bad feeling about it, do not hesitate to bring it up at a family meeting or on a one-on-one basis whichever feels right in your heart (spirit). It could be that the parent is not aware that they are saying things that will keep everyone divided in the home. The adversary is cunning and subtle. The solution is to expose and/or oppose (confront) whatever has the possibility of being destructive.

Starting and forming new habits start in the mind with your choice of words. *Words have power and when released things start to line up with what is said. We will have what we say.* **Pray, declare**

and confess what you desire to see happen in your family not what is negative and currently happening. You will be amazed how hearts start to change towards God's will, and things start to flow smoothly and adjustments seem to be happening supernaturally. Things suddenly work in relationships between the family members that may not have been working before because of the choice of words that were spoken.

Guard against those outside of the immediate family from being allowed to disrespect your spouse by ignoring them; for example, inviting you to a function *without* your new spouse. Games and tactics like these can cause hurt, discord and cause a separation for the blended married couple if it continues to reoccur and no one takes a stand to stop these foolish and selfish acts. Remember, you play right into the adversary's hands if you yield to these devices when he manipulates and uses others to work against your marriage which will eventually affect your family. *A house divided will not stand.*

To maintain unity with the couple and the children, *the parents* need to communicate well with everyone knowing that their words, guidance and strength to do so comes from maintaining their personal relationship with God and praying with each other as a couple daily. **My husband and I began praying together on the telephone before we were married and all these years later we still pray together daily after breakfast. The spirit of agreement delivers** you from backlash and retaliation that is sent to cause stress and serious problems. In addition**, it keeps God first in your marriage** where He is suppose to be, remember marriage is between one man, one woman and God. That forms a threefold cord that is not easily broken.

Matthew 18:19 says,

> Again I tell you, **if two of you on earth agree** (harmonize together, make a symphony together) about whatever [anything and everything] they may ask, it will come to pass and be done for them by My Father in heaven.

To try to break up a marriage especially one that is ordained by God is a serious matter for in His Word He warns, *"What therefore God has united (joined together), let not a man separate or divide" (Mark 10:9).* When people in the family or outside of it allow Satan or other evil forces to use them to come against someone's marriage there are always consequences for wrong decisions that must and will be dealt with.

THE DIFFERENCE BETWEEN DISCIPLINE AND PUNISHMENT:

While moving on we will discuss the structure, discipline and guidelines that will be used for a household. **Realize that there is a difference between discipline and punishment.** *Discipline requires* time, energy, consistency, love, care and reaching out. *Discipline establishes* rules, guidelines, regulations and parameters. *Discipline teaches* godly character and healthy development. *Discipline takes* supernatural wisdom and it will build respect and honor in your children.

Hebrews 12:7, 9, 10 shows why our Heavenly Father disciplines us:

You must submit to and endure [correction] for discipline;

God is dealing with you as with sons. **For what son is there whom his father does not [thus] train and correct and discipline?**

Moreover, we have had earthly fathers who disciplined us and we yielded [to them] and respected [them for training us]. Shall we not much more cheerfully submit to the Father of Spirits and so [truly] live?

For [our earthly fathers] disciplined us for only a short period of time and chastised us as seemed proper and good to them; but He disciplines us for our certain good that we may become sharers in His own holiness.

Whereas punishment is what is done when rules or guidelines are broken. Parents need to be in agreement about the punishment. For example, from giving them one warning or removing things they like for a period of time to spanking appropriately. Each household has to find what works for them. It may vary for different children, within the same household, because of their age and other factors. What may be a suitable punishment for one may not be effective for another child because of their personality, mindset or disposition (their natural attitude towards things). Parents also need to discuss who will administer the punishment; will each correct their biological child only or all the children? This is a decision that will have to be made in each individual household. *What matters is that the two of you* ***are in agreement*** *about the punishment and what each will administer.*

What does the Word of God say about discipline and punishment?

Proverbs 13:24 says,

> He who spares his rod [of *discipline]* hates his son, but he who loves him disciplines diligently and *punishes* him early.

Proverbs 19:18 says,

> *Discipline* your son while there is hope, but do not [indulge your angry resentments by undue *chastisements* and] set yourself to his ruin.

Proverbs 23:13 says,

> Withhold not *discipline* from the child; for if you strike and *punish* him with the [reedlike] rod, he will not die.

Proverbs 29:15, 17 says,

The rod and reproof give wisdom, but a child left *undisciplined* brings his mother to shame. *Correct* your son, and he will give you rest; yes, he will give delight to your heart.

Proverbs 13:24 *above is used often to justify beating children because many do not understand that to spare the "rod" is not always talking about a spanking as if the more you beat or spank the better they will be.* Spanking has its place like everything else. Anything out of order or balance is leaving the protection and wisdom of God. **In the Bible the word rod also means to lead, to protect and to support as well as discipline.** Therefore, at times the parents do not need to spank their child as if it is the only form of discipline when the child is unruly. Maybe that child is crying out for help and the help that is needed is in one of the other areas. Such as **leading them** by giving them guidance, advice and understanding; in **protecting them** by keeping them safe, praying for them and setting boundaries that shows you love them; in **supporting them** by attending school functions or helping with homework or by providing finances for a private school, a good home environment and so forth.

As far as correcting them there is also that called **the "rod of correction,"** (spanking). Foolishness is bound in the heart of a child but God has given us something to pry this foolishness out of their hearts and He calls it a rod of correction. When people in general do so many foolish things it is because they have not been disciplined by God or understand what God's discipline is concerning how one should live and treat others. Born with a sin nature each one of us has this bound in us and occasionally it takes a rod of correction to pry it loose. In addition, a person must be transformed in their mind in order to continue in ways that are upright (Romans 12:2).

When you are leading, protecting and supporting the way the Bible says then the rod of correction will seldom be needed. The child would have learned that they can trust you to be there for them and they will be less rebellious. Children make the association with God through their parents who they see everyday as the authority figure in their lives. *The example we as parents set before our children will be a great influence on how they see a loving God because* **parents symbolically represent God to their children.** If you allow the Lord to discipline you and you treat others with respect before your children then they will listen but when you are not disciplined yourself and you tell them to behave all you are doing is provoking that child to wrath. It takes a person who is disciplined themselves to properly administer discipline to their children or they will more than likely rebel and want to get out from under your poor role model. Never discipline out of anger or embarrassment but let discipline come out of a love response. Do it God's way.

Worldly advice, advice apart from the Word of God, pretty much tells parents not to correct or punish but instead allow their child to do as they please most of the time. In doing this the world's way the Bible says the mother will be brought to shame, there will be no rest in your house and it reminds us to discipline while there is still hope. Once a child knows they will never be corrected or punished they will simply continue in the wrong behavior and sometimes this places a home in such disarray that it could cost the family the peace that they could have enjoyed. It could also contribute to a marriage falling apart from the noise, disorder, confusion, chaos from one or more children in the home who are unruly and undisciplined. **On the other hand, trained children enhance the parent's ability to have peace in their home,** freedom to love one another because they have been taught to give their parents time to have couple time to discuss their day or go on dates together or whatever they plan in order to keep their marital relationship strong. Children that have been taught to contribute to a healthy home environment and to a healthy marriage become very secure within the family as well as learn marital skills and principles for their future homes.

Parents need only to use a little wisdom since the world's system basically comes against parents who choose to do the right things according to the Word of God their standard by which they measure good behavior and all things. They should make sure before they correct with hands-on that it is when they are calm and in an environment that is not going to be quick to yell "child abuse." If your children are normally unruly or curious tell them before hand they need to listen when you say "stop," and if they do not, then you will be leaving the store immediately and taking them home or to a sitter. Eventually they will miss the shopping or fun or whatever and let them know that you will be assigning a punishment because of their behavior. If you follow through they will get the message and each outing will improve because they are being taught right from wrong. It will be a sacrifice for you but well worth it for now and later for both the child and the parents.

Proverbs 22:6 and Ephesians 6:4 are clear about what should be done to have lasting results:

Train up a child in the way he should go [and in keeping with his individual gift or bent], and when he is old he will not depart from it.

Fathers, do not irritate and provoke your children to anger [do not exasperate (annoy) them to resentment], but rear them [tenderly] in the training and discipline and the counsel and admonition of the Lord.

Most parents that really love their children will train them up in the way they should go which means by the example from the One who created us, Who wrote the book, and loves us dearly and truly knows what is best for our lives and our well being. The leading of the Holy Spirit Who has been sent to lead and guide the parent so they are careful not to break the child's spirit, hinder their natural gifts and to be just in how you discipline. It is a matter of choice of where you place your value. Who you choose to listen to whether it will be Almighty God or a person with flaws and problems like anyone else, will be up to you. But remember this, this life has good and evil in it and it does not have to destroy our children or us if we follow the Master's plan instead of our own (Ps. 72:4; Ps.90:16; Ps.102:28; Ps.127:3-5; Luke 10:19; Isa. 49:25-26).

And in addition, if we do not teach those who God entrusted us to, then we as parents are held accountable. Certainly we can be forgiven once we repent for avoiding our responsibilities. However, *the consequences of neglecting to correct, discipline and punish when needed in raising our children will be punishment enough once the child is grown and totally undisciplined to the point they do not respect anyone or anything* and are proud, arrogant and confused, living miserable lives and still searching for the true "love" they did not receive as a child growing up (Ps.103:17).

The above results may be to the extreme but for many it is a reality. At the same time, a lot of our kids will be fine from a warning or punishment every now and then. *For the parents of the countless children and adolescents who did **not** have any or extremely limited discipline or punishment when their child was really crying out for someone to notice, correct and instruct them and let them know that <u>truly someone cared enough to do this for them.</u>* Know that your child still has the option of being restored in whatever area they are struggling in by giving their life to "Daddy" God and receiving His love, acceptance and purpose for their life. As you say a prayer God will move and give your child that which is needed for their future to be brighter.

VISITATION RIGHTS AND CHILDREN LIVING BETWEEN TWO HOMES:

Even though the former marriage has dissolved, when children are involved, in many cases the divorced couple will have to keep a line of communication open via telephone or by other electronic devices. Decisions that concern their children will have to be made to allow both parents to still be a part of their natural children's lives and to comply with visitation rights or joint custody and so forth. Hopefully this can be done with the least amount of drama for the child's peace of mind and well-being. If past hurts and threats become a problem for anyone then new arrangements through the court system will probably need to be made.

Always show respect for all parties involved at all times and this includes your former spouse for three reasons: **(1)** in most cases open communication will be necessary in regards to the children; **(2)** the former spouse is still the child's natural parent and the child knows they are a part of that person and if negative remarks are constantly being made about the other parent the child will associate this with themselves. They could develop the wrong self image especially if they do not know who they are according to what the Bible has to say about them; and **(3)** no one enjoys hearing someone speak badly of their parent regardless of what happened. We all make mistakes and our part is not to judge but to forgive and show love as we continue on with our lives raising a healthy godly family as much as possible.

With regards to visitation rights where children visit the former spouse's home, what kind of arrangements can be made for some cases: a few days out of a month or every other weekend or just for the summer or six months out of a year? Visitation is usually made according to court arrangements and what is in the best interest of the child, however, more time with their child can be arranged if the two families can really communicate with one another and follow through. This can be extremely emotional or confusing especially in the beginning for the children. Adjusting to two households and two sets of parents and maybe additional siblings in each home can be overwhelming and leave the child feeling like they really don't know where they belong. Some kids that are shuffled back and forth feel as if they are not really a part of either family but their life consists of living out of a suitcase with no real roots. But I have learned that people can do all things through Christ who strengthens them. He will keep you sane through it all and give you the strength, knowledge, understanding and wisdom that will be necessary to do what you need to do for that season of your life.

It is important in both households to come to an agreement to have similarities for the child regarding biblical needs, education, homework, the type of diet, bed time, how much television, internet, phone activity is allowed, the type of friends they can see and so forth. **If the parents can have a meeting and discuss what and how the child is being raised in the primary parent's home and comply as much as possible this would make it easier for the child to adjust.** Also if they see that the adults in their lives are able out of maturity and love for them to go the extra distance it would begin to rebuild their trust in their parents, in God and showing them just how much they are loved.

However, because of past hurts and bitterness this may not always be possible especially if the primary parent is not receiving child support or he or she is choosing to punish the former spouse by withholding the child from their visits in hopes that this would cause the former spouse to cooperate. We can also find less cooperation when the visited household is dealing with a very rebellious child towards the new spouse and especially where those parents have heard that the primary parent(s) are really speaking badly about them in front of the children. And when there is constant anger, ignoring instructions, disappearing, use of chemical substances by a child that should not have them in their possession and a number of other behavioral problems, these behaviors could get in the way of how the adults are willing to participate in cooperating between the two households for the sake of that *very* child. Many people are stressed, weary and on the verge of giving up just from dealing with regular life issues let alone added problems of a former spouse with accusations and lies; threats from a child; and the child or children upsetting the peace and structure of their parent's home and new marriage.

While visiting the parent that has visitation rights and not sole custody, the child is sometimes used to spy or report events happening in their home to the primary parent or vice versa and therefore is caught in the middle of the hatred and games which only now add to the child's feelings of confusion, rejection and anger while they are trying to cooperate and please the parent who is making such a request possibly with the false promise that maybe this will aid in getting their family back together or to receive more money and so forth. But when the lies are exposed or the child can sense that the parent's motives are wrong then that child's self-esteem can go to an all time low causing their hopes to become over shadowed by disappointments and depression. Soon rebellion will kick in at another level and their education may be affected as well as their social life, their relationship with God if they had any to begin with and their relationship with both sets of parents. This is a lot for a child or adolescent to take in especially if they are dealing with an unreasonable, immature and a bitter parent(s).

This is why God's ways are always better. We may not feel like forgiving others, or wish to stop blaming each other for our lives and the circumstances we find ourselves in; but when we are able to take our eyes off of ourselves and realize that it is not just about us, but about the assignment on our life or the purpose of why we are here on this earth and that we have a spiritual enemy who is plotting in hopes that we fail and never recover. When we come to that realization that yes our problem may be bigger than we are but it is not bigger than the Almighty, then maybe we will be willing to surrender it into His hands and cast that care on Him (I Peter 5:7) and seek His wisdom and instructions that will lead us out of that dark place and help solve the situation. If we are willing to place our hurts in His hands and say, *Heavenly Father, I cannot do anything with this broken heart, these feelings of rejection and the hurt in my child's heart and the lack of cooperation between the two households so I am going to give them to You in exchange for what You died to give me and that is Your righteousness, Your peace, Your comfort, Your forgiveness, Your grace, Your favor, Your wisdom and Your strength to endure until this situation changes for my family's good in Jesus' name, amen.* Give God the glory and praise Him and be that example and light for your family and for someone else that is in a dark tunnel and cannot see their way out. His ways are greater and He will make a way and deliver your household.

Isaiah 55:8-9:

> For My thoughts are not your thoughts, neither are your ways My ways, says the Lord. For as the heavens are higher than the earth, so are My ways higher than your ways and My thoughts than your thoughts.

We praise God that we did not personally experience having our children living between two households and we are thankful for that. At the same time we still pray for and sympathize with the families who are going through this process. We also realize that many of them will not have major issues attached and for those who do we understand it is an attack against the children and their households/families and as I have said we will be prayerful. **As people learn they have authority they can use and the victory has already been won much of the drama in certain areas of their lives will have to cease at the appointed time.**

ESTABLISH NEW FAMILY CUSTOMS AND TRADITIONS:

By exercising the fruit of the Spirit (Gal. 5:22-23) you can and should establish new family customs that celebrate your Blended Family. If love isn't in your heart for your spouse's natural children or if the children may not be interested in you, you should still show a genuine interest in them and love them with the love of the Lord who will fill your heart with a love for them if you allow Him to. It is important for your spouse to see an effort being made to show love and kindness toward their natural children whom they love.

In the beginning, in our family some of us experienced a supernatural love in our hearts, for bonding with members in each other's family; we had a love for one another that could not be explained. **We later discovered that when God has placed people together He will put a love in their hearts for one another; parent to child, sibling to sibling and child to parent.** For example, in the Bible a great illustration is shown of the love that God places in the hearts of people for someone they do not know well and it can even surpass the love you feel for your natural relatives. *The Spirit of God and what He does will always be stronger than what takes place in the natural. King David and Saul's son, Jonathan, had been knitted together by the Holy Spirit and had a* **brotherly love** *for one another that lasted throughout their lives.* When Jonathan died King David was still loyal to him by blessing Jonathan's only living son as he agreed when they made a covenant together.

I Samuel 20:14-17 shows the actual covenant that was made between the two men:

> While I am still alive you shall not only show me the loving kindness of the Lord, so that I die not, But also you shall not cut off kindness from my house forever—no, not even when the Lord has cut off every enemy of David from the face of the earth. So Jonathan made a covenant with the house of David, saying, And **the Lord will require that this covenant be kept** *at the hands of David's enemies. And Jonathan caused David to swear again by his love for him, for Jonathan loved him as he loved his own life.*

When the Lord brought our two families together we each had one son and they were drawn by the Spirit and had a supernatural brotherly connection before we were married. All of our children received one another and to date I know of no problem that any of them have with each other. They have a strong friendship, love and respect for one another. The love they express to one another including our daughters is a supernatural love that was placed in their hearts before any of them knew they would become related. It was amazing even people from the outside would comment and say things like I did not know you had another sister or I did not know you had a brother. One of my own relatives came by and said to me when he saw the two boys together, I thought you only had one son? There were countless remarks made about how much the children favored one another and so forth. *When God has truly done something He will confirm it in more ways than one.*

On the other hand on occasion a person's mind or flesh may fight against what the Lord has done for various reasons but the love that God places in their heart is still there and whenever they choose to receive and express it to someone in the family they will be able to do so. It was placed there in the first place by God to either fill a need for them and/or to equip them for their assignment from the Lord. It is all to God's glory and He does not do anything in vain, there is a specific reason or purpose for that love and the coming together of certain people by divine connection. If love is in it then God is in it for God is Love!

Many times people are unable to receive the future because they have not let go of the past. When God has sent the "new" they will not be able to receive it unless they let go and are willing to be healed of their past; and during this process one has to realize that the past is over and it is time to move forward into the future or they will be caught (stuck) living in the past and that is unhealthy. **This by no means is saying that one must forget or dismiss the biological parent that left or a sibling from their former family unit, those people will always be a part of your life if you and they desire it to be so, the relationship will only function in a different way.** What it does say is that you understand things have changed, and if it is God's plan and not your own then His plan supersedes all other plans and even though you do not understand it in that moment, it will work out for everyone's good. Therefore, a decision to change with it needs to be made and the necessary adjustments as well, along with outside help if needed or be prepared to be left behind in a world of torment and regrets.

We have the option of benefiting from what God has done or ignoring it and staying the way we are. Remember though, His ways are not our ways and His ways are always better and when we reach out and receive from our heavenly Father what He has done for us, I guarantee it will change your life and your heart and put you in a position to receive abundance from Him in every area of your life because He is able to do exceeding abundantly above all that we ask or think, according to the power that worketh in us.

Ephesians 3:20 says,

> Now to Him Who, by (in consequence of) the [action of His] power that is at work within us, is able to [carry out His purpose and] do superabundantly, far over and above all that we [dare] ask or think [infinitely beyond our highest prayers, desires, thoughts, hopes, or dreams].

God made it clear that as **we build our home on "The Rock"** that when storms come our home will not be easily blown away or leveled. Any building of bits and pieces from a ship wreck or any broken remains (from divorced homes) will never be restored properly without the help of our Savior and Lord and the Holy Spirit. If you try to rebuild without God you will only try in vain and to no avail.

Matthew 7:24-26 says:

> So everyone who hears these words of Mine and acts upon them [obeying them] will be like a sensible (prudent, practical, wise) man who built his house upon the rock. *And the rain fell and the floods came and the winds blew and beat against that house; yet it did not fall, because it had been founded on the rock.* And everyone who hears these words of Mine and does not do them will be like a stupid (foolish) man who built his house upon the sand.

Psalms 127:1 and 3 says very plainly:

> **Except the Lord builds the house, they labor in vain who build it... Behold, children are a heritage a reward.**

Whatever effort you make to follow through with the blessing God has placed before you will be well worth it when it is all said and done.
Therefore, cause your family (whichever type it is) to be strengthened by His Spirit to weather through the storms of life and be found still standing, still trusting and pleasing to God.

Ephesians 3:14-15 KJV is a prayer for your family to be strengthened:

> For this cause I bow my knees unto the Father of our Lord Jesus Christ, Of whom the whole *family* in heaven and earth is named, That He would grant you, according to the riches of His glory, to be strengthened with might by His Spirit in the inner man; That Christ may dwell in your hearts by faith; that ye, being rooted and grounded in love, may be able to comprehend with all saints what is the breadth, and length, and depth, and height; and to know the love of Christ…

ADDITIONAL METHODS ON HOW TO RESOLVE CERTAIN CHALLENGES IN ORDER TO MAKE LIFE IN YOUR HOME A MORE ENJOYABLE ONE:

- Parents remember to be concerned about the deep rooted problems in their child's life as well as their surface needs. If they won't open up, give them time or seek professional help from a Christian counselor who specializes with children if possible. The *American Association of Christian Counselors*, based out of Virginia, President and Founder Dr. Timothy Clinton, is the largest Christian counseling association in our nation. If you do not have a source, they have counselors located all over the nation and resources you can purchase. As a pastor who counsels, I have been a member of the AACC for years and they are upright and really care about restoring families God's way. www.aacc.net *see find a counselor.*

- One of the first things that should happen to begin to deal with the hurt is that **the child needs to accept the situation and flow with it. Of course opposition and rebellion will more than likely be the result** because of all the emotions and unanswered questions and major changes that seem to have in many cases happened suddenly. If your child is blaming themselves and has a lot of guilt, asking "Why me?" They are really speaking to God and questioning His faithfulness. Their thinking may be on these lines, "If God caused this then they cannot trust God or you for ruining their lives." The child is confused and is trying to sort things out with limited experience and knowledge to deal with it all. They need to understand that God did not cause the divorce; people caused it through their choices. The child needs to know that God is on their side and there for them and there is nothing that can separate them from His love (Romans 8:38, 39). When they seek Him expect Him to restore and help them through this and realize that He will not do things the way they would but in the long run what He does will be better than what they could have ever imagined. What the enemy meant for evil God will turn it around for good for everyone involved if they stay with Him (Genesis 50:20). When we listen and follow His plan then all that is done will work together for the child and the family's good (Romans 8:28). As they begin to understand and trust God again they will be able to trust their parents. They should get to the point where they can forgive and discuss the changes. Parents may need the assistance of a counselor to help the child open up to get the relief they need.
- As the child, adolescent or young adult **harbor growing negative feelings toward their blended parent, to release and give the child some relief** they must have someone they can share with without being interrupted,

criticized, condemned or made to feel bad about themselves in any way. Many of them already feel rejected by the parent that left and some may feel the divorce was their fault. They need to open up and be able to share their feelings. If not with any of the parents then find someone who the child will accept and respect. If that person is objective and trustworthy in the eyes of the child this will help them obtain some relief from their pain.

- Another alternative is **a family meeting or open forum** where everyone in the family is given a chance to voice what they really think or feel about all the changes in their lives without them being blamed, condemned or criticized as they vent and say what is on their heart. Let people volunteer to speak and share their ideas, family plans, grievances and complaints. Never try to make them voice their feelings if they are not ready or comfortable with the setting or certain people being in the room that they are not willing to open up in front of. If they sense it is "not for real" they more than likely won't say anything at all until the next family meeting when they now sense this is something they may want to do if only to have a chance to speak their mind and not be persecuted for it. *One way healing comes is when people talk and gain understanding and revelation in a matter.* It is also important after the meeting not to criticize them or make them feel uncomfortable but to continue to show them the love of God that you should be drawing your strength from. As mentioned earlier the family meeting should include a plan of action and a follow-up family meeting to monitor progress in the areas where reasonable change has been requested by a family member.
- **Children that have been rejected by their fathers** may have a hard time relating to any male or they may relate to males in a way that might not be healthy (joining gangs, homosexuality, anger, rebellion and so forth).

They will need to have a good role model to show that all males are not a like and there are many very good fathers, grandfathers, brothers, uncles and cousins out there. The same holds true for the mother, **if the child's mother left** then they usually do not want to have very much to do with any mother, natural, blended, aunt, etc. They will probably choose an older woman they can trust or identify with and attach themselves to her for some of the nurturing they may have missed or still need.

- We all need to feel loved especially by a parent. In the case of a divorce many times the child feels that when the parent left they no longer loved them. **A hug is one way to show your love for someone and especially your child**. When we say we love our children they may not feel loved especially with all of the changes that they blame you for and they may need an expression of that love and to demonstrate that love with a simple hug could do wonders for everyone. Kind words don't hurt either. With blended, foster and adopted children inquire about their history before you try to make physical contact through hugging or a pat on their back to express a good job has been done or I'm proud of you, because if a child has been abused (sexually or physically) they may first resist any type of normal physical contact such as a pat on the shoulder or holding hands or a simple hug. Or they may first resist if they feel you are compelled and it is not out of genuine love for them. This is where the Holy Spirit comes in, He will guide you through all things and He will heal the hearts so love can come forth.
- **When there is deep resentment towards the biological parents for failure to make the former marriage work**, do not defend yourself or justify your mistakes or your part that contributed to the divorce and do not blame the other spouse or anyone (in-laws, employers, etc.). Instead be as truthful as you can about the situation and that you are seeking God for understanding, help,

guidance and strength as well. **God increases us when we show humility** (Psalms 147:6; James 4:10; Psalms 25:9). The child is too young to fully understand and in many cases you as an adult don't understand all the ins and outs of why some things happened the way they did. So in the meantime let your child know that you intend to review the portion that you contributed to the divorce and see what, if any restitution can be done. Owning up to your responsibility will be a good role model for them to see. **As forgiveness is asked for and expressed it opens the door for everyone to forgive and they will in their own time.** To be fully healed and stop torment in a given area they need to forgive their parents unconditionally. This will close the door in their mind where the adversary was sending tormenting thoughts; he will no longer have access with these accusations.

- Divorce makes some kids feel self-conscious or out of place when **others ask them personal or embarrassing questions about their parents.** The child needs to know how to respond in these predicaments or any embarrassment they may feel especially if they are of school age. *First of all let your child know that they do not have to become angry or embarrassed about a decision that someone else made for their life.* If someone comments or asks your child about the parent who no longer lives with him or her one way to respond is to thank the person for asking about their parent and let them know that their parent is still loved but that they are going through something right now and need prayer. And ask the person if they would not mind joining you in praying for them as well; and their conversation with that person is resolved and is over.

- **Your children will have to learn how to function in their new environment even if it is still their old home.** New people some of which you may not know very well are suddenly living in your house. This calls for adjustments from everyone in the home. If all of the adults are working and school age kids come home to an empty house have things for them to do so they won't have time to be involved in things they should not do. Let the child know that it is not because you distrust him or her but it is an opportunity for them to demonstrate how responsible they are by doing the things you request of them until you arrive home. Keep in mind that children need time to adjust to their new environment and adapt emotionally and psychologically or they may show a strong resistance, resentment and rebellion.

- Also have rules that they are not to bring anyone into the house when no adult is present and not to sit in front of a television all afternoon. If the parents can afford a housekeeper or someone they can trust to be with the child after school hours to oversee homework, etc that would be beneficial even if the child says they do not need this because of their age. I personally know that high school kids need supervision as well but in a different way than younger kids. I do not believe that any young person wants to be left alone for hours with their only contact being something that is electronic such as a computer, IPOD and so forth. And this has been proven over the years by the number of children that do not go home to an empty house but will instead hang out at the school, someone else's house or a food establishment or even worse get involved with the wrong crowd. **Guidelines will give them boundaries and show them their restrictions,** even though they may test you, if you follow through the trust and confidence of the child can be rebuilt and it will still show them that you love them enough to do these things that will help them function now and in the future in a productive way. They will thank you for it later (not now unless they are very mature or understand it is for their good).
- **Another solution is to have your children attend a private school** of which there is after school supervision until they are picked up and you all go home together therefore there is no latch key child. This is the option

we were led to do for our children. Long before we met one another our kids were attending private schools. However, our youngest child began home schooling when she was in middle school having been led again by the Holy Spirit and it worked out beautifully.

- If the mother or father is home at the time they arrive or can pick them up on time that would be great to. This will help the child to overcome fear and anxiety caused by the difficult changes in their home life. If the woman feels that she should be home in this season of her children's lives that would be great and God would make the provision and provide abundance even if she and her husband think that they need her salary. Sometimes we just need to downsize our lifestyle a little to accommodate their well being and this is a small sacrifice, compared to the outcome and results that your children will have if you don't. They will have the opportunity to achieve their dreams in life because you chose to be there for them when they needed it.
- Your children must be taught to assume responsibility for their own actions. **Many of them rebel simply to punish the parent for the divorce, remarriage and bringing a new parent into the whole situation.** These young people do not understand they are planting bad seed that will harvest in their own lives one day. They are not operating according to the Word of God and God is no respecter of persons. If they are old enough and have been told that God is with them then they need to ask Him to give them a forgiving spirit, because choosing to forgive all the parents involved will benefit their life and it will be right before God placing Him in a position that can truly help them get pass this to having a wonderful future. Jesus went to the cross and took all the sins of the world so their sins are already forgiven they only need to ask and receive to clear their own sin consciousness and know that they are fully acceptable to God and He is willing to heal their broken heart.

- **Don't ask certain questions of your child if you feel the timing is not right.** But if you are led and in a calm atmosphere and you believe they would be open you can ask them questions that they may have wanted to ask for a long time but did not know how you would respond or how to approach you with the question. *Try not to interrupt the child or adult child or anticipate their answers, put words in their mouths or become angry because it may not be the answer you expected.* And keep in mind the age of the child because that will make a difference in the type of answers you will receive. You could ask them things like: What do you think I could have done to keep my former marriage together? Since I am divorced what do you think I should do now? What do you think God would have us all to do? What kind of future do you think our family will have? What do you really miss about your father/mother? What do you really think about your blended father/mother?

It often takes children and adolescents years to recover after a divorce. The pain and hurt they have if they have not forgiven and are trusting God will carry over into their parent's new marriage and they will find themselves at odds with the blended parent. If they contribute to the breakdown of this marriage they will later have to reap for that (Galatians 6:7-8). The saying is true, what goes around comes around. He who sows iniquity will reap calamity (Proverbs 22:8). God takes all marriages seriously and He defends them because He created them. So when a person takes it upon themselves to play God and fight someone's marriage or interfere to try to cause destruction they are in sin and will need to go before God and ask for forgiveness then repent. Everyone in the household or associated with it has a choice to allow healing to come into their lives or reject it and grow bitter going around saying and doing ugly things and if they choose the latter they will certainly cause the wrong consequences to appear in their own lives at some point.

How can a parent help? Daily seek divine wisdom from God and stay in a state of forgiveness and prayer for your natural and blended children. As each family (regardless of the type) trains their children up in the *way they should go* which causes growth in the Word of God and prepares them for a skill, for their gifts to be released, to have integrity, godly character (fruit of the Spirit) and to impart knowledge to them in various subjects that will carry them through life, they will learn how to be true to themselves. Only godly determination will bring things through until the finish. In the meantime they are showing God that they love Him too by keeping His ways before them. "He leads the humble in what is right, and the humble He teaches His way," (Psalm 25:9).

WAS JESUS A MEMBER OF A BLENDED FAMILY?

Jesus Himself had a Blended (Step) Parent and half brothers and sisters, (Matthew 12:46-50; Mark 3:31-35). His siblings and He shared the same mother but a different father. His half brothers and sister's father was Joseph the son of Jacob the son of Eliud who came through the line of King David and Jesus' Father is Father God, the Divine First Person of the Trinity (Matthew 1:15-16; 18-25). Now some of Jesus' half-brothers were jealous of Him and in some cases even ashamed of Him when He was in His ministry (this was a part of persecution, the only cross we as a people of God are called to bear). An additional reason for Jesus' persecution was the fact that Jesus also functioned as a prophet and the Word says a prophet is not received in his own home. When He returned home to minister He could do little there because people could not in their minds go beyond the fact that He was raised in the home of Joseph and Mary. However, Jesus' Blended Family's brothers and sisters eventually came to some of His meetings while He ministered to the people, Mt. 12:46-50 and Mark 3:31-35.

Joseph, Jacob's son, the grandson of Abraham also came from a family that had additional parents and half brothers and sisters. This was not uncommon, the different variations in families have been from the beginning and it will continue. People will have to make a choice, to either flow with the new or stay stuck in their past; flow with the wonderful works of God or be left behind!

Some may find it very difficult to accept the variations in their family yet if they would yield to His ways they would discover that God has all wisdom and all the answers and once they yield they will find that they can do all things through Christ Jesus who will strengthen them (Phil. 4:13). God in all His wisdom, His answers have never changed, He said to show love because that is Who He is (I John 4:16); and what He is about and how well it is received will give everyone involved the victory in every battle. There is no weapon formed that will defeat true love and *Love* will cast out all fear (I John 4:18). Since He is Love and poured a part of Himself into us when He made us in His image, a little lower than Himself, we have the capacity to show love as well, it is all a matter of choice. The Law of Love will work if you work it by faith (Luke 6:27-36).

Whatever God has asked us to do in His Word as His sons and daughters we have been given the ability to do so and as we believe, receive and do, we will have what He says, no more and no less, (Mark 11:23-24).

Therefore, the answer to receiving the new is to make a decision to flow with the new, show love and trust God and the new will blend into a beautiful thing if you allow it to.

I Peter 1:20-21 NKJV says:

> He indeed was foreordained before the foundation of the world, but was manifest in these last times for you who through Him believe in God, who raised Him from the dead and gave Him glory, so that your faith and hope are in God.

CHAPTER 6

IS YOUR FAMILY FUNCTIONING ACCORDING TO GOD'S ORDER AND THEIR GOD-GIVEN ROLES?

Dominion belongs to God; He establishes ORDER in the heights of Heaven (Job 25:2 NIV). He set up the *order* first in the Heavens the spiritual world then He set up the *order* in our world and delegated it to mankind when He gave us *authority* over all the earth.

Genesis 1:26 says,

> God said, Let Us [Father, Son, and Holy Spirit] make
>
> mankind in Our image, after Our likeness, **and let them have complete authority...over all the earth...**

As we walk in our authority we have the power to take dominion over all of the earth starting within the framework of God's Order in which He first establishes a Family in order to be their

God and for them to be His people. **And within the Family of God He set up an order.**

In Genesis 26:25 it says,

> And [Isaac] **built an altar** there and called on the name of the Lord and **pitched his tent** there; and there Isaac's servants were **digging a well**.

With Isaac God came first. Before doing anything else in the new place, he built an altar and then waited there to call upon the Lord. **His relationship with God came first** Who enabled him with grace to take care of everything else in his life.

His home came second; he pitched his tent. He made provision for his family with a place to live where the family could function and relate to one another.

And his business came third; his servants dug a well. He took care of building his business by giving his servants instructions. He was an entrepreneur.

God's order places people's relationships with others and provision as the second most important thing next to their personal relationship with Him. **Why? Because** *man's relationship with God is his lifeline to everything else.*

The pattern for the **Order of Priorities** set in place by God, are as follows:

- A Personal Relationship with God
- Immediate Family
- Extended Family
- Divine Friendships
- Ministry, Business or Work

Our God is a relational God. He loves to fellowship, He loves to be with people and be included. Notice He placed relationships before the work He purposed for each and every person. If this is so important to Him then it should be important to us!

They are all important to God and one should not be neglected in order to attend to another. He will give you the wisdom as to how and when to attend to each, keeping it all in balance. (For additional information on the importance of our having a personal relationship with God, see Chapter 7, Section Three under A Review of Building and Embracing a Personal Relationship with God).

In the Kingdom of God in order to really serve God and keep Him first not only is a Personal Relationship necessary but is required at all times and is completely opposite to what people are accustomed to doing while living a worldly life (those that are not Born-again Believers). *Most of the time things that you do will not make any sense to someone looking from the outside in with their worldly perspective at your personal relationship with God and how you respond to Him and His instructions* (I Cor. 2:14-16).

One of the reasons God takes first place even before family relationships is so a person will not place anyone or anything before God. And by keeping Him first God is in a position in your life to protect all that concerns you. *Therefore, when the Lord is first before your family members it is for their good for He is the only one that can save everyone.* If you rely on another human being as your main source you are limiting yourself and being unfair to that person because they cannot possibly fill the void in your life the way a loving and living God can. On the other hand if you keep a person first because you are so concerned about them it will turn into worry and fear for their well-being. The more you try to put things in perspective and help others in your own strength the more you are relying on yourself and not on a loving God.

All that is needed is to simply keep Him first in your life and you continually do that by periodically examining your life or reviewing your priorities to make sure God is first before any other person, thing, responsibility or obligation in your daily agenda. Now because He is first in your life and you have chosen to conform to His example of living

He is now in a position where you can cast your care (your burdens) on Him releasing the weight of it and He will sustain you and take care of whatever concerns you, including that parent, spouse or child (Psalm 55:22; I Peter 5:7).

Matthew 10:37-39 says,

> He who loves [and takes more pleasure in] father or mother more than [in] Me is not worthy of Me; and he who loves [and takes more pleasure in] son or daughter more than [in] Me is not worthy of Me; And he who does not take up his cross and follow Me [cleave steadfastly to Me, conforming wholly to My example in living and, if need be, in dying also] is not worthy of Me. **Whoever finds his [lower] life will lose it [the higher life], and whoever loses his [lower] life on My account will find it [the higher life].**
>
> **Jesus' message will not be received by everyone, for the gospel runs at cross purposes with the values and vision of the world. Thus, in some cases it will cause conflict. Its call reverses worldly priorities so that God takes first place even before family relationships.** Family members who do not accept Christ's invitation to the cross will fight against those who do. Jesus did not intend to cause conflict, but the natural reaction of the unbeliever is to oppose all who live out Christ's message [1] Matthew 10:34-39.

You may ask what is the lower life as opposed to the higher life. The lower life is a carnal, in the natural, secular life that one lives day in and day out without much purpose, toward a destiny or future plans. Only their own natural self-centered motives drive them to go forward with their regular routine of life such as: going to school, going to work, going to weddings, funerals, holiday events, endless traveling, etc. and basing their happiness on their circumstances alone. Living basically a defeated life because a real successful life is in Christ and in His will or plan for your life; God measures success differently from the way man does who primarily only bases success on how much material gain he has acquired in life. *There is nothing wrong with wealth and material resources, real or personal properties, but if that is all you have to show for your life you are falling short and don't even know it. "For what does it profit a man to gain the whole world, and forfeit his life [in the eternal Kingdom of God]?"* (Mark 8:36).

The **lower life can be a complicated one** because basically without God in it people are basically selfish and self-centered; frustrated; living in and with their various sins; emotionally and/or physically in pain with no real answers or godly role models in their lives. They are also usually: feeling condemned; feeling guilty about something; living with unforgiveness and bitterness about what someone did to them or the life that they have; having shame about some event that happened and living in lack (poverty or with a poverty mentality even if they have money or resources). The lower life also includes being angry, in fear and not in faith, jealous and envious when they compare themselves to others because they do not know what their purpose in life is. They are in broken relationships or relationships that are in the process of falling apart primarily because other people cannot give you what you need to fill that void in your gut or heart. There is not much hope for the future, everything seems routine and they question, "Is this all there is to life?" *This is a picture of the lower life and when you in your best efforts try to save yourself and make positive changes to obtain the higher life you only continue in your present lifestyle because the higher life is only obtainable one way.*

The Lord said "whoever loses his [lower] life on My account will find it [the higher life]." So what exactly is the higher life? The higher life begins by receiving Jesus Christ as your

Lord and Savior. From there you become a new person on the inside and start to develop in His love and grace as you renew your mind in the things of God and follow His ways which is a process that is learned. You are entitled to live in His promises which are many good things you cannot even imagine. You live your dream. Once you learn the process of how to live a life in the Kingdom of God you will find that it is not one that is full of *inner turmoil,* strife or confusion but at the same time it can **be an exciting life.**

There is peace, joy, righteousness and little effort to sustain contentment as you continue to move higher in the things of God as well as with natural resources and abundance. **You acquire favor** in your life (restoration, assistance, promotion, supernatural increase, honor, real estate and money without sorrow, recognition, victories, policies changed for your good, and so on). You also have **a life of good relationships that are divinely inspired** and connected with you; **a heart to give and help others** instead of being selfish; **health and the power to be healed**; forgiveness, and are more readily able to forgive others rather than live a life full of unforgiveness and bitterness; receiving and living in the blessings of God with the inheritance He has for each one of His children; *worshipping a faithful and true God, not everyone is blessed to have a living and loving God in their life that speaks to them and answers their prayers;* are blessed to have true love, patience and endurance with strength to follow through and your mind free from torment.

With this life also comes an inner joy, something that is not based on outward circumstances to make you happy but a real joy in your heart that gives you hope and strength to go on and one that will enable you to see things from a good perspective. With this higher life you also have the authority given to you in the name of Jesus to remove evil strongholds from your life and the lives of your family and friends. In addition to your family **you will inherit a new family, a Spiritual Family of like minded believing people, not perfect people but people who have the same goal to live and follow**

Jesus' example to the best of their ability. You also have the privilege of fellowshipping or visiting with them on a regular weekly basis in an atmosphere of worship, praise and thanksgiving.

There is so much more to the higher life that it all cannot possibly be explained and for some it will be an unrealistic lifestyle. But the Word of God promises these things and more and many have already obtained them. The Word also says for those who live in the lower life that they will see the higher life as foolishness (I Corinthians 2:14) and something that is unobtainable, a fantasy life and not realistic. *But I assure you it is a very real way of living and it is very easily obtainable and the Comforter (Holy Spirit) will enable you with His grace (power) to maintain and live it everyday of your life.*

Moving along with the next priority set in place by God for our lives are our immediate and extended family and the importance of helping or being there for them; as well as others such as widows, orphans, the elderly and divine friends.

I Timothy 5:8 says,

> If anyone fails to provide for his relatives, and especially for those of his own family, he has disowned the faith [by failing to accompany it with fruits] and is worse than an unbeliever [who performs his obligation in these matters].

I Timothy 5:1-4 says this **in regards to widows and the elderly:**

> Do not sharply censure or rebuke **an older man,** but entreat and plead with him as [you would with] a father. Treat **younger men** like brothers; [Treat] **older women** like mothers [and] **younger women** like sisters, in all purity. [Always] treat with great consideration and give aid to those who are **truly widowed** (solitary and without support). **But if a widow**

has children or grandchildren, see to it that these are first made to understand that *it is their religious duty [to defray their natural obligation to those] at home,* and make return to their parents or grandparents [for all their care by contributing to their maintenance], for this is acceptable in the sight of God.

Isaiah 58:7 says,

Is it not to divide your bread with the hungry and bring the homeless poor into your house – when you see the naked, that you cover him, and that you hide not yourself from [the needs of] your *own* flesh and blood?

In these passages it tells us that we are commanded to not only help the needy (widows and the elderly) but not to forget to help our Immediate Family or our Extended Family members and people in the Kingdom of God who are in God's Family and are our spiritual relatives who may also be in need. *Adult Children and adult grandchildren are to attend to their parents and grandparents with material financial support in addition to other areas of support for the care they received while growing up as a part of showing them honor and respect.* The Lord did not indicate whether this depended upon your parents being the best parents or grandparents, that does not matter because whatever we do it should be done unto God first. This is a part of keeping God and His ways first and you in His will and under His protection with great favor and for your obedience He will reward. Parents like others fall short in many areas this is why we do not look to people to fulfill us or to return what they took from us or could not give to us in the first place because they did not have it in them to give. Therefore, the answer is simple, we look to the One Who is capable of being all things to all those that choose to receive Him.

A **single mother with children in many cases has the same status as a widow** with children if she has no support from her former spouse. She is to be given the same consideration and help. *"If any believing woman or believing man has [relatives or persons in the household who are] widows, let him relieve them..." (I Timothy 5:16).* A household *includes* Extended Family members.

For all those who are Born-again Believers, your first ministry is your family because that is the order of God. Therefore, this comes before our concerns with our place of employment and our businesses.

Why is this the order? Because if the vision God gave you superseded loving and being kind to one another it would come against His own Word. **First** of all, He said that we should love one another, (John 13:34 and I John 4:12). **Second,** if we relied solely on our own works to supply a need we would not need to trust God and we would leave Him out of the equation. We should trust Him and as we are obedient to His Word, expect our business, our ministry or our work to never stop producing and funneling resources. As our need is met with abundance because of our obedience we in turn can continue to be a blessing to our family, friends, widows, orphans, the elderly and others in the Kingdom of God.

Third, when people know that God is their source and the reason they are blessed, it will point them to Him and not to themselves. It is important to give Him all the glory and maintain a relationship with God so people will truly know Who is able and willing to empower them to be blessed or assist in a time of crisis; they would have learned to go to Him first in their time of need just as you did.

Isaiah 58:8 is what God does once verse 7 (listed above) is fulfilled:

> Then shall your light break forth like the morning, and your healing (your restoration and the power of a new life) shall spring forth speedily; your righteousness (your rightness, your justice, and your right relationship with God) shall go before you [conducting you to

peace and prosperity], and the glory of the Lord shall be your rear guard.

We are commanded to help others before we can expect the glorious presence of God to come and continue to bless us. We can expect to receive peace and prosperity for doing what God asks us to do. **His prosperity is designed to make us whole.** It brings provision as well as abundance; a peace of mind; healings in all areas of your life: physical healing, mental healing, emotional healing, financial healing in the form of increase; safety; joy and happiness; good relationships into your life; restoration and miracles. His abundance includes overflowing, over and above, more than enough and above the ordinary. His wholeness includes nothing broken, nothing missing, spiritually, physically nor financially.

We serve a God that is a God of order. Things just don't happen by chance, there is a purpose for doing things a certain way to accomplish or reach a particular goal. God works within the order, pattern and timing that He sets up. Our God moves in seasons which involves His perfect timing and His perfect will. Needless to say if one is outside of God's will and timing there is a strong possibility that you will miss what He has for you simply because of your choice not to be in a position to receive from Him when it is time for certain promises to manifest in your life.

Being conscious of His divine order and keeping balance in our life is God's will and when we are led by His Spirit, receiving divine wisdom, using discernment and setting proper priorities they will enable us to maintain and have a strong upright, peaceful, joyful and orderly life.

ROLES ASSIST US ON HOW TO FUNCTION IN EVERYDAY LIFE:

There is no such thing as a roleless marriage or family and when it is attempted you will discover chaos, resentment and strife will occur. You will find that much is left for assumption and not enough has been defined, people in the family are not clear as to what is expected of them and many will assume someone else will take care of "it."

The ones who are energized will pick up the slack too often for the ones who are passive or lazy. This situation can only lead to major problems as burn out begins to set in and resentment starts to occur. Complete disorder is not godly, therefore if God is not in it then your flesh and/or Satan is.

Some members of a family may view roles as confining, putting people in a box, and limiting people and their choices. Also, if traditional roles are forced on family members and they become locked into a role without any compromises, compensation or flexibility this may lead to rebellion or withdrawal later.

The biblical roles would be the wiser ones to function in. In considering roles, take into consideration what feels right in your heart, who has the interest, the time and other factors that could play a part in deciding a particular role since functions are attached to all roles. As opposed to traditional roles which may be cut and dry, and assigned to a certain gender because it is traditional. *Biblical roles may or may not assign functions that seem right to secular (worldly) people or to even a " religious" person but it is right in their heart for the one who is following the leading of the Holy Spirit and they have a complete peace about it, therefore, it is right before God and that is what matters.*

The biblical role addresses one's responsibility not their status of importance. One role is not better or superior to another making someone else's role inferior. The roles are just different from one another.

The roles between a husband and wife are equal in value and importance. *They are not meant to be the same* but used to help and complement the other, in other words their role helps to complete the other.

The biblical marriage and roles of the husband and wife are patterned after Christ's marriage to the church. Both of their roles include loving one another, with a motive and heart to work together for the good of their family. **They can develop from and bring balance into their roles if they keep the right perspective and motive in their hearts.**

Functioning *first* unto God and not just to seek approval from each other, extended family members, friends, neighbors or even their children; in other words what we do, we do with God in mind seeking to please Him first before pleasing anyone else. Why? Because the desire to please God first keeps things in perspective and it acknowledges and thanks Him for being the One Who gave you the health, the mind, wisdom, provision, family and home in the first place. It will also prevent you from feeling like others are taking you for granted when they are not appreciative because you are not looking to be affirmed by people.

The couple should strive in their daily routine, to bring as much beauty and love into their home as possible letting the light of God shine through them as they endeavor to complete their responsibilities. *As parents they must realize that they symbolically represent God to their children* and when they are doing this to the best of their ability and their children reject them as their parents, the children are not only in disobedience to their parents but they are also rejecting God's established order for family life (Deut. 21:18-21). Parents should speak freely about the Lord in their home; their children should see them reading and honoring His Holy Word (separately or together); let the children see them praying together for the family and other needs; let them see them fellowshipping in their home with other like-minded people and let them see them attempting to live up-right and if they (the parents) make a mistake let the children see them ask for forgiveness, repent and continue to trust and rely on their faith in God's trusted Word. Let the children see their parents being kind to one another; complimenting each other; let them see them making decisions together and let them see you Mom honoring, respecting and listening to your husband and let them see you Dad loving and being considerate to your wife paying attention to her and her needs. Children of all ages should see a strong bond between their parents who have learned to yield to the Holy Spirit, who desires to spend time together and spend time with their family.

Their roles should also include praying for each other, forgiving on a daily basis, communicating at meals or touching bases when they are apart during the day. As they complete their daily tasks with integrity and the right frame of mind it helps to build trust and security in the relationships of family members. It keeps harmony in the home and fills the atmosphere with love and respect for their family and for God. **People of integrity** are preserved, protected, promoted and vindicated according to the Word of God because it keeps you in right standing (Eph. 6:14; Ps 26:1; Ps 25:21; Ps 41:12; Prov.11:3; Prov.19:1; Prov. 20:7).

Many women do not feel appreciated because their husbands and children may not say a simple thank you that they can live in a clean and organized home, have decent and healthy meals to eat, clean clothes to wear, have prayer coverage from Dad's and Mom's prayers and Mom's encouraging words for the day. Not to mention they do not have to come home to find their Mother involved in things that would embarrass the family. It is the little things that Mother's do that are taken for granted but if not done the family could not function without some chaos. If her husband hasn't enough time to completely fill in or if she is a single mom then they would probably resort to functioning on a one-on-one basis, it's everyone for themselves and the older kids helping the younger and the younger pulling their own weight and some not doing anything and with strife breaking out everywhere. The Mother is the heart of the home and it is her responsibility along with the support of her husband to see that it runs smoothly.

Roles allow each person to know what is expected of them. The responsibilities within a role can change rather easily and appropriately when the interest and abilities of an individual changes and it is agreed that the change is for the well-being of the family. This is something that could be requested of the parents and discussed at a family meeting especially if it involves moving into someone else's role or territory within their home.

BIBLICAL INSTRUCTIONS FOR THE ROLE OF A HUSBAND:

In setting up roles in a family and delegating authority, God has made it clear that the husband is the head of his home. The Word says, in Ephesians 5:23 **"For the husband is the head of the wife as <u>Christ</u> is the Head of the church…"** The passage in Eph. 5:21-33 is referring to the similarity of how Jesus led the church as an analogy of how a husband is to lead his wife as the head of his family as Jesus is the Head of the Church. *This is not speaking about male dominance that would force all of his personal beliefs and ways on his wife and children especially those that are not ways and beliefs of God the Father, God the Son and God the Holy Spirit.*

Since Jesus is the example of how a husband is to lead, what were some of Jesus' qualities and attributes: Jesus did not lord over the people; He let them come to Him freely because there is liberty in Christ. He was just and did His share. He laid His life down for those He loved. **He is the King of kings yet, He was humble enough to become a servant** and wash the feet of His disciples. He was supportive and loved to have children around Him. He loved to see justice, was yielded to the Father Himself and obedient unto death taking all the sins of the world upon His shoulders to give us His Righteousness to replace our sin nature. He gave His peace for the torments and brokenness in this world; joy for our sorrow; health instead of sickness and diseases; and wealth as He took poverty and nailed it to the cross. He gave us a wonderful eternal life as well as the Kingdom of God while we are here on this earth instead of a doomed destiny that could have been ours in the pit of hell.

Jesus is also a gentleman, one that is confident, forgiving and is faithful, Who extends grace, is powerful, an excellent protector, an awesome businessman, shows His unconditional love to His family and those not of His family. He keeps His Word and does not break any of His promises, shows mercy, is upright and full of righteousness, looks forward to fellowshipping with those in His family, loves justice, and said He would never leave us nor forsake us.

He knew how to be a true Leader and Head, Someone who is not afraid of responsibility and confrontation. Yet He was there to support and be of service to the church (the people) as He ministered Father God's truths, healed the sick and raised the dead. In addition, **He always kept His purpose and assignment in mind and stayed focused for the good of His bride.**

Jesus is a biblical and prime role model for any man who is serious about being the head of his home in a godly fashion. Of course the man that is a Born-again Believer/Christian and filled with the Infilling of the Holy Spirit as well as devoted to studying the Word of God in order to be better equipped and anointed to walk this walk, would not be required to do it perfectly but with the grace of God he would have the wisdom, ability and favor to do so in an excellent manner as opposed to someone trying to lead in his own strength.

As mentioned earlier on, **the father's presence is extremely important to validate and affirm his wife and children. He is the source and sustainer, the head, the protector, teacher, leader, primary one that disciplines, he is a nurturer,** *and he is the very foundation of his family.* When a father speaks his voice usually commands a certain amount of respect and not out of fear but a reverence for his position in the family. This position was given to him by God and we are to respect God's order. *His way of nurturing his family is to become the source and sustainer as the provider who receives his instructions and resources from his Maker as he yields to God's will for his life.*

A man's wife was never intended to replace him but to help and assist him in his functions and endeavors to achieve the desired results and goals set-up by God for him in his primary role as a *family man as well as other endeavors.*

AS THE PRIEST AND PROTECTOR OF HIS HOME:

As the priest of his home a Christian man is to lead his wife and children into God's presence, pray for them daily, discuss the Word of God with his family especially in areas of God's grace, mercy, forgiveness, obedience to His Word, faith, finances, health/healing and other subjects that the Word of God has to offer. **The husband is not to relinquish his duty to nurture his children in the faith.** Therefore, if he is not familiar with God's Word or desires for his family to be exposed to more than he and his wife's teachings of the Word he can also attend outside Bible study with his family at their local church and at other home Bible studies. There are also Christian television programs available where the entire family can learn and enjoy the Word together as well. In addition, there are thousands of resources available to purchase. There are ministry conferences and events that would give he and his family a strong foundation in the Word of God that they all could benefit from and would enable them to enjoy a prosperous life. The only condition would be to follow the leading of the Holy Spirit for the teaching vehicles that are best for your family.

In Ephesians 6:4 it says,

> Fathers, do not irritate and provoke your children to anger [do not exasperate them to resentment], but **rear them [tenderly] in the training and discipline and the counsel and admonition of the Lord.**

His wife should also be versed in the Bible and permitted to help her husband teach and train up the children in the Word as given to her by God as a part of her role as his wife (Prov. 31:15, 26, 28). Her teaching can also extend to their local church and beyond as she is equipped by God to minister the Word. **However, some men have been taught that "all women" in regards to teaching the Word of God are to be quiet in the home, church and certainly when it comes to teaching men from the Bible.** One of the scriptures used to support this view is I Timothy 2:11-15a:

> Let a woman learn in quietness, in entire submissiveness. I allow no woman to teach or to have authority over men; she is to remain in quietness and keep silence [in religious assemblies]…

It is time for the men who are in bondage in this area to be set free and come up higher in the things of God in order to receive all that God has for them. This would include a help meet who is free to fulfill the mandate God set in order so that she can operate and be in agreement with her husband which will release the dominion (complete authority) over the territory God gave them which would include but is not limited to their home, (Gen. 1:26-28).

In regards to the above passage, Paul wrote this because of the people he was ministering to, he had to deal with them based on their education, where they were spiritually as well as the place and time they lived in.

Further explanation of Paul's message: [3]

> *The ultimate restoration of that regrettable situation (the unnamed woman in I Timothy 2:11-15a) was not to ban all women from public ministry.* No. Instead, in I Timothy 3:11 which says, "[The] women likewise must be worthy of respect and serious, not gossipers, but temperate and self-controlled, [thoroughly] trustworthy in all things;" Paul was stating the qualities necessary for godly women to be released into public ministry. This is exactly the same thing Paul did to counter the harmful influence of the men who were promoting heresy—Hymenaeus and Alexander (I Tim. 1:20). **Just because these two men misused their teaching gifts, Paul didn't eliminate all men from roles of leadership.** No, to prevent further problems, he likewise set down guidelines for men leaders (I Tim. 3:2-10, 12-13). Thus, we see that **Paul dealt with men and women evenhandedly, correcting those of both genders who fell into heresy**, instructing men and women in the ways of spiritual leadership so that they

would not "fall into disgrace and the devil's trap" (I Tim. 3:7).

Are the women of verse 11 deacons or the wives of deacons? The structure of the letter and the content of Paul's message suggest that Paul fully intended women to serve in the leadership of the church. After all, hadn't *Paul begun the ministry in this city with Priscilla and her husband, Aquila?* Nowhere in his writings do we see Paul withholding leadership responsibilities from godly women. On the contrary, we know from his comments concerning Phoebe in Romans 16:1-2 that *he saw her as a fellow servant of the Lord, affirmed her as a deacon, and commended her as an exemplary leader of the church.* (Also see author's addition – Philippians 4:3 where it says, "I exhort you too, [my] genuine yokefellow, help these [two women to keep on cooperating], for they have toiled along with me in [the spreading of] the good news (the Gospel), as have Clement and the rest of my fellow workers whose names are in the Book of Life."

Paul's word to us is not one that makes harsh divisions between men and women, neither with the way they are saved nor with the way they are released into ministry. On the contrary, before the Cross, the playing field is leveled. If we are to fulfill God's forever dream—reaching everyone with the opportunity to be reconciled to Him, everyone of us must pray, profess our faith, and live peaceful and quiet lives. **Everyone of us should follow God's leading into whatever ministry He chooses. This is true for men and likewise for women.**

One more example that comes to mind is the example of Deborah who was a married woman, her husband's name was Lappidoth, she was also a prophet and she judged Israel (Judges 4:4). Deborah prophesied to Barak that God had a mission for him and he was to gather 10,000 men to fight in this battle. This man of war told the prophetess that "If you will go with me, then I will go; but if you will not go with me, I will not go. And she said, I will surely go with you..." (Judges 4:6-8). This man knew that he needed the help of the Lord and he recognized that she was appointed as a prophet and a judge over Israel (the same offices that Samuel the prophet held) and these two offices she could not have walked in without having been appointed with assignments from Almighty God.

Barak further humbled himself knowing that the glory would not go to him but to a woman (Judges 4:9; 22). This man understood it was God's battle and he let go of all pride to cease the victory that was assured if the prophetess was with him to further hear instructions if need be. (In the Old Testament God only spoke through the prophets, priest and kings).

God's thoughts and ways are higher than mans (Isa. 55:9) and we would all see more victories in our lives if we would simply yield to His ways. "...Believe in the Lord your God and you shall be established; believe and remain steadfast to His prophets and you shall prosper," regardless of whether the prophet is a male or female (2 Chronicles 20:20b).

Therefore, the scripture I Timothy 2:11-15a and others like it have been taken out of context and used to silence the female from her God-given rights and role as a person or minister of God. *If there were no other examples showing that God did indeed use women to teach from the Bible then, so be it, but since there are numerous examples of God using women not only to teach but as a leader in His Kingdom man's interpretation of the scriptures is invalid and has no authority in this area because the Greater Authority has already spoken.*

The Biblical Husband is to oversee or supervise his home by keeping himself in line with God's Word. He is to keep all demonic strongholds out and doors closed that evil forces would try to come through to attack his family. When he is not in his set place or doing what God told him to do he has opened a door for spiritual attacks which will manifest in his natural life. He is responsible to keep a hedge of protection around his home by decreeing and speaking life to his family and situation, declaring the blood of Jesus and literally putting on the whole armor of God; and daily walking and living up right while keeping himself pure before God as he continues to develop his personal relationship with the Lord. And above all he is to fully understand that Jesus is the High Priest Who has been given all authority in heaven and on earth (Hebrews 4:15; Matt. 28:18) and as one of His sons and priest *he is to look to* Father God in the name of Jesus and in the power of the Holy Spirit for his help, wisdom, protection and guidance (See Chapter 7 Section Two under Spiritual Weapons).

Even though the husband is the <u>primary</u> provider (he may not be the only provider in the home), which includes where the family lives, provisions for food, clothing and things to keep the family intact and comfortable for daily living. Furthermore, he is to *cast his care and concerns to God, be flexible,* be responsible to do what he knows and has the ability to do as he <u>expects</u> God's wisdom and help to sustain his family by giving him instructions, direction, connections, a means to provide, miracles when needed and abundance in all areas to maintain what God blessed him with and an overflow in order to bless others outside of his home.

What Titus 2:2, 6-8 says about a Christian man's role:

> Urge the older men to be temperate, venerable (serious), sensible, self-controlled, and sound in the faith, in the love, and in the steadfastness and patience [of Christ]. *In a similar way, urge the younger men to be self-restrained and to behave prudently [taking life seriously].* And show your own self in all respects to be a pattern and a model of good deeds and works, teaching what is unadulterated, showing gravity [having the strictest regard for truth and

purity of motive], with dignity and seriousness. And **let your instruction be sound and fit and wise and wholesome, vigorous and irrefutable and above censure**, so that the opponent may be put to shame, finding nothing discrediting or evil to say about us.

It takes true humility to be the support your partner needs you to be. A husband operating in his biblical role would be very supportive of his wife not taking her role lightly or for granted but understanding that her part helps fulfill his part. *That her part is not inferior to the point where he believes that her part in the relationship is unimportant but to simply understand that it is different.* Realizing that if they work together faithfully in their respective roles they will be able to have a peaceful home, and to raise sound, joyful, educated children with godly character who will live within the Kingdom of God yet be ready to function within society as a whole.

Men in general have more responsibility delegated to them by God. The husband may delegate certain decision making to his wife but certainly not all of it. Major decisions should *not* be made without first discussing them with his wife. **The two of them should pray and ask for wisdom, direction and be in agreement about any decision made in the matter;** and this would be the proper order before anything especially major is carried out. **The man should make the final decision even if it is to delegate it to his wife**. He could do this for various reasons: maybe she has the time for the project; or maybe he liked her idea or strategy better or maybe he is overloaded with other responsibilities or not that familiar with the details of this project as his wife is. It does not matter really because they are a team and this is his option and right as the head to delegate recognizing it is in the complete will of God being that God was the one who sent him an equipped help meet to start with.

If the husband decides to make a decision about a matter his wife should be fine with that as well. All decisions should be for the betterment of the entire household. If however, a decision is made by him that would place the home in jeopardy in anyway and his wife is totally against it and not in agreement then the husband needs to yield and seek God for wisdom and direction before doing anything. But if he decides to follow through without being in agreement with his wife, then she needs to release it and give it to God and be prayerful. He needs to understand that the threefold cord has been broken in this area which now gives space to the adversary to operate and the husband should be prepared to deal with the consequences.

Ephesians 5:21 the KJV and the Amplified versions on submission:

> *Submitting yourselves one to another in the fear of God.*

> Be subject to one another out of reverence for Christ (the Messiah, the Anointed One).

When operating properly in their roles, submitting one to another a husband and wife are held accountable to one another and to the Lord. This also brings security and safety to the relationship.

> Mutual submission based upon shared reverence for Christ as Lord is one of three evidences of the Spirit-filled life... Christians in Ephesus were concerned how Christians were to deal with authority in these social institutions.

> **Paul's position was that authentic faith in Christ will enable believer's to be in submission to one another even though social custom expected submission only of women, children and slaves.** [1] Ephesians 5:21

In submitting one to another, they are to honor and respect one another by being supportive of each other and helping one another develop their dreams, gifts and talents that God placed on the inside of each of them. In addition to this, **in a man's eyes the respect that he desires is to be accepted, admired and appreciated by his wife.** He also has a great need to be respected and affirmed in his place of work or business. To feel significant is needed as well to keep his self-esteem and self-worth in tack in order to complete his assignment or purpose in life.

What a husband should understand is that a wife and other people can only fill so much of these needs, if at all. When He goes to his source, His Heavenly Father, every need is met and **he can rest in knowing what God has said about him in His Word and that will be this man's true affirmation and what will make him feel like it is all worth it.** His self-worth won't ever have to be low or suffer because he knows his true worth is not measured by what man says a success is but only by what God declares a successful man is.

Many men have been taught and led to believe that they are the head of "every woman" but that is not what is written by God. **A man is the head of** *his own wife (Eph. 5:23).* If a man were the head of every woman then a man could never have a female employer, supervisor, manager or be comfortable listening to a female judge, teacher, general, doctor, minister, police officer and so on without being in violation of God's Word. He would always have to be in charge over a woman even if he lacked the education, experience, skills, money, connections in a particular work place or in society. Only in his household these things do not make a difference.

God has appointed the male as the head of his house regardless of his education, experience and skills in the work place, how much money or income he has or any connections with certain people, these things do not matter. The man is to be honored and respected in his house as the head of his family in order for his family to function, to be in obedience and under the protection of Almighty God Who is a God of order. Whatever is out of order cannot and will not stand.

When the husband stands in his place as head and is doing all that he knows to do unto God coupled with praying in God's will, not only will his prayers not be hindered, but God will give him the wisdom and all that he will need to be the priest, husband, father, provider, friend, leader and a man of humility in his home. Someone who is not afraid of his responsibilities and secure enough to delegate; he will also respect, listen and seriously consider his wife's opinion and ideas as he so desires his wife to respect his.

I'm sorry to say though, that so many men feel that they must carry on and do it all alone even with help at his disposal because of erroneous teaching that says since they are the head, the provider and so forth they are there to make it comfortable for their wives which includes him keeping all of the problems that come into their home to himself to spare his "poor little weak wife the burden." This kind of thinking is what puts men in an early grave because it is not the will of the Lord. *God sent the man capable help to be of assistance to him and a partner to love, if he found the <u>right wife</u> according to the Bible where it says, "He who finds a [true] wife finds a good thing and obtains favor from the Lord"* (Proverbs 18:22; 19:14; 31:10).

Even though God has built into women in general many attributes to be a help meet the Proverbs 31 woman has a different anointing to do even more and beyond in a more and excellent way. But instead some men believed the lie that was sent straight from the pit to deceive him into missing what God gave him as a gift to make his life easier and better.

A part of the untruth (the fabrication that belittles women and destroys marriages) is that **some men *see women as the weaker vessel in every area of her existence*** and so they treat her as a lesser human being. This makes it difficult for him to see her as a significant other or help meet. It is not necessary for a woman to have large muscles and a great deal of upper body strength (although some female body builders do) for most of the work she is designed to do because women are nurturers at heart.

Men were given upper body strength because he was *designed* to be the provider. Hunting at one time and still is in many parts of the world one avenue or source for the husband to provide for his family. Also planting in the fields and cultivating them was also a primary role for the male. *He is also the builder, the protector, the fighter to guard and keep the home and to serve in the military.* **His strength is needed for so many important roles for his home and in the work place.** *His strength was not intended by God to be used to beat and/or threaten his wife and children as some men have done, but to guard, love and as I have said to protect them.*

I Peter 3:7 addresses the issue of a woman being the physically weaker:

> In the same way you married men should live considerately with [your wives], with an intelligent recognition [of the marriage relation], honoring the woman **as** [physically] the weaker, but *[realizing that you] are joint heirs of the grace (God's unmerited favor) of life, in order that your prayers may not be hindered and cut off.* [Otherwise you cannot pray effectively.]

The scripture says to honor the woman "*as*" physically the weaker vessel... The fact that she does not have a lot of body strength does not mean she is weak in her *mind or in her inner being.* If God sent your wife He knew what was on the "inside of her" would be beneficial to you. For example, women have an inner strength to deal with certain problems and issues that men tend to ignore and one reason is because a woman's brain operates more frequently on both sides so they are better equipped to deal with things that are in great "detail." Whereas this could be more irritating to most men whose brain also operates on both sides but not as frequently so they tend to think more in general terms and would rather not be bothered with too much "detail." Women have an inner strength to not only carry and birth children that men do not have nor do they need since God has chosen the female for this function; *but her inner strength brings about* *an endurance to withstand and tolerate in order to persevere through certain situations and see it through to completion.* Not taking anything away from the man they can certainly follow through to completion but let's understand that a woman can follow through and endure as well. **Remember she was *inside* of a man, a part of him in the form of his "rib" and rib means "hidden support." Therefore, his support system or helper really came from inside of him demonstrating that when God completed His creation mankind was fearfully and wonderfully made,** Psalm 139:14.

If one does not know the purpose of her being there or what she is capable of nor are they willing to find out because they have preconceived ideas of what women can and cannot be or do apart from what God's Word says about them, then more than likely she won't be given the opportunity to work to her fullest potential. *If you do not know the purpose of a wife you will abuse her. This is why some women are labeled aggressive and called all kinds of derogatory names because she in many cases has so much to give and there is no demand for what is on the inside of her or a place to release it.* In most cases she does not fully understand or can she explain what is inside of her but she knows there is more than what is required or expected. So those who do step out of the 'norm' or stereotype or from under the labels to explore or desire to use the gifts and talents that God has placed inside of them are quickly persecuted and made to feel that there is something wrong with them or that they are just rebellious.

A word of caution the scripture above clearly states that a husband is to honor his wife *as* the physically weaker and remember that it has nothing to do with them being joint heirs of the grace of God. Further, the husband can hinder his prayer life which will affect the entire household if he violates the relationship and takes advantage or mistreats his wife because he simply can only see her as a weak vessel and chooses to ignore her inner strength and abilities. In Genesis 1:26 God gave dominion to the two of you and if you are not in agreement you diminish your God-given authority to have the dominion over all that God gave the both of you to have dominion over.

God made males and females different and for different roles and together they make a strong and powerful team to fulfill God's purpose for their lives. *Together honoring, respecting and admiring each other's strengths and picking up the slack where there is a weakness they can win in every battle* **but when divided, comparing, competing and belittling each other because of their differences and weaknesses they will surely fall.** People enter covenants to fill in that part where there are weaknesses by each offering their strengths to make the covenant strong and workable. The male and female sanctioned together by Almighty God is the strongest covenant there is on the face of the planet.

Also a man should not avoid his God-given role to honestly love and treat his wife as a part of himself ("...let each man of you [without exception] love his wife as [being in a sense] his very own self..." Ephesians 5:33). And in addition to this, he will strive to love his wife as Christ loves His own body (His bride, the church). This may be difficult for some men if they do not think well of themselves or feel they have failed as providers for their family. This is why the command from God for everyone to **love their neighbor as [you do] yourself is so important** (Matthew 22:39). **Unless we honestly and in a healthy manner can love ourselves we are incapable of loving anyone else.** *If a man who struggles in this area would believe what the Lord has said about him and how He loves him and made him for Himself to fellowship with; he would be able to compare what God, Someone who cannot lie has said, to the negative things that are sent to his mind by the adversary each and everyday.* Men and women are commanded to cast down the wrong imaginations and thoughts about themselves that are sent to their minds or that others have said and renew their minds in what God has said about them (2 Cor. 10:5 KJV and Romans 12:2).

If God the Father thought you were worth dying for, enough to send His only begotten Son, at least you can find out why He felt this way by taking the time to search it out in the

Word of God for yourself and then repent for believing the lie about yourself and make a decision to follow truth. Once this is resolved the husband will find it easier to love and cherish his wife as Christ loves and cherishes the church as well as be more content in life and open to find and fulfill his purpose.

(See Chapter 1 under Key Tips for a *Successful* Marriage God's Way for information regarding intimacy and Chapter 7 Section Two under Kingdom Economics for financial tips).

BIBLICAL INSTRUCTIONS FOR THE ROLE OF A WIFE:

Before you become a wife, if that is your desire, you should first be a whole and content woman on a journey fulfilling your purpose in life. If you do not know your own purpose how will you expect your husband to know and be supportive? If you are a Christian and you have low self-esteem, feel unworthy, insecure or inferior you will need to educate yourself on who you are in Christ. You can start by seeking God (praying and reading His Word in areas you need answers and to be built-up). Going to God in prayer and asking Him what is your purpose and assignment?

The Lord may not answer you with words but instead place a desire in your heart that will start to equip you by leading you to certain materials to read or listen to; by showing you your gifts and talents (if you are not already aware of them) and by opening doors to make the right connections for you. Being sensitive to His Spirit will definitely help you to find the right path, be with the right people including the right husband for you. This process will also aid if you are already married and are still struggling with the same issues.

The wife's role is significant for the well-being of her family. Her role centers more on her capacity to *nurture* and be *a helper. A helper is not an inferior role but rather describes a "function" and not "worth."* A wife's highest priority is her family and home. The Bible says that "the older women are to give good counsel and be teachers of what is right and noble, so that they will wisely train the young women to be temperate and disciplined and to love their husbands and their children." They are to teach them "to be self-controlled, chaste, homemakers, good-natured, (kindhearted), adapting and subordinating themselves to their husbands, that the Word of God may not be exposed to reproach," Titus 2:3-5 paraphrased.

The Bible says, "She rises while it is yet night and gets *[spiritual] food* for her household and assigns her maids their task." In other words early in the morning she spends time in prayer to receive wisdom and instructions from God and she prepares to delegate work to others for the day (Proverbs 31:15).

It is in those early hours that God so graciously will pour out to her all that she needs for that day. He gives you enough grace (enablement) for each day (Phil. 4:13); from wisdom to the strength that she will need, it can all be found there. For those of you who are not early risers but prefer to stay up late seek Him before going to sleep and during the quiet moments of your day (if you can't find a moment then make time for Him in your schedule) and as you spend that time fellowshipping He will refresh and energize you when you enter into His presence with singing, praying or reading His Word. You can gain wisdom, strength, peace, strategies, instructions, guidance, and encouragement.

Also a married woman's role is to work along side her husband for the betterment of their family. Working unto God and being content and at peace in what she does in the home, with a humble servant-like attitude (a servant's heart) to be of service and assist wherever the help is needed.

In order to fulfill her role she must have the wisdom of God to be creative, active, loving, understanding, humble, dynamic, submissive, and operating many times in the background without any recognition except that which comes from God. Also she can be fulfilled with plenty of satisfaction knowing that decent, loving and kind, god-fearing human beings were being developed for life and the journey ahead of them.

I prefer to follow the biblical definition of what a wife's role is. Since God is the creator of marriage and is the author of all roles and functions within a family, it will be to my benefit to find out what He says a wife's role should be that is pleasing to Him and helpful for her family that He so graciously blessed her with. I have full confidence in His Word because He can back-up every single thing that is written.

The Bible clearly tells a wife how to love her husband in the eyes of God according to Ephesians 5:33:

> ...And let the wife see that she respects and reverences her husband [that she notices him, regards him, honors him, prefers him, venerates, and esteems him; and that she defers to him, praises him, and loves and admires him exceedingly].

THE IMPORTANCE OF A HELP MEET AND SPIRITUAL PARTNER:

I shared the importance and function of a help meet earlier but it needs to be restated somewhat to complete this point. *One of the things God says a married woman is, is a helper meet (help meet in the KJV) someone who is suitable for her husband, adapted, and complementary to her mate (Genesis 2:20). She is one who is capable and equipped sent by God with wisdom, knowledge, gifts and skills to assist her husband. She is her husband's confidante, encourager, an inward strength, comforter; she is his "helper," and sent by God to help him fulfill his purpose and vision.* I like to say, she is in excellent company because one of the names or attributes of the Holy Spirit is "Helper." (Hebrews 13:6 and John 16:7) In Psalm 121:2 God says our Help comes from Him. Here He describes Himself as the Helper as well. God in all His power was still humble (Phil 2:8-9) enough to be called a *Helper* and has placed the wife in a similar position on the earth in the most important institution known to mankind, which is "marriage."

The first marriage took place when a woman was taken from a man's rib or side and God built-up and made the rib into a woman and brought her to the man (Genesis 2:21-22). I once heard a Bishop in regards to a woman being formed from a man's rib say, "*she was taken from under his <u>arm</u> for <u>protection</u>, by his <u>side</u> for <u>fellowship</u> and next to his <u>heart</u> for <u>love</u>.*" In the Hebrew *rib* means a *hidden support*. She is supportive of her husband (as he is supportive of her). She submits to her husband and he submits to her as they honor and respect one another. Again, as was stated in the Biblical Role of a Husband, it says in Eph. 5:21 KJV, **"Submitting yourselves one to another in the fear of God" is accomplished as they honor and respect one another by being supportive of each other by helping one another develop the dreams, gifts and talents that God placed on the inside of each of them.** One way to accomplish this is to adapt, make adjustments, compromise, be flexible and not try to change your spouse to fit into what you think they should be but to help your spouse become all that God has called them to be by helping them develop their potential, gifts, talents and skills through your prayers and asking for wisdom and guidance. For example, either could ask their spouse how they could assist to help where it is needed; do research; make calls; watch; encourage; review information given to them, discuss ideas and so forth.

With wisdom and knowledge ladies, you are equipped as a helper to use your God-giving skills for daily task which are not limited to running the affairs of your household such as: being a mother; planning and preparing meals; managing the household spending plan; cleaning; shopping; organizing schedules; working; planning and executing family functions and events; date nights; doing laundry; dropping-off and picking-up children for school and activities; supervising school homework; using great ideas and giving suggestions and information; *delegating* to a housekeeper, chef, family member or staff and so on as you meet your daily goals. These are only a portion of the functions and more on the nurturing end which we are called, anointed and equipped by God to do.

A wife is to help her husband fulfill the vision and purpose for his life which will ultimately affect their entire household. Since he is a married man this would include his wife sharing in the spiritual development, discipline, structure, guidelines and so forth as a part of the up bringing of their children. To confirm that the Lord would have both parents teach their children His will from His Word He says to the child, "My son, hear the instruction of your father; reject not nor forsake the teaching of your mother" (Proverbs 1:8; Proverbs 6:20). *Also, God entrusted the women to be the first to spread the Good News of the Gospel, that Jesus had risen from the grave. Thereby entrusting the women to take instructions, obey and follow through with the Word of God (Matthew 28:5-10).* This would certainly include their family and home. Therefore, as the husband and wife pray and study the Word of God separately during their own daily prayer and then come together in prayer where the power of agreement is activated and as a result they are in a position to take authority over obstacles and bear good fruit. They can receive instructions, guidance, wisdom, strategies and in some cases miracles from the Lord to help them smoothly manage and keep peace in their household as they gain victory and accomplish the vision not only for their household but the vision given to the head of the house for his life by the Lord which will ultimately affect their entire family.

Therefore, another key function for a wife is to be her husband's Spiritual Partner. The Lord has given the "male" man and the "female" man authority in the earth to take dominion over living creatures, the environment and their circumstances. Genesis 1:26 states that God the Father made a decision that included God the Son and God the Holy Spirit to make mankind in their image and give them complete authority in the earth. Genesis 1:27 says, "**So God created man in His own image, in the image and likeness of** *God He created him; male and female He created them.*" Furthermore, in Genesis 1:28 it says, "And God blessed *them* and said to *them,* Be fruitful, multiply, and fill the earth, and subdue it [using all its vast resources in the service of God and man]; and have dominion…" Being created in His image would include His Spirit giving birth to their spirit as God breathed His Spirit into mankind and gave man the very life that he has (John 4:24, Gen. 2:7 and I Thessalonians 5:23). His image would also reflect His character (the fruit of His Spirit, Gal. 5:22-23) and have reflections of God's glory which was their physical covering before they fell.

Also notice, that God fully recognized the woman's presence from the very beginning when He addressed them both by blessing and speaking to them and giving them instructions even though the only one present in His sight was the "male" Adam (man, mankind or natural man). The "female" Adam at the time was a "hidden support" inside of the male as a *rib* (rib in Hebrew means hidden support) and did not appear until Gen. 2:21-22 when God brought her forth from the male Adam and built her up into a wo-man (man with a womb), Gen. 2:23. **So why was God addressing them both since the "male" man was the only one present?** Because the true person is a spiritual being that lives in a physical body that possesses a soul which is comprised of their mind, will and emotions, therefore, the Lord was communicating with both of their *spirits* as He is a Spirit Himself and communicates with humans from Spirit to spirit as He does to this day. Remember also that a married couple has **supernaturally become one in the spirit** in God's eyes upon marriage, therefore, when He speaks to the husband or wife He is speaking to the plan that He has that would affect them both.

Now because both of them were present in one physical body until the Lord performed surgery on the "male" man and brought the "female" man forth they were both called "Adam" which as previously stated means, man, mankind or natural man, thereby God was expressing that He created all of mankind when He made both the male and female. Furthermore, eventually the "female" man (wo-man), who was also called Adam was renamed "Eve" by her husband and it means Life Spring because she became the mother of all the living (Gen.3:20).

This information is not intended to put one gender down or the other up because neither sex is to be exalted and neither is depreciated but both are meant to complement (complete) the other by recognizing their differences and the purpose for those differences and then respecting, honoring and appreciating the differences.

HER KEY FUNCTIONS ARE NOT HER ONLY FUNCTIONS:

The capacities to nurture and be a helper are both key positions that keep a household lovable, disciplined, organized and functional. **However, these are not her only functions; they are a married woman's key functions.** In the Traditional Nuclear Family as mentioned in Chapter four, a married woman's primary and in most cases *only* role was to support her husband in his career and to help raise their children. And there is nothing wrong with that, it is a part of her function if she is a wife and mother. However, if a wife's value and identity are measured *only* with reference to her husband and children never in terms of herself as an individual with self worth, goals, desires or dreams according to experts she can become and feel increasingly as a person with no identity.

During the fifties and sixties era in the media the Traditional Nuclear Family wife and mom was a person who was unsupported, isolated and considered unimportant by the world's standard and many times bored with the same routine. We understand that God desires that a wife's highest priority is her family and home but is that her only priority? Except for the fulfillment that she was a good wife and mother, **which is highly commended** especially for the strengthening of the family in any society, this is enough for some women *but is it enough for every woman?*

In my personal life I've had the experience of working for years in different corporations doing various types of work which included litigation and banking. I also have years of experience as a homemaker as well as overseeing a home-based business and now running a ministry corporation and as a respected author. I can truly say from experience that each had its own season and I was anointed for each one of those seasons because it was done in God's timing and will for my life. Furthermore, I was anointed to operate in each season with a spirit of wisdom, excellence and provision because *I chose to wait on God.* Waiting on the Lord's timing will change you and renew your strength and power, furthermore, you shall not grow weary or faint (give up), Isaiah 40:31. Being faithful to trust Him will preserve you because "He preserves the faithful," (Ps. 31:23).

This is the key to the Proverbs 31 woman, to move or flow with the Spirit of God in His timing and season and God's wisdom and instructions will preserve and enable you to accomplish what He purposed for your life in each given season. Is that to say we won't ever miss God? Of course not, but if we do, because we are striving to follow His leading, He will place us right back on track and raise us up and give us the victory.

A woman should also have options. God Himself, did not say that being a homemaker like the early sitcom's had indicated was a woman's *only* function and purpose for being on this earth, as important as it is, *but there is a season for everything, she just needs to know what season she is in and yield to the leading of the Holy Spirit. A woman should not have restrictions from people as long as God is clearly speaking or opening doors for opportunities to utilize the skills, gifts and talents He has imparted in that vessel for His purpose.* A woman or wife like anyone else needs to be willing, obedient, available and all that she can be to fulfill her purpose and assignment as she is led by the Spirit of God. *God used women in many capacities other than, and in addition to, the role of a homemaker so who is man to limit her capacity? (Proverbs 31:13-19, 26, 31).* Also, the Bible says, "we must obey God rather than men *(Acts 5:29).*

If this woman is a married woman and she is sensing that God would have her to step out and expand in more areas, then **(1) she and her husband need to seek God, pray and discuss it** so that God's perfect will for their family at that moment, in that season will be done. Also she is to be mindful that this should not be done at the neglect of her present responsibilities. Therefore, to save time and strength **(2) she needs to plan well with divine wisdom** by seeking God early for instructions and **(3) delegate work** and not try to do everything herself so she can plant fruitful vines in her vineyard (so her work will be productive and multiply in a good way and she can still enjoy her life and family), Prov. 31:15-18 Amplified Bible.

Individuals as well as families should be in their "set place" where they are spiritually and physically, for instance where they fellowship (attend church and/or bible study), live, work and so on that is in God's will and timing for that season and where His grace will abound with favor. This will ensure that when God is doing different things in their lives they can **operate with full authority and receive the breakthroughs and victories that come with it.** Does this stop all storms from happening in her family's life? No. God did not say we would not have trials and tribulations, when the storms come we are to resist them and know He will be in them with us to guide us through and at the same time we will become stronger and receive a fresh anointing along with breakthroughs and promises fulfilled.

But on the other hand if a wife is not stepping forward because what people have said has superseded what God has said, then her resistance to God will give place to the adversary and the divine purpose for her life is in jeopardy. For example, she could open a door for delays, hindrances, spiritual attacks on her marriage and home, physical attacks on her health, business and in other areas, simply because through her disobedience she has moved out of the perfect will of God for her life. In other words she is no longer under God's full protection because of her choices. A husband who is hindering his wife from answering any call from God or for fulfilling any assignment God has given her, needs to understand that even though he is the head and priest of their home, **Jesus is the High Priest and final authority in all homes** and she must obey the final authority or it could affect everyone.

God anoints people who are willing and obedient to fulfill His plan. He is not limited to use only adults, or only males, or only females, or even only children. He is not limited to singles or the married. Neither is He limited to gender, age or color **but you can limit God in your life with disobedience to His perfect will and timing**. His only criterion is that they have a willing and obedient heart. This is not intended to add any type of pressure or stress of trying to find His perfect will and timing for your life. God is loving, patient and all knowing. He will gently guide you by His Spirit as you spend time with Him in prayer, in His Word, and are sensitive to His leading as He gives you instructions and directions.

The Traditional Nuclear Family teaches the wife that she is to do all the adapting to her husband in order for their marriage to be successful. **Biblical principles tell us that both partners need to make an effort to adapt and get to know one another.** In Ephesians 5:21 it says "Be subject to <u>one another</u> out of reverence for Christ." Being subject or submitting basically is honoring and respecting one another in the fear of God. *Therefore, the both of them need to know and understand each other's needs, wants and desires to fulfill this mandate.*

The book of Proverbs Chapter 31 has illustrations of the different kinds of options women have. *In other books of the Bible there are recordings of women who were married or single and how God used many beautiful women such as:* **Queen Esther** to save a nation of people by risking her own life (Esth. 4:16); and how He used **Deborah** who was a prophet, a patriotic military advisor who went to war, a ruler of Israel and a married woman, (Judges 4:4-10). God also had **Miriam** lead a nation of women in praise to God (Exod. 15:20, 21), **Hannah,** the ideal mother (I Sam. 1:20; 2:19); **Queen of Sheba,** also referred to as Queen of Ethiopia who was a direct descendant of Ham and of Shem. She was extremely wealthy, was responsible for a kingdom and also gave birth to King Solomon's son Menelek (I Kings 10:1; 2 Chron. 9:1, 9, 12); and lets not forget **Mary Magdalene and Joanna and Mary the mother of James and other women** with them who reported (ministered) the Good News (Gospel) of Jesus Christ for the first time in history by anyone; they were chosen to report the news that Jesus had risen from the grave to the apostles and others (Luke 24: 3-10, 22; Matt. 28:7, 10; John 20:11-18).

There was also a family of women who were honored by God and inherited land when they requested it because their father who had died in the wilderness on the way to the promise land had no sons and his daughters did not want their father's name to be removed from his family by not inheriting his portion of the Promise Land. *So Moses brought it before God and the Lord said* *"the daughters of Zelophehad are justified and speak correctly.* You shall surely give them an inheritance among their father's brethren…" (Numbers 27: 4-8). **This law was then given by God to all that a woman can inherit her father's land if she has no brothers (v. 8).** Unfortunately certain countries and people chose not to listen to this instruction and women were prevented from owning property even if they could afford to purchase it, a plan to keep women at the mercy of men for their livelihood. *Thus another reason many women rebelled because again limitations by man and not by God.* And lastly are the **two women** found in Luke 10:40-42 **one who chose housework and the other who chose according to Jesus** *"the one thing that was needful,* **the good part, which shall not be taken away."** The good part being referred to by Jesus was that she could learn directly from Him the ways of God, who she was in Christ, and what her assignment in this earth would be. She could become the *Proverbs 31 woman* that was so highly spoken of in terms of being an excellent wife, mother, woman of God as well as a businesswoman.

Proverbs 31:10-31 NIV says: [3]

> Women may play many roles in a successful family relationship. This appears to be a composite picture of the ideal wife and mother. One woman could hardly perform all the functions mentioned within one day. The woman is equally active in home and business duties. She is trusted by her husband and seeks to help him at all times. She works hard, makes difficult decisions, earns and invests money well, is compassionate and helpful to the needy, is prepared for the future, and has wisdom to teach other people. She has earned a high reputation in her family, in the business world, and in the community. All of this is possible because her life is centered on God. The Bible thus challenges women to use their talents in as many

areas as possible to bring honor to God, their family, and themselves.

Many women as well as men are not aware of the Biblical order of submission and therefore assume in blind submission that a woman is to be obedient to any male. But the Biblical order of submission is on a broader scale which would bring a greater harvest for obedience. Women are to submit (honor and respect) delegated authority such as submitting to God first; to delegated leaders in Godly appointed authoritative positions; to her government and to her own husband. Submission to God-appointed leadership will always cause God's favor to flow in one's life.

This submission is measured by one's love for God. That love for God gives a woman the grace to submit to the delegated authority in her life once she has done the will of the Father whose authority supersedes any delegated authority in her life because God has all authority in heaven and earth (Mt. 28:18). *In doing for others she is not to be submitted to any type of abuse. Often submission implies a superior/inferior, master/slave, head/foot type of relationship when God never ordained this as part of a woman's role.*

The Lord's submission (because she is doing all unto God) will enable her to be a person who is strong and secure enough with whom she is that she can humble herself in such a way to be submissive to God, to delegated leaders, to the government and to her own husband, not just to any man.

Just like the Lord gave the woman the ability, wisdom and creativity to help her husband, God also gave the man the wisdom and ability to be the head of his family and lead. Therefore, we can help him by doing things to assist and not take over, but help him be the man of the house.

For example, just one of the things a wife can do to honor and show respect to her husband is when you are both *in public* and someone *asks him a question*, let him answer the question. Give him a little time, men process information differently than women and he may need a minute to find out how he feels about something or how he prefers to word his answer.

Most women can be impatient with this because they do not require time to process anything, they hear and they answer, it is as simple as that. However, spiritually mature women have learned to wait and allow their husbands to answer the question. A simple act like this will esteem him, build him up and give him respect in front of others. Sometimes it's alright to take the lead when others are speaking to him but not all the time as some of us will do. Small things like this will keep things in balance and help things continue to flow smoothly in your household.

If you find that you are making nearly all of the decisions that is out of order and it is just a matter of time with reoccurrences like this and others before something collapses. Try building his confidence up and his leadership skills will improve as you step back and allow him to lead.

Some women are probably thinking, well if I step back we will all be in the poor house. Not necessarily unless you are dealing with someone who is doing destructive things that would destroy the home. I am talking about things that will help under normal circumstances occurring in the home.

The Proverbs 31 woman sheds even more light on the role of a wife as we bring this to a close. The following passage describes the woman as a wife, mother and a successful business woman from Proverbs 31:10-31(paraphrased): "She is loved and called blessed by her children (v28) and praised by her husband (v28); she is a homemaker and successful business woman (vv14, 16 and 24). She feeds her family spiritual and natural food as she teaches them the revelation of God's Word (vv14-15). She and her family wear the finest clothing (v13 and vv21-22) and her husband is well known in the city and respected in the community (v23).

She keeps up her physical appearance as she is spiritually, mentally and physically fit (v17); she is a woman that reverently fears the Lord and reaches out her filled-hands to the needy (vv15, 20) and her husband trusts and relies and believes in her securely (v11); she is a woman who in her kindness speaks godly Wisdom as she gives counsel and instruction (v26); she is a person that delegates authority as well as a woman who was not afraid to work (vv15, 19) and she is a woman who is far more precious than jewels and her value is far above rubies or pearls (v10)."

A Proverbs 31 Woman:

> Many daughters have done…nobly and well… but you excel them all. What a glowing description here recorded of this woman in private life, this "capable, intelligent, and virtuous woman…**In what way did she 'excel them all?' In Her spiritual and practical devotion to God, which permeated every area and relationship of her life.** All seven of the Christian virtues (2 Peter 1:5) are there, like colored threads in a tapestry. Her secret, which is open to everyone, is the Holy Spirit's climax to the story, and to this book. In Prov. 31:30, it becomes clear that the "reverent and worshipful fear of the Lord," which is "the beginning (chief and choice part) of **Wisdom**" (Prov. 9:10), **is put forth as the true foundation for a life which is valued by God and her husband as "far above rubies or pearls** v.10, (Taken from the Amplified Bible footnotes).

BIBLICAL INSTRUCTIONS FOR THE ROLE OF A CHILD:

The role of the child may vary with their age as well as their functions in the household may change as given by their delegated authority, their parents.

Overall, a child should have a prayer closet – a time set aside to worship, and talk to God to build their own personal relationship with Him. They should also have time set aside to read the Word of God. This could be after their prayer time or scheduled in before or after homework just to give a few examples. The age to start their personal prayer time can be as young as five, six or seven it depends on the child. My natural daughter was already Born-again, Spirit-filled and praying in her supernatural spiritual prayer language at the age of three and at that time I was surprised because I was not aware that children that young could be filled with the Infilling of the Holy Spirit but the Spirit of God had indeed imparted to her at a very young age. But to be consistent with a regular prayer time I would think a little older would be better for their attention span and understanding.

When my natural son was only nine years old he was up each morning at six a.m. to pray for thirty minutes and this was when he first started hearing the Lord speak to him. He would record what he heard on a pad of paper next to the chair he prayed in. I later encouraged him to write it down after he shared with me what he was hearing. I knew he was truly hearing from God because I heard many of the same prophetic words earlier on the very same morning when I was in my prayer closet. God was confirming what He told me through my son and at the same time He was teaching both of us how to hear His voice and know His ways and will.

After we became a Blended Family and for those children still at home while they were growing up one of the rules or guidelines in our home was that each person had their own daily prayer closet (prayer time). During this time my husband's natural son began having a number of prophetic dreams of which many have already come to pass. Television was not permitted during the early morning hours because that was their time as individuals to spend with God. My husband and I rose up much earlier than the children so we could spend more time in God's presence.

As a result, they all have a relationship with the Lord, and they are Born-again Spirit-filled Christians. They can discern the voice of God or how He communicates with each one of them on a one-on-one basis. Each one has seen God move mightily on their behalf. In addition, they know personally that hell is real and some have heard the voice of Satan try to frighten or deceive them. Our youngest has seen demonic spirits as well as angels. This is something I won't have to convince anyone of in this family.

Some parents make the mistake of not leading the way and directing them towards the will and Word of God that would empower their children. His truth found in the Word will give them a strong foundation in life because they developed their relationship with Him while growing up. God told all parents to do this, train them up the way they should go, meaning train them up the right way, in the Word of God because that is the standard they should live by. Notice I did not say train them up in **"religion" basically knowing there is a God** but show them how to **have a personal relationship so they can know God for themselves** and have the privilege of fellowshipping and learning directly from Him; that is what will make the difference.

Isaiah 54:13 says the Lord will teach your children directly:

> And all your [spiritual] children shall be disciples [taught by the Lord and obedient to His will], and great shall be the peace and undisturbed composure of your children.

Some parents feel they will let their child find their own way and faith after they are older, either teens or young adults. Even though, these same parents will enforce school work, after school activities, sports, music, dance and so on but not enforce and oversee or even introduce the most important part of their upbringing. This happens because they have probably had a bad experience with "church people" themselves, or because they have been told that "religion" is a personal thing that people need to discover for themselves. Wrong! *These parents have been deceived and have left their children to learn the hard way that they will need a Savior in this life and that they can take authority over the evil attacks that come into and against their lives.* In the meantime, for all those that do not know any better they will learn by experience that there is good and evil in this world. Unfortunately they will probably be told they should just flow with whatever life's hand deals them and there is nothing they or anyone can do about it.

Parents the spirit man in your child when they are a Born-again Believer is the same Spirit that is inside of you if you are a Born-again Believer. A spirit has no age and it never dies only our body's age and passes away. Your body is a house or home for your spirit (who is the real person, the real you) and a home for your soul (your mind, will and emotions). Therefore, it is not cruel to help your child develop a relationship with God by taking them to a good Word-based Spirit-filled church; bible study and telling them to pray and read the Bible on their own (2 Tim. 2:15).

The day may come, if you did not teach them, you will wish you had because you would have been able to rest in the fact they had had that foundation to fall back on and remember what is truly important in life (Luke 15). Being exposed to Truth will give them something to compare to when they hear a lot of nonsense from people that do not know the ways of God because His ways will be foolishness to them and something they cannot comprehend (I Corinthians 2:14). As a result they will try to push their unbelief onto your child but if your child is grounded with wisdom and understanding of the Word they should not be moved by other's doctrines (Eph. 4:14).

The Word of God gives specific instructions in the bringing up of our children that will give them a strong foundation for the rest of their lives. One of those scriptures is as follows:

Proverbs 22:6 which says,

Train up a child in the way he should go [and in keeping with his individual gift or bent], and when he is old he will not depart from it.

This is speaking directly to bringing them up the right way, having the righteousness of God (His way of doing and being right – Matthew 6:33). The Word will be the foundation for them to rest upon and make decisions for the rest of their lives if they are taught the principles that are in the Bible.

God commanded the parents to do this, it is not the government's responsibility, nor the schools to teach our children who God is and His ways of doing things, it is ours.

Children are sensitive, trusting and believing in their hearts and are usually not hardened towards the things of God, so it would be easier to teach them while they are young. During this time it would also be good for them to talk to God about their purpose in this life. To ask Him in prayer what His purpose for their life is? So many kids grow up and still do not have a clue as to why they are on the face of this earth. Suicide among teens is enough evidence of that. Young people with *a vision and dream for their future, hope and a personal relationship with God* (I did not say religion or having been forced to church every week) rarely kill themselves. They already know there is more to life than what they have experienced and that life could be exciting if they have truly given it to God.

People are always asking kids and teens, "So what do you want to be when you grow up?" When the question should be what has God said that He has planned for your life? Has He revealed your purpose in life to you yet, (Jerem. 29:11)? When they are young and have heard from the Lord as to what He has planned for their lives this would eliminate a lot of confusion later, also pressure will stop some parents from interfering and trying to dictate what they want their children to be when they grow up and it would give everyone a peace of mind if they are Believers and understand how to live by faith. If it is God's plan for a child to take over the family business then God will let them know and help them run it in an excellent way. *There is such a thing as a generational calling or anointing that God purposed for the offspring to carry on.* God does raise up families to do certain deeds in His Kingdom (His Kingdom includes businesses and work outside of the church building).

As the young person seeks God, He will reveal to him or her what He has in store for his or her life and confirm it in their heart. He could also confirm it through strangers or apparent gifts, talents or interests in certain areas that the child already possesses. Remember though that a person's gift <u>is not always</u> their purpose sometimes the gift is there to help with their purpose. Whatever His plan is it will always be better than any plan he or she or their parents could come up with. God's plan fills the voids, completes and causes one to be content and secure in what they are doing once they make a decision to allow God to enable them to do it. He will also anoint, equip, train and make all the provisions and give the abundance for His purpose in your child's life.

They would only need to rest in Him and follow the leading of His Spirit to make the right connections, be in the right place at the right time and/or attend the right schools for them if that is required. Believe it or not, not everyone is suppose to "go away to college" that is not the plan for everyone. That is worldly thinking that keeps everyone in a box using the same formula to arrive at the same designation and as we can see most end up in dead-end jobs or boring careers that rob them of precious time with their families if they even have time to start one. Why? Because many people never bother to ask God what was His plan and as a result they are operating and functioning in jobs or careers or businesses that they were not anointed or designed or equipped to do and even though they can handle the work they are not fulfilled and many are miserable.

In addition, they are encouraged to get multiple degrees to be able to compete in the market place and so forth. The stress, money and fear of failure all play a part because they are relying solely on what "they can accomplish" according to what man not God says success is. Not to mention that higher education is big business that uses millions of dollars in advertising to pressure people to go in this direction. Higher education is good; if that is something that you have in your heart then it is for you. But let's not make it mandatory for every human being to have in order to be successful. Many times a trade that you love or a small business to help others or running a corporation is best fitted for your child when they become of age. Whatever it is once the young person finds what they were purposed for the contentment, interest and anointing will be there to help them reach their goals. *As long as you are in the will of God and doing what He purposed for your life you are a success!*

Another part of the biblical role of a child is to obey, honor and respect their parents.
Ephesians 6:1-3 says,

> Children, obey your parents in the Lord [as His representatives], for **this is just and right. Honor (esteem and value as precious) your father and your mother** –this is the first commandment with a promise. That all may be well with you and that you may live long on the earth. (Exodus 20:12).

As we are in the last days, a new season has begun and the prophets have foretold the condition and mindset of *those who are not Believers* and of how they including children will treat others and their parents. In I Timothy 3:2 it says that "...they will be abusive (blasphemous, scoffing, disobedient to parents, ungrateful, unholy and profane). When and if we listen to God, Who knows the beginning from the end; Who knows all things and has the power to change things; Who has sent His prophets of whom many were used to record in the Bible warnings for us to take heed to (pay attention to) that would help guide us in life. We can help our children while they are young if we choose to follow simple instructions that are preventive measures for preserving the family. Born-again Believers should not behave in the way of the world, if trained I Timothy 3:2's description does not have to apply to your child.

Studies show that children who have a personal relationship with God at the time of their parents divorce are quicker to recover in a healthier way than those who did not. Because those who did not have a relationship with the heavenly Father, the Savior or Comforter may turn to friends, sex, drugs, alcohol and rebellion for comfort and to pay back those who hurt them (I Cor. 15:33). These things only compounded their problems and as a result they stayed in bondage longer. Whereas the child who has some history with God and knows of His ways and His will, will clearly have the advantage if they turn to Him and do what He says such as to trust Him to make it better and heal their broken heart; forgive and pray for their parents and not turn against all authority and become rebellious making it difficult for the entire family. The child will have an option to do all in the natural or flow with the spiritual and receive supernatural healing and intervention which they in turn can use to help someone else who may be experiencing the same thing.

DOES A PARENT HAVE THE RIGHT TO SPEAK TO THEIR ADULT CHILDREN ABOUT WHAT THEY ARE ACCOMPLISHING IN THEIR LIVES?

- **When the parent is assisting the adult child** with finances and/or other support, as their parent(s) they have a right to speak to them about their lives. The adult child in honoring their father and mother will listen to the advice; however, because they are grown they have a choice of making their own decisions. The Word of God says children obey your parents in the Lord for this is just and right… so that all may be well with you and that you may live long on the earth (Eph. 6:1-3 and Ex. 20:12). However, when the child is now an adult they have the option as an adult to decide which way or what they will do including making other financial arrangements.
- **When the adult child asks for their parent's advice** when they are living at home, or on their own or are now married, parents have a right to answer. Although when the adult child is married the couple should go to God first and their spouse second to try to work things out between them before seeking counsel from the outside with Extended Family members or someone else.
- **When the parent is their adult child's employer** or in some other position of authority not related to home, once again the parent has a right to communicate to

the adult child with work related comments or instructions to secure proper work ethics or to bring a project to completion.
- Under the Old Testament a newly married daughter who was shamed by the lies of her husband was **vindicated by her father and mother** and if her husband was found guilty the elders of that city would fine him and give the money to her father and her husband was whipped for charging her with shameful things (Deut. 22:13-19).
- **As a mentor or <u>spiritual leader</u> in your adult child's life** you are in a position to judge their spiritual life the same as any other person in your congregation and/or that you mentor. When a person calls themselves a Christian then as a spiritual leader it is your responsibility to confront the person caught up in a wayward lifestyle and judge it (I Co. 5:12-13). This is done in order to prevent their blindness (2 Co 4:4) from trapping them into an eternal life of damnation and loosing the benefit of living in the Kingdom of God while still here on this earth (Galatians 5:19-21). **Hebrews 13:17says "Obey your spiritual leaders and submit to them [continually recognizing their authority over you], for they are constantly keeping watch over your souls and guarding your spiritual welfare,** as men who will have to render an account [of their trust]. [Do your part to] let them do this with gladness and not with sighing and groaning, for that would not be profitable to you either]." The spiritual leader can pray for them and point out that they are being deceived and misled! Evil companionships corrupt and deprave good manners and morals and character (I Co. 15:33). *Cultures and societies may change but God's Word never changes just as He never changes. What brought a blessing into your life hundred's of years ago will still bring a blessing today and what brought a curse hundred's of years ago will still bring a curse today.*

The Lord has a hand in the family you are in regardless of whether it is a Biological, Blended, Single-Parent, Adopted, Foster or whatever type. In His Word He does not distinguish between the different types of families. He simply says humble yourself enough to honor your parent(s) by listening to their advice so that your life may be long on this earth. Children of any age are called by God to honor (show respect) to their parents. He did not say if they were perfect or the best parents anyone could have or ask for, but to honor them just because they are in an office that He set up, anointed them for, and placed them in and one that He allowed. Know that God did not send evil works but whatever the devil meant for harm God will turn it around for good (Gen. 50:20). If things were not *perfect* then the adult child is also called to forgive and pray for their parent(s).

He asks us to train them up in the way they should go but **once they are grown continue to love them and now let the Holy Spirit lead and work in their lives.** If they find life hard or a trial is before them, you can assist as you are requested but on the overall move aside by placing them and their situation in the hands of God and watch Him move on their behalf. *He said move out of the way because He doesn't need our help to change and heal their hearts, to give them understanding, peace and direction.* He said trust Him with them so we could have a peace as we exercise our faith which will please Him and allow Him to bless us and our household.

EXTENDED FAMILY AND DIVINE FRIENDSHIPS:

Your Immediate Family is the core that the Extended Family extends from. The Immediate Family is you, your spouse, your children, your children's spouses and your grandchildren. From there the Extended Family is extended from both you and your spouse and includes other relatives related by blood or marriage: your parents, siblings, grandparents, great grandparents, uncles, aunts, cousins and in-laws. Do for each as directed in your heart from the Holy Spirit. Otherwise the Extended Family's needs are attended to after the Immediate Family's needs are met. Draw boundaries and do not allow people to take advantage of your time and resources as you do for others unto the Lord.

Now concerning **in-laws they can be involved as a part of your Immediate Family but actually they are a part of your Extended Family;** and not blood related in about ninety-eight percent of the cases due to the fact that some fourth and fifth cousins can legally marry. In-laws are the parents, siblings, and other relatives of yours or your child's spouse who may have come into the family with different values, morals and so on. In-law problems are one of the largest causes of strife in marriages and the overall family.

Parts of this is the fault of the couple who has not learned to cleave to their spouse yet and is still going to their parent(s) for constant advice and/or help for certain things and sometimes without discussing it first with their spouse (see Chapter 1 for more information on how to cleave to your spouse). This is not good for the entire family because both sets of parents could become involved then hardships, hurt feelings and misunderstandings will more than likely be the result especially if one or both of the **married couple are discussing private issues that could be embarrassing for their spouse which should really stay within their own household for them to work out or decide together to seek outside help.** Otherwise you place your parents in the middle and if you decide to forgive and you have gotten past it but your parents and siblings now have information about your spouse that may make them uncomfortable to be around or difficult to forgive (See Chapter 1 under Cleaving and Becoming One for additional information on cleaving to one another in marriage).

In-laws like to offer help to newlyweds as they are excited for them. They must realize that the adult child and their spouse will need to make their own decisions even if they offer their suggestions. The couple is not to dishonor or disrespect their parents in anyway but realize that they must tactfully suggest to their parents that they relinquish their responsibility to them while they bring their spouse into that position as they become one.

The couple needs to remember to speak well of their spouse and not complain to their parents after all you do not want your parents at odds with your spouse and run the risk of them losing respect for your partner. There is always something good that can be said about most people so choose to say something nice or nothing about them at all. (I am not speaking about abusive situations, of course the abused party should speak to someone that they feel they can trust).

Always honor your in-laws and try to work out any differences in the family with godly principles. Other in-laws such as sisters, brothers, uncles, aunts and cousins add to the family in a wonderful way. It could be an exciting time for the children growing up with family gatherings for birthdays, holidays and major events if everyone makes a conscious effort to do their part, pray more instead of interfering and gossiping and being a robber of peace.

DIVINE FRIENDSHIPS:

Many divine friendships also occur within the family. "Friendship is a close, intimate relationship in which affection can be expressed freely. The heart of such friendship is the willingness even to give one's life for a friend. Families can develop friendship within the established role relationships of husband-wife, parent-child just as Jesus and His disciples became friends even though He never ceased being Lord" 1 (John 15:13-15).

Take care of the concerns for **godly divine friendships** of people outside of your immediate or extended family that you know were placed in your life by God. Even with knowing that certain people were sent into your life continue with prayer, wisdom and caution to keep everything in order and in balance. The Lord will also place people across your path for you to share or minister to by assisting them with their needs from time to time or vice versa that may not have been intended for a long term divine friendship.

There are reasons we emphasize divine friendships, over the years we discover not everyone in your life was sent by the Heavenly Father. There are two ways people come into your life or a cross your path: (1) they are sent by God or (2) they are sent by Satan on assignment. We do not believe anything is just by "accident" and while on your journey certain people will come and go that were destined to be in your life for a season. **God blesses us through each other so do not think it strange that Satan would choose to curse your life or hinder you through others.**

Discern and pray about the people in your life and God will instruct you as to those to help and/or fellowship with and those that are there merely to drain you and pull on the anointing, amongst other things. You will want to avoid weariness, becoming burned out, irritable, or feeling like you are about to loose your mind. We are on the right track for maintaining a right mindset and receiving sound instructions for each day of our lives when God is kept in that first position.

As we realize that a part of God's plan is taking care of the family that He has entrusted and blessed us with and that *He has set in place an order to help it run smoothly* then we should also realize that if we are out of order in any other area this will eventually cause the family to fall apart through no fault of the Lords but our own. His Word says, "Apart from Me you can do nothing" (John 15:5).

God is no respecter of persons, as our family members adjust to His will and timing we will be able to see positive changes, growth, experience joy and peace. On the other hand, if our family members do not adjust and are not willing to work with the guidelines and teachings set down in the Holy Bible then they will experience unnecessary pain, suffering, disappointments, division and sometimes failure. Therefore, discern whether someone is in your life because God sent them or they have ulterior motives that will work against you when given the opportunity.

I Peter 3:17 says,

> For [it is] better to suffer [unjustly] for doing right, if that should be God's will, than to suffer [justly] for doing wrong.

Whether we are with God or not, all people suffer to some degree in this world about something because we live in a fallen world where there is good and *evil.* It was not God's will nor was it ordained by Him that mankind should suffer but once man fell (Adam had a free will to make choices) evil was released through the sin of disobedience: death, sickness, poverty, pain, curses, torment, suffering and so forth came upon the earth (Genesis 3).

WHEN ROLE MODELS ARE OUTSIDE OF YOUR HOME:

Many young children and teens are growing up entirely too quickly and as a result are missing their childhood not only because of wrong choices being made in some of their homes by their parents and/or guardians but **because our society tends to bridge preteens, teens and young adults in the same category**. Different influences in the life of our pre-teens and teens come from role models outside of the home through the mass media which has a great influence. The television, internet, magazines, music, videos and other electronics introduce a whole new lifestyle to children that are too young and immature to handle. A lifestyle which brings confusion, guilt, shame, pain and hurt because they are trying to comprehend information they are not ready to process and to be something they are not and should not become. One example is the influence in dress for our young people.

Adolescents are dressing more like pop stars on a stage for everyday life and losing their own identity and gaining attention in areas that are negative and in many instances dangerous. It is difficult to shop for pre-teens and teenagers because the fashion industry does not and will not recognize that pre-teens and teenagers are not adults and they are very impressionable and under a great deal of pressure to be accepted from their peers. Therefore, the fashion industry capitalizes on this and uses it as an opportunity to increase their sales. [4]

The parent's responsibility is to have raised a child in a holy atmosphere so when they do become of age and are making more decisions for themselves it will be a little easier on everyone because the child would have learned what is right or wrong, and what is appropriate and acceptable.

However, if you are a parent who did not bring your child up in the Word of God and now they are rebelling and will not listen to you and they have no fear of authority of any kind including the reverential fear of God, you must take a stand and let it be known what type of lifestyle and dress is acceptable and not acceptable in your house. **First,** you need to shop with them or if that isn't something you are able to do or wish to do then more than likely you will give the money to the teen to shop for clothing and accessories, but make it clear what type of clothing articles are acceptable. Hold to your standard and don't compromise because you will compromise your child's standards as well. **Second**, When they step out of your front door into the public's eye let them know you are interested in how they dress that they represent the family and if they are a Christian they represent God and it is not so much that you care about what people think (although you should not want people to think the worse because of the appearance of how your child is dressed) but more so that you and your teen should be concerned about what does God think and what kind of message are you sending.

CONTINUE TO SHOW ADOLESCENTS AFFECTION:

Parents and guardians please remember that adolescents (the process or period of growth between childhood and young adult also known as the teenage years), are NOT mature adults. Independence is a part of the growth process and it should be given with supervision realizing of course each child is an individual with different personalities and characteristics and requires a different set of limitations, such as: bedtimes (which are just as important for teens who are still growing and need their rest as much as smaller children), eating dinner with the family as opposed to constantly eating junk food or even eating alone in their room in front of a television or computer most of the time and never having time for family outings, fellowship or other events.

Their social life also needs to be monitored by the parents to know who their teen is actually in contact with and who is an influence in their lives. Some teens may become upset if you seem to be too involved in their "personal life" but never distance yourself too far because that too is not really what they want or need. They still need your love, approval and acceptance as they become a little distant in trying to find their way independent of you as they grow and learn more about themselves and other things in the world. *Some households do not experience the rebellion, the pulling away because the kids like their home and family and enjoy spending time with them. The communication is open and they like doing things together.* All of this depends strictly on the family and the type of upbringing the child was exposed to (sense of security, humility, openness, godly, good communication, balance, roles defined and so on).

Wise parents will listen to and continue to give them attention by being active in their lives in certain areas whether they want it or not using common sense and balance realizing they are individuals and that wise limitations need to be set as mentioned above. In continuing to give them attention show them love with hugs and kisses on the cheek, even a kiss good night is welcomed at most ages. People are never too old for proper affection in expressing love. A little hug here and there or an encouraging pat on their shoulder can be so encouraging and bring healing.

However, each situation will warrant different behavior that is relevant to the type of family you are in. If it is a Blended, Foster or an Adopted Family you may not be dealing with your natural children and unless you know the history of that child, be cautious of how you approach and touch them. Many children in this society and others around the world are experiencing all types of abuse and have been exposed to things beyond their years and need to be healed before they will allow anyone that close so just be aware and not take everything personally.

My kids looked forward to a kiss good night and felt special, loved and for some it offered a sense of security because each child is different with different needs. Many times my husband and I would go into their room together and kiss them good night and this was when most of them at that time were adolescents and some of them even stayed up longer than we did. **We have found that many parents stopped expressing and showing love to their kids in this manner once they became a certain age and frankly that is sad because this is when the need for acceptance is the greatest.** Teens generally will not ask for affection or attention like smaller children instead they act out their need by rebelling or in other ways to receive attention that may be embarrassing or hurtful to their parents or themselves.

If they cannot get the attention, affirmation, love and approval from you that they need they will find someone who will give them the emotional support they desire. Furthermore, it will probably be from the wrong person or source with the wrong advice and motive giving input into your child's life which could be very damaging and cause you and your family great distress for months or even years.

To avoid such problems from the beginning do not give up your role or authority as the parent in your child's life no matter what the age (small child, pre-teen or teenager in some cases young adults who still live at home). Parents should accept their role as parents and their adult responsibilities so their children can remain in their role as children, growing and maturing at a healthy pace for them. They should not be forced too soon into adult roles. Parents should offer comfort and security to their children instead of, as many do, look to their children to comfort and console them and allow or push adult responsibilities on their children.

I believe that teens should help in the home especially with keeping their room and bathroom clean; also pick-up after themselves, organize their wardrobe and put their clothes away. Maintaining the laundry for the younger children is an adult responsibility. When the older children make snacks or meals they should clean up the portion of the kitchen they utilized. They can also have other responsibilities in the household but those that will not drastically interfere with their education, quality family time, play time and their social time nor their time to go to sleep and rest. If possible a housekeeper is always nice to help lighten the load and a part-time chef wouldn't hurt either. But if these don't quite fit into your spending plan (budget) the family can all work together to lighten the load if both parents or a single-parent works outside of the home.

I have a serious problem with parents who assign adolescents the responsibility to take charge, maintain and run the entire household with the planning of meals, and most or all of the cooking, cleaning, shopping, taking care of the younger children, handling the mail and bills, even having a part time job to add to the family income. These are the responsibilities of the parent(s) or an adult in the household. To train a child is one thing but to hand over all or most of your adult responsibilities and duties because you are *too busy* is no excuse and in the end you will have serious consequences including robbing them of precious memories of their childhood. A good healthy balance should apply in every area of your life.

You are responsible to create a loving secure atmosphere and environment in and around your home where your child feels you are in charge, in control of your life and doing your part. You as the parent should know or learn how to adjust your personal schedules and set your priorities following first of all God's instructions and order in which to do things. Ask for wisdom daily as to what He would have you to do in addition to the agenda you have scheduled for yourself and place His request first. Read time management or business information to find out how to set proper priorities and do proper scheduling for your time. It could be that you are involved in too many outside activities, you are running too many unnecessary errands for yourself, your Extended Family or friends, or that you are involved in too much community activity. It could be that you are simply working on a job too many hours; working overtime or week-ends or having a second or third job especially if you are a single parent. **Be aware that this is a trap to wear you out and rob you of years of time that could be spent enjoying your family, friends and yourself.** *And* you would say, "But we have to eat, the bills must be paid!" *And* then I would say, "Yes, but there is a better way!"

God can make provisions for part-time help to come in or move on the hearts of people to help you, whether they are a part of your Spiritual Family or part of an Extended Family or a good friend who will help lighten the load. He can give you such revelation to lead your footsteps on a path where you have every favor and provision met for the need that is before you for the season of your life that you are in at the moment. *The Lord said, He "will liberally supply your every need according to His riches in glory by Christ Jesus"* (Philippians 4:19); He is your Helper (Hebrews 13:6 and John 16:7); God also said that He "...came that they may have and enjoy life, and have it in abundance (to the full, till it overflows," John 10:10). He will make a way for you out of no way and all He asks is that you ask, believe, receive and trust Him to follow through.

As we mentioned in the beginning of this chapter, **if we follow *God's order* He will honor that and help us**. When we set our priorities with His order in mind He will give us divine information and supernatural help to assist us with our family and lifestyle.

Do the things that are in your heart to do for your family. Spending that time to have conversation, or take a walk and walk the dog with your kids, doing simple inexpensive things, where you can give your undivided attention will be greatly appreciated by your children and pleasing to God. Showing acts of love and kindness are attributes of God and when you walk in love, you're walking with God, for God is Love. Remember, He is as close to you as you will let Him be at any given time.

James 4:8 says,

> **Draw nigh (close) to God, and He will draw nigh (close) to you...**

Set your schedule so you will have time once or twice a month or more to spend with each child on a one on one basis offering advice and suggestions that will enable that child or teen to overcome certain obstacles in their lives. For example, James may need advice for a workable schedule and study habits to enable him to complete high school or prepare for college and give praises to him to keep him encouraged during this difficult time. Janet on the other hand has mastered those things and has a great relationship with God and is following His plan for her life, she may need advice or training on her organizational skills, or money management and how to balance a checkbook or how to handle herself in mixed company. Some of these things seem routine to an adult yet they can be extremely stressful to a young person coupled with all the other demands in society today.

Both will need godly and moral training, discipline for proper sleeping and eating habits and so forth. Your child may be a born leader, but a person who is untrained and unloved as a child will more than likely grow up to be a wild, undisciplined and rebellious adult if they are not given an opportunity to develop godly character.

You may say it is too late they are older and rebellious, I'm tired and stressed, and don't know what to do, I do not know God, I do not know the Word of God and I cannot teach them something I do not know myself. On top of all that, my teen is not talking about their personal life or needs with me; they are hiding things, lying about their whereabouts and who their friends are and what they are doing.

Parent(s) just relax, take a deep breath, humble yourself knowing you cannot do this alone, say a simple but sincere prayer from your heart and invite Jesus into your life (if you have not already done so, a prayer for Salvation is at the end of Chapter 7) and ask Him to help you. A simple prayer and a sincere heart will get through to the throne room any day. God and His mercy will expose all, change hearts, conditions and circumstances regarding your child or teen's life before you learn His Word. As you learn of Him God will be faithful to do His part and preserve and keep your family, (Acts 16:31 KJV; 2 Timothy 2:13; 2 Thessalonians 3:3).

He will show you how to meet the need of each of your children, show you their strengths, weaknesses and their concerns as He places them on your heart. **He will begin to give you ideas, guidance, and send people (laborers) across your path that will be a blessing to you and your children in the very area that you need it.**

SUGGESTIONS TO HELP CHILDREN MAKE ADJUSTMENTS (Some may have been listed above but they warrant being mentioned again):

- Learn to really listen to your children; make eye contact as often as possible;
- Help them to feel better about themselves and show them what the Word of God has to say about them (either you do it or find a good bible study);
- You showing them that you have confidence and believe in them and that they are pleasing to God will certainly help them feel more sure about themselves;
- The Word of God will help them develop a strong moral value system, knowing right from wrong where they can make decisions based on truth, facts and God's revelation. As was stated above be a good role model in your home for your family;
- Your family should be aware of your attitudes and habits regarding drugs, alcohol and pre-marital sex. Share

information about these subjects with them and never rely on the schools, their friends or even church meetings to discuss these issues with your children especially without your input;
- Advise them on how to resist peer pressure. Teach them that they cannot please everyone and should not try. They are only obligated to please a loving God with their faith and be themselves. Teach them to say "no" not everyone will like it or like them but they must do what is best for their well-being;
- Encourage and teach them the proper foods to eat. What people eat does affect their behavior especially if there is too much sugar or fast foods in their diet. You as a parent need to plan the meals and lunches and have them participate so they can learn how to select and prepare the better foods for their bodies and future families;
- Talk with other parents who may have children your child's age or a Christian counselor or read Christian materials to keep up with current tips that work in today's society that will help your child grow and mature with godly character and without a lot of drama;
- Teach them not to be self-centered but to care about others. Also teach them to give of their time, and money to help others;
- It is wise to know certain signs that go with certain behaviors. For instance, if your child is involved with drugs or the wrong influences you should know the signs. Notice if there is a sudden change in their behavior in dressing, speech, moods, attitude, withdrawing from authority or being disrespectful to adults. Notice if there has been a change in their sleep patterns and their interests. Be aware and know your child. If you are too busy to do at least half of these suggestions then you are too busy and may need to adjust your schedule and rely more on God and less on yourself.

If you must work, only work one job and trust God for the rest. Tell God, I am doing this Your way and I expect You to help me. He said in His Word that we are to come boldly before His throne. That does not mean with anger or disrespect but come expecting Him to hear you, fellowship and answer.

Hebrews 4:16 says,

> **Let us then fearlessly and confidently and boldly draw near to the throne** of grace (the throne of God's unmerited favor to us sinners), that we may receive mercy [for our failures] **and find grace to help in good time for every good [appropriate help and well-timed help, coming just when we need it].**

James 7:7-8 KJV says,

> **Ask**, and it shall be given you, **seek**, and ye shall find; **knock**, and it shall be opened unto you:
>
> For everyone that asketh receiveth; and he that seeketh findeth; and to him that knocketh it shall be opened.

Yes, He knows what you are in need of before you even ask, but He said to ask (pray), seek (study the Bible) and knock (praise and thanksgiving). Because of your free will and His divine order if you do this His way, you will see the results you desired in your heart.

Because of your effort your family will discover that you genuinely care, are interested and that you are willing to give of yourself with your time, energy and money to have a relationship with them. As you continue to open yourself up and be transparent in order to be as honest as you can they will realize that you are not perfect and that they don't have to be perfect either, but be a person who will put forth the effort to have a better and joyful life with everyone in their household.

When your heart is sincere, they will feel loved and their needs will be met. And any needs that are not met, hopefully, they will know the *One* who will supply all their needs and ask Him, for themselves. It is never too late to come to Him, just as you are.

DELEGATED AUTHORITY IS PART OF GOD'S ORDER:

With God's delegated authority in our lives, our lives flow better; we have better role models, a decent society in which to live and a certain amount of freedom to express our beliefs and practice our rights. As we listen and follow through to give honor and respect to our delegated authority such as: our parents, employers, teachers, public servants, the laws of the land, respect for the office of the President, the government, as well as state and local officials, civil authorities, including our police departments, traffic control, judicial system, school system, and so forth **we set an example of the right attitude and having submission toward authority before our children that we all must obey rules, regulations, and guidelines.** As we respect and pay attention to signs and information posted by these authorities we are recognizing that God placed these authorities before us for our safety and to promote our joy. In addition, because we honor it we will not hinder our ability to hear God's voice and receive His instructions. **We honor God when we honor the authority around us. In this we are exercising** *true freedom and true liberty in Christ.*

> **Romans 13:1-6 is the Biblical recording of our civil delegated authorities:**
>
>> Let every person be loyally subject to the governing (civil) authorities. For there is no authority except from God [by His permission, His sanction], and those that exist do so by God's appointment. Therefore he who resists and <u>sets</u>

himself up against the authorities resists what God has appointed and arranged [in divine order]. And those who resist will bring down judgment upon themselves [receiving the penalty due them]. For civil authorities are not a terror to [people of] good conduct, but to [those of] bad behavior. Would you have no dread of him who is in authority? Then do what is right and you will receive his approval and commendation. For he is God's servant for your good. But if you do wrong, [you should dread him and] be afraid, for he does not bear and wear the sword for nothing. He is God's servant to execute His wrath (punishment, vengeance) on the wrongdoer. Therefore one must be subject, not only to avoid God's wrath and escape punishment, but also as a matter of principle and for the sake of conscience. For this same reason you pay taxes, for [the civil authorities] are official servants under God, devoting themselves to attending to this very service.

I Timothy 2:1-2 tells us that we are to pray for our civil leaders:

First of all, then, I admonish and urge that petitions, prayers, intercessions, and thanksgivings be offered on behalf of all men. For kings and all who are in positions of authority or high responsibility, that [outwardly] we may pass a quiet and undisturbed life [and inwardly] a peaceable one in all godliness and reverence and seriousness in every way.

Hebrews 13:17 is a Biblical recording for our Spiritual Authority:

> Obey your spiritual leaders and submit to them [continually recognizing their authority over you], for they are constantly keeping watch over your souls and guarding your spiritual welfare, as men who will have to render an account [to their trust]. **[Do your part to] let them do this with gladness and not with sighing and groaning, for that would not be profitable to you [either].**

2 Corinthians 1:24 contains more on Spiritual Authority:

> Not that we have dominion [over you] and lord it over your faith, but [rather that **we work with you as] fellow laborers [to promote] your joy, for in [your] faith** (in your strong and welcome conviction or belief that Jesus is the Messiah, through Whom we obtain eternal salvation in the Kingdom of God) you stand firm.

One reason spiritual authority exists is to increase our strength and joy, to help us remain sensitive to the leading of the Holy Spirit so we can hear instructions and directions as well as fellowship with God. **As we learn to obey and submit to the delegated authorities God has placed in our lives we also learn how to be in authority. In other words, we must know both how to be under authority and be in authority to be effective in the Kingdom of God.** True leaders first have learned how to submit to authority before they attempt to lead. When we really have learned to yield to His authority in the land it will become easier to recognize it whether it is in our home, work place, schools, military, courts or any other institution. As we yield out of respect for the office that God has set in place God will honor our obedience. **Realize that you are not being subject to the <u>person</u> in the office but to the <u>anointing on the office</u> that God has ordained for a person to oversee.**

Hebrews 5:8-9 says that the Son of God learned obedience by the things which he suffered. Some of us never learned to yield to spiritual or civil authority and in not doing so ever achieved the destiny that was purposed for our lives. God is no respecter of persons what He asks of one He asks of all and that is to respect what He has put into place for the good of all people. **If we are subject to our Heavenly Father then we must also be subject to His delegated authority for they represent Him** and are responsible for their assignments from Him, therefore, in God's eyes if we reject His delegated authority we are rejecting God.

Furthermore, God will not entrust His authority to self-righteous prideful people who seek the glory for themselves. Hidden pride always comes out. But He will entrust His authority to those who are set apart and sanctified for His use. *People in authority are often alone because they are set apart and cannot do as others do in many things and still be mightily used of God.*

We are to appoint, elect and vote people into leadership roles that know Him (His will, His ways and that believe His Word) so good leaders will rule over the people and the people will rejoice otherwise they will groan and sigh. This God-given instruction works together for the good and protection of all. Proverbs 29:2 says, **"When the [uncompromisingly] righteous are in authority, the people rejoice; but when the wicked man rules, the people groan and sigh."** That is why we are called to pray for our civil leaders (I Timothy 2:1-2).

True freedom is to have peace while obeying the authority God has placed in your life. **True freedom is not doing whatever and whenever you wish to do something, that will only lead to misery and a sense of loss of control for your life and cause your life to eventually lose meaning.** True freedom is liberty in Christ; to set forth to accomplish your vision and fulfill the purpose of your life as it is given by God while obeying the laws of the land and delegated authority in your life. Most people need guidelines and boundaries in order to be held accountable to someone other than themselves. People also need a meaningful support system of others in their lives. *The God that we serve is a God of relationship; therefore, He desires that we fellowship, love and help one another. The first people on earth had a personal relationship with each other and with God.*

We as parents should obey and pray for our leaders, judges, employers, our children's teachers, community business owners and politicians instead of criticizing and judging them especially in front of our children, this will add to being a positive role model. This will show them a constructive way of living even though there may be unpleasant conditions in our lives because of certain policies and laws. Let them see that you are still trusting God to make the necessary changes to improve any given situation or unfair policies or regulations that are beyond your control. God has the answers to all problems and as we continue to pray and wait for the right way with the right attitude and expectations about decisions of those in authority over and around us, God will move in the situation and cause the necessary changes to policies and rules and for improvements.

God is willing to change the hearts of men and to give instructions to show them a better way, and open new doors as He performs miracles. As we watch Him work on our behalf because we decided to obey the laws of the land and respect the authority in our own lives, we become the role models our spouses, children, extended family, neighbors, co-workers, associates, and friends need to see and have in their lives.

Realize those in authority won't always validate or appreciate you, but you can receive affirmation and appreciation somewhere else such as from your spouse, family or friends. Right now be a blessing and learn what God would have you to learn while you are under certain authority, pass the test and move on.

On the other hand a poor example of not respecting delegated authority before your children would be to live unholy, cursing your jobs, employers, supervisors, managers, teachers and civil authorities and coming against the very provisions that were made for you. This would also extend to working in your career or if you own your own business if you are always upset with your employees or the government because of the taxes or whatever that is affecting your business.

In any event as we make a conscious decision to honor delegated authority and operate within God's guidelines it will add to our lives, set an example for our families as it teaches them godly principles and integrity while building godly character.

INFORMATION REGARDING FAMILY ORDER AND ROLES:

(General and Miscellaneous Information)

Parents should be able to come in agreement, especially in areas of guidance and discipline for their children and how they will bring them up in the Word of God. Parents should want to see their offspring with a better life, living obedient in the will of God so that they won't be lead astray by false doctrine, the occult, worldly living and any type of peer pressure.

The parents can express what they expect from God, expect from each other and expect from each of their children as individuals or as a unit. This will aid in the making of a workable family that loves, is healthy and that will be supportive of one another.

Overall realize, that the parents are still the parents and they should be respected in their home and the parents in turn should give respect to the children. Remember neither you nor they placed themselves in these roles nor position and all of you have *Someone* greater than yourselves to be held accountable to with what you have been entrusted with. We are referring here to families that are together by a divine connection.

Transparency is a key element in the healing process. Create a Christ-centered forum where children feel safe and secure to meet and have the freedom to speak and express their emotions without running the risk of being criticized, judged, punished, laughed at or made to feel that what they have to say is

not important. God loves and cares about all that are involved regardless of their role, position or age.

The parents should set up house rules or guidelines for their home that will be shared at a family meeting. These guidelines should be carried out by each member of your family. Even though the parents initially set them up they should feel free to ask everyone about the guidelines and discuss them before putting them into action. Parents should not compromise their godly beliefs, morals, or show favoritism concerning the family guidelines.

Hold family meetings as often as your family believes it is necessary, once a week, once every two weeks or once a month. This is an effective way for members of the family to hear announcements, changes in schedules, updates, family goals, discuss family vacations, changes in guidelines (house rules), outings, events, complaints, give their opinions, express or vent their feelings, concerns, grievances and release their frustrations freely. They should also be able to discuss their hopes, visions and dreams if they choose to do so.

Family meetings are an excellent way to keep the lines of communication open especially if they were shut at one point. Everyone is included in discussing family vacations, short and long term goals, plans for the family and how it will function as a whole and as individuals in certain areas. I placed a huge monthly calendar in the kitchen during our first year together and called it the message center. This reminded everyone and kept them informed of what events, house responsibilities or goals we were looking to complete as a family for that particular month or with certain family members e.g. a prom or meeting with a tutor or an art class, etc.

During the meetings **all family members should be listened to and taken seriously** and no one taken for granted or made fun of. At the same time everyone in the family is learning each other's likes and dislikes. During the course of a family meeting, Dad and Mom are also free to express themselves as well as be able to admit that they are not perfect and have faults and make mistakes too. The parents should be humble enough to show their children that they need God as much as the next person. Understand that their parents are also learning and they should have patience with them as well. If someone had a concern in between meetings of course they could come to either of us at anytime. If they had a suggestion that involved others then we would bring it up at the next family meeting.

Family meetings also help in preventing family members from having to go outside of the family to acquire the attention or a listening ear that they sometimes so desperately need from within the family circle. Confidential matters should not be discussed in an open forum but with a one-on-one or the child with either parent(s) or someone they can confide in. The important thing is to release and not harbor bitterness or unanswered questions. When they ask a question and you do not have an answer, you and the child can pray about that need and do research to find an answer; otherwise trust God to give you the revelation to be able to explain it.

Schedules are used basically as a guideline not to become rigid but as a flexible schedule to help things flow a little better as well as to show routines that are set in place where there should be order or consistency. *They help reduce stress, overload, and burnout* in some people that could eventually lead to a nervous breakdown. Schedules are also *used to instill self discipline*, to assist in *setting up a daily agenda* and give *direction for your daily activities.* These are tools which aid in accomplishing things of significance on a daily basis. *These tools are especially needed in a blended household. Many times you are living and functioning in a home where you may not know the people you live with very well.*

It also offers, as I briefly mentioned above, that one can learn their place or role in their family. For example, **in a Blended Family an** *only* **child may now have siblings or an** *older* **child has now become a middle child or even the youngest.** Responsibilities and roles have shifted, a new older sibling may now have your responsibilities simply because they are now the oldest in the family. A new parent is making major decisions that may affect your life and you may feel threatened or confused because it may seem as though you no longer have control over your life in certain areas or with the parent you thought would always be there. Please note that whether your role model parent(s) is a good or a poor role model, realize that parents are human, they are operating in God-given roles and they will make mistakes. Furthermore, whether they are holy or not, all they can do is the best that they know to do, with the knowledge they have at the time they are raising you and your siblings. Pray for them whether they are a good or bad role model and give God space to work in their lives to improve and enlighten them which will also improve your life as well.

These adjustments may not always come about easily. The children could find themselves sharing their natural parent, home, room and space with someone they may consider to be a stranger at best. Or their present homes may be for sale looking to purchase one large enough to accommodate everyone. Things that were taken for granted in a smaller family such as space to relax and be alone to read, talk on the telephone, take care of personal needs and so on, that is no longer available could bring out hidden emotions that were not foreseen or considered an issue before. Everyone should really try to be considerate of one another's space; aware of others bed times and any noise they make; remember to knock on doors before entering a room and do not borrow anything without permission. Of course these are the kind of reminders that should be in your family guideline.

If the parents have done all that they know to do and to the best of their ability, knowledge and skills, they can then have a clear conscious even if one or more of their children strayed or became rebellious. After all God the Father is an excellent parent yet many of His children rebelled as well. *People are attacked by demonic forces when they are doing what is right and they are attacked when they sin. The difference is when you know who you are in Christ you can resist it and be victorious, meaning it will turn around for your good.*

The Bible says that when a child does not respect or honor their parents the child may cut their own life short but if they show respect they will live long on the earth. Children should obey their parents and adult children should listen to their parent's advice but make the final decision themselves and all ages are to honor and show respect to their parents.

Even though a passage is addressed to the father, whom the responsibility was given, the mother is to assist the father in the bringing up of their children:

Exodus 20:12 KJV says,

> Honour thy father and thy mother: that thy days may be long upon the land which the Lord thy God giveth thee.

Ephesians 6:1-3 KJV says,

> Children, obey your parents in the Lord for this is right.

> Honour thy father and mother, which is the first commandment with promise; That it may be well with thee, and thou mayest live long on the earth.

Ephesians 6:4 says,

> Fathers do not irritate and provoke your children to anger [do not exasperate them to resentment], but rear them [tenderly] in the training and discipline and the counsel and admonition of the Lord.

Everyone is born with a free will. If their choices lead them off the path of righteousness then our God through our prayers will do everything in His power to direct them back into His will simply because He loves them and loves us and will honor our seed (our child) and prayers according to His Word (Prov. 11:21).

Psalms 146:8 tells us that the Lord opens the eyes of the blind and He lifts up those who are bowed down. He will make the crooked things straight again as it says in:

Isaiah 42:16,
> And I will bring the blind by a way that they know not; I will lead them in paths that they have not known. I will make darkness into light before them and make uneven places into a plain. These things I have determined to do [for them]; and I will not leave them forsaken.

However, the ultimate choice and decision still rests with each individual whether they receive this free gift of love and salvation or not. Parents this is where your compassion and your spiritual maturity comes in to aid your child if they got off track until they can see the light again. Therefore, do all that you know to do in the sight of God, then pray and leave the battle to Him, (2 Chron. 20:15). Continue in Him following His instructions and do not live with condemnation or guilt, (Romans 8:1). If you are a child of the King leave it in His hands and watch Him do a mighty work for your family.

CHAPTER 7

WALK IN VICTORY AND AUTHORITY THROUGH EFFECTIVE SPIRITUAL WARFARE AGAINST DEMONIC ATTACKS ASSIGNED TO YOUR MARRIAGE AND FAMILY

IT'S NOT OVER TILL GOD SAYS IT'S OVER!

First of all in order to maintain the victory already won by our Savior in every battle against demonic attacks we must know there is a True and Living God, and who we are in relation to Him. Then we need to understand who the enemy, the adversary is and acknowledge that there is a war taking place for the possession of our souls and the souls of our loved ones.

Secondly, you will need to know in your heart that you want the victory in your life and to know where you and your loved ones will spend eternity. However, **in order to live the kind of life God intended for you it is not enough to know that the**

victory is yours, you will have to earnestly desire it and stay focused in order to keep it. Because it is going to cost you something, in some cases it may cost you *everything*. **Thirdly,** once we receive the manifestation of the victory how do we maintain that success?

This chapter was added for one reason, to give families the advantage over the "Destroyer." We learned first hand as we were taught by the Holy Spirit how to fight for what belonged to us; how to fight in the spirit and win against attacks that threaten the unity and success of our family. **Your enemy ultimately wants one thing and that is your faith, the faith that you use to stand against him and the kingdom of darkness**. Therefore, he will attack your mind to take your faith in God then try to annihilate (destroy) you and all that belongs to you until he has your soul.

Well, that is *his* plan anyway. Many of us already know that there is a God Who is able all by Himself to expose and destroy the works of the enemy. We know that ultimately vengeance is God's and once we have followed His instructions and at the appointed time, He will Himself bring justice to the situation, will deliver us from our enemies who are basically controlled by the adversary our true enemy and give us total restoration and recompense. This will involve our spirit, mind, body, finances and social life being blessed once the Lord turns it around (Ps. 94:1-15; Isa. 34:8; Jeremiah 51:6).

The Holy Spirit will execute vengeance and He will cover every base not missing anyone or anything that was in place to stop our progress in God. He will do this out of love for His child who has been robbed, wronged, held-up, hindered, slandered and who is trusting Him in faith to turn the situation around (Ps. 105:15; Gen. 50:20). In other words **He will move on our behalf because He loves us and is a God of Justice**.

Isaiah 61:8 God's Justice is at hand,

> For I the Lord love justice; I hate robbery and wrong with violence or a burnt offering. And

> I will faithfully give them their recompense in truth, and I will make an everlasting covenant or league with them.

Hebrews 10:30 God's Justice involves His Vengeance,

> For we know Him Who said, Vengeance is Mine [retribution and the meting out of full justice rest with Me]; I will repay [I will exact the compensation], says the Lord. And again, The Lord will judge and determine and solve and settle the cause and the cases of His people. Also see Deut. 32:35 and Romans 12:17-19).

In the meantime, we have all authority to control a situation or spiritual attacks that are in our territory and still get the victory in the battle until the war is won. At that time God releases "The Blessing" into our lives.

Even though I direct much of my attention to the Blended Family, know that the tools shared are for *any type of family* whether they are a Traditional Nuclear Family; a Single-Parent Family; Family by Adoption; a Child-Free Family; Foster Parent Family or members of an Extended Family. **The type of family you have does not matter, what does matter is, if the family chooses God they will acquire authority and learn strategies that can only be taught by the Master Strategist on how to effectively fight against the destruction that has targeted their household.** These strategies will ultimately show you how to win the battles and the war and save your family which is a gift and a blessing from Almighty God in heaven. And since families are the foundation of all societies throughout the world the more families that have this knowledge will contribute their part in taking back what was stolen from all people in the earth as well as build the Kingdom of God.

Many Blended Families start with strikes against them with deadly emotions such as anger, unforgiveness, bitterness, depression, baggage from their past and other negative emotions. These emotions may not only be generated from the married couple but also from their children, because *this type of family is the only type that involves adjustments from everyone at the onset of the marriage.*

I experienced the enemy's ugly ways and devices before I knew who I was in Christ and that I had authority over such destructive things. My husband and I shared how years before we met we both watched the enemy destroy our lives, our finances, our reputations and steal both of our physical homes right from under us. And how years later we met by divine connection and were married two years after that. The enemy attempted to devour our **new Blended Family** that God had blessed my husband and me with but because of the Holy Spirit instructing us it was to no avail.

At this point God opened our eyes and began teaching us one-on-one combat. We became bolder, courageous, and determined to resist and stop the enemy. My husband who is my number one prayer partner and I pray and come in agreement *daily* and with the help of the Holy Spirit, to date we have been able to stand against and win every battle that has been launched against our family.

Every time Satan raised his ugly head with some type of crisis God sent help right on time every time. In the beginning we learned as a God-Blended Family a few things about how to operate in the spiritual realm (things the both of us did not have a clue about during our former marriages). And now in addition to the both of us, our children are also in the Word of God and filled with His Spirit, praying in their supernatural spiritual prayer language of the Holy Spirit and coming in agreement. When the devil would try to rob us of something God planned for our lives especially in major areas (where we lived, our transportation, divine connections and favor) God would supernaturally block it or give us grace to go through the test and be strengthened because of it. Of all the things that we do that are considered warfare tactics against the enemy our commitment to pray everyday as a couple and several times in a given week in specific areas confess the Word of God together has been two of the most effective because we are in agreement and in God's will; **it is not easy to break a threefold cord.** In addition, we are pulling down demonic strongholds in the spiritual realm and keeping our hedge of protection strong as we continue with our personal relationship with God while operating in His Word.

Ecclesiastes 4:12 says:

And though a man might prevail against him who is alone, two will withstand him. A *threefold cord is not quickly broken.*

We were willing to be trained by the Holy Spirit because we were determined that Satan would not rob us in this area of our lives, the well being of our family and home again. Whatever we went through we did not give Satan any glory by complaining against God because of our test and trials. When we went through them, we kept our joy as much as possible, and encouraged one another, knowing we would be stronger and better because of it. We knew we were forerunners and had to experience some things first hand because we were becoming more effective as ministers of the Gospel of Jesus Christ. **We were determined that we would have the victory and God would receive all the Glory.**

James 1:2 in the Message Bible addresses it this way,

Consider it a sheer gift, friends when test and challenges come at you from all sides. You know that under pressure, your faith-life is forced into the open and shows its true colors. So don't try to get out of anything prematurely. Let it do its work so you become mature and well developed, not deficient in any way.

Listed in three separate sections in this chapter is information, tools, skills, spiritual weapons and strategies we were taught from the Word of God and by the Holy Spirit on how to fight spiritual battles that were sent to cause division, destruction, to ruin us financially, cause strife, affliction and anguish in our family and how these tools or spiritual weapons turned it around and gave us total victory in each case.

Section One: When we decided to breakthrough (go through and beyond), it was **a decision to train for spiritual warfare that was very real.** We learned that evil forces were using devices, tactics and weapons designed to take our family out permanently. Therefore, one of the first things *we must know is who our adversary is* because we cannot effectively fight if we do not know who the enemy is. And we need *to be aware of devices, tactics and weapons that are sent to destroy our family.*

Section Two: We must *decide we want the victory and then take it by force as we discover the weapons, tools and strategies that the Master Strategist has given us to use.* Also, *wisdom with finances* is used as a tool or weapon *to block giving place to the enemy* who uses a lack of finances as a means to destroy marriages and households.

Section Three: In a spiritual war like any other war we must decide which side we will be on. Who will we give our allegiance and our loyalty to? *Discover through Effective Spiritual Warfare Who has the real power to change hearts, lives and circumstances; as well as the power to restore, revive and reconstruct?* In short, *we must know Who God is and Who we are in relation* *to Him, know His Holy Spirit* and how He functions and **uses angels**. Also, in this section is a review of what is necessary to build and embrace a strong personal relationship with God; also included is a brief history of the King of kings.

First of all unless we humble ourselves and acknowledge that without God we can do nothing we will stay right where we are (John 15:5). It will take a humble person, one who is thankful and has a tender conscience that is sensitive to the leading of the Holy Spirit and knows that He will lead them through the path that is designed for their purpose in life while preserving them if they will keep their peace and joy as they flow or stay in step with His Spirit.

If you are prideful and think you can do it all by yourself, then you are headed for disaster before you even start; *haughtiness comes before disaster, but humility before honor* (Proverbs 18:12).

Apostle Paul wrote in Romans 7:18-25:

> For I know that nothing good dwells within me, that is, in my flesh. I can will what is right, but I cannot perform it. [I have the intention and urge to do what is right, but no power to carry it out.]
>
> For I fail to practice the good deeds, I desire to do, but the evil deeds that I do not desire to do are what I am [ever] doing. Now if I do what I do not desire to do, it is no longer I doing it [it is not myself that acts], **but the sin [principle] which dwells within me [fixed and operating in my soul]. So I find it to be a law (rule of action of my being) that when I want to do what is right and good, evil is ever present with me and I am subject to its insistent demands.**

> For I endorse and delight in the Law of God in my inmost self [with my new nature]. But I discern in my bodily members [in the sensitive appetites and wills of the flesh] a different law (rule of action) *at war against the law of my mind* (my reason) and making me a prisoner to the law of sin that dwells in my bodily organs [in the sensitive appetites and will of the flesh]. **O unhappy and pitiable and wretched man that I am! Who will release and deliver me from this body of death?**
>
> **O thank God! [He will!] through Jesus Christ (the Anointed One) our Lord!** So then indeed I, of myself with the mind and heart, serve the Law of God, but with the flesh the law of sin.

Apostle Paul was *humble and wise* enough to realize that sin was a part of him because of his sin nature and therefore, in his own strength he was powerless against the evils in this world that came to influence him and that were around him that caused him to trespass. In other words **the sin nature that he was born with made him a "sinner" and the trespassing was what he did.** *But through Christ he found that he could indeed overcome.* *This was a man that was well educated with the law and found that it was no help against a sin nature and he discovered it was more important that he had become educated in the things of the Spirit.*

In Galatians 2:20 Paul further states:

> I have been crucified with Christ [in Him I have shared His Crucifixion]; *it is no longer I who live but Christ* **(the Messiah) lives** *in me*; **and the life I now live in the body I live by**

faith in the Son of God, Who loved me and gave Himself up for me.

Paul realized that *only God could help him be free, he could not do it alone;* the spirit is willing but the flesh is weak. We have an enemy whose job is to bring chaos, disorder, pain, division and destruction any way he can to make our lives a living hell. **Paul found the answer, more of Christ and less of him, more of the Spirit and less of the flesh. Build yourself up by building up your spirit man, conquer your flesh (your way of thinking) which is so easily tempted and led astray which means as the mind thinks the body will respond.** Then guard and keep yourself in the love of God (Jude 20-21). Paul realized that apart from God he could do nothing.

We must guard and protect our soul which consists of our mind (intellect and imagination), will and emotions from the influence and oppression from Satan and his evil demon spirits who need a human body to work through on this earth to do evil deeds and who will oppress and/or take possession of human bodies from time to time.

SECTION ONE

WHO IS THE ADVERSARY AND WHAT ARE HIS DEVICES?

WE MUST KNOW WHO OUR ENEMY IS:

Satan began as "Lucifer," from the Latin version of Scripture, and Lucifer means "light-bringer" or "shining one" as it is translated in the King James Version. He was the most beautiful anointed cherub in heaven and he was over praise and worship. He was beautiful, every precious stone was his covering (a part of his body) the carnelian, topaz, jasper, chrysolite, beryl, onyx, sapphire, carbuncle and emerald, (Ezekiel 28:13-14) and out of his body came the most beautiful music to glorify God. Of course all of that changed once he attempted to approach God to over throw Him and take His place. The archangel Michael threw him out of heaven and as a result he hates everything that has been taken from him and given to mankind as much as he hates God Himself.

The definition of Lucifer from *The Everyday Life Bible*, by Author and Apostle, Joyce Meyer, in Isaiah Chapter 14, the footnote states that:

> Lucifer, the light-bringer, is the Latin equivalent of the Greek word "Phosphoros," which is used as a title of Christ in II Peter 1:19 and corresponds to the name "radiant and brilliant Morning Star" in Rev. 22:16, a name Jesus called Himself. This passage here in Isa. 14:13 clearly applies to the king of Babylon.

Lucifer was given the name Satan in the third century AD, and is based on the supposition that Luke 10:18 is an explanation of Isaiah 14:12. Lucifer's name changed from Lucifer to Satan after he was thrown out of heaven.

Isaiah 14:12-15 NKJV and the AMP says,

> How have you fallen from heaven, O Lucifer, son of the Morning! How you are cut down to the ground you who weakened the nations!
> For you have said in your heart:
> I will ascend into heaven,

> I will exalt my throne above the stars of God;
> I will also sit on the mount of the congregation
> On the farthest sides of the north;
> I will ascend above the heights of the clouds,
> I will be like the Most High
> Yet you shall be brought down to Sheol (Hades), to the lowest depths of the Pit (the region of the dead).

It was an act of Lucifer's *will* that was generated by his pride in wanting to take God's place. He at that moment became the "age-old serpent, who is called the Devil and Satan, he who is a seducer (deceiver) of all humanity the world over; he was forced out and down to the earth, and his angels were flung out along with him" (Revelation 12:9). They are now fallen angels who at one time lived in heaven. The theory is before the first flood on the earth these fallen angels ruled on the earth with Lucifer over a species known today as demons, principalities, familiar spirits, evil powers, master spirits who are the world rulers of this present darkness in the earth (Ephesians 6:12, Emphases added). **Lucifer did not begin this way but this is how he chose to finish.**

These evil forces once had a body that was part human and part animal and are now disembodied and in need of a body to function on this earth. <u>They lost their bodies when Satan was thrown back to the earth the day he thought he would over power God and take His place</u>. Isaiah 14:13 above says that Lucifer said to himself, "I will **ascend** to heaven." He would not have needed to ascend (move upward) if he were already in heaven. God had already given him the earth to rule over with a third of the angels and Lucifer ruled over the beings that inhabited the earth at that time which were as mentioned above, beings that were part human and part animal as the theory is taught. Confirmation may well be the drawings of lesser gods of pagans as they appeared in the people's dreams and they recorded what they were shown.

When Lucifer fell to the earth with his fallen angels a flood occurred and water covered the earth and the sun was moved and the earth was frozen, which accounts for the "Ice Age" that was discovered by scientist years ago. Also discovered were prehistoric bones of monster size animals that once lived on this earth <u>before</u> the first flood. After the first flood the earth was left without form and an empty waste until God spoke to it and said "Let there be…" and the Holy Spirit Who was hovering over the face of the waters restored the earth as the Creative mind of Father God spoke it back into existence.

Genesis 1:1-3 states:

> **In the beginning God (prepared, formed, fashioned, and) created the heavens and the earth. (v.2) The earth was without form and an empty waste, and darkness was upon the face of the very great deep. The Spirit of God was moving (hovering, brooding) over the face of the waters. (v.3) And God said, Let there be…**

In the book of Genesis it clearly states that God created the heavens and the earth and something happened between the time He created it and billions of years later we see it had become a void and empty place with great darkness of water upon it. And then God brought it back to life: "He created the great sea monsters (whales) and every living creature that moves, which the waters brought forth abundantly…and every winged bird according to its kind…" He told "the earth to bring forth living creatures according to their kinds: livestock, creeping things and [wild] beasts on the earth…" And then He created mankind to rule over it all (Genesis 1:3-27). And "by faith we understand that the worlds [during the successive ages] were framed (fashioned, put in order, and equipped for their intended purpose) by the Word of God, so that what we see was not made out of things which are visible" (Hebrews 11:3).

Remember all three of the Godhead (the Father, the Son and the Holy Spirit) were together before the earth was formed, John 1:1-3 says, "In the beginning [before all time]

was the Word (Christ), and the Word was with God, and the Word was God Himself. He was present originally with God. All things were made and came into existence through Him; and without Him was not even one thing made that has come into being."

These disembodied spirits that lost their bodies in the first flood long for a body so they take possession of human beings whenever they find an entrance that a person gives them to come and live inside of them. Thus the person is now possessed and in need of these demons to be cast or driven out of them by Born-again Believers who have the authority to do so in the name of Jesus (Luke 9:38-42; Mark 1:23-26). It says in Mark 16:17, "And these attesting signs will accompany those who believe: in My name they will drive out demons…; and in Luke 10:19 it says,

> Behold! I have given you authority and power to trample upon serpents and scorpions, and [physical and mental strength and ability] over all the power that the enemy [possesses]; and nothing shall in any way harm you.

We are called to deal with these wicked spirits on the earth and exercise our authority over them or they will take dominion over us. Notice I did not say that only fivefold ministers had the authority to drive or cast them out, <u>all Believers</u> (true Christians) have been given that authority by the One we follow and call Lord. We must use the authority given to us in the name of Jesus in our homes regarding our spouse, children and extended family or Satan and evil spirits will oppress them with torment and influence them and us to do wrong or work through us to cause constant chaos, strife, disorder and other evil works in our homes, churches, businesses, work places, schools, economy, government, the media, arts and entertainment, politics, and so on. **They are sent to rob us of our joy which is our strength and rob us of our peace of mind in hopes of hindering or stopping our faith in God altogether.** When we are truly trusting God we resist evil, we cast our care and keep our peace and joy in the Holy Spirit daily as we seek Father God in the presence of His Son for fellowship, instructions and direction before starting our day.

Lucifer was blameless in his ways from the day he was created until iniquity (wickedness) and guilt were found in him. He was filled with lawlessness and violence, and he sinned, therefore God cast him out as a profane thing from the mountain of God as the guardian cherub drove him out. Lucifer's heart was proud and lifted up because of his beauty and he corrupted his wisdom, he profaned his sanctuaries by the multitude of his iniquities and the enormity of his guilt. **God reduced him to ashes on the earth, stripping him of all authority and giving it to mankind** (Ezekiel 28:15-19). This is one reason why he hates people so much. He was the closest thing to God before he was thrown out and people were placed above the angels. **He also hates mankind because God loves us and created us in His image. Satan hates God and everything that God loves. He also knows that his time is short, (Revelation 12:12)!**

Lucifer turned himself into Satan because of his wicked ways and deeds. **Satan** *himself masquerades as an angel of light* (2 Co. 11:14). He is deceptive as he assumes the form of an angel to deceive people. *As we exercise the gift of discernment, spiritual maturity and insight these help to protect us from the master of deceit, his lies and tricks.* We must remember that he is a spirit and spirits do not die. When people take on Satan's attributes they open a door to allow him to use, oppress or possess them with evil spirits. If any evil spirit possesses a body it will come in and control that person to carry out evil against those who are righteous in God.

"The Hebrew language has two spellings for Satan, seen-tet-nun, and samech-tet-nun. The former is the one used in Scripture, in Num, 22:22, 32, 1 Sam. 29:4, 2 Sam. 19:22, 1 Kings. 5:4; 11:14, 23, 25, Zech. 3:1,2, Ps. 109:6, Job 1:6,7,8,9,12; Job 2:1,2,3,4,6,7, and 1 Chr. 21:1. The latter spelling, samech-tet-nun, which does not appear in Scripture, means slander, slanderer, accuser. The former means adversary, archenemy, foe, devil, the Evil One, and hinderer, accuser. The verb form means to hate, denounce, condemn, speak against and is used several times in Scripture. The difference between these words is not great, but it is significant that Scripture uses the stronger word because it includes, but is not limited to, accusing, but goes far beyond that in actively pursuing evil ends. **Creatures, including the dragon and serpent of Revelation, symbolize the results of Satan's endeavors. In Isa. 27:1 those symbols are called Leviathan referring to the evils of the modern world,"** (The One New Man Bible).

The second flood came about because of the gross wickedness on the earth started by Satan and spread by demons and fallen angels. Fallen angels were sleeping with human women and producing giants as their off-springs, a form of man God did not ordain or create so the second flood came about to destroy all of this wickedness. (Another theory is that the giants who died were not redeemed by God so their spirits went to hell and they are believed to be a part of the demonic world of demons that influences and oppresses people today). So God instructed "Noah to build the ark (which was a model for the very first ship) and along with his immediate family which included his daughter in-laws and <u>for every clean beast</u> he took seven pairs, male and female; and of the <u>beast that were not clean</u> he took a pair of each kind and he took birds of the air seven pairs of male and female to keep their kind alive" (Genesis 7:2-3 Paraphrased). "They all went into the ark as God had commanded Noah and the Lord shut him in and closed the door. The flood was forty days upon the earth and as the waters increased and bore up the ark, it was lifted [high] above the land until even all the high hills under the whole sky were covered with the water being fifteen cubits higher and all flesh ceased to breathe that moved upon the earth…" (Genesis 7:16-21 Paraphrased).

I mentioned this flood in detail because once this flood was over, <u>the earth was not void and dark as after the first flood (Genesis 1:2) but it was light and everything was still in place that God had spoken into existence including day and night as seen in Genesis chapter one</u>. When Noah and those with him walked out of the ark there was no other living person or creatures on the face of the earth except those that were on the ark (Genesis 7:23; Matthew 24:37-44).

Moving on, Satan enjoys destroying marriages in order to rob the parents and attempt to rob the children of their childhood and everyone in the family of their joy, peace of mind and homes. He causes dysfunction in families and works hard at destroying these homes so he can tear our communities, cities and overall societies apart. He also loves to oppress or possess the people who have the most influence such as heads of ministries, church leaders, kings, presidents, prime ministers, generals, leaders, judges and entrepreneurs. These are some of the people who make decisions that affect masses of people.

In the book of Ezekiel 28:1-12, it tells of a king who was possessed with an evil spirit, who gained increase, wealth and power through his own wisdom and understanding and who was lifted up in pride and thought of himself as a *god*. The end result was God Almighty caused him to be totally destroyed by bringing him down to the pit of destruction. The true God demonstrated that the king may have thought of himself as a god but he was only a man made from the dust of the earth. He was not given the authority to prosper or have power in the earth, which was given to God's family (Prov. 10:22). Those who possess wealth without permission usually find sorrow in their lives as a result of it.

This is why **God has asked His people to pray for our leaders** so they can receive salvation so their minds will be free to follow Him and to make righteous decisions based on the Word of God. We also pray for them to have God's wisdom and to be covered with God's protection as they work to fulfill His will and purpose and not their own. The Word of God is the foundation and instruction manual on how we are to live in order to have joyous and fulfilled lives that are in right standing with God.

2 Chronicles 7:14 says,

> If My people, **who are called by My name**, shall humble themselves**,** pray, seek, crave, and require of necessity My face and turn

> from their wicked ways, then will I hear from
> heaven, forgive their sin, and heal their land.

God says He will heal their land. First of all He will heal people, we are from the land having come from the dust of the earth. He will also heal the land itself from disasters caused by storms, earthquakes and so forth and He will restore property to the rightful owner (Ezekiel 21:27) because whoever owns the land will control it. He is prepared to make us the head and not the tail, the lender and not the borrower, if we would only pray.

This is another reason why humility is so important, it will keep you balanced. It will bring you to a place where you are pliable and moldable in the hands of God to do what God says and not what we think, feel or want to do apart from Him.

John 10:10 says,

> **The thief comes only in order to steal and kill and destroy...**

This is the enemy's sole purpose towards mankind especially those who have chosen to receive and follow the Lord Jesus Christ.

Luke 10:17-20 says, [1]

> Satan's defeat and ouster from heaven became sure when Christ gave His power over satanic forces to His church (Mark 3:15). The church must be intent on defeating Satan and participating in the heavenly kingdom, not on proudly exhibiting its power on earth. It is time for the church to confess God's power and certain victory over all that opposes Him.

Our adversary is a spirit that is in rebellion and as a result has fallen from the grace of God and His Kingdom. His final destination is the Lake of Fire for eternity; he loses and we win (Rev. 20:10). As we learn who he is we will have a clearer understanding of why the Lord gives certain strategic instructions the way He does. The Bible says, do not be ignorant of the devil's devices, in Ephesians 4:27 it says, "Leave no [such] room or foothold for the devil [give no opportunity to him];" "Neither give place to the devil," (Eph. 4:27 KJV).

Always remember we are dealing with evil spirits that can be conquered by a person who is filled with the Holy Spirit, Who is greater ("...greater is He that is in you than He that is in the world," I John 4:4 KJV). The Holy Spirit will deal with Satan through the prayers and declarations of the Believers who are filled with His Spirit. If we are not Born-again Believers with the Infilling of the Holy Spirit aka the Baptism in the Holy Ghost, then it will be difficult to maneuver in the spiritual realm with our words and faith and take back the dominion that was given to us.

If we do not deal with evil spirits by using our authority and declare the Blood of Jesus, rebuke, bind up, cast out, renounce, dismantle, or decree and declare God's words, then evil spirits will dominate. Walk in the full authority that Jesus paid the price to give to you. We take dominion or they will dominate; we overthrow or be overthrown; we overtake of be overtaken, that is how it works.

ORDER AND INFORMATION ABOUT THE SATANIC KINGDOM OF DARKNESS: [9] (Emphasis added)

> **Satan** – god of this world and the prince of the power of the air. Also known as Beelzebub the chief of the devils; and in Greek – Beelzeboul, the prince of demons (Luke 11:15 KJV and NLT). He is the archenemy of God, but he does not work alone. His demons walk in a dedicated order with uncompromising commitment to him. They fear breaking rank, and every position gets the respect that it is due.

> **Beelzebub**– the prince of the devils, answers directly and only to Satan. Princes of devils are

assigned by era. During Jesus' life, Beelzebub was the prince of the devils. During Elijah's life, Baal was it. (Baal – a ruler, owner, or master of another person or people. As well as a title for pagan deities in and around Canaan).

Principalities – princes of the four corners of the earth (continents, countries, states, cities, counties), arch magistrates or principal demons; first in rank.

Powers–organizations (*exousia*–special ability, highly competent; liberty in jurisdiction). When other demonic spirits cannot get a job done, Satan dispatches power spirits against God's people.

Ruler spirits –neighborhoods, families, individuals (kosmokrator–world ruler, spirits with direct contact with their targets). Called rulers of the darkness of this world, these are demons of the cosmos or world rulers. The ruler hides the truth and blinds the minds of people through cosmetic deception. They rule over regions and make fetishes look like fads and witchcraft look like family traditions. They make murder look like a life choice and homosexuality look like a lifestyle. To break peer pressure off of our children, we must dismantle the power of world rulers from over their heads.

Spiritual wickedness in high places–idolatry (Hezekiah tore down the high places) (*poneria*–iniquity and malice, sin and idolatrous activity. Demonic activity and influence from the second heaven. It affects the world because it influences those who have positions in high places with great influence. They manipulate and rule from the second heaven (outer space). The word wicked means to degenerate or to become worse in state (Eph. 6:12 and Matt. 12:45).

Satan also has ground-level devils or disembodied spirits (imps, watchers, scanners, eavesdroppers and so forth) some possess people. These demonic spirits are the ones found when demons are cast out of people. Eph. 2:2 speaks of how the prince of the power of the air rules over the children of *disobedience (people who are careless, rebellious and unbelieving who go against the purposes of God) they are connected to the second heaven just as people are seated in heavenly places with Christ Jesus in the third heaven (Eph. 2:6). People must be disconnected from the second heaven activity in order to receive full deliverance.*

BE AWARE OF DEVICES, TACTICS AND WEAPONS THAT ARE SENT TO DESTROY YOUR FAMILY:

Below are listed many of the devices used to cause problems in families and in people's lives in general that could lead to destruction and devastation if not stopped. Some may seem insignificant and very trivial but the adversary is subtle to say the least. Many people are unaware that they are living and operating daily using devices and tactics of Satan. If they are a Believer they are out of the will of God and most haven't a clue that they are no longer under His hedge of protection. It is only by God's mercy, grace and sovereignty that many are even alive and are in their right minds today.

When you do not resist evil you are cooperating with it. In the book of James 4:7 it says *"So be subject to God. Resist the devil [stand firm against him], and he will flee from you."* Believe this by faith as you believed when you asked Jesus to be your Lord and Savior and you knew in your heart you were saved at that very moment. It is all by faith, believe He is pleased and is moving immediately on your behalf, as it is done first in the spiritual realm then in the natural realm expect the manifestation at the appointed time on earth and whether it is instant or for a set time, just know that it is done.

2 Corinthians 2:11 KJV says:

Lest Satan should get an advantage of us: for we are not ignorant of his devices: [13] (Paraphrased)

- Fear; Unforgiveness; Doubt; Not Praying; Complaining; Murmuring; Gossip; Bitterness; Strife; Stress; Abuser; Lack of Communication; Grumbling; Jealously; Pride; Sexual Immorality (Fornication; Adultery); Idolatry; Heavy Drinking; Lazy; Lying; Procrastination; Rebellion; Offense; Depression; Not Thankful; Selfishness; Shame; Self-Pity; Guilt; Condemnation; Judging Others; Criticism; Hatred; Not Showing God's Love; Prejudice; Resentment; Lust; Poverty Mentality; Violence; Illegal Drugs; Greed; Proud Look Toward Others; Controlling; Faultfinding; Worry; Wicked Thoughts & Plans; Suffering; Infirmity/Sickness; Unequally Yoked; Betrayal; Treacherous; Unfaithful; Disloyal; Cursing; Suicide; Confusion; Demonic Agenda Enforced; Retaliation; Revenge; Slander; Discouragement; Deception; Despair; Division/Sowing Discord; Gluttony; Rude; Yoga; Sin While Angry; Vengeance; Suspicion; Envy; Murder (slander or physical); Lasciviousness; Uncleanness;

Astrology; Tarot Cards; Quija Board; Horoscopes; Black Magic; White Magic; Reincarnation; Palm Reading; Crystal Ball; Séances; Tea Leaf Reading; Hypnosis; Witchcraft; Medium(s); Occult Literature; Rejecting Godly Knowledge and Wisdom.

Some are actions and others are words but they **all lead to destruction, damage, disorders, disaster, devastation, people being mistreated, abused, cut-off, ruined and lives in complete disarray.** Many of these devices or weapons are sent to us, therefore, as we discern what is happening and when we are submitted to God (James 4:7) we have the authority and the right to resist any evil. According to the Bible we have authority over our own life, therefore, we rebuke evil, bind it up and cast it out by faith (Luke 10:19). Many of these devices are actually demons that have watched and studied people for generations through their forefathers and have been assigned to them to bring the same problems or worse into their lives. These are called generational curses but the good news is, there is no name that is above the name of Jesus, and it was all dealt with on Calvary so all we need to do is walk in (exercise) our authority.

When we cast out demonic spirits, the person who is now set free from that yoke of bondage has to be ready to follow the Lord and read the Word of God so the evil spirits will not have the same entry again.

Matthew 12:43-45 says,

> **But when the unclean spirit has gone out of a man, it roams through dry [arid] places in search of rest,** but it does not find any.
>
> Then it says, **I will go back to my house from which I came out.** And when it arrives, it finds the place unoccupied, swept, put in order, and decorated.

Then it goes and brings with it seven other spirits more wicked than itself, and they go in and make their home there. And the last condition of that man becomes worse than the first...

Satan also likes to distort and pervert *music* **because it was given by God for us to enjoy and to use appropriately.** As I mentioned earlier Satan was over praise and worship when he lived in heaven and is jealous that we have those gifts and he attempts to destroy us by using it against us. **Even when music is perverted especially music directed towards our children and teens it can draw them into corrupt and abusive behavior and many times suicidal behavior is the result of certain lyrics in songs** by artists they admire and are under their influence. Music can touch our emotions and influence us to act a certain way. Is all music bad, of course not, we love music it is a gift from God. At the same time we have to guard what we listen to and oversee what our children and teens are listening to that would pull them in the wrong direction and cause havoc in their lives. With today's electronics this is no small task. The best safe guard is to bring them up aware of these devices and the strength that is in the Word and Spirit of God to resist and overcome so that they can draw from them because it will be impossible to resist in their own strength some of the evil things they will be tempted with.

We always have a responsibility to guard what we see, hear and speak. If we choose to do, watch and hear whatever then we take our chances and later deal with the consequences of our choices and actions. *What we allow into our soul will accumulate and show up later and because there is a change in us our path in life will change and our footsteps will lead us across the path of people that the Lord did not send into our lives. As a result we may find ourselves in undesirable situations depending upon what our soul is full of and who is acting as lord over our lives.*

Remember our soul consists of our will, emotions and mind (intellect and imagination). We make choices with the part of our soul called, *the mind*, and we may regret our choices later if what was dominating our soul was not the Word of God and as a result we were influenced to make the wrong choices. Be careful because we do not want to plant something in the spiritual realm we will have to confront and deal with later once it harvests. Whatever seeds we plant they will harvest unless we dig them up quickly with words, ask for forgiveness and with true repentance in our hearts put them under the blood of Jesus. Therefore, words that were spoken that should not have been, once you dig them up by declaring you did not intend to say those words this should stop the negative harvest from manifesting or curtail the fullness of it.

The Holy Spirit will expose and reveal and give us the strategy needed to be successful. When God's righteous Word is our strong foundation we will make choices based on the Word of God and be able to avoid a lot of unnecessary trauma and drama in our lives.

Deuteronomy 30:19 tells us that we can make a choice to continue with the grace of God in our lives:

> I call heaven and earth to witness this day against you that I have set before you life and death, the blessings and the curses; therefore choose life, which you and your descendants may live.

If we have made wrong choices and made terrible mistakes that caused major problems for ourselves, a family member or someone else, the remedy is the same. Understand first "for all have sinned and fall short of the glory of God" (Romans 3:23 NKJV); and "There is no condemnation to those who are in Christ Jesus… "(Romans 8:1 NKJV). Therefore, we can go before God and ask for forgiveness, repent and receive His forgiveness.

However, if you choose to participate with certain devices that are wicked and *live in it* and *not* ask God for forgiveness or repent then you should know, that the Bible also says in Romans 6:23, "for the wages which sin pays is death…" (First there is a "spiritual death" that takes place immediately and sometimes this will also include a physical death as well of which the timing is unknown), (See Chapter 2 under Clarifying Sin). God speaks of death as being our last enemy to subdue and abolish (I Co. 15:26).

He also said in Isaiah 25:8:

> **He will swallow up death [in victory**; He will abolish death forever]. And the Lord God will wipe away tears from all faces; and the reproach of His people He will take away from off all the earth; for the Lord has spoken it.

God already took care of death for all those who will choose His Son, Jesus, as their Lord and Savior. Death is something that no Believer will ever have to face. When a person passes there is a separation that takes place of their spirit and soul leaving their physical body. The Believer continues to live even a greater life with Jesus in heaven until it is time for all humans in heaven to return to earth and rule with Jesus for the next one thousand years during the Millennial Reign (Rev. 20:4).

Satan uses tricks, tactics and out right attacks to discourage people, cause illness, depression and to wear them down until they are exhausted and at the point of giving up all hope. It is all a part of his strategy to intensify the hardship he is afflicting in order to steal, kill and destroy homes, marriages and families or an attempt to rob them of any breakthroughs and a better life. It is also an attempt to control societies by using government or state agencies to inflict more hardships by taking Christian children out of their homes as is happening in some countries and placing them in institutions for various negative reasons and financial gain. These and other negative practices which are occurring in some societies today come about when families are in a weakened state which causes the society overall to become weak because the family is the backbone of all societies and if there is no Awakening to prayer for that society it will eventually collapse.

TACTICS AND ATTACKS DESIGNED TO WEAR PEOPLE OUT:

Dysfunctional home (parents separated; strife; rebellion, etc.);

Bad and non-loving parent(s); parents who drink heavily and use drugs;

Abusive, cruel, battered and uncaring acts toward children;

Financial problems that need professional assistance;

Accidents (vehicle, airplane, etc.);

Distractions that rob you of precious time needed for quality things;

Sudden illnesses; babies aborted and tormented mothers;

Sudden death in the family (grief, sadness, depression);

Extremely poor diet, health issues;

Betrayal and slander; hopelessness;

Working extensive hours causing family neglect;

Child custody battles and kidnapping; using children as a weapon;

Rejection; abandoned babies or small children left in dumpsters, alleys and vacant buildings;

Loss of employment or a business;

Unexpected move or you were not able to acquire the desire of your heart;

Tax issues out of control;

Television programs which belittle the family structure and its members;

Graphic violence through the media which encourages murders and violence;

Constant stressful changes; unpredictable attitudes and moods of others;

Sexual abuse; family members tortured;

And the list goes on and on.

Of course we have to cooperate with the adversary for his devices to actually be successful over us if we are a child of the King. We are called to be subject to God and resist Satan and God is faithful and will restore us. Also realize that suffering is temporary, God will rescue His people and give them a way of escape. Godly people can draw strength and gain courage knowing that God has not forgotten them and they know that they do not yield to fear, anxiety and doubt like those in the world.

I Peter 5:8-10 NIV gives hope to the hopeless:

> Be self-controlled and alert. Your enemy the devil prowls around like a roaring lion looking for someone to devour. Resist him, standing firm in the faith, because you know that your brothers throughout the world are undergoing the same kind of sufferings. And the God of all grace, who called you to His eternal glory in Christ, after you have suffered a little while, will himself restore you and make you strong, firm and steadfast.

In Hebrews 13:5 God said that He will never leave us:

> …For He [God] Himself has said, I will not in any way fail you nor give you up nor leave you without support. [I will] not, [I will] not, [I will] not in any degree leave you helpless nor forsake nor let [you] down (relax My hold on you)! [Assuredly not!] [Josh. 1:5.]

One word of caution, when you are emotionally, physically, mentally and spiritually tired that is when Satan sends his attacks the most (this is why keeping balance in our lives is so vital). He will usually start with negative thoughts or voices and/or some kind of tactic to catch you off guard. Do not entertain negative thoughts or voices it is not the Lord but an evil presence that has come to speak into your life and hopefully set up a stronghold in your mind to cause your thinking and your own words to defeat you; so as a man thinks, so is he.

Instead, when the thoughts or voices come, stop it and address it, **never repeat what it is saying to you** but answer or cast it down with the Word of God. Do not ignore it because it will continue until it sets up a stronghold in your mind (Luke 11:21; 2 Cor. 10:5). After which you will more than likely need prayer to bring you out from under the spirits of heaviness, fear or depression.

For example, after I was separated but still in my former marriage my son was in a Bible school with another child at this child's church and it was just my daughter with me when *I heard a voice say to me "this is all the family you have." I heard this very clearly, and I knew it was referring to my daughter and myself and <u>I never repeated what was said to me</u> (the devil wanted me to use my mouth to put that lie in the atmosphere and to place it in my heart to come in agreement with his lie).* But instead I answered and said "that is a lie, I have a husband and children." Every time I heard this my answer was the same and after that day I never heard that lie again. <u>I declared and spoke what I expected God to do even though it wasn't what I was experiencing at the time.</u> I was not moved by my circumstances but only moved by the truth, God had given me a husband and children so that is what I declared regardless of the fact that my former husband at that time had left home. According to the Bible, you will have what you say and I was keeping my mouth lined up with what I was praying and believing God for.

Words proclaimed in the natural realm reach into the realm of the Spirit where your miracle is. Your words come in agreement with God's Word and call forth the miracle God promised, I John 5:14.

Words that are rooted in your heart have the power to save your soul; carefully watch over your words. James 1:21.

The more time you spend meditating on God's Word, the more you will reap from it. The more Word you read and hear, the more power and ability you will have. How much you get from the Word of God will depend on the time and effort you put into studying, digesting and putting it to use.

As you speak forth words that are released into the atmosphere, they are then activated by the Holy Spirit Who will cause your words to come to pass at the appointed time in the correct season chosen by God simply because He said His Word shall not return to Him void.

Isaiah 55:11 says:

> So shall My word be that goes forth out of My mouth: it shall not return to Me void [without producing any effect, useless], but it shall accomplish that which I please and purpose, and it shall prosper in the thing for which I sent it.

Therefore, choose and guard the words that exit your mouth with all diligence knowing that you <u>will</u> have exactly what you say. A well known quote, quoted by Joyce Meyer says, "Complain and Remain; Praise and Be Raised!"

The Word of God is Truth and it will change facts presented before you in any area of your life.

Numbers 23:19 says:

> **God is not a man, that He should tell or act a lie,** neither the son of man, that He should feel repentance or compunction [for what He has promised]. Has He said and shall He not do it? Or has He spoken and shall He not make it good?

Confess God's Word and watch Him work. **His Word will drive the devil back and give you the victory every time.** The Bible says, "How can I curse those God has not cursed? Or how can I denounce those the Lord has not denounced?" Numbers 23:8. The Bible further says, "That no one can deliver out of My hand, I will work and who can hinder or reverse it?" Isaiah 43:13; so, "Be Still and Know that I AM God," Ps 46:10.

SECTION TWO

TAKE THE VICTORY BY FORCE USING GOD'S SPIRITUAL WARFARE WEAPONS

AND FROM THE DAYS OF JOHN THE BAPTIST UNTIL NOW THE KINGDOM OF HEAVEN SUFFERS VIOLENCE, AND THE VIOLENT TAKE IT BY FORCE
Matthew 11:12 NKJV

WE MUST DECIDE *WE WANT* THE VICTORY THEN TAKE IT BY FORCE:

When God tells you it is time and He has given you the victory, now all you have to do is decide whether or not you are going to go up and pursue and take back everything that was stolen as you continue on your way to your destiny (I Samuel 30:8). For many of us this is exciting and we are ready to go up and pursue all, and all we ask is that God lead us and give us instructions in order to recover everything. Simple, but maybe not easy for all because of certain trials in life which are evil and designed by Satan to destroy, many have lost all hope and are very weary. But **God will turn it around for our good and the trial or tribulation will actually be used to build-up our spiritual muscles, stretch our faith, give us strength to endure and patience as we become established and firm in purpose (Gen. 50:20).** Not to mention that it could also develop godly character and cause spiritual maturity as we become sons of God and glorify His name (Romans 8:14; Hebrews 12:7).

It seems as if only the remnant, the faithful obedient worshipers, who have been faithful till the end will enjoy the spoils until the others wake-up, shake-off and get delivered from spiritual blindness and a compromising lifestyle so they to can enjoy the rewards of the Kingdom of God.

James 1:3-4 clarifies that trials can help in strengthening us,

> Be assured and understand that the trials and proving of your faith bring out endurance and steadfastness and patience. But let endurance and steadfastness and patience have full play

and do a thorough work, so that you may be [people] perfectly and fully developed [with no defects], lacking in nothing.

This is the season (set time, age and decade) where all of the preparation, training and standing through the wilderness will be compensated and rewarded. It is double portion time, double for your trouble, time for the manifestation of His glory to shine like never before. It is time to finish and take back what was stolen (Isaiah 61:7; Isaiah 43:18-19).

We have met people who have grown content in the state that they are in and are no longer pursuing the dream God placed on the inside of them and they are willing and ready to settle for second best or for some even less. **The Lord has said that "the just (righteous servant) shall live by faith" and He also said "if he draws back and shrinks in fear, My soul has no delight or pleasure in him" (Hebrews 10:38).** He will help us stay focused on the mission if we take our eyes off of what is surrounding us and not look to the right or to the left but set our minds on what is above (the higher things), Colossians 3:2 and Philippians 4:8. As we realize that *"to whom much is given much is required,"* that whatever we may go through, know that God is with us and the situation will turn around for our good if we keep the right attitude, stay in faith, and know that *"...He [can be trusted] not to let you be tempted and tried and assayed beyond your <u>ability and strength of resistance and power to endure</u>, but with the temptation He will [always] also provide the way out (the means of escape to a landing place), that you may be capable and strong and powerful to bear up under it patiently,"* I Cor. 10:13. We fight *from* a place of victory not for it because we already have it!

You have to make a decision of whether you are going to settle and say this is good, this is enough or are you going to believe and trust God and say I want everything You have purposed for my life. When you settle you start to level off and you are no longer pursuing or climbing. Therefore, you will start to decline, for nothing stays the same. We are not talking about only pursing material gain, we are talking about pursuing God given dreams that can become a reality and when they do God will add all of His promises which will give you your heart's desires.

It is time for Satan to give it back seven fold because the thief has been found (Proverbs 6:31). In addition, be ready for the hundred fold return as well. It is time for us to walk in our authority, it is time for the "closet Christians" to step out and voice the Word of the Lord for His name sake!

Luke 10:19 tells us we are equipped to take it back!

> Behold! I have given you authority and power to trample upon serpents and scorpions, and [physical and mental strength and ability] over all the power that the enemy [possesses]; and nothing shall in any way harm you.

Realize that what you have been through is really not about you but about others that God chooses to bless through you because of your steadfastness, determination, obedience and love for Him. When you pray and cooperate the Holy Spirit will enable you to have a will, desire and the strength to begin or continue in the process of your recovery which will include your household. Why does it include your household? Because when the Holy Spirit restores He restores everything that was stolen and more, nothing missing and nothing broken. *Stop going around the same mountain and go forward, it is time to go into your promise land, it is time to take your Jericho, it is time for victory and "The Blessing" to manifest in your life. (Deut. 2:3; Joshua 6:15-16).*

Once you have established in your heart that you *want* the victory then Your Heavenly Father, the Master Strategist Who has already prepared and equipped you to receive it will enable you to take it by force. As it says in our opening scripture for this section "And from the days of John the Baptist until now **the Kingdom of Heaven suffers violence, and the violent take it by force"** basically means *when you have done all that you were* *instructed by the Holy Spirit to do to the best of your ability and you have made a decision that you want the victory and total restoration* then **taking it by force is next. This will transition you into a position where God is ready to give you the final instructions to make the right connections to go forth and receive.** (Matt. 11:12).

To take it by force means: to **Continue** to Praise Him; **Continue** to listen and follow through (obey) Him; **Continue** to thank Him and truly have the right attitude; **Continue** to love and help others; **Continue** to give tithes and offerings; **Continue** to do the right thing as you seek first the Kingdom of God; **Continue** to resist demonic strongholds and evil spirits with the Word of God and through prayer. James 4:7 gives you the order for this victory: "So be **subject** to God. **Resist** the devil [stand firm against him], and he will flee from you." And as you **Continue** in faith in spite of whatever type of difficulties are before or around you your faith is what will keep you. As you **Continue** because of it and remain persistent you will take back all that was stolen from you out of the devil's hands with the power of God on your side because you know Who God is, who you are in relation to God and who your real enemy is (Eph. 6:11-12). As we **Continue,** when He returns we may have and enjoy perfect confidence, boldness and assurance in Who He is and who we are in Him (I John 2:28, Romans 11:22).

Ephesians 6:11 KJV says,

> Put on the whole armour of God, that ye may be able to stand against the wiles of the devil.

The wiles of the devil are his lies, deception, his strategies and deceits. He is the father of lies and this is all he is working with since Jesus defeated him in the finished work at the cross (John 8:44). The battle will be won, basically with spiritual weapons and not carnal ones. In reality, when Jesus was raised from the dead He stripped Satan of his authority over mankind nearly two thousand years ago. That authority was originally given to men and women by God Almighty (Genesis

1:26) before Satan deceived and robbed them of it. Now it has been delegated to the Body of Christ in the earth (Mark 16:17-18) and we can bind Satan in the name of Jesus, the name that is above every name. We are not under a curse of any kind once we receive Jesus as our Lord and Savior. However, we still must resist any evil that is on the earth by listening and following the Lords teachings, then by taking authority over evil with the Word of God (Luke 10:19; James 4:7).

Matthew 16:19 KJV says,

> And I will give unto thee the keys of the Kingdom of heaven: and whatsoever thou shalt bind on earth shall be bound in heaven: and whatsoever thou shalt loose on earth shall be loosed in heaven.

The prayer of binding and loosing halts Satan's activities. God intends for the Body of Christ to watch and pray and use their authority in His name to control and defeat evil forces in this world. We are to change circumstances and cause them to line up with God's will and put Satan under our feet through the power of Almighty God. We are to spoil Satan's plans, plots, strategies and maneuvers against God's people. "Lest Satan should get an advantage of us; for we are not ignorant of his devices" (2 Cor. 2:11 KJV).

Remember, the devil can't hurt you but he can deceive you and cause you to destroy yourself. "We resist the devil not by focusing on resisting him, but by being established in the faith that we are made right with God through Jesus' blood, that we are the righteousness of God in Christ," [8] 2 Cor. 5:21.

Your Heavenly Father will give you a plan of action that will cause you to make divine connections at the appointed times and He will direct you in such a way that you will seize the victory at different intervals in your life. A lot of it, will come "suddenly," some of it by "miracles," some will come quickly and then consistently and as you continue in Him, He will continue in you. God is a *now* God, place a demand on His *Prophetic Word* for your personal life and ask (petition) boldly for the things already promised in His Word for you in this season to manifest in your life *Now!*

As you press in Father God sees your faith and at the appointed time releases whatever is necessary to bring you into what He promised. This also includes Him removing your enemies from your open door of opportunity and causing justice to be done (Hebrews 10:30).

Revelation 3:8 says,

> I know your [record of] works and what you are doing. See! I have set before you a door wide open which no one is able to shut; I know that you have but little power, and yet you have kept My Word and guarded My message and have not renounced or denied My name.

Keep in mind that Father God, Jesus and the Holy Spirit know that we come from dust (Gen. 2:7), we are not perfect, nor will we do all that we have been assigned to do perfectly, so what am I saying? I am saying that in this hour God is releasing what He has promised for His name sake and the fact that He is a God that cannot lie. As we strive to continue in Him He asks us to do one thing that would allow Him to manifest His promises and that one thing is to "Believe."

John 6:28-29 explains,

> They then said, What are we to do, that we may [habitually] be working the works of God? [What are we to do to carry out what God requires?] Jesus replied, **This is the work (service) that God asks of you: that you believe in the One Whom He has sent** [that you cleave to, trust, rely on, and have faith in His Messenger]. (Also see Mark 11:23-24).

DISCOVER "26" SPIRITUAL WARFARE WEAPONS, TOOLS AND STRATEGIES THE MASTER STRATEGIST HAS GIVEN US *TO USE:*

2 Corinthians 10:3-5 explains that our weapons are not carnal but mighty:

> For though we walk (live) in the flesh, we are not carrying on our warfare according to the flesh and using mere human weapons. For the weapons of our warfare are not physical [weapons of flesh and blood], but they are mighty before God for the overthrow and destruction of strongholds. [Inasmuch as we] refute arguments and theories and reasonings and every proud and lofty thing that sets itself up against the [true] knowledge of God; and we lead every thought and purpose away captive into the obedience of Christ (the Messiah, the Anointed One).

The Master Strategist will prepare you to do a work for Him that will benefit your family as well as His Kingdom. He will train, equip, and anoint you with His Spirit, giving you wisdom, tools, skills, the gift of discernment and much more to work toward the total deliverance of your family.

The greatest weapon is number three the "Word of God," working in conjunction with numbers two, four, six and seven. The purpose for all of the spiritual warfare weapons is to cause you to live a life of excellence with liberty in Christ Jesus, free from all bondage. Further, to know who you are in Christ and the confidence you should walk (live) in. Also, you need to know how to live before a Holy God with boldness and might as you exercise your rights as sons of God. When Satan shows his ugly head you will have the faith and confidence to put him and his followers back under your feet where they belong.

The gift of discernment which includes wisdom, knowledge and understanding will help you avoid deception; it will bring clarity into your hearing from God; it will give you "the ability to discern and distinguish between [the utterances of true] spirits [and false ones]." I Corinthians 12:10.

Ephesians 1:17, 19, a Word Confession and Prayer with personal emphases added:

> "[For I will always pray to] the God of our Lord Jesus Christ, the Father of glory, that He may grant me a spirit of **wisdom and revelation [of insight into mysteries and secrets] in the [deep and intimate] knowledge of Him**... [so that you can know and understand] what is the immeasurable and unlimited and surpassing greatness of His power in and for me and all who believe, as demonstrated in the working of His mighty strength," and as I advance, I am divinely empowered with skills and understanding, as I thank You for the fruit of the Spirit that is demonstrated in my life today.

The Following is a List of "26" Spiritual Warfare Weapons, Tools and Strategies to use for Success:

1. Build and Maintain a Close and Personal Relationship with God
2. Develop a Daily Prayer Lifestyle
3. The Word of God is the Greatest Spiritual Warfare Weapon
4. Develop Your Supernatural Spiritual Prayer Language aka Tongues
5. Develop Your Hearing from God for it is Important to Receive Clear Instructions
6. Develop a Strong Love Walk
7. Resting in the Lord; Trusting Him by Faith
8. Anointed and Consecrated to Live a Godly Lifestyle
9. Ask for Godly Wisdom and Follow the Leadership of the Holy Spirit
10. Build a Hedge of Protection
11. Choose to Forgive Others, Yourself and God

12. As you Develop and Walk in the Fruit of the Spirit you become a Weapon
13. Become sons of God (male or female) it will Open Doors for the Spiritual Gifts to Flow in your Life
14. Develop Godly Character
15. Dispatch Angels for Others and Yourself
16. Take Communion
17. Walk (live) in your Authority; Take Territory; Cast out Demons
18. Be Aware of the Times and Seasons You are in; Are You in Your Set Place in the Natural and in the Spiritual Realm?
19. Focus and Endurance, Key Attributes to Completing your Assignment or Goals
20. A Prophetic Word to You is a Powerful Spiritual Warfare Weapon
21. Kingdom Economics (Godly Principles) Resist the Enemy and Allows Financial Progress
22. Proper Rest for your Temple (body) and Eating Properly will Strengthen you for Spiritual Warfare and Life in General
23. Utilize Time Management and Maintain Balance
24. Thankfulness, a Spiritual Warfare Weapon that Changes Hearts and Gives Victory
25. Develop a Spirit of Humility
26. Walking in Peace/Shalom (wholeness) is a Strong Spiritual Warfare Weapon and a Part of our Armor

Ephesians 6:10-12 records preparation and who we are actually fighting in the spiritual realm:

> ...be strong in the Lord [be empowered through your union with Him]; draw your strength from Him [that strength which His boundless might provides]. Put on God's whole armor [the armor of a heavy-armed soldier which God supplies], that you may be able successfully to stand up against [all] the strategies and the deceits of the devil.

> *For we are not wrestling with flesh and blood [contending only with physical opponents], but against the despotisms, against the powers, against [the master spirits who are] the world rulers of this present darkness, against the spirit forces of wickedness in the heavenly (supernatural) sphere.*

When Jesus was raised from the dead He took the keys to death, hell and the grave which took Satan's authority over mankind from him and Jesus returned it back to mankind. He took Satan's authority over mankind back when He took the keys to death, hell and the grave. **This authority was given to both men and women by God from the beginning (Gen. 1:26) and it has been delegated to the Body of Christ in the earth (Mark 16:17-18).** We bind Satan in the name of Jesus, the name that is above every name. We are not under a curse of any kind once we receive Jesus as our Lord and Savior, however, we still must resist any evil that is on the earth by listening and following the Lords teachings then by taking authority over that evil (Luke 10:19). As we rebuke and bind from the root (the strongman) we seal the manifestation of evil assignments sent through master spirits to work against us and our family, nation, judicial system, educational system, Godly leaders, the arts and entertainment industry, the political system and so forth (Colossians 2:15; Isa. 54:17; Luke 11:21-22; Deut. 18:9-14; Prov. 28:10; James 4:7; Psalms 91: 7, 10-11).

DETAILS REGARDING OUR SPIRITUAL WARFARE WEAPONS, TOOLS AND STRATEGIES:

(1) Build and Maintain a Close and Personal Relationship with God:

- Each person determines their own level of intimacy with God. You are as close to Him as you *want* to be (Hebrew 4:16 and James 4:8).

- When you live a life keeping God first, one of His rewards is to bless you with the spirit of Favor. Favor will bring restoration, assistance and support, promotion, supernatural increase, honor, real estate opportunities, recognition, the change of policies and rules in your favor and other benefits.
- See *Section Three* of this Chapter under A Review of Building and Embracing a Personal Relationship with God.

(2) Develop a Daily Prayer Lifestyle:
- **Develop a consistent prayer time morning or night and pray on and off as you are led during the day.** In your prayer "closet" wherever you spend time to pray (talk to God) you can utilize different methods of prayer. This will vary according to the person and how they are led by the Spirit of God. *A part of one's prayer time could consist of one or more of the following methods or styles being utilized in one session of prayer : praise and worship; adoration; thanksgiving; petition; supplication; intercession; forgiveness; binding and loosing; pleading the blood and putting on the whole armor of God; communion; and word confessions (confessing scriptures out loud).* During this time you may also speak to God in the understanding (your natural language) or in the Spirit as we call it (your supernatural spiritual language also referred to as tongues). *Another part of your time with God would simply be to be still in His presence to listen and be sensitive to His Spirit and enjoy His presence as He speaks and/or imparts to you. Reading the Word of God and receiving revelation or instructions is another way of seeking Him during your prayer time.* Outside of your private prayer closet you may desire to *come in agreement or participate in corporate prayer* with others.

- There are so many ways to communicate with the Spirit of God and it can be very exciting when He responds with His presence; His voice; an unction so we may have an inner knowing; or confirmation. But **whether you sense or feel the tangible presence of God or not, it will not make any difference in His hearing you.** "And this is the confidence that we have in Him, if we ask anything according to His will, **He heareth us**" (I John 5:14 KJV). All He asks is that you believe (have faith) that He heard you, pray according to His will, then be in a state of expectancy, Mark 11:24.
- **"Prayer releases the power of God into our daily lives when we are Born-again…The power of prayer can move the hand of God.** God can change an individual heart, free a person from bondage and torment, overturn disappointments and devastations, break the power of an addiction, or heal a person's emotions. God's power can restore a marriage, impact a sense of value and purpose, bring peace and joy, grant wisdom, and work miracles… the greatest power in the universe, is released in our lives through simple, believing prayer." [3]
- **Intercede daily for others, including leaders in your nation, in the Kingdom of God, your church and around the world.** Target different people or subjects in your prayers spending whatever time on each as the Holy Spirit leads you. Intercession is one major area where your supernatural prayer language is a great benefit because we do not always know what to pray especially for someone else's situation. As you pray in an unknown tongue the Holy Spirit will then pray through you as He prays for you and the concerns you have for others (I Corinthians 14:2, 4, 14) .

- **If two or more shall agree it shall be done by My Father in heaven** (Matthew 18:19). The first two to agree and work together for the good of the earth was God the Father and His Word (Gen. 1:2-3). ...The *Spirit* of God was moving (hovering, brooding) over the face of the waters (He was waiting) and *God said,* as He spoke His *Word* and because the two were in agreement, God and the Word, God the Holy Spirit brought it to pass. **When a husband and wife agree it is one of the most powerful tools you can use against the enemy.** When we agree with our spouse, it looses spiritual authority and binds up backlash and revenge. A threefold cord is not easily broken when we are in agreement God will perform His Word because His Word shall not return to Him void.
- **The "Binding and Loosing Prayer" is another form of a prayer** for protection. James 4:7 says, "So be subject to God. **Resist the devil [stand firm against him], and he will flee from you.**" See also Mark 16:17-18; Luke 10:19; Psalms 91:1-16. In order to spoil Satan's plans and evil deeds, subject yourself to God first (seek His Kingdom) then bind the devil's works and render him helpless in the name of Jesus. **Resist him at the onset, rebuke and bind the strongman,** do not receive his lies but plead the blood of Jesus and put on the whole armor of God (Matthew 12:29; Luke 11:21-22; Heb.10:19 and Eph. 6:10-18). Matthew 18:18 tells us that whatever we forbid and declare to be improper on earth must be what is already forbidden in heaven... and **"whatsoever we bind on earth shall be bound in heaven and whatsoever we loose on earth shall be loosed in heaven"** (Matthew 16:19 KJV).

- Journal – keep a journal to record notes and instructions from the Holy Spirit and to record praise reports (testimonies).
- **Prayer Night Watches.** "The rendering of some form of the Hebrew (to "protect") may mean a day or night watch; thus there was a guard of the king's house and in Jerusalem under Nehemiah. The Greeks and Romans, like the Jews divided the night into military watches instead of hours, each watch representing the period for which sentinels or pickets remained on duty (Ps. 90:4)." In Hebrew Shaqad "(to "be alert") is to be wakeful, and so watchful, either for good or evil."[2]
- **The Jewish calendar recognized only three such watches**: First or beginning of the Night watches: 6:00 p.m. to 10:00 p.m.; Middle watch: 10:00 p.m. to 2:00 a.m.; and the Morning watch: 2:00 a.m. to 6:00 a.m. (Lam. 2:19; Judges 7:19; Ex. 14:24; I Sam. 11:11).[2]
- "The night hours in first century Israel were divided into watches, with the First Watch extending from sundown until midnight. The Second Watch was from midnight until 3:00 A.M., and the Third Watch from 3:00 A.M. to 6:00 A.M., Matthew 14:25 and Mark 6:48 use the Roman time of the fourth watch..." (The One New Man Bible).
- **The Romans recognized four watches**: Evening watch: 6:00 p.m. to 9:00 p.m.; Midnight watch: 9:00 p.m. to midnight; Cockcrowing watch: 12:00 a.m. to 3:00 a.m.; and the Fourth watch 3:00 a.m. to 6:00 a.m.[2]
- I have included parts of the spiritual meanings of the night watches so we can understand what prayer will accomplish when done in accordance with God's timing and His way. It will be more effective but keep in mind *whenever* you pray

with a pure heart and the right motive God will hear your prayer. According to Apostle Kimberly Daniels in her book "*Give It Back*" the **spiritual meaning of all the watches (paraphrased) are as follows:** The *First watch* "is the apostolic watch that was put in place during the time that God's people considered the beginning of the day, sundown. **Under the O.T.** it was a time to pray for your children; a time that darkness could be easily shaken. **Under the N.T.** 6:00 p.m. to 9:00 p.m. was a watch in which the sun sets. It is the time to carry out the anointing of the day (Mark 1:32). Those who gird their loins on the first watch must have the anointing to break into new territories. This is a time of miracles and the breaking of barriers, a time to be strong and do exploits."

- "The *Middle watches* under the **O.T.** were to set the strategy, Judges 7:19. It means "womb of the watch," or the central watch that everything else was built around. It was also the watch during which evil seed was planted against the righteous. **Under the N.T.** 9:00 p.m. to 12:00 a.m. strong intercessors should be on the second watch who know how to move in the Spirit in order to jump ahead of the enemy before the midnight hour. And the 12:00 a.m. to 3:00 a.m. watch will require disciplined, stable intercessors who are willing to pray which will render witchcraft useless and take back from the enemy the authority that he has attempted to steal when witches plant seeds of witchcraft during this time."

- "The *Morning watch* is considered the last watch. **Under the O. T.** it was the watch where you gained victory over your enemies. In the morning you break through or plowed through. The faithful and dedicated can expect victory over their enemies every time." Ex. 14:24; I Sam. 11:11; Ps. 49:14. **Under the N.T.** The Fourth is the watch 3:00 a.m. to 6:00 a.m. of the early risers and commanders of the morning. The activities of the day are established during this watch. A time to declare the prosperity of our days. It was the fourth watch when Jesus walked on the water (Matthew 14:25-33). Jesus also prayed in the morning watch as well as other times of the day. "And in the morning, long before daylight, He got up and went out to a deserted place, and there He prayed" (Mark 1:35). In the last days God is placing a mandate on His church to wake up, to watch and pray. Prov. 8:17 says, "…and those who seek Me early and diligently shall find me."

- Use *Word Confessions*: Let the Word of God work for you. Pull scriptures to say out loud once or twice a day in areas where you need to see change or need to be strengthened. As you decree and declare the Word into the atmosphere where the Holy Spirit and the angels are, the Holy Spirit will move on your behalf and also dispatch angels to your assistance in addition to the ones already assigned to you and your household. The Word is spirit and alive, therefore, you can call those things which be not as though they were, Romans 4:17.

(3) The Word of God is the Greatest Spiritual Warfare Weapon:
- **Effective prayer always involves God's Word. It is a powerful weapon and if used properly it will literally give you victory over attacks from Satan and circumstances that happen in life because of wrong choices.** The devil is no match for the followers of Christ Jesus who are filled with the Spirit of God and armed with the Word of God and a willingness to obey what God wants them to do.

- **Jesus used the Word to defeat Satan when Jesus was being tested in the wilderness (Matthew 4:4, 7, 10).** Jesus is the Son of God and still Satan approached Him in the wilderness while He was fasting (read Matthew 4:1-11 to see the process of how Satan tempted Jesus physically, emotionally and spiritually). The enemy comes to attack you <u>physically</u> like he did Jesus when Jesus was physically hungry. He attacks people tempting them with all kinds of things that will destroy their lives (immorality, drugs, stealing and so forth). He also attacks people <u>emotionally</u> (with wrong desires) and <u>spiritually</u> by tempting them to worship any god except the true and living God.
- **The way Jesus defeated Satan in that moment is our example of the way we are to defeat him, with the Word of God.** Satan had to listen and obey not just because He was Jesus but because of His lifestyle. He was anointed, righteous, consecrated and obedient. **We have that same authority** because of the name of Jesus. As we use His name in prayer because of the "righteousness" we have in Him that was acquired at the cross we have authority over Satan. (That is why the world fights so hard to remove His name from being used in the public square). **Believers are to exercise their God-given rights and authority and use the Word of God along with His name to defeat Satan** in every area of their lives. The other spiritual warfare weapons keep us in balance and in His will so when we do use the Word Satan must obey.
- Also Jesus did not reason with Satan, He did not have to think over Satan's offer to Him. Jesus did not negotiate with Satan and agree to try something "just this one time." No, the Word says do not give Satan any place.

- **Knowing the Word of God is a form of protection.** It is also an instruction manual for Christians, those who "Believe" the Good News of the Gospel. When you **read the Holy Bible ask God for revelation** and He will reveal mysteries (hidden truths) to you within the pages of His Book. As you read the words in the Bible they will come alive because the words are living words and give life by constantly revealing layers of revelation as you continue to read and study. Read where you are led by the Holy Spirit or where you have a concern in life or an area where you need to be strengthened. Do not hesitate to use the table of contents or the concordance to help you find scriptures. Learn ways to **study the Bible** that work for you and it will successfully renew your mind in the principles of God (2 Timothy 2:15, Romans 12:2). There are books in Christian bookstores and some secular stores that will instruct you on how to study.
- Remember *"ALL* **scripture is given by inspiration of God,** and is profitable for doctrine, for reproof, for correction, for instruction in righteousness" (2 Timothy 3:16 KJV).
- Use different versions of the Bible to aid in receiving understanding from a different perspective. The more Word you have in you the stronger you will be. The Word of God is progressive and it has layers of revelation. As we mature in Him and continue to read the Word mysteries (revelation) is revealed to us on deeper levels and we gain understanding to what we could not previously comprehend. **The devil comes immediately to steal the Word of God from you in hopes of stealing your faith, the covenant and ultimately your soul.** He cannot break the covenant you have with God but he knows that you

- won't operate in something if you are not aware that it exist or how powerful it is (Mark 4:15-20).
- A Bible Dictionary or a Strongs Concordance would be a good investment. Suggested versions of the Holy Bible to read and obtain scriptures are: The New King James Version; The New International Version; The Amplified Version; The New Living Translation; and The New American Standard Bible. You can also use an *electronic bible* to locate scriptures quickly. A Parallel Bible version will give you the King James Version plus another version of your choice if you so desire to have the King James Version along with another version without the sixteenth century language.
- Christian books and articles will feed or enhance your spirit man with fresh revelation as well energize you with strength.

(4) Develop Your Supernatural Spiritual Prayer Language aka Tongues:
- **This is a language of men and angels (I Corinthians 13:1). It is for every Born-again Christian** that has said a prayer (asked) to receive the Infilling (Baptism) of the Holy Spirit who desires to speak (pray) in their supernatural spiritual language (tongues). When people began receiving Salvation, directly following that they were baptized in the Holy Spirit and immediately experienced speaking in foreign or unknown tongues (languages) and prophesied (Acts 2:4 and Acts 19:5-6). **And this is the standard that Believers should follow that which is written in God's Word**, and they should <u>follow it above</u> the standard of men's doctrines or certain denominations that do not favor praying in the (Holy) Spirit. Acts 5:29 says, **"We must obey God rather than men."**

- **The very first thing that God does for people once they are saved is to send "The Promise"** that Jesus instructed the disciples to wait for (Acts 1:4). That Promise was the *Holy Spirit* to be with them and in them. As they were filled with His Spirit and "began to speak in other (different, foreign) languages (tongues), as the Spirit kept giving them clear and loud expression [in each tongue in appropriate words]" (Acts 2:4). Other or unknown tongues were the beginning of something wonderful. *This was the one gift that covered everything.* You could worship, intercede for others, build yourself up (strengthen yourself spiritually), receive divine wisdom and strategies, increase your intimacy with God, rest in God and increase your ability to hear His voice. All was the *result of praying in tongues or in the Spirit with your spiritual language;* or however you wish to refer to it. The Bible also says, "And these attesting signs will accompany those who believe…they will speak with new tongues" (Mark 16:17 KJV).
- *There are many reasons and benefits as to why Believers should speak (pray) in their spiritual language in addition to what has already been listed.* Praying in the Spirit is a form of praying from your heart. **You can also pray from your heart in your natural everyday language the only <u>difference is</u> your natural language does not go directly into the throne room to speak to God like your heavenly language (I Corinthians 14:2) because evil forces can block what they understand but they cannot understand tongues therefore they cannot block it. Your supernatural language reveals mysteries and Satan and evil forces do not understand the mysteries of God (Luke 10:21). But he <u>can</u> understand every single word of your natural**

tongue (language) and send evil forces to cause a delay or hinder your answers to prayer.
- And in your natural language it is not the Holy Spirit making intercession for you, you are praying with your own mind in your own understanding which is limited compared to the Holy Spirit. Romans 8:27 explains how this works, "And He Who searches the hearts of men knows what is in the mind of the [Holy] Spirit [what His intent is], because the Spirit intercedes and pleads [before God] in behalf of the saints according to and in harmony with God's will." **In other words the Holy Spirit will pray perfect prayers through you as you speak in a language that is unknown to you that involves your spirit expressing specific thoughts that your mind is unaware of.**
- **There are two types of tongues that are a gift from God and given only as He wills** and they are (**1**) *Divers kinds of tongues* (different types of tongues, speaking in foreign languages you do not know (Acts 2:4) and (**2**) the *Interpretation of tongues* (I Corinthians 12:10). These are the only supernatural tongues that are not for everyone but for those who God chooses to give them to.
- **There are four ways your supernatural spiritual language can operate**: (**1**) God through a person, I Co. 14:3-5; (**2**) A person to God, I Co.14:2; 2:4-5 (**3**) Singing in the Holy Spirit, I Co. 14:15; and (**4**) Building up your spirit man. "...Build yourselves up [founded] on your most holy faith [make progress, rise like an edifice higher and higher], praying in the Holy Spirit" Jude 1:20.
- **More benefits of praying in your supernatural spiritual language** are: You are receiving the Promise that God sent to you and He will bring power into your life (Acts 1:4; 8; I Cor. 2:4); you

are releasing spiritual gifts that may be lying dormant inside of you (I Co.12:4-11); praying with your mind in your natural language and praying in the Spirit results in an alert and keen mind (I Co. 14:15); You are speaking mysteries, something that can only be known by revelation as well as receiving divine wisdom, understanding and instructions (I Co. 14:2); You are praying the will and mind of God; you are prophesying your future; the saints are praying in unity; you are praying for family and others, including the nations and lot's more.

- It also allows a person to enter into the rest of God as they pray in the Spirit. Ephesians 6:17-18, in v.17 **"...and the sword that the Spirit wields, which is the Word of God." The sword of the Spirit is the Holy Spirit Who effectively uses the Word of God (Jesus) inside of you.** The Holy Spirit is the Spirit of the Father and of the Son. In v.18 it says to, "Pray at all times (on every occasion, in every season) in the Spirit..." Why? Because as mentioned, there are so many benefits to gain from this gift for every Believer. As you pray you **literally enter into the rest of God** (trusting Him) and as a result experience more peace, revelation, become more aware of spiritual matters, as it releases other gifts inside of you that the Father has bestowed upon you. In addition you become stronger and can resist sin much better. Remember, Apostle Paul, said that it was the spiritual that he needed not rules and traditions to help with his sin nature, Romans 7:16-25.
- Have you ever been led by the Holy Spirit into <u>unrighteousness</u> or something that was meant to harm you? Of course not. The weapon of tongues is a two-edged sword, is multi-purpose and it is

one that Satan cannot understand nor interfere with. Yet it can add to your protection and give you strategies to defeat the enemy every time.

(5) **Develop Your Hearing from God for it is Important to Receive Clear Instructions:**
- "**When we are Born-again, we are made alive in our spirit to be sensitive to the voice of God.** We hear His whisper even though we cannot tell where it comes from. He whispers to convict, correct, and direct us by a still, small voice deep within our heart...God speaks to our inner being through direct communion, through our intuition (a sense of unexplainable discernment), and through our conscience (our base convictions of right and wrong)," [4] and He also whispers to convey and reveal His love for us.
- God also speaks to us to **edify** or to build us up; for **exhortation:** to encourage us and to give us instructions, guidance, knowledge and warnings and to bring **comfort** (restoration) (I Co. 14:3 emphases added).
- **To help us step out of our comfort zone (comfortable surroundings) and to help us stay on track (continue to flow with the Holy Spirit to stay in the will of God for our lives) we need to hear from God, therefore, we need to learn how He speaks to us.** The things He tells us will also include strategies to use and warnings about our enemies so we can be victorious. **God speaks to us:** in a still small voice that we hear through our spirit man; He also speaks through His written Word, visions, dreams, a thought, Godly counsel, prophets as well as Born-again Christians who have a gift of prophecy or through a person He chooses to give a prophetic word to you by the inspiration of the Holy Spirit. He also speaks through circumstances; our peace in our inner being or the lack

of it; through wisdom and common sense; an unction; <u>right</u> doors opening in our lives to listening to ministers on television, the internet, in person at our local churches or conferences as well as in the market place or wherever He chooses to show up and speak.
- God speaks to us in many different ways and it is a commandment that we hear Him. **The best way to hear Him clearly and accurately** is to spend time fellowshipping with Him; learning about Him through His Word so that we become familiar with how He communicates with us. When we obey we become more sensitive to the Holy Spirit which is the heart of God. He asks us to open our hearts and be willing to hear because God is a Spirit and He communicates with us directly to our spirit, (John 4:24; I Thess. 5:23).
- I like to get a **good night's sleep** and ask the Holy Spirit to wake and refresh me early so we can spend quality time together and so I can complete certain projects that have been assigned by the Spirit of God. The Holy Spirit will reveal mysteries and tell you what the Father and Son are saying to you and you can sense His presence or sometimes not feel anything at all. It all happens by faith. He said He would never leave me so I choose to believe that, therefore, I know He hears me when I speak to Him. It is also a good idea to **sleep with a pad of paper and pencil near you to capture those divine thoughts, messages or instructions that can come to you upon awakening** and after awhile you will know which ideas are from God, you or thoughts that the adversary has tried to plant in your mind. The adversary's won't line up with scripture but on the other hand anything that God gives you

one can find a scripture that exemplifies the principle that confirms what God has given you.
- **During worship with music is another time when many people hear from the Lord and experience His presence to a great degree.** At this time healing and miracles could also take place. The Lord inhabits the praises of His people and His Spirit moves in the midst of this type of worship especially from people with a pure heart and motive wanting only to spend time with Him and enjoy His presence (John 4:23). Another form of worship is done in everyday life as we follow His teachings to be pleasing to Him.
- **God will speak to you in a tone and with the words that the hearer can identify with and understand.** He spoke to Abraham like he was a friend He even visited with him and ate with him. God spoke to Moses through a burning bush as he heard an audible voice. When God spoke to Saul (later called Paul) God spoke with great authority and demonstration when Saul was knocked to the ground and blinded. Saul understood authority and Jesus showed up with plenty of it. **To each man God spoke in a way that they would be able to receive Him.** On each it made such an impact or impression that they were able to carry through with their assignments on earth. He will do the same for each one of us when He communicates with us.
- **Many times God's still small voice will sound like your own voice or the voice of someone you know.** This happens because you are familiar with those voices so certain thoughts will come through the voice you either heard it in or that you are familiar with. God does speak in an audible voice (Acts 9:7) but most of the time He speaks to us from within. Many times that audible

voice is still coming from within you and it may sound loud but no one else can hear it. When it comes from your spirit there is less opportunity for interference from some other spirit to cause deception. When it comes from within you most of the time you just know that you know it is the spirit of God speaking. **He will also confirm His words to you.** Over a period of time you are well familiar with how God communicates with you. This is not to say He may decide to speak to you in a different way, do not limit God. In a time of growth or testing you may not hear as easily or as frequently. A part of this is to cause your faith to stretch and for you to know that He is there on standby. **His ways are not our ways so, what and when He speaks to you is what you need to hear and when you need to hear it.**

- **What are some of the things that will hinder your hearing from God?** Sin in your life that has not been confessed to God and repented of. Unforgiveness, bitterness and disbelief; a hardened conscience from watching graphic violence repeatedly from entertainment because it reduces our sensitivity to God's voice. Hardened hearts also stop the flow of the anointing and therefore hinders our ability to hear and be sensitive to the leading of the Holy Spirit. A hardened heart can also indicate that you have shut down some of your feelings and emotions possibly because of hurt in a certain area and this will also limit your sensitivity to God because you are trying to protect yourself instead of receiving healing and staying open and free. When we ignore the promptings or the unction of the Holy Spirit each time He approaches us it becomes a little more faint and harder to hear until we can no longer hear. This is exactly what the adversary wants and it will sooner or later backfire on you. Still there are others whose ears are uncircumcised: "To whom shall I [Jeremiah] speak and give warning, that they may hear? Behold, their ears are uncircumcised [never brought into covenant with God or consecrated to His service], and they cannot hear or obey. Behold, the Word of the Lord has become to them a reproach and the object of their scorn…" (Jeremiah 6:10).

(6) Develop a Strong Love Walk:
- **There is no weapon that can successfully fight against** *Love* **and win over a child of the King.** The Word says to "guard and keep yourselves in the love of God" (Jude 1:21), Why? Because "… anyone born of God does not [deliberately and knowingly] practice committing (live-in) sin, but *the One Who was begotten of God carefully watches over and protects him [Christ's divine presence within him preserves him against the evil], and the wicked one does not lay hold (get a grip) on him or touch [him]"* I John 5:18). God said He watches over and protects him who is born of God, well according to I John 4:15-16 that would be "anyone who confesses (acknowledges, owns) that Jesus is the Son of God, God abides (lives, make His home) in him and he [abides, lives, makes his home] in God…and **he who dwells and continues in love dwells and continues in God, and God dwells and continues in him."**
- The Lord specially told us what to do to show or express our love for Him and what to do to be His friend. In John 14:15 to love Him, He said: "If you [really] love Me, you will keep (obey) My commandments." And in John 15:14 in order to be his friend He said: "You are My friends if you

keep on doing the things which I command you to do." *He told us to keep His commandments which are basically His ways, His teachings, His precepts and His principles because that is the way to stay in fellowship with a Holy God and the way to have success and victory in your life.*

- I Corinthians 13:1-8, of the *Love Chapter*, we see the *character of love in vv. 4-7* which demonstrates how God has given us to love one another unconditionally with compassion for each other. When you have true compassion for others it generates miracles, (Mk 12:29-31). **"God is love" and "we are of God" so we are to love**; **His love is the very source of our love** (I John 4:16; I John 4:7-8). **Love is a spiritual weapon and there is nothing that can stand against it.** Therefore, "if anyone says, I love God, and hates (detests, abominates) his brother [in Christ], he is a liar; for he who does not love his brother, whom he has seen, cannot love God, Whom he has not seen. And this command we have from Him: that he who loves God shall love his brother [believer] also," (I John 4:20-21).
- We are also **called to love our enemies** which will require us to operate in **the law of love** and to express the Golden Rule. God has asked all Believers to "invoke blessings upon and pray for the happiness of those who curse you, implore God's blessing (favor) upon those who abuse you" and most of all "as you would like and desire that men would do to you, do exactly so to them" (Luke 6:27-36). When you pray for your enemies to be blessed you are praying for their salvation if they do not have it and praying for them to have a forgiving spirit and the help that they need. Most people who try to hurt others are usually people who are unhappy and are hurting themselves and they need compassion. (For those in

abusive and dangerous relationships you can forgive and pray for others from "afar").
- **"The Golden Rule is the key to understanding the demands of love** of neighbor. For the disciple, to love a neighbor would include every person, even enemies. Such love is not partial, nor is it selfish. Mercy controls the disciple's life, not justice or greed. The disciple asks not what is due me but what can I do for someone else." [1]
- The word **love is depreciated** as we claim we love "things," our house, our car, our work, and so on. God told us to love Him and people. He gave us *things* to enjoy and function with on this earth. We *enjoy* things and *love* people.

(7) Resting in the Lord; Trusting Him by Faith:
- **We are able to rest in Him for He is the Believer's Sabbath.** With the New Covenant the **Sabbath is not merely a physical day but a Person who offers a place where we can take refuge as we rest in Him at any given time, on any given day.** "So then, there is still awaiting a full and complete Sabbath-rest reserved for the [true] people of God; For he who has once entered [God's] rest also has ceased from [the weariness and pain] of human labors… Let us therefore be zealous and exert ourselves and strive diligently to enter that rest [of God, to know and experience it for ourselves], that no one may fall or perish by the same kind of unbelief and disobedience [into which those in the wilderness fell]" Hebrews 4:9-11.
- As we cast our care and not worry about things but give it to Him He will fight the battle and give us the wisdom and strength to get through it victoriously ((I Peter 5:7; 2 Chronicles 20:15). As we commit our ways to the Lord and trust Him (leaning on, relying on and having confidence in

Him) then He will bring whatever we are believing for, that is in His will, to pass at the appointed time (Psalm 37:5; I Thessalonians 5:24). Why? **Because our faith in trusting Him pleases Him** (Hebrews 11:6) and as we become a doer of the Word of God and not merely listeners we will put action with our faith and that is what will move the hand of God (James 1:22 and Hebrews 4:2).
- **Fully trusting God will enable us to rest in Him.** Trusting Him brings our confidence and faith to a level that we can come boldly to His throne to fellowship and make our requests known. Years ago when I started on this journey one of the first things the Lord spoke to me about in an audible voice was trust. He said, "Audrey, I want you to know that you can trust Me." Over the years through difficult times I would think back on those words and realize He knows, He cares, He's right there gently guiding and leading as I find my way towards my destiny while watching things turn around for my good along the path. I knew in my heart He would never leave even in those silent and lean years when one hears very little as you are learning to trust Him at His Word as He stretches and builds your faith, strengthening you for your journey.
- **We enter God's Rest by faith in the gospel, giving up our works as the way to salvation and receiving it by His Grace.** The message of the gospel must be <u>mixed with faith</u> in order for us to benefit from it (Heb. 4:2). "For by grace you have been saved through faith, and that not of yourselves; it is the gift of God, not of works, lest anyone should boast" (Eph. 2:8-9 NKJV). **Faith** is activated by **Love** and it is the **Grace** of God that enables us to receive our salvation by faith. Furthermore, one powerful way to enter God's

rest is simply to pray in the Spirit (tongues) which is also received by faith. And you will experience rest as the Holy Spirit prays through you, it will literally remove yokes and bondages from you. **This may not make a lot of sense to the natural mind, it may even seem crazy but please realize that your "faith does not rest in the wisdom of men (human philosophy), but in the power of God" (I Cor. 2:5). If He said it, then it is so.**

- **What is faith? Acting on the Word of God as we take it at face value by simply believing and trusting in it as we move with His Spirit;** it is also believing in the unseen; trusting Him to bring the unseen prayer or promise and His Word to pass by Him doing what He said He would do. *Faith comes by hearing the Word of God, so faith hears, faith speaks, faith believes, faith receives and faith takes it back from the enemy. Faith is a Spirit.* Faith says what God says when it comes in agreement with His Word. Faith speaks about the end result from the beginning. **Without faith it is impossible to please God,** therefore, your begging, self-pity, complaining, hunger, poverty and your need will not move His steady hand but your faith will (Heb.11:6). "Just as it is impossible for God to operate in your life without faith, it is also impossible for Satan to operate without fear. Faith will enter you into rest while fear will enter you into torment." **As you ask, believe, receive and take action; are patient with confidence; take authority in His name; bind and loose; and thank and praise Him you are living out and exercising your faith to the fullest.**

- **The Bible says "Now Faith is the assurance** (the confirmation, the title deed) **of the things [we]** *hope for,* **being the proof of things [we] do not see** and the conviction of their reality [faith perceiving as real fact what is not revealed to the senses]. By faith we understand that the worlds [during the successive ages] were framed (fashioned, put in order, and equipped for their intended purpose) by the Word of God, so that what we see was not made out of things which are visible." The famous King James Version records it, "**Now Faith is the substance of things hoped for, the evidence of things not seen…so that things which are seen were not made of things which do appear,**" (Heb.11:1, 3).

- **Faith is made complete by what we do.** *To believe only is not enough for even the demons believe.* Faith without deeds (works) is useless, for example: "…Abraham was considered righteous for what he did when he offered his son Isaac on the altar. His faith and his actions were working together, and his faith was made complete by what he did…Abraham believed God and it was credited to him as righteousness…you see a person is justified by what he does and not by faith alone," James 2:21-24, paraphrased. A Christian is saved and justified before God by faith, but it is a "living faith" through which God accomplishes His purposes by good works."

- **According to my faith, be it unto me (Mt. 9:29). The promises of God and His blessings all operate and are received by exercising our faith.** Salvation is received by faith; deliverance is received by faith; the Infilling of the Holy Spirit is received by faith; provision, abundance and prosperity are all received by faith. **Faith is believing and declaring what God has already done and is now manifesting in your life.** The Bible says that "God has dealt to each one a measure of faith" (Romans 12:3 NKJV). We all have faith to believe in the finished work at the cross (Jesus came, died rose and is alive today) and we can increase our faith as we choose to hear the Word of God. Once increased we will have the faith to accomplish and receive more for the Kingdom of God.

- **Our covenant with God is not in an insurance policy against problems and challenges; but our covenant is a commitment from God that through the exercising of our faith we can overcome any hardship or problem we face because faith believes we receive because "God said."** He said, according to your faith be it unto you not according to your education, nor your race, nor your religion, nor your finances or connections, but according to your faith in God, be it unto you. **For example, if you pray to be healed in your body and debt free but you can only "see with your spiritual eyes or visualize" yourself sick and in debt and can only confess with your mouth what you see in the natural then that is what you will have.** *But on the other hand "…whatever things you ask when you pray, believe that you receive them, and you will have them."* **You do not receive what you pray for when you pray, you will acquire what you can believe and receive (take into your heart and visualize yourself having it), (Mark 11:24 NKJV).**
- Once you move in faith to believe and receive then be thankful, forgiving, patient until it manifests and do not stop believing or quit and you will surely acquire that thing which you asked for. Everyone else can give up on you and your dream; just make sure *you* don't give up on you and your dream.
- **The enemy of life wants us to miss what we can do something about** by having us to try to change or be concerned about something we have no control over. Distractions and smoke screens are to remove our focus off of our assignments

and off of our harvest or what God promised. We must **acknowledge that there is nothing we can do to change things that are out of our control**. That is the perfect time to Release our concerns and give them to God leaving it with Him as we pray for instructions and continue with His purpose for our lives. He will handle it because He is faithful (2 Tim. 2:13 Message Bible). When you take a stand to handle it God's way of course the **persecution will rise against you but His Word says He will deliver you out of it all (2 Tim. 3:11).**

- When we are faithful to trust Him He will preserve us for the Word says "He preserves the faithful… (Ps. 31:23); we will abound with blessings (Prov. 28:20); and He will answer a faithful person (Ps.143:1). **God will also strengthen and empower us to accomplish and finish our course:** for example, Apostle Paul said, "there is no unbelief or distrust made him waver (doubtingly question) concerning the promise of God, but **he grew strong and was empowered by faith** as he gave praise and glory to God" (Romans 4:20). And "because of faith **Sarah herself received physical power** to conceive a child…long past the age for it" Heb. 11:11).
- "Because of our faith in Him, we dare to have the boldness (coverage and confidence) of free access (an unreserved approach to God with freedom and without fear" to approach Him and ask in prayer for whatsoever in His Son's name and receive it, (Eph. 3:12).
- As I seek first the Kingdom of God, I realize "**it is no longer I who live, but Christ (the Messiah) lives in me; and the life I now live in the body I live by faith in the Son of God**" Who is enabling

me to live by faith, to have strength and to keep my peace and joy (Gal. 2:20).
- **"For we walk by faith, not by sight,"** (2 Cor. 5:7 NKJV), is the scripture motto that our precious and dynamic man of God, **Apostle Frederick K.C. Price,** used to end each session of his teaching which instilled faith and integrity in us and millions over the years. One that has carried us, given us courage and helped us to remain steadfast as we were reminded to trust God and not be moved by our circumstances. I trust it will do the same for you as you step out in faith and receive all that God has purposed for your life!

(8) Anointed and Consecrated to Live a Godly Lifestyle:
- **The anointing is basically the authority and power of God flowing in your life.** All Christians become anointed at the time they receive their Salvation. Over time they receive different anointings to do things in life that God has commissioned or assigned them to do. Authority and power come with being anointed and you need to guard and protect the anointing on your life. It is the very presence of God in and with you.
- Joyce Meyer wrote about **protecting the anointing** in her book, *Ending Your Day Right*, (emphasis added): "A godly response to those in authority over you provides you with spiritual safety. If you submit to authority for the sake of honoring God and His Word, you will enjoy a free flow of His anointing in your life. If you rebel and refuse to submit, you will block the anointing. Submission protects you from demonic attacks, while rebellion opens the doors for the enemy. You protect the anointing on your life realizing God has given it to you to help you in all that you

do. Remember that things are accomplished by the Spirit of God and not by might nor by power (man's power) Zech. 4:6. Therefore, to guard your anointing: be obedient; stay peaceful and calm; be quick to forgive, slow to anger, patient and kind. There are other things that also protect your anointing but by doing these few things your anointing will be stronger."

- Submission is basically giving honor and respect and in this case to His Word and those in authority in your life. However, when an authoritative figure (an individual, a party, a government, a state or a city, etc.) is not submitting themselves to the Will of God, then **to continue to protect the anointing on your life you are at liberty to go with the Word of God because God is the final Authority and the One that is given the highest respect and honor**. (To read further about the *anointing*, what it is and does; plus other ways to protect it see the end of Chapter 4).
- **To Consecrate** basically means to make or declare holy. God has called each one of His children to be holy, why? Because it is written, **"You shall be holy, for I am holy"** 1 Peter 1:16. Our righteousness is in Christ and we acquired it because of the finished work at the cross when He took our sins and gave us His Righteousness. **Our part is to live righteous (choosing to do the right thing) before Him so we can remain in a *consecrated* lifestyle before Him which will allow the anointing to continue to flow in our lives unhindered.**
- Draw nigh to God and He will draw nigh to you (James 4:8). Be drawn to fellowship with like Believers even though you minister to non-Believers. The Word of God plainly says to not be unequally yoked…for what partnership have right living and right standing with God with iniquity

and lawlessness? Or how can light have fellowship with darkness? ... (2 Cor. 6:14-16). People that are Born-again have the Light; people who are not are unaware that they are living in darkness.
- Whether **your assignment** from God is a ministry, to be an employee, have a professional career, business or to reach certain goals in life, keep the order God has set-up so the anointing for each position or role will flow correctly through you, not being hindered in any way that would prevent you from carrying out your assignment.

(9) Ask for Godly Wisdom and Follow the Leadership of the Holy Spirit:
- A wise person will always be knowledgeable, but not all knowledgeable people are wise. **The fear of the Lord is the beginning of real wisdom as wisdom is the principle thing** (Prov. 4:7-8). The reverent fear and worship of the Lord is the beginning of Wisdom and skill (Prov. 1:7; Prov. 9:10). **Ask God for Godly wisdom then follow His instructions when it has been imparted to you.** The more you listen and are willing to follow through the more wisdom you will receive. Reading the Bible consistently regardless of how much you know is divine wisdom (Ephesians 1:17, 19; Prov. 3:5-7; Prov. 8:35 and James 3:17). Blessed is the man who finds skillful and godly Wisdom, and the man who understands...it is more precious than rubies; and nothing you can wish for is to be compared to her... (Prov. 3:13-17).
- **Following the Leading of the Holy Spirit is divine wisdom.** When you choose to follow the leading of the Holy Spirit you have chosen to seek first the Kingdom of God because that is where He will lead you. He will only lead you into

righteousness (right standing with God), **peace** (completeness and wholeness) and **joy** (strength and endurance) in the Holy Ghost (Spirit), (Matthew 6:33). In Deut. 34:9 Joshua was filled with the spirit of wisdom because Moses had laid his hands on him…The Holy Spirit will share or impart the spirit of wisdom aka the gift of wisdom, which in this case the anointing imparted understanding, judgment, and insight to Joshua.

- **There is liberty in Christ Jesus when you "walk and live [habitually] in the [Holy] Spirit [responsive to and controlled and guided by the Spirit];** then you will certainly not gratify the cravings and desires of the flesh (of human nature without God). For the desires of the flesh are opposed to the [Holy] Spirit… (Gal 5:16-17). "But if you are guided (led) by the [Holy] Spirit, you are not subject to the Law"…because "by the Holy Spirit we have our life in God, let us go forward walking in line, our conduct controlled by the Spirit." (Gal. 5:18, 25). In other words, **when we live and are led by Jesus' Spirit, the Holy Spirit will bring balance to the written Word and we will not live under rules and regulations but live with God's teachings with the guidance and strength from His Spirit to do so.**
- The Holy Spirit was sent to us with several attributes that will bring success and victory into our lives. He is the designated "power source" of the Trinity and through Him you can do all things. (John 14:16, 26; Phil. 4:13). (See more about this Amazing Person of the Trinity in Section Three of this Chapter).

(10) Build a Hedge of Protection:
- Plead the Blood of Jesus over yourself, your family and others daily (Heb. 10:19);

- Put on the Whole Armor of God daily (Ephesians 6:10-18);
- Continue to Pray in the Spirit building up your spirit man (Jude 1:20);
- Put on Love and have the right attitude throughout your day and respect others (I Co. 13:4-8);
- Enter into His Rest by simply praying in the Spirit, casting your care and trusting Him (I Peter 5:7; Jude 1:20);
- Do not walk in Fear, Isaiah 41:10, 13...there is nothing to fear... I am with you; (Prov. 29:25; Ps. 91:4-6; Isaiah 51:12 NIV).
- Establish your hedge with Psalm 91. Remain stable & fixed under the shadow of the Almighty [Whose power no foe can withstand];
- Command the Peace of God to be in your house daily (Isaiah 32:18);
- Continue in Truth as you endure to wait for instructions (John 8:31-32).

(11) Choose to Forgive Others, Yourself and God:
- As a matter of using forgiveness as a spiritual weapon, 2 Corinthians 2:9-10, forgiveness went forth to keep Satan from getting the advantage over us (2 Corinthians 2:11). God said do not be ignorant of his wiles and intentions.
- We are called to choose between life and death and feelings have nothing to do with it, it is about making a conscience choice to do things God's way (Deut. 30:19). When we choose we are making a decision. We can choose to forgive when we do not feel like doing so and that would be a decision to choose life. **The Bible instructs us to choose life and once a decision is made for *life* the Holy Spirit and angels get involved to start the healing process for the situation as well as bring forth that which is requested and/or needed.** In this life we always have the option to choose life or

to choose death, blessings or curses, forgiveness or bitterness, joy or misery, peace or torment, to be a giver or selfish, to be faithful or unfaithful, to be thankful or complain, to live a righteous holy life or to live in sin. If you choose what is not of God then evil forces will bring that choice to pass as well, it is all up to you. (See Chapter 2 for further information on Forgiveness).

(12) As You Develop and Walk in the Fruit of the Spirit you become a Weapon:
- The fruit is Love, Joy, Peace, Patience, Gentleness, Goodness, Faithfulness, Kindness (humility, meekness) and Self-control (Galatians 5:22-23).
- They are all extremely important. **Patience** will help develop Godly character and teach you how to wait on God so you will not go out ahead of Him or lag behind. Patience works with our faith and **faith** is the only thing that pleases God (Hebrews 10:36 and Hebrews 11:6).
- As you learn to keep your **joy,** you will experience a supernatural inner knowing that everything is alright. It is not based on outer circumstances to make you happy. You will keep your strength and out last the Devil. Your strength is important to keep you in step with the Holy Spirit so you will not grow weary and fall into the snare of the enemy.
- The fruit of **peace** will bring wholeness into your life. Jesus said He left us **His peace not the worlds** (John 14:27). See spiritual warfare weapon number 26.
- **We become weapons when we are living sacrifices and pliable in the hands of Almighty God.** When we are focused and strong in His might and come in the name of the Lord we defeat the enemy with the power and might that has been

bestowed upon us by Father God through the Holy Spirit. We become a living weapon when our hearts are sincere and we operate with the fruit of the Spirit whose foundation is love. We quickly realize no weapon that is formed against us shall prosper. Note: it may form but it shall not prosper, (Isa. 54:17).
- Many times our foes or enemies are in our own households because of varies reasons: strife, misunderstandings, division, lack of communication and so forth (Matthew 10:36). But when we choose to walk in love and forgiveness we become a spiritual weapon that God can use to dissolve the plan or destroy the plots of the adversary who is at the foundation and in the midst of any turmoil. One person can also be used as a weapon to cause division and destruction such as was done in Babylon to bring destruction for the wrong it had done to Zion (Jeremiah 51:20-24).

(13) Become sons of God (Mature Christians, male or female) it will Open Doors for the Spiritual Gifts to Flow in Your Life:
- "But as many as received Him, to them gave He power to become the **sons of God,** even to them that believe on His name," John 1:12 KJV. The Amplified Bible says "But to as many as did receive and welcome Him, He gave the **authority** (power, privilege, right) to become the children of God, that is, to those who believe in (adhere to, trust in, and rely on) His name who owe their birth neither to bloods nor to the will of the flesh [that of physical impulse] nor to the will of man [that of a natural father, but to God. [They are born of God!]" vv.12-13.
- **To become mature Christians aka sons of God** "you must submit to and endure [correction] for

discipline; **God is dealing with you as with sons.** For what son is there whom his father does not [thus] train and correct and discipline? Now if you are exempt from correction and left without discipline in which all [of God's children] share, then you are illegitimate offspring and not true sons [at all]. Moreover, we have had earthly fathers who disciplined us and we yielded [to them] and respected [them for training us]. Shall we not much more cheerfully submit to the Father of spirits and so [truly] live?" Hebrews 12:7-9.

- I Corinthians 2:6 explains, that **mature Christians** are given a **higher wisdom** that had been previously hidden. And in Hebrews 5:13-14 it tells us that mature Christians **eat solid food** whereas immature Christians feed on milk. It is the **sons of God who are the mature Believers** that will be in a position for God to operate more consistently by using His spiritual gifts. These mature Believers will understand their **right to exercise full authority** in the earth and take back dominion that God intended for the Body of Christ, the people within His Kingdom. (See the information that follows spiritual warfare weapon number twenty-six).

- As stated by Joyce Meyer, "The gifts are supernatural endowments of power given to Believers to help us live our natural lives in supernatural ways."

- **God can operate His gifts through any Saint or Believer as He wills, however, some of His gifts can only be entrusted to certain people that are mature in the spirit and/or people of the five fold ministry** for "the perfecting and the full equipping of the saints (His consecrated people), [that they should do] the work of ministering..."

As you can see some spiritual gifts will require a certain level of maturity in the spiritual realm before God releases them to operate through a person. He alone decides what gifts will be used, when they will be used, with whom and/or which ministry office, (Eph. 4:11).

- In regards to leadership and gifts in the church: "Leadership authority is based on God's grace and His gifts. Humans do not deserve or earn leadership roles. God does not give every gift to each church member. Members are to serve in accordance with the gifts they possess and are not to run after other people's gifts. The key is for various members to use their gifts cooperatively and to give place to others when they exercise a different gift." [1] (Romans 12:3-8).
- All of the gifts are necessary and important. In the matter of spiritual warfare next to the spiritual warfare weapon of "Love" I would think that the gift of Discernment would be extremely helpful because it will help you avoid deception, bring clear hearing from God and the ability to discern and distinguish between true and false spirits (I Corinthians 12:10).
- All of the gifts and callings appointed by God are without repentance. Which means "For God's gifts and His call are irrevocable. **[He never withdraws them when once they are given, and He does not change His mind about those to whom He gives His grace or to whom He sends His call.]"(Romans 11:29)**. If someone makes a decision to withdraw from God, give up their "free gift of Salvation" and renounce Him as their Lord and Savior still their spiritual gifts are not removed and taken back, however, their gifts will begin to be perverted and used by Satan for destruction instead of what they were intended for.

Continuation of Number 13: The Spiritual Gifts appointed by God for the perfecting of the Saints (Believers) are as follows:

I Corinthians 12:7-11 specific gifts used by God for the perfecting of the Saints:
- *Gifts of Revelation:* The Word of Wisdom, Word of Knowledge and Discerning of Spirits
- *Gifts of Utterance:* Prophecy, Divers Kinds of Tongues, Interpretation of Tongues
- *Gifts of Power:* Special Faith, Working of Miracles, Gifts of Healing

In Ephesians 4:11-12 are gifts appointed by God for the perfecting of the Saints:
- They are the offices of the Apostle, Prophet, Evangelist, Pastor and Teacher

In Romans 12:**6-15** all seven gifts are given for the edifying of the church:
- Gifts of prophecy/ preaching; serving; teaching; exhorting; giving; ruling/administration; and mercy

(14) Develop Godly Character:
- **When you are spiritually mature and the glory of God is upon you because you are not compromising the Word of God but working the principles found in the Bible as well as developing the fruit of the Spirit in your life you are expressing the character of God.** This person is a son or daughter in the faith because of their maturity. They are comfortable with God and they know that He will always come through for them as they are willing to trust and wait on His timing.
- **Having integrity is a part of Godly character.** The Lord said that your integrity will vindicate you, protect you, your children would be blessed

because of it and it would cause promotion in your life. It will also preserve you and it is vital to your life. Ps 26:1; Eph. 6:14.
- As we learn to walk upright with integrity before God and man with godly character and the love of God in our hearts for people regardless of what is going on in our lives whether it is positive or negative, one of the things assured us is that we will be vindicated by the Holy Spirit if the need arises.

(15) Dispatch Angels for Others as well as Yourself:
- **With faith in God and coupled with the ministry of angels we can overcome every obstacle.** God has commanded His angels to minister to us and take charge over us which simply means they accompany, defend and preserve us as we speak the Word of God and remain in right standing with Him. (Psalm 91:11).
- Angels as protectors is expressed by **Dr. Billy Graham in his book,** *Angels God's Secret Agents,* where he writes, **"Somehow it has always been easier for people to believe in demons than in the brighter side of the unseen world, the world of God's protecting angels...angels have a much more important place in the Bible than the devil and his demons."** He further says that "An angel is a spiritual creature without a body created by God for the service of Christendom and the church." [12]
- Furthermore, Dr. Graham says that "every true believer in Christ should be encouraged and strengthened! Angels are watching; they mark our path. They superintend the events of our lives and protect the interest of the Lord God, always working to promote His plans and to bring about His highest will for us." He says that "the most important characteristic of angels is not that they have power to exercise control over

our lives, or that they are beautiful, but that they work on our behalf." [12]
- **See the "Angel Movement Chart" in this Chapter, Section Three** for additional information about angels: what they are, how they function and their rank in the spiritual realm.

(16) Take Communion:
- When we take communion at home, at church or anywhere we are remembering the sacrifice that was made and that we were bought with a huge price and made His own. **When we take communion we are honoring what God did for us and He in turn honors our faith and sincere heart for remembering Him and our blood covenant.** He expressed His love and our worth to Him that day on Calvary. We are also reminded that our bodies are the temple (the very sanctuary) of the Holy Spirit Who lives within us. Whom we have received [as a Gift] from God. Therefore, we are not our own but bought with a price and should honor God as we bring glory to Him in our bodies when we shun immorality and other sins committed with our bodies" (I Corinthians 6:18-20 paraphrased).
- Taking communion is a time of getting free, a time to receive healing, a time to reach new anointings and a time of strengthening and being energized. As well as **it is a time to simply believe God, to fellowship and be intimate with Him.** It is also a time to remember that we have been redeemed, healed and made whole, and that we have access to abundance and authority, and all the promises of God.
- **The communion represents Jesus' broken body and the blood that was shed as He made Himself a sacrifice so that humanity could be**

reconciled back to God, in other words brought back into proper relationship with our Father in heaven. Through this relationship a covenant was made for eternal life and the promises of God in our lives for all those who partook of the bread and cup. Jesus declared in Matthew 26:26-29 and in I Corinthians 11:23-26, that **as often as you took the bread and the cup you were doing this in remembrance of Him**. He did not say it *was* Him or that the elements transformed into Him but that *it represented Him* as we partook. Luke 22:18-20 says, "For I say to you that from now on I shall not drink of the fruit of the vine at all until the Kingdom of God comes. Then He took a loaf [of bread], and when He had given thanks, He broke [it] and gave it to them saying, *This is My body which is given for you; do this in remembrance of Me.* And in like manner, He took the cup after supper, saying, *This cup is the new testament or covenant [ratified] in My blood which is shed (poured out) for you."* It also says in I Cor. 11:26, "For every time you eat this bread and drink this cup, **you are representing and signifying and proclaiming the fact of the Lord's death until He comes (again)."** Believers receive the communion sacrament or elements (bread and grape juice) as a reminder of Christ's finished work on the cross.

- **The bread should not have any leaven in it.** At Passover most Jewish people and Christians/ Believers use matzo bread for communion. Matzo bread is baked; it is thin with brown spots and tiny holes and feels and tastes like a cracker. The Christians use it because of what it represents. The thin unleavened bread symbolizes that there was no sin His body; the brown spots symbolizes the

body was broken and bruised for them; and the tiny holes symbolizes that He was nailed to the cross and made a curse so we could be free, made righteous, and blessed.
- For convenience churches will use the pre-filled cups of grape juice with a wafer. Still others will use some type of bread and juice. Some of the traditional churches will use red wine instead of grape juice. The bottom line is it is perfectly alright to have communion anywhere, anytime and it is alright to use whatever elements you may have because it is done by faith and as you bless the sacraments God sees the sincerity of your heart and is honoring your faith because you believe.
- Taking communion is a powerful weapon against the enemy because you are recognizing the Finished Work at the Cross by Christ Jesus Who triumphed over Satan and took back what was stolen when He went to the cross. The very first recorded communion involved Melchizedek king of Salem (Jerusalem at the time) of which His Hebrew name was made up of two Hebrew words: Melech **(king)** and Zadok **(righteousness)** for he was both king and priest. God confirmed His covenant with King Melchizedek and Abraham in Jerusalem with a blood covenant (wine represented the blood). This king was a type and shadow of our Lord Jesus who is the King of Righteousness.
- **When communion is taken with the understanding that there is power in intimacy with Christ through the bread and cup it will yield benefits such as:** (1) Reminding you of what Christ did for you and who you are to Him each time you partake; (2) He sees your faith in action which pleases Him as you remember your covenant with Him; (3) *Reminds you that the Lord is your*

Salvation and in that you have eternal life, provision, abundance, protection, deliverance and His promises; (4) It causes you to examine and judge yourself (are you saved, have you asked for forgiveness and have you repented) I Cor. 11:27-28; (5) It causes you to purify your heart and release all unforgiveness towards others; (6) It limits the power of the enemy from operating in your life; (7) It brings you in closer communication or fellowship with the Lord; (8) Because of your faith it becomes spiritual medicine to help you walk in healing: spiritually, mentally, emotionally, physically, financially, and socially; (9) It brings greater unity to your marriage and family; (10) And it reminds you of His promises, one being that if you believe (have faith) in the Lord Jesus, He will save you and your household (Acts 16:31).

(17) Walk (live) in Your Authority; Take Territory; Cast out Demons:

- Revelation 3:7-8 tells us that God is the Holy One, the True One, He Who has the key (authority) of the house of David, "He shall open and no one shall shut, and He shut and no one shall open" (Isaiah 22:22; Rev. 3:8). *He is the same One that gave the key of authority from the house of David to His church, His people, in His name.* Therefore, we have the right to command and renounce and rebuke. **As we exercise the authority given to us it releases God's ability or power into the situation.** For example: when you take authority and bind and loose, things move in the spiritual realm first then manifest in the earth. God said "let them have dominion (complete authority and ruler ship)... over all the earth" (Gen. 1:26). He especially gave us authority in the territory given to each of us. That territory includes our

physical body; our household; and wherever He has instructed us to fellowship, live, work, travel to, etc. we are to speak life and protection with His Word and to resist evil for we are empowered by the Holy Spirit with His authority to do so (Mark 16:17-18; Luke 10:19).
- He has given us authority over the works of His hands and in order to be effective you must recognize your authority and use it through prayer. (For resources regarding warfare prayers and clarification of different types of evil spirits and strongholds and to bring them under subjection see materials by Dr. N. Cindy Trimm at www.cindytrimm.com. [14]
- According to Isaiah 54:17 **No weapon formed against you shall prosper** (it may be formed but it does not have to destroy or do any great harm) if you resist it. Mark 16:17 says that **authority is given in the name of Jesus to cast out demons**. Remember when the thief is found he has to restore to you seven times what he stole (Proverbs 6:31). As you learn the names of certain evil strongholds such as the spirits of sabotage, fear, jezebel, strife, infirmity, affliction and others and how they operate then come against them in the name of Jesus, the name that is above every name (Phil. 2:9-11) with all power and authority. **(I do not suggest anyone other than a Born-again Spirit-filled Christian who knows who they are in Christ come against these or other strongholds or master spirits because you do not have the authority and they know it and will retaliate against you, (Acts 19:15-16).**
- Sample prayers: **Prayer of Jabez** to seek God to bless, enlarge your territory and for protection: See I Chronicles 4:10 NKJV; Ps. 91. **A Prayer for peace to rest in your home**: I have authority in

this house and *I have the right to set the atmosphere here,* therefore, I decree, declare and command the Peace, Rest, Heart, Will and Joy of the Lord to come into this house where the presence of the Lord is welcome. For it says in the book of Isaiah 32:18 that *my home is suppose to be a peaceable habitation, a quiet resting place and the house of the [uncompromisingly] righteous shall stand,* (Prov. 12:7; Isaiah. 22:22; Galatians 5:22-23 and Luke 10:19).
- See below after number 26 for an explanation of who has the right to use the authority given in the name of Jesus.

(18) Be Aware of the Times and Seasons You are in; are You in Your Set Place in the Natural and in the Spiritual Realm?
- **Knowing the season you are in is a spiritual weapon because you can fight back by keeping your peace and with assurance that whatever God said will come to pass.** He is able and willing to bring it all to pass by Himself right "on time" at the "appointed time." Therefore, use this weapon to remain calm and at peace so you can successfully hear from the Holy Spirit. When you know the season you are in you can be at rest and peace knowing that nothing has caught God by surprise. He will be there for you to instruct and deliver as promised.
- **God does not live in "Time," He created it** for the earth when He separated day from night and light from darkness (Gen. 1:4). But He lives in eternity. "Eternity is not simply unlimited time, forever extending backwards and forwards. Eternity is another dimension of existence and belongs solely to God. **Time itself is a creation of God. Time is the experience of a succession of events and experiences for a created being.** God existed in the dimension of eternity when

He had not created time. As eternal, God stands above time just as He stands above matter and persons whom He also has created... If God had a beginning, He too would be a creature, and we would want to worship the one who brought Him into existence" [1] (Genesis 1:1).

- **He set it up and we are to use our precious time wisely because once we spend it we cannot get it back.** God can redeem our time but that will be a time in our future, the old time is gone. Ecclesiastes 3:1-8 says there is a time for everything. **God moves in seasons and He reveals what time it is by the season you are in.** *When He reveals the season it is an indication that He is ready to bring whatever is due for that season into existence at its appointed time.*
- **For an example**, Noah was surrounded with evil yet he was a righteous man. God revealed the season and then did something about it. He instructed Noah to build an ark (represented a safe place) and at the appointed time only he, his family and the chosen animals and birds went in and were saved from the flood that destroyed every living thing on earth at that time and they stayed in it for one year and ten days (Gen. 1:18; Gen. 8:21, 22). **Likewise we are now living in the last of the Last Days and God has shown many the season we are in and what will occur** as a result of being in this season because He ultimately is in full control of the times and seasons regardless of who is in leadership in any nation of the world. Whatever God has declared that is what will take place (Mt. 24; 2 Tim. 3:1-7; I Co. 15:51-54). Additional examples in reference to the Bible: **This is an hour or season we need to be grounded, rooted and strong in the Word** is 2 Tim. 3:1-9; "**Pray at all times** (on every occasion,

in every season) in the Spirit..." (Eph. 6:18); and Mark 10:29 refers to the time in **your individual season** according to what sacrifices you made for the Kingdom of God as to how you will reap your harvest. Demons even know there is an appointed time for them to be tormented for eternity (Mt. 8:29).

- **When He opens a door in a space of time that door becomes an opportunity, for He is our opportunities (I stand at the door and knock... Rev.3:20)** When He knocks we should be prepared to answer the knock and open the door. If we are sensitive to the Holy Spirit God will reveal what season we are in so that we will be ready to receive our knock at the door. *He is the only One who sets the times and the seasons and the only One who can open the door to our true destiny and purpose.*
- **"An appointed time"** is a space of time appointed and definite, period fixed by God. **"A season"** primarily "due measure, fitness, proportion," is used in the New Testament to signify "a season, a time, a period" possessed of certain characteristics frequently rendered "time" or "times." The word "season" was sometimes substituted for "time."[5] **"Due season"** meant it was the "most opportune time," "perfect time," "proper or right time" in which to plant or to harvest, time and opportunity to sow or to receive. **"Day"** meant set time or period of time.
- **Terms used for appointed seasons and times are**: "Day," "An appointed time;" "a set time;" "set or appointed time"[2] "a set hour;" "today;" and "due season;" "a season;" "a space of time" (Ex. 9:5; Ps. 102:13; Ro. 5:6; Heb. 4:7; Mark 10:29; Dan. 2:16-21; Titus 1:3). Also the word "cycle" refers to a set time.

(19) **Focus and Endurance Key Attributes to Completing your Assignment or Goal(s):**
- **Focus on the Lord and His plan for your life or current project or assignment from Him first,** (Jeremiah 29:11; Eph. 2:10). What assignments or projects are in your heart to start and complete? What you receive in your heart through a still small voice; an unction; a very strong impression with great peace, or even an audible voice, vision or dream, write it down. The Bible says write the vision down and make it plan (Habakkuk 2:2). If you are not one hundred percent sure of what is in your heart, then *ask God to confirm His Word.* Seek God for instructions and wisdom. Make a list and set your priorities in place. Once the plan is in order begin to execute it in God's timing. If it is His will and done in His timing all of the provisions will be made as you step forward and step out.
- **Next pray that your mind stays focused and bind and rebuke distractions** not only sent to your mind but those assigned to your day. In the name of Jesus let it be known that no demonic force is going to stop you from completing your assignment for today. Ask and thank God for wisdom, insight, revelation knowledge, instructions and discipline to help you complete your project or assignment. If you need to delegate speak to God about the kind of help you desire, the type of people or just ask Him to send you the help that you need.
- **Staying focused with God's plan is the road to fulfillment, accomplishment and success.** As you seek God He will faithfully give you instructions, strategies and enable you to finish what He started in you. Apostle Paul declared **"And I am convinced and sure of this very thing, that He**

Who began a good work in you will continue until the day of Jesus Christ, developing [that good work] and **perfecting and bringing it to full completion in you**" (Philippians 1:6). In I Peter 5:10 also spoken by Apostle Paul in regards to finishing strong it says "...the God of all grace [Who imparts all blessing and favor], Who has called you to His [own] eternal glory in Christ Jesus, **will Himself complete and make you what you ought to be, establish and ground you securely, and strengthen, and settle you.**"

- **There is power in staying focused.** It requires discipline and putting aside distractions, hearing and obeying God in a timely fashion, avoiding procrastination, setting healthy boundaries, staying on track and in step with the Holy Spirit, taking proper care of your temple and being stable and trustworthy. *This is not a time to dwell on the pass with regrets but to set new goals for the future.*
- Remember that Satan comes only to steal, kill and destroy (John 10:10). Being that he is a deceiver he will try to tempt your flesh and if possible he will pull you off track away from the plan of God onto a plan that will cause destruction in your life. If you allow distractions to take your focus you could become discouraged from falling behind time limits, lose interest, lose work, miss important connections and possibly be set back or off course for years. **The key is to *resist him and begin again*** as often as you need to, to stay on track spiritually and in the natural to remain in God's timing.
- **Many times we would like to wait for the perfect time or convenient season to follow through with certain projects** (Acts 24:25). But this kind of attitude or thinking will cause you to miss opportunities because **more than likely** *there*

will never be a perfect or favorable season. We have to make or schedule in the time and sometimes that requires leaving our comfort zone or being inconvenienced in order to accomplish what is at hand. It may never seem like the right time but **if we will step out in God's timing we will find that much of what was done to stop or discourage us will lift as we move forward.** When we take a step, God takes a step if we do our part He will do His.

- **...For you have need of <u>endurance</u> so that when you have done the will of God you may receive what was promised** (Hebrews 10:36 NAS). The Bible also says if we will not fling away our fearless confidence, it carries a great and glories compensation of reward (v35). Some of those promises are a part of our reward for our endurance: favor, peace, deliverance, restoration, salvation for our loved ones, wealth, miracles, health, breakthroughs, property as well as blessings and protection for our children. *The prize goes to the one who can endure,* **crosses the finish line and finishes the race;** don't ever give up, Heb.12:1-3. In 2 Chron.15:7 it says, "Be strong, therefore, let not your hands be weak and slack, for your work shall be rewarded." The Word further says, "If we endure, we shall also reign with Him" (2 Tim. 2:12).

- As we are **determined to finish** our course it pleases God because He has given us all that we need to be finishers like Him. After He completed His finished work at the cross He said, "It is finished." Those that wait on Him for instructions and follow His leading shall renew their strength and power (Isa. 40:31). He will refresh and gift you with a particular spiritual talent, a gracious divine endowment through His grace to

continue (I Peter 4:10). He has done all of this to assist you in finishing and using what He placed inside of you to complete your purpose.
- Yet others will benefit and become stronger and even more determined when they **remember the vision and use it as a point of contact to stand on and believe God for it to come to pass.**
- **Pray for God to strengthen you to continue.** For example one could pray: "May God grant me out of the rich treasury of His glory to be strengthened and reinforced with mighty power in the inner man by the [Holy] Spirit [Himself indwelling my innermost being and personality]" Eph. 3:16. I am the just (the up right), therefore, I will live by faith, and if I draw back and shrink in fear, God's soul has no delight or pleasure in me (Hebrews 10:38).
- **The Lord desires that we do not draw back in fear but pursue, overtake and conquer as we remember that we can do all things in Christ who strengthens us and that He is with us,** (Phil. 4:13). Therefore, there is nothing to fear or escape from but only *to run* the *race* and *finish*.

(20) A Prophetic Word to You is a Powerful Spiritual Warfare Weapon:
- Prophetic basically means hearing from God. If you have received a personal prophecy (a prophetic word) for your life either through a prophet, a Godly upright Believer or directly from God know that **opposition will come when it is a true Word from the Lord because the Word has to be tried.** You must exercise your faith and stand on that prophetic word (hold on to it until God brings it to pass) even when you are being attacked in your mind with negative thoughts because it has not happened

yet. **Use the prophecy as a reminder of what God said which supersedes the lies being sent to your mind.** In this way the prophetic word becomes a spiritual weapon to fight the evil thoughts sent to bring doubt into your mind with hopes of you giving up on what God told you. **The devil only wants to steal the prophetic word so he can steal your faith and destiny.** The prophecy will help you endure and remain in faith when the devil wages war and battles against your calling or purpose in life (I Timothy 4:13-16 NIV and I Cor. 14:3).

- People who believe the Promises of God, which were prophesied and recorded by the prophets in the Bible are challenged when Satan comes immediately to steal the Word from them (Mark 14:15). **Read the Bible for yourself and use prophecy as a tool to stay on course and not be deceived (I Timothy 4:1-3).** Knowing the future as it was recorded in the Bible (which has been proven by the prophetic words that have already come to pass and those that are manifesting today) and as it is told by true prophets today working in conjunction with the Holy Spirit they can help protect you from false prophets, false prophecy and deception. I Thessalonians 5:20 says, "False prophets may seek to lead the church astray. Nevertheless, prophecy is not to be undervalued, resented, or ignored. We must not hamper the guidance of the Spirit in the community." [1]
- **Today we have excellent Bible Prophecy Teachers who are anointed** and sent by God to inform the church of the End Time Prophecies and how we should handle it and what we should expect. Bible Prophecy is a tool to evangelize a dying world.

- 2 Chronicles 20:20 says "...Believe in the Lord your God and you shall be established; **believe and remain steadfast to His prophets and you shall prosper.**" To be "steadfast" is to be established, immovable, firm in purpose and rooted in your set place where your enemies have no power to stand against you. **It also says you will prosper because you believe the Word of the Lord through His chosen prophets.**
- Also people are <u>not to search out prophets</u> for a prophetic word because if you are Born-again you are filled with His Spirit and can hear for yourself from the One who is the Revealer (the Holy Spirit, John 15:16) and He will confirm His Word by the Spirit. God knows how to bring certain people into church or conference meetings or across someone's path to receive what He has for them.
- **When Prophets speak into your life.** Establish that they are a "true" prophet that has been placed across your path from God. Many people can operate in the supernatural, but Jesus said He is the Door, the only Way and anyone operating apart from the true and living God is not who you would want speaking into your life (John 10:9; John 14:6). Judge the words spoken by the Bible, they should line up with the written Word. The Bible tells us that we do not judge a prophet by how well they prophesy **as to whether or not they are a true or false prophet but by the person's fruit (Godly or ungodly lifestyle) you shall know them** (Matthew 7:16). Ask God to show you who they are or confirm the words they have given to you. Ask God for discernment (I Cor. 12:10). If what they say does not witness in your spirit, (your own heart) and/or it is **not** confirmation then do not come in agreement

with it but do ask the Lord to reveal it to you and to give you other confirmation, I Thess. 5:21. **If it is truly God and you are still walking in obedience, the prophetic word will manifest at the appointed time because His Word will not return to Him void** (Isa. 55:11). We do not need to try to make anything happen, if it is God He will instruct you while on your journey with Him and ultimately what He said will come to fruition. When it comes to pass however long it takes the Holy Spirit will bring it to your remembrance that this is what He said He would do.

- **Realize that prophets only have a part of the whole picture and that gifts of the Spirit and the anointing vary from person to person.** We are dealing with people who are imperfect vessels, we all are, **Jesus was the only One who was perfect**. Do not concentrate on the *messenger* so much that you are unwilling to hear the message (unless it is obvious that the person is not living an upright lifestyle). If you have a peace and/or it is confirmation then receive the prophetic word. You should, however, ask God to confirm it again especially if it concerns a major decision for your life, I Cor. 13:8-10.

- **Sometimes prophets miss the timing of God** because they prophesy the present (Word of Knowledge), the future (Word of Wisdom) and the gift could reveal a person's past as they speak by the inspiration of the Holy Spirit. But because each vessel or messenger is not perfect and can perceive so much in their spirit they can miss the exact timing but very rarely miss the season. **God communicates more with people about the season than the exact appointed time within the season. When a person is in the appointed season it will come to pass if the person has been obedient** to follow God's instructions. Even if the person isn't doing everything right some things will come to pass at the appointed time because it has to in order for God's overall plan which could include several elements yours being one of them that has to be in place in order for God to manifest the larger picture which maybe something that has been prophesied by His prophets or something in His written Word.

- So if the prophet missed the **EXACT** timing that does not mean that the prophet that gave the prophetic word is a "false" prophet; but it may mean that **God did not give the exact timing (the appointed day) to the prophet because God desires for people to stand in faith and believe until they see the manifestation.** When a prophetic word is given one should try the spirit by the spirit, in other words, discern if the word is from God, as mentioned above. Ask God to confirm His word and when and if it is confirmed then stand on it and believe Him. Also follow instructions and if the word is tried (as mentioned earlier) continue to believe until it comes to pass.
- **Keep in mind that none of the five fold ministry gifts are perfect because the gifts flow through imperfect vessels. Therefore, the Apostles, Evangelists, Pastors and Teachers of the five fold ministry gifts (Ephesians 4:11) have all missed it to some degree as well.** That by no means makes them false men and women of God anymore than missing dates makes a prophet a false one. Sometimes it is the disobedience of a person who received a prophecy and did not follow through on their end as to why something has not come to pass or still yet maybe it was not the time for it to manifest. Many, many times prophetic

words will come to pass days, weeks, months or even years after they have been given. However, based on the current season of harvest we have entered in, things spoken will manifest quicker because the hour is great. Another way to put it is the Church is being prepared for His coming, therefore, people are on a prophetic time table and certain things that have already been spoken must come to pass so the person can move forward and complete their assignment from God. God Himself will see to it that the faithful obedient person will not be stopped, they will be compensated and justice will be done for them (Ps. 94:12-18; Hebrews 10:30).

(21) Kingdom Economics (Godly Principles) Resist the Enemy and Allows Financial Progress:
- Finances are discussed in this Chapter, Section Two under Kingdom Economics (Godly Principles) Resist the Enemy…

(22) Proper Rest for your Temple (body) and Eating Properly will Strengthen you for Spiritual Warfare and Life in General:
- First of all <u>what did God intend for your body</u> which is the house for your spirit man and your soul? He said in 3 John 2, "Beloved, I pray that you may prosper in every way and [<u>that your body] may keep well</u>, even as [I know] your soul keeps well and prospers." He further said, "**You were bought with a price** [purchased with a preciousness and paid for, made His own]. So then, honor God and bring **glory to Him in your body**" (I Corinthians 6:20). Therefore, "food [is intended] for the stomach and the stomach for food, but God will finally end [the functions of] both and bring them to nothing. **The body is not intended for sexual immorality,**

but [is intended] for the Lord, and the Lord [is intended] for the body [to save, sanctify, and raise it again]. **And God both raised the Lord to life and will also raise us up by His power**" (I Corinthians 6:13-14).
- **We are to respect the Temple of God and give it proper rest.** When we are properly rested we think more clearly and function better. We will have the strength to obey and follow through. God will supernaturally strengthen us for certain projects or tasks but over all we are to remain in a place where we are not weary physically, emotionally or spiritually so that we are ready to move forward at a moments notice. He never tells us to do anything He has not equipped, made provision for or anointed us to do. Even if He tells you to step out in faith at the appointed time with nothing you must believe that as you step forward He will take the next step. Living by faith takes strength and determination. See spiritual warfare weapon number four (4) regarding your Supernatural Spiritual Prayer Language which will assist you in entering into God's rest and being strengthened by His Spirit.
- However, **if we do become weary in well doing the Lord said**, "Come to Me, all you who labor and are heavy-laden and overburdened, and **I will cause you to rest**" (Matthew 11:28). Another way to rest is to sleep at night especially between the hours of 10:00 p.m. and 2:00 a.m. which allows the Holy Spirit to rejuvenate your body. According to Dr. Don Colbert in his book, *The Seven Pillars of Health*, what he says **about sleep** is very enlightening, "During those precious hours your body shuts down and repairs itself. Your immune system recharges. Your major organs are restored. Old cells are being replaced with new

ones. Your mind relaxes and orders its thoughts, creating a healthy mental state."
- **Sleep is so vital for a number of reasons**, in addition to the reasons listed above with at least six (6) hours, seven (7) being a better number of hours a night for sleeping according to sleep experts you will avoid sleep debt. Before television people slept about nine hours a night. And in our society today there are a number of businesses and activities going on twenty-four (24) hours a day and because of this people are losing sight of night and day as God designed it. Proper sleep will help you wake up rested and stay alert during the day. You will also have fewer accidents; you will be healthier and have less stress and overall better function of your mind and body. **Without proper sleep** there may be an increase in errors, accidents, irritability, difficulty in handling stress, day time sleeping, fatigue, aging, weight gain, high blood pressure and/or insomnia may develop as well as other diseases because the lack of sleep will take its toll on your health. **Psalm 127:2 says that, "…He gives [blessings] to His beloved in sleep."** The term get your "beauty sleep" was probably coined after this passage.
- Dr. Colbert gives key points on the importance of sleep, natural supplements to help with sleep for those who may need this in order to change old or bad habits with their sleep pattern. He also gives suggestions or tips on how to prepare your room for a good night's sleep. For more information go to www.drcolbert.com.
- **We must guard and protect our bodies with the proper rest staying in balance and using discipline to do so.** Dr. Don Colbert further says in his book, *The Seven Pillars of Health* that, "Busyness comes at a high price. Many people have lost

their health, marriages, and relationships as they strive to achieve more. But by abandoning rest we violate one of God's most basic principles: the Sabbath of rest...He said to rest one day out of every week. No exceptions...God knew what our bodies and minds are capable of and what they need to function properly. **A Sabbath rest does what sleep does: it lets the body and mind relax, unwind, and recuperate.** It helps to maintain our strength, energy, and youthfulness. It even humbles us by reminding us that, after all is said and done, God is the source of our strength."

- **Under our New Covenant the *Sabbath of Rest* is in Christ and at anytime on any given day we can rest in Him.** Furthermore, the Lord will honor it if we take one day a week and use it as a rest day to preserve our bodies as well as honor Him by doing other things besides work. For many Christians our worship day is different from a day of rest; although we can rest on the day that we worship. The Lord once told me to choose a day and rest on that day. After experiencing that I found that it will literally refresh you for the entire week.

- **To do what God has called and anointed each Believer to do we must be rested and in good health.** To have the strength to pray, praise, and worship the Lord, fight in the spirit through prayer, praise and interceding, to raise our families, to help others, run our businesses, to put in a honest days work, to travel and to be fruitful accomplishing meaningful tasks and our purpose in life, we need to be healthy, strong, alert, full of wisdom and might. **Some key reminders on keeping ourselves healthy are to**: Rest properly as mentioned above, drink plenty of water, get fresh air, get sunlight, exercise, take the proper supplements (because the soil which the food is raised in is no longer able to give us the nutrients we need), eat properly and avoid foods that are harmful for our bodies. Spending time in the presence of the Lord will keep us consistent, with wisdom, faith, strength and fresh ideas.

- **The Bible tells us what foods are the better foods that will agree with the system (body) that God created.** Some of them are vegetables and fruits; oats and grains, whole wheat; nuts and beans, and other foods with fiber, protein, and good fats. In addition to telling us what foods are compatible with our body it also says which meats are clean and unclean (Gen. 1:29-30; Deut. 14:3-21; Lev. 11:9-47 and I Cor. 8:8-13). **Certain animals and fish were created to be eaten and others were created to keep the environment clean.** Because the covenant changed from old to new it did not change the purpose for the animals or fish, what was considered unclean then is still unclean and not good for the human body today. Not to mention that certain companies use all kinds of chemicals in their meat to fatten it up, for color and so forth for presentation. When you eat this fattened meat the same chemicals used to fatten the meat will cause you to gain weight and eventually start to put your health at risk. Purchasing organic foods and meats does make a difference. I like to say pay now for the better foods or pay the doctors later, either way you will pay. Once again the choice is ours.
- As far as what is considered clean and unclean the following are examples: **a <u>clean</u> red meat would be**: beef, lamb, mutton, veal and an <u>**unclean**</u> **red meat would be**: pork, dog, cat,

horse and mule. **Clean poultry would be**: capon, chicken, turkey, Cornish hen, etc. and an **unclean** poultry would be: eagle, falcon, goose and osprey. A **clean** fish or sea food would be: salmon, halibut, bass, red snapper, kipper, tilapia, other cold water fish and so forth whereas an **unclean** fish or sea food would be: shrimp, catfish, oysters, scallops, swordfish, crab, lobster, mackerel, eel, dolphin, and blue marlin. I've listed a few of each to give an idea of what is considered clean and unclean meat or fish according to the Word of God.

- **Unhealthy fast foods** such as french fries, certain chips and donuts prepared in oils that release free radicals into your body. These same foods prepared in the proper oils at home would be healthier. Pizza with white bread and pepperoni, cold cuts (lunch meat), hamburgers, hot dogs, white sugar, white flour, sodas and other fast foods some have been bleached, others chemicals have been added that cause addiction to the food so people will return and spend their money. Also avoid pork, shellfish, aspartame, hydrogenated or partially hydrogenated oils, caffeine, and alcohol which reduce the body's ability to burn fat by about one third and increases high risk of cancer of the liver and pancreas. These and similar foods are not healthy and contribute to many diseases including high blood pressure, cancer, diabetes, obesity, asthma, allergies not to mention the destruction to the body organs, cells and immune system. The results of poor eating can be seen in all ages in today's society.
- **Material is available that will educate anyone interested in eating better and taking care of their body for the glory of God.** I have listed four

Christian doctors who have a mandate on their lives to educate the Body of Christ and whoever is interested in their health about good nutrition. They are Don Colbert, M.D., www.drcolbert.com; Dr.Valerie Saxion, Nutritionist, www.valeriesaxion.com; Eric Braverman, M.D., www.pathmed.com; & Scott Hannen, D.C. www.hannenhealth.com; A good nutritional cookbook by Sharon Broer with Dr. Ted Broer called "The Maximum Energy Cookbook" will save you time by giving you ideas for quick and nutritional meals, plus valuable information on nutrition. There are many other Christian doctors and nutritionist available and to locate one near you call or go on-line for referrals from Trinity Broadcasting Network (TBN) www.tbn.org or call 714.832.2950. You can also watch doctor programs on their network.

- A product that my family uses that will build the immune system; removes inflammation out of the body (which is at the root of all diseases); causes you to sleep better; stops pain or stiffness in the joints (arthritis); increases energy levels; has a great taste and successfully reverses most *major* diseases when consumed as directed. It is *an excellent supplement, an all natural fruit juice* made from the **Mangosteen fruit and its "rind."** Much research has been done and the conclusion was that healing agents from the Mangosteen fruit *rind* which is patented and located in 'Xango Juice' has over forty anti-oxidants in this one product. Some retail business stores offer a Mangosteen Juice *without the rind* and because of this it will not have the same results. For further information visit, www.xango.com or www.xango-juice.com . It is time for the Kingdom of God to rise up and make a difference in our families,

- communities and nations around the world, something one cannot successfully do while in poor health.
- To add one note, **even if we did all the right things in the natural to improve our health it will only go so far if we are harboring deadly emotions.** Deadly emotions as they are called by Dr. Colbert are located in your soul and if they are active you are out of balance and will be **hindered in all other efforts to maintain excellent health.** The objective of these emotions is to destroy you and rob you of your future with your family, your purpose, destiny and to make your life miserable in your attempts to achieve and succeed. Not to mention you will not be able to enjoy the Kingdom of God and all of its benefits right now.
- **Some of these deadly emotions are**: **strife, unforgiveness, contention, offense, bitterness, complaining, having a critical judgmental spirit towards others, faultfinding, lying, anger that is not righteous indignation, and anything that is done that robs you of your peace. We are to be aware of his devices and not receive but resist them at all times.** (2 Cor. 2:11; John 10:10; Ephesians 4:31-32; Hebrews 12:15; Mark 4:16-17; Prov. 6:16-19; I Cor. 10:10; 2 Tim. 2:23-24; 2 Peter 2:20-21; Luke 22:31).
- For example: when we are **offended it is actually a trap** that is designed to bring us out of the will of God into a state of anger, unforgiveness or bitterness which like the others will block the flow of the anointing on our lives and **prevent us from obtaining all the benefits of sleeping properly, eating the right foods, exercising, and so forth.**
- Healing is one of the things that God died for us to have. **All we need to do is receive it.** But when

we are full of condemnation, sin, unforgiveness, unrighteousness, revenge, envy and strife it makes it harder to use our faith which will produce the results that we need and is already available for us to have. *It also makes it difficult to receive the goodness of God and what He has prepared for us because we are so preoccupied with the "junk" that the adversary has used to ensnare some of us.* We are to be aware of his devices and not receive but resist them at all times.

(23) Utilize Time Management and Maintain Balance:
- *Shhh, I'll tell you a secret but only if you promise you will share it with everyone.* The way to get most things done is for you to have the ability to prioritize. *But this time set your priorities and trust God with your time.* After all He created time and set it in place so I would think that He knew a little something about it. **Seek Him and what He would have you to accomplish and work on that *first* because what is important to Him should be what is most important to you.** *The key to accomplishing the other things on your agenda is when you place His request first the rest of your day will fall in line and you should accomplish much.* He will give you the strength, energy, ideas, strategy, the anointing to finish, remove distractions, send you help, equipment, and supplies that will be necessary to complete any given work. **Whatever it takes, if it is His assignment or project to you He will make the provision to take care of it. Your part is to stay in balance, focused and sensitive to His Spirit**. He said we could do all things in Christ Who empowers us… (Phil 4:13).
- Ephesians 5:15-16 basically says that we are to "live purposefully and worthily and accurately, not as the unwise and witless, but as wise

(sensible, intelligent people)" and in that **v.16 speaks about us redeeming our time (making the very most of it)** knowing that the days are evil and a transition will eventually take place, however, in the meantime we should be **investing our time in the Kingdom of God as opposed to distracting busywork.** Wisdom redeems our time and connects us with opportunities we may have forfeited by being unwise. **God is the only One who can give us the wisdom and teach us to plan our lives and use our time in such a way that we will reach our full potential.** (Psalms 90:12).

- In order to successfully achieve operating according to God's timing, order and to have a godly balanced life, there are certain spiritual and natural things that need to be considered **to simplify and accomplish** our assignments and/or goals.
- **When working on special projects God gave me the idea to rise up earlier than my usual time.** So I started each morning at 2:00 a.m. and not only was I refreshed and ready to start my morning prayer before starting my project, but before I could rise up for the morning He had given me instructions, many times *an order of priority to follow* **for working on a current project** or certain materials to review so that I could get the work done speedily. *Plus I had hours of quiet uninterrupted time.* In addition, I knew if I were going to rise up earlier I also needed to rest properly. *We must keep all things in balance and use wisdom.* I found this advice of rising earlier and keeping a balanced lifestyle as much as possible to be true for all projects He places on my heart to do. He will give us the strategy and if we cooperate we will be successful, Luke 10:40-42.

- Your vision could entail owning a business, work, career, having a wonderful and prosperous family or using your gifts and talents to the fullest as directed through open doors of opportunity. **The Lord told all of us to occupy till He comes**, therefore, we are to utilize the gifts and talents God gave us while we continue to seek Him for further instructions and directions. The key is to use them wisely and keep everything in order and balance. Try not to hurry so much as you are going about your day because this could hinder your sensitivity to the Holy Spirit and block your hearing from God.
- **We are to be productive and fruitful not just busy all the time**. Spinning our wheels wasting precious time and really accomplishing nothing significant that really needs to be done. Doing works that do not accomplish anything or bring any type of progress is a robber of time, time that you cannot get back. Time is a resource that needs to be managed. Do not follow the world's system where there will never be enough time but there will be a lot of hurrying, stress and guilt for not doing everything you think you need to do. Being guided daily by the Holy Spirit will cause you to make the right connections and to accomplish what is really necessary for that day. I have found that **keeping a weekly schedule that list each day with certain items to be done works well as a guideline so time won't be wasted, a routine is set up and good habits can be formed**. Since I use it as a guideline, **flexibility is always available** to do things God is asking of me; for emergencies that may come up; or to be able to attend or participate in special events. What it does is it keeps things flowing in my home so certain things will be done and not forgotten and

control of work hours will not be out of balance since I have a tendency to work long hours. The Word says, *"When you bear (produce) much fruit, My Father is honored and glorified, and you show and prove yourselves to be true followers of Mine"* (John 15:8). He further says, **"You have not chosen Me, but I have chosen you I have appointed you** [I have planted you], that you might **go and bear fruit** and keep on bearing, and that your fruit may be lasting [that it may remain, abide], so that *whatever you ask the Father in My Name [as presenting all that I AM]*, He may give it to you" (John 15:16). He is saying when you ask in the name of Jesus you are going before God the Father with all that is in Jesus not in you but in Him that will determine the answer to your prayer.

- **I Peter 5:8 speaks about being well balanced and being cautious because we have an enemy and robber of time, energy, health, finances, and relationships seeking to devour us.** When we are out of balance we are caught off guard more easily, we make more errors and usually because we are too tired to deal with things. My weekly schedule helps to **keep my time balanced.** When I designate time with God in the morning; with family; work; rest and relaxation; overseeing my home; study; socializing; shopping and so forth **it keeps me in balance and also helps to prevent burn out.** I have never been a people pleaser but I enjoy giving and helping others. As I have come into the Word of God **I do all unto Him and I have found that He meets the family and people's needs through me that He wants to reach in a well balanced way.** We all need to say no to people sometimes if that is what it will take to keep us in balance.

- I would like to add that *even though I designate early morning time to my Heavenly Father I commune with Him on and off all day everyday because He is a part of my life (my life source) and I enjoy my personal relationship with Jesus.*
- For my daily agenda I initially review my monthly calendar which is located in my organizer. From there I see my weekly schedule, my project to do list, and call sheet (calls I may need to make) all located in my organizer. After which I usually check the in box on my desk. Once I review each source I transfer the information for the day onto a "3x5" ruled index card as a reminder. I review this card periodically during the day as well as take it with me if I am in the field. This avoids my having to carry my organizer and run the risk of misplacing it. This is an idea that God gave to me years ago and it works very well for me. On this card I list things to accomplish by priority on the left side. On the right side, I list phone calls to make that day and on the bottom right encouraging words from a daily devotional. On the reverse side of the card I have reminders to family, staff or others. *Note:* If I have an extended list for either side I will use a 5x8 sheet of paper in addition to the card. By doing this I do not have to refer to my organizer or weekly schedule during the day nor try to remember what it is that I need to accomplish and run the risk of forgetting something that is very important. This system helps my day run smoother and more efficiently.
- **Some people work two and three jobs to make ends meet which can have tragic results.** Not only will it rob you of time with God, your family and any type of social life, rest, relaxation and

peace but it will eventually take its toll on your health and possibly ruin your marriage and so forth. I find the best way is to *pray about employment, work where you have a peace about it knowing that God is in it* and then pray and trust God for the provisions not covered in your pay check. **It also helps to realize that our pay checks are not designed for us to "live on" but to provide seed in the Kingdom of God and allow God to multiply a return on our seed.** In the Kingdom of God the return on your seed could branch out into areas where there is a need that money alone cannot solve. (See Spiritual Warfare Weapon number 21).

(24) Thankfulness, a Spiritual Warfare Weapon that Changes Hearts and Gives Victory:
- **God's will for us all is to literally be grateful and acknowledge Him in our circumstances.** It is a command that we are to be thankful. *Are we to thank Him for the hard, bad and ugly things that happen as a result of "circumstances" in our lives? Of course not;* but **we are to see and be aware of His power, ability and willingness to bring us through it and be thankful for His love, mercy, grace and willingness to use His resources to help us in all of our circumstances.** The Bible says "Thank [God] in everything [no matter what the circumstances may be, be thankful and give thanks], for this is the will of God for you [who are] in Christ Jesus [the Revealer and Mediator of that will]" I Thessalonians 5:18. We should be thankful because no matter how bad a situation may be you can always find someone else with a situation worse than yours. The Lord does not allow any test or trial that we cannot bear and if we just go through it trusting Him we will come

out victorious and strengthened. With that kind of an end we can rejoice and be thankful "right now."
- The Word of God says that **we have the responsibility of maintaining our hearts, guarding over them and not allowing them to be troubled but kept in the right condition** (John 14:27). We can pray and ask God to create in us a clean heart and renew a right spirit within us, one that is not fearful, hard and stony but pure and pliable as we delight ourselves in Him (Ps. 51:10; Ps 37:4). With the right heart we can be grateful and thankful.
- **Part of guarding our heart is to know what complaining does, not to mention complaining is the opposite of being thankful.** Therefore, since to be thankful is the will of God and complaining is a sin before God (Phil. 2:14) when we complain we defeat ourselves and our purpose. **The way out of a terrible situation or circumstance** is not through complaining but through offering thanksgiving and praise. God's ways and thoughts are higher and yield more success!
- **The effects of murmuring and complaining:** It will keep you in the same position because it will nullify your progress even set you back; it will grieve the Holy Spirit and block the flow of the anointing as it works to destroy the anointing in your life; it will rob you of divine wisdom which is one of the principle things God desires for you to have; it will cause you to lose confidence in yourself and in the faith that you have; it will pull the hedge of protection down until destruction occurs (I Cor. 10:10); it will cause you to lose and destroy the favor in your life; it will cause unforgiveness and bitterness to be able to block your blessings; it will nullify your

Word confessions to God; it will impact others watching your walk with God in the wrong way and may even lead them astray to the point where they lose heart because they thought you had something that was real and worth pursuing. Complaining does not discriminate between jokes, decrees and seriousness because once you release complaining words they will have the same effect regardless of whether you were joking or not; you are ensnared by your own words.

- **We are to be thankful for all things from the greatest to the least.** For example: We can be thankful that **God was willing to redeem us from Sheol or Hell which contrary to what many (Christians and non-Christians) believe that Hell is not a "real physical place,"** *I assure you that Hell is a very real place, not only because "God said" it exists and He is a God that cannot lie (Luke 10:15; Isaiah 14:9; Amos 9:2); but there is documented proof of engineers who were drilling in the earth's curst when they heard and recorded people screaming in great pain. Still there were others that have had near death experiences and have gone there after being escorted by demons but were released back into their bodies when revived.* And because of His love for us and the fact that He created us in His likeness and image and redeemed us whereas other created beings such as fallen angels and beings that lost their bodies in the first flood and are now disembodied spirits were not redeemed and are now all doomed for the Lake of Fire. Thank God we were redeemed, restored, rescued and made whole by the Blood of the Lamb who took our sins and saved us from this horrible end.

- **Another major thing to be thankful for is the fact that we can draw near to His throne of grace (the throne of God's unmerited favor to us… Hebrews 4:16). He asks us to draw near to Him (James 4:8);** He desires to be our Friend, He loves relationships especially family relationships and says He freely enters into relationship with His people whom He calls His family. He wishes and knows His own and to be known by them (Genesis 9:8-17). We should be thankful that we have the opportunity to be in relationship with such a loving God and <u>not</u> one that hates and tells his followers to murder others because they believe or think differently or that their culture is different. There is liberty in Christ Jesus and we should be so thankful that we can experience it especially when so many are prevented through spiritual blindness or the laws of their land.
- **Those of us in the Lord that have found our true purpose in life should all be thankful that our lives have purpose and meaning.** That God took the time to create a destiny for each one of us and that the work He started in us He will perform, continue and develop that good work until He brings it to completion (Philippians 1:6; Jeremiah 29:11).
- **We are also thankful for the presence of the Holy Spirit** and that He has given: His guidance, teachings, revelations for revealing mysteries, for strength to endure to the finish line, for shelter, the fruit of the Spirit, for the gifts of the Spirit, for good health, for divine relationships, for provision, for the abundance and prosperity, for a sound mind, for opportunities, for increase, thankful that our enemies cannot defeat us or for whatever you want to thank Him for. The point is to be thankful and realize that God is

moving (working) in your life and it does not matter whether you see or feel it just know that He is.
- Being grateful and giving praise and thanksgiving to God (Psalms 100, 149-150) when the enemy wants you to be depressed, withdrawn, ill, broke, in a mindset of giving up or committing suicide, know that you can praise Him anyway, and in spite of your circumstances. This will get the attention of the Holy angels, the fallen angels and demons. But because you decided to praise Him the Holy angels begin to move on your behalf. But if you cannot be thankful and would rather have a pity party then the fallen angels and demons have an opportunity or an open door to move against you and bring you deeper into despair. The choice of your outcome is always yours to make.
- Therefore, if you choose life then praise Him! "Praise God in His sanctuary; praise Him in the heavens of His power! Praise Him for His mighty acts; praise Him according to the abundance of His greatness! ...Let everything that has breath and every breath of life praise the Lord! Praise the Lord!" (Psalm 150:1-2, 6).

(25) Develop a Spirit of Humility:
- Have you become the standard for everyone you know? **Should not the Bible be our standard in how we view others?** Humility involves meekness, kindness and self-control, all of which are a part of the fruit of the Spirit. It is a part of godly character that is essential to your walk with God. **A humble person is teachable, thankful, sensitive to the Holy Spirit, they don't mind asking for help, they are not full of themselves or prideful.** A humble person is quick to forgive, and slow

to take offense, they are usually patient, they are peacemakers and will give credit to others when it is due them, they do not mind building someone else up by complimenting them. And most importantly they are a giver and know how to treat others. **The most humble person who ever lived was Jesus Christ; and because He lowered Himself so low, "God has highly exalted Him and has freely bestowed on Him the name that is above every name"** (Phil. 2:8-9).

- **A humble person** can usually wait for God to vindicate he or she; they can pray for their enemies; they know they are not perfect and are aware of their weaknesses but does not allow that to slow them down; they realize everyone does not show love the same way nor does everyone know how to show love; they do not mind giving a compliment to others; they strive to build others up; they do not mind helping others obtain their goals in life and so forth. Humility is a part of godly character and that is why it has so many godly attributes.
- "…For **God sets Himself against the proud** (the insolent, the overbearing, the disdainful, the presumptuous, the boastful) [and He opposes, frustrates, and defeats them], but gives grace (favor, blessing) to the humble," I Peter 5:5. In Luke 14:11 it says that "For everyone who exalts himself will be humbled (ranked below others who are honored or rewarded), and he who humbles himself (keeps a modest opinion of himself and behaves accordingly will be exalted (elevated in rank)." "Haughtiness (proud, overbearing, arrogant) comes before disaster (destruction), but humility before honor (good name, outward respect, a person of superior standing, purity and integrity (reverence, and obedience)" Proverbs

18:12 emphases added. If you are full of yourself there is no room for the Holy Spirit to live inside of you to the fullest and without the help of the Holy Spirit you will end up being lead astray.
- Pride is a spirit that causes people to respond in certain ways. Satan uses pride to cause division. It causes people to be very critical and judgmental of others. Prideful people cannot be easily corrected; they usually think they are always right and everyone else is always wrong. It causes people to mistreat others and spiritually, prideful people want the credit or glory that only belongs to God. In Proverbs 6:16-17 the Lord says that one of the six things that He hates is "a proud look [the spirit that makes one overestimate himself and underestimate others]…"
- **You should desire to change if you are not a humble person** because the Holy Spirit will work with you and not against you. It is better to have the favor of God than have Him frustrate you because you are working against His plan. There are **three ways that people learn**: (1) they learn from other people's mistakes; (2) they learn the hard way from their own mistakes; or (3) they learn the tragic way by not learning from either. We all learn from experience but it is not the only teacher, the Holy Spirit was sent to teach and lead us and even though it may be difficult at times you have the assurance that He is with you and will always cause you to triumph if you endure to the end.
- **Humility has its rewards:** If you have a reverential fear of the Lord that is the beginning of wisdom. Humility gives us access to God's wisdom and favor. It could empower you to have wealth because a yielded person to God's way will listen, learn and seek to serve and is rewarded for

their obedience. We can maintain good health and good relationships in our lives as a result of choosing to humble ourselves to His Word and His Way.

(26) Walking in Peace/Shalom (Wholeness) is a Strong Spiritual Warfare Weapon and a Part of our Armor:
- **With His Peace we are whole.** *Shalom* in Hebrew means completeness, contentment, safety, health, well-being, prosperity, success and peace in our covenant. When we have His peace we have everything we need. To be whole would include your mind being at rest, your health in excellent condition, your relationships with family and friends are successful and in order. Your lifestyle is in a place where your finances are in abundance with overflow to the point you can be of help to others and meet some of their needs large or small. To be whole is to be prosperous (nothing missing); to be content with joy in your heart knowing that your "Source" will never run dry, will never fail nor ever leave you.
- **What is the secret to having a peaceful soul?** The answer to this question and any other pertaining to your life is the same – Jesus, He makes the difference. If you do not agree with me then you do not know Him, at lease not to the fullest. **He is called the "Prince of Peace"** (Isaiah 9:6). He continued to bless others with "His Peace" after He rose from the dead and walked the earth (John 20:11-23). He left His Peace for all of us today, one of His best gifts to partake in as it is stated in John 14:27 *"Peace I leave with you; My [own] peace I now give and bequeath to you. Not as the world gives do I give to you. Do not let your hearts be troubled, neither let them be afraid. [Stop allowing yourselves to*

be agitated and disturbed; and do not permit yourselves to be fearful and intimidated and cowardly and unsettled]."
- Simple trust leaves you with total peace if you have learned to cast the cares of this world on Him. Walking in peace is loving God, being sensitive to Him and what He is doing in your life even when you do not understand it. As your soul is quiet you can reflect on The Lord in relation to others and how He would have you to help, respond or meet a need. We all need to have our needs met and He knows all of our needs but His ways to acquire them are different from ours, His ways and thoughts are higher. Walking and living in His peace will cause provision and abundance to be met naturally and supernaturally.
- If you are in the Will of God, abiding with His plan to the best of your knowledge and you are within His timing and order, **even when there are trials, tests, hardships, sufferings, challenges, persecutions, obstacles, hindrances and delays,** *you will be able to maintain a peace,* keep a sound mind and have joy as you continue in Him. These are signs that you are honoring, trusting God and that you have made Him first in your life. Doing the last thing He told you to do while still waiting for your manifestation (promises to manifest, show up, become visible, and come to pass or to materialize) will keep you in a calm state with confidence and assurance in Whom you believe.
- When you go through a process of what is necessary to win the battle, keep your peace (which is important to have in order to hear God), and ultimately stand and *keep standing after you have done all you know to do.* In other words continue with His instructions and leading no matter what

you are facing. **Most of what the enemy sends your way is only a bluff or a smoke screen and will disappear or move out of your way as you continue to move forward keeping your peace and living by faith, with hope and with unconditional love** (Mark 11:23; I Cor. 13). As you become grounded in His Word to the point you cannot be moved and blown here and there with every doctrine, you will avoid being double minded (for "a double-minded man is unstable and unreliable and uncertain" in all his ways) (James 1:6-8 paraphrased).

- One last note, **when we are troubled we are allowing the adversary to rob us. God has instructed us on how to stay in peace** even when dealing with our enemies. Remember the adversary cannot do anything with a peaceful person who is truly trusting. God said in Proverbs 16:7 NLT "When the ways of people please the Lord, he makes even their enemies live at peace with them." **During this process He will guard and keep the minds that are stayed on Him in perfect and constant peace** (Isaiah 26:3). He also said in Psalms 37:1-2, 12, 13 basically not to worry about the wicked because the Lord is laughing at them for He sees their day of judgment and as long as we continue to trust Him and seek first His righteousness, joy and peace we will live a prosperous (whole) life, (Matt. 6:33).

Who has the Right to use the Authority given in the Name of Jesus? (An Addition to Spiritual Warfare Weapon number 17).

Only a Born-again Christian has the right to use the authority given in the name of Jesus (Mark 16:16-18). "Physical birth is not enough; one must be Born-again spiritually to enter the Kingdom of heaven. **There is a difference between a water baptism and Jesus' spiritual baptism.** In Christ all things are new."

[1] *A spiritual baptism takes place only after a person has acknowledged and confessed with their mouth that Jesus is Lord and in their heart believes that God raised Him from the dead* (Romans 10:9; John 3:5-6). By the age of accountability (usually somewhere around the age of twelve) a person can receive their Salvation even though this is possible at a younger or older age. When a person gives their life to the Savior and receives Him as their Lord they have acquired a life full of power and authority because of the Holy Spirit that dwells in them. However, one must grow in divine knowledge and wisdom in the things and ways of God. Once they are prepared and trained to operate in the authority that comes with the name of Jesus/Yeshua, they will acquire an anointing for their assignment and be able to use and appreciate the authority, power, benefits and gifts that have been imparted to them to a greater degree.

In addition, they can acquire greater benefits in their spiritual walk with the Lord as they say the prayer for the *spiritual baptism* (the Infilling of the Holy Spirit with the evidence of speaking in their supernatural spiritual language) as well as publicly affirm this transition with a *water baptism* of which both should be done at the time they receive their salvation or shortly thereafter to receive the maximum of what the Lord has sent to each one of His to begin their walk with Him, (Ro.10:9-10; John 3:17; Acts 2:4; John 3: 22-23). (A prayer for Salvation and the Infilling of the Holy Spirit is at the end of this chapter as well as at the end of this resource).

John 3:3, 7 records the following in regard to being Born-again:

> **...I assure you, most solemnly I tell you, that unless a person is born-again (anew, from above), he cannot ever see (know, be acquainted with, and experience) the kingdom of God. Marvel not [do not be surprised, astonished] at My telling you, You must all be born anew (from above).**

Now that we have established according to the Word of God that one must be Born-again to be saved which automatically gives them authority and dominion, **I would like to take this one step further. Even though any Believer has authority most of them are not aware of this and thus do not exercise their authority in His name.** Most of them are constantly beat down by life and unhappy waiting for their circumstances to change just like the world (unbelievers) so they can be happy. But when they are Believers they are entitled to have a peace in the midst of a storm, their health and so much more.

This brings me to the Believers that God calls His "sons of God" they are the mature Christians who walk (live) in their authority (See Spiritual Warfare Weapons numbers 13 and 17).

I Corinthians 2:6-7 says the following about the mature Christian:

> **Yet when we are among the full-grown (spiritually mature Christians who are ripe in understanding), we do impart a [higher] wisdom (the knowledge of the divine plan previously hidden);** but it is indeed not a wisdom of this present age or of this world nor of the leaders and rulers of this age, who are being brought to nothing and are doomed to pass away. But rather **what we are setting forth is a wisdom of God once hidden [from the human understanding] and now revealed to us by God** [that wisdom] which God devised and decreed before the ages for our glorification [to lift us into the glory of His presence].

"The Father our Creator in His eternal wisdom planned Salvation before time began. Christ the Lord was crucified to provide that Salvation. The Spirit is present among us to teach us the wisdom of God's Salvation and how to communicate this to others. He gives us the mind of Christ."[1] Galatians 4:4-7 explains that "when the proper time had fully come, God sent His Son, born of a woman…to purchase the freedom of (to ransom, to redeem, to atone for) those who were subject to the Law, that we might be **adopted and have sonship conferred upon us** [and be recognized as God's sons]. And because you [really] are [His] sons, **God has sent the [Holy] Spirit of His Son into our hearts,** crying, Abba (Father)! Father! Therefore, you are no longer a slave but a son; and **if a son, then [it follows that you are] an heir by the aid of God, through Christ."**

For clarity sake, when the Word of God says "sons of God" or in some cases uses the words "man," "men," "him" or "Bishop" as found in 1 Timothy 3:1-2 we realize that when God has given authority He is not recognizing or always referring to the "male" man but to both the "male and female" man. **He is referring to the real person who is a spiritual being that lives in our physical body, our spirit which is of no gender and is referred to as our spirit "man."** God said, **"He is a Spirit"** (John 4:24) even though He came in the body of a "male" man. To legally operate on the earth you must have a body and since He was a Spirit He came legally to exercise His authority in the earth in the body that was prepared for Him by His Father. But His true *being* is a Spirit which is neither male nor female. In regards to the usage of the title **"Bishop"** it is addressing only the male because of the era in which it was written. For we are well aware that females are confirmed into the office of Bishop across denominational lines. Paul gave instructions for godly women to move forth in ministry in the same passage I Timothy 3:11. Therefore, the guidelines for a Bishop would apply to her as well. For example, she is to have one husband and so forth.

When the Bible refers to the **"sons of God"** in John 1:12 KJV and it refers to **"children of God"** in John 1:12 in the Amplified Bible we can see this same passage is referring to all Born-again Christians or Believers regardless of their gender. The term "sons of God" as explained earlier is usually referring to a mature Christian.

This is important so that men and women alike understand that God speaks to both; increases both; loves both unconditionally; has given His authority to both; both have a free will;

both have access to His wisdom and can come boldly before His throne; both have power to heal in His name; both are heirs; and last but not least He died for them both and took away their sins and gave them both His righteousness and eternal life.

As a Believer there are certain rights and authority that you have access to because of your Salvation. Authority over the enemy is one. The Bible says the authority is yours whether you feel like you have it or not because the authority God gives you is not based on feelings but in His name. He is a God that cannot lie and if He says you have something whether you feel like you have it or not, that is not the point, the fact is, you do have it as a Believer in Jesus (Yeshua).

In their immaturity, not having the full revelation of who God was Adam and Eve fell as many Believers do today. But we have a chance to mature and become "sons" of God as our God is a God of chances.

Hebrews 5:13-14 has recorded the distinction between the mature and immature. It says that some Believers are immature and still feed on milk whereas mature Believers eat solid food:

> For everyone who continues to feed on milk is obviously inexperienced and unskilled in the doctrine of righteousness (of conformity to the divine will in purpose, thought, and action), for he is a mere infant [not able to talk yet]! **But solid food is for full-grown men**, for those whose sense and mental faculties are trained by practice to **discriminate and distinguish between what is morally good and noble and what is evil and contrary either to divine or human law.**

The Bible also says **we have authority to change our circumstances and lifestyle if we choose to do so.** In Genesis 1:26, it says, "…Let them have complete authority over the fish of the sea, the birds of the air, the [tame] beasts, and over all of the earth, and over everything that creeps upon the earth." God said, "…He created him; male and female He created them." And told them to fill the earth, and subdue it [using all its vast resources...and have dominion over...every living creature that moves upon the earth," (Gen. 1:27, 28).

God recognized that the female was present from the beginning because they were both created at the same time (Genesis 1:27) and **that is why He blessed and spoke to them both even though Adam was the only one present in His sight** (Gen. 1:28). God knew and fully intended to bring forth the *hidden* "female" man from Adam's body at the appointed time, which God did when Adam discovered his need for a spouse (Gen. 2:21, 22) and God called them both "Adam" which means "man, mankind or natural man." (See Chapter 6, under The Importance of a Help Meet and Spiritual Partner, for additional information on how God gave dominion to both the male and female at the same time so they could have full authority and take dominion over the earth).

God declared they would have authority and they did until they lost it after they were deceived but it was restored as we know when the second Adam (Christ Jesus) took it back. Now as mature Believers we exercise our authority and take back what was stolen by force from the hands of the enemy through acknowledging Jesus as Lord and Savior, praising God and following through with His will in our lives.

CLARITY ABOUT SPIRITS AND THE SPIRITUAL KINGDOM:

When some people think or hear the words *spirits and/or the spiritual realm* **they become fearful.** Probably because the words imply and/or produce an image of the unknown, uncertainties, something vague and possibly harmful. It implies that something is in the atmosphere that we cannot see with our natural eyesight or apply our natural senses to. In this type of sphere (realm or kingdom) the environment or surroundings is one that is not of this world but another, it is a kingdom in and of itself one that has good and evil involved as well and one that is greatly misunderstood for a lack of knowledge, (Hosea 4:6; Prov. 4:7).

We live in two worlds: one we can see and one that we cannot see. We live in a world that is visible and one that is invisible to the natural eye. We can see, smell, taste, touch, hear and sense things in the natural or visible world and in the invisible one we cannot do any of these except *sense* that there may be a presence near us. But if we are Born-again we can function in spiritual gifts as well as see, smell, touch, hear and sense things in the spiritual sphere as God wills. **Which world is more real? Which one should we heavily rely on for truth and understanding?**

2 Corinthians 4:18 says,

> Since we consider and look not to the things that are seen but to the things that are unseen; for the things that are visible are temporal (brief and fleeting), but the things that are invisible are deathless and everlasting.

The Word of God answers the question in this scripture. What we can see with our natural eye is only temporary and will pass rapidly and the things that we cannot see are everlasting and will never die.

The invisible world is populated by *spiritual beings* known as angels and demons. **God also lives in the invisible spiritual world or kingdom because He declared He is a Spirit** (John 4:24). When God created mankind He blew or breathed His Spirit into the first man and brought his created body to life. **All *human beings* are part spirit** because we were made in God's image (I Thessalonians 5:23; Gen. 1:26-27). We were made a little lower than God and He has crowned us with glory and honor (Psalm 8:5). Since we consist of three parts: spirit, soul and body, when we pass from this life our spirit and soul never die, as spirits live forever. Only our body will decay and return to dust where it came from (Gen. 3:19). Our spirit will return to heaven because it belongs to God who gave it to us to live in a mortal body. Our soul, well that is the question, where is our soul going to spend eternity? That decision is strictly up to the person, they must decide.

In the spiritual kingdom or realm there are mysteries and when they are revealed they are more real than what you will ever sense with your five natural senses. Why is it more real? Because everything that a human being can see, smell, taste, touch, or hear came *first* from the spiritual realm.

When The Holy *Spirit* communicates with humans that are Born-again Christians He speaks to the part of us that is spirit and the spirit within us sends the message to our mind which is a part of our soul. We can communicate back to Him in our everyday language or for those filled with the *Infilling of the Holy Spirit* (Baptized in the Holy Spirit) we can communicate with His Spirit and speak directly to God in our supernatural spiritual prayer language of tongues (I Corinthians 14:2). For those who are not aware anytime we are speaking to God it is a form of prayer. (See this Chapter, Section Two under Spiritual Warfare Weapon no. 4).

The spiritual kingdom or realm is not as uncertain as many may think. There is perfect and scientific order in the spiritual realm. Many things, events and miracles have been proven time and time again to have taken place. Many of these events were already recorded in the Holy Bible and confirmed by scientists. **Science is finally catching up to the Bible.** Many unanswered questions have already been answered in the Word of God. In other words prophecy was fulfilled and proof has been discovered to confirm it. Some simply choose to believe God and others choose to continue to live in unbelief and fear of the so called "unknown."

The spirits that exist in the spiritual realm or kingdom are angels that God the Father has sent forth and assigned to Believers to assist, protect and preserve them while they are on this earth (Ps. 91:11) and to do various types of work for Him. They are strong and mighty and can take on the form of humans and can be seen with the natural eye and move about on the earth or they can remain invisible while completing their assignment. (See this Chapter in Section Three under *Angels Movement Chart* for additional information about angels.).

Other spirits that exist on this earth are fallen angels who are sent by the direction of Satan to complete an assignment against human beings. They primarily live in the second heaven that which we call outer space. The fallen angels that slept with women before the second flood of Noah and caused giants to be birthed on the earth are now chained up in the underworld in a region called Tartarus (a prison for wicked angels). **Demons (disembodied spirits)** are also moving about on the earth at the direction of Satan. They come to deceive and possess human bodies because they do not have a body and are in need of one to function with their evil deeds on earth. They primarily stay in the underworld region called the pit or the abyss which is located inside the earth (Ps. 30:3; Isaiah 38:17-18; Ezekiel 32:23).

Many people think that "Ghosts" are dead people that have come back to earth. They are afraid that a *ghost* is going to "harm them." **Ghost is an English word for "Spirit" and a spirit is not a dead person coming back to the earth to haunt someone.** I have described the spirits that are on this earth. When someone dies their spirit (the real person) and their soul both go to be in heaven with the Lord (2 Corinthians 5:8); however, if the person had refused to receive salvation when he or she was alive then their soul (their mind, will and emotions) have made their new home in Hell also known as Sheol (Hebrew) or Hades (Greek), (Isaiah 14:15, 19).

2 Corinthians 5:6 and 8 explain that the "true" person (their spirit) is either at home in the body on earth or at home with the Lord in heaven:

> So then, we are always full of good and hopeful and confident courage; **we know that while we are at home in the body, we are abroad from the home with the Lord** [that is promised us]. [Yes] we have confident and hopeful courage and **are pleased rather to be away from home out of the body and be at home with the Lord.**

Therefore, when someone claims that they have seen a loved one who has passed (died) or someone appeared and frightened them and they looked like someone they knew that had died; they are dealing with demonic spirits that can transform into human form and look like a person that once lived. (See this Chapter in Section One under *Who is the Adversary and What Are His Devices* and also see this Chapter in Section Three under the *Angel Movement Chart* which will cover how Holy angels also transform and appear as humans but not to frighten but to help people when necessary).

The Bible clearly tells us in the book of Deuteronomy that we are not to indulge in detestable practices that will open a door and allow demonic forces into our lives where we can become deceived, harmed or possessed by these evil spirits. Some of these practices include: attending a **Séances where Mediums** claim to bring someone who has died for a visit to speak to loved ones who wish to converse with them. At that point they are **entertaining familiar spirits** who can answer your questions about the person, they can sound like the person and look like the person because that spirit is familiar with your family. It is a disembodied spirit, they do not die, it has watched your family for generations and it has essential specific knowledge about the person who died and the family.

Another detestable practice that the Bible tells us not to engage in is to see psychics for the reading of our palms. These people at one time may have had a true gift that has now been perverted and they hear and speak half truths and half lies which they pick up from demonic forces or spirits to bring confusion and deception into your life. Plus it opens a wide door for Satan and other evil spirits to operate his devices in your life and with your family. In addition, spirits can transfer to you as you participate in these practices. We are also to stay away from such devices or practices such as the occult, horoscopes, tarot cards, quija boards, the dungeon and dragon game, astrology, hypnosis and all forms of witchcraft which would include the practice of making spells which are taught in the Harry Potter series of books and films that children do not need to read or watch (Read Acts 19:11-19).

Acts 19:18-19 illustrates that Christians should discard books and materials that contain witchcraft:

> Many also of those who were now Believers came making full confession and thoroughly exposing their [former deceptive and evil] practices. And many of those who had practiced curious, magical arts collected their books and [throwing them, book after book, on the pile] burned them in the sight of everybody. When they counted the value of them, they found it amounted to 50,000 pieces of silver (about $9,300).

Deuteronomy 18:9-12 NIV forbids the use of certain practices used to communicate with the spiritual realm that leads people in the wrong direction and into torment:

> **When you enter the land the Lord your God is giving you, do not learn to imitate the detestable ways of the nations there. Let no one be found among you who sacrifices his son or daughter in the fire, who practices divination or sorcery, interprets omens, engages in witchcraft, or casts spells, or who is a medium or spiritist (a person who practices sorcery), or who consults the dead. Anyone who does these things is detestable to the Lord, and because of these detestable practices the Lord your God will drive out those nations before you.**

People are not to seek and participate in these practices to reach loved ones who have passed or to know the future for their lives. It can lead to danger for that person. ***People are to seek God through prayer and reading His Word, they are to be led by His "Holy" Spirit for guidance and come into the house of the Lord for spiritual strength, fellowship and growth.*** Seek God about the place of worship that will be right for you and when you find it you will have a peace and words from the pulpit that witnesses in your heart. Deuteronomy says in 18:14-15 NIV, "The nations you will dispossess listen to those who practice sorcery or divination. But as for you, the Lord your God has not permitted you to do so. The Lord your God will raise up for you a *prophet* like me from among your own brothers. You must listen to him."

Under the New Covenant or New Testament people are not to seek out prophets for direction and use them as if they were psychics which they are not. People are suppose to seek God in the name of Jesus and the Holy Spirit will guide and teach them all things (John 14:26). God has sent His prophets to His people with specific words of wisdom, knowledge, comfort, instructions, warnings and so forth as He wills. There are men and women of God who walk in the five fold office of the Prophet that was set up by God for the perfecting and the full equipping of the Saints (His consecrated people), Ephesians 4:11-12. **The prophet speaks by the inspiration of the Holy Spirit and reveals mysteries (secrets) of the future and events by divine guidance. Amos 3:7 says, "Surely the Lord God will do nothing without revealing His secret to His servants the prophets."** The Bible further says in 2 Chron. 20:20b, "... *Believe in the Lord your God and you shall be established; believe and remain steadfast to His prophets and you shall prosper."* The prophet comes to bring and declare a word that is going to make a difference in your life. God will get an answer to you when you seek Him first. (See this Chapter in Section Two, under *Spiritual Warfare Weapon number 20* which deals with the Prophetic Word).

You have protection from the Holy Spirit and the angels because His Word says, "Fear not [there is nothing to fear], for I am with you" (Isaiah 41:10). Therefore, there is really nothing to fear about the spiritual realm especially when you are a Child of God. So when you think of the spiritual realm first think of our Gracious Heavenly Father, His Beloved Son and our Precious Holy Spirit and that it is a Kingdom in which they also dwell and put your mind at rest. **As a Believer we have full authority and power over demonic spirits in the name of Jesus** (Mark 16:17; Luke 10:19). "Little children, you are of God [you belong to Him] and have [already] defeated and overcome them [the agents of the antichrist], because He Who lives in you is greater (mightier) than he who is in the world" (I John 4:4). When you are saved and filled with the Holy Spirit you need only to bind and rebuke evil spirits and plead the blood of Jesus. God has already given you victory nearly two thousand years ago at the Finished Work at the Cross. Just walk in your authority and remember Holy angels work in conjunction with the Holy Spirit on your behalf so there is no reason to fear.

2 Timothy 1:7 NKJV says,

> For God has not given us a spirit of fear, but of power and of love and of a sound mind.

People want to know the answers to everything before hand to make sure they do not have to go through anything or try to avoid as much as possible. **Those that have a personal relationship with the One and true God understand that they must live by faith and continue to trust the Almighty**; He really knows what He is doing. His ways and thoughts are so different from ours because they are much, much higher. He has already spoken forth what is happening in the earth and its outcome. He is aware, He is not asleep and He will never leave us nor forsake us (Hebrew 13:5; Deut. 31:6).

I Corinthians 2:12-23 says,

> **Now we have not received the spirit [that belongs to] the world, but the [Holy] Spirit Who is from God,** [given to us] that we might realize and comprehend and appreciate the gifts [of divine favor and blessing so freely and lavishly] bestowed on us by God. **And we are setting these truths forth in words not taught**

by human wisdom but taught by the [Holy] Spirit, combining and interpreting spiritual truths with spiritual language [to those who possess the Holy Spirit].

When we become acquainted with Him and His ways we understand that the natural world is a reflection of the spiritual world except in the spiritual kingdom all is permanent and it will be perfected at the appointed time when Satan and his followers are removed to the Lake of Fire (Rev. 20:10, 15).

Restoration will take place and "many will be constituted righteous (made acceptable to God, brought into right standing with Him)" at the appointed time because of the obedience of One Man, the Christ. The world's system has fallen because of sinful men who do not know Him and His ways and is in a corrupt state because of the disobedience of one man, the first Adam (Romans 5:19). *The things of the spirit are foolishness to the worldly man (mankind) and unfortunately unless He surrenders his life to Christ he will remain in this state.*

I Corinthians 2:14 says:

> But the natural, nonspiritual man does not accept or welcome or admit into his heart the gifts and teachings and revelations of the Spirit of God, for they are folly (meaningless nonsense to him; and he is incapable of knowing them [of progressively recognizing, understanding, and becoming better acquainted with them] because they are *spiritually discerned* and estimated and appreciated.

KINGDOM ECONOMICS (GODLY PRINCIPLES) RESIST THE ENEMY AND ALLOWS FINANCIAL PROGRESS:

Biblical or Kingdom Economics is another major area required in order for a family to be healthy and strong. How a couple manages their finances is extremely important, because a great number of marriages dissolve as a direct result of poor management of the family income(s). Marriage is a partnership *between a husband, a wife and God*; therefore, *all that concerns the couple is also a concern to God*. His principles when applied to their finances will assist tremendously in giving the wisdom needed for management.

Once a couple realizes that everything belongs to God and He makes them trustees of His possessions, that they are stewards (they are His partners who manage what He has entrusted to them) it will be easier to operate within His economic system. *They must also be aware that the battle for their finances is a spiritual one and Satan hopes to destroy their finances which will destroy their ability to produce and gain fruit in the Kingdom.* He wants to rob you of any faith you may have in God for a turn around in your circumstances so much so to the point that you are depressed and feel hopeless.

They should also understand that if they honor Him with what He has given them He will bless and increase them. How do you honor God with your capital or money? When you give money where He tells you: to help family, others, widows and orphans; to give to your local church, to ministries involved in international rescue; to schools, orphanages, homes for the homeless, and so on, when you give money it is the same as giving a part of yourself because you earned it with your time and talents and when you do this you are honoring God. By the way this is an excellent investment into the Kingdom of God.

There are two types of success "in life, there is **good success** and **bad success.** Bad success is the kind of success which robs you of time with your family, friends and church, and destroys your health and relationships. With good success, on the other hand, you see prosperity in every area of your life. God wants you to enjoy good success." [8]

God never plans for anyone to fail. His plan includes your purpose and with that comes **good success!**

Joshua 1:8 says,

> This Book of the Law shall not depart out of your mouth, but you shall meditate (speak the Word of God) on it day and night, that you may observe and do according to all that is written in it. **For then you shall make your way prosperous, and then you shall deal wisely and have** *good success.*

Joshua served God all of his life and towards the end of his life he said something that is a primary scripture that our family stands on in our own home and that is, "But as for me and my house, we will serve the Lord" (Joshua 24:15; 31). Your family on one accord loving and serving God together is the greatest success your household could ever achieve. *God's good success leads to His prosperity* and not necessarily to what a culture dictates as success and prosperity based on their limited views of what success is.

In this section of Kingdom Economics we will address three subject matters regarding finances. First, The World's System and Why Some Suffer Lack; Secondly, God's Prosperity is a part of His Kingdom and Differs from the World's System; and Thirdly, When Income is Applied to Biblical Truths and Principles it will resist the Adversary and Allow Supernatural Increase and Financial Progress.

THE WORLD'S ECONOMIC SYSTEM AND WHY SOME SUFFER LACK:

Unfortunately in our society most people have learned to operate with the world's economy and have worked towards what the world defines as success and prosperity and not on what God says it is. John 17:14-16 speaks of the difference between the worldly and godly. God is not of this world and neither are those that are in Christ, therefore, we need not be subject to the world's system. Many families struggle financially for years until it may become a major area that causes great stress and pressure to the point of separation and/or divorce. *More than half of dissolved marriages had an issue with how finances were managed in the home. There is either a lack of finances or miscommunication between the couple, along with misunderstandings of what was meant to be of importance or not and the setting up of priorities for the use of their income.* It could be a problem because: of separate accounts, lack of trust, lack of faith, over indulgence, loss of employment, loss of medical and dental benefits, high interest rates and inflation, having a poverty mentality (everything is for a rainy day), not enough money coming into the household in comparison of what is going out, and so on.

What most families and people in general do not realize is that there are two types of economic systems in the earth today. **One is the "World's Economic System" and the other is the "Kingdom's Economic System." Both are a type of government,** one has its own interest at heart while the other has the interest and well-being of people. One is based on human wisdom and might, trying to meets its needs without God while the other is based on Biblical principles (2 Colossians 2:8; I Cor. 2:14).

I Corinthians 3:18-20 says,

> Let no person deceive himself. If anyone among you supposes that he is wise in this age, let him become a fool [let him discard his worldly discernment and recognize himself as dull, stupid, and foolish, without true learning and scholarship], that he may become [really] wise. For this world's wisdom is foolishness (absurdity and stupidity) with

God, for it is written, He lays hold of the wise in their [own] craftiness. And again, The Lord knows the thoughts and reasonings of the [humanly] wise and recognizes how futile they are.

Comparing the World's Economic System with the Kingdom's Economic System is an eye opener to say the least. God's ways and thoughts are much higher and greater than those of mortal men (Isaiah 55:8-9). *When the World's Economic System is in decline the Kingdom of God's Economic System, which is of the Kingdom of Light is on the rise and will empower us to prosper.* It says in Prov. 13:22, "… the wealth of the sinner [finds its way eventually] into the hands of the righteous, for whom it was laid up." **The World's Economic System has failed. It belongs to the kingdom of darkness and is not designed to prosper anyone but to control and suppress lives.** The World's Economic System has lack, poverty, sickness and bondage; it is a Babylonian type of *Worldly System that God sent a deliverer into to set His captives free.* In doing so God instructed that a lamb without blemish be roasted and the blood from that lamb be placed on the door post and the lamb eaten and nothing of the meat remain. **God was breaking the world's curse off of His people, setting them free from bondage and establishing a new Kingdom in their lives.** For all those who ate of the lamb were healed and it's blood that was placed on the door post caused the **spirit of death to *pass*** **over them as they were saved from destruction and they left that same night wealthy, healthy and free from bondage** (Ex. 12:3-14; 35-36; 41).

Because of Jesus' Finished Work at the Cross where He became our Passover Lamb the Kingdom Economic System was birthed at that point into the earth. *As the World's Economic System is in a steady decline the Kingdom's Economic System is on the rise.* As with the Israelites, which is our example, when God delivered them out of bondage from the Babylonian World's System He empowered them that same night to have wealth and healing in all those who partook of the lamb. Today, for all those who receive the Lamb of God, He has sent a Deliverer to set the captives free. When they leave the World's System they will be healed and empowered to get wealth, (Deut. 8:18; Ro. 8:17); to have health and be prosperous (3 John 2; I Peter 2:24); to have liberty and freedom in Christ (2 Cor. 3:17; Romans 6:14). When we apply His blood by declaring it, it covers us so that destructive assignments must pass over us.

Let's explore for a moment what operating in the World's Economy has taught us. Most people that have learned to diligently operate within the World's Economy and do not practice the principles of the Kingdom of God usually directly or indirectly <u>make money their god</u>. Greed (in love with money), selfishness (stingy), cheating, pride, lack of integrity and so on accompanies the world's way of thinking and doing things. As a matter of fact taking advantage of others is seen in today's business world as operating with good business strategy.

The World's Economic System is a system based in "fear of lack" and therefore teaches one how to hold their money (hoard), keeping it even when others could be blessed with a little help. This system does teach you to save and invest but just for your own interest and purposes. Investing in the Stock Market requires a lot of research, primarily because the system is set up for you to gamble with your income or investment money. Therefore, proper research is necessary to avoid unnecessary risk as much as possible. One reason it is a high risk is because you can lose your principle as well as the interest when the Stock Market collapses or crashes every few years when a shaking goes on with the economy. Whatever is not created by God when the shaking starts it will fall a part (Hebrews 12:25-29). This is not how the Kingdom Economic System functions; it is not designed to cause you to risk your hard earned income that is meant for other things. But once again, if you choose to invest in the Stock Market be well informed and not only relying on a broker to make all major decisions with your finances.

The world's system encourages gambling and playing the lottery, two vices with the purpose of gaining and increasing at others expense as well as accomplishing their "get rich scheme." Most corporations that at one time did business with the people's best interest at heart are now seeking ways to charge more for less product and quality of service. Business is conducted with the lust of the eye, lies, broken promises and failure to follow through on items agreed upon. Many companies or civil businesses act like they are doing you a favor for calling them to give them business. As well as some businesses over charging for basic goods and/or services, adding hidden charges and cost. Government and State agencies are at an all time high of exercising usury by over taxing and charging high interest and penalties (Luke 19:7-8; Neh.5:1-12; Ps. 15:5). Nowadays, it is the norm "to get over on someone else." In other words it is the norm for so many to gamble, cheat and steal from whoever they can.

I Timothy 6:17-18, mistreating people for uncertain riches,

> As for the rich in this world, charge them not to be proud and arrogant and contemptuous of others, nor to set their hopes on uncertain riches, but on God, Who richly and ceaselessly provides us with everything for [our] enjoyment.
>
> [Charge them] to do good, to be rich in good works, to be liberal and generous of heart, ready to share [with others], In this way laying up for themselves [the riches that endure forever as] a good foundation for the future, so that they may grasp that which is life indeed.

It is common and taken for granted that you can put your trust in uncertain riches or how well you can scheme and trick others. **This information is <u>not about all</u> of the rich or well to do because all of the rich or well to do people are not practicing** these things or ways. This message is for anyone who feels it is alright to take advantage of someone else. Employees can benefit from this information too because many of them are the ones with the attitudes when you call these companies, but they forget so easily that God loves people and when you come against, especially godly people, and take advantage of them you are surely setting yourself up to have things taken from you (Galatians 6:7). Many times people are acting certain ways at their place of employment or business because the world's system does not offer much hope and the routine of day in and day out without motivation or hope of a brighter future does not give people anything to look forward to and thus there is no fulfillment.

A person who lays up riches for himself just to hoard them never gives thanks to God or thinks of anyone to bless. "And I will say to my soul, Soul, you have many good things laid up, [enough] for many years. Take your ease; eat, drink, and enjoy yourself merrily. But God said to him, You fool! This very night they [the messengers of God] will demand your soul of you; and all the things that you prepared, whose will they be? So it is with the one who continues to lay up and hoard possessions for himself and is not rich [in his relation] to God [this is how he fares]" (Luke 12:19-21). *Notice we are not simply talking about someone who has riches that is not the point, we are talking about the attitude that some have who have riches and how empty many of their lives really are.* **Further, notice the money by itself** cannot fill any void in your life and give you a healthy and wonderful outcome. If you think it can just speak to past lottery winners.

Because of his or her selfishness, what was stored up will be given to the righteous: "A good man leaves an inheritance [of moral stability and goodness] to his children's children, and the wealth of the sinner [finds its way eventually] into the hands of the righteous, for whom it was laid up" (Proverbs 13:22). **God believes in blessing with riches He does not believe in riches being your god and replacing Him.** So whoever does this because of the influences of the world's economy it will eventually be transferred to someone who remembered to keep God first, honoring Him with his or her capital by blessing others and living well themselves being thankful and humble.

An unsaved or any Saved person for that matter that embraces the world's economy leaves God out of the picture. Either they do not believe that He exists or they do not believe that including Him in their finances is necessary. They do not believe that He could possibly contribute anything substantial to money issues. *The Bible has this to say about people who are a friend to the world's system, "You [are like] unfaithful wives [having illicit love affairs with the world and breaking your marriage vow to God]! Do you not know that being the world's friend is being God's enemy? So whoever chooses to be a friend of the world takes his stand as an enemy of God" (James 4:4).*

The world's thinking is that they tend to trust in their own intellect for all strategies, schemes, plots and arrangements for the management of money and business. How foolish it is to trust only in the knowledge of men when God has created the very tree where man makes his paper that makes his money. *How foolish it is to not know that in the Bible God discusses money more than any other topic because He knew it would be a major issue for people since it is the primary way to exchange goods and services.*

God said, "He frustrates the devices of the crafty, so that their hands cannot perform their enterprise or anything of [lasting] worth. He catches the [so-called] wise in their own trickiness, and the counsel of the schemers is brought to a quick end" (Job 5:12-13).

The world's system teaches that people who belong to the Kingdom of God are not supposed to have wealth or even desire it because according to them "Money is Evil." But in spite of them believing that money is evil the ungodly uses plenty of it for all of their selfish gain, illicit sexual immoral businesses, films, and so on.

What does the Bible say about money and its relationship with Believers and are Christians living without what God intended for their lives? Money has been called everything that represents evil that is designed to destroy your life. I have seen and heard of *people with money* who have had tragic lives with poor health, poor relationships, with bad attitudes and who are just plain wicked. Some of them have committed suicide and have left all of their millions behind. **On the other hand** I have heard of *people living in poverty* who have had tragic lives with poor health, poor relationships, with bad attitudes and are just plain wicked. Some of them have committed suicide and left their poverty stricken lives behind and their families in debt. **So what is the difference if money is supposed to solve everyone's problems, why do we see the same sad stories for both the rich and the poor?**

Money in and of its self is not good or evil. *It is a tool given by God for mankind to advance the Kingdom of God with the good news of Christ; to live on; to help others and exchange goods and services, no more and no less.* It is for everyone and it was not designed only for those with a profession, but for those with a trade, skill, business, a homemaker, farmer, business person, anyone who has a dream and dares to put it into action. **Whose hands the money falls into will determine whether it is used for good or evil purposes.** If it is in the hands of righteous people in Christ and they are taught according to the Word of God to give their tithes and offerings into the house of God then the money will be used for good because as they give the tithe, ten percent, God will bless the ninety percent that is left over. If it is in the hands of greedy and selfish self-centered people doing things that are unlawful then it will be used for wicked purposes.

I Timothy 6:10 says,

> For the **love of money** is a root of all evils; it is through this craving that some have been led astray and have wandered from the faith and pierced themselves through with many acute [mental] pangs.

During the Dark Middle Ages there was an attack on the Church through a Roman Emperor named Constantine who wanted to destroy the Church and stop the people from being prosperous. There was an attempt to remove God out of everything, similar to what is happening in these Last Days (2 Tim. 3:19; Matt. 24:1-44). But, *God is still here* and I do not believe that He is going anywhere! Constantine did a number of wicked things but one that comes to mind is the fact that **he changed the calendar for Believers from the Biblical calendar (aka the Jewish calendar) to a Western or Gregorian calendar around 325 A.D. which starts in January.** This was done so followers of Jesus would not be aware of the Feasts the Lord told His people to observe, in other words, he was blocking the way for God's people to be blessed.

Constantine made it a law that no one could pay their tithes. He also noticed how the people were blessed when they gave first fruit offerings when they acknowledged God on His Feasts (appointed times for God to meet with man) especially at Passover (Pesach); Pentecost (Shavuot); and the Feast of Tabernacles (Sukkot). The Day of Atonement (Yom Kippur) is also very significant. When these Feast were acknowledged the windows of heaven were opened and much revelation was given (Malachi 3:10). *The priests and leaders in the church were also told to take a vow of "poverty." Because the people were not permitted to give for so long it became a habit and the bad habit or disobedience became the norm therefore future generations were not familiar with giving tithes and offerings to the church.* Subsequently many of the churches became poor and now that is what the world (the unsaved) as well as many saved people and churches expect and believe is the correct thing for the church and those that are a part of it. So the thought of giving the tithe or having prosperity (wholeness which includes good health, peace of mind, good relationships, having an abundance of money and so forth) seems like something that was never meant for the church or the Kingdom of God's people.

It was never God's will for families to live in poverty and/or lack. The blood covenant that Believers have with God redeems us from the spirit of poverty because Jesus took poverty to the Cross along with sin and sickness. *To have been released from poverty by a great sacrifice then to choose it, is a slap in the face to the One Who paid the price to remove it from us.* Jesus said, "The thief comes only in order to steal and kill and destroy. I came that they may have and enjoy life, and have it in abundance (to the full, till it overflows)," John 10:10. John prayed, "...that you may prosper in all things and be in health, just as your soul prospers" (3 John 2 NKJV).

Many "religious" institutions teach that it is wrong to have money based on scriptures that have been taken out of context, like the story of the rich young ruler (Mark 10:17-27). Jesus was pointing out that this man's true god had become his money and his possessions that is why he could not part with his "things" to follow Christ like the others did (Mark 10:28; Matt. 19:27-29). *Jesus was asking him to give it up not because it was wrong to have money and nice things but so this young man could receive revelation of what was really important for his life. Once, that had occurred, it would have been restored to him in greater measure* (Mark 10:29-30; Luke 18:28-30; Job 42:10-17). *Using scripture to confirm what Satan wants instead of what Jesus has declared as a part of our covenant with Him, those things He desired and came and died for us to have, to take a stand against His will for His people is wrong.* Especially when there are so many biblical examples that are very clear about what the Lord has done and has given to His people to bless them. **The Word of God reveals many people God empowered to be rich and they stayed rich** until they died and then it was passed on as an inheritance for their descendants (Prov. 13:22).

Many Christians who struggle financially need to stop living in fear of success and with the fear of having money. This theology is a trap to keep you out of a place of prosperity that God has chosen for you to dwell in so your life will be blessed and you will be in a position to bless others. **The scripture <u>does not say</u> that money is evil** what it says is "the <u>love</u> of money is a root of all evils," (I Tim. 6:10). Again, if God is out of the picture or if He is in the picture but not first in your life then something other than God's will, will become first in your life. In most cases since money is used practically everyday to meet some sort of need it won't be long before it takes the place of Almighty God if the money is first in your life. **Moving money out of its place as a tool or device used to: advance the Kingdom of God; to take care of you and your family's needs, wants and desires; and to help others (I Tim. 5:1-5, 8, 16); if money is moved from a place of righteousness it will be moved to a place that allows the money to dictate and control you.** You must **choose** to guard yourself against the love of money. If you begin to love money above all else ignoring the command from God to love Him with all your heart, all your soul, all your strength and all your mind; then love others as you love yourself (Luke 10:27) then you have been deceived into doing dead works. You run the risk of living in fear, worry, fretting, reasoning and analyzing, trying to put your plan together to achieve success and fulfillment. **God never told us to love things but to enjoy them. Money is a "thing" not a person, we control it, and it does not control us.** However, if we give it first place in our lives we can fall into the traps of greed, pride and covetousness (start to wrongly desire the possessions of others). To help us guard against this we are to remember to seek God first and know that if we do this His way all these "things" will be added to us (things taken together will be given to us besides, Matt. 6:33).

When you guard your heart you are keeping it pure and your motives will remain pure before God. When your heart is not pure or what you are doing even for the Kingdom of God is done with the wrong motives it is not rewarded by God, for He looks on the heart of a person not like men who look at the person and their outward actions alone. Therefore, keep a check in this area of your life, **yet don't shun money that can be used for good.** *When you keep God first you won't have to live in fear of greed, pride, guilt and covetousness destroying you.*

Another area to guard your mind and heart from is deceitfulness of riches. **People get caught up in the perceived power that comes with money.** If you do not guard your heart by being selective of what you watch and listen to (especially in the media) and who you fellowship with, deceiving ideas can get into your heart and your heart can begin to change as you become more manipulative using impure motives to gain wealth. This leads to having sorrow that comes when one acquires wealth with means other than ordained by God. For instance: The Bible says that Judas, Lot, Achan and Ananias and Sapphira among others lied, stole, had a lustful eye for things and did whatever was necessary to acquire money and things. All of them had a miserable life and ending. They fell into the trap which changed their hearts and motives and they ended up with impure hearts which led to desires and ways that were not pure. Remember when you wheel and deal with your plots and plans that are not godly, but inspired by the adversary through your thoughts or others, you are only deceiving yourself in an attempt to deceive others by using devices that are crafty, and that are full of tricks and schemes. How? Because our Lord sees all and His Word tries the Word. To put it another way, no one really gets away with underhanded dealings, what you put out there, you will have to answer for, (Job 5:12-13).

John 12:47-48 explains, **He does not judge but Saves, and His Word will judge you**:

> If anyone hears My teachings and fails to observe them [does not keep them, but disregards them], it is not I who judges him. For I have not come to judge and to condemn and to pass sentence and to inflict penalty on the world, but to save the world. Anyone who rejects Me and persistently sets Me at naught, refusing to accept My teachings, has his judge [however]; **for the [very] message that I have spoken will itself judge and convict him at the last day.**

The following passage **demonstrates what happens when you hear the Word of God but you do not receive it into your heart where it could become rooted.** *Because it is not rooted in your heart making a strong foundation to stand on, it in turn is stolen from you. This leads to compromising the Word and will of God, being unwilling or unable to stand for righteousness because you failed to guard your heart from outside voices and deceptive teachings and worldly influences.*

Below Mark 4:16-20 states the interpretation of the parable given in vv. 3-8:

> And in the same way the ones sown upon stony ground are those who, when they hear the Word, at once receive and accept and welcome it with joy; and they have no real root in themselves, and so they endure for a little while; then when trouble or persecution arises on account of the Word, they immediately are offended (become displeased, indignant, resentful) and they stumble and fall away. And the ones sown among the thorns are others who hear the Word; then the cares and anxieties of the world and distractions of the age, and the pleasure and delight and false glamour and deceitfulness of riches, and the craving and passionate desire for other things creep in and choke and suffocate the Word, and it becomes fruitless. And those sown on the good (well-adapted) soil are the ones who hear the Word and receive and accept and welcome it and bear fruit – some thirty times as much as was sown, some sixty times as much, and some [even] a hundred times as much.

When grounded in the Word you will be able to do things God's way. Otherwise, yes, you will acquire but it will bring bad success not good success. God's prosperity may come with persecution but not with sorrow, "The blessing of the Lord –it makes [truly] rich, and He adds no sorrow with it [neither does toiling increase it]," Prov. 10:22. But when it comes without God a host of sorrows will accompany what you have because of how you obtained and made use of it.

When there is a lack of finances most believe that additional work will solve the problem because it will bring in additional money. Though with it may come added stress, time away from your family, lack of a social life and proper rest. All of these will cause problems in other areas of your life. It is as if you solve one problem and add ten more. That is a part of the world's economic system to solving money problems. **Furthermore, the problem is a spiritual one which is not commonly known or known how to be dealt with. When things are out of order and out of balance it is first affected in the spiritual realm then we see the results in the natural.**

The lack of an anointing (power of God) to acquire finances is missing. He said that He empowers us to get wealth (Deut. 8:18). He blesses us with all things and finances are a part of all things. Jesus had the *anointing of multiplication* working in His life. He multiplied two fish and five loaves of bread and fed over five thousand people (Matt. 14:17-21) and on another occasion He took seven loaves and a few fish and fed over four thousand (Matt. 15:36-37). We must understand that because we are saved and a part of Him, we operate with the same anointing that is on His life. Therefore, we have the ability by faith to operate in the anointing of multiplication for any situation, meaning we can apply it in our home, work place, ministry, business or for a project. If the early church (Christians: a combination of Jews and Gentiles, Galatians 4:3; Eph. 2:14) operated in the anointing of multiplication and since God is the same yesterday, today and forever (Heb.13:8) and He said we would do greater works than He did then by the Spirit of God we should be operating in this anointing today at a greater degree (John 14:12).

The following is another example of the *anointing of multiplication* at work. Peter preached about the outpouring of the Holy Spirit and 3,000 people (Jews) got saved that day (Acts 2). A few days after that 5,000 people got saved. We must remember that the same principle of operating by faith applies in every area. By the way, a person receiving their salvation is a greater miracle than producing finances. In the eyes of God one type of miracle is no more difficult than another. The anointing is what makes the difference and that is activated by our faith and our faith is activated by our love. What am I saying? It goes back to the basic principle when we put God first and decide to do things His way (seeking first the Kingdom of God Matt. 6:33) we will have the results of all types of miracles and good things we are looking for as long as our motives for certain things are pure in our hearts.

In order for the anointing of multiplication to be applied to your life you must activate it with the giving of tithes and offerings. Placing your giving into Jesus' hands through His storehouse is the same principle as when they placed the two fish and five loaves in Jesus' hands so that when He gave thanks to His Father the anointing of multiplication was released. When we are thankful coupled with our obedience to give in faith as we release what belongs to God (the tithe which is holy unto God and offerings) at the appointed time then it produces a harvest and will be multiplied back to us. In the meantime, because of the release to conform with His teaching the hedge of protection is strong and as we go through our daily lives we are protected and given favor.

We have concluded that people, Christians included, suffer lack for various reasons. In the natural on the surface it appears that poor management of ones income is the main problem but in reality the lack and problem started in the spiritual realm first as mentioned above. **A person or family may be dealing with a poverty mentality or mind set as the result of a poverty spirit that has been in their generational blood line for decades. This makes it spiritual** because you are in a battle with demonic forces that are on assignment to block your increase. With this type of mindset you are unable or unwilling to battle successfully. One reason being, you are unable or unwilling to see God for who He is and are unable or unwilling to fully trust and believe that He will come through for you. You are unable to wait on His timing. You have a poverty conversation and confession such as, I can't afford this; we can't do that; it cost too much; I can't see myself living in that house or that neighborhood or having a vehicle like that; it is a waste of money to eat out on occasions; and so forth. **When you speak in lack you reinforce the stronghold spirit of poverty that is working against you and you prevent angels from moving on your behalf.**

There are other spirits or behaviors that also contribute to poverty or struggling financially. Some of those have already been mentioned but will be mentioned again in order to group them altogether and they are: the fear of lack which will prevent you from giving; fear of success; doubt in God's ability or desire to help you; pride during times when you are prosperous; guilt and condemnation; sin and sin consciousness; laziness; procrastination; jealousy; envy; strife; heavy drinking; being wasteful; making money your god; unthankful; selfishness; constant worry about money and things; seeking things *first* above God; bitterness; unforgiveness; impure motives; ignoring the laws of the land; plots and plans against others; not taking care of what has already been entrusted to you and withholding tithes and offerings are to name a few that block the anointing from flowing and bringing consistency to you in way of empowering you to be blessed.

Whatever has been attempted to resolve the financial problem (higher education, starting a business, promotion at work, second and third jobs and so on) nothing seems to work to really change the situation. It is because you are fighting demonic spirits that are working against your fruit and harvest coming to fruition. Basically the adversary desires for the Children of God to live in ruins. He wants their focus to be on the cares of the world, how we are going to eat, where we are going to live, what we are going to wear, etc. Because their entire concentration is on their personal and immediate needs instead of where it belongs, on their assignment or purpose from God to bring glory to His name, they run the risk of growing weak and being overtaken by evil assignments working against them. They will not be in a position to fight against the kingdom of darkness and cause it any real damage. Ephesians 4:27 says, "Leave no [such] room or foothold for the devil [give no opportunity to him]. A change needs to take place but not just any change you devise on your own because as you have seen that does not guarantee any real change.

The world's way is in the natural you speak what you see and hear. In the Kingdom of God you line your words up with the Word of God in spite of what you see and hear. Words are spirit and have power, so when we speak them we will have what we say. Therefore, in lieu of the negative report from your mouth change it and use godly positive words. For example: instead of saying "I can't afford it" say "I do not have the funds set aside for that right now so I will do it later;" or you could say, "my money is already allotted for something else at this time so I'll make a note and take care of that at some other time." You are not lying you are still admitting you do not have the funds for something but you are *not confessing that you do not have any money nor will you ever have it.* What you are saying is not working against you in the spiritual realm. By confessing that you will do it later you can activate something in the spiritual realm that is now going to move on your behalf if you believed it when you said it. If you really did believe then you activated your faith and now angelic forces will start to move on your behalf instead of demonic forces moving against your finances. The Bible says that "death and life are in the power of the tongue, and they who indulge in it shall eat the fruit of it," you choose (Prov. 18:21). Be mindful of the words you put into the spiritual realm (the atmosphere) because angels and demons are waiting for instructions to move on your words. Angelic angels pick your words up to bring the manifestation when your words come from the Word of God, (Psalm 103:20; Isa. 55:11). Demons pick them up when they are negative words full of doubt and unbelief and bring those to pass. (See this Chapter under Clarity about Spirits and the Spiritual Realm and this Chapter under Spiritual Warfare Weapons number 3).

GOD'S PROSPERITY IS A PART OF HIS KINGDOM AND IT DIFFERS FROM THE WORLD'S ECONOMIC SYSTEM:

The Hebrew word for prosperity is "Shalom" because *God's prosperity includes wholeness, peace, provision, safety, favor, good relationships with family and friends and wellness in every area of your life; nothing broken or lacking and nothing missing, things are functioning and operating in your life the way it should according to the Word of God.* **Shalom starts with God's plan for your life.** In Jeremiah 29:11 is God's future for us: "For I know the thoughts and plans that I have for you, says the Lord, thoughts and plans for welfare and peace and not for evil, to give you hope in your final outcome."

Ephesians 2:10 says God prearranged and made ready for us the "good life:"

> For we are God's [own] handiwork (His workmanship), recreated in Christ Jesus, [born a new] that we may do those good works God predestined (planned beforehand) for us [taking paths which He prepared ahead of time], that we should walk in them [living the good life which He prearranged and made ready for us to live.

God's plan for prosperity is different from the world. *His plan may include gold, money, silver, great things to posses but it does not necessarily start or stop there.*

Prosperity and welfare are in His house, and His righteousness endures forever.

One way He honors us is to prosper us. John prayed, "that you may prosper in every way and [that your body] may keep well, even as [I know] your soul keeps well and prospers" (3 John 2). *God's prosperity includes the whole man. He is concerned about us beyond our finances. His prosperity covers every part of our lives, our overall well-being, our health, our peacefulness, happiness, safety, the relationships in our lives, are we fulfilling our purpose, the assignment He has given each of us that will bring us into the abundant life He intended for us to have?* John 10:10 declares that He came that we may have and enjoy life, and have it in abundance (to the full, till it overflows). *His financial plan is to bring us into His Shalom, His completion. His plan is to prosper us and not do us harm.* This prosperous life will be the result of dedication to God in keeping Him first. Being committed will cause us to have a quality life with an ongoing progressive state of good success.

Christian Believers are anointed at the time of salvation. When we need wisdom in a particular area we ask for it. God's way of managing money and finances in His economic system is different from the world's economic system which basically teaches that money is your god and it is better to store it up for yourself, increase and multiply your assets for you, your family and no more. God's economic system teaches us to store up as well but at the same time to give where He is asking us to give. By giving the anointing not only continues to flow but it causes multiplication. His economic system meets all of our needs even when something supernatural has to take place in order to make sure our needs are met. As His sons and daughters (mature Christians) trust the leading of the Holy Spirit in regards to what He has entrusted to them to manage they will not have to be concerned about money issues because they have learned to rest (trust) in Him. **They will pray and cast their care and trust God for an answer that will manifest on time whether through favor or resources and it will be on time for God's purpose not theirs.**

As we ask for wisdom and guidance He grants it to us. He will give us skillful and godly Wisdom, for from His mouth comes knowledge and understanding. He says that, "He hides away sound and godly Wisdom and stores it for the righteous (those who are upright and in right standing with Him). **His knowledge is not the world's knowledge. His knowledge is divine revelation and understanding (Prov. 2:6-7; 3:5-6).** The Word of God says, "The reverent and worshipful fear of the Lord is the beginning and the principal and choice part of knowledge [its starting point and its essence]; but fools despise skillful and godly Wisdom, instruction, and discipline" (Prov. 1:7).

Proverbs 115:13-14 says, "He will bless those who reverently and worshipfully fear the Lord, both small and great. *May the Lord give you increase more and more, you and your children."* As far as your children are concerned He continues by saying, "*A good man leaves an inheritance [of moral stability and goodness] to his children's children..."* Prov. 13:22. In other words, a good man (righteous in Christ) will leave goodness which is the manifestation of the glory of God and what God blessed him with (tangible, wisdom, love or whatever he had that blessed and enhanced) that will not only be able to bless his children but his grandchildren as well. It became a generational blessing which was handed down because of the person's salvation and receiving God's glory on their life. "For my thoughts are not your thoughts, neither are your ways my ways, saith the Lord."

"Jesus was always conscious of abundance. His eyes were on the Kingdom of God where there is always abundance. God does not want you to be conscious of the lack in your natural circumstances. He does not want you to live by how much you earn or how much you have in the bank. He wants you to be conscious of the abundance of resources in His Kingdom; be conscious first of the abundance inside of you. Then, what is inside of you will become a reality on the outside." [8] Emphasis added.

The Lord delights in making you rich according to Deut. 8:18 which says,

"But you shall [earnestly] remember the Lord your God, for **it is He Who gives you power to get wealth**, that He may establish

His covenant which He swore to your fathers, as it is this day."

Deuteronomy 28:1-14, He commands the blessing upon you:

> v.8 ...**The Lord shall command the blessing upon you in your storehouse** and in all that you undertake. And He will bless you in the land which the Lord your God gives you...

Those who truly worship shall not want nor lack any beneficial thing Ps. 34: 9-10:

> O fear the Lord, you His saints [revere and worship Him]! For **there is no want to those who truly revere and worship Him with godly fear.** The young lions lack food and suffer hunger, but they who seek (inquire of and require) the Lord [by right of their need and on the authority of His Word], **none of them shall lack any beneficial thing.**

The Father will keep His word to our forefathers, Abraham, Isaac and Jacob because of the blood covenant He established through the line of King David and ratified in the Blood of Jesus.

COVENANT PEOPLE THAT GOD MADE RICH:

The Bible is full of covenant people that God made rich and they remained so until their deaths and then it was passed to their children (Prov. 13:22). He is always looking ahead beyond just their needs or mission and looking at the future generations in that person's life. For instance, with **Abraham He made him extremely wealthy**, "And I will make of you a great nation, and I will bless you [with abundant increase of favors] and make your name famous and distinguished, and you will be blessed [dispensing good to others]. And I will bless those who bless you [who confer prosperity or happiness upon you] and curse him who curses or uses insolent language toward you; *in you will all the families and kindred of the earth be blessed [and by you they will bless themselves]" Gen. 12:2-3.* **The Blessing of Abraham is a material blessing (land, money, goods) for you to live a good life while on the earth.** *Because of Jesus we inherited the Spiritual Blessings which included spiritual authority in His name to resist and destroy evil that comes to rob us of the good successful life that Jesus acquired for us.*

Others that the Lord made rich were Abraham's seed, **Isaac** (Gen. 26:12-14; 24-25) and grandson **Joseph** (Gen. 41:39-44) who became the second most powerful and wealthiest man in Egypt. Joseph was the son of Jacob who was one of Isaac's sons, also had favor on his life for prosperity. Then there was **Solomon** who was the richest man in the world then and still holds that record. "The temple he built for the Lord was estimated at $87 billion and this does not include his personal wealth (according to a report by the Illinois Society of Architects in 1925)." [8] He asked God for wisdom and knowledge to go out and come in before God's people. He wanted to rule in the eyes of God and be pleasing to God as He took care of the people. So God not only granted him with the wisdom but because he was not asking for riches for himself, God also granted Him wealth, "Solomon, because this was in your heart and you have not asked for riches, possessions, honor, and glory, or the life of your foes, even for long life, but have asked wisdom and knowledge for yourself, that you may rule and judge My people... **wisdom and knowledge are granted you. And I will give you riches, possessions, honor, and glory such as none of the kings had before you, and none after you shall have their equal**" 2 Chron. 1:9-12. God made Solomon the wealthiest man in the world for all time after He had made him king over His people. Another was, **Job,** it tells us that the Lord blessed the latter days of

Job's life and he had double what he had before his life changed (Job 1:1-3; 42:12) .

You may think that those are all Old Testament wealthy people but does God still bless and/or provide wealth for His people today? God never changes (Heb.13:8), those that are descendants of Abraham through the line of King David were given, as mentioned earlier, "The Abrahamic Blessing" because of the covenant sealed by the Blood of the Lamb of God. So yes, it is for today. The Word of God makes it clear that what God did for Abraham was for his descendants forever through an everlasting pledge by God. In Genesis 17:7 it says, "And I will establish My covenant between Me and you and your descendants after you through their generations for an everlasting, solemn pledge, to be a God to you and to your posterity after you." Galatians 3:16 is the New Testament version of this scripture. Also in Galatians 3:28-29 it says, "There is [now no distinction] neither Jew nor Greek, there is neither slave nor free, there is not male and female; for you are all one in Christ Jesus. *And if you belong to Christ [are in Him Who is Abraham's Seed], then you are Abraham's offspring and [spiritual] heirs according to promise."*

The Bible says in 2 Corinthians 9:10 – He will increase the fruits of your righteousness [which manifests in active **goodness...**]; and in Proverbs 13:22 where it says a good man leaves an inheritance [of moral stability and **goodness]...** in both of these verses the word *goodness* is God actually manifesting His goodness in a way that you can experience it with your five senses: you can see it, smell it, taste it, hear it and touch it because it is a tangible, visible thing that shows the evidence of what God has promised and told you that He would do. Your proof has been revealed by the manifestation of His goodness.

How can you leave an inheritance to your children's children if you are suppose to be broke, busted and in lack all of your life? **God never said that His children, the Saints, the covenant people of God, had to live with lack or in poor health to please Him. That gives Him no glory and who would**

desire to serve a God like that? Poverty is not from God it is a demonic force/spirit and God is not glorified when His people live in poverty or lack. The Bible says that it is our faith that pleases God not demonic attacks that come against us. It also says that the wealth of the sinner (someone who is *not* Born-again) finds its way eventually into the hands of the righteous (those who *are* Born-again) because acquiring wealth without God is illegal and therefore what has been robbed has to be returned to its rightful owner (Prov. 6:31). God is the owner of all and has placed all things under man's feet as He has empowered His people to get wealth (Ps 8:6; Deut. 8:18).

Jesus came to fulfill the 'Law' not to do away with it, and in fulfilling it He became the curse on the tree so we do not have to endure the curse. *Jesus did not change the order of blessing or do away with it. What empowered a person to receive a blessing from God under the Old Testament will empower a person to receive a blessing today.* We are not excluding trials, test, tribulations, problems, attacks, broken hearts, betrayal, and so forth because bad things happen to everyone; but how one handles them and how one receives the victory over them is the difference in regard to those who just acquire or accumulate money as oppose to those who have <u>God's prosperity and true wealth which supersedes only having money.</u>

There are numerous scriptures in the Word of God located in the New Testament as well as the Old Testament that support the fact that God has always desired for His people, His children to prosper. He told us to choose life or death and in life there is God's prosperity when you are walking with the Almighty.

My point is this, the world's people expect those who have a personal relationship with God to be poor. But that was never God's plan for His people. Throughout history those that dared to follow the Lord and not yield to the world's system were not in lack and quite prosperous according to God's definition of prosperity.

However, the thought that Christians are suppose to be poor or just have enough to live and get by on, is received and well known because of a belief that has circulated for centuries. **People see Jesus as someone who is Holy and since He is seen as the "Christian's God and Role Model," the thought is, since Jesus was poor then poverty must be holy and for a Christian to have wealth is considered a curse or a sin** *(which is completely false). Needless to say this goes against everything written from God to His people from the book of Genesis to the book of Revelation.* This is one of the greatest lies that were introduced to the Body of Christ (His church) and to the world. In addition, with **certain "religious" institutions taking a vow of poverty** (even though it was forced on the church during the Middle Ages) did not help the situation. There needs to be a renewing of the mind and people reeducated about what the Bible says about money (Romans 12:2).

Jesus left a great abundance of wealth in heaven to come to earth. In comparison to what He had is what made Him appear poor. But on earth He did not *become what was considered poor* **until he took our poverty and gave us His wealth at the Cross on Calvary (Galatians 3:13-14).**

2 Corinthians 8:9 says,

> "...though He was [so very] rich, yet for your sakes He became [so very] poor, in order that by His poverty you might become enriched (abundantly supplied) (See also John 10:10).

However, "before the cross, Jesus was given great gifts of gold, frankincense and myrrh when he was a toddler in his home with His family (Matt. 2:7-12). When the disciples who were a combination of commercial fishermen, a doctor and a tax collector set aside their businesses to follow Him for a season and later they preached the Gospel, these men nor their ministry ever lacked for anything. Jesus' ministry even had a treasurer (Judas) something you do not need if there is no money. He also told His disciples not to take money with them on some of their trips so they could increase their faith and rely on God to take care of them one hundred percent. Jesus clothes were so fine that the Roman solders gambled over His garment" [10] (Emphasis added to reference).

Jesus was an extremely humble man but also straight to the point (Phil. 2:8-9). What He did not have in their travels He simply prayed and the wisdom was imparted along with signs and wonders to get the work done or whatever was needed to be fulfilled.

God's Economic System is opposite from the World's Economic System because it is managed with the wisdom of God and not mere intellect that does not offer the divine. God knows all things and is all powerful, therefore, we would rather place our trust in *a proven system* that has never failed than keep pouring into one that is *failing more* and more each and everyday.

WHEN INCOME IS APPLIED TO BIBLICAL TRUTHS AND PRINCIPLES YOUR SEED WILL RESIST THE ADVERSARY AND ALLOW SUPERNATURAL INCREASE OR FINANCIAL PROGRESS:

In the Kingdom the people are instructed through the Word God to give their Tithes and Offering (Mal. 3:8-12), to have savings, to give to ministries that have international outreaches that reach out to help people all over the world and to other types of ministries as directed by the Holy Spirit. We are asked to be good stewards over what we have already been entrusted with so God can give the increase. We are to remain righteous before the Lord so He can bless our children and our children' children.

A godly plan of action is needed to stop the spiritual battle over finances and to begin recovery from financial loss. A Biblical Spending Plan (BSP) is one way to get back on track.

But before we discuss a biblical plan to handle finances lets look at the instruments used in the "natural" by most people

and when not coupled with biblical principles it will usually lead to debt because divine wisdom has not been included.

Many blended families will start their marriages in debt. Unlike some first time marriages where the couple acquire together and could make wrong choices that lead to debt second and third marriages inherit these debts from their former marriages which compound the problems of overcoming debt during the early stages of their marriage. After prayer and listing debts, most should be able to manage with the proper advice or training. Some will need to seek out financial advisors such as a Christian accountant, banker, financial planner, broker, CPA or an insurance agent. In some cases an attorney may be needed if you feel you must file bankruptcy (not God's perfect will) or you are dealing with some other type of financial litigation or contract. *Because there are so many options it is best to seek God first and receive in your heart which plan of action or help would be better for you and your family in order to set your records back in order and come out of debt.*

The Master Strategist can be your financial planner. Seeking Him through His Word by studying out scriptures regarding money issues as well as reading Christian material regarding finances will impart the wisdom of God to you in this area.

Proverbs 21:30 states:

> There is no [human] wisdom or understanding or counsel [that can prevail] against the Lord.

Before long with diligence and discipline you will be directed out of debt through natural means or supernatural miracles with the anointing of multiplication, increase or debt cancellation done on your behalf. The old will be behind you and new methods and strategies for managing your income will be in place. Because of the renewing of your mind in the Word of God and having a heart for Him with the right attitude, hindrances will be removed and deliverance in your finances can take place at the appointed time. Because of your decision to do things His way you have opened yourself up to hear new and better ways of handling your finances.

It takes time to build wealth especially in the natural. Therefore, take your time and learn the best protection and type of entity; structure; tax strategy; what is the proper insurance for you and your family; learn about capital; how to best invest to protect your principle; record and keep good records; remove distractions and do not allow zeal to cause you to over extend yourself or make decisions too fast. Some things will require a long term approach. **Even when cooperating with the spiritual aspects you will continue to use natural instruments or storehouses** (checking and savings accounts, money market accounts, certificates of deposit, mutual funds, insurance plans and so forth) for your finances, Deut. 28:8. Remember a successful financial plan does not start with a Biblical Spending Plan (budget), savings, building and investing in different properties or corporations, but rather it begins in the spiritual realm first through your prayers so you can receive divine wisdom, instructions and direction for your financial well being.

When it is **spiritual it starts with a plan – God's plan of prosperity that is tailor made for you if you are in His family. It may come through a dream or a vision or directly from the mouth of God.** You will need faith, strength, the gifts and skills He has allotted to you and His connections to make it a reality. You will need to be sensitive to His leading so you can move forth in the right season with the right people in the correct location or whatever is required to bring it to fruition. You will need to maintain your personal relationship with Jesus who will communicate with you by His Spirit. Giving you sound advice and an unction that will warn if a wrong decision is about to be made or if it is the right decision and to move on it quickly. You will need to plant seed (give) in good ground (the ministry you are directed to give into that will cause a prosperous return to you because of their obedience to God to be good ground) in order to build a harvest. You will also have an advantage operating with the Spirit of God, His Word and angles at your disposal regarding finances that the world just does not have. He will empower you with His grace to enable you to become wealthy in more areas than money. You will be blessed and live a blessed life.

HOW TO COME OUT OF DEBT BY USING SPIRITUAL AND NATURAL INSTRUMENTS:

- Believing and trusting God and doing things His way by allowing the anointing of the Holy Spirit to flow in your life daily to guide and teach you;
- By consistently giving your tithes and offerings where you are being fed the Word of God and built up in the Spirit. Giving tithes and offerings is an avenue to prosperity as well. It will keep you protected as a part of your hedge of protection (Malachi 3:11). We are to give offerings into good ground where the Holy Spirit is directing us to do so. Giving your **tithe and offerings is a Godly principle; and it is the connection that releases "The Blessing" that was placed on mankind all the way back to the book of Genesis. Giving started <u>before</u> the "Law" and it is for today (2 Cor. 9:6-11 and I Cor. 3:6-11). For example: The very reason Cain killed Abel was the fact that God received Abel's "Offering" and Cain became angry. This shows that God was receiving from people long before the Law was ever known (Gen. 4:1-8; Heb. 11-4).** Abram was blessed by Melchizedek when Abram gave the tithe (10th) to Him (Gen. 14:18-20).You only rob yourself of the blessings it brings when you *reason with your mind* that tithing and giving offerings is outdated or not

intended for the church when the Bible and much evidence says otherwise.
- **Some do not give because they feel they cannot afford it**, well you cannot afford not to give. It is all a matter of how much you are able to trust God to come through for you. He said when you give the tenth that it is holy and furthermore it belongs to Him. In addition, when we give our tithe God blesses the ninety percent because we honored the tenth as it is holy unto Him. As you give the tenth one way that He blesses the rest is to supernaturally stretch or increase it. Another way is to give you great discounts, connections, favor and miracles.
- When you give to God's house you are not giving to the people, the leadership or the preacher (minister), you are obeying a commandment to give to God's house so there will be food (resources) in His house (Mal. 3:10). **Many people do not tithe nor give offerings because they feel they are supporting a preacher's lifestyle. However, the Bible says that if you preach the Gospel you are to be paid by the Gospel (I Cor. 9:13-14; Num. 18:21).** People in the congregation have a *kingly anointing*, to work and prosper, and as they give into the *priestly anointing*, the man or woman of God are freed up to pray, study, seek and receive fresh revelation from God to feed the people's spirit man so they will remain in a place of strength, growth and prosperity. Also, God has anointed many preachers **(ministers of the Gospel) in this hour to have** *both, a priestly and kingly anointing,* **to manage and prosper in the blessings and businesses God is transferring to His Kingdom during these End Times in order to prosper the people of God in all walks of life.** As you take

care of God's house, He will take care of yours! (Proverbs 13:22; Matthew 24:1-44).
- Tithing teaches you how to respect your money and keep a balanced life. If you respect money and use it as a tool for the Kingdom of God, living expenses, investments and helping others and not make it a god you will keep it in the right perspective and have balance in your financial life.
- *As already mentioned we should always remember to give first fruit offerings during the time of God's three major feast where the windows of heaven are open and He is pouring out blessings of revelation, promises being fulfilled and so forth* (Malachi 3:10). God's Feasts which are times God selected to meet with man are: The Feast of Passover; the Feast of Pentecost; and the Feast of Tabernacles. Also the Feast of Rosh Hashanah (Trumpets) is a time to be aware of for it is the beginning of the Biblical Civil New Year as Passover is the beginning of the Biblical Spiritual New Year. Beautiful Biblical calendars that will help you become familiar with God's appointed days to meet with mankind and timing plus information regarding His Feast and other topics are available for those who are led to honor God on His important days can be purchased by going online at www.store.jewsforjesus.org or call (877) 463-7742. You can also go online at www.ifcj.org for the International Fellowship of Christians and Jews to acquire teachings regarding God's Feast, other information and prayer request for His chosen people.
- All Christians at one time celebrated these appointed times but they were removed from them when the calendar was changed by the Roman Emperor Constantine around 325 A.D. now in these last of the last days God is opening the minds of His people and giving revelation

as well as restoration of those things which were stolen. The Lord gives us power to get wealth (Deut. 8:18), it is a sign of His covenant with us. Whatever amount is entrusted to you, you have a responsibility to preserve it and grow it and extend the Kingdom of God, realizing it is not just for you to be comfortable but for you to make a difference in other people's lives as you are led by the Holy Spirit.

- Repent for being in debt and receive God's forgiveness.
- An example of a **"Biblical Spending Plan"** (budget) would include: 10% Tithe; 10% Savings; Offerings, Taxes, Emergency Fund, and Expenditures. **Savings is a major part of God's spending plan.** It is used to set aside money for various reasons including paying or giving to yourself and/or for your household. It is extremely important to set up savings accounts and designate them for short or long term goals as well as being specific to name what the savings account is for. Note: Even though many tithe on their gross income, savings and offerings are planned from the net income.
- **Commit to something you can save consistently.** It is better to save less consistently than to save more inconsistently. Always place saving at the top of the debt list or you may never have a chance to save. Keep in mind that **spending habits change for people during the summer months and holidays,** therefore, for your business, plan ahead for those times. Your biblical example –the ant gathers in the summer to make provision for the winter, Prov. 6:6-8. [11]
- It is a godly principle to **take savings and pay off old debts.** You should not save money for yourself while you still owe money to others. Save for

the purpose of paying off old debts, or whatever your specific goal is. [11]
- **Do not touch savings that is designated for long term goals** such as taxes, investments, large purchases unless it is a real emergency like life or death so the money can be used for what it is designated for – use wisdom. [11]
- **Use different accounts without an attachment to ATM or some other form of quick withdrawal.** *Designate accounts for different purposes.* [11]
- Since money decreases in value over a period of time it is wise to **transfer it from cash to an asset that will increase in value** such as real property (home or commercial), stocks, bonds, mutual funds, gold, CD accounts, owning a business and other types of investments.[11]
- **Withdrawing from your heavenly account or spiritual storehouse**: Once you pray over and release your tithe and offerings there is a corresponding deposit into your heavenly account. That deposit is multiplied so when you make a withdrawal it is always given back to you in greater measure, "And [God] Who provides seed for the sower and bread for eating *will also provide and multiply your [resources* for] sowing and increase the fruits of your righteousness…" 2 Cor. 9-10. It could be returned in money, or opportunities, open doors that have been closed to you, a healing, a breakthrough or whatever your need is. **Because by faith you planted something now God has something in His hands from you that He can work with; like Jesus was given the two fish and five loaves and fed five thousand men plus** thousands more with women and children (Matthew 14:17-21). That same anointing of multiplication will be on your seed when it is manifested, because you

gave and placed it in the hands of a living God. When it comes back it will come to you in areas that you really need a breakthrough or possibly a miracle.

- **Our motive for giving and the measure by which we give play a key role in the rewards we receive.** Luke 6:38 NIV says, "Give, and it will be given to you. A good measure, pressed down, shaken together and running over, will be poured into your lap. For with the measure you use, it will be measured to you." "Our motives for giving usually determine the rewards we expect. Like a generous merchant who dispenses a heaping measure of grain, God pours out love and blessings to those who exhibit love for others by gracious giving. The greatest reward to the faithful giver is the joy of participating in Christ's ministry and seeing the results. Christ taught that rewards are gifts from God." [1]

- **When withdrawing from your heavenly account be specific about the amount or deed requested**; lay hold of it by faith (Mark 11:24); come in agreement with another Believer (Matt. 18:19); use your authority in Jesus' name and bind the devil and his forces by standing on Mark 16:17 and then tell him not to come back in that area of your life (Mark 9:25). Now loose the forces of heaven, "whatever I forbid and declare to be improper and unlawful on earth must be what is already forbidden in heaven, and whatever I permit and declare proper and lawful on earth must be what is already permitted in heaven" (Matt. 18:18); now send the angels to get what it is that you are requesting that is in God's will. Thank God by praising Him for the manifestation. We serve a "now" God (Ps 118:25).

Trust Him and praise Him for it being done even though you have not seen it yet.
- No matter how much you save, unless you **change your mentality about the amount you have saved** it will never be what you think it should be, so do not fall into the trap that you do not have enough to give or do what God is saying because He made the provision for whatever it is you have. [11]
- When your income is lined up with godly principles, wisdom will follow. As you continue with the Biblical Spending Plan your savings will become greater and your assets will increase and/or your liabilities will decrease.

ALL SOCIETIES ARE IN THE PROCESS OF EXPERIENCING A TRANSFER OF WEALTH:

Hebrews 12:27-29 NKJV says,

> Now this, "Yet once more," indicates the removal of those things that are being shaken, as of things that are made, that the things which cannot be shaken may remain. Therefore, since we are receiving a Kingdom which cannot be shaken, let us have grace, by which we may serve God acceptably with reverence and godly fear. For our God is a consuming fire.

This will consist of God transferring wealth from the unrighteous to the righteous in Christ at the appointed time within the season we are currently in (Prov. 13:22). **One strong indication that it has begun is that a shaking takes place in the land and everything that is not of God will not stand.** This indicates that God is in the midst of doing a work that He has already declared in His Word. Darkness will continue in the land and grow even worse but the Kingdom of Light will shine as the people of God will live in God's true prosperity of having wholeness in every area of their lives which will include health, peace, relationships, provision, safety and so forth. They will inherit the ideas, strategies and inventions that will be needed to sustain in this hour. They will have a stream of wisdom that will be needed for the times we are living in. God will transfer more than financial wealth, He will transfer whatever it is going to take to make His people the head and not the tail, the lender and not the borrower (Deut. 28:13 and Prov. 22:7).

Whereas with God He said "For I know the thoughts and plans that I have for you, says the Lord, thoughts and plans for welfare and peace and not for evil, to give you hope in your final outcome." The NIV says, "...plans to give you hope and a future" (Jeremiah 29:11). God's plans for His people always includes grace (the ability to do things you could not do, have what you could not have before and to receive what you could not receive). The Kingdom of God's economic system is designed to empower its followers to prosper in every area of their lives and that includes finances contrary to what most Christians and Non-Christians believe.

The importance of this point was shared earlier but it needs to be re-emphasized. In the Kingdom the people are instructed through the Word to give their Tithes and Offerings (Mal. 3:8-12), to have savings, to give to ministries that have international outreaches that reach out to help people all over the world and to other types of ministries as directed by the Holy Spirit. We are asked to be good stewards over what we have already been entrusted with so God can give increase. We are to remain righteous before the Lord so He can bless our children and our children's children (Prov. 13:22).

The Kingdom's Economic System, which is a higher system, teaches us to give and be fruitful and productive with our resources and finances and to bless others. In doing so we are following the ways of Christ.

This brief quote defines *Christian Economics, those in the Kingdom of God who incorporate God's plan in their finances and everyday living:* [7]

> Since economics is the science that deals with production, distribution, and consumption of goods and services, Christian Economics is the "discipline that studies the application of Biblical principles or laws to the production, distribution, and consumption of goods and services." It entails "how men use God-given natural resources, ideas, and energy to meet their human needs and glorify Him.
>
> Christianity produces internal liberty in man, which is the foundation for a Christian economy. The internal change of heart that Christ brings produces Christian character and self-government which is necessary for an economy to be prosperous. Christian character and self-government: People who will not steal; People with a strong work ethic who will labor hard and be productive. This will cause an economy to grow; People who save and invest to acquire greater return later; and People who have concern for their posterity and will seek to pass on a greater estate than they received.
>
> The truth of the gospel also imparts new ideas and creativity to man which assists him in increasing his material welfare. This occurs as man creates new and better tools. In addition, man gains the understanding that God has given him an abundance to rule the earth and if he seeks His supply, he will find it.

When we do things God's way He will prosper us and we will not have sorrows come with it that the world has. "The blessing of the Lord, it makes [truly] rich, and He adds no sorrow with it [neither does toiling increase it], Prov. 10:22. We can increase God's way and keep our joy, peace, and have good relationships with our family and friends while we have rich and nice things. Why is this possible? Because our focus is not on the things because we realize they are only things to enjoy. We are called to love God and people. If we keep the correct perspective the "things" that are added as a part of the reward and blessing for making the decision to handle our finances the way God intended for them to be handled won't get out of balance and cause us to stray. "For the Kingdom of God is not meat and drink; but righteousness, and peace, and joy in the Holy Ghost (Spirit)" (Romans 14:17 KJV).

We are instructed to seek His righteousness. Righteousness is "that state which makes a person acceptable to God." Righteousness is the force of absolute rightness; where integrity is expressed and is a part of your life because our righteousness is in Christ. We know that apart from Him we can do nothing except run the risk of being pulled off track by deception (John 15:5). As long as there is peace the Holy Spirit is able to dwell and communicate with us. His joy gives us strength which is necessary as we trust God day by day. In Matthew 6:33 KJV says, "But seek ye first the Kingdom of God, and His righteousness; and *all these things shall be added unto you.*" It goes on to say in v34, "**So do not worry or be anxious about tomorrow**, for tomorrow will have worries and anxieties of its own. Sufficient for each day is its own trouble." Instead remember, "if God so clothes the grass of the field, which today is alive and green and tomorrow is tossed into the furnace, will He not much more surely clothe you…?" (v30).

If you are dealing with generational curses of poverty over your finances the following are instructions that will help to set them free and remove the strongholds so that your will regarding money will line up with the will of God and manifestation can take place. **How do we fight and break these generational curses regarding finances?** When we receive our salvation the blood that was shed to seal our covenant with God breaks the curse (Romans 10:9). Next we should receive the Infilling of the Holy Spirit so we can successfully battle in the spirit without demonic agents knowing what we are praying about or what strategies God is revealing (Acts 2:2-4; I Cor. 2:4-5). Learn of Him by renewing our minds in the Word of God (Romans 12:2) and as we learn of Him begin to use the authority He has given us in His name. We realize we are not fighting against flesh and blood so we put on the whole armor of God to do battle (Eph. 6:10-18). We fight with the Word of God which "is quick, and powerful, and sharper than any two edged sword, piercing even to the dividing asunder of soul and spirit, and of the joints and marrow, and is a discerner of the thoughts and intents of the heart," (Hebrews 4:12 KJV).

Next, we do not receive the reports that come from the World's Economic System declaring a recession or any other thing that is negative regarding finances because those reports are for the unbelievers to instill fear and affect whatever little faith they have in any goodness or fairness in the laws of the land or the banking institutions. Christians are not under that economic system and therefore do not need to take heed to their reports in their hearts. Because we walk by faith and not by sight and we will not be moved from our place of increase. We recognize that we need to be in position as God is transferring the wealth to His Kingdom's Economic System. We are to remember His ways so that our "faith might not rest in the wisdom of men (human philosophy), but in the power of God," (Prov. 13:22; 1 Co 2:5; Gal. 3:11; Heb.19:11; 2 Co. 5:7; Hab. 2:4).

Last but certainly not least know that there is a name that is above every name including the names of want, lack, poverty, past due notice, foreclosure and the like that will be removed from our lives once and for all as we conquer operating in the Kingdom's system and break curses. Therefore, stop being a borrower and become a lender, Prov. 22:7. *We give thanks because of His sacrifice where He became very poor, "He laid aside His existence with the Father to be born for our salvation…giving up the riches of heaven, that we might be made rich with His blessings" (2 Cor. 8:9).*[1]

SECTION THREE

DISCOVER WHO HAS THE REAL POWER TO CHANGE HEARTS, LIVES AND CIRCUMSTANCES AS WELL AS THE POWER TO RESTORE, REVIVE AND RECONSTRUCT

IF GOD IS FOR US, WHO [CAN BE] AGAINST US? WHO CAN BE OUR FOE, IF GOD IS ON OUR SIDE? THE LORD CONTENDS WITH THOSE WHO CONTEND WITH US; HE FIGHTS AGAINST THOSE WHO WAR AGAINST US UNTIL THEY ARE AS NOTHING. HE SAYS FEAR NOT, I WILL HELP YOU! Romans 8:31; Isaiah 49:25; Isaiah 41:12-13 (Paraphrased)

The real power to change hearts, lives and circumstances then restore, revive and reconstruct can only be fulfilled by One God and that is the Trinity: The Father, The Son and The Holy Spirit. Three distinct personalities with unique responsibilities working together with all power and wisdom for your good.

As most Blended families ours started as well with some of the baggage most people bring into new relationships. Learning each other and sorting through years of hurt and negative emotions from both families was not an easy task. But we basically had an advantage because we were divinely connected, a supernatural love had been released by the Holy Spirit thus we had God on our side and we were all on His. We also experienced a lot of wonderful days and family time in spite of prior years of great disappointments.

Because we were a **God-Blended Family** we were aware that we were all divinely brought together and trusting God. And because of trusting Him, the "Comforter" was sent and He did a supernatural work in all those who would receive it.

Our "Helper," The Holy Spirit had a strong hand in changing hearts, guiding, shaping, and structuring not only the outer appearance but the very soul of our immediate family. He orchestrated deliverance for each family member His way and in His timing to ensure success and to bring completion to each ones process of healing. We understood that it was only God through His mercy, grace and teachings that would bring us to certain points in the reconstruction or building of our **God-Blended Family** that was needed to maintain and endure until full recovery and restoration were manifested in each member.

In addition, to building godly character and trusting in God The Holy Spirit taught us strategies on how to walk by faith and not by sight by allowing Him to develop our faith so we could follow through with instructions; by developing our spiritual weapons and tools as well as developing the fruit of the Spirit; and by forgiveness and expressing love in our lives. *This was the foundation of our strategy, fighting in the spirit by continuing in faith, praising, being obedient and ultimately being patient until we won every battle no matter how long it took.*

My God is Sovereign, always at work carrying out His purpose and no opposition can defeat His plan. The angels also worked with the Holy Spirit to accomplish the assignment of restoring our family.

Psalm 91:11 says,

> For He will give His angels [especial] charge over you to accompany and defend and preserve you in all your ways [of obedience and service].

Who is the "Comforter," our "Helper" the Holy Spirit Who has all *power and might* **and is the Spirit of the Living God?** Who preserved and kept us as He taught us about Himself and who our true enemy was and still is. *The Holy Spirit is worthy to be praised!*

John 16:7, 13 sheds light on some of the Holy Spirit's attributes:

> Jesus said, I am telling you nothing but the truth when I say it is profitable (good, expedient, advantageous) for you that I go away. **Because if I do not go away, the Comforter (Counselor, Helper, Advocate, Intercessor, Strengthener, Standby) will not come to you [into close fellowship with you]; but if I go**

away, I will send Him to you [to be in <u>close fellowship with you</u>].

But when He, the Spirit of Truth (the Truth-giving Spirit) comes, **He will guide you into all the Truth** (the whole, full Truth). **For He will not speak His own message [on His own authority]; but He will tell whatever He hears [from the Father;** He will give the message that has been given to Him], and **He will announce and declare to you the things that are to come [that will happen in the future].**

WHO IS THE HOLY SPIRIT?

We know Who sent Him;
We know why He came and what He does;
But, Who is He? Who is this Holy Spirit?

The subject and Person of The Holy Spirit is one of the most misunderstood and misinterpreted in the Christian faith because many believe <u>what</u> He does is <u>who</u> He is and that is not the case.

The Holy Spirit was sent by God The Father to the earth for all those, both Jews and Gentiles who *after* they have received His Son, Jesus as their Lord and Savior and become the "One New Man" are now in a position to receive the Infilling of the Holy Spirit (Ephesians 2:14; Galatians 3:28 and Acts 2:4). The Holy Spirit is the most valuable asset to Christian living and is the very Spirit of Jesus (who was the ultimate sacrifice to redeem mankind from his destiny in Sheol and ultimately the "Lake of Fire"). Next to Jesus, The Holy Spirit is the best Friend you will ever have (John 14:16, 26 and John 16:7, 13).

Because The Holy Spirit is in charge of the affairs of the Kingdom of God in the earth, He is responsible for bringing mankind into the knowledge and things of God giving them true life, vision, guidance, protection and shalom (wholeness) by literally transforming the lives of all those He comes in contact with. Those with a life of routine, greed, lust, hopelessness and fear are brought to a life that is full and one that includes love, joy, peace, patience and so forth, when they choose to follow His leading. **Life can be very exciting, different, full and complete as you realize Who The Holy Spirit is and Who He is in reference to you.** He can help you in this world with assignments and missions from God The Father by giving you insight, direction, instructions, miracles, weapons to defeat the adversary by revealing mysteries/revelation (hidden treasures; discovering God's truths) and much more.

Begin to fellowship and form a relationship with The Holy Spirit, which is primarily done by glorifying Jesus, the only begotten Son of God. True worship is seeking God and His Kingdom of righteousness, peace and joy in The Holy Spirit *first* then The Holy Spirit is able to guide, lead, help, strengthen, heal, encourage, warn, protect and intercede on your behalf. He will also give you insight, ability, boldness, freedom in liberty with Christ and a new life that has been completely transformed by the power of God. The Holy Spirit will give you a desire to learn more about God the Father and God the Son as you seek God through prayer and reading His Word. The Holy Bible will renew your mind and your heart so that you will become a new person as you learn and begin to take on His attributes, His ways and have His character.

You'll come into all Truth as The Holy Spirit teaches and convicts you when necessary in order to help you remain in God's will, so you can be all that God The Father purposed for you to be. Because He dwells in you, you will be able to do things beyond your intellect, become bolder, rejuvenated, strengthened and operate with spiritual gifts as you mature in the things of the spirit and can be trusted with them. **Remember, The Holy Spirit wants to be made welcome and He yearns for fellowship with you. Do not allow work, careers, family, friends, money, projects or success to take His rightful place in your life.**

Furthermore, if you ignore Him, ignore His voice, His unction, His convictions, His confirmations, His will and His plans of action and decide not to fellowship with Him *and you deny Him, deny His presence and deny His power you will grieve The Holy Spirit and that is a sin* (I Thessalonians 5:19). It is a commandment that you do not grieve Him; in short, it could become very dangerous for you because you are left on your own to handle all of life and what it holds for you by yourself. Let's face it, by yourself you are no match for Satan, but with the help of God you will win whatever battle or circumstance you are facing.

Now we have covered briefly Who sent Him and some of the functions on earth of what He does, but the question still remains: Who is He?

Many of us know The Holy Spirit as the **"Divine Third Person of the Trinity."** He is a personality in the order of the Godhead. As the Father and the Son is God, so is The Holy Spirit who also has divine attributes, such as knowledge, sovereignty, and eternity. The Holy Spirit is the same in substance and equal in power and glory with the Father and the Son. *However, He operates from a position that is subordinate to both The Father and The Son, as He proceeds from them and is sent by them and they operate through Him.* The Holy Spirit is also known by these Biblical symbols that represent Him, a dove, the wind, fire, water and the anointing oil.

We also know Him primarily as a **"Helper"** the help that He supplies particularly as a defense against adversaries. He will help you stay focused on where you are going and not on your past. He will give you instructions and a plan of action to help you stay in order by balancing and setting priorities in your life in hopes of accomplishing much that will glorify God The Father and Jesus through you. A helper is a strong person who supports and provides assistance to any person with a need whether they themselves are weak, strong or self-sufficient. Humility enables one to understand that they need this kind of help and are grateful that it is available to them.

We also know Him as a **"Comforter"** someone who will bring the comfort of peace into a terrible situation or bring peace and comfort in the midst of a storm or circumstance that is beyond our control. The real comfort that The Holy Spirit brings is restoration as He begins to rebuild our broken lives.

The Holy Spirit is a **"Person"** without a body, who is a **"Spirit;"** a Spirit with feelings and emotions who can be grieved and upset, but who can also be joyous and excited about things. He has His own will, He perceives and responds. He also has the ability to love and have wrath which is the ability to hate because of righteous indignation (anger aroused by something that is unjust).

The **"Gifts"** are a part of the Holy Spirit. When people fall under the power of God, or they are instantly healed, miracles occur, doors of opportunity are opened, or when blessings come and they know, that they know it is from God, this is all a part of *what* the Holy Spirit does and it is a part of Who He is. The emotional events in the church are the aftermath of knowing He has been there, knowing that you have been in the *presence* of Almighty God. The Holy Spirit is with you, in you and comes upon you to empower you, to heal you, to bless you and keep you. Before you knew Him He was already with you; but once you know Him and invite Him into your heart, He is in you; then He comes upon you with glory and great power to do a work through you.

The Holy Spirit came to reveal the power of "Love" not the love of power! He is the power source and He shows us that power is Love. When you exercise, show and walk in love you are bringing forth Who God is and showing His true character. **He is LOVE and He is ALL POWER!** (I John 4:16; Acts 1:8).

The Holy Spirit is the **"Power"** of The Father and of The Son. The Father is the Creative Mind and the Son is the Agent who is called the Word of God. And when the Father spoke the Word, all came into being by the *Power* of The Holy Spirit. The Hebrew word *Ruach* refers to God's Spirit, the spirit of a person, breath or wind. The Spirit of God is everywhere in association with power and life, both of which are important in creation. God's Spirit moved or hovered over the waters which covered the earth and kept the chaotic forces in check as it manifested all at the commands of God the Father (Genesis 1).

Hebrews 4:12 speaks of the Power of the Word through the Holy Spirit:

> **For the Word that God speaks is alive and full of power** [making it active, operative, energizing, and effective]; it is **sharper than any two-edged sword**, penetrating to the dividing line of the breath of life (soul) and [the immortal] spirit, and of joints and marrow [of the deepest parts of our nature], exposing and sifting and analyzing and judging the very thoughts and purposes of the heart.

If you are filled with His Spirit the Power of creation is inside of you. *Who* is He, He is Power. He is the Power that upholds the Word. He causes the Word to come alive. The **Holy Spirit is the manifestation of the Power of God.** Everything The Holy Spirit does is based on Almighty God's Word.

Acts 1:8 says,

> But you shall receive *power* (ability, efficiency, and might) when The Holy Spirit has come upon you, and you shall be My witnesses in Jerusalem and all Judea and Samaria and to the ends (the very bounds) of the earth.

In addition to the above **"His fruit"** is *Who* He is as well. His fruit is His character. His fruit is the same fruit that He imparts unto all those who ask Him to come and live inside of them which is: Love, Joy, Peace, Patience/Endurance, Gentleness, Goodness, Faithfulness, Meekness/Humility and Self-Control (Galatians 5:22-23). In this regard, this is how we are truly made in His image as spirit beings and as we take on the fruit of the Spirit, we are being like our Maker. Like Him, we are also a spirit that possesses a soul (mind, will and emotions) the difference of course, as humans we are spirit, soul *and body* (I Thessalonians 5:23). Because we are limited in these bodies, it is the power and gifts of the Holy Spirit inside of us that makes the difference in our lives.

As we know Him by His fruit which will show us His character, that in turn will help us understand and appreciate His attributes. His attributes are powerful and they have the ability to change a person's heart among other difficult things and because of this, He is able to change a person's life.

The fruit of the Spirit will help us to develop and have the strength to stand and project godlike character that will give us integrity, boldness, and a life worth living. The fruit of the Spirit will also help us with everyday life, our attitude about life and aid us in exercising gratitude and giving. These qualities only come from knowing God and taking on His character that will literally change our life for the better and teach us how to trust God and rely on Him as our source. *Jesus was a total man, perfect, yet the scriptures say He would not make a move without the Holy Spirit.* (Isa. 40:13-14; I Co. 2:16; and Ro. 11:34-36).

Jesus' ministry did not meet the Jewish leader's expectations. It did, however, meet God's expectations. The Spirit directed Jesus' ministry and fulfilled Old Testament expectations of the Messiah – Luke 4:16-19. Jesus affirmed the Spirit's role in His life by quoting Isaiah 61:1, 2 when He read it and sat down and said "Today this scripture is fulfilled in your hearing."

Your life has a chance of becoming the example God Almighty would want it to be merely because you allowed The Holy Spirit to come into your life, dwell inside of you and show you the way through The Father and through our Lord and Savior, Jesus Christ.

ATTRIBUTES OF GOD THE HOLY SPIRIT

God is a Spirit (John 4:23-23)
Holy (1 Peter 1:15-16)
The Head of every man is Christ (1 Cor. 11:3)
Helper (John 14:16, 26; John 16:7) (Helps you reach your destiny)
Counselor (John 16:7)
Advocate (John 16:7) (Takes charge with us)
Anointing Oil (Isaiah 10:27; Psalms 23:5; Ex. 37:29) (symbol)
Intercessor (John 16:7; Ro 8:26-27)
Teacher (John 14:26; John 2:20-27)
Spirit of Truth (John 16:13)
Comforter (John 16:7)
Strengthener (John 16:7)
Deliverer (Ro 11:26)
Standby (John 16:7) (One that can be relied on, ready to act)
Vindicator (Ro 12:19) (He will fight your battles)
Convicts (John 16:7-8) (Helps to keep you in His will)
Revealer (John 16:15) (Reveals mysteries)
Preserves (1 John 5:18)
All Power (Ro 13:1-2)
Our Guide (Gal. 5:16; 25; Acts 13:2; Ro 8:14)
Justifier (Ro 3:26) (Not condemned)
Fruit of the Spirit (Gal. 5:22-23) (His character in us)
Our Joy (Ps 51:12)
Promoter of Jesus Christ (John 15:26)
Miracle Working God (Gal. 3:5)
The Promise of the Father (Acts 1:4)
Anoints one for service (1 John 2:20)
The Spirit that comes upon you when anointed (Isaiah 61:1)
Fills you with His Holy Spirit (Acts 4:7-8)
By My Spirit (Zech 4:6) (Not by might, nor by human power)
Jehovah M'Kaddesh (Ex. 31:13) (God My Sanctifier)
Jehovah Rophe (Ex. 15:26) (God My Healer)
Jehovah Nissi (1 Cor. 15:57; Ex. 17:15) (My Banner of Victory)
Jehovah Shammah (Ezek. 48:35) (God the Abiding Presence)
Omnipresent (Ps 139:1-13) (everywhere/ever present)

Omnipotent (Jerm. 32:17, 27) (all powerful)
Omniscient (1 John 3:20) (all knowing)
Guarantee of Eternal Life (Eph. 1:13-14)
Ability to work through you as you yield to His Spirit (Zech. 4:6)
Ability to create a new heart in you (Ps 51:10)
Renews the right spirit in you (Ps 51:10)
Gives you the will, strength and desire to obey (1 Peter 1:22)
Gives you rest (Isa. 63:14)
Beautified the Heavens and the Earth (Job 26:13; Gen. 1:1-2)
Glory of the Father (Romans 8:11)
Glory Cloud (Ps 105:39; Ps 78:14)
Always leads you in triumph (2 Cor. 2:14)
Holy Spirit is greater in me than he that is in the world (1 Jn. 4:4)
He searches diligently, examining everything (1 Cor 2:10)
He lives inside of me (Acts 1:5; John 14:17; Ro 8:9, 11)
He seals (2 Cor.1:22; Eph 1:13; 4:30; Ro 8:16) (Marks us as His)
The Holy Spirit is given to us by God (Acts 2:39; Luke 11:13)
He regenerates us (John 3:3-8; Titus 3:5) (Makes us alive spiritually)
He fills us (Eph. 5:18; Acts 4:8, 31; 6:3; 9:17; 11:24) (Empowers us)
Warns not to grieve or quench the Holy Spirit (1 Thess. 5:19)
Spirit will not strive with man forever, for he is flesh (Gen. 6:3)

Biblical Symbols that Represent the Holy Spirit:

A Dove (Gentle and Kind)
The Wind (Spirit)
Fire (Holy)
Water (Holy Spirit)
Anointing Oil (The Lord would anoint His "sheep" with the Holy Spirit, Whom oil symbolizes, to empower them to engage more freely in His service and run in the way He directs, in heavenly fellowship with Him).

Isaiah 40:13-14 NKJV:
…who as His counselor has taught Him? With whom did He take counsel, that instructions might be given Him? Who taught Him the path of justice and taught Him knowledge and showed Him the way of understanding?

The Unpardonable sin, blasphemy against The Holy Spirit is the only sin that is **not** forgiven, see Matthew 12:31-32; and Luke 12:10.

Unpardonable = every evil, abusive, injurious speaking or indignity against sacred things. **Indignity** = an offense against personal dignity or self-respect; to humiliate.

The Holy Spirit should be given the appropriate respect and love as He is God and is Worthy of all Honor and Praise!

ILLUSTRATION OF PROGRESS IN ONE'S LIFE WITH THE HOLY SPIRIT

This is an illustration of the different levels or stages of Christians (Believers) as they start and complete their life or walk with God by the leading of The Holy Spirit Who is on this earth to help them reach a certain level of maturity, their potential and purpose designed for them by God The Father.

1	2	3	4	5	6
Baby	Toddler	Child	Adolescent	Young Adult	Mature

1. **Baby Christian** - they know that something has happened and they may have a sudden love for God that they did not have before but they don't know how nor in most cases can they explain it. Usually still a carnal Christian, still acting like people not Born-again, not living by faith but instead living by their feelings and emotions. But in reality they have the authority as sons (a mature Christian) because of the Holy Spirit who dwells in them yet many are not aware of it nor are they in a position to utilize it, (Gal. 4:1-7; John 1:12 KJV and AMP).

2. **Toddler** – someone filled with the Holy Spirit but not developed yet, they sense a difference in their strength and ability. There is an inner knowing that there has been a change.
3. **Child** – learning the Word of God, experiencing miracles, joy, and are usually on fire for God. There is an awareness of The Holy Spirit present in their lives.
4. **Adolescent** – learning how to walk by faith while going through the wilderness of life's experiences and at the same time being strengthened and developing in the fruit of the Spirit (Gal. 5:22-23). Also learning more about the adversary (Satan) and how he functions and how to fight him in the spiritual realm.
5. **Young Adult** – continuing in the ways of God regardless of the trials, trusting God and striving to be obedient in all they do. Not moved by what they see, walking by faith and learning more of who God is.
6. **Mature Adult** – is a son or daughter and a friend of the Lord (I Cor. 2:6-7; John 15:14). Is comfortable with God and knows God will always come through for them. They are willing to wait on God's timing and accepts the way God chooses to do things. A place of perfection (maturity) in the things of God. A place of hearing and obeying no matter what the cost may be. Having become a hearer and a doer, realizing faith without works is dead and not pleasing to Almighty God.

ANGEL MOVEMENT CHART

Angels assist The Holy Spirit in changing lives. They have been dispatched or sent by Jehovah Tsabaoth the Lord of Host (of Angels) to bring forth "The Blessing of Abraham."

As God's *Angels* are commissioned to come forth, the adversary has hindrances to block "The Blessing of Abraham" nevertheless God has enabled and empowered us to receive "The

Blessing." We have the authority to cast out evil in the name of Jesus and send forth angels. As we remember who we are in Christ and exercise any of the following tools or spiritual warfare weapons such as: walking in Love; seeking first the Kingdom of God; praying in the name of Jesus; offering up praise and thanksgiving; to declare the Blood of Jesus; declare we have on the Whole Armor of God; read; hear; believe; receive; act; study and confess the Word of God we will use our level of authority regardless of any circumstance or whatever device the enemy is using and it shall not prevail against us! (Random list below).

ANGELS ARE SENT	EVIL RESPONSE	PEOPLE STAND
With "The Blessing"	Blockage/Hindrance	Continue/Stand/Wait to Receive
Favor	Unforgiveness	Stay in God's Will
Grace, Mercy	Fear, Doubt	Move in God's Timing
His Glory	Not Praying	**Favor releases:**
Manifestation of Promises:	Strife, Complaining	Restoration, Support
Double Portion	Bitterness, Gossip	Assist, Promotion
Financial Breakthrough	Rejection, Jealousy	Supernatural Increase
Restoration of all stolen	Immorality, Lying	Honor in the Midst of your Enemies
Miracles	Grumbling, Murmuring	Unmerited Favor
Divine Presence	Not Walking in Love	Bring you Real Estate
Sons & Daughters Blessed	Procrastination	Greater Victories

Deliverance	Not Thankful	Special Privileges
Family Saved	Witchcraft, Rebellion	Petitions Granted
Breakthroughs	Offense, Pride, Lazy	Recognition
Healing	Depression	Prominence
Protection	Not Walking in Peace	Preferential Treatment
Provision	Sin while Angry	Policies and Rules Changed
Fight your battles	Selfishness	Battles Won

With faith in God's Word, showing honor and trusting The Father, The Son and The Holy Spirit, coupled with the ministry of angels we can overcome every obstacle. God has commanded His angels to minister to us, it says in Psalm 91:11 that "God will give His angels charge over you to accompany and defend and preserve you in all your ways [of obedience and service]." When we speak the Word of God the angels are not only strengthened but they have been instructed to heed to the **voice** of His Word and do what we say in the name of Jesus, *the name that is above every name.* Praise Him! (Psalm 103:20).

This is the season and the *time to take back what was stolen,* as you open your mouth and **use your tongue which is a weapon, declare God's Word and expect The Holy Spirit and a host of angels to move on your behalf.** Angels are dispatched when the Kingdom of God is preached (spoken). Life and death are in the power of *your* tongue (Prov. 18:21).

Take heed and know that this is the start of a new season, be aware that **thousands upon thousands of angels have been dispatched on the earth by the Lord to do a mighty work for this season of harvest** as God brings us into His Glory and manifest the promises many of us have waited years to receive. Angels will play a huge part in the transfer of wealth and deliverance in our lives in the last of the Last Days (the season we are currently in, see 2 Timothy 3:1-9 and Matthew 24:1-44). Remember that *angels move according to your words not your needs because things are done according to your faith.*

Psalm 103:20 says that angels hearken to the voice of the Lord, well we are that voice. God doesn't go past our conversation, **angels are on assignment and assigned to bring us into the impossible, but they are waiting on the voice of God,** waiting for us to speak the **Word of God** and as we do and continue to do so especially in this season, the Word will tear down the demonic strongholds, those areas that were captured, dominated and controlled by evil forces.

The following information about these mysterious creatures called "Angels" is to give some insight about angelic beings: What they are? How do they function? What is their chain of command and much more? However, *I would like to caution the unbeliever that what is written is directed to a Child of God who should be able to receive the revelation of God's work and plan.* For it will be **a challenge to the unbeliever** because you are probably in doubt or unbelief about God and His host of angels and because of that you will more than likely be hindered and unable to see with spiritual eyes largely due to spiritual blindness of the truth; or you may simply believe this is all foolishness (2 Corinthians 4:4; I Corinthians 2:14). Note: People are hurting and need answers and they do not have time for "foolishness" but will make time for "Truth" that will rise up in the hearts of those who choose to receive and go forth towards their victory.

John 14:17 says,

> The Spirit of Truth, Whom the world (unbelievers) cannot receive (welcome, take to its heart), because it does not see Him or know and recognize Him…

THE FIVE DIVISIONS OF ANGELS:
There are five divisions of angels: (1) Seraphim; (2) Cherubim; (3) Living Creatures; (4) Archangels; and (5) Common Angels:

(1) *The Seraphim's* located in Isaiah 6:1-9, declare the glory of God.

(2) *The Cherubim's* located in Ezekiel 1:4-28 are to protect the glory of God. They are also called Living Creatures. "And this was their appearance: they had the likeness of a man, but each one had four faces and four wings," vv. 5-6. **Their four faces are the same pattern as the emblems for the tribes of ancient Israel and the four major federal buildings in Washington, D.C. in the U.S.A.** according to research done by Evangelist and author Perry Stone. Those faces are as follows: **the face of a man** (Jefferson Memorial and the tribe of Ruben); **the face of an eagle** (The White House and the tribe of Dan); **the face of a lion** (The Capitol Building and the tribe of Judah) and **the face of an ox** (Lincoln Memorial and the tribe of Manasseh). This is largely because the U.S.A. is the only country in the world that has Hebraic connections. The States ranging from the east coast to the west coast are in the same pattern as the ancient tabernacle which means God has ordained a place for Himself to tabernacle, to dwell. Some call U.S.A. the sister nation to Israel. Note: Nothing God does is without purpose and significance.

(3) *Living Creatures* located in Revelations 4:6 are angels of judgment. "And around the throne, in the center at each side of the throne, were four living creatures (beings) who were full of eyes in front and behind [with intelligence as to what is before and at the rear of them]." In v. 8, These living creatures, individually having six wings, were full of eyes all over...and day and night they never stop saying, Holy, holy, holy is the Lord God Almighty..."

(4) *The archangels* located in Revelation 12:7 defend the glory of God; they are warring angels such as Michael and Gabriel; Lucifer was the top archangel before he fell and became Satan.

(5) *Common Angels* located in Psalm 103:20; 2 Thessalonians 1:7 and Hebrews 12:22 are millions of angels (without wings) who defend, guard and protect those in the Kingdom of God whom are gathered from the church or the Body of Christ which is composed of the people of God/The One New Man/ God's Blended Family. These angels travel from heaven to earth frequently and are seen often but not recognized while on assignments from God. Once their mission is completed they may leave as suddenly as they came leaving people to think about certain events then later they usually realize there was something different about "those people or that man, woman or child."

For instance during the 911 attack in New York city there were several reports of "people" who appeared and were extremely calm and giving directions on leaving the building and once the people were safely out those "people" left "suddenly."

I personally have had encounters where I later realized that many of the head-on collision accidents that were avoided in my life were the result of help from angels. I experienced my hands moving much faster on the steering wheel than normal and turning out of danger. On one occasion I was in my minivan with Kevin one of my sons when I was distracted watching some teens that had been pulled over by the police and I had an accident. My son later told me that just moments before the accident he heard a voice tell him to put on his seat belt (something we always did but for some reason it was not done that day). Just as he listened and put the seat belt on I turned to face the traffic and saw that it had stopped and I was still driving at least 40 miles an hour and as I started to break my foot slipped and was caught between the peddles (something that has never happened to me before or since). **Needless to say I did not break and the impact was so strong that it was a four vehicle collision. It was so loud that the police with the teens ran over to our accident. We all got out of our vehicles safely and without a scratch. Then we all noticed that not one of the cars were damaged in any way.** All of the drivers in front of me involved in the collision once seeing there wasn't any damage to their vehicles returned to their cars and drove off.

The police refused to even take my name and then they left. So I drove on to the store. I did realize though that a miracle (the supernatural) had taken place and that angels had cushioned between each vehicle so there were no damages and no injuries. **My son who was about ten or eleven at this time was prevented from going through the windshield** *because he heard a voice* **tell him to put on his seat belt.**

Notice that God did not stop the accident but was in the midst of it with us and prevented us from any harm. At that time I was going through a separation which led to financial problems and my vehicle was not insured or registered and the police could have taken it had they asked for my name. So, what the devil meant for evil God turned it around for my good with the help of His angels who will assist in delivering you from danger or harm, Acts 5:19; 12:6-11 as well as protect you Dan. 3:28; Matt. 26:53.

A DESCRIPTION OF ANGELS AND WHAT THEIR PURPOSE IS:

Angels are created beings (Psalm 148:2-5) **and many of them are with immeasurable beauty and brilliance shinning like the sun, colorful and glorious** (Daniel 10:6; Rev. 10:1). Angels look different and have different functions depending upon their rank. Some have wings, and some do not; some look like children while others are like giants mighty and strong (Rev. 18:21). **They have the ability to change their appearance to physical bodies taking on human form** when God appoints them to special task or assignments on earth (Gen. 18:2; Dan. 10:18; Zech. 2:1; Mt. 28:2-6; Luke 24:4 and Judges 13:6). For instance, "**God uses angels to work out the destinies of men and nations.** He has altered the courses of the busy political and social arenas of our society and directed the destinies of men by angelic visitation many times over. We must be aware that angels keep in close and vital contact with all that is happening on the earth. Their knowledge of earthly matters exceeds that of men. We must attest to their invisible presence and unceasing labors.

Let us believe that they are here among us. They may not laugh or cry with us, but we do know they delight with us over every victory in our evangelistic endeavors. Jesus taught that 'there is joy in the presence of the angels of God when one sinner repents' (Luke 15:10, TLB)."[12]

They are spirits that are visible or invisible, they do not age nor do they reproduce their own kind (Mark 12:25 and Matthew 22:30). They can only be in one place at a time not like The Holy Spirit Who is omnipresent (everywhere). Millions of angels are at God's command and these spiritual forces are available to all Christians (Believers) as well. Many times angels are protecting you even before you are "Born- again" because you are marked and sealed by The Holy Spirit because God already knows the day and the hour that you will confess His Son as Lord and Savior of your life (2 Cor. 1:22).

The Angel of the Lord is believed to be God Himself inasmuch as He has powers and the characteristics which belong only to God in Heaven (Gen. 16:7; 18:1-2; 22:11; 31:11; Exo. 14:19-20). Many believe that the Angel of the Lord is Jesus and that Jesus is the pre-incarnate Word that was here from the very beginning (John 1:1, 14).

Angels were also present and played a role in the events surrounding Jesus' birth and resurrection (Mt. 1:20; 2:13, 19; 28:2; Luke 1:11-38; 2:9-15; 22:43; 24:23 and John 20:12).

Angels are also worshippers and messengers for Almighty God. As worshippers they are called to bless the Lord with worship around His throne (Ps 148:2-5; Ps. 103:21; Rev. 5:11-13). "And the four living creatures, individually having six wings, were full of eyes all over and within [underneath their wings]; and **day and night they never stop saying, holy, holy, holy, is the Lord God Almighty** (Omnipotent), Who was and Who is and Who is to come" (Revelation 4:8).

They serve men as ministering angels as well as assist human beings as messengers. When there is spiritual conflict in the lives of the Believers as they pray and commission angels they are sent on assignment by Almighty God and follow the instructions of The Holy Spirit as they come to the Believer's aid in struggles against Satan. They intervene in the affairs of nations as well as execute judgment on nations, Gen. 19:1, 11, 13, 15-17; 2 Sam. 24:16. They also participate in bringing about signs and wonders. The angel's part in the Believers life isn't as much since the Holy Spirit is present but the Holy Spirit does work with the angels for the people's good.

Angels bring comfort, they guide and prepare the way or go before you (Gen. 24:7) as they protect and preserve (Psalm 91:11; I Kings 6:14-17). They strengthen and inspire you; warn and deliver you; and they provide for the people of God in the midst of suffering persecution (I Kings 19:5-8). Furthermore, **angels escort Believers to heaven** when they pass from this life on earth (Luke 16:22).

People do not *become* angels when they go to heaven because angels are an entirely different "Being." Once people go to heaven they are only *like* angels in two ways: **(1)** People will not marry neither do angels marry. Jesus said people will not marry in heaven in Luke 20:34-35 which says, "The people of this world and present age marry and are given in marriage; But those who are considered worthy to gain that other world and that future age and to attain to the resurrection from the dead neither marry nor are given in marriage;" and **(2)** People will not ever die again neither do angels die. In Luke 20:36 it says, "For they **cannot die again, but are *angel-like* and equal to the angels.** And being sons of and sharers in the resurrection, they are sons of God." Angels are spirits and we are part spirit, soul and body (I Thess. 5:23). The body goes back to dust from which it came and the soul (mind, will and emotions) goes either to heaven with your spirit or your soul goes to outer darkness for all eternity depending upon the choice you made in choosing life or death, life being in Christ, (Deut. 30:19; John 14:6; and Matt. 25:30).

Angels do not receive revelation from the Word of God (I Cor. 2:7-8) they know of God by watching and observing the Believers because revelation is revealed only to the redeemed. **Angels do have a free will** that is why a third of them when deceived by Satan chose and did follow him to their eternal destruction.

I might add that the angels that fell with Satan were not redeemed by God. One reason being is that "life" is in the blood and blood was shed to redeem mankind but angels have no blood for they are spirits. In addition, they were not made in God's likeness or image. Furthermore, as mentioned, God Himself is a Spirit and that is why a body with prefect blood was prepared for Jesus which was used to redeem **humans who are of spirit, soul and body (flesh and blood)** (Hebrews 2:16; Hebrews 10:5-12; I Thessalonians 5:23).

Angels speak to people (Luke 2:8-12; Zech 2:1-4; Luke 1:19; Mt. 28:6; Judges 13:6-7); **they also have their own language** (I Co. 13:1). They praise God (Luke 2:13-14) and they sing (Rev. 5:11, 12). They have wisdom and knowledge men do not have (2 Sam. 14:20). They also have the ability to plan and make decisions and they can be emotional creatures as seen when they are full of joy and rejoice when one wicked person (sinner) is Born-again or rededicates their life to Christ and repents (Luke 15:10).

Angels have their own food (Ps.78:25). Elijah ate their food and had strength for forty days (I Kings 19:5-8). **They can also eat human food** as demonstrated when God appeared in human form as an Angel along with two other angels and they all shared a meal with Abraham (Gen. 18:1-8). Also Lot prepared a meal for two angels as they visited his home (Gen. 19:3).

Angels realize that God has placed man in a high position (Hebrews 2:5-8) and in Psalm 8:5 it says "Yet You have made him but a little lower than God [or heavenly beings], and You have crowned him with glory and honor. Angels were the first and only sons of God until Genesis two when man was created and are now called sons of God. When people reign with Jesus after the rapture (I Cor. 15:51-55; Rev. 4:1; Gen. 5:21-24; 2 Kings 2:11) and the Tribulation Period is over, during the Millennial Reign (Rev. 20) man will judge the common angels as well as rule with Christ on the earth.

Angels do not possess human bodies like disembodied demons do when they find an entrance into someone's life. This is why Jesus had to cast demons out of people and why His followers do the same (Mark 16:17). The Holy Spirit seals and indwells men when they belong to the Kingdom of God but He does not do this for the angels.

Many people wonder if they are supposed to pray and worship angels? We are not to pray to or worship angels because they are not all-powerful and all-knowing only God is (Ps. 103:20; 2 Thess. 1:7). We are to pray and worship our Father in Heaven and the King of kings and the Lord of lords, our Savior Christ Jesus as we also acknowledge and worship the Holy Spirit in all His power.

A REVIEW OF BUILDING AND EMBRACING A PERSONAL RELATIONSHIP WITH GOD:

> Jesus said, "...if I go away, I will send Him to you" [to be in *close fellowship* with you].
> John 16:7

In Order to Build and Maintain a Close Fellowship through the Divine Third Person of the Trinity, The Holy Spirit, and in Order to **Embrace a Personal Relationship** *with Our Heavenly Father and His Beloved Son, Christ Jesus:*

We are to have a close and personal relationship with The Holy Spirit which will bring us closer to our Heavenly Father and to His Son, Christ Jesus. This is accomplished as we fellowship with The Holy Spirit Who speaks to us on their behalf.

With a personal relationship with Jesus, God's purpose for your life, vision, dream or assignment will come alive with clarity, instructions, provision, power and the enablement to fulfill it because of your intimate relationship with Him. The Bible says without revelation knowledge My people perish, they are destroyed, they can become confused, their mind wanders, they become wild and have a lack of purpose and live with a life full of regrets (Hosea 4:6). By staying close to Jesus keeping their eyes on Him their vision will stay alive and come forth at the appointed time (Habakkuk 2:2-3).

As you and your family follow God's order each day, a complete work will be accomplished in your life. In order to have true success and victory in your life make a choice to follow Jesus, stay focused and live holy before Him. Remember that Jesus will not force anyone to choose Him or His ways. For those who decide to follow, He will empower you to be blessed and become a blessing to others. He will place divine connections across your path to enable you to prosper and some of these connections will be in positions of authority, in different businesses, civil agencies, at your work place and so on. Many times these people will be complete strangers and as you respect the delegated authority before you God will open doors of opportunity.

In order to successfully follow Him and have a personal relationship you must not only be willing to allow God's standard and order to operate in your life but be willing to have certain things or people pruned from your life and lifestyle as well. This would entail putting off the "old man" the old person and learning how to renew your mind in Christ and dying to fleshly desires that are there to tempt you into bondage and sin. This does not mean it will be permanent some things and/or people will be reinstated at the appointed time and it will be better than it previously was.

One reason people fall short of His glory is because religion and tradition have taught us how to operate in the family and in the church. But the church, the Kingdom of God, God's family belongs to Christ the Anointed One not to religion or traditions of men because God does not function within religion or traditions. He is Anointed and is outside of the "box." Therefore, let Him through the power of The Holy Spirit teach you how to function both within the family and the Kingdom of God. This is one of the paramount reasons we must have a close and personal relationship with Christ.

A QUICK REVIEW OF WHAT *SHOULD* BE IN PLACE TO KEEP GOD FIRST:

- **Receive Jesus/Yeshua** as your Lord and Savior (Romans 10:9; Acts 2:21; John 10:9). (See this Section, What is Salvation).
- **Receive the "Infilling of the Holy Spirit"** also known as the "Baptism in the Holy Spirit" with the evidence of speaking in your supernatural spiritual prayer language aka tongues (Acts 2:1-8; Romans 8:9-11; I Corinthians 14:2; 2:4-5). (See Section Two, under Spiritual Warfare Weapon number 4).
- **Develop a personal relationship with Him through your prayer life** as you commune with Him through His Holy Spirit; read and study His Word; and as you pay attention and follow His teachings you will be blessed (Matthew 7:7; 2 Tim. 2:15; Deut. 28:1-14). (See Section Two, under Spiritual Warfare Weapon number 2).
- **Join a local Christian Church one that is Spirit-filled and studies the Word through the Holy Bible**, to have the proper covering you need as you begin your walk or journey with God. It is important to have people to come in agreement with you who are mature in the things of God and who can feed you the Word with revelation on a regular basis to help you acquire understanding and unfold mysteries. "…Christ brings us together as a family. Christians seek ways to encourage one another to express love through good deeds. Communal worship is one way we gain strength and motivation from other disciples." [1] Hebrews 10:24-25.

Hebrews 10:25 KJV tells us not to give up meeting together: "Not forsaking the assembling of ourselves together, as the manner of some is; but exhorting one another: and so much the more, as ye see the day approaching."

- As you are learning of Him and **renewing your mind in the Word of God** (Romans 12:2) seek Him for His purpose and will for your life. Stay open and receive confirmation and once you start to receive information about your assignment (purpose or vision) write it down so it can be clear and so Satan cannot come and steal it from your memory over a period of time (Habakkuk 2:2-3). Now ask God for His instructions, directions, will, strength and desire while you are on your journey to ensure reaching your destiny.
- Attend a good **Bible study class regularly**. Also attend **conferences and conventions as you are led by The Holy Spirit. Watch Christian programs,** there are many available if you do not know of any may I suggest (*Trinity Broadcasting Network*, TBN.org) it is the largest Christian television network in the world and the owner of other Christian networks that reach children, teens, families, churches and countries around the world as well as being on the internet and other electronics). **Read Christian books; listen to CD's and DVD's** and develop relationships with people that God has placed across your path to become mentors, prayer partners, friends and to possibly form a Spiritual Family within the Body of Christ. In addition, reading and using **materials that are non-Christian are fine**; everything is from above but realize that some materials have become twisted, perverted and are demonic so guard what you allow into your soul through your eyes and ears. Some **self-help**

books and materials are alright, most of them are biblically based but <u>without</u> scripture references and mixed with a lot of *opinions of men* which is not the biblical standard to live by.
- Allow the Holy Spirit to train you up to **fight and/or resist evil in this spiritual war** so you will walk in the victory that has already been given to you over the kingdom of darkness (Ps 119:115; I John 4:4). Because of your covenant with God when you **use your authority acquired because of the finished work at the cross realize He has already "disarmed the principalities and powers** that were ranged against you and made a bold display and public example of them..." (Col.2:15) paraphrased.
- Declare daily that you are **covered with the Blood of Jesus** (Revelation 12:11; Exodus 12:13) and that you **have on the Whole Armor of God** which does include your supernatural spiritual prayer language aka tongues as shown in v. 18 of Ephesians 6:10-18.
- **Be mindful that walking with the fruit of the Spirit is expressing the character of God.** Others will see the glory of God on you even if they do not know what it is they are seeing. They will know that there is something different about you.

As you do your part, be confident that He will fulfill His. He has made certain promises that He cannot break because He is a God that cannot lie so see to it that <u>you</u> do not break the covenant by <u>living</u> outside of His will with an unrepentant heart. **Claim your protection** with verses such as *Psalm 91:1 which says, "He who dwells in the secret place of the Most High shall remain stable and fixed under the shadow of the Almighty [whose power no foe can withstand]." And in Psalm 91:7 "A thousand may fall at my side and ten thousand at my right hand, but it shall not come near you."* Also see Psalms 23 for comfort.

Remember that **complaining and murmuring removes your divine protection and favor and it has the power to set you back in your endeavors** (Phil 2:14; I Co 10:10; Prov.18:20-21). It is a sin before God and one should repent. It will push you further away from His presence than bring you closer. *Since words are "spirit" the spirit realm takes every word as a command or a mandate that we speak.* How the word is expressed does not make any difference, for example, if it is said seriously, as a joke, as a decree or demand it does not matter because the words have been released into the

atmosphere (the spiritual realm) and they will eventually bring you a harvest of whatever you are speaking.

Therefore, guard what you say because the harvest of your words will manifest whether they were godly words or negative words. By your words you establish life or death, success or failure, peace and chaos, blessings or curses. In addition, when others speak negative, evil words over you and your destiny do not believe them, do not come in agreement with them because that is not what God spoke about you or your destiny and His Word is the standard we measure all other words by. Simply forgive them then reverse their words when you pray and cast them down, bind them up and place them under the blood of Jesus.

While seeking God and you are not sure which way to go or what to do, be still and continue to wait for clear instructions, confirmation, guidance and peace. Continue doing what He has already shown you to do, and as you do you will walk right into all and more than you hoped for you and your family at the appointed time.

Remember God speaks when, where and how He chooses to speak. If He chooses to speak through a vessel He has raised up by His Spirit remember people are not perfect and they only have a part of the whole picture and that gifts of the Spirit and the anointing vary from person to person. (See Section 2, under Spiritual Warfare Weapons numbers 5, 20 and 13).

A BRIEF HISTORY AND THE WONDERFUL WORKS OF THE KING OF KINGS:

Yeshua ha Mashiach, Jesus the Messiah, is known to most as "Jesus Christ," our Lord and Savior; our High Priest and the King of Glory.

His Personal name is Jesus, which signifies Savior. A name that was given to the archangel Gabriel to give to Mary (Miriam in Hebrew), Jesus' mother (Luke 1:31). He was also so named by the angel to Joseph in his supernatural dream in respect to Mary and the Child (Matthew 1:21). This is the name that was given before he was conceived in the womb of Mary by The Holy Spirit (Matthew 1:18).

To know Him better one must understand His identity. Jesus Christ is not His first and last name (His given name and family name). Jesus is the Greek translation of His Hebrew name Yeshua which in Hebrew means Salvation or God Saves. Why this name? Because His purpose was to save His people from their sins through Salvation. Throughout the Old Testament when reference is made to Salvation it is referring to Yeshua or Jesus (Psalm 62:2 and Isaiah 12:2).

Christ is not His last name, Christ is His official title and it means **"Anointed One."** The Greek word Christos comes from the Hebrew word Mashiach (Christos – Christ– the Anointed) The Hebrew word Mashiach or Messiah – the Anointed, (Isaiah 61:1). Jesus was anointed to minister on this earth (John 1:33) and to bring forth through His atonement on the cross Salvation for all those in the world who will receive this gift.

Even though Jesus is fully God, He needed to be anointed for His assignment because He literally emptied Himself, when "He made Himself of no reputation (poured Himself out), and took upon Him the form of a servant (assumes that He forsook another role), and was made in the likeness of men and had to do things by the power of The Holy Spirit (Phil. 2:7 KJV). He is the Anointed One and every person Born-again is anointed as well because once you are Born-again His Holy Spirit dwells inside of you.

A love for the Anointed One will compel you to constrain yourself from doing something that will quench the anointing on your life (2 Cor. 5:14). *If you have had the privilege of being in the presence of the Anointed One all sense of time leaves as you bask in His presence.* **Because you have experienced His tangible love it will cause you to be conscious of His presence at times when you do not feel a tangible presence but you have a knowing that He is there living inside of you with all power, joy, peace and the freedom that comes with knowing Him.** As you become more and more acquainted with Him (learning of Jesus) your love for Him will deepen and you will want to choose not to do the things that will grieve the Holy Spirit which is the Spirit of Jesus. You will know the importance and value of not coming in agreement with things that you are aware of that are enemies of the anointing such as unholy alliances (See Chapter 4 under Defining the Anointing of God).

He claimed identity with the Father in the unique Trinitarian relationship they share, Matthew 12:44-50:

> But Jesus loudly declared, The one who believes in Me does not [only] believe in and trust in and rely on Me, but **[in believing in Me he believes] in Him Who sent Me. And whoever sees Me sees Him Who sent Me.** I have come as a Light into the world, so that whoever believes in Me [whoever cleaves to and trusts in and relies on Me] may not continue to live in darkness. If anyone hears My teachings and fails to observe them [does not keep them, but disregards them], it is not I who judges him. *For I have not come to judge and to condemn and to pass sentence and to inflict penalty on the world, but to save the world.* Anyone who rejects Me and persistently sets Me at naught, refusing to accept My teachings, has his judge [however]; for the [very] message that I have spoken will itself judge and convict him at the last day.

This is because I have never spoken on My own authority or of My own accord or as self-appointed, but the Father Who sent Me has Himself given Me orders [concerning] what to say and what to tell. **And I know that His commandment is (means) eternal life.** So whatever I speak, I am saying [exactly] what My Father has told Me to say and in accordance with His instructions.

"He was born in Bethlehem of Judea (Luke 2:11; Mic. 5:2) in the days of King Herod who after finding out from wise men that they were there to worship the King of the Jews, King Herod was disturbed about this and tried to convince the wise men after they located the Child to share the news with him so he could worship Jesus to. But he was only plotting to do harm. When they saw the star (Num. 24:17) that was guiding them they went into the Child's house who was with His mother, Mary, and they fell down and worshipped the Child and brought gifts of gold and frankincense and myrrh, three different types of gifts by numerous wise men. After their visit to Jesus' home the wise men were divinely instructed and warned in a dream not to go back to Herod" (Paraphrased Matthew 2:1-12; Jeremiah 23:5-6; Zech. 9:9; John 19:19).

What was the purpose of Jesus being born in Bethlehem? Bethlehem means the House of Bread (Bethlehem comes from two Hebrew words Beth or Beit =house or household and lehem or le-chem=bread). **Jesus referred to Himself as the Bread of Life** (John 6:48). Bethlehem is part of the land that was given to Judah. **Bethlehem is in the region that was part of the territory that was given to Judah which represents the kingly line.** When Jacob (Israel) was blessing his children he declared that Judah would be the kingly line. **Jesus is from the tribe of Judah this establishes His Kingly line.** *"He stripped Himself [of all privileges and rightful dignity], so as to assume the guise of a servant, in that He became like men and was born a human being" (Philippians 2:7).* He came into this world as a Jew and He will return as "the Lion of the tribe of Judah, the Root (source) of David..." (Rev. 5:5).

The next reason why it was significant for His birth to take place in Bethlehem is that it was the original home of Naomi and the dwelling place of **Ruth the Moab woman** who became a part of Israel when she declared to Naomi "…**Your people shall be my people and your God my God…and they came to Bethlehem**" (Ruth 1:16-19). **This relates to the nations to the Gentiles coming to know the True God of Israel by embracing Yeshua/Jesus.** In Isaiah 42:6 it says that the Messiah would be a light to the nations (the Gentiles) and give them a covenant. The heart of Ruth was grateful that she has come to know the God of Israel, **this represented the ingrafting of the Gentiles (2 Co. 5:17) into the family of God and becoming the "One New Man"** (Eph. 2:14; I Cor. 12:12-13).

Her life is a demonstration of an attitude to bless the people who brought us the Messiah which by the way came through one of her descendants after she married Boaz and had a child named Obed who was the grandfather of King David (Matthew 1:5-6) demonstrating further that God honored her for honoring her Jewish mother-in-law and *God blessed her life when she herself honored the God of Israel*. Another reason for Jesus being born in Bethlehem was the fact that **King David was also born there** as well as anointed there by the Prophet Samuel to be Saul's successor. Jesus was called the *Son of David* (Isaiah 9:6-7) which is an important part of His identity as the Jewish Messiah as shown in Matthew 21:9 where the Jewish crowds welcomed Him as *Hosanna in the Highest.*

He is the promised "Seed" of the woman that shall bruise the head of Satan (Genesis 3:15; Gal. 4:4). His assignment or mission as a perfect man who never sinned was the **"Redeemer" of the lost** (those without a covenant through Salvation). While on the earth, He was an Orthodox Jewish Rabbi, A Prophet, Priest and King (John 4:42-44; John 18:37; Matt. 13:57; Matt. 21:11; 2 Sam. 7:16; Ps. 89:29). **He is now our High Priest** (Hebrew 4:15) **and at His second coming, Christ will set up the Davidic mediatorial kingdom and reign as King-Priest** (Zech. 6:11-13; Rev. 19:16; Matt. 2:2; I Tim. 1:17).

The Jews and many Christians observe seven feasts that are appointed days that God has set to meet with man. "The Passover, Unleavened Bread, Firstfruits, Pentecost, Trumpets, Atonement and Tabernacles. **The first four have been fulfilled literally by Jesus.** He was the Passover Lamb (I Cor. 5:7), the Bread of Life (John 6:35) and the firstfruits of those who have fallen asleep (I Cor. 15:20). And when Pentecost had fully come after His ascension, He sent us the Holy Spirit (Acts 2:1-4)." [8]

"So the next feast we are waiting for Jesus to fulfill literally is the Feast of Trumpets...the rapture of the church (Body of Christ). When the trumpet sounds, 'in the twinkling of an eye,' we who are alive will be changed. We will put on new bodies that will be like Jesus' body! Those who are dead in Christ will rise and also receive new bodies. They will go up first followed by us who are alive, and we will all meet the Lord in the air" (I Cor. 15:51-55). [8]

> Matthew 28:18 Jesus declared all authority was His before He gave the Great Commission:
>
> **...All authority (all power of rule) in heaven and on earth has been given to Me** (See Matt. 28:19-20).

Yet, even having been given all authority in heaven and on earth, He was the true most humble person whoever walked the face of the earth. "And after He had appeared in human form, **He abased and humbled Himself [still further] and carried His obedience to the extreme of death even the death of the cross!** Therefore, [because He stooped so low] God has highly exalted Him and has freely *bestowed on Him the name that is above every name"* (Philippians 2:8-9; Gal. 3:13).

"That in (at) the name of Jesus every knee should (must) bow, in heaven and on earth and under the earth..." (Philippians 2:10). He has great compassion yet He never compromised His position or His Word. This is one of the reasons we can have total confidence in His name.

"His Kingdom is not of this world, His was not a physical kingdom based on war and violence. **His is a Spiritual Kingdom establishing the truth in the world**. Being part of His Kingdom is knowing God, who is Truth, and whom we know as we know Jesus" [1] (John 18:33-37; 1 John 2:3).

Always know and be aware of how much our Lord and Savior loves you. *He is concerned about His family and He is concerned about His Kingdom as He oversees them both.* He is the One that is merging the two together especially in this last hour as one strong and magnificent body of people that will rise up and be a voice, the church without spot or wrinkle. He will restore us to a position of power that will take back what the enemy has stolen by giving us great favor, with spiritual weapons, strategies and gifts in operation to use for His will and purposes to do good.

As our Savior He is our High Priest, Good Shepherd, Groom and Eldest Brother. He is the Head of His family as we are His body, children, flock of sheep, bride and joint heirs.

As King He is our Lord, Master, Commander-in-Chief, Chief Apostle, and Bishop that will rule His Kingdom with justice and might as He leads and instructs His church to govern, legislate and manage His Kingdom on the earth. Because He is our King and we are a remnant, those true worshippers that will live for and in Christ Jesus, in His Kingdom we function as sons of God, His partners, citizens, soldiers, a government and all those that walk in His authority.

His name and attributes describe and refer to His character. **Yet Jesus/Yeshua or Y'shua** is the One name that is above every name. When Moses asked for God's name so he could go "to the Israelites and say to them, The God of your fathers has sent me to you," the Lord replied and said to Moses, **"I AM THAT I AM"** (In Hebrew it is, ehyeh asher ehyeh), "you shall say this to the Israelites: I AM has sent me to you!" (Exodus 3:13-14 KJV and AMP). I AM means He is able to take care of anything you encounter. *He is saying whatever you need, I AM.* In addition, "wherever you see the I AM you know that He is speaking about something that He is determined to do, something very purposeful" (The One New Man Bible).

Furthermore, according to the Complete Jewish Bible by David H. Stern in Exodus 6:3, His name is Yud-Heh-Vav-Heh or as some would spell it, Yod-Hey-Vav-Hey (YHVH), is the name of God which the Jews do not speak because "the third commandment prohibits taking God's name in vain, and the man who used it in a curse was put to death at God's explicit instruction." Because it is Holy the Jews substitute Adonay (Adonai) for the name of God which means Lord. Also, the English rendering of the Tetragrammaton, YHVH is either Yahweh or Yahveh or Jehovah. Adonay Yahweh (my Lord, my God).

Additional names or attributes that He is frequently referred to are as follows: Savior; Lord; El Shadday (Shaddai); Almighty God; Immanuel; Wonderful; Elohim Elyon; Master of All; Prince of Peace; Redeemer; The Holy One of Israel; Good Shepherd; Hashem; Rock of Salvation; Lamb of God; Bread of Life; Son of David; Healer; Son of God; The Last Adam; The Door; The True Vine; Faithful and True; King of the Ages; Eternal Life; The Author and the Finisher of our faith; Holy Lord of Glory; Light of the World; The Lion of Judah; Our Passover Lamb; Comforter; Teacher; Strengthener; Deliverer; Omniscient; Omnipotent; Omnipresent; King of kings and Lord of lords; The Resurrection and the Life; the Bridegroom; the Great Shepherd of the sheep; I am the Way, the Truth and the Life; Amen (which means the Beginning and the End); and The Word of God, just to name a few of the precious names and attributes that are used in referring to our Endearing Friend (John 15:14).

THE PROPHETIC scripture, the subject of the prophetic word and the scripture showing that it was truly fulfilled just as it was prophesied demonstrates that "Every Scripture is God-breathed (given by His inspiration) and profitable for instruction, for reproof and conviction of sin, for correction of error and discipline in obedience, [and] for training in righteousness (in holy living, in conformity to God's will in thought, purpose, and action) so that the man of God may be complete and proficient, well fitted and thoroughly equipped for every good work" (2 Timothy 3:16-17).

PROPHECIES OF THE MESSIAH FULFILLED IN JESUS CHRIST PRESENTED HERE IN THEIR ORDER OF FULFILLMENT: [6]

(The Scriptures are not written out in this text)

PROPHETIC SCRIPTURE	SUBJECT	FULFILLED
Gen. 3:15	Seed of a woman	Gal. 4:4
Gen. 12:3	Descendant of Abraham	Matt. 1:1
Gen. 17:19	Descendant of Isaac	Luke 3:34
Num. 24:17	Descendant of Jacob	Matt. 1:2
Gen. 49:10	From the tribe of Judah	Luke 3:33
Is. 9:7	Heir to the throne of David	Luke 1:32, 33
Ps. 45:6, 7; 102:25-27	Anointed and eternal	Heb. 1:8-12
Mic. 5:2	Born in Bethlehem	Luke 2:4, 5, 7
Dan. 9:25	Time for His birth	Luke 2:1, 2
Is. 7:14	To be born of a virgin	Luke 1:26, 30, 31
Jer. 31:15	Slaughter of children	Matt. 2:16-18
Hos. 11:1	Flight to Egypt	Matt. 2:14, 15
Is. 40:3-5	The way prepared	Luke.3:3-6
Mal. 3:1	Preceded by a forerunner	Luke 7:24, 27
Mal. 4:5, 6	Preceded by Elijah	Matt. 11:13, 14
Ps. 2:7	Declared the Son of God	Matt. 3:17
Is. 9:1, 2	Galilean ministry	Matt.4:13-16
Ps. 78:2-4	Speak in parables	Matt. 13:34, 35
Deut. 18:15	A Prophet	Acts 3:20, 22
Is. 61:1	To Heal the brokenhearted	Lk. 4:18, 19
Is. 53:3	Rejected by His own people, the Jews	John 1:11; Luke 23:18

Ps. 110:4	Priest after order of Melchizedek	Heb. 5:5, 6
Zech. 9:9	Triumphal entry	Mark 11:7, 9, 11
Ps. 8:2	Adored by infants	Matt. 21:15, 16
Is. 53:1	Not Believed	John 12:37, 38
Ps. 41:9	Betrayed by a close friend	Luke 22:47, 48
Zech. 11:12	Betrayed for thirty pieces of silver	Matt. 26:14, 15
Ps. 35:11	Accused by false witnesses	Mark 14:57, 58
Is. 53:7	Silent to accusations	Mark 15:4,5
Is. 50:6	Spat on and struck	Matt. 26:67
Ps. 35:19	Hated without reason	John 15:24, 25
Is. 53:5	Vicarious sacrifice	Rom. 5:6, 8
Is. 53:12	Crucified with malefactors	Mark 15:27, 28
Zech. 12:10	Pierced through hands and feet	John 20:27
Ps. 22:7, 8	Scorned and mocked	Luke 23:35
Ps. 69:9	Was reproached	Rom. 15:3
Ps. 109:4	Prayer for His enemies	Luke 23:34
Ps. 22:17, 18	Soldiers gambled for His clothing	Matt. 27:35, 36
Ps. 22:1	Forsaken by God	Matt. 27:46
Ps. 34:20	No bones broken	John 19:32, 33, 36
Zech. 12:10	His side pierced	John 19:34
Is. 53:9	Buried with the rich	Matt. 27:57-60
Ps. 16:10; 49:15	To be resurrected	Mark 16:6, 7
Ps. 68:18	His ascension to God's right hand	Mark 16:19; I Cor. 15:4; Eph. 4:8

Described below is much of what Jesus endured and why *Jesus would understand* **what everyday people endure or tolerate as a result of some type of persecution or attack because of their faith:** [8]

From an early age, as a carpenter, He knew all about working hard with His hands, standing on His feet all day long and returning home with aches in His body.

He continues to say that, the religious leaders of His day made life difficult for Him. **They challenged His authority (Matt. 21:23) and tested His teachings** (Matt. 19:3). They also called Him a glutton, winebibber, friend of tax collectors and sinners (Matt. 11:19, and blasphemer (Mark 2:7). They said that He was demon-possessed and mad (John 10:20), put Him on the spot when they brought an adulterous woman to Him (John 8:2-11), attempted to stone Him (John 8:59, 10:31-39) and accused Him of perverting the nation (Luke 23:2). He was also chased out of His own hometown (Luke 4:29).

He experienced the pain of being denied by a loved one (Luke 22:54-62) and betrayed by one considered close to Him (vv.47-48). He also knows all about the sickness you are suffering because He bore your sickness and pains on the cross (Isaiah 53:4). He endured His sufferings for our sakes, so that we can have His peace and the anointing to rise above the troubles we are facing.

My friend, **you may feel that no one understands your struggles. Listen, while this may be true of man, it is not true of Jesus.** He knows exactly what you are going through and He can sympathize with your weaknesses because He was in all points tempted as we are, yet without sin.

None of us have been tempted in all points. But God allowed Jesus to be tempted in all points so that He can understand and identify with the struggles of every single

person on this earth. He can be touched by our humanity –our weaknesses, tears, disappointments, griefs...

All points!

There is no trial, difficulty, challenge or temptation that you face that Jesus cannot identify with. My friend, the moment you go through it, right there and then, He feels it too. That is the kind of representative you have in Jesus! That is the love of God so that you will draw near to His throne of grace (not judgment) to find mercy and grace in time of need! (Hebrews 4:15-16).[8]

WHAT WAS FINISHED AND ACCOMPLISHED AT THE CROSS?

The Finished Work at the Cross is where His endurance of persecution and suffering produced a great work beyond measure and no other person has ever done as much for people as our Savior. He stayed focused on His assignment knowing that it was a work that would last for eternity and because of His suffering and the price that was paid He knew of the joy that would come out of it and bring Light into the world. He declared **"...It is finished!** And He bowed His head and gave up His Spirit" (John 19:30). Furthermore, the proof of His death was a pierced side where blood and water flowed indicating His heart had ruptured before He died (John 19:34).

Hebrews 12:2 KJV says,

> Looking unto Jesus, the Author and Finisher of our faith, who for the joy that was set before Him endured the cross, despising the shame, and has sat down at the right hand of the throne of God.

What was accomplished because of His love, humility and determination to save a dying world on that day at Calvary?

He gave us **His Righteousness** and He took **our Sins**	2 Co. 5:21; John 1:29
He gave us **Eternal Life** and **He conquered Death**	John 3:16; Rev. 1:18
He gave us **Health** and took our **Sickness**	1 Peter 2:24; 3 John 2
He gave us **A Peace of Mind and took Confusion and Torment**	John 14:27; Ro. 8:1
He gave us **Wealth** and took our **Poverty**	Deut. 8:18; Gal. 3:14; 2 Cor. 8:9
He gave us **Forgiveness** and took the **Punishment**	Eph. 1:17
He gave us **His Strength** and took our **Weaknesses**	Isaiah 40:31
He gave us **Blessings** and took the **Curses**	Deut. 28:1-14 and 15-68
He made us **sons of God** as He became the **Son of man**	Romans 8:14-16
He gave us **Deliverance** and **Punished the Wicked**	Prov. 11:21
He gave us **Wisdom** while **others** were **Spiritually Blind**	2 Co. 4:4; I Co. 2:7-8
He gave us **Reconciliation to God** as **He was separated from Him**	Ro. 10:9; Acts 2:21; Matt. 27:46
He gave us **Wholeness** and took **our Brokenness**	Mark 10:52

He gave us **Victory** and **Scattered our Enemies**	Luke 23:12; Deut. 28:7
He gave us **Power in the Holy Spirit & Tongues**	Acts 2:4 and 19:6
He made us **the Head and not the Tail**	Deut. 28:13
He gave us **Authority in His name**	Mark 16:17; Luke 10:19
He gave us **Prosperity** and took our **Lack**	Job 36:11; Prov. 10:22
He caused us to be **Heirs of God**	Romans 8:17
He caused us to be **Overcomers**	Rev. 12:10-11
He caused us to be the **Lender and not the Borrower**	Prov. 22:7
He gave us **All of the Promises in His Word**	2 Cor. 1:20

"The works of the Lord are great, sought out by all those who have delight in them. His work is honorable and glorious, and His righteousness endures forever" (Ps. 111:2-3). The Lord was declaring that He will work miracles in your life as a Believer when He said, **"I will be their God, and they shall be My people** (Hebrews 8:10). When the Lord went about doing good He did great miracles which included to raise the dead, cleanse the lepers, drive out demons and heal the sick: the lame walked, the blind could see, the deaf could hear and much more, (Matt. 10:8; John 5:4-9; Luke 8:43-48; Luke 8:49-56; John 9:6-9; Luke 13:10-13; John 5:4-9; Mark 1:31, 34; Matthew 9:14-25).

He prayed for all types of sickness and all that came to Him were healed. His first miracle entailed turning water into wine for a wedding at the request of His Mother (John 2:1-11). He was also a comfort to those who mourned; He operated in the anointing of multiplication and as He gave thanks He fed five thousand plus men (not counting the women and children) with five loaves of bread and two small fish and when He fed four thousand men (again not counting the women and children) with seven loaves of bread and a few small fish with food left over in both cases (Matthew 14:17-21; Matthew 15:36-37; John 6:9-14). He walked on water and He calmed the seas, He is truly the Son of God, the Anointed One.

He had a great compassion for people and was grateful in His heart and very thankful. He only did and said what He was sent to do and say by the Father in heaven and as a result many benefited from His obedience and miracles (the supernatural went forth). He also dealt with the demonic realm, casting demons out of people and setting them free. Many people say they want to be like Jesus but in order to be like Him you must be ready to love others, be willing to lay hands on the sick, be available to pray for others, and anointed to cast out demons that only bow to the name and authority of Christ Jesus. Therefore, when He sent His disciples on a mission "He gave them power and authority over unclean spirits, to drive them out, and to cure all kinds of disease and all kinds of weakness and infirmity" (Matt. 10:1). When Jesus' disciples were saved and filled with the Infilling of the Holy Spirit on the Day of Pentecost (Acts 2:1-4) they went about as well ministering the Gospel and laying hands on the sick with boldness and signs and wonders followed, (Acts 4:29-20).

Signs and wonders follow those who believe (Mark 16:17). When these signs and wonders followed Jesus' ministry there were those who were offended by it and opposed it greatly. It actually caused those who were "spiritually blind" (I Cor. 2:14; 2 Cor. 4:4) to hate instead of love and be happy that people were being set free from long term illnesses and bondages. **"...But now they have seen these miracles, and yet they have hated both Me and My Father. But this is to fulfill what is written in the law: 'They hated Me without reason (a cause)' "** John 15:24-25 NIV.

"God sent Moses as the mediator of His covenant, but as great as Moses was, he was merely a servant in God's house. Jesus is the

Son (Heb. 3:5-6), the Mediator of the new and final covenant (Heb. 8:6). He comes with a message of judgment for those who will not repent, but he has grace and mercy for all who come to the Father through Him. He intercedes for us before the Father's throne, and he invites people from all nations –men and women, young and old – to receive the blessings of the new covenant. In Him, and through Him, we are able to enter God's presence and dwell with Him forever," (NLT Parallel Study Bible).

The most profound expression of the love of God for us is the gift of His only Son to be our Savior. **It is love that seeks the best interest of an individual while seeking nothing for itself in return**. God's purpose was to save over judgment or condemnation and for this reason **God is declared to be "Love"** (I John 4:8, 16). As we follow His example and choose to love without expecting anything in return our marriages and families will blossom beyond our expectations because there won't be any selfish motive involved and therefore sincerity will shine and true healing of the heart will come forth.

John 3:16-17 NIV,

> *For God so loved the world that He gave His one and only Son, that whoever believes in Him shall not perish but have eternal life. For God did not send His Son into the world to condemn the world, but to save the world through Him.*

WHAT IS SALVATION?

Isaiah 43:3-6; 10-12, speaks about God as our Savior and the fact that there is *no other God before or after Him:*

> **For I am the Lord your God, the Holy One of Israel, your Savior**…Because you are precious in My sight and honored, and because I love you, I will give men in return for you and peoples in exchange for your life. **Fear not, for I am with you**…I will say to the north, Give

up! and to the south Keep not back. Bring My sons from afar and My daughters from the ends of the earth...You are my witnesses, says the Lord, and My servant whom I have chosen, that you may know Me, believe Me and remain steadfast to Me, and understand that I am He. **Before Me there was no God formed, neither shall there be after Me. I, even I, am the Lord, and besides Me there is no Savior.** I have declared [the future] and have saved the nation in times of danger], and **I have shown [that I am God]** – when there was no strange and alien god among you; therefore, you are My witnesses, says the Lord, that I am God.

Salvation is a gift for anyone who makes a decision for life over death. In it is everything a person would need but you will also receive an abundance that goes beyond your need. The most important thing about receiving Salvation is that it offers the gift of eternal life, eternal existence. "*Eternal life* ...is the present possession, as well as a future hope, for all persons who believe in the Son of God. God loves the world so much that He sent His Son to die on the cross to give eternal life to those who trust in Him. He does not want anyone to perish in sin, but those who reject His Son are already living under the wrath of God." [1] John 3:15, 16, 36 (Paraphrased).

In our Salvation we have His promises: health, preservation, protection, provision, prosperity, peace, shalom (wholeness), good relationships, wellness, purpose, assignment, help, favor, deliverance, authority, strength, mercy, guidance, angelic help, increase, wealth and much more. **It also includes our covenant with God**; it cleanses our conscience of dead works, shame, guilt and sin. But most of all we are thankful because "in Him we have redemption (deliverance and salvation) through His blood, remission (forgiveness) of our offenses, in accordance with the riches and the generosity of His gracious favor" (Eph. 1:7). **The Gospel is the power of God unto Salvation to the Jew first then to the world.** "I am the Way, and the Truth and the Life. No one comes to the Father except through Me. If you really knew Me you would know My Father as well" (John 14:6-7 NIV). For the work of the Father and of the Son flow into one another; *the work One does is the work of the Other.*

There is but One name and One way to Eternal Life and Jesus is the way God has provided for us. To *know* God and not just know *about* Him requires a personal relationship – John 17:3 NLT says:

> And this is the way to have eternal life – to know You, the only true God, and Jesus Christ, the One You sent to earth.

If you are not a Born-again Christian with the Infilling (Baptism) of the Holy Spirit or you are a Christian Believer and would like to rededicate your life to Jesus just say the following Prayer and tell someone of the Decision you have made regarding the Good News!

A PRAYER FOR SALVATION AND THE INFILLING OF THE HOLY SPIRIT

Dear Heavenly Father,
I come to You now, just as I am in the name of Jesus and ask for forgiveness. Your Word says, "…Whosoever shall call on the name of the Lord shall be saved" and if you confess with your mouth Jesus is Lord and in your heart believe that God raised Him from the dead, you will be saved (Acts 2:21; Romans 10:9).

I believe and confess now that Jesus Christ is the Son of God and He is alive today. I receive Him as my personal Lord and Savior. Thank You Father God that Your Son has set me free from eternal darkness (I John 2:2, 12). I now declare that I am redeemed, I am healed, I am blessed and I am whole. Therefore, I now have a renewed, abundant and confident life in Christ Jesus.

Father God, You said my Salvation would be the result of Your Holy Spirit giving me new birth by coming to live in me (Romans 8:9-11). So I ask You now for the Infilling of Your Holy Spirit as you have promised. Thank You for the gift to speak in other tongues, my supernatural spiritual prayer language that is unknown to man but known to God according to Acts 2:4 and I Corinthians 14:2. Now I bind the strong man that was sent to rob me and I plead the Blood of Jesus over my mind and mouth as I now release from my spirit my supernatural spiritual prayer language in Jesus' Mighty name. Amen!

The above Prayer is based on Romans 10:9-10 which says:

If you acknowledge and confess with your lips that Jesus is Lord and in your heart believe that God raised Him from the dead, you will be saved. For with the heart a person believes and so is *justified*, and with the mouth he confesses (declares openly and speaks out freely his faith) and confirms [his] salvation.

I John 2:2, 12 says:

And He [that same Jesus Himself] is the propitiation (the atoning sacrifice) for our sins, and not for ours alone but also for [the sins of] the whole world. *...because for His name's sake your sins are forgiven [pardoned through His name and on account of confessing His name].*

"Justified" – We are as if we never sinned! We are declared righteous, acceptable to God because of the Finished Work at the Cross where Jesus took our sins and gave us His Righteousness because in Him we have redemption through His blood! Hallelujah for a God Who Saves! (Ephesians 1:7).

In closing the following poem by a man of God of whom I never had the pleasure of meeting or hearing minister the Word, the late, Dr. S. M. Lockridge, who seems to have captured and divinely expounded on revelation of Who the King of kings really *is*:

THAT'S MY KING

The Bible says my King is a seven-way king.
He's the King of the Jews; that's a racial king.
He's the King of Israel; that's a national king.
He's the King of Righteousness. He's the King of the Ages.
He's the King of Heaven. He's the King of Glory.
He's the King of kings, and He's the Lord of lords.
That's my King
Well, I wonder do you know Him?

David said, "The Heavens declare the glory of God and the
Firmament shows His handiwork."
My King is a sovereign King.
No means of measure can define His limitless love.
No far seeing telescope can bring into visibility the coastline
of His
shoreless supply.
No barrier can hinder Him from pouring out His blessings.
He's enduringly strong. He's entirely sincere.
He's eternally steadfast. He's immortally graceful.
He's imperially powerful. He's impartially merciful.
Do you know Him?

He's the greatest phenomenon that ever crossed the horizon of
This world. He's God's Son.
He's the sinner's Savior. He's the centerpiece of civilization.
He stands in the solitude of Himself.

He's august. He's unique. He's unparalleled. He's unprecedented.
He's the loftiest idea in literature.
He's the highest personality in philosophy.
He's the supreme problem in higher criticism.
He's the fundamental doctrine of true theology.
He's the cardinal necessity for spiritual religion.
He's the miracle of the age.
He's the superlative of everything good that you choose to call Him. He's the only one qualified to be the all sufficient Savior.
I wonder if you know Him today.

He supplies strength for the weak. He's available for the tempted
and the tried. He sympathizes and He saves.
He strengthens and sustains. He guards and He guides.
He heals the sick. He cleanses lepers. He forgives sinners.
He discharges debtors. He delivers captives. He defends the feeble. He blesses the young. He serves the unfortunate.
He regards the aged.
He rewards the diligent and He beautifies the meek.
I wonder if you know Him.

Well, my King is the King.
He's the key to knowledge. He's the wellspring to wisdom.
He's the doorway of deliverance. He's the pathway of peace.
He's the roadway of righteousness.
He's the highway of holiness. He's the gateway of glory.
Do you know Him?

He's the master of the mighty. He's the captain of the conquerors.
He's the head of the heroes. He's the leader of the legislators.
He's the overseer of the over comers.
He's the governor of governors. He's the prince of princes.
He's the King of kings and He's the Lord of lords.
That's my King.

Well, His office is manifold. His promise is sure.
His light is matchless. His goodness is limitless.
His mercy is everlasting. His love never changes.
His word is enough. His grace is sufficient.
His reign is righteousness, His yoke is easy, and his burden is light.
I wish I could describe Him to you, but He's indescribable.
He's incomprehensible. He's invincible. He's irresistible.

I'm coming to tell you, the heavens cannot contain Him,
Let alone a man explain Him.
Well, you can't get Him out of your mind.
You can't get Him off of your hand.
You can't out live Him, and you can't live without Him.
The Pharisees couldn't stand Him,
But they found out they couldn't stop Him.
Pilate couldn't find any fault in Him. The witnesses couldn't get their testimonies to agree.
Herod couldn't kill Him.
Death couldn't handle Him, and the grave couldn't hold Him.
Yea, that's my King, that's my King.

He always has been and He always will be. He had no predecessor and He'll have no successor. There was nobody before Him and there'll be nobody after Him.
You can't impeach Him and He's not going to resign.
That's my King!
Father, thine is the kingdom and the power and the glory forever and ever,
and ever, and ever, and ever. How long is that?
And ever, and ever, and when you get through with all the forevers, then
AMEN!

APPENDIX

OUR BLENDED FAMILY'S TESTIMONY:

HOW GOD BLENDED AND BONDED OUR TWO FAMILIES TOGETHER THROUGH OBSTACLES AND LOVE WITH A PRE-SCHOOLER, THREE TEENS, ONE YOUNG ADULT AND GAVE US A NEW BEGINNING

INTRODUCTION TO OUR TESTIMONY:

Our testimony is the making of a family that God formed from two separate families where not only we the parents had a divine call on our lives and were chosen to do a work for God in the five fold ministry, but we discovered that all five of our children were also called, chosen and operated in the five fold ministry gifts.

The Bible says this about divine calls:

I Corinthians 12:28 says:

> So God has appointed some in the church [for His own use]: first apostles (special messengers); second prophets (inspired preachers and expounders); third teachers; then wonder-workers (miracles); then those with ability to heal the sick; helpers; administrators; [speakers in] different (unknown) tongues.

Ephesians 4:11-12 also describes the five fold ministry office gifts:

> And His gifts were [varied; He Himself appointed and gave men to us] some to be apostles (special messengers), some prophets (inspired preachers and expounders), some evangelists (preachers of the Gospel, traveling missionaries), some pastors (shepherds of His flock) and teachers. His intention was the perfecting and the full equipping of the saints (His consecrated people), [that they should do] the work of ministering toward building up Christ's body (the church). (Author's addition - The word "men" used in this passage is speaking of "mankind" for those of you wondering if wo-men are called to serve God in this capacity).

God sets ministry gifts in the Church – not man. God is the only one Who does the setting and the calling. *"Now there are distinctive varieties and distributions of endowments (gifts, extraordinary powers distinguishing certain Christians, due to the power of divine grace operating in their souls by the Holy Spirit) and they vary, but the [Holy] Spirit remains the same"* (I Cor. 12:4). A person does not enter the ministry just because they *feel* like it. You cannot make yourself a five fold ministry gift from God and many that have tried have found this could be very dangerous. Just seeing a "need" is not necessarily a divine call from God into the five fold ministry offices. That is not scriptural but what is scriptural is the fact that God commanded each one of us to love one another and that would also entail having compassion on another in *need* which does not necessarily mean one has to be of the five fold ministry to fulfill but rather is a general command to all saints (John 15:17).

When God chooses someone for the five fold ministry He also anoints, empowers and equips them to do a work or an assignment for Him. Also each ministry gift is equipped with spiritual gifts necessary to stand in the office in which they are called that will enable the man or woman of God to go forth and accomplish an assignment or a work in the Body of Christ for His Glory. "All these [gifts, achievements, abilities] are inspired and brought to pass by one and the same [Holy] Spirit, Who apportions to each person individually [exactly] as He chooses." God *equips* them to minister regularly with these gifts and it is not to be confused with laymen who have spiritual gifts operating *through* them on occasion (I Corinthians 12:1-11).

All that are used by God are first chosen. Keep in mind that God chooses people for more than the five fold ministry. He has anointed people to accomplish various tasks, to be parents, run businesses and professions of all sorts. Our concentration is in the area of ministry because we are giving our testimony and our testimony is how God chose, equipped, trained, anointed and blended our families together to do a work in ministry for Him.

John 15:16 says this about being *chosen*:

> You have not chosen Me, but I have chosen you and I have appointed you [I have planted you], that you might go and bear fruit and keep on bearing, and that your fruit may be lasting [that it may remain, abide], so that whatever you ask the Father in My Name [as presenting all that I AM], He may give it to you.

Revelation 17:14 says this,

> …for He is Lord of lords and King of kings – and those with Him and on His side are *chosen* and *called* and loyal and faithful followers.

The Lord said He was raising our family up to do a great work for Him. This is not anything new for God; He has always raised up families to do a work for Him. From biblical days to modern times the pattern has not changed. Does He do this with every family, of course not, just the ones He has chosen for this type of mission to accomplish a specific vision He has imparted to them for His purpose.

This may not only include the **Immediate Family** with sons and daughter in-laws and daughters and son in-laws but with the parent's parents, siblings, cousins and other **Extended Family** members. **In the Bible there are variations of families that were used of God.** For example: Abraham and Sarah were a family of two, a ***Child-Free Family*** for many years before God blessed them with a son named Isaac. Their family was used to instill great faith in God's people. One of Isaac's sons named Jacob (later renamed Israel) had a large ***Blended Family,*** consisting of his biological children by two different wives and concubines which created blended (step) children with blended mothers within his household. The family had twelve sons which formed the twelve tribes of Israel and they worked closely with their father. We know the story of God setting apart one of Jacob's sons, Joseph, for a while to be prepared for the ministry and vision or assignment God had imparted to him. Later he was reunited with them and used of God to save his family from a famine in the land and to give way for the Israelites to live in Egypt. Then there was Esther and her cousin Mordecai an *Extended Family (Esther 2:7)* working together and ultimately being used by God to save the nation of Jewish people from their enemy Haman. Of course as we look at Noah and his family, *a Biological Family,* his immediate family was comprised of a wife, three sons and three daughter in-laws; *again a family that was used by God except this time God used a family to preserve mankind for the entire world.*

Some of the modern day family role models and mentors that the Lord has given to our family are men and women of God with integrity, faith and a great love for Him. We have been raised up by God as a family ministry and each of the following ministries represents a family ministry that the Lord gave to us as an example and which we have partnered with over the years: *Fred and Betty Price; Kenneth and Gloria Copeland; Dave and Joyce Meyer; Bill and Veronica Winston* and it was all possible because of *Paul and Jan Crouch.* The Crouchs were obedient to the vision that God imparted to them to start Trinity Broadcasting Network (TBN.org) which is now the largest Christian television system of networks in the world. They too, are a family ministry and a blessing to the entire human race.

These are all faithful, powerful family ministries that the Holy Spirit directed us to receive as role models, as an example of family ministries who were walking/living by faith and integrity. *They are Anointed Biological Families of God and one is an Anointed God-Blended Family* called into the service of the King of kings. They are a blessing in the Kingdom of God as each person is appointed, equipped and anointed as a five fold ministry gift (Ephesians 4:11). They have all been a tremendous blessing in our lives! Each one of these ministries employs their sons and daughter in-laws as well as their daughters and son in-laws, grandchildren and other extended family members to work on staff. Each one of these ministries is successful in their own right having been obedient and faithful to the divine call and assignment from God for their lives. We as a family thank God for their example and steadfastness to encourage those behind them to never give up but always continue in the things of God knowing He will prove Himself strong and faithful!

We have been ordained for sometime and primarily functioning within the five fold ministry office gifts as God wills and for His sole purpose. Our family is an *Anointed God-Blended Family* called to the service of the King. There are thousands upon thousands of Blended Families in the earth but the distinction being made is that not every Blended Family is called, chosen and anointed to serve God in the five fold ministry.

In chapter four **we described the Anointed Family as a Family of God that has placed God first in their lives;** the God-fearing family, Psalms 128:1-6. It functions by the Word of God and is obedient to move forward as a unit in the will of God.

God's Blended Family as described in chapter four is an anointed family. It is formed from one man with or without children and one woman with one or more children or vice versa who are Born-again Christians, have the Infilling of the Holy Spirit, Anointed with the Authority and Power of God who are blended together in marriage under the direction of the Holy Spirit. Also in Chapter four under 'Family Types that Exist in the Kingdom of God Today…' we give **the Divine Perspective of 'God's Blended Family' which is larger than what we perceive or consider as within the limits of a usual or customary family.**

OUR BLENDED FAMILY'S TESTIMONY:

The process over the years was all God as the Holy Spirit instructed my husband and me. Neither one of us knew anything about blended/step families both having come from intact biological two-parent families. We had absolutely no knowledge of what to expect about blended families, what to notice, what to avoid, what were the pitfalls or danger points, or zones if you will, therefore, *the Holy Spirit literally took us by the hand and walked us through some of the most difficult and painful years of our lives and some of the greatest!* We basically kept our joy knowing God was at the head of our family and giving us strength. We knew that if we would remain obedient to the Holy Spirit we would emerge the better for it and come out victorious.

My husband's parents were married for forty plus years until his mother passed and he is the youngest of three sons. My parents were married for fifty-eight years until my father passed and I am the eldest of ten children, three sons and seven daughters.

Both of our backgrounds included bishops, pastors, professionals and blue collar workers and our entire immediate family and most of our extended family are Born-again Christians. I have siblings who are also prophets and called to pastor as well as being fourth generation spirit-filled Believers. Much of my family's position with Christ is credited to praying parents, grandparents and great-grand parents.

God is moving and equipping families, He is taking back territory, transferring wealth *and He is doing much of it through one of the very things He used to replenish the earth when it was in the post-deluvian era (meaning once the earth was replenished after the flood of Noah), and that was "A Family!"*

Our Testimony begins at the end of my former marriage and tells of the journey my children and I traveled that brought us into our new beginning as a Blended Family. It was impressed upon me that it was important to start here because so many women and some men are raising their children alone and need to understand that they do not have to rely on a social system or a natural person for help if they are willing to rely on God. He is the only *Person or Source* they will need during this transition in their lives and he will supply all of their needs if they choose to trust Him.

I had been standing and believing God to restore my former marriage for approximately five years when I received a telephone call from a young prophet, fifteen years of age during the fall of 1992. He told me that God was doing a new thing and that He had a ram in the bush along with some other information. I told him that I would not stop waiting for God to restore my marriage and he said, "Then you will wait in vain." After I heard this shocking word, I prayed because I knew what God had spoken to me about my marriage. God told me there would be no divorce. What I did not know at the time was that God moves in seasons. His purpose will go on, and everyone has a free will to make their own choices. We must know how to discern when the Lord is done with something especially if He did not ordain it in the first place. "To everything there is a season, and a time for every matter or purpose under the heaven…" Ecclesiastes 3:1-8.

God was about to do something new and different in my life, and I had to decide whether I would stay in the past and continue with the old or flow with the Holy Spirit and move forward with the new. I thought about the prophetic words God had personally given to me and how He had confirmed them regarding my former marriage, a marriage that I had been standing and believing Him to restore for nearly seven years. By this time my former husband and I were approaching seventeen years of marriage with two children who loved him dearly. One of the problems was, he did not have enough Word in him to stay home and he would refuse to pray for himself until he was overwhelmed with the things of the world that kept pulling on him and suddenly he would leave. **Over the years the Lord would tell me He was sending my husband home and to prepare a place for his things and within two weeks he would be home.**

Every time the Lord spoke that my husband would return and when he did he would ask me, "how did you know I was coming home when I did not know?" He would ask this question because he had decided not to come back. I told him because I am listening to God and you are listening to the devil.

God would send ministers across his path to minister to him, and God would change his heart, and show him the way, and free him up to make the right choices and it was during this time that God was answering our prayer that he would return home. Unfortunately he would stay for a while and without a renewed mind in Christ and a complete healing in his soul, thinking on the old things constantly and being drawn by the "world" and what it had to offer after a few weeks or months he would leave home again. After five years of going and coming and trying to stay home in his own strength without the help of the Holy Spirit, at the appointed time God said, enough is enough and God shut the door (Revelation 3:7).

I also learned that even though God instituted marriage and that He hates divorce, He will permit it, sometimes order it. I further understood that God was releasing me to go forth with His purpose for my life and the lives of my children. The Lord was not going to cause anyone including my former spouse to stay in a marriage he no longer desired. The Lord will not go against anyone's will. As I've already mentioned, God will send help and change hearts, open doors and give chances but *the final decision is yours* to obey and go through the door God has opened and prepared for you.

Some choose to make their *own way* which generally leads them into a trap of some kind because they cannot see what is ahead. God gives chances but they eventually run out and we are left with the consequences of our choices. Romans 1:28 says, "And so, since they did not see fit to acknowledge God or approve of Him or consider Him worth the knowing, God gave them over to a base and condemned mind to do things not proper or decent but loathsome." In the KJV it says that God gave the person over to a reprobate mind; v.29 "being filled with all unrighteousness, fornication, wickedness..." (Titus 1:15-16; 2 Tim. 3:8-9).

Furthermore, because it was our own plan and because Satan is so subtle we were not aware he was operating in our lives due to the deception and spiritual blindness that had entered in because of disobedience and rebellion.

2 Corinthians 4:3-4 says this about *spiritual blindness:*

But even if our Gospel (the glad tidings) also be hidden (obscured and covered up with a veil that hinders the knowledge of God), it is hidden [only] to those who are perishing and obscured [only] to those who are spiritually dying and veiled [only] to those who are lost.

For the god of this world has blinded the unbelievers' minds [that they should not discern the truth], preventing them from seeing the illuminating light of the Gospel of the glory of Christ (the Messiah), Who is the Image and Likeness of God.

"All the ways of a man are pure in his own eyes..." (Proverbs 16:2 NKJV); "There is a way that seems right to a man, but its end is the way of death..." (Proverbs 14:12 NKJV); "The backslider in heart will be filled with his own ways..." (Proverbs 14:14 KJV); "Pride goes before destruction, and a haughty spirit before a fall" (Proverbs 16:18 AMP); "A fool has no delight in understanding, but in expressing his own heart" (Proverbs 18:2 NKJV).

Proverbs 18:1-2 says,

> **He who willfully separates and estranges himself [from God and man] seeks his own desire and pretext to break out against all wise and sound judgment. A [self-confident] fool has no delight in understanding but only in revealing his personal opinions and himself.**

My former spouse's heart was hardened about staying home for good. Even though there was an effort made on his and my part using our own strength, because in the beginning of the trouble that led to our separation neither one of us had turned to God for help. We were warring against spirits we did not know even existed. *There were generational curses and spirits of separation and divorce that had been assigned to our marriage which we were not aware of at the time because we did not read the Word of God nor did we pray or attend church on a regular basis to understand these things or to get answers.* Furthermore, there were very few Christian television programs on the air during this time and to be truthful we did not watch those either. We were baby Christians and were learning as all of this was taking place. So whatever we did to save our marriage was what we came up with in our natural minds and in the flesh or some poor advice from another worldly person. There were a few people including family that did tell me to pray but I could not see or understand how that alone could quickly help my current situation and looking back that was simply because I did not know the Word of God for myself.

God says that He has a better plan for us if we would only seek Him for it. His plan would also involve solutions to problems because He knows how to bring what He begins to a finish.

Please read Jeremiah 29:11 through 14 and see the follow below:

> For I know the thoughts and plans that I have for you, says, the Lord, thoughts and plans for welfare and peace and not for evil, to give you hope in your final outcome...
>
> v14 – I will be found by you, says the Lord, and I will release you from captivity and gather you from all the nations and all the places to which I have driven you, says the Lord, and I will bring you back to the place from which I caused you to be carried away captive.

If you have missed God (you will know because you will be frustrated and upset much of the time and you may even be worn out) all that is necessary is to ask for forgiveness and repent with a sincere heart and He will remove the blinders so you can see clearly and get on the right path, which is His plan for your life.

One of the things that we tried to do one year after the initial separation (our communication was very open especially because of the children, so we stayed in touch and there was a series of breaking up and going back together as I mentioned earlier) at one time the both of us left our employment and moved across the country to Atlanta with our children for a fresh start. (I want to speak a word of caution: you cannot run from your problems they will only follow you).

After being in Atlanta, Georgia for a month and making progress with new employment, schools and sitters, he made contact with his former girlfriend who was also his chemical dependency connection in Los Angeles. I assumed the urge came and he did not know where to buy anything in a new place so he decided he would return to Los Angeles. However, I was not aware that he wanted to return to Los Angeles until he told me to call and tell them to keep our Volvo automobile and his motorcycle in Los Angeles (we had a moving company ready to transport all of our belongings, furniture and our other vehicle and what not). When I asked him what was going on he would not say anything. When I asked about the vehicle he said he was going to sell it from L.A. but he had no response about his motorcycle which became a part of his new lifestyle when he was going back and forth. So I telephoned the storage company where one of my girlfriends was overseeing the process at the storage and she said the moving company was there at that very moment and they were pulling everything out to place on the moving van to ship all of our belongings to Atlanta. I then told her to have them put everything back in storage until I knew what was going on. He never made it clear as to why He was returning to Los Angeles but he did ask me to come with him and I refused to leave therefore he left.

He left the children and me with the minivan and he decided to take the Greyhound Bus back and while in route I telephoned the bus line and left a message and he called and I told him to come back and that we could return together but he refused and kept going. So there I was abandoned in a city I really did not know, with two small children (a son ten years of age and a daughter who had just turned two years old a few days prior). I was not really aware of the seriousness of the addiction he had, I did not know he was taking anything until after we had been married for over ten years. In the beginning when we met again after not seeing one another since Junior High School, He told me at that time that he had been using substance abuse chemicals while he was in Vietnam but had not used them since the war and I believed him. As did the rest of his immediate family, no one knew he was using anything; he went to great lengths to hide his addiction.

My not knowing anything about the use of drugs nor the affect it had on people I was unaware of the signs which would have indicated he was using something and how addicted he was. **I probably did not notice because he was a devoted husband and father up until this point. Whatever he was involved in he kept it away from our home and family. He decided to leave after he saw he could no longer control the addiction and he needed his salary to support his habit.** There was a drastic change in his personality and character noticed by his family, co-workers and friends. None of us suspected chemical abuse because it did not really fit his character. He eventually lost everything: his family, home, employment, self respect, friends, associates and all that was connected with our life together.

As I was saying, **I now found myself abandoned in another state across country with my two small children and living with one of my cousins on my mother's side of the family.** I decided to return to Los Angeles because it was my home and my family was there. I was invited to stay in Los Angeles with an elderly lady who took care of our children when they were small while my former husband and I worked. She had asked me to stay in touch and a day or so after he left I decided to call her. She was in her seventies and lived in a home she inherited for which she gave God all the glory for giving it to her. A home in which God knew one day I would need to pass through while on my journey. This sweet lady invited me to stay with her when I told her what had happened. I asked her if she had the room and she said yes.

So now that I had somewhere to live in Los Angeles while I looked for new employment and a place to live for my children and myself, I went to the Automobile Club in Atlanta and had a map made for my route back to Los Angeles. I told the lady I wanted the fastest route back and she asked me if my husband was going to drive because the fastest was the hardest route and I told her yes and she prepared the map. I let my cousin who we were staying with in Atlanta know we were leaving, I telephoned my family in Los Angeles and I spoke to my former husband's grandmother and let her know as well. I packed our things, bought fruit and plenty of snacks and my children and I began our three day trip across country. I drove all day, an average of ten hours a day starting approximately 7:00 a.m. until night only stopping for gas (I did not want anyone to notice I was alone with two children). Then I would rent a room in whatever city we were in, feed and bathe the kids they would watch television then go to sleep and we would start again the next day. Our spirits were up, we sang along with the only praise tape I had in our minivan and enjoyed snacks. Kevin who was ten at the time read our map as I drove, while Melinda sat in her baby car seat looking around and enjoying the scenery.

We encountered one major obstacle while traveling across country. While driving through Mississippi there was a fire on a part of the road, a few cars were going through and some were turning back, I had a map with a specific route drawn out for us (God will lead us on a path that is narrow if we will not look to the left or to the right but continue never turning back) and I did not know any other way but I knew that I was not going back, so I made a decision to go through the fire. I told Kevin to roll up his window, I checked the rest of the windows and looked at Melinda then I proceeded to drive through the fire in order to continue on my journey home. (God will ask us to do the same in our spiritual walk with Him. We must go through the fire asking Him for wisdom and strength to endure whatever the test or trial may be).

Some would refer to this time as a storm or being in the wilderness, it is a time when you put off the old things of your flesh (die to your flesh, your old way of thinking) and start to learn of God and the more you learn of Him the more you'll trust Him and the more peace you will acquire. **During this time, you cannot go over the fire, around the fire or under the fire;** *you must go through the fire.* *Afterwards you will be strengthened and know that God is faithful and true to His Word. You will know that He will never leave you nor forsake you.* As you are strengthened and continue to increase in faith you will also start to grow spiritually as well as mature in the natural. You will gain history with God through each experience which is another way to strengthen your faith.

At the time all of this was taking place I was new in my walk with God, I did not know anything about the anointing, the blood of Jesus, angels, God's promises, the armor of God, His fruit or gifts. After it was all said and done and as I looked back over the years I discovered that God was protecting me and keeping me alive. He was helping me all along even during the times when I had no knowledge of His goodness or mercy or that His Holy Spirit was with me. This reminds me of a poem called "Footprints," the person telling the story is an unknown author who said he was walking along a beach with Jesus when he asked the Lord why there was only one set of footprints in the sand at the most difficult times of his life. Whereas there were two sets of footprints in the sand before it became difficult. Jesus explained that during the hard times it was then that ***He carried him*** and that is why there was only one set of footprints in the sand during the hard and difficult times of his life.

Many times we are not aware that the Holy Spirit is with us before we even know who Jesus is. For example, He brought me through six operations all basically female problems, endometriosis, two cesarean sections, two DNC'S after miscarriages, and so on. Now I am aware and know that the Lord was with me through each surgery because looking back I healed and recovered extremely fast, I was walking sooner than most and standing upright without any pain. People in the hospital would ask what I was there for and when I said surgery they assumed I had not had it yet and I explained that I had already had surgery and most of them could hardly believe it. And the many near head on car accidents that I never had as I reflect back and realize it was because of angelic assistance. God is good and think about it, He has sealed us as His when He didn't have to do it!

Continuing on with my testimony, after my children and I arrived in Los Angeles from our three day trip across country and visiting with my parents and extended family we continued on and arrived at the elderly lady's home I spoke about earlier. I found that this lady really did not have any extra room but that she had made room in her home for my children and me by giving us her bedroom while she slept on a roll-a-way bed in her dinning room because her son and grandson were living with her and they had the other two bedrooms. She knew that if I had known this I probably would not have come. But God had already prepared a way for me by placing it in her heart to give me unmerited favor. Some of my family members said they did not have any room for us at that time, but God said He had hardened their hearts so they would know that He walked with me and He would get the glory and not them.

Within two weeks of being in her home I was employed again in a law firm and God lead me to a two bedroom house that was for lease in a lovely area with a large yard, He gave me favor with the owners of the property who were my neighbors before I moved across country. They were not aware that we had been separated because we signed the lease together (he was back and forth). When they were told they were extremely nice and I lived on their property for the next year and a half. This was the first house I had lived in since selling our home to relocate to the suburbs which was for a short while and then we had one other move before going across country for our supposedly new start. I was living in this two bedroom house when I found out about the divine call on my life and then God stopped me from working and I went into full-time ministry in August of 1989.

In my last secular employment position before coming into full-time ministry I was working in a law firm in downtown Los Angeles, I witnessed many healings when I prayed for people on my breaks and at lunch. I really did not know the extent of my calling at that time, all I knew was that I loved God, I loved going to church and I loved ministering to hurting people and seeing their lives changed and their bodies healed. The Lord spoke to me when I arrived home from **my last day at this office** after being laid off with no warning. I received a phone call from my sister Jackie for prayer and when I was praying for her and gave a prophetic word included in that was a word for me as well and God said "…they thought that they had done something, but I saw how weary you were working for man and working for Me, so now you just work for Me." **The very next day** the owner of the two bedroom house that I was living in, who with her husband (who has now passed), originally said I could stay as long as I wanted came over and gave me a three month notice to move because her daughter wanted the house. **Shortly after that the Lord spoke to me and said, "Audrey, I want you to know that you can trust Me."** Within the month I spoke with my former husband who had returned home and encouraged him that we should stand through this time and trust God but he told me, "you stand, I am leaving." While living in this house he had come and left a few times as well.

I lived in this house for the next few months without any income, just trusting God. The Lord did not tell me to apply for any aid and place my trust in any social services so I did not. I put my faith and trust in God (for some God may send that route, but He did not tell me to receive any aid, He clearly told me to trust Him). **The Lord spoke at that time and said nothing would be turned off and He told my son, Kevin to "Tell your Mother that you will always have shelter and you will never starve."** As we received notices to disconnect our lights, water, gas and telephone I called for extensions and received favor, but when it was time to pay I still did not have any money, so when the final notices came I could do nothing but trust God and take Him at His Word.

I began to experience the supernatural as God kept His Word. He demonstrated that He was in control of my situation and life and that all I needed to do was to continue in Him by trusting Him by faith, be thankful and receive what He was doing. On the day that one of the utilities was scheduled to be cut off the service man came out to our house and he left an extension notice on the house and simply left. I never called to make any additional extensions and as far as I know the field employee does not have the authority to do this but it happened over and over for the next seven months. *Meanwhile I attended church, revivals, conferences and ministered to whomever God put across my path. I received phone calls and knocks at my door from people that were sent by God to bring food, money, and things that were needed for my family. Many of them called me on the phone and asked for my address and said God told them to send me money. I was taking care of His business and trusting Him to take care of mine and He did.*

After a few weeks the Holy Spirit told me to pack and He directed me as to which room to pack and when. He was preparing me to leave that place and when I did it was the beginning of a journey that would last for the next few years as I learned I could truly trust God no matter what the circumstance. I kept a journal as I grew in my relationship with the Lord, it was an exciting journey, one that I will never forget and one that I thank God for. Many people were not able to understand my positive attitude about all of this. However, if you would stop and consider that I was conversing with the Creator of the heavens and the universe and watching Him bring things to pass before my very eyes the things He said He would do. I cannot begin to tell you how exciting and amazing all of this was at that time in my life.

Once my son whispered, I am hungry, I did not hear him, but our neighbor came to the door and said my wife and I are going to the store make out a shopping list. Kevin told me what he had said and how fast God answered him.

A three month notice was given but I stayed seven months. During that time God was proving to me He could take care of me and the kids without having to rely on having a husband in my life or any government assistance of which I never did receive. Which brings to mind a short story about a year before moving into this house and before God spoke and told me to trust Him, I was advised by other women in ministry to go to Social Services and have them make my husband (at that time) contribute to his household while we were separated. So I followed their advice because of my two small children and I sat there all day and just before five o'clock someone finally called me in to tell me that there wasn't anything they could do for me. This was only confirmation that this was not the will of the Lord for my life. However, while I was there in the waiting room I did have an opportunity to minister to other people who were there and hurting emotionally. I left and that was the extent of my experience with that. **God told me in an audible voice that He wanted me to know that I could trust *Him*.** God also said in His Word that He is my Husband.

Isaiah 54:4-5 says,

> Fear not, for you shall not be ashamed, neither be confounded and depressed, for you shall not be put to shame. For you shall forget the shame of your youth, and you shall not [seriously] remember the reproach of your widowhood any more.
>
> **For your Maker is your Husband** – the Lord of hosts is His Name – and the Holy One of Israel is your Redeemer; the God of the whole earth He is called.

I finally received an eviction notice to move and I responded to it but the time had elapsed by the time I found the notice. It had been lodged down in the front door and the time had already passed according to the agency I took it to in order to respond.

Just before we moved out of this house there were a series of spiritual attacks on my family. For instance, one morning while

I was in the living room praying my son saw a girl's face appear in the bedroom and her mouth was wide open and a dark hole was in the center of it. Kevin and Melinda were in that room and Kevin pleaded the Blood of Jesus and got up and came to get me, it had left by the time I arrived. Another time the light bulbs, one after another would blow out and one lamp caught on fire and Melinda noticed that and came and told me. After a few more instances the co-pastor of the church I attended at that time came over and we prayed over the property and those activities stopped. It was all a part of the early days of ministry training with the Holy Spirit and I thank God for it.

Many people in the church and Christians do not believe that Satan or the dark side is real. Well I am here to tell you, from first hand experience, it is very real, that it does exist and you need to know who you are in Christ and what your authority is in order to protect your family and yourself against such evil.

After I moved out of this house I telephoned the utility companies and the telephone company to cancel our services and the operators were shocked that the services were still on after not receiving any payments for seven months. From there the Lord opened a door for me to live with my uncle, my mother's brother who was nearly seventy. He told me that he was glad I was there and how lonely he was and that he had just let another young lady and her two small children move in one week before I arrived, she was the daughter of some friends of his that had passed.

She later told me that she was about to leave her children and go to San Francisco but decided to stay after I moved in. I led her to the Lord and my uncle went to church with us. I found out later she was a survivor of the Jim Jones massive killing years ago. Her immediate family was murdered but she over heard the people say they could not touch her. She confided in me she could hear God and the Holy Spirit revealed she was a prophet. We studied the Bible together and received a lot of revelation and instructions from the Holy Spirit.

In the midst of all of this my former husband came back again, this time to my uncle's house. Without my knowledge he spoke to the elderly lady that I lived with when I came back from across country and she was now living alone so he asked her if we could move in for one month until we saved for a place of our own and she agreed.

After moving in with her he left again. Of course, people thought I was crazy at this point for taking him back again, but the Lord was speaking to me and telling me when to take him back. The Lord was merciful and giving him chances, he had a divine call on his life too and the devil was trying to rob him as well. But he made a choice and his choice remains to the time of this manuscript to continue to live a worldly lifestyle, in other words to live outside of the Kingdom of God.

I was living with the elderly lady who was a retired housekeeper that had taken care of families for a living for over thirty years and was now taking care of small children in her home. Furthermore, having been anointed to serve allowed my children and me to benefit from her gift. God knew I needed the rest especially after five years of chaos with one test and trial after another and in many cases several at once.

She cooked most of our meals; after I washed my family's clothes and set them aside to be ironed she would iron them when I was doing other things and before I realized she had done it. She screened my calls without my asking her to which were frequent from various people wanting prayer and so forth, and if I offered to help her she declined the help. Even though she did help with those things I still took full charge of my two children. My point is this, God always knows what we need because He is our source and He knows how to protect what belongs to Him. I was at the end of this cycle of events for this period of my life but did not realize it. God will give you a rest before you go on another assignment or mission so to speak.

My former husband returned again to us at this elderly lady's home only to leave again and this time it would be for the last time. He had been warned by five prophets of God, all in the same week prior to his leaving. Three of them did not know one another, one was our daughter, Melinda, whom God had been using since the age of four to deliver prophetic words, and the other was me. **The warning said, "If you leave again the door will shut from the north, east, south and west and you will never get back again."** One of the warnings that came through another prophetess at a bible study gave him an illustration and said, "In a kitchen a mother may have a cookie jar full of cookies and the child may take one when she isn't there, the child may keep taking a cookie until they are all gone. Well the cookie jar is now empty, there are no more cookies, and there are no more chances for you to leave again…"

One evening during this same week two days before he left for the last time, he told the children and me he was going to leave and they were very upset and crying. Then all of a sudden Melinda became very composed, the Spirit of God rested upon her and she spoke by the inspiration of the Holy Spirit and prophesied about his leaving again, (we could tell clearly it was not a five year old speaking because of the words and her mannerism). My former husband told the children after Melinda gave him that word from the Lord that he would not leave again. Two days later after they were asleep, I will never forget how he was standing near a dresser in our room in the elderly lady's house when he turned and looked at me and smiled and started packing. I warned him then, in a calm voice, that if he walked out of that door he would never walk through it again, because the door is shut from the north, east, south and west and he walked out of the door in front of the elderly lady and me with his things.

This was a very painful and difficult experience for the entire family, our extended family included. It was demonic, there was nothing normal about the way he would change and suddenly leave and it was not all drug related. It went deeper than that and it had little to do with our marriage. He had deep hurts from his past that I was not aware of at the time that led him to substance abuse to cover up his pain. All these things played a part but the biggest thing was something we could not see or understand that was pulling at him and it was beyond our control. Even when he left home for the first time on June 6, 1986 in the **6th month**, on the **6th day** in year **1986** we learned it was a **strategic demonic move (666)** the same number assigned to the beast or the Anti-Christ (Rev. 13:18). At the time he first left we were making long range plans and had just had a new baby and suddenly out of nowhere when I came home from work one Friday evening he told me he was leaving home the next day and I thought he was joking because he joked from time to time and he liked to laugh a lot.

How do I know this was demonic, because God Almighty stepped into the situation and sent supernatural help at my request once I started seeking Him. Anything God asks you to do, He has already equipped and enabled you to do it. If God said don't leave and you leave, that is a choice you have made because you have a free will, but it also means you had the *strength and power* to stay. We always have a choice especially in matters like these. **People need to realize that there are consequences with each choice they make. Good consequences with the right choices and bad consequences with the wrong choices.** *I believe he thought he could return anytime he desired after the warnings. He was in disbelief that it was God who was giving him chances to return to God and return home to his family. For the past five years he thought it was me who was giving him these chances to come home and stay but he soon learned that it was not me but a loving God working through me.*

Now the door was shut, and so it began, the prophetic words were starting to manifest and come to pass. It started with the elderly lady as she came to me and told me that even though he was my husband she did not want him in her home again, not even on her front porch. So I telephoned him at his work place and told him that I was going to honor her request because it was her home, therefore God had closed this door. It is amazing that he originally left June 6, 1986 and five years to the month June 25, 1991 he had the grace of God before the door shut for good. (Note: The date 6-25-1991 adds up to number 33, the same age Jesus was when He was on the cross and said "It is Finished" (John 19:30). It is as if the Lord was saying that this cycle had run its course and now it was finished). I also learned that five is the number of grace and the number to establish. It was God's grace that moved on my heart to give him the opportunity over and over to keep his family and together with me be in a position to serve God in the ministry. But once he made a decision in his heart that he wanted both worlds, at the appointed time the Lord Himself shut the door for good. You see it is impossible for anyone to serve two masters, "for either he will hate the one and love the other, or he will stand by and be devoted to the one and despise and be against the other." You cannot serve God and whatever you are placing your trust in at the same time (Matthew 6:24).

A few months later he called and asked me to leave her home and find another place to live so he could come back again and **I told him I was sorry but the Lord told me to be still. I could not move out until God told me to and he could not come back because God shut the door to where I was living.**

Then the Lord spoke to me and said my husband would take me away from this house. I did not understand what He meant since He had closed the door, but I remained still. People like my children's former instructor from a Christian school they had attended who was also a prophetess, telephoned me and confirmed the same message that God had given me, "to be still and do not move." This teacher did not know what the Lord had spoken to me. In this season of my life the Lord had a number of prophets both male and female but mostly females who were either ministering in full time ministry or still employed who spoke into my life. He was leading them across my path and would use many of them to confirm the instructions He had already given to me.

Many times the Lord would give me directions or a word in the early morning hours when I was in prayer and then confirm it through one of my children the same day by giving them the same word when they prayed after they woke up. He was doing a quick work. I would have needed to have been deaf, blind and stupid to miss God in this stage of my life because He was speaking very clearly. I'm not saying I never missed God, everyone misses Him at some point regardless of how much they seek Him or how well they can hear Him. Although I have found that if you do miss an instruction when you ask for forgiveness, repent and continue, He will continue with you. Note: Some people become full of condemnation or regret and find it difficult to continue with God. They need to change their perspective and realize that missing God is a part of their walk and training. He already knew we would miss Him. But in His mercy He will forgive, restore and raise us up again and put us on the right path again as long as we continue to desire Him to be our God and not give up).

While waiting for further instructions from the Holy Spirit, I respected the elderly lady's home. I took care of my children, prayed, studied the Word and helped her where I could. I also prayed with my children, studied the word with them and made sure that Kevin had personal time with God as well. I was very conscious to remain in the will of the Lord because I knew it was the only way I was going to get out of this situation, so I remained obedient to His Word as the Holy Spirit led and prepared me for the ministry.

From the time the children and I were left by my former husband at the elderly lady's home and God spoke to me to be still and later said that my husband would take me away from there, to the time the Lord confirmed His Word through others that I was to stay there until my husband came for me, it was hard to imagine that my former husband would come for me because I had not heard of any change with him even though I knew God could work miracles and the fact that God said the door was shut from the north, east, south and west.

In the meantime the elderly lady was growing tired of my being in her home and even though she did not ask me to leave she started doing things to make us uncomfortable in her home. **God was now closing this door His way and I had to make a decision to obey Him and be still or look at the circumstances and leave. I had no choice but to remain until God** spoke either through her to tell me directly to leave or send my husband to remove me.

It was at this point that Robert and I were about to meet. The Lord had directed Robert to a small Christian school through one of his patients who was the owner of the school. Robert was looking for a school for his son, Brandon, to remove him from some of his peers at his present high school. Shortly after Robert enrolled his son in this private Christian school, Robert became a member on the Board of Directors there. I in turn, learned of this same school from a woman who I met in church and who was also Robert's patient. This lady's daughter was attending a youth ministry connected with this same Christian school and Robert's daughter, Christa, was the founder of this youth ministry. The lady from the church had asked me to call this school and pray for the owner, so I did. I also prayed for him with the co-pastor of the church I was attending at the time who was also a powerful prophet in the Body of Christ. Later she telephoned me to say God said your children are to attend that school with the long name (this particular Christian school had a long title). Weeks before my former husband left for the final time on June 25, 1991, I had made an appointment to meet with the owner and visit the school to follow through with the instruction given to me by the prophet.

We went to the school to meet with the owner. We did not like the location or the size of the school it was small with a very small playground. We went in and met with the owner with our minds pretty much made up that we would see him and then leave. While inside we spoke to the owner and went on a tour of the school which taught grades pre-school through twelfth grade. **In one of the buildings I began to pray for the owner of the school and he fell under the power of God and my former husband caught him as he was falling. Then as I turned around, I saw a vision of Jesus standing on the other side of the room and He was just standing there smiling at me. I knew then that God was in this place and the anointing and presence of God was very strong there.** At that point I told my former husband that our children would be attending this school and he was in agreement.

In the month of July I spoke to the owner of the school and made arrangements for my children to attend their summer school. When I arrived at the school the owner told me God showed him that I was suppose to work there and I said I know I had seen visions of myself speaking with the students and their parents and to the student body. So that summer I started to work at the Christian school as a volunteer. He had asked me to do public relations work for the school which included speaking and praying with the parents and students as they came to the school to consider enrollment. I would also take them on a tour of the school and explain the programs the school offered. In addition, since I had a background as a paralegal, a law office manager, a legal secretary and an executive assistant, as well as some trust officer banking experience and experience working in insurance companies, I offered to organize his administrative office and he was very happy about this arrangement. (I listed some of my experience to demonstrate that I could have looked for employment in an area I was familiar with and made a decent salary to support my family but in 1989 the Lord shut the door to secular employment and told me I only worked for Him. Being in full-time ministry does not always mean one has to leave their regular employment it depends on your assignment and what path God has you on. So follow the leading of the Holy Spirit, and do not step out ahead of Him nor lag behind just stay in step and flow with His Spirit. This is one of the things you will learn as you follow His leading).

At this point I was in full time ministry and to have acquired employment for the sake of supporting myself when God was preparing and training me to lean on Him and trust Him: (1) I would have been out of the will of God in that season for my life and gotten out of His timing; (2) I would not have past the test that God had placed before me nor been promoted by God to the next level in the spirit; and (3) I would have come from under my hedge of protection and opened the door for the adversary to place further obstacles in my path. Furthermore, I needed to know on this level that no matter what, God would come through for me. He never failed me once and it was all well worth it to follow His ways in spite of the temporary inconveniences. It is all about your perspective so if you chose Him then let Him lead. He will do wonderful works beyond whatever you could imagine. "Now unto Him that is able to do exceeding abundantly above all that we ask or think, according to the power that worketh in us," (Ephesians 3:20 KJV). Also see Phil. 4:13 "… [I am ready for anything and equal to anything through Him Who infuses inner strength into me; *I am self-sufficient in Christ's sufficiency].*"

A number of the parents informed me that this school was their last hope, that they had tried many other schools and they were led here as a last chance for their child's education in the upper grade levels. At this Christian school the Lord revealed to me how gifted and anointed some of the children were and that He had chosen many of them to do a great work for His Kingdom and that many of these children held offices in the five fold ministry and some of them had international ministries in their futures. This was truly a training ground that would change some of our lives forever and God was training us up in the enemy's territory (the area the school was located in and some of the demonic activity that was attacking some of these children's homes).

It was **July 12, 1991**, while Kevin, my natural son was away for three weeks at a Bible school with a friend and his family that I decided to work late at the Christian school and complete organizing the administrative office. At this time **Robert** and Brandon his natural son, came to the school that evening to visit with the owner who had stepped out. Melinda was playing in the classroom while I worked in the office located just off the classroom. When Robert and Brandon came into the classroom and met Melinda first, she called Robert, daddy, this was something Melinda had never done before (later we learned that God had given her this revelation for He knew what His plan was and He was revealing a part of it at that time to Melinda). Robert and Brandon noticed how much she favored Robert's oldest daughter Camille when she was that age. Then Brandon came to the office door which was open and where I was working and he knocked and simply said hi and I in turn said hi and came out to meet them. Melinda called Robert daddy again, in my presence this time and I told her not to say that and we just assumed it was a child playing. Melinda had never called anyone else daddy except her natural father, not her grandfather or my brothers nor any of my brother in-laws.

After we met we spoke briefly and decided to pray together with our children. The Lord used me to give some prophetic words to them that evening. I also saw a vision of his wife as she would have appeared in the late fifties or early sixties and she was carrying a suitcase in her hand. After I described what I saw, Robert said that is my wife you are describing. At the time we all believed she would return to her family. She had left Robert and their three children three years prior to that time and Robert believed God for her return home as I believed God for my husband to return.

However, in my case the Lord had already declared that He had shut the door from the north, east, south and west and he would never return again. But I was still learning of God and His ways so at that point, I still believed that God would heal my former husband and he would return home for good. God had also given chances to Robert's former spouse to return home, to no avail. God will not violate someone's free will. Still I had hope, primarily because my children were so young and I wanted them to know, love and be raised by their natural father. I really did not think anyone else could love them like their biological father but the Holy Spirit proved me wrong.

This same evening I had a strong desire come into my heart for Brandon to become friends with my son Kevin. I knew Brandon was older and wiser about natural things and that they were very different in that regard and this could hinder them from becoming friends. But in my spirit God was already alerting me of the connection and bond that would later take place

OUR BLENDED FAMILY'S TESTIMONY

between the two of them that I could have not possibly known. It was like the revelation Melinda had in her heart as a five year old calling Robert daddy as soon as she saw him. Later the Holy Spirit did reveal that Brandon and Kevin's hearts were knitted together like King David and Saul's son Jonathan. Within the next few months they had become extremely close, closer than any two blood brothers. There is a saying that blood is thicker than water, I would like to add that the Spirit is "thicker" and more powerful than the blood in our bodies because the Spirit created the blood.

I Samuel 20:42, gives an illustration of David and Jonathan's hearts toward one another:

> And Jonathan told David, Go in peace, forasmuch as we have sworn to each other in the name of the Lord, saying, the Lord shall be between me and you, and between my descendants and yours forever. And Jonathan arose and departed into the city.

I worked at this school for the rest of the summer and just before the fall semester began, when the staff was to meet with the parents, **God spoke to me regarding a prophetic conference in Florida and He told me "if I take care of His business, He would take care of mine"** I did not want to leave my children to go to Florida so I had to make a decision, to obey God or to ignore God. Needless to say I chose to obey. So, I went to Florida and left my two children with the elderly lady I lived with at the time and who already knew and at one time had cared for my children (before all of this began this lady was my babysitter when my former husband and I were at our places of work). It was a successful conference and God mightily used the prophetic ministry that I was a part of at that time. Several witches were sent to that prophetic conference but to no avail. God's work was done. (Witches are people who have made Satan their god. They are on assignment by Satan to do the evil works that he tells them to do. On the other hand,

Believers are people who chose the Most High God and will do what He tells us to do. I cannot understand fully what is so difficult to understand about this. We do not need spiritual eyes to see the wickedness in the world. It is being generated from somewhere. It does not benefit anyone to ignore it, to be caught up in it or allow themselves to be used by the enemy. If God has said, and He has, that Satan exists and there is evil in the world then who are we to say that Satan is just a cartoon figure and evil does not exist? Those who say God is wrong or He is missing it have been deceived and blinded by the enemy and they cannot see truth, 2 Cor. 4:4; I Cor. 2:14).

In returning home from the conference five of us left a day before the rest of them and I was among that five. **While on the plane the Lord spoke to me and said "I have saved you." I was wondering what He *meant* because I was already "saved," then I heard "airplane crash," then I heard "I have protected you." What I wondered now was, is the Lord going to save me in the air or on the ground, either way I knew I would be alright.**

I looked at the other four women with me amongst the plane filled with passengers. These women had also received the word from the Holy Spirit about the crash. The lady next to me said Audrey, look at your hands. I had not noticed but both of the palms of my hands were both very red as if they were on fire. She told me to place one hand on the plane and one hand on her stomach (she needed a healing that I was not aware of and a week later her stomach was flat).

As I placed my hand on the plane I heard a choir singing, it was beautiful, nothing like I had ever heard before, I realized it was angels that I heard singing. At that point all five of us began to pray, one prophet prayed very loud in tongues, her supernatural prayer language, two of them were praying softly in tongues, another quoted Psalms 91as she read the Bible out loud, and I prayed aloud as well in English declaring and demanding that the plane line up and that it was covered with the blood of Jesus and so on. We continued to pray and not one person on that flight said a word to us about praying about the impending danger that the plane was in. Even up unto that point the flight attendants had never left their seats from the start of the flight and the seat belt light had never gone off, which it does when it is safe to walk around the cabin.

As we continued to pray the plane suddenly dropped, the pressure was so great we could no longer speak but only hold hands. As suddenly as it dropped, it suddenly stopped in the air and we were flying again. We were told later it stopped just before it hit the ocean and the plane never ascended again but rather flew all the way to Houston, Texas just above the ocean. Once we reached Houston the second attack came and we had to pray for the plane to land and land safely because it was raining and the plane kept circling longer than the pilot said it would. The flight attendants never left their seats the entire flight. As we continued to pray out loud the plane finally landed. Later the Lord informed one of the prophetesses that something was wrong with the pilot. We boarded another plane and the Lord said it would be a good flight and it was very smooth and we enjoyed dinner on the next flight to Los Angeles.

Meanwhile after we arrived home I received a call from our co-pastor and prophet who was scheduled to leave Florida the following day with the others, they were praying for us as well. God had alerted them about the crash that the devil had planned. I also received a call about two days later from a prayer partner I had in Gary, Indiana who asked me if I was on a plane recently and I told her yes, she too had been alerted to pray and was shown the plane. She told me she asked God whenever someone she loved or cared about was in danger to inform her so she could pray. **God is faithful, He alerted us and raised up intercessors to pray for us. Prayer works!**

I am sharing some of the miracles (supernatural works) that happened for my family and me that took place as God was moving me from the old to the new, preparing me for destiny and building my faith in Him. Whenever the enemy would attack I was told by God to continue and as I continued with His instructions to me He protected me and gave me the victory. He did whatever was necessary for me to continue. **Remember the Lord took me** off of my employment and told me He wanted me to know I could *trust* Him. For four years I had no income and for four years, until I remarried it was God and me and he never let me down. He told my son "you will never starve and you will always have shelter" and we did. We did not always eat what we wanted or live where we thought we should but He was true to His Word and I learned I could trust Him to do His part if I would do mine. That is a covenant and there is power in a covenant especially if you are in one with the King of kings. This is another reason why the marriage covenant is not to be taken lightly, God is a part of that covenant and He will do His part when we do ours and yield to His ways!

You hear people say I pray all the time. *My question is do you act once the answer or instruction has come into your heart* and you know, that you know God is about to move on your behalf, *or do you ignore the voice of God?* If you act you will see miracles (a supernatural move of God). If you do not it shows a lack of faith and God is not pleased with that and He is unable to move for you the way you may need Him to. You see the atmosphere has to be one of faith and confidence believing God is going to do what He said He would do. You limit Him when you fail to step out and simply do what He says. God has no pleasure in those who draw back and shrink in fear (Hebrews 10:38).

After being home about a week from my trip to Florida God performed another miracle. This time it was regarding my minivan which had been towed because the registration was not current then it was transferred to the legal owners. This happened just before I left for Florida when I was attending a prayer meeting in Pomona, California. The legal owners of the minivan informed me in a letter that they would auction my minivan if I did not pay the back car payments to bring my account current. So I called them and said "I don't know what you are going to do, but God told me the van was coming back to me." I was informed they would go forth with the auction. After the auction I received a call from the same agent at the Credit Union, which was the legal owner of the minivan and he informed me that for *some reason* they could not touch my van but that they had rescheduled the van to be auctioned off again. I told him the same thing again, that God said the van was coming back to me. At that point I also had an opportunity to speak with him about the Lord and he received it and I prayed for him. After the next auction, I received another telephone call, again they could not touch the minivan and they did not know why, I told him the same thing again. The man told me this is what we are going to do, we will keep the van and when you have the money you come and pick it up.

Toward the end, I believe of the same week, I received a telephone call from my attorney regarding a personal injury case that had been pending for five years. He informed me they had finally settled the case and I discovered it was almost enough money for me to pick up my minivan but I was short seven hundred dollars. So as I sat on the porch and while sipping a cup of tea, the Lord impressed upon me to call my attorney back and tell him what I needed to pick up my minivan. The attorney said there was a check for seven hundred dollars still waiting to be claimed by one of the doctors who never called so he said he would give it to me and if they telephoned later they could contact me directly and I would be responsible to pay them, to this date they have never called.

My point – God told me to go to Florida when I did not want to leave my children, and He told me if I took care of His business, He would take care of mine. Notice how many miracles I received just from this one act of obedience. I just want to praise Him and continue to encourage you that God is faithful and He is not a man that He should lie. If we are willing and obedient, He will do His part, when we do ours. Not only did lives change in Florida but God saved my life at a time a major breakthrough was about to occur in my life and He restored my minivan with a miracle that witnessed to unbelievers involved in the process at the Credit Union and with the people who gave me a ride to the Credit Union to pick it up.

Now summer is over and it is time for the first day of school at the place our two families met and God showed Himself strong. The owner of the Christian school is running late, the staff and students are in one of the larger classrooms, so one of the instructors sent for me from the administrative office. I went over, introduced myself to the students and staff, I discussed some things about the school and then asked everyone who knew how to pray in tongues to do so and those who did not to praise God as we prayed for this first day of school.

I was not accustomed to working in a school and since we had been praying in the Spirit all summer with students and parents, and I was told that is what we do and believe, after all it was a *Christian* school, I was very open with it and comfortable asking everyone to pray in their supernatural spiritual prayer language from the Holy Spirit. I of course was later told that very few of them were baptized in the Holy Spirit and were offended because they considered this something to do in private or at church and not at a school. Even some of the people that did pray in tongues were shocked. I knew by the Holy Spirit that this was more than a school, it was also a training ground for God's people. I also knew that children could be saved and baptized in the Holy Spirit at a very young age because my two children were. The Christian preschool that Melinda attended their students prayed in the Spirit (in tongues) in their classroom everyday. Those children learned early about the power of God and the school and the church that owned the school benefited from their prayers as well. However, later at this small Christian school all of the students would be saved and most received the infilling of the Holy Spirit with the evidence of praying in tongues before they left the school for good and this included some of their parents.

What I did not realize was that God was forming lifetime relationships for others and myself at this school with some of the staff and students that would literally change all of our lives forever. We had many challenges at this small Christian school that brought us all closer together over the next seven months. **We laughed, shared, played, cried, prayed, bonded and worshipped as we experienced miracles and heard praise reports of lives being changed, restored, deliverance coming forth, children suddenly having hope who were hopeless and learning** how to pray for their families and seeing results such as parents coming off of drugs, families buying new homes, some moving to a better place and parents who were separated coming back together, as well as healings coming forth, it was amazing!!!

In approximately the sixth month, God began instructing one of the instructors and me to take her class of students between the ninth and twelfth grade to the park which was two blocks away from the school. There they played basketball and board games and we were also led to pray with them in the open space on the grass. Furthermore, she and I wore the same colors each day without the others knowledge of what we were going to wear to school that day, (God was bringing us into agreement in a powerful way, God uses colors, visions, words whatever necessary to complete His will).

At one of these outings the Lord gave me a vision of boys in a classroom at this particular instructor's home and then God spoke seven boys names to me and I knew very strongly it was the Lord because two of the boys I did not know because they were new. When I mentioned two other boys to God He said, "No not James, no not Michael." I knew without a shadow of doubt it was the Father of the universe through the Holy Spirit giving me these names. The Lord also said these seven boys had international ministries.

I mentioned it to the instructor and told her about the vision, at the time she was surprised and did not say much about it. I wrote the names down and told her if she started a school for boys I would help her. Later she told me that about five years prior another woman had prophesied to her that she would have a boy's school in her home ninth to twelfth grade. The Lord had sent her to this little Christian school to begin her ministry and through her willingness and obedience He could now move her to the next level and work in these student's lives.

We should never despise small beginnings, God is watching over His Word and ready to perform it at all times. Remember, some of "your lowest points are launching pads to God's greatest promotions."

As we continued at the school, my natural children and Robert's natural children were drawn closer together by the Holy Spirit, others kept mistaking them to be brothers and sisters all the while the Holy Spirit was bonding them together.

For example: Parents would come into the office where I worked and referred to Brandon as my son saying, "Your son with the pony tail he did..." I would then inform them I did not have a son with a pony tail (Brandon looked more like my natural daughter than my natural son did, both Brandon and Melinda had long hair, favored one another, were about the same complexion, they even had similar personalities and were both full of energy).

This continued for weeks, I heard this from parents, other staff members, students and many of them knew that he was not my natural child but they kept coming to me regarding him as if he were. It became so noticeable and in addition to all of this I was having visions which showed Brandon living with my family, shopping with us and doing things with our family other than school activities. God confirmed these visions were from Him when one of the students who also operated in the gifts of the spirit told me the visions he was having and they were the exact visions I was having regarding Brandon. I stopped explaining that he was not my child and started answering the questions when people approached me about him.

It was clear that I had developed a mother's love for Brandon. Although I did not understand why the Lord would place a mother's love in my heart for this young boy who was sixteen at the time when in the natural I had no voice whatsoever about his well being. I found myself praying for him with other prayer partners constantly and wondering how he was when school was closed for the weekends. I was concerned with whether or not he was eating properly, getting enough rest, doing his homework, wondering who was taking care of his needs. I knew his father worked long hours at his dental practice, he had a housekeeper and one of his daughters was helping him oversee things at the house as well. He was doing the best he could. Nevertheless, these concerns continued to bother me.

I got a little relief when arrangements were made for me to take Brandon to his father's dental office after school. Brandon would stay after school and talk to Kevin and other students until it was time for us to leave and instead of him taking public transportation or on occasions leave with his sister, Christa, I drove him to his father's dental practice and treated him like one of my own children.

I finally asked God, why was this child in my life? The Lord spoke to me and said, "For I have given unto you a son to nurture and bring up in the things of the Spirit." I thought to myself, "Oh, the Lord has given me someone else to minister to." The Lord repeated this statement to me many times over the next few weeks because I had not comprehended nor gotten the revelation of what He was actually telling me. He started confirming this prophetic word through different people and some were total strangers that prophesied Brandon was my son. Needless to say I did not understand what the Lord was doing.

I taught adult Bible study on Friday nights at the request of the owner of this Christian school. It was the same night the youth ministry met at this school. I volunteered to help drive kids home after the youth meetings and Christa said she had prayed for someone to help with the driving. So after I finished teaching the adult Bible class I would go to the youth ministry classroom, where my children were also participating and I waited until it was over to help drive children home. It was at one of these meetings that Christa, who was the founder of the youth ministry and one of Robert's daughters, told me that the Lord told her that I was her spiritual mother and I received that because I also had a love in my heart for her as well. (When a prophetic word comes forth, usually it is confirmation for the person who is receiving the word).

Robert was usually the only other parent at these youth meetings. We did not converse much, usually while waiting for our children we read our own Bibles and spoke to other students. On occasion Robert and I would participate in teaching the youth from the Word of God. Also on occasion after the meetings were over we prayed together for parents who were picking up their children. When it was time to leave Robert would take children in his SUV and I would take children in my minivan and drive them to their homes. This time was particularly difficult for his children and me because we would not be able to see one another again until school resumed on Monday.

I later discovered that God had a bigger plan than my loving and nurturing Robert's children. The Lord spoke to me at the end of 1991 and said **"I am merging these two families together."** We must be careful when God speaks, so often we assume what He means. When it is not clear to us be careful not to imagine that He is saying something that He really isn't. *The interpretation could be wrong and then we make up in our own minds as to how He is going to do that which He said, whereas He never really said what we thought He did to begin with. And some of us become angry because He does not do things the way we think He should.* One of the best things to do is be still and wait for clarity and confirmation when you are not sure or if you don't have a peace or the revelation of what is taking place.

When the Lord said to me that He was merging these two families together, *I assumed* He was merging the two families together to fellowship in church and develop a friendship after both of our spouses returned home. Later He revealed that was not His plan at all! Again I didn't catch the revelation because I was in a mindset that my former husband would be with me and our children, in other words I wasn't prepared to hear the future because I was holding on to a part of my past. God was merging our two families, the Dickeys and the Creightons, together in marriage. **The Holy Spirit even brought it to my remembrance that He had sent other prophets across my path years prior to tell me that He had another husband for me.** I rejected and did not receive those words from them; however, I must tell you, that if you continue with God, and are striving to be obedient, the words that He sends will come to pass in the season they are appointed because you are in His will and timing and He is a God that cannot lie.

Isaiah 55:11 says,

> So shall My word be that goes forth out of My mouth:
>
> it shall not return to Me void [without producing any effect, useless], but it shall accomplish that which I please and purpose, and it shall prosper in the thing for which I sent it.

Even though I did not come in agreement with the words that came forth, but because I chose to continue with God and listen to Him, I still saw the results because God had spoken this for my life. His ways are not our ways and we must be careful not to limit God but be willing and obedient to His Spirit as we keep our joy which is our strength to follow Him.

Isaiah 55:8 says,

> For My thoughts are not your thoughts, neither are your ways My ways, says the Lord.

Isaiah 1:19-20 says,

> If you are willing and obedient, you shall eat the good of the land; But if you refuse and rebel, you will be devoured by the sword. For the mouth of the Lord has spoken it.

God is not obligated to support what we think or what was misunderstood but He supports His plan and His purpose which is better for all of us in the long run.

Neither Robert nor I were dating anyone; we took care of our children, I was working full time in the ministry and one of my assignments at that time was the Christian school where I was a volunteer (someone who shares their gifts and talents for the glory of God). Robert was operating his dental practice which he had owned for over twenty-two years at that time and he was serving God by praying with his patients and being active in his church. His patients reported little if no pain when he treated them, some received healing of cancer and other diseases while in his dental chair. They also received words of wisdom as they visited his dental office. We were both content taking care of our families and working for the Lord as He chose to use us.

We later discovered, that before we met, we both had confessed to the Lord, that if our spouses did not choose to line up with God's will then we were ready to go forth and serve Him without them. Unknowingly we had shown and proved that God came first in our lives and we trusted Him above all even our families not being restored with our former spouses. We both left this in the hands of God. All we knew at that point was that we wanted to serve God. We also discovered after this decision was made, that is when God brought us across each other's path by first bonding our children together. I want to add that even though I fought this *new thing* God was doing in my life I never gave up on God's plan even though I had a battle existing in my mind. Also, because of the Lord's intervention and my having enough Word in my heart plus prayer coverage from Robert and others it was enough to sustain me and keep me in God's will until the victory was won!

When we asked to go on with God even if it meant forsaking our marriages to do His will, God showed us that it was His will for our families to have an earthly father and an earthly mother, even if He had to send someone else to fulfill His purpose. **God had given us a family ministry and it would take both of us and our children to fulfill His purpose.** He later showed us that it was destined from the beginning that we would all be together. He was preparing our families to be a *God-Blended Family.*

Up until now I had never heard of a Spiritual Family. The Lord showed me in His Word that **He created the Spiritual Family** and in many cases it superseded many of the various family types especially those without Jesus in their lives.

Matthew 12:46-50 shows a type of Spiritual Family,

> Jesus was still speaking to the people when behold, His mother and brothers stood outside, seeking to speak to Him. Someone said to Him, Listen! Your mother and Your brothers are standing outside, seeking to speak to You.
>
> But He replied to the man who told Him, Who is My mother, and who are My brothers?
>
> And stretching out His hand toward [not only the twelve disciples but all] His adherents, He said, Here are My mother and My brothers. For whoever does the will of My Father in heaven is My brother and sister and mother! (Mark 3:31-35).

A Spiritual Family, Saved people who are divinely connected as a family by God, that may or may not be biologically related; that may or may not be related by marriage; that may or may not dwell in the same home and "does the things God wills..." (Matthew 12:46-50; Mark 3:31-35).

The Lord has shown us time and time again that a family which He develops will stand. **He will create new hearts, give new beginnings, cause bonding, joy, peace, healing and genuine love to come forth every time and as the family receives they will be successful because it's members turned to Him and kept Him first. Once a family is formed by the Holy Spirit and they operate with a willing heart there is nothing that cannot be forgiven or accomplished because they know that they can do all things through Christ who will strengthen them, Phil 4:13.**

> Psalms 51:10-12 says this about a new heart and the right spirit:
>
>> Create in me a clean heart, O God, and renew a right, persevering, and steadfast spirit within me.

> Cast me not away from Your presence and take not Your Holy Spirit from me. Restore to me the joy of Your salvation and uphold me with a willing spirit.

Now the time had come in February 1992, it was time to leave this small Christian school. The Lord had said he was removing some of the students and the owner of the school did not believe it was a word from the Lord and asked me to leave. I told him I was not leaving until I directly heard from God. This took place on a Friday in the seventh month after I had arrived to work at the school. *Over the weekend the Lord did speak to me and informed me that it was time to leave. The Lord had done a new thing and the owner of the school's heart had changed toward me and that door was now closed so God's will would prevail.*

The owner of the school had *not* been obedient to what God had entrusted to him and I believe it was only for a season that the school would be in operation in order for God's purpose to merge us and others together. The student's parents suddenly started removing the students from the school over the next few weeks and months. Prophetic words were given to some of the students still there by other students who were also prophetic as to the dates kids would be leaving and they were removed on those dates by their parents without the parents having heard the dates that were foretold. The school closed one year after the prophecy went forth that I had given and it is closed to this day.

Now back to that weekend, once I had heard from the Lord confirming it was time to leave, on that following Monday I returned to the small Christian school to say goodbye to the high school instructor that I ministered closely with and to say goodbye to the students. The instructor informed me that the following Friday would be her last day and it was confirmed by one of the students who had heard from the Lord and had written it down without having any knowledge of this and showed it to her that morning. She spoke with her husband and decided to open the school with the seven boys the Lord had given that day at the park. Once again I volunteered as I was led by the

Holy Spirit to help her with this school. I used my minivan to pick-up and drop-off the students, for the Friday field trips, and for their driving lessons. I also organized and assisted her with her administrative office. This is another reason God gave the minivan back to me, He knew that I would use it for His purpose and glory.

Later that morning the instructor and I took the seven boys aside and shared what God had done and informed them that we would be contacting their parents for them to begin classes at the high school instructor's home. To make a long story short all seven attended her school beginning in the next few weeks through the following year starting at the appointed time for each one of them. Melinda prophesied that Brandon would be the last one to enroll and the first one to graduate. Thanks to God's divine connections the instructor's Christian school located in her home was accredited by the Los Angeles Unified School District ISP, within the first year of her starting her school ministry. She was also able to relocate to a commercial building to house her school within the first year.

And yes, Brandon was the last to enroll and the first to graduate as God had said and prophesied through Melinda. He walked across the stage with the last high school class he attended before transferring to the Christian school where all of us met. On the day that he left his old high school he announced and declared he would be back and graduate (he prophesied and declared his end at his former high school and it came to pass). On the very day of graduation he appeared in cap and gown and walked across the stage with his class. Of course many of the other students were surprised. Afterwards we had a great graduation dinner with our family and some of his friends. God is Good and Faithful!

The devil fought this transfer for him to attend the school God ordained because he knew there would be victory there for him. However, **God still had a greater plan in mind which was a merger of two families becoming one and birthing a powerful ministry.** Before Brandon transferred, however and part of the reason he was the last to enroll in her school was because his father, Robert, refused to allow him to attend the instructor's Christian school because of the lies he had heard from the owner of the small Christian school upon our leaving about how I prophesied the school would close. Robert was only trying to protect his son but at the same time it was keeping him out of God's perfect will and hindering his progress to graduate. Brandon would not have been able to graduate from the small Christian school he was previously in because the owner of the old school never received accreditation. Therefore, none of his students would have been able to graduate with a high school diploma. The parents were not aware of this and neither were the instructors or myself, but God knew that the owner had lied and God shut it down!

    Ultimately this situation of Brandon transferring to the new school caused a wedge between his father, Robert, and me and so we all continued to pray until God gave us a breakthrough about Brandon's transfer. The Lord gave us instructions later that would allow Robert and me to communicate again, instructions I was not at all thrilled with.

    In the meantime, **the purpose for my minivan was finished** and the Lord allowed it to be removed and all that was connected with my former marriage was removed as well. The reason I said the Lord was finished with these things was because He made no further provision for me to keep them, they were a part of my past and God was now doing a new thing in this new season of my life. This new thing would include preparing me to be removed from the elderly lady's house as well. The minivan was repossessed and everything that my former husband and I owned together for the past fifteen years plus items I owned before we married that were in storage were auctioned off.

    I requested through the storage manager that the new owners set aside my photo albums, books and file cabinet with important records because they had no use for those things. She informed me that they said they would not. At the same time one of the students from the new Christian school who was very prophetic prophesied to me in so many words that anyone who touched my things would bring a curse on themselves and I would have those things I requested. Well to make a long story short, I received a phone call from the storage manager who said she had never seen anything like this in her life; she related that the new owner of my things who owned and operated a furniture store came and picked everything up and drove to his store only to find it was burned down to the ground when he arrived (this was during the time of the Los Angeles riots in the early nineties). So he returned and placed everything back in the storage and separated out all of the items I had previously requested and journals I had forgotten I had (Psalm 105:15). I did not like the outcome for the store owner but God will stand by and prove His Word. In this case it was the prophetic word that was given to me through a student who grew up and became a minister that said I would have those things that I requested.

As I stated earlier a prophet instructed me that *at an appointed time the Lord was going to give me the words to say to Brandon's father in the way of asking for forgiveness.* I did not understand why I needed to do this since I was only trying to help his children and doing what God had directed me to do. She explained that he saw me as a person that was interfering with his children and since he did not know me that well and because of certain things that had been said about me disturbed him. These accusations were told to prevent Robert from trusting the new instructor and myself. Later he discovered the truth and that the owner of the old school had lied to him about many other things pertaining to the school as well. It was also prophesied by a young boy that I would receive a breakthrough in the month of August.

Two days later the Lord did speak to me and He gave me the words to say. I wrote them down and called Robert and read it to him as it had been given to me by the Holy Spirit (I wanted to make sure that I repeated everything that was given by the Lord) and **Robert's heart was changed towards me and we could once again communicate.** Even though I did not understand it, I did it. If we obey without trying to figure everything out, but drop our pride and stop reasoning and simply do what the Lord has instructed, we will save so much time and heartache for ourselves as we make progress.

As it was prophesied, now it was **time for the breakthroughs** that were going to happen in the month of August concerning the matter of Brandon's transfer. On August 1, 1992, I needed a babysitter for Melinda but my relatives were busy so I took her with me and on the way to where we were going my brother Harold was driving through the area of the Dickey home and I thought about Christa babysitting Melinda for a couple of hours and I asked him to drive over there. I told Melinda to get out of the car and go to the door and ask for Christa. Well, Robert answered the door and Melinda asked if mom could speak to Christa then Robert looked at the car and told me that if I wanted to talk to Christa I would have to come in. I looked at my brother with an expression of I don't know what to expect and got out of the car and proceeded to the door. Robert greeted me with a big hug and called Christa from her room, she said she thought she had heard my voice but couldn't believe it was me in her home knowing how in the past her father and I did not see eye to eye when it came to Brandon's situation and Christa and I were happy to see one another and she Melinda. I asked her to babysit and she did. Later that day she asked me if Melinda could spend the night and I let her. I always felt good about Kevin or Melinda staying in their home but as a rule they did not spend the night out often and never with people that I barely knew. But God had already prepared our hearts in the spirit to make the transition a little easier. After this day Robert and I were able to communicate more about all of our children. And once again I began helping with the youth ministry that was founded by Christa which had been moved to their home from that small Christian school which at that time was its last few months before it shut down for good.

Shortly after Christa was preparing to leave for college I went to her home to say goodbye and met her natural mother who was also there visiting her before she left. Later I met with both of them to talk about Brandon attending the new school.

They both agreed that Brandon could start after meeting with the owner and myself, we further agreed that Brandon would be brought to where I lived (which was with the elderly lady) and he and Kevin would travel to school together with Melinda and myself and we all traveled on public transportation to the school which was located in another city.

This is the same private Christian school we covered earlier that he transferred to as one of the seven boys who God had chosen to attend and that he graduated from and walked across the stage with his former high school class. This is the part of the story of how God used the new school in the beginning to further bridge the two families together by *Robert and I helping each other with our children so they would be able to finish high school.*

Shortly after the new semester began the Lord removed Melinda and me from the new Christian school and our sons traveled to the school together. They would return together to where I was living after school, eat dinner and start their homework before Brandon's other sister, Camille, would pick up Brandon and take him home.

Our stay in the elderly lady's house was coming to a close. God told me I was no longer the head of this family. (Since my former husband was gone, God spoke through someone else that God made me the head of my immediate family. This would curtail some of the demonic attacks on our family that we were experiencing because of the open doors due to the lifestyle of my former spouse. Note: When the head of the house is out of the will of God this opens a door for the devil to attack the rest of the family. But now God had said that I was no longer the head of my family). **The elderly lady's heart began to change towards me, one moment I had great favor and now the door was closing because the Lord was about to keep His word and move me out and forward.** When God moves or works on something it will not be the way you think. When He moves sometimes it seems as if it is in a totally different direction of how you would have chosen to do things. He will usually move for you in your darkest hour or right on time, giving you a miracle so you and others will know that it was He and He alone who made the change. It won't always involve a miracle but in my case there was no other way because I was trusting Him and He made sure that I and others would give Him the glory. This is important so people looking on will know where to go for help when they need it and by this time there were a lot of eyes on my situation.

I informed Robert that I was going to move to Lake Ellsinore with my cousin and I could no longer keep Brandon after school (I was going to leave so the elderly lady could have her home back). He asked me if Kevin could come and stay at his home so he could complete his high school education, Kevin had one year left, he was covering part of the eleventh and the twelfth grade in one year and he would graduate early at the age of sixteen. Robert said he wanted to help me with Kevin especially since I had helped with his son's education and daughter's youth ministry. I agreed which was strange for me, I had never been separated from my children for any length of time not even when my former mother-in-law offered to keep our children for us when we moved to Atlanta, Georgia until we were settled, in hopes of a fresh start but we declined her offer and took our children with us. But with Robert keeping him I had a peace about it.

Kevin did not mind going to Robert's home he and Brandon were friends at this point and he liked it there plus I had reassured him that I would come and get him later. So Robert picked Kevin and his things up and we went over to his home, we all spoke with Brandon about it and he agreed that it was okay with him as well and Camille did not seem to mind. About a week had gone by and my cousin did not come or call, and on top of that, **the Lord was still telling me to be still that my husband would pick me up from here**. I received a call from the owner of the new Christian school where the boys attended she and others confirmed that I was to continue to be still and wait for God to move. So I did.

Robert telephoned me to let me know how things were going at his home with the boys. They were arriving at his home hours before Robert and not really doing their homework and having any dinner until he arrived if they did not find something in the freezer to eat (Robert would prepare food and store it in the freezer for the kids to eat after school). I telephoned Brandon's natural mother and asked her to help me by going over to the house and cooking dinner for the boys and overseeing their homework, after all, her natural son was about to graduate and he needed to get good grades and complete his courses. I told her we could alternate days until he graduated. She informed me that she worked long hours and that she was not available to help. So I told her I would do it alone.

In the beginning Camille would leave the dental office to come over after school and pick up the boys, Melinda and me and take us to the house so I could be there for the boys, oversee their homework and cook dinner for the family. Later Robert offered to bring me his vehicle in the mornings before he went to his office because he needed Camille at the dental chair in the afternoons (she was his dental assistant) and so I could keep the vehicle to run errands for our children's needs while I was still living at the elderly lady's house. Robert, some of the children and I shopped together on the weekends to have the necessities at his home during the week.

So during the week Robert and the boys would pick Melinda and me up from the home I lived in, in the mornings and he would drive to his office to work and Camille would meet him there. I would then drive the boys to school so they no longer had to take public transportation all the way to another city. Next I would take Melinda to school, take care of the banking, shopping and other daily errands if they needed to be done, started dinner and then picked everyone up from school, supervised their homework and continued preparing dinner.

Brandon would pick Robert up from the office later that evening and we would all eat dinner together. After dinner I would clear the table and do the dishes, sometimes we would have dessert together and then Robert would drive Melinda and me back to the house where I was staying with the elderly lady.

On one occasion after dinner I was feeling perfectly fine and suddenly I lost all of my strength and energy and collapsed on the living room floor. I heard the Holy Spirit say "the death angel is on the way." I told Robert and the kids and the boys began to pray in tongues while Robert spoke the written Word over my life. I then heard two names of people to call. Robert called them and one explained it was an assignment against my life and the other person had heard the same thing I heard "that the death angel is on the way" and that person had instructions for me as well. He told Robert to go with me to the elderly lady's house where I lived and put anointing oil on the walk way to the house and go in. So Robert drove me over to the house and assisted me because I had very little strength on my own. Once the oil was dropped on the walk way as we made our way to the front door and *when I reached the door "suddenly" all of my strength returned just as suddenly as it had left.* I was stronger than ever and very angry about the attack because the devil had tried to kill me.

The elderly lady expressed that she still wanted her house back so I began to look for somewhere else to go. Robert's former wife asked Robert's next door neighbor, who was a missionary and took people in, if she had any room for Melinda and me so I could be close for the kids when they came home from school but the lady did not have any room. There did not seem to be any open door, with my relatives, friends or acquaintances as I called around looking for somewhere to go with my daughter. **Now the elderly lady wanted Melinda and me to move; we had been in her home for two and half years and her son wanted to move back home. The door was closing fast and the only thing the Lord would say was "your husband will move you."** So, I stayed in God's will even though I made phone calls in hopes of finding somewhere else to move and to show respect for the elderly lady because she had asked me to move but because there just did not seem to be an open door anywhere I remained physically still and she knew I was looking to comply with her wishes.

One evening after dinner when Robert was about to drive Melinda and me back to the house, I telephoned to tell the elderly lady I was coming so she could be prepared to open the door because the key she had given me when I moved in was no longer working but she never answered the telephone. So we took the boys with us because they were going to Robert's office after they dropped Melinda and me off to make copies of their book reports that were due for school. Robert walked Melinda and me to the door and we knocked and rang the bell for nearly fifteen minutes, and the only key that I had did not work. It was late, about nine or so, cold and dark and Robert refused to leave my daughter and me in that state on the front porch, so he said "why don't you just come home?" I looked at him and thought to myself, "what do you mean come home? Your house is not my home." At that point it was either sleep on her front porch with my seven year old daughter in the dark and cold or sleep on the sofa downstairs in his home. So we returned to the car where the boys were and went on to the office to make copies for their reports and then went back to Robert's house.

I had seen a pastor who was also prophetic and I prayed with her and others about the situation and she told me the Lord said it was of Him for me to move to Robert's home. I spoke to others and prayed and had a peace about it. I even spoke to his former wife (who he had been separated from for years at this point) who told me that I was over there helping all the time anyway so I may as well move in and we told our children who were surprised but supportive because they knew the situation.

I was very disturbed about being in a married man's home and the fact that I was married also, even though both of us had been separated for years from our spouses it still did not look right regardless of the circumstances. God clearly showed others and me through confirmation that this was the only door He was opening for my children and me at this time. I spoke to the elderly lady and she wanted me to move, it was her home, the door was closed to me and since that door was now closed that meant God had opened another door. (Remember, the Lord told Kevin years prior to this, to tell your Mother you will always have shelter and you will never starve. I always held on to this and knew God would be faithful to His Word and this was one of the things that gave me the strength and determination not to do anything on my own like get a job or seek welfare for the kids. I knew I could trust God to turn the situation around for me *His way* and complete the training He was doing in me for the ministry).

Camille came with me to move my things later in that week because I did not want Robert to help me even though he offered. I continued to pray and seek God for another door to open while I took care of our families. We all barely knew one another yet we were living under the same roof and functioning "*as a*" family even though we were not one in the natural, yet. Melinda and I slept on the downstairs sofa, Kevin and Brandon shared Brandon's room upstairs across from Robert's room and Camille slept in the downstairs bedroom while Christa was away at the university.

Robert thought he was helping a friend and her children out of gratitude for me being there for his children. But only God knew that He had a far greater plan than that. God was doing a quick work as we were all bonding together as a family. A house full of strangers in the natural but mending together in the spirit.

During the next few weeks that followed I continued to take care of the family and slept on the sofa in the living room. However, Melinda was now sleeping in the room with Camille. Even though Camille offered to share her room with me I declined because I did not want to impose and I felt it best that I was in full view at night. While Christa was on a school break and back at home I remember she coming in with a girl friend at night once while I was asleep and I either heard the girl or Christa told me later that she wanted to know why I was sleeping on the sofa and Christa told her because they are not married. It was important for us to keep this relationship holy before our children and God. (Note: Our engagement is explained further on).

We had been accused of things and by some spoken about very badly, even by some of the ones who told us they *knew* by the Spirit it was God who sent me there. I discovered that people will believe what they want to believe and many choose to believe the worst while others will try to find good in a given situation. *There are certain people God can trust in a situation like this and it is His business, the opinions of others do not really matter when God has spoken and has done a thing. Nothing will change the fact that the Lord chose to move this way for us and He gave us a beautiful testimony, a great ministry, a wonderful family and victory in our lives.*

CAUTION: Robert and I are not suggesting that people make these type of arrangements on their own before marriage because there is a need to help someone, or for any other reason. What we are saying is to be led by the Holy Spirit and be obedient to Him and He will turn it around and work through whatever the problem is, *just let Him do it His way*. **The bottom line with our situation is that God knows, my husband knows and I know the truth.**

The Lord spoke to me when I first moved into their house and said "if you keep it holy I will bless it." I shared this word with Robert and we both knew the danger involved and we had been celibate for years while our spouses were gone. We knew we had to continue to be holy before God and not jeopardize what He was doing for us in this hour. I am here to tell you that with the wisdom of God, His grace and power anything can be done in Christ. We were not about to miss our blessing because of adultery or any other spirit. *We were not alone in the house before we wed with four kids at home and their friends visiting, the youth ministry meeting there and adults coming over for prayer made this possible.* We always tried to have one or more of our children with us even when we had to shop on the weekends for our families and we went to restaurants and the theatre with our children as well. I continued to sleep on the sofa until the wedding so everyone knew where I was. We wanted especially to demonstrate to our children that one can keep a situation or relationship holy and do things God's way no matter what the circumstances are.

Some people will remain faithful and do things decent and in order till the proper time without a great struggle. Whereas, for certain people the temptation would be too great and God knowing their flesh He would not have led them in this direction. However, anyone is capable of falling or making mistakes, missing the mark or willfully sinning. It is a part of life ("For all have sinned, and come short of the glory of God," Romans 3:23). Keep in mind though **Jesus made provision in His Word to enable you not to fall or stumble** (2 Peter 1:3-10), but if you do, He has also made provision at the cross where He took your sins and if you ask for forgiveness, receive it and repent you are forgiven (I John 2:2, 12).

Both Robert and I ministered to people and knew the appearance we were giving and we felt badly about it. I struggled with the appearance of this arrangement because the Bible says in I Thessalonians 5:22 KJV says, *"Abstain from all appearance of evil."* So this really bothered me and I was somewhat upset with Robert because I felt terrible about being in his home and how I appeared to others and I was upset with God for not opening another door for my children and me.

Then the Lord took me to the book of John 7:24 KJV and AMP:

> Judge not according to the appearance, but judge righteous judgment.
>
> Be honest in your judgment and do not decide at a glance (superficially and by appearances); but judge fairly and righteously.

God also revealed that in the Old Testament many men brought their future wives into their homes before they married but they were not to touch them until after the marriage vows were said which was the final stage that consummated their marriage. Remember the engagement period was the first stage of marriage and was binding. Up until a few years ago if a person was engaged but did not show up for their wedding to consummate the marriage the party left had a right to sue the person for a breach of contract, breach of *promise* and in some cases this law may still be in affect.

Genesis 24:1-7, 14, 27, 38, 40, 51, 58, 63 and 62-67 tells the story of how Abraham sent his servant to take a wife for his son Isaac. How the servant prayed and thanked God for the right wife (vv.14, 27 and 40) as he followed the leading of the Holy Spirit to bring her back to his master's home. In vv. 62-67 it tells how Isaac met her when the servant was in route to bring her to him and how he took her into his mother's tent that had died and she became his wife and comforted him after his mother's death. I am sure they did not wed the day she arrived.

God also commanded that *if a man wanted to marry a captive woman he must bring her into his home and wait* for one full month before he married her.

Deut. 21:10-14 NLT, see verse 13 as follows:

> ...Then she must remain in your home for a full month, mourning for her father and mother. After that you may marry her...

The Lord moves in seasons and my time with the elderly lady was over, I needed a covering because of my walk with God and prayer coverage for my life which was under spiritual attack and I had come near death many times for what appeared to be no apparent reason. We knew the adversary was trying to kill me before we came into the knowledge of our reason for being together. Just as he had tried to kill me while in route on a plane to Los Angeles from Florida, it was directly after this trip that I met Robert. **As long as I am saved and striving to be in God's will and set place for my life regardless of how it *appears*, I will be under the protection of the Holy Spirit.**

It was also time for our sons to prepare to graduate from high school which would enable them to go on to college and continue in God's will for their lives. We knew God's will was for them to attend college because He said they would graduate from high school and college, therefore, He made the provisions for it to happen. At this stage of our children's lives they needed two parents a mother in the home and a father who needed to be freed up to work and know his house was in order. Furthermore, at this point we had no choice but to continue and follow the instructions and the leading of the Holy Spirit and keep our relationship holy.

We were unable to marry right away being married to our former spouses because we were believing God for them to return home even though at that point Robert had been separated between three and four years and I had been separated between six and seven years.

Some questioned that God placed us in the same house before we were married even though we had confirmation from true prophets and pastors, it witnessed in our spirits and we had a peace about it. We knew what God had said and our children's needs were being met. I admit I was very uncomfortable with this decision but I also knew that I had to put that aside and continue for the sake of the children and what God was doing for all of us. *I needed to take the focus off of my reputation and how I was perceived and see the larger picture, vision and what God was building and doing for His Kingdom,* (Phil 2:7 says "...But stripped Himself [of all privileges and rightful dignity]...)." In other words, **He made Himself of no reputation.** His assignment, *is His assignment.* He calls the shots and makes all the provisions for His purposes. We won't always understand His plan nevertheless all we have to do is yield and reap the harvest and when it is all said and done His plan will always lead us to victory.

Therefore, because of what has been stated above, this is the conclusion that we have arrived to: don't assign your values, weaknesses or expectations to someone else who is on an assignment from God. Nor judge by appearances only. God will and does vindicate His own. He will keep and preserve them who are misunderstood, slandered, lied upon and persecuted as they dare to step out and take action on what they believe

their instructions are from Almighty God. He will anoint and equip people to do whatever He has given them to accomplish. So let God handle each couple according to what He placed in them and has instructed them to do. If their assignment is not from God then their true motive will eventually be exposed.

Basically, I was functioning in Robert's household as a nanny. Men or women who are divorced, separated or widowed will in many cases hire a housekeeper, nanny, cook or all three when they need the extra help and they can afford it and nothing is said about it. God placed me in the house with the elderly lady who was a housekeeper for thirty years and now ran a Day Care. She was a blessing for us for two and a half years. Why shouldn't God do the same for Robert?

When I moved into his home he had a housekeeper but no nanny or someone that was involved with the concerns of his children nor someone that could prepare meals or that could take care of other errands during the day. God sent Him the help he needed, in his future "wife to be." Furthermore, things were in order for us to operate in God's will, meaning we had grown and matured to a certain level and with His grace and anointing as we were able to finish this assignment and remain holy before God.

The Lord will send some Believers into night clubs, drug houses, bars, on the streets to witness to wayward women and men as well as other places you shouldn't find saints, why? Because God is interested in people and giving them the life He died for them to have. Everyone is not equipped or anointed for the mission field but you can pray for those who are and have stepped out into their assignment instead of sending ill wishes, gossip and complaining.

As I stated earlier, my husband knows, I know and God knows and that is all that matters, that we were pleasing to God. I wanted to take the time to explain this because *religious spirits* don't understand how to flow with the Holy Spirit. Yes His Word says certain things about our being under the same roof as I have explained but His Spirit will balance that Word and bring clarity and power where necessary to carry out His Word or assignment.

Now having said that, I will resume with the rest of my testimony. My former husband and his girl friend filed for his divorce and had me served. I ignored it at first thinking we will only stop it again, but the Lord sent a young woman, the same prophet He sent shortly after I had moved into Robert's home at a time when I was asking the Lord where was I suppose to be? And this prophet showed up thirty minutes after I had asked God and she said that she was on her way to her daughter's school to pick her up and the Lord told her to come and see me. Once she was there she voluntarily told me "I was where I was supposed to be" and answered the question I had asked the Lord not thirty minutes prior.

Now God had sent the same prophetess again to my door and she told me that the Lord told her to go to Audrey's house (God referred to Robert's house as Audrey's house) and tell her that the divorce was going to go through this time. After she said that and to my knowledge she did not know that I had been served any papers, I pulled those papers from my files and read them all the way through for the first time and discovered that my former husband was filing for joint custody of our children and I only had a short time to respond. I immediately telephoned a friend of mine that I had worked with when I was a paralegal and law office manager and asked her to send me a Dissolution Package so I could respond to the petition. I responded and handled the divorce in Pro Per which means I represented myself in the Superior Court and when the divorce process was over the Lord had given me the victory (I was awarded Soul and Legal Custody of both children) and once again the Lord brought a promise He had made to me to pass! Thanks to His mercy to send a prophet across my path to give me instructions "right on time" to save my children from having to go into a situation that would have come against all of their beliefs in God, caused confusion and one that would have made our lives miserable and interfered with God's plan for our family.

As we continue, during the time we were attending the youth ministry which had moved to Robert's home from the small Christian school the youth meetings were attended by so many adults that by the third Friday in February of 1993 the adults were told by Christa long distance (she was away at college and had left someone else in charge of the youth ministry) had to hold their meeting in another location. **On that particular Friday the Lord began sending confirmation to confirm that Robert and I were to be married.** There were no less than twelve different people many of them prophets that we knew contacted us throughout the same day and some the following day by either telephone or by coming over to the house and giving us a word from God that we were to be husband and wife. Two of the women that came over together did not have the address of where I was living and they said the Lord directed them to the house.

Even the new Christian school instructor's sister who lived in another state who I had never met was talking with her and had a word for me and I spoke to her over the phone and in so many words she told me the that my marriage had become dead weight and God was removing it. These confirmations confirmed what the Holy Spirit had done for Robert in early November of 1992. At that time he and I had become prayer partners and we were on the phone praying for our kids and others when **the Holy Spirit according to Robert, poured into him starting from his head to his toes what seemed like an oil of love that filled his entire being.** This was so profound that he said he did not know what happened to him but we needed to get off the phone, but before we did, he told me that from this point on our relationship has changed and he needed time to seek the Lord. Two weeks later he called and explained how the Holy Spirit poured into him a love for me and that our relationship could not be the same any longer. These conversations took place when I was still at the elderly lady's home.

On that eventful Friday after we arrived at the adult Bible study we were told by one of the participants who said that everyone here knows that you two are suppose to be together but you. So after the Bible study Robert told me that because that was enough confirmation for him he would meet with his former wife to determine where she was with any efforts toward reconciliation. If the forgoing confirmations were from God then the final confirmation would come from her mouth. Indeed he met with her the following Sunday to discuss reconciliation and how she felt about it. When the question was put to her she said that it was not possible and she did not want any man over her again. At this point Robert asked her if she wanted a divorce and she said she did not care. Robert informed her that he would file for the divorce and she said Okay.

Shortly after all of this Robert and I continued receiving prophetic words that we were *suppose* to be together but because many of these people knew us and what we had been through it may have caused them to speak out of their emotions or their own spirit. So Robert and I agreed to continue to pray for our spouses to return until the Lord told us directly and made it absolutely clear that we were to be together. We were not interested in being in a new marriage that God had not ordained. I wanted to hear it directly from God for myself. I had not heard this directly and I knew I could hear from God, and since there were so many people, most of them prophets, prophesying this to us, **I asked God to confirm His word through people that did not know us, I wanted a confirmation from a total stranger. Within the next week or so three different pastors that did not know one another or knew us confirmed that we had a ministry together and it was God's will. Shortly after that Robert proposed marriage and I accepted because we knew it was God's will for our lives.**

*Three weeks later we were invited by some friends to a meeting a Prophet was having at the Holiday Inn in Hollywood. The Prophet called me up to the front and said, "three weeks ago I was headed in one direction and the Lord changed my life and did a one hundred and eighty degree turn and **if I had not gone with it I would have missed God's blessings," and it had been three weeks since Robert proposed marriage.**

We cannot go by what we see or think when the Holy Spirit has spoken. "The Lord said my husband would move me" and even though that is not what it appeared to be at the time, and we did not understand what God was doing, we had no choice but to go forth because prayer had gone forth and one door was shut and another one opened. *Nine months later Robert was my husband, so you see, my husband did move me from the elderly lady's home even though it was not the way I thought it would be. (Isaiah 55:8-9).*

Now we both found ourselves going through divorces after all those years of praying for our spouses to return home. *Later we received revelation that God's purpose will go forth and if certain individuals decide that they do not want to go on with God and His purpose they will eventually be removed (run out of chances). If anyone is in the way of God's plan, becoming dead weight, God will remove them and send the willing and obedient ones so His purpose can be fulfilled.* It is all about God's will and plan for His people. If you are willing and obedient as He is fulfilling His purpose He will be in a position to bless you as you work with Him and not against Him (Isaiah 1:19).

As I drove for hours each day the kids and I bonded together in the car. We prayed together, laughed together, had conversations about their lives and needs and our walk with the Lord Jesus Christ. I also ran errands with them in the car to make the most of our time, so we did some shopping together as well. The needs of the family brought us all closer together as we shared and helped one another during the day. *And the visions of Brandon shopping and spending time with our family was another manifestation of God's Word that had come to pass.*

OVER THE NEXT FEW PAGES I WILL SHARE HOW THE LORD FURTHER BONDED US TOGETHER. PLEASE KEEP IN MIND THAT SOME OF THESE EVENTS ARE NOT IN CHRONOLOGICAL ORDER, THEREFORE, I COULD BE SPEAKING OF TIMES BEFORE OR AFTER

WE WED. HOWEVER, I WILL DO MY BEST TO INDICATE WHICH IT IS.

Two small families are now operating as one large family with seven members and it all seemed to work fairly well. The children knew each other from school and had become friends and some of them were referring to themselves as brothers and sisters. As I have stated the Lord started merging our families together with the children first, then with me and the children and then Robert and the children. Later our families were having outings together, Robert and the boys played board games and he was helping the kids with their homework.

With our divorces in progress, planning a formal wedding, preparing breakfast, and lunches, taking Robert to the office and dropping the kids off at school in three different cities, running errands at the market, bank, cleaners, malls in preparation for the prom and other events approaching and then preparing dinner before picking everyone up, it seemed to work very well but only because the Holy Spirit anointed us to do it. Camille worked at the dental office with Robert while Christa was away at a university in another state. Brandon was preparing for a prom and his high school graduation and looking forward to starting college in the fall; Kevin was taking a computer and an art class that was located at another facility for the Christian high school he was attending while completing the twelfth grade; Melinda was now eight and enrolled in elementary school. We made many trips to the Beverly Hills Library for various reports and study time and on certain days all three were enrolled in karate classes for a short time in yet another city. Needless to say we spent a lot of time in the car.

Each location was miles a part we had one car and it was serviced for brakes at least every two to three months because of the wear and tear of all the driving. The dealership informed me that during the week I was driving an average of two hundred miles a day. We did have a housekeeper and this was a great help during those first few months leading up to our wedding.

The Lord knew what He was doing, the children and I had no choice but to spend time together and in the process we learned of each other, prayed for each other, wounds were healed and voids filled. With our children (teens included) we attended church every week and had Bible study every week in our home or we attended other Bible studies as well as ministry conferences as we were led. In addition, Robert and I along with our children also spent leisure time together mostly out to dinner and a movie on the week-ends. Also on occasion we visited amusement parks and went horseback riding.

I strongly believe in families eating meals together having been raised that way. In our household my father, Henry W. Jones, did the Sunday dinners, any major events, holiday and some of the regular week day cooking having been a Head Chef and requested personally by the Admiral in the United States Navy during World War II. My father had a gift and joy for cooking even though he had a scholarship to college to study math and accounting. He was an extremely kind and soft spoken man who had a love for God and family along with having high morals and standards. He took every opportunity to instill in each one of his ten children the importance of education and so forth. He was always available to help with homework. He walked us to school in the mornings as he worked in the evenings. He spent recreational time with the family as well as did the laundry and much of the major grocery shopping so my mother could be with the children and do other things in the home. He was a wonderful role model of strength, integrity and endurance.

Whereas my mother, Lillian C. Jones, had not been exposed to any cooking or housework having grown up in a privileged home with a father who was a Bishop, a businessman and doctor she and her siblings were not required to do housework of any kind leaving that work to the housekeepers. Over the years, however, my Dad taught my mom how to prepare a few dishes and she liked to bake pies and sweets for the holidays. She had a gift for counseling because she could sit for hours and listen to other people's problems and then give wise biblical advice. She held these sessions in our kitchen as she gave her undivided attention to those who came that were hurting emotionally to seek her listening ear. Both of my parents had a giving heart and loved to feed and help others. My parents raised us the way they had been raised, over protected but very much loved. So my siblings and I, as most children will do once grown, basically raised our children the same way.

Therefore, when I moved into Robert's house I treated his children the same way I treated mine, the only way I knew how. My natural children were younger than his natural children and I simply did not know how to relate to older kids so I did what was natural and comfortable for me and treated them all the same. Just like my parents, I did not believe that children should take on adult responsibilities. Cleaning their rooms and helping with other little things around the house was fine. Even though I knew his natural children's ages it still did not dawn on me to let them take on more responsibilities because as far as I was concerned they were still children, just older children. So I continued doing for them as if they were younger. I did not follow Robert's suggestion when he said that I should let the kids help more especially with dinner and clearing the table afterwards. I just could not see that as being an option. My thoughts and feelings were, we were the parents and we were to take care of them. I failed to realize that they consisted of a young adult and adolescents that were capable of doing a lot more for themselves. Melinda really was the only one that was truly very young as I was reminded by others looking in from the outside. Bob later said yes they can do these things but for now they needed a mother's love and he thanked me.

As far as I remember the older children never said anything to me that was negative about the way I treated them. I would hold them on my lap, and kiss them good night, I did most of the shopping, prepared the meals, set the table, and cleared the table afterwards, I drove them to the doctors for check-ups when necessary, oversaw their homework and even washed everyone's hair at least once and for two of them on a regular basis. A couple of the children required my help with their hair because their hair was very long. Inasmuch as Camille was a cosmetology student at the time she also helped keep their heads trimmed and looking nice. I drove all of them for their dental check-ups except Camille who was already at the dental office during the day with Robert. Even though some of them had driver's licenses I still drove them various places. They didn't seem to mind it and I was told that they liked the changes that were done to their house and Bob and I could see that they were enjoying the fellowship and outings we did as a family. Sometimes Camille and Kevin would walk to the video store a couple of blocks away and rent a movie for all of us to watch after dinner.

During those first few months together while still in the process of going through our divorces and planning our formal wedding, we rearranged the furniture, bought new appliances for the house we were leasing, painting was done inside of the house in various rooms, carpet and tile was laid, we cleaned out closets, and cleaned out the garage which had boxes stored for years. The whole family participated in these projects and it helped to bring further closure to things that had been lingering for years. Even his former wife came over and participated as well and got things that had been in the garage in boxes for years. It was a joy for my natural children and me to help especially because all of our things had been auctioned in storage the year before so it was nice to have a chance to help them distribute and take care of their belongings.

One of Robert's natural children thanked me and told me I turned their house into a home. I give all the glory to God because He showed me what needed to be done and with Robert's cooperation because he was now ready to move forward with his life, was a key factor in my being able to do what needed to be done. He initiated most of the changes when he told me whatever needed to be done just do it. God gave us the wisdom and made provisions for it to be done. The both of us worked out a spending plan for the family to make the necessary changes to the house (even though it was a rented house we wanted it to be a home for the kids). Robert added that his natural children, though they were older and knew how to do most of these things still allowed me to do it because at the time they needed a mother's love. One of them told me that they did not know how much they needed a mother until I came, having been without a mother in their home for a few years.

Christa was with us only during school breaks and Camille was about to leave and take care of an elderly aunt in her nineties who was bedridden. She would also later marry and is now the mother of three wonderful children herself.

On the other hand Robert was a great father to my natural children and still is. He did not make a difference and treated them all the same as well. God placed a love in his heart for my natural children just as He had placed a love in my heart for his.

Robert built a basketball court for Kevin in his back yard and on occasion he and Brandon played basketball with Kevin and sometimes the girls played as well while Melinda and I watched. All of the kids enjoyed board games with Robert such as chess, backgammon and other games. Robert over the years also taught Melinda how to skate, ride a bike, how to swim, some front office dental work and to drive a vehicle as he taught all five of our children how to drive even though the two youngest also attended driving school. He helped all of the kids with their homework after he had worked long hours at the office. He also did science projects with Melinda and she received a ribbon for first place for one of them. In one of our homes there were not enough bedrooms for Melinda to have her own bedroom who was eight years old at the time, so Robert built a wall off of the family room and put in a shelf for her belongings, I purchased a day bed and between the two of us turned it into a cozy bedroom for her. He accompanied Christa across country when she started college and was very supportive of Camille in her endeavors including training her to be a dental assistant.

Robert is very much a family man. His background included parents who were family oriented as well. For instance his father, Lloyd DuQuesne Dickey, II, was Superintendent of an Elementary School District in Los Angeles County for many years. He was also involved as a Scout Master spending time taking young boys camping. During his career he was also employed as a pharmacist and was a carpenter, who Robert as a child would help and observe. That is where Robert learned to do a number of carpentry jobs around the house and his Dad also left him all of this tools. His father's role model for he and his two brothers was one of a high achiever, who had determination and discipline to accomplish and at the same time was well respected, liked and sought after because of his kind demeanor and his philosophical views of life which were biblically based. His favorite scripture was in the Book of Revelation regarding the church at Philadelphia especially chapter three verse twelve.

Robert's mother, Juanita U. Dickey, was a stay at home Mom who operated a Day Care Center from their home. She loved this work and poured a lot into the children, supplying small tables and chairs so they could also learn while in her care. She was also heavily involved in the Social Society of Los Angeles as a member of Jack and Jill and the Links. I would like to add that as a member of Jack and Jill this social group of women reached out and really spent time with the younger people and children of all ages to help shape and prepare them to function successfully in society at large.

There are many fathers who are also raising children alone and not by choice. When Robert was left with his three children he told me he had found a great respect for single women raising children and all that was involved in running a house. He had to operate in the role of a wife as well as his own. Robert is a very strong person with parenting skills and business knowledge as well but God did not call him to be both the husband and the wife so it became a challenge. Sure he could function but he was not really equipped to handle the emotional needs and demands of the family from a more detailed perspective as a woman may have been able to in the same position. Overseeing the household and his dental practice was a great responsibility and he handled it quite well even though it was taking its toll.

God knew what He was doing when He gave two parents, one male and one female, a father and a mother. Together they brought balance, power, wisdom and an anointing that is needed to properly raise children and run a household. If God intended for people to fill both shoes He would not have sent two separate people of two different genders to do it. With the balance of two they will respond to issues differently adding a wider perspective to things.

I also operated as mother and father, I was not designed to be the head of a family but I walked in those shoes for nearly seven years. Many women do this very successfully, but if it had not been for the Lord and His anointing and impartation of wisdom, skills and gifts I do not know how successful I really would have been. To be honest, it was one of the hardest things I have ever done because I was not designed to be the head but the help meet.

I became drained, I missed having a partner and the children missed having a father. It is better to have someone to share the responsibilities and decision making. I enjoyed marriage and being a wife and mother but having to do it all is no picnic and I think after speaking to a number of women in this position many would agree.

When Robert and I were praying for our spouses to return, as I look back I think it was more so for the sake of the children than anything else. While praying, God answered as He always did and He answered His way. The Bible says in Isaiah 55:8-9, that His thoughts are not our thoughts and His ways not ours but His are higher than ours. Give Him the freedom to move in your life in all areas that will benefit the entire family.

In short when the children needed a mother's love or attention they spent time with me in the kitchen helping to prepare meals and doing other things around the house even visiting with me in my home study while I was working and/or studying. I taught each of those at home how to use their checking account, read their bank statements and organize and file their papers, and so forth. They all helped on occasion with chopping and preparing ingredients especially during the holidays when I used my Mother's recipes for sweet potato pie and potato salad.

When they needed a father's love or attention they spent a lot more time with Robert. Kevin learned a lot over the years about carpentry work watching and helping Robert build or assemble things for our home. Brandon loved to discuss business with Robert or me and talk about things regarding electronics. Robert also trained both of our sons to be dental assistants and gentlemen. We tried to have as much interaction with our children as possible especially since three were adolescents and would be grown soon. We wanted them to have good memories in addition to the ones they had before their former families went through the dissolution process.

God had anointed Robert and me to meet our children's needs. But we knew that they loved and missed their natural parents that were absent as well. Robert and I were in agreement that the other parents could visit whenever they chose to but even that was seldom on their part.

We had family meetings with open forums so all could speak openly and freely about their concerns; to keep everyone informed about family plans; and to allow every one to give suggestions and input. We used a set of written guidelines (rules) that were first discussed and prayed about between my husband and myself before we presented them to our children. These guidelines were incorporated so everyone would know what was expected of them in the family. Each person initialed a master copy indicating they received a copy of their Guidelines. This was followed through with those still living at home.

Everyone had written schedules for school and homework that were *flexible* to accommodate sudden changes nothing rigid or forced. These schedules were also used to help teach discipline, responsibility, set priorities and organize their time. We knew the most important thing next to teaching our children the Word of God and God's ways, was open communication within the family. We were also mindful that we were adjusting to a different size family other than what we were both originally accustomed to. Robert had three children and I had two, individually those were considered small families but now we were a family of seven, with different ranges of ages and that was a big adjustment.

Some of our guidelines or rules required that we stay a family of faith going to church and Bible study plus everyone was encouraged to have personal prayer time in the morning as well as read the Word for themselves during the week; everyone was responsible to keep their room and personal affairs in an orderly manner; respect one another's property and privacy; knock on a door before entering and do not borrow anything from anyone until you ask them first. They were told to calendar in, time for family and business meetings, family functions and vacations; no one of the opposite sex other than a family member was allowed in a bedroom unless there were three people in the room; unacceptable films, programs and music should not be shown or heard by anyone. These requests were mandatory in order to keep our home a home of faith and to maintain a certain level of holiness. We even purchased from our sons their worldly rap music (to discard) and suggested they buy Christian rap if they needed an alternative.

Because some of them were older we gave them the option to participate in family outings and things on that order. We also asked them to calendar as a reminder functions we would like to do together.

Living a life of faith requires waiting on God and continuing in His ways. If you wait on God you will develop the fruit of patience which will instill and build godly character in you. *Godly character is one of the main ingredients the Lord is striving to build in His people so they will have the integrity, faithfulness and other attributes that are necessary to live the kind of life He has for them. They in turn will be able to be an example and role model for someone else by showing them the way.*

Looking back before we were married, even with the housekeeper that was employed by Robert before I arrived along with the children and Robert who were doing their share and even with the above tools at work, the schedule I had for myself was still very demanding. I am very organized and somewhat of a perfectionist. Things were being accomplished and our family enjoyed seeing the progress. We knew our children had come out of dysfunctional homes and had been through a lot with the separations and divorces, therefore, Robert and I wanted so much to give them the home they had been robbed of over the last few years.

However, there were still lessons yet to be learned. With some events still in progress or having passed I needed to be very careful and only do what I was anointed to do, (that which God empowered me to do). As I mentioned earlier I was fine with the planning of my formal wedding and going through the divorces at the same time (and I was responding and handling my own divorce in pro per). The family was still bonding and learning one another, I was still overseeing the home and the heavy schedules for their schools which were in different cities and activities for the kids which required a lot of driving. Plus one child about to go to the prom and graduate and with all the other activities in the works I was fine with it.

But when I started helping with calls from home for the dental practice, having some of the calls forwarded in order to help out, well needless to say it was beginning to over tax me and take its toll.

I began receiving instructions and warnings to get more rest but I felt fine and continued with my long daily schedule anyway. I learned later that whenever the Lord sends specific instructions it is always for our good whether we recognize it or not. God knew when to rest and advises us to rest also. His rest is a realm where we are in a position to receive anytime because we place our trust in Him and not in our own efforts. He has all wisdom and knowledge and it pays to listen. If I had listened and physically rested more my mind and body would have had a chance to rejuvenate itself while I was asleep (Psalm 127:2). The cells in ones body rejuvenate as you sleep between the hours of ten p.m. and two a.m. and you need at least seven hours of sleep to be refreshed. This would have helped me to *maintain* balance much better, by resting properly, eating properly and having fun as well as working hard I would have been more in tune with the Holy Spirit and had more time for prayer and reading as I had prior to this new schedule.

I went from four to five hours or more in prayer, reading and studying in the early hours of each day to about two hours or less and this was not good in my case, (Proverbs 8:17). To whom much is given, much is required. God would have sent additional help and done whatever was necessary to help us, but because I chose to take on more than I should have during this season I probably missed some instructions that could have made all the difference in the world. The slightest bit of disobedience or missing valuable instructions from the Holy Spirit could have consequences even though it could be rectified later. **It was also a learning experience and as I have stated these events took place nearly twenty years ago and I am sharing them as helpful tips for others who maybe currently having a similar experience.**

Because I was not getting my proper rest it was easier to become irritable, frustrated and just burned out. I was leaving too much room for the adversary to get in. Even if it is for good things like taking care of your family or doing ministry work everything requires balance and direction from the Holy Spirit, otherwise you will get out of balance and start to give ground to the enemy. The devil works hard at trying to wear us out to the point of exhaustion. Becoming weary is a trap and he can intensify his attack to bring us down. We can lose our focus, energy and time with God which is extremely important to stay built up in the spirit and receive fresh revelation (mysteries or truths) from Him.

The Lord says in Matthew 11:28 NIV,

> Come to Me all you who are weary and burdened and I will give you rest.

Galatians 6:9 says,

> And let us not lose heart and grow weary and faint in acting nobly and doing right, for in due time and at the appointed season we shall reap, if we do not loosen and relax our courage and faint.

At one point early in our first year of marriage I felt like I was burned out when the family and a friend of Robert's employee who was a minister prayed for me and God revealed to her that I was tired. Immediately God showed me a vision of which things He did not give me the grace to do and that was, the dental office work. He showed me a vision of the file cabinet where I kept the dental office files in the home. I needed to return those files back to the office and delegate more work to others and not try to do so much myself. Because of prayer God answered and showed me what needed to be done. **It is important not to do the things God never instructed you to do. He will give you the grace and the enablement to do what He has asked you to do.** Does this mean one should pray about every single thing they do in a given day? No that is not what I am saying. I am saying pray about what God would have you to do, what He has equipped and assigned you to do. And if you have a problem or lose your peace then ask Him what is it that you maybe doing that you do not have the grace to do. You are strengthened (He is your strength) for your gifts, talents, assignments, and the things that He purposed for you to accomplish.

Philippians 4:13 says,

> **I have strength for all things in Christ Who empowers me** [I am ready for anything and equal to anything through Him Who infuses inner strength into me; I am self-sufficient in Christ's sufficiency].

To illustrate how a battle in your mind can intensify when anything is out of balance or order lets go back before Robert and I married. I was anointed to take care of the family and home but the dental office files and some other projects I was not told to do began to cause me to become weary. A trick of the enemy is for you to do things just because there is a need. You should never allow yourself to become too tired, hungry, angry or lonely for they open doors to the enemy. The adversary had been fighting this marriage before the onset and with us both very busy and out of balance because of our schedules and not having enough rest the battle within my mind started to intensify. Plus I was still a little upset about being in Robert's home and how others perceived it and in addition to that whether I loved him enough to marry him which led me again to contemplating whether or not I should leave in spite of not having anywhere to go. I had mentioned this to my natural children and Kevin informed me that if I left Bob that he could not guarantee that he would stay with Melinda and me. (Bob was the name most of us used when referring to Robert, now of course for years Kevin simply calls him Dad like all the other children). Kevin never wanted me to remarry or have a stepfather primarily because of the close relationship he had had with his natural father *but now* he was telling me that if I left Bob he did not know if he could stay with me. Melinda was not in favor of my leaving Robert either.

At a family meeting I announced I was leaving, I informed Robert that he could hire someone to do what I was doing. Brandon his natural son spoke up, this was the first he had heard of this and he said, yes, he can hire someone to do what you are doing but he cannot pay someone to pray for me or kiss me good night and he went on and on until my eyes were teary, so because of the three children, again I decided to stay.

Closer to the date of the wedding the spiritual attacks against my mind grew worse and just before we were to send out our wedding invitations I was again contemplating leaving but this time I did not mention it to anyone, not even my children.

That in and of itself was out of character for me because I am a very open and straight forward person that confronted when necessary or followed through with whatever it was I needed to do. But nevertheless, I was contemplating leaving because I was not sure if I loved Robert enough to spend the rest of my life with him.

When God tells you to do something He has already equipped you to do it. The thing I was struggling with was a battle in my mind of whether I loved him or not. It was a demonic attack to stop the marriage and ultimately stop the family ministry God had given us together.

There was one thing that I knew without a shadow of doubt, and that is according to the Bible, that if you watch (discern) and pray He said He would give you a way of escape. God will not allow you to fall into a trap when you are diligently seeking Him. After discerning what spirits are in operation around you then you can say spiritual warfare prayers such as the prayer of Binding and Loosing to halt Satan's activities and assignments. You can also plead the blood of Jesus and put on the whole armor of God daily to protect yourself and your loved ones.

Matthew 26:41 says,

> All of you must keep awake (give strict attention, be cautious and active) and watch and pray, that you may not come into temptation. The spirit indeed is willing, but the flesh is weak.

I Corinthians 10:13 writes it this way,

> For no temptation (no trial regarded as enticing to sin), [no matter how it comes or where it leads] has overtaken you and laid hold on you that is not common to man [that is, no temptation or trial has come to you that is beyond human resistance and that is not adjusted and adapted and belonging

to human experience, and such as man can bear].

> *But God is faithful [to His Word and to His compassionate nature], and He [can be trusted] not to let you be tempted and tried and assayed beyond your ability and strength of resistance and power to endure, but with the temptation He will [always] also provide the way out (the means of escape to a landing place, that you may be capable and strong and powerful to bear up under it patiently.*

While we were engaged through everything we went through Robert and I **never** stopped praying together nor did we ever stop spending private time with God in the early morning hours in our separate prayer closets. At four-thirty every morning the entire house could hear Robert upstairs singing praises to God. I could always hear him downstairs because I was also up spending my time worshipping the Lord and studying His Word.

James 1:12 says,

> Blessed (happy, to be envied) is the man who is patient under trial and stands up under temptation, for when he Has stood the test and been approved, he will receive [the victor's] crown of life which God has promised to those who love Him.

To complete the story, when I was about to leave before the wedding as I had mentioned earlier, I had decided not to tell anyone, not even my children. One evening while I was waiting in my vehicle with Melinda to pickup Kevin and his cousin Gregory from the movie theatre she said something that changed my life. Melinda who at the time was eight years of age, filled with the Infilling of the Holy Spirit with the evidence of speaking in tongues since the age of three, prophesying by the age of four and who God used to minister under the anointing and prophetic in a church at the age of five and later at prophetic conferences when she was only six or seven years of age asked me could she sing a song to me, the Lord gave her new songs that she would sing under the inspiration of the Holy Spirit. I said all of that about Melinda to say this, I knew what God was doing in her life and I had seen lives changed and many things come to pass as a result of her ministry and the Lord knew when He spoke through her by the inspiration of the Holy Spirit, **I would listen.**

So as I sat there waiting for Kevin to come out of the theatre on October 30, 1993, I was tired, engaged and scheduled to marry Robert on December 28th and now again I was making plans to leave. In the midst of all of this going on in my thoughts, as I said, Melinda calmly asked me could she sing a song to me and I said yes. As she began to sing to me the anointing filled the car with the tangible presence of God that was so thick you could not miss it if you tried. It was one of the heaviest I had ever felt in my life to this day. Then she instructed me to get my pad and a pencil (which I always kept in the vehicle) and said "the Lord wants to tell you something." Ready with pad and pencil she began to prophesy to me and said these words from the Lord:

> "**My child, My child I have given you a husband and a family, receive it. Have given you a car and family that will treat you right, a real family. Robert has been here for you My child. I love you. Brandon is your son, Kevin is your son, Christa is your daughter.** (Melinda stopped and I *thought* but I did not say anything, Lord, what about Camille and no sooner than I thought it Melinda continued to speak under the inspiration of the Holy Spirit and said) **Camille loves you very much deep inside her heart. Camille misses you, misses that love…**"

Other people have given us prophetic words to confirm we were to be together and that we had a ministry together but none of those words touched my heart as the one given by Melinda, because Melinda did not know nor could she understand that I was planning to leave the relationship within the next few days and the word spoken under the anointing was right on time and just what I needed to hear. Even though she was young God had already proven that she was His prophet because nearly every thing she spoke under the inspiration of the Holy Spirit came to pass. She is a blessing in our lives and we thank God for her.

To date I have over seventy journals full of God's words to us and others and this is the only prophecy I carry in my purse because it is the one that changed my life and kept me on the right course for good. It broke yokes off of my life, I could no longer fight what God was doing nor did I desire to do so.

The next morning while I was spending time in prayer I heard a still small voice speak to me and say, "I have given unto you a husband." I asked God then to give me the love for him and God said the love was already in my heart and I told God I did not feel that love for him and God said *"because you have not let go of the old."*

When I submitted to God's will to do what He wanted me to do I realized that what He had done was for my good and the good of both our families. **As I yielded and received God's plan I felt a love come into my heart for Robert. Over the years it has grown more and more** and I thank God for doing all that He did so I would not miss His plan for my life and our household. I also thank God for my husband's character and the anointing on his life that enabled him to have the patience, wisdom and understanding that was needed while waiting on God to move on my heart.

I could not hear nor could I receive because I had not let go of the past. You cannot receive *the new thing* **until you release the old.** Even though my mind was attacked with thoughts to leave because Satan wanted us both to miss our blessing, but because the Word of God was in my heart and not only in my mind along with prayer from others it was enough to sustain and keep me as long as I did not give up and was willing to continue in God and because I was willing, God was willing to continue in me.

Isaiah 43:18-19 says,

> Do not [earnestly] remember the former things; neither consider the things of old.
>
> Behold, I am doing a new thing! Now it springs forth; do you not perceive and know it and will you not give heed to it? I will even make a way in the wilderness and rivers in the desert.

2 Corinthians 5:17 says,

> Therefore if any person is [ingrafted] in Christ the Messiah) he is a new creation (a new creature altogether); the old [previous moral and spiritual condition] has passed away. Behold, the fresh and new has come!

Just before we wed on December 28, 1993, a date given by the Holy Spirit which was three days after Christmas and three days before New Years, we completed twelve marital classes at the church we were members of at the time; both of our divorces were final two months before the wedding; one of our sons had graduated from high school and was enrolled in college and our other children were settled and we had a beautiful Christmas that year just before the big event.

All of our children originally were scheduled to be in our wedding, later Camille left for personal reasons. One of our spiritual children, a son, named Ron was also in the wedding. The wedding party consisted of those that the Lord placed in our hearts. It was a beautiful wedding and all of our children were included in our wedding vows. Our reception followed immediately at the Los Angeles Airport Marriot Hotel and the following day we flew to Hawaii for our honeymoon. Everything was done as planned and as seen in visions long ago, prophecy was fulfilled; and things God had spoken came to pass all for His Glory and purpose.

As we began to share more with one another we discovered over the years our paths had crossed but we never met nor knew one another until the *appointed time.* For example, we discovered that we were neighbors for one year living three blocks a part on the same street; our sons attended the same junior high school in Hancock Park but during different years; we had used the same real estate company to purchase our homes; we shopped in some of the same stores; and Robert and I graduated from the same high school only in different years. Even the church building that Robert and I were married in I had considered marrying in that same church many years prior with my former husband but the Lord had reserved that church for Robert and me so for whatever reason my former wedding location was changed to the Wayfarers Chapel, a glass chapel on a hill over looking the ocean in Rancho Palos Verdes. The church we wed in was destined for Robert and me and it was confirmed by our church home at that time, not performing December weddings so we had to locate another church that did December weddings when we were directed to the very one I had considered many, many years prior.

Furthermore, because our divorces were so close to the wedding date, and because of all the obstacles we encountered, it was truly a miracle that we were married by the end of the year as it had been prophesied.

As long as you are continuing with God changes will come in God's perfect timing, not yours. Yield and become sensitive to the leading of the Holy Spirit so God can do a wonderful work in your life.

Now with some of our hardest obstacles at the time behind us and only two months after our wedding **the Lord uplift's us as one family** from our dwelling and we embarked on a journey that would last for the next eighteen years. Through the next eighteen years we would encounter trials, be equipped, tested, anointed and prepared for the ministry assignment God had spoken to us.

The same vision given to Robert was also given to me. We were given different parts and details but basically the same assignment. This confirmed that Robert was the head of this family and I was his help meet.

The Lord once said to me that there would be some things I would have to experience first hand in order to do the work He prepared for me to do (Acts 9:15-16). In some cases this included my husband and children experiencing some difficult things as well because we are one unit. The Holy Spirit leads us during good times and difficult times. For example, we know that God does not send poverty, lack, infirmity (sickness), and so forth; however, people will experience trials and storms in their lives whether they are saved or not. Those that build their homes on the Rock (on Jesus) as opposed to those who build their homes on sand is the determining factor of how they will fair during the storms of life and if they will succeed or fail (Matt. 7:24-26).

Some of the negative things we experienced over the next few years as a family were broken hearts, being homeless, living in hotels, living with relatives and so forth. These things were sent by the adversary to try to destroy us; but God would turn it around for our good every time. "As for you, you thought evil against me, but God meant if for good, to bring about that many people should be kept alive, as they are this day" (Gen. 50:20). Part of our journey was to plant seed for our vision and home by moving and living where the Lord sent us to do a work and to turn a house into a home for whoever was moving in after us. Even though God would tell us when to move God did not send the storms but while in the midst of a storm, as we continued to trust Him knowing He would never leave us nor forsake us, our faith grew, our joy was sustained, we continued to give, and didn't complain (Heb. 13:5). We also continued to reach out to help others and minister. At the appointed time He always came through, telling us where to go and then giving us favor, provision and a nice home.

Without tests, your faith will never manifest (James 1:3-4). His Word will be tested and as you believe and act on what you believe knowing He will never leave you, you will find He is *Someone* you can trust. He is about building your faith not destroying your life. We were hated and rejected, isolated and persecuted by others for His name sake; simply not being understood, thought to be crazy for refusing to follow the norm or compromise our beliefs. We were being prepared to minister to the brokenhearted and to set the captives free. The Lord told us years ago there would be many homeless people and now we see cities being destroyed and everyone in it homeless and some times these things coming about in one day. God has prepared some to be able to minister to these hurting people. As we stood the test of faith we were strengthened and our fruit of the Spirit increased, the anointing increased, wisdom increased, and so on. With the wisdom of Jesus, you will have blessings beyond what you can imagine and you will be able to keep the blessings that have come into your life. You will have success when following Christ, Psalm 90:17 NLT says, "And may the Lord our God show us His approval and make our efforts successful. Yes make our efforts successful!" (Psalm 44:3 NLT).

God is faithful and even though we have trials like anyone else, we learned to cast our care, praise God in the midst and live as much as possible with the fruit of the Spirit in our lives. We learned that our joy and peace was important in order to keep 'The Blessing' in our lives. We experienced victory in God with our family, home, ministry and businesses, finishing the race and taking the prize! The Lord has blessed our family mightily and our family is a blessing to the Kingdom of God. We are a blessing to one another and all that we do is blessed, Praise God!

As you follow God begin to declare 'The Blessing' of the Lord as we did. *We Confess and Declare that we are Blessed (increased) and are a Blessing to Others!*

Genesis 12:3, **Blessed according to our Covenant:**

> And I will *bless* those who *bless* you [who confer prosperity or happiness upon you] and curse him who curses or uses insolent language

toward you; in you will all the families and kindred of the earth be *blessed* [and by you they will *bless* themselves]. We are also *blessed* through God's promises of *blessings* in Deut. 28:1-14.

Galatians 3:6-9 NLT, **Blessed because our Faith is in Christ:**

In the same way, "Abraham believed God, so God declared him righteous because of his faith." The real children of Abraham, then, are all those who put their faith in God. What's more, the Scriptures looked forward to this time when God would accept the Gentiles, too, on the basis of their faith. God promised this good news to Abraham long ago when he said, "All nations will be *blessed* through you.

And so it is: All who put their faith in Christ share the same *blessing* Abraham received because of his faith.

Ephesians 1:3-5 NLT, **Blessed with the Spiritual and Material:**

How we praise God, the Father of our Lord Jesus Christ, who has *blessed* us with every spiritual *blessing* in the heavenly realms because we belong to Christ. Long ago, even before He made the world, God loved us and chose us in Christ to be holy and without fault in His eyes. His unchanging plan has always been to adopt us into His own family by bringing us to Himself through Jesus Christ. And this gave Him great pleasure. *Proverbs 10:22 NKJV* The *blessing* of the Lord makes one rich, and He adds no *sorrow* with it.

Isaiah 61:7, 9 NLT, **Blessed and Honored as a People:**

Instead of shame and dishonor, you will inherit a double portion of prosperity and everlasting joy. Their descendants will be known and honored among the nations. Everyone will realize that they are a people the Lord has *blessed.*

Ephesians 3:20-21 NKJV, **He will Exceed our Expectations!**

Now to Him who is able to do exceedingly abundantly above all that we ask or think, according to the power that works in us, to Him be glory in the church by Christ Jesus to all generations, forever and ever. Amen.

A SCRIPTURE PASSAGE THAT QUALIFIES AN ANOINTED FAMILY OF GOD:

Isaiah 61:1:

The Spirit of the Lord God is upon me, because the Lord has anointed and qualified me to preach the Gospel of good tidings to the meek, the poor, and afflicted; He has sent me to bind up and heal the broken hearted, to proclaim liberty to the [physical and spiritual] captives and the opening of the prison and of the eyes to those who are bound, (Luke 4:18).

Unless you understand great loss, persecution, failure and being broken hearted, for God's sake and purposes, (I Peter 4:12-19; Mark 10:29-30), it would be difficult in many instances for you to be able to relate to the needs of the people with compassion in your heart, with the right kind of Spirit and attitude. Many people who go through these things live in unforgiveness and bitterness never coming to that place of *peace* knowing God is able and willing to restore and resurrect their lives by faith (Matthew 9:29 and Romans 1:17).

Mark 10:29-30 says,

> Jesus said, Truly I tell you, there is no one who has given up and left house or brothers or sisters or mother or father or children or lands for My sake and for the Gospel's, Who will not receive a hundred times as much now in this time: houses and brothers and sisters and mothers and children and lands, with persecutions—and in this age to come, eternal life.

I Corinthians 2:14 says,

> But the natural, nonspiritual man does not accept or welcome or admit into his heart the gifts and teachings and revelation of the Spirit of God, for they are folly (meaningless nonsense) to him; and he is incapable of knowing them [of progressively recognizing, understanding, and becoming better acquainted with them] because they are spiritually discerned and estimated and appreciated.

The more in tune or in step you are with the Holy Spirit the better you will be able to tell someone of God's goodness and to demonstrate it through His fruit: love, joy, peace, patience, gentleness, goodness, faithfulness, kindness and self control. You will be better able to help them move forward with hope, faith and instructions that will help them reach their goals.

People need to know that God can and will bring them through the storms of life, the circumstances of life keeping their mind and giving them complete restoration and a knowing that you know, that you know it is going to be alright.

It is good for others to hear your testimony or see what God has done in your life. To witness to them that He is no respecter of persons and what He did for us and our children,

He will do for you. You have to know you can go through trials, troubles and heartaches with a knowing that you will be able in the midst of it all to grow, be strengthened, have a peace of mind, your joy and hope instead of depression, doubt, torment or fear that you will never recover.

Through your experiences you can teach others that the way out is *through*: loving God enough to obey Him; showing the love of God to yourself and to others; exercising your faith; giving into God's Kingdom; sharing your testimony (your story) and of course by declaring the Blood of the Lamb!

Revelation 12:11 says,

> And they have overcome (conquered) him by means of the Blood of the Lamb and by the **utterance of their testimony...**

As you learn to trust (lean on, rely on and be confident) in God and discover who He is and how He functions, it will become easier and easier to follow Him. The more and sooner you listen and respond the less chance there is of the Holy Spirit's voice growing faint in your hearing which would cause great regrets in missing God and His perfect will and timing for your life. He will enable you to avoid traps, set backs, moving off track or out of His will when you are in communication with Him. You can begin to live and move with confidence, boldness and Godly love. As you obey God the strongholds, bondages and yokes will start to fall off as you are delivered from generational curses, sin, pass mistakes and wrong choices. You will be freed up to walk in love, joy, forgiveness and obedience with a willing heart. **You are now in a position to pray and see major breakthroughs and changes in your life and the lives of those you pray for, beginning with your "*family.*"**

I pray that, *God's Blended Family*, has been a blessing to you. Always remember that the battle is not yours but God's, cast your care on Him, receive His victory and enjoy your life!

If you are <u>not</u> a Born-again Christian with the Infilling (Baptism) of the Holy Spirit <u>or</u> you are a Christian Believer and would like to rededicate your life to Jesus just say the following Prayer and tell someone of the Decision you have made regarding the Good News!

A PRAYER FOR SALVATION AND THE INFILLING OF THE HOLY SPIRIT

Dear Heavenly Father,

I come to You now, just as I am in the name of Jesus and ask for forgiveness. Your Word says, "…Whosoever shall call on the name of the Lord shall be saved" and if you confess with your mouth Jesus is Lord and in your heart believe that God raised Him from the dead, you will be saved (Acts 2:21; Ro.10:9).

I believe and confess now that Jesus Christ is the Son of God and He is alive today. I receive Him as my personal Lord and Savior. Thank You Father God that Your Son has set me free from eternal darkness (I John 2:2, 12). I now declare that I am redeemed, I am healed, I am blessed and I am whole. Therefore, I now have a renewed, abundant and confident life in Christ Jesus.

Father God, You said my Salvation would be the result of Your Holy Spirit giving me new birth by coming to live in me (Romans 8:9,11). So I ask You now for the Infilling of Your Holy Spirit as you have promised. Thank You for the gift to speak in other tongues, my supernatural spiritual prayer language that is unknown to man but known to God according to Acts 2:4 and I Corinthians 14:2. Now I bind the strong man that was sent to rob me and I plead the Blood of Jesus over my mind and mouth as I now release from my spirit my supernatural spiritual prayer language in Jesus' Mighty name. Amen!

This Prayer is based on Romans 10:9-10 which says:

If you acknowledge and confess with your lips that Jesus is Lord and in your heart believe that God raised Him from the dead, you will be saved. For with the heart a person believes and so is *justified,* and with the mouth he confesses (declares openly and speaks out freely his faith) and confirms [his] salvation.

I John 2:2, 12 says:

And He [that same Jesus Himself] is the propitiation (the atoning sacrifice) for our sins, and not for ours alone but also for [the sins of] the whole world. ...*because for His name's sake your sins are forgiven [pardoned through His name and on account of confessing His name].*

"Justified" – We are as if we never sinned! We are declared righteous, acceptable to God because of the Finished Work at the Cross where Jesus took our sins and gave us His Righteousness because in Him we have redemption through His blood! Hallelujah for a God Who Saves! (Ephesians 1:7).

ENDNOTES

CHAPTER ONE
What is the Biblical Definition for Marriage?
(And How God by His Grace Gave us a Covenant to Seal it)
1. The New Unger's Bible Dictionary. Chicago: Moody Press, 1988
2. Vine's Complete Expository Dictionary with Topical Index. Nashville: Thomas Nelson Publishers, 1984, 1996
3. Disciple's Study Bible, NIV Footnote. Nashville: Holman Bible Publishers, 1988
4. H. A. Maxwell Whyte, *The Power of the Blood.* New Kensington: Whitaker House, 1973
5. Ed Young, *The 10 Commandments of Marriage.* Chicago: Moody Publishers, 2003
6. Perry Stone, *The Ancient Jewish Wedding—A Revelation on the Rapture; The Mystery of the Four Passover Cups.* Http://www.perrystone.org/store/index.php/dvds-all/dvds/dv094: DVD DV094
7. Rev. William J. Morford, *The One New Man Bible.* Travelers Rest: True Potential Publishing, Inc., 2011

CHAPTER TWO
What is the Biblical Definition for Divorce?
(And Things the Bible has to Say about it)
1. The New Unger's Bible Dictionary. Chicago: Moody Press, 1988

2. Vine's Complete Expository Dictionary with Topical Index. Nashville: Thomas Nelson Publishers, 1984, 1996
3. Disciple's Study Bible, NIV Footnote. Nashville: Holman Bible Publishers, 1988
4. R. T. Kendall, *How to Forgive Ourselves Totally*. Lake Mary: Charisma House: A Strang Company, 2007.
5. The New Webster's Dictionary of the English Language, International Edition. New York: Lexicon Publications, Inc., 1991
6. Joseph Prince, *Destined To Reign, Devotional*. Tulsa: Harrison House, 2008
7. Bryan, Christina, and DeVault Strong, *The Marriage and Family Experience*. 6th Ed., St. Paul: West Publishing Company, 1995
8. David Hocking, *Marrying Again*, Old Tappan: Power Books, 1983
9. Tim Clinton and John Trent, *Marriage & Family Counseling*. Grand Rapids: Baker Books, 2009 www.aacc.net

CHAPTER THREE
What is the Biblical Definition for Family?
(Also Healthy and Strong Qualities it *Should* Possess)
1. The New Unger's Bible Dictionary. Chicago: Moody Press, 1988
2. Vine's Complete Expository Dictionary with Topical Index. Nashville: Thomas Nelson Publishers, 1984, 1996
3. Disciple's Study Bible, NIV Footnote. Nashville: Holman Bible Publishers, 1988

CHAPTER FOUR
Various Family Types that Exist in *Our Society* Today.
1. The New Unger's Bible Dictionary. Chicago: Moody Press, 1988
2. Vine's Complete Expository Dictionary with Topical Index. Nashville: Thomas Nelson Publishers, 1984, 1996
3. Disciple's Study Bible, NIV Footnote. Nashville: Holman Bible Publishers, 1988

4. Robert Lewis and William Hendricks, *Rocking the Roles*. Colorado Springs: NAVPRESS, 1991, 1998
5. Loren Cunningham, David Joel Hamilton with Janice Rogers, *Why Not Women?* Seattle: YWAM Publishing, 2000
6. Joyce Meyer, *Hearing from God Each Morning*. New York: Faith Words, 2010

CHAPTER SIX
Is your Family Functioning According to God's Order and their God-Given Roles?
1. Disciple's Study Bible, NIV Footnote. Nashville: Holman Bible Publishers, 1988
2. Watchman Nee, *Spiritual Authority*. New York: Christian Fellowship Publishers, Inc., 1972
3. Loren Cunningham, David Joel Hamilton with Janice Rogers, *Why Not Women?* Seattle: YWAM Publishing, 2000.
4. John Townsend, *Boundaries with Teens*. Grand Rapids: Zondervan, 1984

CHAPTER SEVEN
Walk in Victory and Authority through Effective Spiritual Warfare Against Demonic Attacks Assigned to Your Marriage and Family; It's Not Over Till God Says It's Over!
1. Disciple's Study Bible, NIV Footnote. Nashville: Holman Bible Publishers, 1988
2. The New Unger's Bible Dictionary. Chicago: Moody Press, 1988
3. Joyce Meyer, *Hearing from God Each Morning*. New York: Faith Words, 2010
4. Joyce Meyer, *How to Hear From God*. Warner Faith A Division of AOL Time Warner Book Group, 2003
5. Vine's Complete Expository Dictionary with Topical Index. Nashville: Thomas Nelson Publishers, 1984, 1996
6. Ever Increasing Faith Study Bible, NKJV. Los Angeles: Faith One Publishing, 1994 and Nashville: Thomas Nelson Publishers, 1982

7. Mark A. Beliles and Stephen K. McDowell, *America's Providential History*. Charlottesville: Providence Foundation, 1989, 1991
8. Joseph Prince, *Destined To Reign, Devotional*. Tulsa: Harrison House, 2008
9. Kimberly Daniels, *Give it Back*. Lake Mary: Charisma House: A Strang Company, 2007
10. Valerie K. Brown, *Miseducation of the Christian*. Lake Mary: Creation House, 2007
11. Deena Marie Carr, *Building Godly Wealth*. DVD regarding Financial Planning, www.financeaccordingtoyourfaith.org
12. Billy Graham, *Angels, God's Secret Agents*. Waco: Word Books, 1986
13. Cindy Trimm, *The Rules of Engagement Volume II: Binding the Strongman*. Ft. Lauderdale: Kingdom Life Publishing, 2005
14. Cindy Trimm, *The Rules of Engagement Volume I*. Ft. Lauderdale: Kingdom Life Publishing, 2003

ABOUT THE AUTHOR

Audrey L. Dickey, D. Min., Ph.D., is a Prophet and Pastor along with her husband, Dr. Robert L. Dickey, Prophet, Pastor and Dentist. They are the founders of Christian Love Fellowship Church, Inc. in Los Angeles, California. Dr. Audrey L. Dickey has a Doctorate of Philosophy in Religious Studies and a Doctorate of Ministry with an Emphasis in Biblical Counseling. She is also a member of the American Association of Christian Counselors (AACC) which includes membership in the Marriage and Family Network Division as well as the Black African-American Christian Counselors Division. For over thirty years she has studied relationships and counseled married couples, families and singles as she has a heart for marriages and families to be prosperous and successful. Since being in full time ministry for over twenty-two years she has taught from the Holy Bible as well as spoken at prophetic conferences and meetings throughout the United States and abroad. She has operated in the gifts of the Spirit since her youth and over the years has seen signs and wonders, healings and prophecies come to pass as well as lives changed through the power of God. Drs. Robert and Audrey Dickey are a God-Blended Family with five grown children, two sons, Brandon and Kevin and three daughters, Camille, Christa and Melinda all of whom are saved and have received the Infilling of the Holy Spirit.

To Contact the Author:

Dr. Audrey L. Dickey
P. O. Box 48288
Los Angeles, CA 90048

Godsblendedfamily@yahoo.com

You may include your prayer request or comments

GOD'S BLENDED FAMILY

STUDY NOTES

STUDY NOTES